lonely planet

P9-EFJ-971

Croatia

Zagreb
p42

Inland Croatia
p72

Kvarner
p136

Istria
p99

Northern Dalmatia
p171

Split & Central Dalmatia
p199

Dubrovnik & Southern Dalmatia
p253

THIS EDITION WRITTEN AND RESEARCHED BY
Peter Dragicevich
Marc Di Duca, Anja Mutić

Contents

PLAN YOUR TRIP

MEREDITH ANDREWS / LONELY PLANET ©

CROATIAN GELATO, KOMIŽA
P251

WIKIPEDIACOMMONS / BUDGET TRAVEL ©

PLITVICE LAKES NATIONAL
PARK P173

ON THE ROAD

Contents

Welcome to Croatia

If your Mediterranean fantasies feature balmy days by sapphire waters in the shade of ancient walled towns, Croatia is the place to turn them into reality.

Coastal Croatia

Croatia's extraordinary island-speckled coastline is indisputably its main attraction. The first thing that strikes you is the clarity of the water. When it's set against a dazzling white pebbly beach, it sparkles with a jewel-like intensity in shades of emerald and sapphire. There are long sandy and shingly stretches too – perfect for lazy days spent lounging and devouring trashy holiday novels. If that all sounds too relaxing, there are myriad water-based activities at hand to lure you off your sun-lounger – snorkelling, diving, kayaking, windsurfing and sailing, just for starters.

The Edge of Empires

Precariously poised between the Balkans and central Europe, this land has been passed between competing kingdoms, empires and republics for millennia. If there's an upside to this continual dislocation, it's in the rich cultural legacy that each has left behind. Venetian palazzi snuggle up to Napoleonic forts, Roman columns protrude from early Slavic churches, and Viennese mansions face off with Socialist Realist sculpture. Excellent museums showcase treasures that cover the gamut of European history, from the prehistoric to the post-communist, telling a story that is in equal parts fascinating and horrifying.

Beauty on the Inside

Shift your gaze for just a moment from the glittering waters, and chances are an almighty mountain will loom into view. The Dinaric Alps, which stretch all the way from Italy to Albania, hug much of the coast. The limestone karst has bequeathed a wonderland of craggy peaks, caverns, river canyons, waterfalls and ridiculously picturesque lakes. Head further inland and things flatten out again into rolling farmland. Active types will find plenty of chances to get among it on the numerous hiking and biking trails – while the more adventurous can have a go at rock climbing, rafting and ziplining.

Cultural Feast

If you're lucky enough to cross the tourist/guest barrier and be invited into a local's home, you'll soon become acquainted with the refrain *'Jedi! Jedi! Jedi!'* (Eat! Eat! Eat!). Sharing food and drink plays a big part in the culture here, which speaks both to the nature of Croatian hospitality and to the quality of local produce. Simple home-style cooking is a feature of family-run taverns, but increasingly a new breed of chefs are bringing a more adventurous approach to the table. Meanwhile, Croatian wines and olive oils are making their mark on the world stage, garnering top awards.

Why I Love Croatia

By Peter Dragicevich, Writer

I'll admit, I'm more than a little biased, but Croatia is quite simply my favourite country to visit. It offers a unique combination of all the things I love: breathtaking natural beauty, great swimming, summertime sun, oodles of history, interesting architecture, incredible wine, delicious seafood...I could go on. True, Croats don't always present the sunniest face to complete strangers, but break through that initial reserve and you'll discover the friendliest, most hospitable people you could hope to meet. I'm sure that even if my grandparents didn't hail from here, I'd still adore the place.

For more about our writers, see p352

For more about our writers, see p352

Above: Dubrovnik (p255)

Croatia

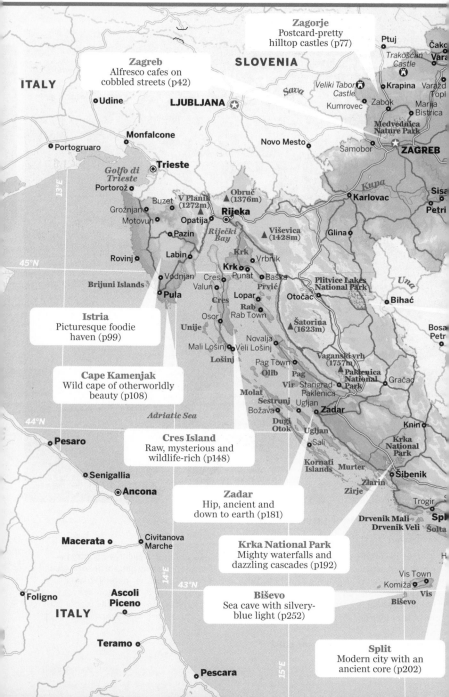

Zagorje
Postcard-pretty
hilltop castles (p77)

Ptuj

Čakc

*Trakošćan
Castle*

Vara

Zagreb
Alfresco cafes on
cobbled streets (p42)

SLOVENIA

*Veliki Tabor
Castle*

Krapina Varažd
Topl

ITALY

Kumrovec Zabok

Marija
Bistrica

Udine

Sava

LJUBLJANA

Novo Mesto

Samobor

**Medvednica
Nature Park**

ZAGREB

Monfalcone

Portogruaro

Trieste

*Golfo di
Trieste*

Portorož

Kupa

Sisa

Karlovac

Petri

13°E

Buzet

*V Planik
(1272m)*

*Obruč
(1376m)*

Rijeka

Grožnjan

Motovun

Opatija

*Riječki
Bay*

*Viševica
(1428m)*

Glina

45°N

Pazin

Labin

Rovinj

Krk

Vrbnik

Krk

**Plitvice Lakes
National Park**

Una

Vodnjan

Cres

Punat

Baška

Valun

Prvić

Otočac

Bihać

Brijuni Islands

Pula

Cres

Lopar

Rab

Rab Town

*Šatorina
(1623m)*

Bosa
Petr

Osor

Istria
Picturesque foodie
haven (p99)

Unije

Novalja

Mali Lošinj Veli Lošinj

Lošinj

Pag Town

Olib

Pag

*Vaganski vrh
(1757m)*

Cape Kamenjak
Wild cape of otherworldly
beauty (p108)

Adriatic Sea

Molat

Vir

Starigrad-
Paklenica

**Paklenica
National
Park**

Gračac

Sestrunj

Ugljan

Božava

Zadar

44°N

Pesaro

Dugi
Otok

Ugljan

Sali

Knin

Cres Island
Raw, mysterious and
wildlife-rich (p148)

**Krka
National
Park**

Senigallia

Ancona

Zadar
Hip, ancient and
down to earth (p181)

**Kornati
Islands** Murter

Zlarin

Šibenik

Zirje

Macerata

Civitanova
Marche

Trogir

Krka National Park
Mighty waterfalls and
dazzling cascades (p192)

**Drvenik Mali
Drvenik Veli** Šolta

Sp

14°E

H

Vis Town

Foligno

Komiža

43°N

Biševo
Sea cave with silvery-
blue light (p252)

Vis

Biševo

**Ascoli
Piceno**

ITALY

Teramo

Split
Modern city with an
ancient core (p202)

15°E

Pescara

0 — 100 km
0 — 50 miles

HUNGARY

Nagykanizsa

Koprivnica

Pécs

Bjelovar

Mohács

Virovitica

Drava

Drava

Duna v

Danube

Subotica

Kopački Rit
Wetland heaven for
birdwatchers (p93)

Kutina

Kapovac
(790m)▲

Osijek

Slavonska
Požega

Nova
Gradiška

Našice

Vukovar

Bačka
Palanka

**Novi
Sad**

Slavonski
Brod

Vinkovci

Ilok

Sremska
Mitrovica

Bosut

Tisa

Danube

Dunav

rijedor

Bosna

Brčko

Sava

Šabac

BELGRADE

Banja Luka

Plitvice Lakes National Park
Lush paradise laced
with waterfalls (p173)

Vrbas

Drina

Sava

SERBIA

**BOSNIA &
HERCEGOVINA**

Jajce

Travnik

Bol
Glorious beach and wind-
surfers' playground (p236)

Čačak

Livno

nj

SARAJEVO

Goražde

Konjić

Mljet Island
Heavenly isle with cobalt-
coloured lakes (p276)

Neretva

Pljevlja

ar

Breša

č

Makarska

Mostar

Bol

ri Grad

Jelsa

Hvar

Piva

Dubrovnik
Dazzlingly beautiful
walled old town (p255)

Tara

Korčula

Korčula
Town

Metković

Peljašac
Peninsula

Neum

Vela

Lumbarda

uka

Ston

Mljet

Lastovo

Elafiti
Islands

Trsteno
Gardens

Trebinje

MONTENEGRO

Nikšić

Hvar Town
Island hot spot for
beach parties (p239)

Dubrovnik

Cavtat

Herceg Novi

Kotor

PODGORICA

18°E

ELEVATION

1500m
1000m
700m
500m
300m
200m
100m
0

Croatia's
Top 17

Majestic Dubrovnik

1 Croatia's most popular attraction, the extraordinary walled city of Dubrovnik (p255), is a Unesco World Heritage Site for good reason. Despite being relentlessly shelled in the 1990s during Croatia's Homeland War, its mighty walls, sturdy towers, medieval monasteries, baroque churches, graceful squares and fascinating residential quarters all look magnificent again. For an unrivalled perspective of this Adriatic pearl, take the cable car up to Mt Srđ. For a more intimate glimpse, circle the city walls and peer into hidden gardens and ancient lanes strung with laundry.

Plitvice Paradise

2 A turquoise ribbon of lakes linked by gushing waterfalls in the forested heart of continental Croatia, Plitvice Lakes National Park (p173) is an awe-inspiring sight. There are dozens of lakes – from 4km-long Kozjak to reed-fringed ponds – their startling colours a product of the karstic terrain. Travertine expanses covered with mossy plants divide the lakes, while boardwalks allow you to easily traverse this exquisite watery world. Follow hiking trails through beech, spruce, fir and pine forest to escape the crowds by the water.

ANDREY OMELYANCHUK / 500PX ©

KELLY CHENG TRAVEL PHOTOGRAPHY / GETTY IMAGES ©

MARCOS MESA SAM WORDLEY / SHUTTERSTOCK ©

Marvellous Mljet

3 Cloaked in dense pine forests, marvellous Mljet (p276) is an island paradise. Legend has it that Odysseus was marooned here for seven years, and it's easy to appreciate why he'd take his time leaving. The entire western section is a national park, where you'll find two sublime cobalt-coloured lakes, an island monastery and the sleepy little port of Pomena, which is as pretty as a picture. Don't neglect eastern Mljet, home to some tranquil little bays, brilliant beaches and a couple of excellent eateries.

Wining & Dining in Istria

4 *La dolce vita* reigns supreme in Istria (p99), Croatia's top foodie destination. The seafood, truffles, wild asparagus and a rare breed of Istrian beef called *boškarin* all stand out, as do myriad regional specialities and award-winning olive oils and wines by small local producers. Slow food is a hit here: you can sample the ritual in upmarket restaurants in seafront towns, in traditional family-run taverns in medieval hilltop villages, and in converted olive mills high up in the hills of the peninsula's verdant interior. Top right: Seafood risotto in Rovinj (p111)

A Zagreb Coffee Fix

5 Elevated to the status of ritual, having coffee in one of Zagreb's outdoor cafes (p63) is a must, involving hours of people-watching, gossiping and soul-searching, unhurried by waiters. To experience the truly European and vibrant cafe culture, grab a table on the cobbled car-free Tkalčićeva, with its endless streetside cafes, or one of the pavement tables on Trg Petra Preradovića or Bogovićeva (pictured). Don't miss the Saturday morning *špica*, the coffee-drinking and people-watching ritual in the city centre that forms the peak of Zagreb's weekly social calendar.

Flashy, Trashy Hvar

6 Come high summer, there's no better place to dress up and get your groove on than Hvar Town (p239). Gorgeous tanned people descend from their yachts in droves, rubbing shoulders with up-for-it backpackers at après-beach parties as the sun drops below the horizon. While the cashed-up yachtie types keep the town's top-notch restaurants and cocktail bars in business, sun-dazed young revellers do the same for the little dance bars that are the mainstay of the scene. Pack beach gear and shoes suitable for dancing on tables and you'll be sorted.

Unmissable Vis

7 The most remote of Croatia's main islands, Vis (p248) is also one of its most charming. A duo of attractive towns adds historic interest to its northern and western coasts, while hidden to the south and east are some of the nation's most idyllic little coves – some pebbly and some sandy, and all completely irresistible. Scattered around the island in villages, on farms and at isolated beaches are some excellent traditional eateries, while Vis Town has one of the best contemporary restaurants in the whole of Croatia. Bottom: View of Komiža (p251)

The Soul of Split

8 Experience life as it's been lived for thousands of years in Diocletian's Palace (p202; pictured below), one of the world's most imposing Roman remains. The mazelike streets of this buzzing quarter, the living heart and soul of Split, are chock-full of bars, shops and restaurants. Getting lost in the labyrinth of narrow streets, passageways and courtyards is one of Croatia's most enchanting experiences – and it's small enough for you to always find your way out again easily. Escape the palace walls for a drink on the marble-paved, palm-fringed Riva along the water's edge.

Spectacular Korčula

9 Like Dubrovnik in miniature, the sweet little seaside town of Korčula (p282) has its own set of imposing walls and towers but only a fraction of the tourists of its more famous sibling. The highlight is its extraordinary cathedral, adorned with a downright kooky set of carvings. You can walk every one of the marbled streets of its compact old town in an hour, leaving plenty of time for lazing on the beach or heading into the hinterland for a memorable meal a a village *konoba* (tavern). Bottom: Veliki Reveli Tower (p283)

Breezy, Beachy Bol

10 Bol, on the southern coast of Brač Island, is home to the illustrious Zlatni Rat beach (p236; pictured above), with its hornlike shape and golden pebbles. The town is a favourite among windsurfers: the channel between the islands of Brač and Hvar provides ideal wind conditions, thanks to the westerly *maestral* that typically blows between April and October. The wind picks up slowly in the morning, an excellent time for beginners to hit the water. By early afternoon, the winds are strong – perfect for those looking for a real-deal adrenalin kick.

Cracking Krka

11 There are Roman ruins, historic watermills and two fascinating monasteries (one on an island and one built over ancient catacombs), but the star of this highly scenic national park (p192) is the Krka River itself, rushing through canyons, broadening into lakes and splashing over numerous falls and cascades. You can stroll along boardwalks and marvel at the multitude of fish darting through the emerald waters, and then cap off your visit with a dip in a lake at the foot of a mighty waterfall.

Wild Cape Kamenjak

12 It's the wild rugged beauty and end-of-the-world vibe of this small peninsula, just south of Pula, that have earned it cult status among Croatian beach-goers. An undeveloped protected nature reserve, Cape Kamenjak (p108) showcases a carpet of heath plants, shrubs and wildflowers, criss-crossed by a maze of dirt tracks. It's fringed by a string of pebble bays and secluded rocky beaches, surrounded by a crystalline blue-green sea. It gets busy in summer, but there's always an empty beach to escape to, plus a fun beach bar for socialising.

PAUL PRESCOTT / SHUTTERSTOCK ©

Biševo Blue Magic

13 Of the numerous caves on the islets surrounding Vis, Biševo's Blue Grotto (Modra Špilja; p252; pictured above) is the most spectacular. The light show produced by this rare natural phenomenon will amaze you. On a clear morning, the sun's rays penetrate through an underwater hole in this coastal cave, bathing the interior in a mesmerising silvery-blue light. Beneath the iridescent water, rocks glimmer silver and pink, creating an unearthly effect. It's so popular that it's often impossible to swim here in summer, but come later in the season for an unmissable experience.

Kopački Rit – a Wetland Wonder

14 A flood plain of the Danube and Drava Rivers, Kopački Rit (p93), part of a Unesco biosphere reserve, offers breathtaking scenery and some of Europe's best birdwatching. Join a boat trip and keep your eyes peeled for white-tailed and imperial eagles, black storks, purple herons and woodpeckers – just some of the nearly 300 species recorded here. Mammals such as red deer and wild boar are common, too. Explore a flooded forest by canoe, hike the nature trails or saddle up and ride a horse.

De-Stressing on Cres

15 Leafy, sparsely populated and never overwhelmed by tourists, the island of Cres (p148) is unique among Croatia's Adriatic isles. Strolling through the Tramuntana region in the north you might even begin to believe the old people's stories about elves lurking in the ancient forests. At the other end of the island, tiny Osor is a walled town as sleepy as you'll find on the entire coast. Scattered in between are gorgeous beaches, lost-in-time hilltop villages and the pretty pastel-hued harbour of Cres Town.

Storybook Castles of Zagorje

16 The postcard-perfect medieval castles of Zagorje are a prime spot for some time travel. Journey back to 1334 in Trakošćan Castle (p80), although its present-day neo-Gothic exterior is the result of a 19th-century makeover. Learn about Croatian aristocracy in its well-presented museum and wander the 215-acre castle grounds landscaped into a romantic English-style park. Enter the 16th century via the hilltop castle of Veliki Tabor (p80; pictured below), worth a visit for its pentagonal towers and turrets, atmospheric interiors, and the bucolic landscapes that surround it.

Discovering Zadar

17 Set on a peninsula shaped like a hitch-hiker's thumb, the old town of Zadar (p181) has history and culture in spades. Roman ruins protrude haphazardly from the city streets, while museums and churches lurk around every other corner. Artsy types and style-mavens rub shoulders in bars ranging from utterly classy to deliciously divey, while food-lovers frequent the many excellent eateries. Backpackers are well served by some brilliant hostels, while families gravitate to the surrounding beach resorts, and charming boutique hotels reel in the romantics. Bottom: Sun Salutation (p185), architect Nikola Bašić

16

17

Need to Know

For more information, see Survival Guide (p327)

Currency
Kuna (KN)

Language
Croatian

Visas
Generally not required for stays of up to 90 days. Some nationalities (such as Chinese, Indian, Russian, South African, Turkish and Ukrainian) do need them.

Money
ATMs are widely available. Credit cards are accepted in most hotels and restaurants. Smaller restaurants, shops and private accommodation owners only take cash.

Mobile Phones
Users with unlocked phones can buy a local SIM card, which are easy to find. Otherwise, you may be charged roaming rates.

Time
Central European Time (GMT/UTC plus one hour)

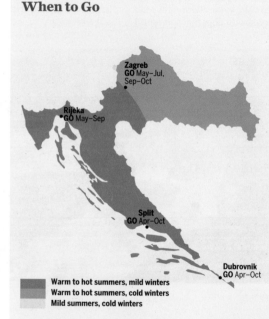

When to Go

Zagreb
GO May–Jul, Sep–Oct

Rijeka
GO May–Sep

Split
GO Apr–Oct

Dubrovnik
GO Apr–Oct

Warm to hot summers, mild winters
Warm to hot summers, cold winters
Mild summers, cold winters

High Season
(Jul & Aug)

➡ Peak season brings the best weather. Hvar Island gets the most sun, followed by Split, Korčula Island and Dubrovnik.

➡ Prices are at their highest and coastal destinations at their busiest.

Shoulder
(May–Jun & Sep)

➡ The coast is gorgeous, the Adriatic is warm enough for swimming, the crowds are sparser and prices are lower.

➡ In spring and early summer, the steady *maestral* wind makes sailing great.

Low Season
(Oct–Apr)

➡ Winters in continental Croatia are cold and prices are low.

➡ Christmas brings a buzz to Zagreb's streets, even with the snow, plus there's skiing too.

Useful Websites

Croatian Tourism (www.croatia.hr) The best starting point to plan your holiday.

Like Croatia (www.likecroatia.hr) An information-packed online guide to Croatia.

Taste of Croatia (www.tasteofcroatia.org) Excellent and informative culinary website.

Parks of Croatia (www.parkovihrvatske.hr) Covers Croatia's national parks and nature parks.

Chasing the Donkey (www.chasingthedonkey.com) Entertaining travel blog by an Aussie family of Croatian extraction living in Dalmatia.

Lonely Planet (www.lonelyplanet.com/croatia) Destination information, hotel bookings, a traveller forum and more.

Important Numbers

To call from outside Croatia, dial your international access code, then the Croatian country code, the area code (without the initial ✆0) and the local number.

Country code	✆385
International access code	✆00
General emergency	✆112
Ambulance	✆194
Roadside assistance	✆1987

Exchange Rates

Australia	A$1	5.24KN
Canada	C$1	5.13KN
Europe	€1	7.50KN
Japan	¥100	6.47KN
New Zealand	NZ$1	4.92KN
UK	UK£1	8.71KN
US	US$1	6.95KN

For current exchange rates, see www.xe.com.

Daily Costs

Budget: Less than 450KN

➡ Dorm bed: 100–325KN

➡ Tent site for two: 100–360KN

➡ Meal in a local tavern: 60KN

➡ Bus, tram or train ticket: 10–150KN

Midrange: 450–1400KN

➡ Double room in a hotel: 450–800KN

➡ Meal in a decent restaurant: 120KN

➡ A city tour by bike: 175KN

➡ Short taxi trip: 30KN

Top End: More than 1400KN

➡ Double room in a luxury hotel: from 800KN

➡ Meal in a top-tier restaurant: 300KN

➡ Private sailing trip: 1000KN

➡ Car rental per day: 450KN

Opening Hours

Opening hours vary throughout the year. We've provided high-season opening hours; hours generally decrease in the shoulder and low seasons.

Banks 8am/9am to 8pm weekdays and 7am–1pm or 8am–2pm Saturdays.

Cafes and Bars 8am/9am to midnight.

Offices 8am–4pm or 8.30am–4.30pm weekdays.

Post Offices 7am–8pm weekdays and 7am–1pm Saturdays. Longer hours in coastal towns in summer.

Restaurants Noon to 11pm/midnight. Often closed Sundays outside peak season.

Shops 8am–8pm weekdays, 8am to 2pm/3pm Saturdays. Some take a 2pm–5pm break. Shopping malls have longer hours.

Arriving in Croatia

Zagreb Airport (p69) Croatia Airlines bus (30KN) leaves from the airport every half-hour or hour from about 4.30am to 8pm. Taxis to the centre cost between 110KN and 200KN (20 minutes).

Split Airport (p217) An airport shuttle bus heads to the main bus station at least 14 times a day (35KN, 30 minutes). Local buses 37 and 38 stop near the airport every 20 minutes, heading to Split (17KN) or Trogir (13KN). Taxis to Split cost between 200KN and 250KN.

Dubrovnik Airport (p272) Atlas runs the airport bus service (40KN, 30 minutes), timed around flights. Buses to Dubrovnik stop at the Pile Gate and the bus station. A taxi costs 250KN to 280KN.

Getting Around

Transport in Croatia is reasonably priced, quick and generally efficient.

Car Useful for travelling at your own pace, or for visiting regions with minimal public transport. Cars can be hired in every city or larger town. Drive on the right.

Bus Reasonably priced, with extensive coverage of the country and frequent departures.

Boat Extensive network of car ferries and faster catamarans all along the coast and the islands.

Air A surprisingly extensive schedule of domestic flights, especially in summer.

Train Less frequent and much slower than buses, with a limited network.

For much more on **getting around**, see p336 ➡

What's New

Zipline, Omiš

Whiz across the mighty Cetina River canyon on a 150m-high zipline. There are eight cables in total, the longest of which runs for 700 scream-inducing metres. (p225)

Obonjan Island

A brand-new holiday resort on a tiny car-free island near Šibenik, Obonjan is a quirky concept, with accommodation in safari-style tents combined with a summer-long festival. (p195)

Buggy Safari Dubrovnik

Catch the cable car up Mt Srđ, high above Dubrovnik, and take a dusty blast in a buggy to a farm and a fort. (p263)

Game of Thrones Tours

It seems that everyone in Dubrovnik's offering one these days, much to the delight of fans of the HBO-produced TV series. You'll run a gauntlet of touts before you even reach Pile Gate.

Vučedol Culture Museum, Slavonia

It may be devoted to a prehistoric culture that most people have never heard of, but that doesn't stop this new museum, 4km down river from Vukovar, from being highly interesting. (p96)

Hostels Galore

Croatia's independent hostel scene continues to improve year-on-year. Our favourite new places include the Pula Art Hostel (p103), Hostel Bol (p237) and Hvar's Earthers Hostel (p243).

Casual Hvar Dining

A couple of chilled-out new eateries offer a tasty alternative to Hvar's swanky dining scene. Fig Cafe Bar (p244) serves delicious breakfasts, while 50 Hvar (p244) offers gourmet burgers with a view.

Zlatna Greda, Slavonia

A new adventure park and accommodation complex have been added to the Zlatna Greda eco-centre, based in a deserted village in Kopački Rit Nature Park in northeastern Slavonia. (p93)

Kopački Rit Nature Park Interpretation Centre

A brace of straw-roofed wooden huts houses Kopački Rit Nature Park's whiz-bang new interpretation centre, with interactive exhibits and a cafe. (p93)

Zagreb's Bistro Explosion

Zagreb has gone bistro crazy over the last couple of years, adding a touch of variety to a dining scene dominated by local-pleasing Croatian and Italian eateries.

Grič Tunnel

Built as an air-raid shelter during WWII, this 350m-long tunnel in Zagreb's Upper Town is now open to the public as a subterranean footpath. (p50)

Museum of Illusion

Kids will love this museum in a converted Zagreb apartment, featuring all sorts of tricksy optical illusions, puzzles and games. (p47)

For more recommendations and reviews, see **lonelyplanet.com/ Croatia**

If You Like...

Walled Towns

Built for defence but breathtakingly picturesque, Croatia's walled towns are among the nation's greatest treasures.

Dubrovnik One of Europe's most visually arresting cities, ringed by monumental defensive walls. (p255)

Ston Dubrovnik aside, this is Croatia's most impressive set of walls – stretching over a mountainside. (p279)

Rovinj The atmospheric old town still has some of its seaward walls and three original gates. (p111)

Trogir Pocket-sized seaside town full of well-preserved Romanesque and Renaissance buildings, and a lovely cathedral. (p219)

Korčula Town One of Croatia's most charming old towns, jutting into the sea enclosed by sturdy walls. (p282)

Osor Small, unassuming and obscure, but gorgeous nonetheless. (p153)

Krk Town Walls still surround the labyrinthine old-town centre. (p160)

Rab Town A profusion of picturesque church towers rises above the walls on its seaward side. (p166)

Poreč An ancient Roman street runs straight through its centre. (p118)

Šibenik Not much wall remains, but its cathedral is the architectural glory of the Dalmatian coast. (p193)

Beaches

Get your kit off or don the latest designer swimsuit on one of the many gorgeous beaches that dot Croatia's coastline and islands.

Zlatni Rat A protrusion of golden pebbles packed with beach bodies and activities galore. (p236)

Stiniva A spectacular and secluded cove of white pebbles within a circle of high cliffs. (p249)

Dubovica Blue waters dazzle against white pebbles in this isolated spot on the island of Hvar. (p241)

Pakleni Islands Pine-shaded beaches for naturists and swimsuit wearers alike. (p246)

Zrće Croatia's summer clubbing capital. (p181)

Lubenice Small, secluded, sensational and difficult to reach. (p152)

Prapratno A pretty, sandy bay on the Pelješac Peninsula. (p279)

Paradise Beach A sandy stunner with shallow waters and the shade of pine trees. (p170)

Brela A string of pine-fringed coves with pebbles. (p225)

Cape Kamenjak Thirty wild kilometres of inlets, coves, pebbles and rocks. (p108)

Local Culinary Specialities

For a real taste of Croatia, hunt down the nation's best homegrown ingredients and traditional dishes.

Truffles Experience Istria's most famous culinary bounty on a truffle hunt in Paladini. (p129)

Olive oil Call ahead to sample Ipša Estate's award-winning olive oils. (p129)

Pršut Sample delicious local prosciutto while sipping on fine wine at Hvar Town's 3 Pršuta. (p245)

Pag cheese and lamb Konoba Figurica is a great place to try Pag Island's renowned specialities. (p181)

Octopus, fish or meat peka Roki's on Vis are masters of this traditional metal-dome cooking technique. (p251)

Dalmatian-style grilled fish A ubiquitous coastal dish, done exceptionally well at Split's Konoba Matejuška. (p214)

Pašticada Dalmatia's meaty stew finds its apotheosis at Trogir's Konoba Trs. (p222)

Brodet/brujet/brodetto We rate Stermasi's version of this classic Dalmatian fish stew. (p279)

Čobanac A traditional Slavonian meat stew; try it at Kod Ruže in Osijek. (p91)

Kremšnite U Prolazu is the best place to try Samobor's famous custard pies. (p73)

Roman Remains

Once positioned near the very heart of the Empire, Croatia has some of the very best Roman structures still standing today.

Split Diocletian's 4th-century palace, complete with an intact temple and mausoleum, remains the city's living heart. (p202)

Pula Along with its magnificent 1st-century amphitheatre, Pula has a complete temple and a triumphal arch. (p101)

Salona Ruins of an entire ancient city, including basilicas, baths, gates and an amphitheatre. (p221)

Brač An intact domed mausoleum is hidden within a museum in the village of Škrip. (p233)

Mljet National Park The remains of a huge palace dominate the town of Polače. (p277)

Krka National Park A secluded corner contains the remains of a military amphitheatre and an aqueduct. (p192)

Poreč Wander through the remains of the forum, including the Temple of Neptune. (p118)

Zadar Roman ruins protrude from the most unlikely places in this ancient city. (p181)

Varaždinske Toplice This still-popular spa centre contains the ruins of Aqua Iasae, a Roman bathhouse. (p81)

Outdoor Activities

There's plenty for active and outdoorsy types to do in

Top: Pag cheese, *pršut* (proscuitto), bread and figs
Bottom: Plitvice Lakes National Park (p173)

Croatia. Start with swimming in the Adriatic and progress to mountain biking, windsurfing, kayaking, climbing, rafting and more.

Paklenica National Park Croatia's prime rock-climbing destination, plus lots of hiking trails. (p176)

Bol Brilliant for windsurfing, swimming, sailing, diving and, in the hinterland, hiking and mountain biking. (p236)

Kopački Rit Nature Park Birdwatching, canoeing, horse riding and a family-friendly adventure park with ziplines. (p93)

Rovinj Great for snorkelling, diving, kayaking, cycling and rock climbing. (p111)

Vis Fascinating sites for advanced divers, great beaches and superb hiking and kayaking. (p248)

Omiš Rafting on and ziplining over the Cetina River, good beaches and mountain hikes. (p224)

Split Sailing, kayaking, and hiking and rock climbing on Marjan Hill. (p202)

Poreč Excellent cycling and hiking trails in the hinterland, plus dive sites nearby. (p118)

Dubrovnik Picturesque kayaking, brilliant beaches and a cable-car ride up to a dusty buggy safari. (p255)

Mt Medvednica Hiking in summer and skiing in winter. (p76)

Nightlife

Croatia has become a hot ticket on Europe's nightlife circuit, pulsating with a variety of options – from beach parties to mega-clubs.

Hvar Town A brilliant bar scene that starts pumping before sunset and doesn't let up. (p245)

Zrće Beach Croatia's answer to Ibiza, this summertime clubbing mecca provides round-the-clock beats. (p181)

Tisno Host to a series of high-profile music festivals in summer, but a sleepy place otherwise. (p191)

Split Tops for nightlife, its palace walls throb with music, especially in the summer months. (p214)

Poreč Istria's party capital has nightlife hawks coming to let loose in its late-night clubs. (p118)

Zagreb Croatia's capital offers cafe-bars galore and a developing artsy music scene. (p63)

National Parks

Croatia's appeal is grounded in nature – its waterfalls, forests, mountains and the dazzling Adriatic coast. Thankfully, much of it is protected – Croatia has eight national parks covering 961 sq km.

Plitvice Lakes This startling natural phenomenon contains forest-fringed waterfalls and turquoise lakes. (p173)

Krka Explore sublime waterfalls and visit a remote monastery. (p192)

Paklenica Experience nature on a big scale, hiking and climbing alongside mountains and canyons. (p176)

Risnjak Shady trails through dense forests and meadows rich in wildflowers. (p143)

Kornati Islands The isles' stark otherworldly beauty is the ultimate resort-free Adriatic escape. (p190)

Mljet Find Mediterranean paradise on this serene and unspoilt island. (p276)

Brijuni This archipelago off the coast of Istria is the most cultivated of Croatia's national parks. (p109)

Islands

Croatia's coast is speckled with a multitude of magnificent islands that range from tiny, verdant and unpopulated to massive, arid and buzzing.

Hvar People come to party on Croatia's sunniest isle, thanks to its glam hub Hvar Town. (p238)

Vis Remote and off-limits to foreigners for decades, it has top beaches, seaside towns and food. (p248)

Mljet Long, slender and beguiling, with a lagoonlike saltwater lake, an island monastery and superb scenery. (p276)

Cres Among Croatia's least touristy islands, with awe-inspiring landscapes, medieval villages and a pretty port. (p148)

Brač Sports Croatia's most famous beach, the alluring Zlatni Rat in the pretty town of Bol. (p232)

Rab The Kvarner isle with the most diverse landscapes, plus beaches and enchantingly ancient Rab Town. (p165)

Pag Sun-scorched scenery akin to the moon, famously pungent cheese and beach clubs. (p178)

Korčula Rich in vineyards, olive groves and scenic hamlets, and featuring the marvellous medieval Korčula Town. (p282)

Kornati Comprised of 140 uninhabited islets and reefs, it's the Adriatic's largest and densest archipelago. (p190)

Lošinj Beautiful bays, lush vegetation and a pair of pretty port towns. (p148)

Month by Month

January

As the country goes back to work after the holidays, snow makes inland roads difficult to tackle, while strong winds on the coast and islands limit the ferry schedule.

🏃 Skiing on Sljeme

Hit the downhill slopes right outside Zagreb at Sljeme, the main peak of Mt Medvednica, complete with ski runs and lifts. Skiing is a popular pastime for sporty Croats. (p76)

◉ Beat the Crowds on the Coast

If you want to explore Croatia's coastal cities, this is the prime time to save some cash. Many hotels offer discounts of up to 50% at this time.

◉ Night of Museums

Dozens of Zagreb's museums and galleries throw open their doors to the public on 31 January for a free slice of culture.

February

Enjoy scenic snowy hikes in continental Croatia but still be mindful on the roads. Bura winds blow along the Adriatic, ferries run infrequently and many hotels in coastal towns shut down.

🎭 Feast of St Blaise

On 3 February each year, the streets of Dubrovnik perk up with folk dancing, concerts, food, processions and lots of street action, all happening in honour of St Blaise, the city's patron saint.

🎭 Carnival

To fully experience the colourful costumes and revelry associated with this pre-Lent celebration, head to Rijeka, where Carnival is the pinnacle of the year's calendar. Zadar, Split, Dubrovnik and Samobor host colourful Carnival celebrations, too. (p141)

March

Days start to get longer and temperatures begin to rise, especially on the seaside. As winter ice melts, it's a great time to catch the waterfalls in Plitvice and Krka. Most action is still indoors.

☆ Zagrebdox

Catch documentary films from around the globe during this annual international festival in Zagreb. Zagrebdox starts in late February and continues into March, drawing a small crowd of avid doco lovers.

April

Soak up some sunshine and enjoy the solitude on southern islands and the coastline. Continental Croatia is still chilly, but trees start to blossom and, as rivers swell with water, rafting and kayaking are tops.

☆ Music Biennale Zagreb

Held in the capital city each April during odd-numbered years since the 1960s, this is Croatia's most high-profile contemporary music event. By 'contemporary', do not read 'pop' – this prestigious fest celebrates modern-day classical music.

🍴 Wild Asparagus Harvest

During early spring, the fields and meadows of inland Istria become dotted with wild asparagus. Do like the locals do and head out to pick some, and then cook up a mean asparagus *fritaja* (omelette).

✴ Holy Week

Holy Week celebrations are particularly elaborate in Korčula. The entire week before Easter is devoted to ceremonies and processions organised by the local religious brotherhoods dressed in traditional costumes.

May

It's sunny and warm on the coast, and you can take a dip in the sea. Hotels are cheaper, too, and crowds have yet to come. Cafe life in Zagreb and Split kicks into full gear.

✴ Sudamja, Split

The 7 May feast of St Domnius, Split's patron saint, is stretched out into a two-week extravaganza starting at the beginning of the month. Expect concerts, rowing races, religious rituals and fireworks. (p211)

✴ Subversive Festival

Mingle with Europe's activists and revolutionaries, who storm Zagreb for this two-week festival each May. The first week hosts a series of film screenings, while the second week's program includes lectures and panels by left-leaning movers and shakers.

✴ Ljeto na Štrosu, Zagreb

Kicking off in late May is this ultra-fun summer-long event that features free outdoor film screenings, concerts by local bands, artsy work-

shops, best-in-show mongrel dog competitions and other quirky happenings, all along the leafy Strossmayer promenade.

🍷 Open Wine Cellar Day

On the last Sunday in May each year, renowned winemakers and winegrowers of Istria open the doors to their wine cellars for free tastings and wine-fuelled merrymaking.

June

Swim in the Adriatic, take in great festivals across the country and enjoy outdoor activities galore. Ferries start their summer schedule, peak-season prices haven't quite kicked in and hotels are still not packed.

✴ Cest is D'Best

For several days in late May through early June, Zagreb's streets come alive with music, dance, theatre, art, sports and other fun events. This street festival is a much-loved affair, with several stages around the city centre and around 200 international performers.

☆ INmusic Festival

Get your groove on during this three-day music extravaganza, which takes over leafy Jarun Lake with multiple stages and spots for camping. This is Zagreb's highest-profile music festival; The Black Keys and Pixies fronted a recent year's line-up. (p57)

🔒 Design District Zagreb

All sorts of things pop up (shops, workshops, studios,

concerts) on Martićeva street during this mini design festival, held over three days in June. (p57)

July

Tourist season is in full swing: hotels along the coast get booked out and beaches are full. Ferries run on their maximum schedule and there are festivals aplenty. A good time to explore Croatia's crowd-free interior.

☆ Hideout

The festival that put Zrće on the electronic-dance-music map takes over the beach bars and clubs in late June/early July. Expect big-name DJs and multiple nights of mayhem. (p180)

☆ Courtyards, Zagreb

For this 10-day festival many of the Upper Town's hidden courtyards are flung open to the public as settings for concerts and other performances. (p57)

☆ Dubrovnik Summer Festival

Kicking off in the middle of July and lasting into late August, this festival has been taking place in Dubrovnik since the 1950s. It features classical music, theatre and dance at different venues around town, including Fort Lawrence. (p265)

☆ Split Summer Festival

Open-air stages are set up for plays, ballet, opera and concerts all over the harbourside city. The festival runs from 15 July right through until 15 August.

☆ Motovun Film Festival, Istria

This film festival, Croatia's most fun and glamorous, presents a roster of independent and avant-garde films in late July each year. Nonstop outdoor and indoor screenings, concerts and parties take over the medieval streets of the hilltop town of Motovun. (p127)

☆ Dance & Nonverbal Theatre Festival

The otherwise sleepy Istrian town of Svetvinčenat comes alive during this late-July festival, which showcases contemporary dance pieces, street theatre, circus and mime acts, and other nonverbal forms of expression. (p133)

☆ Ultra Europe

One of the world's largest electronic-music festivals takes over Split's Poljud stadium for three days in July, before heading to Bol, Hvar and Vis for the rest of the week. (p211)

☆ Full Moon Festival

During this festival held on the night of the full moon, Zadar's quays are lit with torches and candles, stalls sell local delicacies and boats lining the quays become floating fish markets.

August

Tourist season peaks in the Adriatic, with the hottest days and sea temperatures, swarming beaches and highest prices. Zagreb is hot but empty, as people escape to the coast.

☆ Obonjan Island

It spills over into July and September as well, but every day and night during August, this resort island hosts a month-long cultural program including DJ sets, live music, comedy, workshops, talks and yoga. (p195)

☆ Soundwave, Tisno

Kicking off for five nights in August, this dance-music extravaganza features live acts from the alternative, dub and world-music end of the dance-music spectrum. (p191)

☆ Sonus

Five days and nights of electronic music in mid-August take over Pag Island's iconic Zrće Beach. In previous years the festival has featured the likes of John Digweed and Laurent Garnier. (p180)

☆ Vukovar Film Festival

The annual Vukovar Film Festival in late August shows features, documentaries and shorts, mainly from Danubian countries. Visiting is a great way to support this city, as it is still recovering from the war. (p97)

☆ Špancirfest

In late August this eclectic festival enlivens the parks and squares of Varaždin with a rich repertoire of events that range from world music (Afro-Cuban, gypsy, tango and more) to acrobats, theatre, traditional crafts and illusionists. (p83)

September

The summer rush is over, but sunshine is still plentiful, the sea is warm and the crowds have largely gone – it's a great time to visit Croatia. Zagreb becomes alive again after the summer exodus to the coast.

☓ Festival of Subotina, Buzet

The white-truffle season is kicked off with this one-day festival on the second Saturday in September. Stick around to help consume the giant truffle omelette.

☆ Varaždin Baroque Evenings

Baroque music takes over the baroque city of Varaždin for two weeks each September. Local and international orchestras play in the cathedral, churches and theatres around town. (p83)

☆ World Theatre Festival

High-quality contemporary theatre comes to Zagreb for a couple of weeks each year, often extending into early October and delighting the country's die-hard theatre buffs.

October

Children are back in school, parents are at work and the country sways to its regular rhythms. Ferries change to their winter schedule but the weather is still pretty mild.

☆ Zagreb Film Festival

Don't miss this major cultural event that takes place in mid-October each year, with film screenings, accompanying parties, and international film directors

competing for the coveted Golden Pram award.

✕ Truffle Hunting

Go hunting for the prized white and black truffles that grow in the forests around Motovun and Buzet in Istria's interior. Then cook up the smelly fungus and eat it in risotto, pasta and omelettes. (p129)

November

The continent chills but the seaside can still be sunny, albeit not warm. Many hotels along the coast shut their doors for the season, as do many restaurants.

♀ Feast of St Martin

Martinje (St Martin's Day) is celebrated in all the wine-producing regions across Croatia on 11 November. There are wine celebrations and lots of feasting and sampling of new wines.

December

It's freezing everywhere, but marginally less so on the coast. In this deeply Catholic country the churches are fill to bursting for midnight mass on Christmas morning.

☆ Human Rights Film Festival

This film festival sheds light on human rights issues around the world, and takes place for a week each December at Zagreb's Kino Europa.

♀ Fuliranje

Zagrebians brave the freezing temperatures for the mulled wine and street food at this site-shifting Advent market. (p58)

Top: Špancirfest, Varaždin (p83)
Bottom: Christmas ice park, Zagreb (p42)

Itineraries

BOSNIA & HERCEGOVINA

Trogir

Split

Brač

Bol

Hvar Town

Hvar

Korčula Town

Korčula

Dubrovnik

ADRIATIC SEA

1 WEEK Essential Croatia

This itinerary focuses on the essential Croatian experience – a sunny island-hopping trip along the Dalmatian coast. We've envisaged it as a journey that can be made predominantly by ferry. Start with a stroll through the marbled streets of **Trogir**. Either stay for the night or continue on to Croatia's exuberant second city **Split** for a day or two of sightseeing and nightlife. Hop on a passenger ferry to **Bol** on the island of Brač (or alternatively a car ferry to Supetar and then a bus). This pretty little port town is most famous for its striking beach.

Next, catch the fast catamaran to historic **Hvar Town**, the vibrant capital of Hvar Island (alternatively, catch the cat to Jelsa and connect by bus). This picturesque place offers an intriguing mix of European glamour and raucous bars. From Hvar there are year-round connections to **Korčula Town** – a highly photogenic walled town jutting out into the Adriatic. In summer, there are direct fast ferries to Dubrovnik from here, otherwise you'll need to catch the car ferry to Orebić and continue by bus. Your first sight of the magnificent old town of **Dubrovnik** is bound to blow you away. Spend two days taking in its sights.

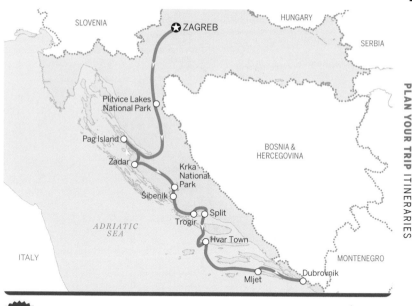

Capital to Coast

Take in the heavyweights of Croatia in this two-week journey, including the capital city, three national parks and the gems of the Dalmatian coast.

Start in the capital, **Zagreb**, and set aside two days to delve into its booming cafe culture, cutting-edge art scene, simmering nightlife and interesting museums. En route south, spend the day at the World Heritage–listed **Plitvice Lakes National Park**, exploring its verdant maze of turquoise lakes and cascading waterfalls. Cut down through the Velebit mountains to the coast and cross onto **Pag Island** to try some of its famously pungent cheese and indulge in its summertime beach club scene. Continue on to **Zadar**, one of Croatia's most underrated cities. It's simultaneously ancient and modern, and packed with attractions.

The following day, stop en route at **Krka National Park** and do the hour-long loop along the boardwalks connecting the little islands in the emerald-green river. End the outing with a swim at the lake below Skradinski Buk, the park's largest waterfall. Continue on to **Šibenik**, another gem of an old town with a truly magnificent cathedral. Next day, stop at **Trogir** to admire the World Heritage–listed walled town sitting on its own little island, then travel south to the buzzing Dalmatian city of **Split** for a two-day fling focused on Diocletian's Palace. If you hired a car, return it here and hop over to chic **Hvar Town** by ferry for a taste of its happening nightlife and for some clothing-optional sunbathing on the Pakleni Islands, immediately offshore.

Catch another ferry to Pomena on the gorgeous island of **Mljet**, gateway to Mljet National Park – you'll get a great view of spectacular Korčula Town from the boat. Walk through the forest and around the salt lakes before hiring a car to drive to the eastern end of the island to spend the night. The following morning, return the car to Pomena and catch the ferry on to **Dubrovnik**. Spend the next two days exploring its old town's gleaming marble lanes, vibrant street life and fine architecture. Note that the Hvar–Pomena–Dubrovnik ferries only operate from May to October. At other times it's easiest to omit Mljet, ferry back to Split and catch the bus to Dubrovnik.

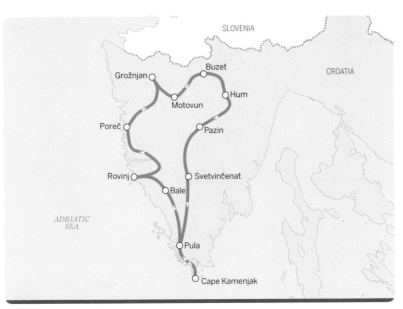

 Highlights of Istria

Explore the Istrian peninsula for its coastal resorts, pretty beaches, hilltop medieval towns, top-rated food, award-winning wines and lovely rural hotels.

Start your trip in **Pula**, the peninsula's coastal capital, home to the remarkably well-preserved Roman amphitheatre that overlooks the city's harbour. Arena, as it's known locally, once hosted gladiatorial contests, seating up to 20,000 spectators; today you can tour its remains and take in the small museum in the chambers downstairs. Base yourself in Pula for two days to see the smattering of other Roman ruins and take at least an afternoon to explore nearby **Cape Kamenjak** by bike or on foot. This entirely uninhabited cape, Istria's southernmost point, features rolling hills, wildflowers (including 30 species of orchid), medicinal herbs and around 30km of virgin beaches and coves.

Stop to check out the captivating town of **Bale**, an offbeat place and one of Istria's best-kept secrets. Push on to **Rovinj** and set aside at least two days for the coast's showpiece resort town. Its steep cobbled streets and piazzas lead up to the Church of St Euphemia, an imposing construction with a 60m-high tower that punctuates the peninsula. Take time to explore the verdant beaches and some of the 14 green islands that make up the Rovinj archipelago just offshore. Zip up the coast to **Poreč** to gape at its World Heritage–listed Euphrasian Basilica, one of Europe's finest intact examples of Byzantine art, with magnificent 6th-century frescoes.

Spend the rest of your trip exploring the peninsula's wooded interior. Drop into music-filled **Grožnjan** before continuing on through to **Motovun**, a similarly artsy hilltop settlement known for its summer film festival. The hilltop town of **Buzet**, known as Istria's truffle epicentre, makes for a good base for exploring the villages of Croatia's foodie heartland, where you can try *pršut* (air-dried ham), olives, excellent wine and, of course, truffles. Stop to wander around the world's smallest town, the adorable **Hum**. Head southwest towards **Pazin** to walk through its famous chasm, which once inspired Jules Verne. On your way back to Pula, make a final stop to stroll through scenic **Svetvinčenat**, with its Renaissance-era square and castle.

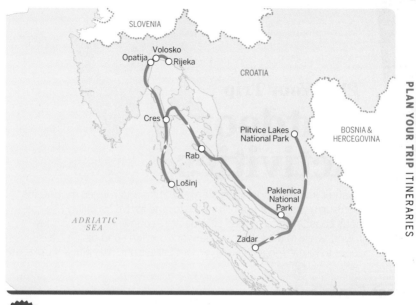

10 DAYS Kvarner & Northern Dalmatia

Take in the delights of Croatia's northern coastal stretches and their wild hinterland, starting with the Kvarner Gulf and moving south to northern Dalmatia with its wide spectrum of appealing sights.

Start in the capital of Kvarner, **Rijeka**, Croatia's third-largest city and a thriving port with a laid-back vibe and a lively cafe scene. Take a day to explore this under-visited city and another to visit the elegant seaside resort town of **Opatija**. Its beautiful belle époque villas date from the dying days of the Austro-Hungarian Empire, when the town was the stomping ground of the Viennese elite. While you're at it, take time to stroll Lungomare, a picturesque path that winds along the coast through exotic bushes and thickets of bamboo to **Volosko**, a pretty fishing village that's become one of Croatia's gastronomic meccas; make sure you have lunch or dinner in one of its acclaimed restaurants.

Next, hop over to one of the Kvarner islands for two days – the interconnected **Cres** and **Lošinj** are the most offbeat. Wilder, greener Cres has remote camping grounds, pristine beaches, a handful of medieval villages and an off-the-radar feel. More populated and touristy Lošinj sports a pair of pretty port towns, a string of beautiful bays and lush and varied vegetation throughout, with 1100 plant species and 230 medicinal herbs, many brought from faraway lands by sea captains. Spend another two days chilling on **Rab**, lounging on the sandy beaches of Lopar peninsula and exploring the postcard-pretty Rab Town with its ancient stone alleys and four bell towers that rise from them.

Back on the mainland, if you're feeling adventurous, don't miss a hike through the alpine trails and stunning canyons of **Paklenica National Park**. Next head down to **Zadar** for an amble through this vibrant coastal city with its medley of Roman ruins, Habsburg architecture and a lovely seafront; stick around for two days to take it all in. Head back inland to spend a day exploring the dazzling natural wonderland of **Plitvice Lakes National Park**, with its gorgeous turquoise lakes linked by a series of waterfalls and cascades.

Plan Your Trip

Outdoor Activities

Croatia's juxtaposition of crystalline waters and rugged mountains opens up a wealth of opportunities for the active traveller. The gorgeous coastline and myriad islands are a renowned boaties' playground, while in the interior, a network of hiking and biking trails gives access to forest-fringed lakes, verdant valleys and magnificent uplands.

Best Experiences

Vis
Swimming in the secluded bays.

Plitvice Lakes National Park
Strolling the lakeside paths – preferably when it's not too busy.

Parenzana Bike Trail
Cycling the 78km Croatian section of this off-road trail in Istria.

Crveni Otok
Snorkelling around the rocky coast of this island near Rovinj.

Split
Shooting the breeze on a day's sailing.

Dubrovnik
Watching the sunset over the old town from atop a kayak.

Bol
Trying your hand at windsurfing on the island of Brač.

Paklenica National Park
Tackling the park's rock-climbing routes.

Cetina River
Rafting along the river near Omiš.

Swimming

If there's just one activity you're planning to partake in during a Croatian holiday, we'd put money on it being this one. Croatia's clear waters are nigh on irresistible on a hot day, and the European Environment Agency rates 94% of Croatia's bathing sites as having excellent water quality. In summer the water temperature can reach over 25°C, and it's usually over 20°C from June right through to October.

There are good swimming spots along the entire coast and throughout the islands. Beaches come in a variety of textures: sandy, shingly, rocky. Some of the best, like blissful little Stiniva (p249), on Vis, and Dubovica (p241), on Hvar, have large smooth white pebbles. Locals tend to favour the pebbly beaches, partly because many of the sandy beaches are extremely shallow. This is especially true of those around Lopar (p170) on Rab, although less so for the sandy beaches at the eastern end of Vis (p248) and places like Prapratno (p279) on the Pelješac Peninsula.

In summer, the Adriatic can more closely resemble a millpond than the sea, but the waves pick up when the wild wind known as the *bora* arrives in winter. During the peak season, however, conditions are generally safe and the main hazards are the sea urchins that reside in the rocky

ADRENALINE-INDUCING ACTIVITIES

Visiting daredevils will find activities scattered throughout the country to satisfy their adrenaline needs.

Starting at the gentler end of things, Dubrovnik's cable car (p261) heads up to a height of 405m, offering an unbeatable eagle's-eye view of the famous old town. Another one suitable for the whole family is the new set of ziplines at Zlatna Greda (p93) in Kopački Rit Nature Park. On a similar theme, but more hair-raising, are the eight ziplines (p225) over the Cetina canyon near Omiš; the highest is 150m up, while the longest stretches for 700m. There's also a zipline over the 100m-deep Pazin Chasm (p131) in Istria.

Paragliding Kvarner (p139), based in Crikvenica near Rijeka, offers tandem flights taking off from 770m above the Adriatic. In Istria, you can take a tandem paragliding ride from Motovun (p126), while in Slavonia, Parafreek (www.parafreek.hr) offers jumps from a launch site near Japetić (879m), the highest peak of the Samoborsko range.

On the island of Krk, the Cable Krk Wakeboard Center (p162) offers both wakeboarding and waterskiing. If you fancy trying skydiving, contact the Croatian Aeronautical Federation (www.caf.hr). Another worthwhile contact is the local extreme-sports association Cro Challenge (www.crochallenge.com).

As with all activities in Croatia, it's often easiest to arrange them though a specialist adventure agency. Here are some worthwhile operators:

Alter Natura (p252) Vis-based adventure specialists, offering trekking, kayaking and abseiling.

Biokovo Active Holidays (p226) Hiking, cycling, canyoning, rafting and kayaking trips.

Huck Finn (www.huckfinncroatia.com) Specialises in adventure travel and runs the gamut of adrenaline-lifting tours around Croatia: river and sea kayaking, rafting, canoeing, caving, cycling, fishing, hiking and sailing.

Hvar Adventure (p241) Sailing, cycling, climbing, hiking, windsurfing, sky-diving, jeep safaris and triathlon training.

Outdoor (www.outdoor.hr) Adventure and team-building travel.

Portal Trogir (p222) Quad-bike safaris, rafting, diving, canyoning.

Red Adventures (p209) Based in Split and offering sea kayaking, rock climbing, hiking and bike tours.

Zagreb Tours (p56) Adventure tours, among other offerings.

---

shallows. Many people wear plastic swimming shoes as a precaution.

Away from the coast, popular swimming spots include the lakes at Krka National Park (p192), Zagreb's Bundek (p56) and Jarun (p55) lakes, and the island of Ada (p97), on the Danube, near Vukovar.

Hiking

Hiking in Croatia can be as untaxing as a slow stroll around the boardwalks and well-maintained lakeside trails of Plitvice (p173) or as challenging as an assault on the high reaches of Paklenica (p176). Lo-

cal tourist and national-park offices are well equipped to recommend a walk to suit your time constraints and level of ability. Many produce their own free walking maps or sell detailed maps for more remote areas. If you're contemplating a serious expedition, consider contacting the Croatian Mountaineering Association (p73), which can provide information and access to a network of mountain huts, or joining a guided walk organised by one of the many agencies specialising in adventure tourism.

Spring, early summer and autumn are prime hiking times, beating the worst of both the crowds and the summer sun. The karstic coastal mountains roast in July and

August, offering very little shade or water – while the leafy trails of Plitvice and Krka get clogged with people. In these months, try less-visited Risnjak National Park (p143) or head even further inland.

The mountains near Samobor (p73) offer the best hiking in Croatia's interior, featuring forests, caves, river canyons, waterfalls and nine mountain huts. Medvednica Nature Park (p76), north of Zagreb, is also good.

In Istria, there are trails around Buzet (p128) and Poreč (p120), and a well-marked 11.5km circular hiking track leading from Gračišće (p133). The Kvarner region offers off-the-beaten-track hiking in both Učka Nature Park (p148) and Risnjak National Park (p143). Risnjak's Leska Path is a recommended, easy 4.2km trail through the forest where you might even spot wildlife. The islands of Cres (p148), Lošinj (p148) and Rab (p165) also have a wealth of good trails.

Dalmatia is spoilt for choice, but the most obvious hiking highlights are the national parks Plitvice (p173), Krka (p192) and Paklenica (p176), and Biokovo Nature Park (p232). The first two offer plenty of easy lakeside strolls, although they do get insanely busy in summer. Paklenica and Biokovo are both mountainous terrains, offering superb views over the coast and islands. There are also brilliant walks on the islands of Brač (p232), Hvar (p238), Vis (p248), Lastovo (p287) and Mljet (p276), and in the mountains above Omiš (p224) and Orebić (p280).

Cycling

Bicycle touring is increasingly popular in Croatia, both independently or with organised groups. Bike hire is easy to arrange and there are plenty of relatively quiet roads to explore, especially on the islands. Try to avoid the main Adriatic highway – there are no bike lanes, few passing spaces and it's extremely busy. Thankfully much of it can be bypassed by catching ferries; bikes can be taken on car ferries for a small additional charge but not on most catamarans.

March, April, September and October are the best cycling months, with mild, mostly dry weather. The traffic is much busier from June to August, and it can get extremely hot.

Slavonia has a couple of excellent long-distance trails (p93): the 80km Pannonian Peace Route between Osijek and Sombor in Serbia, and the 138km Danube Route, tracing the Hungarian and Serbian border.

The best route, however, is the Parenzana Bike Trail (p124), which follows a former railway line between the Italian city of Trieste and Poreč in Istria (the Croatian section is 78km long). Also in Istria, there are bike trails around Buzet, Pazin, Poreč and Rovinj, and an unchallenging 41km cycling trail from Pula to Medulin.

Kvarner is another great region for cyclists, with 19 routes around Opatija, Učka Nature Park and the islands of Cres, Lošinj, Krk and Rab detailed in the *Kvarner by Bicycle* brochure, available from local tourist offices.

In Dalmatia, there are scenic cycling trails on the islands of Mljet and Lastovo. The *Central Dalmatia Bike* brochure details six routes on the Makarska Riviera, ranging from an easy 15km ride around Makarska to a gruelling 61km climb up Biokovo to a height of 1749m. Biokovo is also good for mountain bikers, as are the islands of Korčula and Brač, where trails lead to the island's highest point, Vidova Gora (778m).

Useful websites with information for cyclists (not all in English) include www.mojbicikl.hr, www.pedala.hr and www.istria-bike.com.

Diving & Snorkelling

The most striking thing about the Adriatic coast is the clarity of the water. Snorkelling is a worthwhile exercise pretty much everywhere, although there are some extra special spots, such as Crveni Otok (p101) near Rovinj.

The area's turbulent history has also bequeathed it with numerous interesting underwater sights, from wrecks dating to antiquity through to a downed WWII plane. The latter is off the coast of Vis (p249), where there's also an amphorae field and shipwrecks to explore – although the most interesting sites here are at depths that require technical diving skills.

Other famous wrecks include: the *Taranto*, an 1899 Italian merchant ship sunk by a WWII mine off Dubrovnik; a 3rd-century Roman ship and a German

Above: Krka National Park (p192)

Right: Pilgrim hervia (sea slug) in the Adriatic sea

DAVID HAVEL / SHUTTERSTOCK ©

Rock climbing in Paklenica National Park (p176)

Sailing was once the exclusive preserve of the rich, but Croatia now offers plenty of more affordable opportunities for both day sails and organised multiday tours. Operators such as Sail Croatia (www.sail-croatia.com) even target cruises to young backpacker types.

If you'd prefer to go it alone, it's an easy matter to charter a boat, either with a skipper or, if you're suitably experienced, on a 'bareboat' basis. Useful contacts include the Adriatic Croatia International Club (www.aci-marinas.com), which manages 22 marinas, and the following charter companies: Cosmos Yachting (www.cosmosyachting.com), Nautical Centre Nava (p211), Sunsail (p265), Ultra Sailing (p211), White Dust Sailing (p103), Yacht Rent (p139) and Yacht Charter Croatia (www.croatiacharter.com).

Kayaking

Kayaking, of both the sea and the river varieties, is a popular activity in Croatia. Kayaks can be hired from numerous locations, and there are many specialist operators offering both short paddles and multiday island-hopping expeditions.

It's particularly popular in Dubrovnik, where you'll see great shoals of kayakers heading out on guided trips – with sunset paddles being especially well subscribed. There are also good crews operating out of Makarska, Split, Cape Kamenjak, Rovinj and the islands of Korčula, Vis and Rab.

Inland, don't miss the opportunity to kayak on the Danube at Vukovar, and on Zagreb's Jarun Lake.

Windsurfing

Croatia's two prime windsurfing locations are Bol (p236) on the island of Brač and Viganj (p281), near Orebić on the Pelješac Peninsula. Both are exposed to the *maestral*, a strong constant westerly that generally blows from morning to early afternoon from April to October. The optimum conditions tend to be at the end of May/early June and the end of July/early August.

Other good spots include Hvar Town, Makarska, Mali Lošinj, Cape Kamenjak and Poreč, and you can even windsurf inland on Zagreb's Jarun Lake. At all of these locales you can hire boards and take lessons.

WWII torpedo boat off the island of Mljet; the *Rosa,* off Rab; the *Peltastis,* a 60m Greek cargo ship, off Krk; and the *Baron Gautsch,* an Austrian passenger steamer sunk by a mine near Rovinj during WWI.

On top of that there are plenty of reefs, drop-offs and caves to investigate. Marine life includes scorpionfish, conger eels, sea snails, sea slugs, octopuses, lobsters, the rare giant mussel, red coral, red gorgonian fans and colourful sponges.

There are diving centres all along the coast, with particular hot spots being Poreč, Pula and Rovinj in Istria; the islands of Krk, Cres, Lošinj and Rab in the Kvarner area; the Dalmatian islands of Dugi Otok, Brač, Hvar, Vis and Mljet; and Dubrovnik. For further information, refer to the Croatian-only website of the Croatian Diving Association (www.diving-hrs.hr).

Sailing

Could there be a more blissful holiday than gliding between remote islets and otherwise hard-to-access beaches all day, before finding a pretty spot to moor for the night?

Rock Climbing

Croatia's best rock climbing is in Paklenica National Park (p176), with graded climbs for all levels of ability including 72 short sports routes and 250 longer routes. A rescue service is also available. Sticking in Dalmatia, there are climbing crags on Marjan hill, right in the centre of Split.

Heading up the coast, there are a couple of sites near Baška (p162) on Krk Island. The best climbing in Istria is in the Punta Corrente Forest Park (p113) near Rovinj, which has 80 climbing routes in a defunct Venetian stone quarry. Free climbing is also possible near Buzet and Pazin.

There's also a famous rock-climbing area in the Plešivica section of the Samoborsko Gorje range (p73), west of Zagreb.

March, April and May are the best months for climbing, before the summer heat kicks in. The wind tends to pick up in autumn and winter.

The easiest way to get started is to enquire at local tourist offices or to contact one of the local agencies specialising in adventure tourism. The Croatian Mountaineering Association (p73) also has some information on their website (in Croatian).

Rafting

Croatia's prime rafting locale is the Cetina River (p224), which spills through a steep gorge and into the Adriatic at Omiš. It's an easy matter to join a trip in the pretty little town, as operators tout for business by the riverside. Otherwise, specialist adventure agencies in Split and Makarska organise transfers and expeditions with reputable rafting companies.

Trips are possible from around April to October, with the fastest flows in April and after heavy rains. In summer it's a more gentle experience, of more interest to first-timers.

Skiing

Only 20 minutes from Zagreb, the Sljeme Ski Resort (p76) has lifts heading up to five downhill runs on the side of Mt Medvednica. The best snow cover is in February, but the season can stretch for three to four months with the use of snow-making equipment. Night skiing is also possible.

Wildlife Watching

Croatia's premier wildlife-watching spot is Kopački Rit Nature Park (p93) in Slavonia, a significant wetlands on the flood plain of the rivers Danube and Drava. Nearly 300 species of bird have been spotted here, including white-tailed and imperial eagles, black storks, great crested grebes, purple herons, spoonbills, wild geese and woodpeckers. They're joined by 44 species of fish and 21 different kinds of mosquito (bring repellent). If you're extremely lucky, you might spot some of its mammalian inhabitants, such as red deer, wild boar, beavers, pine martens and foxes. The best time for spotting birdlife is during the spring (March to May) and autumn (September to November) migrations.

The Kvarner region is also rich in wildlife. The mighty griffon vulture roosts on the islands of Cres, Krk and Prvić, while Lošinj has centres devoted to the preservation of sea turtles and dolphins. Risnjak National Park (p143) is named after the lynx, which lives in the virgin forest here alongside brown bears, wolves, chamois and wild boar. You're unlikely to see these superstars of the forest, but you might spot deer at feeding stations along the tracks and you're bound to see some of the 500 species of butterfly.

Despite the summertime hordes, Plitvice Lakes National Park (p173) hides bears, wolves, deer and boar, alongside rabbits, foxes and badgers. If you can divert your gaze from the waterfalls, you might spot hawks, owls, cuckoos, kingfishers, wild ducks, herons, black storks and ospreys.

In Dalmatia, Paklenica National Park (p176) is home to various birds of prey, while Krka National Park (p192) has eagles and migratory marsh birds.

Plan Your Trip
Travel with Children

With safe beaches, hiking and biking tracks to suit all abilities, a clutch of interactive museums, and lots of ancient towns and fortresses for would-be knights and princesses to explore, Croatia offers entertainment aplenty for those with children in tow.

Best Regions for Kids

Dubrovnik & Southern Dalmatia
Offers lots of beach action and unique experiences; let the littl'uns off the leash in the car-free old towns of Dubrovnik and Korčula.

Split & Central Dalmatia
Wander the maze that is Diocletian's Palace and then head to the beaches of the Makarska Riviera.

Northern Dalmatia
Kids are fascinated by Zadar's nature-powered Sun Salutation and Sea Organ. Šibenik hosts an excellent children's festival.

Istria
Poreč and Rovinj are great bases for exploring nearby caves, dinosaur parks and beaches.

Zagreb
Ride the funicular, check out the many museums, get active at Jarun and Bundek, and hike up to the mountain peak of Sljeme.

Inland Croatia
Savour a slice of Croatian country life at Vuglec Breg and Grešna Gorica, tour the interactive Neanderthal museum in Krapina and visit medieval castles.

Croatia for Kids

Croatia has a lot of open spaces, playgrounds aplenty and pedestrian zones where there's no danger of traffic. Most seaside towns have a *riva* (seafront promenade) away from the water's edge that's perfect for strolling and letting the toddlers run around.

There are beaches galore, although some of what are referred to as 'beaches' are rocky indentations with steep drop-offs. Many of the sandy beaches are extremely shallow: perfect for toddlers but not so great for the teens. The numerous pebbly beaches tend to offer better swimming.

Keep in mind that some of Croatia's smaller seaside towns can be too quiet for fun-seeking teenagers. They (and you in turn) will be a lot happier in the more happening coastal destinations where there are buzzy cafes and seasonal funfair rides.

Children's discounts are widely available for everything from museum admissions to hotel accommodation. The cut-off age is often nine, when student discounts kick in. Many attractions offer free entry for the little ones.

Eating with Kids

The generally relaxed dining scene means that you can take the children almost anywhere. Even the more upmarket restaurants will have a kid-friendly pasta, pizza or rice dish on the menu. Children's portions are easily arranged. However, you won't often find high chairs for the tinier tots, and dining establishments are rarely equipped with nappy-changing facilities.

Locals are quite happy to take their children out for dinner to restaurants, and you'll often see kids running around on the square while the adults are eating, drinking and chatting. Children eat mostly the same food as the adults, and everyone tucks into an ice cream at the end of the meal.

Babies

Breastfeeding in public is uncommon, but is generally accepted if done discreetly. Specific baby-friendly facilities are still thin on the ground, although that is slowly changing.

Baby food, disposable nappies and powdered baby formulas are easily found at supermarkets and pharmacies.

Hazards

Those spending a lot of time in forests during spring, summer or early autumn should make sure that they check the kids for ticks. If you do find one, go to a doctor immediately. Be mindful of the numerous sea urchins in the shallows, particularly on rocky beaches; invest in some plastic water shoes for safer playing.

Children's Highlights

Beaches

Baška, Krk Island (p162) A 2km-long crescent of beach with a little waterpark at one end.

Cres & Lošinj Islands (p148) Lots of family-friendly campsites set right by the beach.

Crveni Otok, Rovinj (p117) Two connected islets awash with pebble beaches.

Lopar, Rab Island (p170) Shallow, sandy beaches that are perfect for toddlers.

Mljet National Park, Mljet Island (p277) The smaller of the saltwater lakes is warm and perfect for babies.

Museums & Sights

Technical Museum Nikola Tesla, Zagreb (p55) A quirky museum with a planetarium and a replica mine.

Museum of the Krapina Neanderthal, Krapina (p80) Get up close and personal with our ancestors.

Sun Salutation, Zadar (p185) Come sunset, tots have a ball racing around this marvellous light display.

Batana House, Rovinj (p113) Multimedia interactive displays illustrate Rovinj's fishing history.

Kumrovec Staro Selo Museum (p77) An entertaining slice of traditional village life.

Istralandia, Istria (www.istralandia.hr) Shoot down the slides and ride the waves in this big water park.

Planning

Consider renting a private apartment – they're usually cheaper than a hotel room and give you more flexibility. Make sure you ask for specifics about the facilities – whether there's air-conditioning, a full kitchen and laundry facilities, and how far the beach is, for example.

Hotels may have cots, but numbers are usually limited and sometimes there's a surcharge. Kids under three often stay for free, while those under nine get a considerable discount. Most properties in Croatia are family-friendly but few are family specialists. Of those, the best are Club Funimation Borik (p186) near Zadar and Hotel Vespera (p155) in Mali Lošinj.

When to Go

The coastal city of Šibenik hosts a renowned International Children's Festival (p196) in late June/early July, with craft workshops, music, dance, children's film and theatre, puppets and parades. July and August coincide with the European school holidays, so they tend to have the most laid on for kids. If you'd prefer fewer people and lower prices, June and September are the best times, as the sea is warm enough for swimming and the days are sunny.

Regions at a Glance

Zagreb

Cafes
Museums
Food

Cafe Culture

Zagreb is a bastion of Europe's famed cafe culture. The prime time to experience the peak of its social calendar is during the coffee-sipping and people-watching ritual known as *špica,* which happens on warm-weather Saturday mornings, when everyone and their mother comes out to show off their latest outfits.

Eclectic Collections

Zagreb's cultural flagship, the Museum of Contemporary Art, has brought an artistic flavour to the city's streetscape, while the quirky Museum of Broken Relationships has quickly become a favourite since opening a few years ago.

Modern Croatian Cuisine

On the food front, there is plenty to explore in Croatia's capital, where the culinary scene has diversified in recent years. A handful of destination restaurants showcase Croatia's unique style of cooking, prepared with high-quality ingredients from around the country.

p42

Inland Croatia

Architecture
Wildlife
Scenery

Castles

Fairy-tale castles dot the wooded hills of this bucolic region. The neo-Gothic Trakošćan offers an intimate insight into the life of former Croatian nobility, while the formidable Veliki Tabor, complete with towers, turrets and other castle trimmings, looks down from a hilltop. There are further examples in Varaždin, Varaždinske Toplice, Vukovar and Ilok.

Birdwatching

One of Europe's most important wetlands, Kopački Rit Nature Park occupies the floodplain where the Danube meets the Drava. Internationally famed for its diverse birdlife, the park is best visited during the spring or autumn migrations.

Rural Vistas

The pretty pastoral panoramas of Zagorje's vineyard-covered hills and dense forests, and Slavonia's verdant fields and gingerbread cottages are the stuff of storybooks. Savour traditional Croatian farm life as it unfolds away from the tourist hullabaloo down south.

p72

Istria

Food
Architecture
Coast

Istrian Cuisine

Indulge in *la dolce vita* Istrian-style, feasting on meals prepared in creative ways using top-quality local ingredients. From white truffles and wild asparagus to award-winning olive oils and wines, dining and wining is a highlight of any stay in Istria, Croatia's most foodie-friendly place.

Historic Buildings

Istria's hotchpotch of architecture includes a world-famous Roman amphitheatre and a Byzantine basilica, along with Venetian-style town houses and medieval hilltop towns, all packed tightly and prettily into one small peninsula.

Beaches

From pine-fringed, activity-packed pebbly beaches a hop and a skip from Pula, Rovinj and Poreč, to the wild landscapes of Cape Kamenjak and its string of secluded coves, Istria has some wonderful beaches – just no sandy ones.

p99

Kvarner

Architecture
Wildlife
Food

Medieval Towns

Krk Town has a beautifully preserved medieval core, while the small but perfectly formed Rab Town features a string of historic churches and bell towers. The town houses in Cres Town, Veli Lošinj and Mali Lošinj all show strong Venetian influences.

Marine Life

The connected islands of Lošinj and Cres each boast excellent wildlife projects: in tiny Veli Lošinj you'll find a fascinating Adriatic dolphin research centre, while up in Mali Lošinj there's a centre devoted to rescuing sea turtles.

Gourmet Villages

The tiny villages of Volosko and Kastav, between Opatija and Rijeka, are gastronomic hotbeds of Croatian cooking – both traditional and modern – with a clutch of high-quality, atmospheric *konobas* (taverns) and restaurants.

p136

Northern Dalmatia

Nature
Cities
Sailing

Mountains & Lakes

Most visitors come to Dalmatia for the coast, but this region also has a highly appealing hinterland. Krka and Plitvice showcase lovely lakes and exquisite waterfalls. Head to Paklenica for soaring mountains and great hiking.

Living Historic Cities

Northern Dalmatia's two cities both offer culture and history while being far from touristy. Šibenik arguably has Croatia's most elegant cathedral and a remarkable old quarter, while the walled town of Zadar offers up Roman ruins, intriguing sights, hip bars and restaurants.

Island-Dotted Waters

See the Mediterranean as it looked to the ancients, sailing between the isles of Kornati National Park, the largest and densest archipelago in the Adriatic, with 140 uninhabited islands.

p171

Split & Central Dalmatia

Coast
Architecture
Activities

Beaches

From fun-filled Bačvice, Split's adored city beach, to horn-shaped Zlatni Rat on Brač Island, to the adorable pebbly and sandy coves of Vis Island, Central Dalmatia has some of Croatia's best beaches – both popular and off the well-worn trail.

Ancient Town Centres

Two Unesco World Heritage Sites sit a quick drive from one another in Central Dalmatia: the buzzing Roman-era quarter that is Diocletian's Palace in Split, and the architectural medley of Trogir's compact old walled town, set on its own tiny island.

Outdoor Pursuits

Be it sailing, mountain biking, sea kayaking, diving, hiking, rafting, rock climbing, ziplining or windsurfing, active travellers will find plenty of distraction in Central Dalmatia's varied environment.

p199

Dubrovnik & Southern Dalmatia

History
Nature
Wine

Walled Towns

One of the world's most evocatively situated and historic cities, Dubrovnik is a dream to look at, a delight to explore and a wrench to leave. The much smaller but gorgeous Korčula Town offers a similarly affecting experience.

Islands

The thinly populated, pine-forested islands of Mljet and Korčula are rightfully acclaimed for their natural beauty and beaches. But don't neglect little Lokrum and the lovely Elafitis.

Dalmatian Varietals

The unspoilt Pelješac Peninsula is Croatia's premier wine region. Try the rich, vibrant, local red *plavac mali* while visiting vineyards in the prestigious appellations of Postup and Dingač. Neighbouring Korčula is renowned for its white wines from the *pošip* and *grk* grapes, while the Konavle region, south of Dubrovnik, has its own endemic white, *malvasija*.

p253

On the Road

Zagreb

♪ 01 / POP 790,000

Best Places to Eat

➜ Vinodol (p62)

➜ Mundoaka Street Food (p62)

➜ Zinfandel's (p62)

➜ Bistro 75 (p60)

➜ Mali Bar (p62)

Best Places to Sleep

➜ Studio Kairos (p58)

➜ Esplanade Zagreb Hotel (p59)

➜ Swanky Mint Hostel (p59)

➜ Hotel Jägerhorn (p59)

Why Go?

Zagreb has culture, arts, music, architecture, gastronomy and all the other things that make a quality capital city – it's no surprise that the number of visitors has risen sharply in recent years. Croatia's coastal attractions aside, Zagreb has finally been discovered as a popular city-break destination in its own right.

Visually, Zagreb is a mixture of straight-laced Austro-Hungarian architecture and rough-around-the-edges socialist structures, its character a sometimes uneasy combination of the two elements. This small metropolis is made for strolling the streets, drinking coffee in the permanently full cafes, popping into museums and galleries, and enjoying the theatres, concerts and cinema. It's a year-round outdoor city: in spring and summer everyone scurries to Jarun Lake in the southwest to swim or sail, or dance the night away at lakeside discos, while in winter Zagrebians go skiing at Mt Medvednica (only a tram or bus ride away).

When to Go
Zagreb

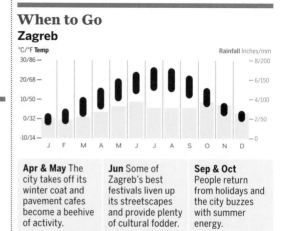

Apr & May The city takes off its winter coat and pavement cafes become a beehive of activity.

Jun Some of Zagreb's best festivals liven up its streetscapes and provide plenty of cultural fodder.

Sep & Oct People return from holidays and the city buzzes with summer energy.

History

Zagreb's known history begins in medieval times with two hills: Kaptol, now the site of Zagreb's cathedral, and Gradec. When the two settlements merged in 1850, Zagreb was officially born.

The space now known as Trg Bana Jelačića became the site of Zagreb's lucrative trade fairs, spurring construction around its edges. In the 19th century the economy expanded with the development of a prosperous clothing trade and a rail link connecting Zagreb with Vienna and Budapest. The city's cultural life blossomed, too.

Zagreb also became the centre for the Illyrian movement. Count Janko Drašković, lord of Trakošćan Castle, published a manifesto in Illyrian in 1832 and his call for a national revival resounded throughout Croatia. Drašković's dream came to fruition when Croatia and its capital joined the Kingdom of Serbs, Croats and Slovenes after WWI.

Between the two world wars, working-class neighbourhoods emerged in Zagreb between the railway and the Sava River, and new residential quarters were built on the southern slopes of Mt Medvednica. In April 1941 the Germans invaded Yugoslavia and entered Zagreb without resistance. Ante Pavelić and the Ustaše moved quickly to proclaim the establishment of the Independent State of Croatia (Nezavisna Država Hrvatska), with Zagreb as its capital. Although Pavelić ran his fascist state from Zagreb until 1944, he never enjoyed a great deal of support within the capital, which maintained support for Tito's Partisans.

In postwar Yugoslavia, Zagreb (to its chagrin) took second place to Belgrade but continued to expand. Zagreb was made the capital of Croatia in 1991, the same year that the country became independent.

◎ Sights

As the oldest part of Zagreb, the Upper Town (Gornji Grad), which includes the neighbourhoods of Gradec and Kaptol, has landmark buildings and churches from the earlier centuries of Zagreb's history. The Lower Town (Donji Grad), which runs between the Upper Town and the train station, has the city's most interesting art museums and fine examples of 19th- and 20th-century architecture.

◎ Lower Town

Trg Bana Jelačića   SQUARE

Zagreb's main orientation point and its geographic heart is Trg Bana Jelačića – it's where most people arrange to meet up. If you enjoy people-watching, sit in one of the cafes and watch the tramloads of people getting out, greeting each other and dispersing among the newspaper- and flower-sellers.

The square's name comes from Ban Jelačić, the 19th-century *ban* (viceroy or governor) who led Croatian troops into an unsuccessful battle with Hungary in the hope of winning more autonomy for his people. The **equestrian statue** of Jelačić stood in the square from 1866 until 1947, when Tito ordered its removal because it was too closely linked with Croatian nationalism. Franjo Tuđman's government dug it up out of storage in 1990 and returned it to the square.

Archaeological Museum   MUSEUM

(Arheološki Muzej; ☑ 01-48 73 101; www.amz.hr; Trg Nikole Šubića Zrinskog 19; adult/concession/family 20/10/30KN; ⊙ 10am-6pm Tue, Wed, Fri & Sat, to 8pm Thu, to 1pm Sun) The artefacts housed here stem from prehistoric times onwards. Among the most interesting are the **Vučedolska golubica** (Vučedol Dove), a 4000-year-old ceramic censer found near the town of Vukovar – the 'bird' has since become a symbol of Vukovar and peace. The courtyard has a collection of **Roman monuments** dating from the 5th to 4th centuries BC.

Also inside are some fascinating Egyptian mummies, with ambient sounds and light designed to provoke pondering. The collection of some 260,000 coins, medals and medallions is one of the most important in Europe.

Zrinjevac   SQUARE

Officially called Trg Nikole Šubića Zrinskog but lovingly known as Zrinjevac, this verdant square at the heart of the city has become a vital part of Zagreb. It's filled with stalls almost year round, and features festivals and events, be it summer or winter. Most are centred on the music pavilion (dating from 1891).

Zrinjevac is part of the Green Horseshoe, also known as Lenuci Horseshoe, a U-shaped series of seven city squares with parks.

Gallery of Modern Art   GALLERY

(Moderna Galerija; ☑ 01-60 41 040; www.moderna-galerija.hr; Andrije Hebranga 1; adult/concession 40/20KN; ⊙ 11am-7pm Tue-Fri, to 2pm Sat & Sun)

ZAGREB SIGHTS

Zagreb Highlights

1 **Tkalčićeva**
(p63) Sipping coffee and cocktails alfresco-style along this chic strip.

2 **Museum of Broken Relationships**
(p52) Gaping at the remains of failed romances at this quirky museum.

3 **Upper Town**
(p43) Strolling along the winding streets of this ancient part of town.

4 **Museum of Contemporary Art**
(p55) Tapping into Croatia's current art beat in this stunning city icon.

5 **Maksimir Park**
(p54) Picnicking and strolling in the rambling wooded enclave.

6 **Mirogoj** (p54) Contemplating mortality amid the trees and tombs.

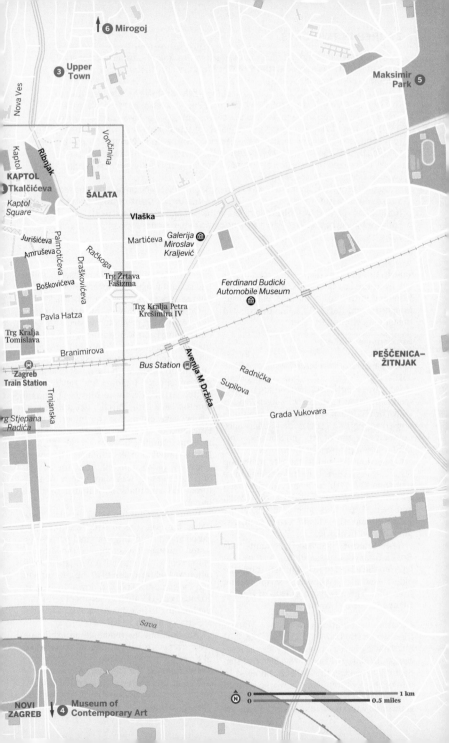

6 **Mirogoj**

3 **Upper Town**

Maksimir Park 5

Nova Ves

Vončinina

KAPTOL

Kaptol

Ribnjak

Tkalčićeva

Kaptol Square

ŠALATA

Vlaška

Jurišićeva

Palmotićeva

Amruševa

Martićeva

Galerija Miroslav Kraljević

Draškovićeva

Račkoga

Boškovićeva

Trg Žrtava Fašizma

Ferdinand Budicki Automobile Museum

Pavla Hatza

Trg Kralja Petra Krešimira IV

Trg Kralja Tomislava

Branimirova

PEŠČENICA–ŽITNJAK

Bus Station

Avenija M. Držića

Radnička

Zagreb Train Station

Supilova

Trnjanska

Grada Vukovara

rg Stjepana Radića

Sava

NOVI ZAGREB

4 **Museum of Contemporary Art**

N

0   1 km
0   0.5 miles

ZAGREB IN TWO DAYS

Start your day with a stroll through Strossmayerov trg, Zagreb's oasis of greenery. Take a look at the **Strossmayer Gallery of Old Masters** and then walk to **Trg Bana Jelačića** (p43), the city's centre.

Head up to **Kaptol Square** for a look at the **Cathedral of the Assumption of the Blessed Virgin Mary** (p54), the centre of Zagreb's religious life. While in the Upper Town, pick up some fruit at the **Dolac Market** (p54) or have lunch at **Amfora** (p62). Then get to know the work of Croatia's best sculptor at **Meštrović Atelier** (p52) and see its naive art legacy at the **Croatian Museum of Naïve Art** (p52), followed by a visit to the quirky **Museum of Broken Relationships** (p52). See the lay of the land from the top of **Lotrščak Tower** (p51), then spend the evening bar-crawling along Tkalčićeva (p63).

On the second day, tour the Lower Town museums, reserving an hour for the **Museum Mimara** (p47) and another one for the **Museum of Contemporary Art** (p55). Lunch at **Vinodol** (p62) and digest in the **Botanical Garden** (p47). Early evening is best at **Trg Petra Preradovića** before dining and sampling some of Zagreb's nightlife.

Take in this glorious display of Croatian artists from the last 200 years, including such 19th- and 20th-century masters as Bukovac, Mihanović and Račić. It's a fine overview of the nation's vibrant arts scene.

Strossmayer Gallery of Old Masters
GALLERY

(Strossmayerova Galerija Starih Majstora; ☎ 01-48 95 117; http://info.hazu.hr/the_strossmayer_gallery_of_old_masters; Trg Nikole Šubića Zrinskog 11; adult/concession/family 30/10/50KN; ⊘ 10am-7pm Tue, to 4pm Wed-Fri, to 1pm Sat & Sun) This museum is housed in the 19th-century neo-Renaissance Croatian Academy of Arts and Sciences – this lovely building showcases the impressive fine-art collection donated to the city by Bishop Strossmayer in 1884. It includes Italian masters from the 14th to 19th centuries, such as Tintoretto, Veronese and Tiepolo; Dutch and Flemish painters such as Brueghel the Younger; and the classic Croatian artists Medulić and Benković.

The interior courtyard contains the **Baška Slab** (Bašćanska Ploča), a stone tablet from the island of Krk, which features the oldest example of Glagolitic script, dating from 1102. There is also a **statue of Bishop Strossmayer** by Ivan Meštrović.

Croatian Association of Artists
GALLERY

(Hrvatsko Društvo Likovnih Umjetnika; ☎ 01-46 11 818; www.hdlu.hr; Trg Žrtava Fašizma 16; adult/concession 20/10KN; ⊘ 10am-1pm & 4-8pm Wed-Sun) East of the centre, this gallery is housed in one of the few architectural works by Ivan Meštrović and has a diverse repertoire of art shows and various events – a must on the art circuit of Zagreb. The building itself has also had several fascinating incarnations, reflecting the region's history in a nutshell.

Originally designed by Meštrović in 1938 as an exhibition pavilion, the structure honoured King Petar Karađorđević, the ruler of the Kingdom of Serbs, Croats and Slovenes – which grated against the sensibilities of Croatia's nationalists. With the onset of a fascist government, the building was renamed the Zagreb Artists' Centre in May 1941; several months later Ante Pavelić, Croatia's fascist leader, gave orders for the building to be evacuated of all artwork and turned into a mosque (claiming it was to make the local Muslim population feel at home). There were murmurs of disapproval from the artists, but the building was significantly restructured and eventually surrounded by three minarets.

With the establishment of socialist Yugoslavia, however, the mosque was promptly closed and the building's original purpose restored – though it was renamed the Museum of the People's Liberation. A permanent exhibition was set up and in 1949 the government had the minarets knocked down. In 1951 an architect called V Richter set about returning the building to its original state according to Meštrović's design.

The building has remained an exhibition space ever since, with a nonprofit association of Croatian artists making use of it. Despite being renamed the Croatian Association of Artists in 1991 by the country's new government, everyone in Zagreb still knows it as 'the old mosque'.

Ferdinand Budicki
Automobile Museum   MUSEUM
(www.otk-ferdinandbudicki.hr; Ulica kneza Ljudevita Posavskog 48; adult/concession 30/20KN;
⊙10am-7pm) Croatia's first automobile museum, it showcases more than 50 classic cars
(including a 1922 Ford Model T) and motorcycles in 1500 sq metres of a former cork factory in east Zagreb. The museum was named
after the man who in 1901 brought the first
car to Croatia. A must for car aficionados.

Art Pavilion   GALLERY
(Umjetnički Paviljon; ☑01-48 41 070; www.umjet
nicki-paviljon.hr; Trg Kralja Tomislava 22; adult/con-
cession 40/25KN; ⊙11am-8pm Tue-Thu, Sat & Sun,
to 9pm Fri) The yellow Art Pavilion presents
changing exhibitions of contemporary art.
Constructed in 1897 in stunning art-nouveau
style, the pavilion is the only space in Zagreb
that was specifically designed to host large
exhibitions.

Botanical Garden   GARDENS
(Botanički Vrt; ☑01-48 98 060; Marulićev trg 9a;
⊙9am-2.30pm Mon & Tue, to 7pm Wed-Sun Apr-
Oct) FREE If you need a change from museums and galleries, take a break in this lovely,
verdant retreat. Laid out in 1890, the garden
has 10,000 species of plants and plenty of
restful corners and paths.

Museum Mimara   MUSEUM
(Muzej Mimara; ☑01-48 28 100; www.mimara.
hr; Rooseveltov trg 5; adult/concession 40/30KN;
⊙10am-7pm Tue-Fri, to 5pm Sat, to 2pm Sun Jul-
Sep, 10am-5pm Tue, Wed, Fri & Sat, to 7pm Thu, to
2pm Sun Oct-Jun) This is the diverse private
art collection – Zagreb's best – of Ante Topić
Mimara, who donated over 3750 priceless
objects to his native Zagreb (even though he
spent much of his life in Salzburg, Austria).
Housed in a neo-Renaissance former school
building (1883), the collection spans a wide
range of periods and regions.

Inside you'll find an archaeological section with 200 items; exhibits of ancient Far
Eastern artworks; a glass, textile and furniture collection that spans centuries; and
1000 European art objects. In the painting
collection, check out works by Raphael,
Caravaggio, Rembrandt, Bosch, Velázquez,
Goya, Manet, Renoir and Degas.

Ethnographic Museum   MUSEUM
(Etnografski Muzej; ☑01-48 26 220; www.emz.hr;
Mažuranićev trg 14; adult/concession 20/15KN;
⊙10am-6pm Tue-Fri, to 1pm Sat & Sun) The ethnographic heritage of Croatia is catalogued

in this museum housed in a domed 1903
building. Out of 70,000 items, about 2750 are
on display, including ceramics, jewellery, musical instruments, tools, weapons and folk
costumes, such as gold-embroidered scarves
from Slavonia and lace from the island of
Pag. Thanks to donations from the Croatian
explorers Mirko and Stevo Seljan, there are
also artefacts from South America, Ethiopia,
China, Japan and Australia.

Arts & Crafts Museum   MUSEUM
(Muzej za Umjetnost i Obrt; ☑01-48 82 123; www.
muo.hr; Trg Maršala Tita 10; adult/concession/family
40/30/70KN; ⊙10am-7pm Tue-Sat, to 2pm Sun)
Built between 1882 and 1892, this museum
exhibits furniture, textiles, metal, ceramic
and glass ranging from the Middle Ages
to today. You can see Gothic and baroque
sculptures from northern Croatia, as well as
paintings, prints, bells, stoves, rings, clocks,
bound books, toys, photos and industrial design. The museum hosts frequent temporary
exhibitions.

Museum of Illusion   MUSEUM
(www.muzejiluzija.com; Ilica 72; adult/concession/
family 40/25/100KN; ⊙9am-10pm; 🖝) Housed
in an apartment building, this newcomer
delivers a fantastic sensory adventure to visitors of all ages. Children in particular are in
for a great time. The Slanted Room or the

ZAGREB'S CONTEMPORARY ART GALLERIES

Zagreb's palpable creative energy is
driven by a host of young ambitious
artists and curators who think outside
the box. The city has a variety of places
where you can catch home-grown
art. If you want to discover new art
trends in Croatia, check out **Galerija
Greta** (www.greta.hr; Ilica 92; ⊙5-8pm)
FREE, **Galerija Studentski Centar**
(☑01-45 93 602; galerija.sczg.hr; Savska
25; ⊙noon-8pm Mon-Fri, 10am-1pm Sat)
FREE, **Galerija Nova** (☑01-48 72
582; www.whw.hr/galerija-nova; Teslina 7;
⊙noon-8pm Tue-Fri, 11am-2pm Sat) FREE,
Lauba (p55), **Galerija Miroslav
Kraljević** (www.g-mk.hr; Šubićeva 29;
⊙noon-7pm Tue-Fri, 11am-1pm Sat) FREE
and the Croatian Association of Artists
(p46). Note that many of these shut
their doors in August so check before
you head there.

Zagreb

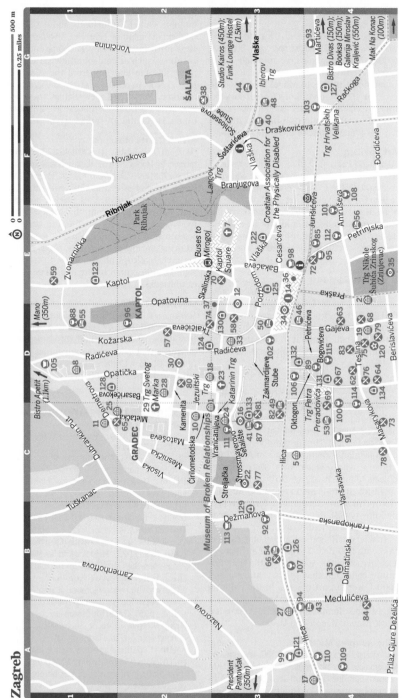

N

0   0.25 miles
0   500 m

ŠALATA

Vončinina

Novakova

Ribnjak

Park
Ribnjak

Zamenhoffova

Studio Kairos (450m);
Funk Lounge Hostel (1.5km)

Vlaška

Iblerov
Trg

Marticéva

Bistro Divas (150m);
Booksa (150m);
Galerija Miroslav
Kraljević (550m)

Mak Na Konac (100m)

Račkoga

127

103

Schlosserove
Stube

Draškovićeva

Trg Hrvatskih
Velikana

Đorđeva

Šoštarićeva

Langov
Trg

Branjugova

Vlaška

Croatian Association for
the Physically Disabled

Jurišićeva

Amruševa

101

108

Petrinjska

56

Buses to
Mirogoj

Kaptol
Square

Vlaška

Cesarčeva

Bakačeva

85

112

95

Trg Nikole
Šubića Zrinskog
(Zrinjevac)

35

KAPTOL

Zvonarnička

Kaptol

Opatovina

Skalinska

Podrtom Vlaška

Praška

GRADEC

Mano (350m)

Kožarska

Radićeva

Tkalčićeva

Opatička

Bistro Apetit
(1.1km)

Dubravkin Put

Basaričekova

Dimitrova

Mletačka

Visoka

Mesnička

Ćirilometodska

Opatička

Trg Svetog
Marka

Kamenita

Jezuitski
Trg

Katarinin Trg

Matoševa

Vranicanijeva

Strossmayerovo
Šetalište

Museum of Broken Relationships

Streljačka

Zakmardijeve
Stube

Petra
Preradovića

Bogovićeva

Gajeva

Teslina

Berislavićeva

Trg Petra
Preradovića

Oktogon

Petrićeva

Ilica

Ilica

Varšavská

Frankopanska

Dežmanova

Medulićeva

Masarykova

Dalmatinska

Prilaz Gjure Deželića

Tuškanac

Nazorova

President
Pantovčak
(350m)

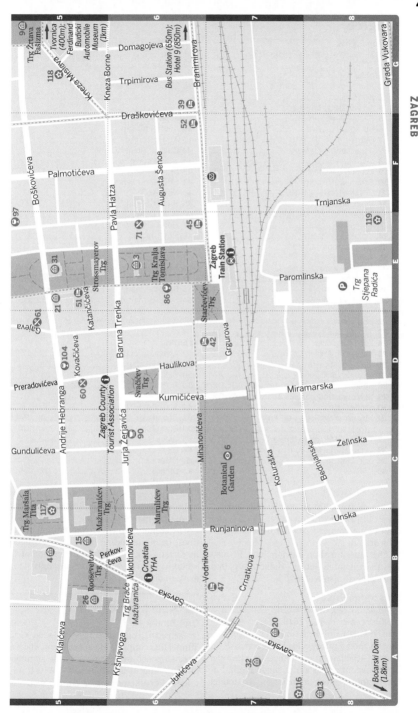

Trg Žrtava Fašizma

Tvornica (400m); Ferdinand Budicki Automobile Museum (1km)

Kneza Mislava

Kneza Borne

Domagojeva

Trpimirova

Draškovićeva

Bus Station (650m); Hotel 9 (850m)

Branimirova

Grada Vukovara

Palmotićeva

Boškovićeva

Pavla Hatza

Augusta Šenoe

Trnjanska

Strossmayerov Trg

Katančićeva

Baruna Trenka

Trg Kralja Tomislava

Zagreb Train Station

Paromlinska

Trg Stjepana Radića

Preradovićeva

Kovačićeva

Andrije Hebranga

Zagreb County Tourist Association

Gundulićeva

Jurja Žerjavića

Haulikova

Starčevićev Trg

Kumičićeva

Grgurova

Miramarska

Mihanovićeva

Koturaška

Bedrijanska

Zelinska

Botanical Garden

Trg Maršala Tita

Mažuranićev Trg

Marulićev Trg

Runjaninova

Unska

Klaićeva

Rooseveltov Trg

Perkovčeva

Vukotinovićeva

Savska

Croatian YHA

Vodnikova

Crnatkova

Trg Braće Mažuranića

Kršnjavoga

Jukićeva

Savska

Bočarski Dom (1.8km)

Zagreb

Mirror of Truth are among 70-plus intriguing exhibits, hologram pictures, puzzles and educational games that offer up a fun mental workout.

The museum shop has fabulous 3D puzzles and Dilemma Games – didactic toys that make a perfect souvenir.

Backo Mini Express   MUSEUM
(☑ 01-48 33 226; www.backo.hr; Gundulićeva 4; adult/concession/family 20/15/55KN; ⊙ 10am-6pm Fri & Sat) Children and tech lovers fall for this model railway displayed across 75 sq metres – the largest in southeastern Europe. The museum consists of a single room, but the hypnotic effect of gazing at 102 model trains choo-chooing across 1050m of railway more than makes up for it.

The scenery is meticulously crafted to the finest detail, including tiny people engaged in various activities. The 'wow' moment is seeing a train through a transparent floor drive underneath your feet.

⊙ Upper Town

Grič Tunnel   TUNNEL
(⊙ 9am-9pm) FREE The mystery-laden Grič Tunnel that connects Mesnička and Radićeva streets opened to the public in the summer of 2016. Built in 1943 for use as a WWII air-raid shelter and rarely used since – except for

the legendary rave party that took place here in 1993 – it is now yours to cross.

At the time of research there wasn't much to see inside this 350m-long tunnel, though walking under the Upper Town is a great way to beat the heat. Enter from Mesnička or by the new Art Park below Stross and get out in a passageway just off Ilica, next door to NAMA department store. There are ambitious plans to turn the tunnel into an interactive Museum of the Senses.

Lotrščak Tower　　　　HISTORIC BUILDING
(Kula Lotrščak; Strossmayerovo Šetalište 9; adult/concession 20/10KN; ⊙9am-9pm Mon-Fri, 10am-9pm Sat & Sun) The tower was built in the middle of the 13th century in order to protect the southern city gate. Climb it for a sweeping 360-degree view of the city. Near the tower is a **funicular railway** (ticket 4KN; ⊙6.30am-10pm), constructed in 1888, which connects the Lower and Upper Towns.

For the last 100 years a cannon has been fired from the tower every day at noon, allegedly to commemorate one day in the mid-15th century when the cannon was fired at noon at the Turks, who were camped across the Sava River. On its way down, the cannonball happened to hit a rooster, which was blown to bits – according to legend, this was so demoralising for the Turks that they decided not to attack the city. (A less fanciful explanation is that the cannon shot allows churches to synchronise their clocks.)

★ Museum of Broken Relationships
MUSEUM

(www.brokenships.com; Ćirilometodska 2; adult/concession 30/20KN; ☺9am-10.30pm Jun-Sep, 9am-9pm Oct-May) Explore mementoes that remain after a relationship ends at Zagreb's quirkiest museum. The innovative exhibit toured the world until it settled here in its permanent home (it recently opened a second location in Hollywood, too!). On display are donations from around the globe, in a string of all-white rooms with vaulted ceilings and epoxy-resin floors.

Exhibits hit on a range of emotions, from a vinyl record that was played during a teen-age breakup 40 years ago to a stun gun that never got to be used. Check out the lovely adjacent store – the 'bad memories eraser' is a bestseller – and the cosy cafe with side-walk tables. There are jazz nights on Thursdays during summer and fall.

Jesuit Church of St Catherine
CHURCH

(Crkva Svete Katarine; Katarinin trg bb; ☺Mass 6pm Mon-Fri, 11am Sun) This fine baroque church was built between 1620 and 1632. Although battered by fire and earthquake, the facade still gleams and the interior contains a fine altar dating from 1762; the interior stucco work dates from 1720. Look for the 18th-century medallions depicting the life of St Catherine on the ceiling of the nave.

Galerija Klovićevi Dvori
GALLERY

(☑01-48 51 926; www.gkd.hr; Jezuitski trg 4; entry varies by exhibit, up to 40KN; ☺11am-7pm Tue-Sun) Housed in a former Jesuit monastery, the gallery is among the city's most prestigious spaces for exhibiting modern Croatian and international art. Past exhibits have in-cluded Picasso and Chagall, as well as col-lections by prominent Croatian fine artists. The gallery's atrium hosts concerts in July as part of the Evenings on Grič festival. There's a nice cafe here also.

Croatian Museum of Naïve Art
MUSEUM

(Hrvatski Muzej Naivne Umjetnosti; ☑01-48 51 911; www.hmnu.hr; Ćirilometodska 3; adult/concession 25/15KN; ☺10am-6pm Mon-Sat, to 1pm Sun) If you like Croatia's naive art – a form that was highly fashionable locally and worldwide during the 1960s and 1970s and has de-clined somewhat since – this small museum will be a feast. It houses around 1900 paint-ings, drawings and some sculptures by the discipline's most important artists, such as Generalić, Mraz, Rabuzin and Smajić.

St Mark's Church
CHURCH

(Crkva Svetog Marka; Trg Svetog Marka 5; ☺Mass 7.30am & 6pm Mon-Fri, 7.30am Sat, 10am, 11am & 6pm Sun) This 13th-century church is one of Zagreb's most emblematic buildings. Its col-ourful tiled roof, constructed in 1880, has the medieval coat of arms of Croatia, Dalmatia and Slavonia on the left side, and the emblem of Zagreb on the right. The Gothic portal, composed of 15 figures in shallow niches, was sculpted in the 14th century. The interior contains sculptures by Ivan Meštrović. You can enter the anteroom only during opening hours; the church is open only at Mass times.

From late April to October there's a guard-changing ceremony outside the church every Saturday and Sunday at noon.

Sabor
HISTORIC BUILDING

(Trg Svetog Marka 6) The eastern side of Trg Svetog Marka is taken up by the Croatian *sabor* (parliament), built in 1910 on the site of baroque 17th- and 18th-century town houses. Its neoclassical style is quite incongruous on the square, but the historical importance of this building is undeniable – Croatia's seces-sion from the Austro-Hungarian Empire was proclaimed from its balcony in 1918.

Meštrović Atelier
GALLERY

(☑01-48 51 123; www.mestrovic.hr; Mletačka 8; adult/concession 30/15KN; ☺10am-6pm Tue-Fri, to 2pm Sat & Sun) Croatia's most recognised art-ist is Ivan Meštrović. This 17th-century build-ing is his former home, where he worked and lived from 1922 to 1942; the excellent collection it houses has some 100 sculptures, drawings, lithographs and pieces of furniture from the first four decades of his artistic life. Meštrović, who also worked as an architect, designed many parts of the house himself.

Croatian Natural History Museum
MUSEUM

(Hrvatski Prirodoslovni Muzej; ☑01-48 51 700; www.hpm.hr; Demetrova 1; adult/concession 20/15KN; ☺10am-5pm Tue, Wed & Fri, to 8pm Thu, to 7pm Sat, to 1pm Sun) This museum houses a collec-tion of prehistoric tools and bones excavated from the Krapina cave, as well as exhibits showing the evolution of animal and plant life in Croatia. Temporary exhibits often fo-cus on specific regions.

City Museum
MUSEUM

(Muzej Grada Zagreba; ☑01-48 51 926; www.mgz.hr; Opatička 20; adult/concession/family 30/20/50KN; ☺10am-6pm Tue-Fri, 11am-7pm Sat, 10am-2pm Sun; ⛶) Since 1907, the 17th-century Convent of St Claire has housed this historical museum,

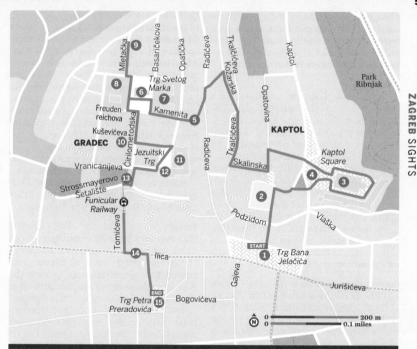

Walking Tour
Architecture, Art & Street Life

START TRG BANA JELAČIĆA
END TRG PETRA PRERADOVIĆA
LENGTH 1KM; 1½ HOURS

The natural starting point of any walk in Zagreb is buzzing ① **Trg Bana Jelačića** (p43), the city's main meeting point. Climb the steps up to ② **Dolac Market** (p54) and pick up some fruit or a quick snack before heading for the neo-Gothic ③ **Cathedral of the Assumption of the Blessed Virgin Mary** (p54). Cross ④ **Kaptol Square**, lined with 17th-century buildings, walk down Skalinska and come out at Tkalčićeva. Wander up the street, then climb the stairs that will take you up to ⑤ **Stone Gate** (p54), a fascinating shrine and the eastern gate to medieval Gradec Town. Next, go up Kamenita and you'll come out at Trg Svetog Marka, the site of the 13th-century ⑥ **St Mark's Church** (p52), which has a colourful tiled roof; the ⑦ **Sabor** (p52), the country's parliament; and ⑧ **Banski Dvori**, the presidential palace. Wander through the winding streets of the Upper Town, and find out more about

Ivan Meštrović, Croatia's most renowned artist, in ⑨ **Meštrović Atelier** (p52). Walk back across Trg Svetog Marka and down Ćirilometodska, stepping into one of the country's most singular museums, the ⑩ **Croatian Museum of Naïve Art** (p52). Cross Jezuitski trg and enter ⑪ **Galerija Klovićevi Dvori** (p52), where local and international contemporary art exhibitions await. When you're finished with art, gaze up at the gorgeous ⑫ **Jesuit Church of St Catherine** (p52), before finally emerging at ⑬ **Lotrščak Tower** (p51), built in the middle of the 13th century and today offering dazzling 360-degree vistas of the city. Near the tower is a historic funicular railway, constructed in 1888, which connects the Lower and Upper Towns. Take in the cityscape then go down in the funicular, or take the verdant stairway – either will leave you on the side of ⑭ **Ilica**, Zagreb's commercial artery.

Cross Ilica and walk to ⑮ **Trg Petra Preradovića**, known to locals as Cvjetni trg, where you can take a break at one of the many outdoor cafes.

which presents the history of Zagreb through documents, artwork and crafts, as well as interactive exhibits that fascinate kids. Look for the scale model of old Gradec. Summaries of the exhibits are posted in English.

Stone Gate   GATE

(Kamenita Vrata) Make sure you take a peek at the Stone Gate, the eastern gate to medieval Gradec Town, now a shrine. According to legend, a great fire in 1731 destroyed every part of the wooden gate except for the painting of the Virgin and Child (by an unknown 17th-century artist). People believe that the painting possesses magical powers and come regularly to pray, light candles and leave flowers. Square stone slabs are engraved with thanks and praise to the Virgin.

On the western facade of the Stone Gate you'll see a statue of Dora, the hero of an 18th-century historical novel, who lived with her father next to the Stone Gate.

Tortureum – Museum of Torture   MUSEUM

(📝 01-64 59 803; www.tortureum.com; Radićeva 14, 1st fl; adult/concession/family 40/25/100KN; ⏥ 11am-7pm) Horror buffs will love the display of 70-plus full-scale historic instruments of torture. But seeing, touching and trying out the 1792 guillotine replica, pendulum, rack or iron maiden gives more than a sensationalist take on violence. Experiencing the museum's multisensory rooms, such as the semi-dark Cabinet of Wonders or the Dungeon, will prompt questions about human vulnerability and the issues of today's hidden forms of torture, such as bullying or domestic violence.

You can also enter from Tkalčićeva 13.

Dolac Market   MARKET

(⏥ open-air market 6.30am-3pm Mon-Sat, to 1pm Sun, covered market 7am-2pm Mon-Fri, 7am-3pm Sat, 7am-1pm Sun) Zagreb's colourful fruit and vegetable market is just north of Trg Bana Jelačića. Traders from all over Croatia come to sell their products at this buzzing centre of activity. Dolac has been heaving since the 1930s, when the city authorities set up a market space on the 'border' between the Upper and Lower Towns.

The main part is on an elevated square; the street level has indoor stalls selling meat and dairy products and (a little further towards the square) flowers. The stalls at the northern end of the market are packed with locally produced honey, handmade ornaments and cheap food.

Cathedral of the Assumption of the Blessed Virgin Mary   CHURCH

(Katedrala Marijina Uznešenja; Kaptol 31; ⏥ 10am-5pm Mon-Sat, 1-5pm Sun) Kaptol Sq is dominated by this cathedral, formerly known as St Stephen's. Its twin spires – seemingly permanently under repair – soar over the city. Although the cathedral's original Gothic structure has been transformed many times over, the sacristy still contains a cycle of **frescoes** dating from the 13th century. An earthquake in 1880 badly damaged the cathedral; reconstruction in a neo-Gothic style began around the turn of the 20th century.

Inside, don't miss the baroque marble altars, statues and pulpit, or the tomb of Cardinal Alojzije Stepinac by Ivan Meštrović.

Mirogoj   CEMETERY

(Aleja Hermanna Bollea 27; ⏥ 6am-8pm Apr-Oct, 7.30am-6pm Nov-Mar) A 10-minute ride north of the city centre (or a 30-minute walk through leafy streets) takes you to one of the most beautiful cemeteries in Europe, sited at the base of Mt Medvednica. It was designed in 1876 by Austrian-born architect Herman Bollé, who created numerous buildings around Zagreb. The majestic arcade, topped by a string of cupolas, looks like a fortress from the outside, but feels calm and graceful on the inside.

The lush cemetery is criss-crossed by paths and dotted with sculptures and artfully designed tombs. Highlights include the grave of poet Petar Preradović and the bust of Vladimir Becić by Ivan Meštrović.

Take bus 106 from the Cathedral of the Assumption of the Blessed Virgin Mary.

◉ Maksimir

Maksimir Park   PARK

(📝 01-23 20 460; www.park-maksimir.hr; Maksimirski perivoj bb; ⏥ info centre 10am-4pm Tue-Fri, to 6pm Sat & Sun) The park, a peaceful wooded enclave covering 18 hectares, is easily accessible by trams 11 and 12 from Jelačić square. Opened to the public in 1794, it was the first public promenade in southeastern Europe. It's landscaped like an English garden, with alleys, lawns and artificial lakes.

The most photographed structure in the park is the exquisite Bellevue Pavilion, constructed in 1843. Also here is the Echo Pavilion, as well as a house built to resemble a rustic Swiss cottage. Zagreb Zoo (www.zoo.hr; adult/child/under 7yr 30/20KN/free; ⏥ 9am-8pm, ticket booth to 6.30pm) has a modest collection of the world's fauna and daily feeding times for seals, sea lions, otters and piranhas.

Novi Zagreb

Museum of Contemporary Art MUSEUM
(Muzej Suvremene Umjetnosti; ☑ 01-60 52 700; www.msu.hr; Avenija Dubrovnik 17; adult/concession 30/15KN; ⊙ 11am-6pm Tue-Fri & Sun, to 8pm Sat) Housed in a stunning city icon designed by local star architect Igor Franić, this swanky museum displays both solo and thematic group shows by Croatian and international artists in its 17,000 sq metres. The permanent display, *Collection in Motion*, showcases 620 edgy works by 240 artists, roughly half of whom are Croatian. There's a packed year-round schedule of film, theatre, concerts and performance art.

Inside, note the fun interactive *Double Slide* piece by Belgian artist Carsten Holler, and the stirring *Ženska Kuća* installation by Croatia's foremost artist, Sanja Iveković, dealing with the theme of violence against women.

Admission is free on the first Wednesday of each month. On summer Saturdays catch concerts on the rooftop.

Western Zagreb

Lauba GALLERY
(☑ 01-63 02 115; www.lauba.hr; Baruna Filipovića 23a; adult/concession 25/10KN; ⊙ 3-11pm Mon-Fri & Sun, 11am-11pm Sat) This private art collection, housed in a former textile-weaving mill in an industrial area of western Zagreb, provides an insight into Croatian contemporary art from the 1950s to today. Works on display change frequently, with an exciting roster of events, and there's the cool Lauba Bistro (p63) on site.

Technical Museum Nikola Tesla MUSEUM
(Tehnički Muzej Nikola Tesla; www.tehnicki-muzej. hr; Savska 18; adult/concession 20/15KN; ⊙ 9am-5pm Tue-Fri, to 1pm Sat & Sun; ⊞) Take your kids to the Technical Museum, which features a **planetarium** (entry 15KN, not recommended for children under seven), steam-engine locomotives, scale models of satellites and space ships, and a replica of a mine, as well as departments of agriculture, geology, energy and transport. Free admission for children under seven.

Dražen Petrović Memorial Museum MUSEUM
(☑ 01-48 43 146; www.drazenpetrovic.net; Trg Dražena Petrovića 3; adult/child 20/10KN; ⊙ 10am-

5pm Mon-Fri, to 2pm Sat) Basketball is popular in Zagreb, which is home to the Cibona basketball team. Pay homage to the team's most famous player at the Dražen Petrović Memorial Museum, next to the Technical Museum. Games take place frequently at the Cibona Tower (p67) nearby.

🏃 Activities

Jarun Lake WATER SPORTS
Jarun Lake in south Zagreb is a popular getaway for residents at any time of the year, but especially in summer, when the clear waters are ideal for swimming. Although part of the lake is marked off for boating competitions, there is plenty of space to enjoy a leisurely swim. Other recreational options include biking, rollerblading and kids' parks.

On arrival, head left to Malo Jezero for swimming and canoe or pedal-boat rental, or right to Veliko Jezero, where there's a pebble beach and windsurfing.

Take tram 5 or 17 to Jarun and follow signs to the *jezero* (lake).

Sports Park Mladost SWIMMING
(☑ 01-36 58 553; Jarunska 5, Jarun; day ticket adult/child/family weekend 30/25/100KN, weekday 25/20/60KN; ⊙ noon-7pm Mon-Fri, 10am-7pm Sat & Sun; ⊞) Set by the Sava River, this park has outdoor and indoor Olympic-size swimming pools, as well as smaller pools for children, a gym, volleyball and basketball courts and tennis courts. To get to Jarun, take tram 5 or 17.

Sports & Recreational Centre Šalata SWIMMING
(☑ 01-46 17 255; Schlosserove Stube 2; day ticket adult/child/family weekend 30/20/60KN, weekday 20/15/40KN; ⊙ 1.30-6pm Mon-Fri, 11am-7pm Sat & Sun; ⊞) The centre offers outdoor and indoor

tennis courts, a gym, a winter ice-skating rink and two outdoor swimming pools (open June through September). There's also an indoor ice-skating rink that rents out skates.

👉 Tours

Secret Zagreb TOURS

(www.secret-zagreb.com; per person 75KN) A thorough ethnographer and inspiring story-teller, Iva Silla is the guide who reveals the Zagreb of curious myths and legends and peculiar historical personalities. Take her hit walking tour Zagreb Ghosts and Drag-ons (which runs year round) to peek into the city's hidden corners or forgotten grave-yards, all set in the city centre.

Seasonal tours include 13 Days of Hallow-een, Zagreb Christmas Carol and Into the Forest; the last is a perfect way to explore Mt Medvednica.

Blue Bike Tours CYCLING

(📞098 18 83 344; www.zagrebbybike.com; Trg Bana Jelačića 15) To experience Zagreb on a bike, book one of the tours that run twice daily at 10am and 5pm from May through September (2pm only from October to April); choose between Ancient or Novi Zagreb. Tours last around 2½ hours and cost 190KN. The four-

hour combo tour of both options costs 290KN. They also rent bikes for 100KN per day between 10am and 8pm.

Funky Zagreb Tours TOURS

(www.funky-zagreb.com) Personalised tours that range in theme from wine tasting (450KN for 2½ to three hours) to hiking in Zagreb's sur-roundings, mainly the hills around Samobor (from 865KN per person for a day trip).

Zagreb Bites FOOD & DRINK

(📞091 52 88 723; www.zagrebites.com) For a guided tour of Zagreb food, wine and craft-beer hot spots you wouldn't easily find your-self, book with this venture started by a pair of renowned Croatian food bloggers. They also run excursions to the wine regions near Zagreb and organise supper-club dinners on request.

Segway City Tour TOURS

(www.zagreb.segwaycitytour.hr) See Zagreb by riding a Segway. This tour has daily depar-tures, by prior booking, starting at 250KN for a 50-minute ride.

Zagreb Tours TOURS

(📞01-48 25 035; www.zagreb-tours.com) Offers trips from Zagreb to Zagorje, specialising in cultural, spa and adventure tourism.

ZAGREB FOR CHILDREN

Zagreb has some wonderful attractions for kids, but getting around with small children can be a challenge. Between the tram tracks, high curbs and cars, manoeuvring a stroller on the streets isn't easy. Buses and trams are usually too crowded to accommodate strollers, even though buses have a designated stroller spot. Up to the age of seven, children travel free on public transport. If you choose taxis, make sure they have working seat belts for the kids. Ekotaxi (p71) has car seats for babies and toddlers but you must book at least two hours before and specify the age of your little one.

Kids will be fascinated by the bug collection at the Croatian Natural History Museum (p52). The Technical Museum Nikola Tesla (p55) features a planetarium and col-lections including steam-engine locomotives, scale models of satellites and space ships, and a replica of a mine; note that the planetarium might not appeal to very young kids. The little ones love the slide at the Museum of Contemporary Art (p55) though, and the interactive exhibits at the City Museum (p52).

For open-air activity, the best place for tots to work off some steam is Bočarski Dom (Prisavlje 2; 🏠). The park has the best in playground equipment, playing fields and a rollerblading ramp, and the relaxing path along the Sava River can be enjoyed by parents. To get there, take tram 17 west to the Prisavlje stop.

Another good spot is Bundek Lake in Novi Zagreb, with water fit for swimming (in summer) and two playgrounds, one for children up to seven years and another for those seven-plus. To get there, take tram 14 from Jelačić square.

There are two playgrounds and a zoo inside Maksimir Park (p54), which are all great for little ones. Aquatically minded kids will like the pools in the Sports Park Mla-dost (p55) and Sports & Recreational Centre Šalata (p55). Head to Jarun Lake (p55) for other recreational options, such as biking, rollerblading and kids' parks.

🍲 Courses

Kuhaona
COOKING

(☑️01-41 04 841; www.kuhaona.com; Opatovina 13) A gastro-educational centre steps from Dolac Market, Kuhaona offers cooking classes, the shortest of which takes two hours and involves preparing typical Zagreb dishes like *eingemachtes* (chicken minestrone), Zagreb steak (veal escalope filled with ham and cheese) and *jabuke u šlafroku* (apple fritters).

Longer classes take you on a gastro tour of Croatia, showcasing dishes like the Dalmatian black-squid risotto. Prices range from 200KN to 600KN per person, depending on the number of participants and whether the prep involves a trip to the market to pick the ingredients.

iCroatiaTravel
FOOD & DRINK

(☑️01-23 01 405; www.icroatiatravel.com/zagreb-gourmet-experience) iCroatiaTravel organises a five-hour Zagreb gourmet experience, which costs 900KN per person and includes a chef-led cooking class and lunch.

🎊 Festivals & Events

For a complete listing of Zagreb events, see www.infozagreb.hr. Croatia's largest international fairs are the Zagreb spring (mid-April) and autumn (mid-September) grand trade fairs.

Night of Museums
CULTURAL

On the last day of January, more than 40 cultural institutions in Zagreb, from museums and galleries to private collections, open their doors for free and stay open till 1am. It's the one night everyone in Zagreb hits the museums.

Zagrebdox
FILM

(www.zagrebdox.net; ⊙ late Feb-early Mar) This annual Zagreb festival celebrates documentary film.

Music Biennale Zagreb
MUSIC

(www.mbz.hr) Croatia's most important contemporary music event is held in April during odd-numbered years. By 'contemporary', do not read 'pop' – this prestigious fest celebrates modern-day classical music.

Subversive Festival
CULTURAL

(www.subversivefestival.com) Europe's activists and philosophers descend on Zagreb in droves for film screenings and lectures over two weeks in May.

Ljeto na Štrosu
CULTURAL

(www.ljetonastrosu.com) From late May through mid-September, this quirky annual event stages free outdoor film screenings, concerts, art workshops and best-in-show mongrel dog competitions, all along the leafy Strossmayer Šetalište.

Cest is D'Best
CULTURAL

(www.cestisdbest.com) This street festival delights Zagreb citizens for a few days in late May through early June each year, with six stages around the city centre, around 200 international performers, and acts that include music, dance, theatre, art and sports.

INmusic Festival
MUSIC

(www.inmusicfestival.com) A three-day extravaganza every June, this is Zagreb's highest-profile music festival. Previous years have seen PJ Harvey, New Order and Franz Ferdinand take to the Jarun Lake main stage.

Design District Zagreb
CULTURAL

(www.designdistrict.hr) For a few days each June, Zagreb's newly minted 'design district' around Martićeva street comes alive with a curated program of pop-up shops, workshops, studio visits, concerts and dining events, which take place all around the neighbourhood – in private apartments, courtyards and otherwise empty storefronts.

World Festival of Animated Film
FILM

(www.animafest.hr) Held in June, this prestigious festival has taken place in Zagreb since 1972 – odd-numbered years are devoted to feature films and even-numbered ones to short films.

Courtyards
CULTURAL

(Dvorišta; www.dvorista.in) For 10 days each July, Zagreb's historic Upper Town courtyards, many of which are normally off-limits, open their doors for a string of concerts and performances, combined with food, booze and merrymaking.

International Folklore Festival
CULTURAL

(www.msf.hr) Taking place in Zagreb since 1966, this festival, held in July, features folk dancers and singers from Croatia and other countries dressed in traditional costumes. There are free workshops designed to introduce you to Croatian folk culture.

Evenings on Grič
MUSIC

This festival presents a cycle of concerts in the Upper Town each July. The atrium of Galerija Klovićevi Dvori (p52), on Jezuitski trg, and the Gradec stage are used for performances of classical music, jazz, blues and world tunes.

Puppet
International Festival
PERFORMING ARTS
(www.pif.hr) Typically taking place during the month of September, this prominent puppetry festival, around since 1968, showcases star ensembles, workshops on puppet making and puppetry exhibits.

World Theatre Festival
THEATRE
(www.zagrebtheatrefestival.hr) High-quality contemporary theatre comes to Zagreb for a couple of weeks each September, sometimes extending into early October.

25 FPS – International
Experimental Film & Video Festival
FILM
(www.25fps.hr) This offbeat festival presents alternative visual expressions during one week of screenings, typically in late September/early October.

Zagreb Film Festival
FILM
(www.zagrebfilmfestival.com) If you're in Zagreb in mid-October, don't miss this major cultural event, with film screenings and accompanying parties. Directors compete for the Golden Pram award.

Human Rights Film Festival
FILM
(www.humanrightsfestival.org) Screenings of films that shed light on human rights issues around the world, taking place for a week each December in Kino Europa.

Fuliranje
CHRISTMAS MARKET
(www.facebook.com/fuliranje) This alfresco holiday market, which uses various locations around the city centre, is held from late November though December, as part of the increasingly popular Advent program in Zagreb. The focus is on street food, mulled wine and much merriment despite the below-zero temperatures. Check their Facebook page for this year's location.

🛏 Sleeping

Zagreb's accommodation scene has been undergoing a noticeable change with the arrival of budget airlines. Hostels have mushroomed in the last couple of years – at the time of research there were over 45 in Zagreb, from cheap backpacker digs to more stylish hideaways. Many are in the Lower and Upper Town but lodgings are scattered all over Zagreb, including in some outlying neighbourhoods.

🛏 Lower Town

Chillout Hostel Zagreb Downtown
HOSTEL €
(☏ 01-48 49 605; www.chillout-hostel-zagreb.com; Tomićeva 5a; dm 105-140KN; s/d 300/400KN; P ❄ @ 🛜) Located in the tiny pedestrian street with the funicular railway, this cheerful spot has no less than 170 beds just steps away from Trg Bana Jelačića. The trimmings are plentiful, and the vibe friendly. Breakfast is available.

Shappy Hostel
HOSTEL €
(☏ 01-48 30 483; www.hostel-shappy.com; Varšavska 8; dm 137-190KN, d from 530KN; P ❄ @ 🛜) This 14-room hostel is a peaceful oasis tucked away in a courtyard. Rooms range in size and theme – from the Romantic for Two and a six-bed Happy Room to a 10-person dorm; there's also a two-room apartment. On site is a bar with a terrace.

Hostel 63
HOSTEL €
(☏ 01-55 20 557; www.hostel63.eu; Vlaška 63/7; dm/s/d 129/380/418KN) Swank hostel to the east of the main square, in a cheerful courtyard with great company – Zagreb's best pizza place, Karijola (p61); one of the city's best restaurants, Mali Bar (p62); and a fantastic wine shop, Vintesa (p67). Dorms sleep up to four. Breakfast is charged extra but you get towels and soaps.

Hobo Bear Hostel
HOSTEL €
(☏ 091 90 54 427; www.hobobearhostel.com; Medulićeva 4; dm/d from 153/436KN; ❄ @ 🛜) Inside a duplex apartment, this sparkling five-dorm hostel has exposed brick walls, hardwood floors, free lockers, a kitchen with free tea and coffee, a common room and book exchange. The three doubles are across the street. Take tram 1, 6 or 11 from Trg Bana Jelačića.

Palmers Lodge Hostel Zagreb
HOSTEL €
(☏ 01-88 92 868; www.palmerslodge.com.hr; Kneza Branimira 25; dm 120-150KN, d from 450KN; P ❄ @ 🛜) Convenient for late arrivals, this hostel – part of the namesake British hostel chain – is mere steps from the train station. The dorms aren't spectacular, but each comes with its own bathroom, plus there's a common space, a shared kitchen and excursions.

⭐ Studio Kairos
B&B €€
(☏ 01-46 40 680; www.studio-kairos.com; Vlaška 92; s 340-420KN, d 520-620KN; ❄ 🛜) This adorable B&B in a street-level apartment has four

well-appointed rooms decked out by theme – Writers', Crafts, Music and Granny's – and there's a cosy common space where a delicious breakfast is served. The interior design is gorgeous and the friendly owners are a fountain of knowledge. Bikes are also available for rent.

Swanky Mint Hostel HOSTEL €€
(☑ 01-40 04 248; www.swanky-hostel.com/mint; Ilica 50; dm from 150KN, s/d 360/520KN, apt 650-800KN; ❄@❀🏊) Inside a restored textile-dye factory from the 19th century, this cool hostel in the heart of town combines industrial chic with creature comforts in its rooms, dorms and apartments. Freebies include wi-fi, lockers, towels and a welcome shot of *rakija* (grappa). The garden bar serves breakfast and drinks, and there's even a small pool on site.

Art Hotel Like HOTEL €€
(☑ 01-46 16 610; www.arthotellike.hr; Vlaška 44; s/d 675/713KN; ❄❀) This artsy three-star hotel is so central that you can see the Zagreb cathedral from the window of any upper-floor crispy white room. The interiors are a lovely blend of a classic Austro-Hungarian town house and modern designer furniture, including original commissioned photography and light installations by Croatian artist Hamo Čavrk.

Hotel Jadran HOTEL €€
(☑ 01-45 53 777; www.hotel-jadran.com.hr; Vlaška 50; s/d 420/560KN; P❄@❀) This six-storey hotel has a superb location only minutes from Jelačić square. The 49 rooms are laid out in a cheery style and the service is friendly. Rates are negotiable depending on availability.

Hotel Central HOTEL €€
(☑ 01-48 41 122; www.hotel-central.hr; Branimirova 3; s/d 490/640KN; ❄@❀) The best mid-priced place to stay if you have a train to catch, Hotel Central is in a square concrete building with 76 comfy, if a little poky, rooms. The larger top-floor rooms face the leafy courtyard.

Hotel Garden HOTEL €€
(☑ 01-48 43 720; www.gardenhotel.hr; Vodnikova 13; s/d 471/560KN; ❄❀) This contemporary three-star has clean-lined rooms with a full range of amenities. It's right by the Botanical Garden, hence the name. A great midrange choice, with a convenient location near the train station and the main square.

★ Esplanade Zagreb Hotel HOTEL €€€
(☑ 01-45 66 666; www.esplanade.hr; Mihanovićeva 1; s/d 1165/1700KN; P❄@❀) Drenched in history, this six-storey hotel was built next to the train station in 1925 to welcome the *Orient Express* crowd in grand style. It has hosted kings, artists, journalists and politicians ever since. The art deco masterpiece is replete with walls of swirling marble, immense staircases and wood-panelled lifts.

Hotel Jägerhorn HOTEL €€€
(☑ 01-48 33 877; www.hotel-jagerhorn.hr; Ilica 14; s/d/apt 890/1000/1300KN; P❄@❀) A charming little hotel that sits right underneath Lotrščak Tower (p51), the 'Hunter's Horn' has friendly service and 18 spacious, classic rooms with good views (you can gaze over leafy Gradec from the top-floor attic rooms). The downstairs terrace cafe is lovely. It's the oldest hotel in Zagreb, around since 1827.

Hotel Dubrovnik HOTEL €€€
(☑ 01-48 63 555; www.hotel-dubrovnik.hr; Gajeva 1; s/d from 645/800KN; P❄❀) Smack on Zagreb's main square, this glass New York–wannabe is a city landmark, and the 245 well-appointed units have old-school, classic style. It buzzes with business travellers who

ⓘ A ZAGREB HOME OF YOUR OWN
Short-term apartment rentals in Zagreb are becoming increasingly popular, as they are a good way to experience the city like a local. You can book prior to arrival through an agency or directly from the owners. The choice of apartments can be dizzying, so go to either **ZIGZAG Integrated Hotel** (☑ 01-88 95 433; www.zigzag.hr; Petrinjska 9; r/apt from 450/720KN; P❄❀) for a choice of apartments in the city centre or the agency **InZagreb** (☑ 01-65 23 201; www.inzagreb.com; apt 455-670KN; ❄❀). There's also a terrific private apartment right on the main square, fittingly called **Main Square Apartment** (☑ 098 494 212; www.accrommodation.com; Trg Bana Jelačića 3; 2/3/4 people 600/675/750KN; ❄❀). Plus there's a sweet cottage a short drive outside the city, **Kućica** (☑ 099 62 92 985; www.kuchica.com; cottage weekdays/weekends 450/750KN; P), for those who want a taste of the Croatian countryside. Note that one-night stays sometimes have a surcharge.

love being at the centre of the action – try to get a view of Trg Bana Jelačića and watch Zagreb pass by under your window. Enquire about packages and specials.

Palace Hotel   HOTEL €€€
(📞01-48 99 600; www.palace.hr; Strossmayerov trg 10; s/d from 779/890KN; 🅿 ✳ @ 🛜) This classy hotel oozes European charm. Its grand Secessionist mansion (built in 1891) has elegant rooms and suites outfitted with the latest modern comforts. Try to get a front room for fantastic views over the park. Look for the frescoes in the back of the ground-floor cafe, which has unique Austro-Hungarian finesse.

Arcotel Allegra   HOTEL €€€
(📞01-46 96 000; www.arcotelhotels.com; Branimirova 29; s/d from 730/840KN; 🅿 ✳ @ 🛜) Zagreb's first designer hotel has 150 airy rooms and a marble reception area accessorised with exotic fish. The bed throws are printed with faces of Kafka, Kahlo, Freud and other iconic personalities. The top-floor wellness and workout area has great city views.

Hotel 9   HOTEL €€€
(📞01-56 25 040; www.hotel9.hr; Avenija Marina Držića 9; s/d 680/900KN; ✳ 🛜) This recent hotel addition, steps from the main bus station, is also Zagreb's most boutiquey option – its 20 swanky rooms on three floors are ideal for design hawks. Breakfast with all the trimmings is served on the rooftop terrace.

🛏 Upper Town

Taban Hostel   HOSTEL €
(📞01-55 33 527; www.tabanzagreb.com; Tkalčićeva 82; dm/s/d/apt 100/200/400/450KN; 🅿 @ 🛜✳) Great location for partying, right on Tkalčićeva. Some rooms come with TVs, fridges and private bathrooms. A one-bedroom apartment is also available. There's a buzzing bar downstairs with live-music events.

President Pantovčak   BOUTIQUE HOTEL €€€
(📞01-48 81 480; www.president-zagreb.com; Pantovčak 52; s/d 742/891KN; 🅿 ✳ 🛜) This four-star boutique hotel, snuggled in the leafy hills just moments from the city's bustle, is an art- and design-lovers' oasis. Showcasing hand-picked artwork by well-known Croatian painters and sculptors such as Edo Murtić and Dušan Džamonja, rooms open to the landscaped gardens via floor-to-ceiling windows. For a proper luxe stay, request the personal chef and butler services.

🛏 Maksimir

Funk Lounge Hostel   HOSTEL €
(📞01-55 52 707; www.funklounge.hr; Rendićeva 28; dm 135-180KN; s & d 450KN; ✳ @ 🛜) Located steps from Maksimir Park, this outpost of the original Funk Hostel (southwest of the centre) has friendly staff, neat rooms and a range of freebies, including breakfast, a shot of *rakija,* toiletries and lockers. On site is a restaurant and bar, and a full kitchen.

Ravnice Rooms & Apartments   HOSTEL €
(📞01-23 32 325; www.ravnice-youth-hostel.hr; Prve Ravnice 38d; dm/s/d 110/150/260KN; 🅿 @ 🛜) A 20-minute tram ride (on lines 11 or 12) from the centre, this pioneer of Zagreb hostels has clean rooms, a rambling garden and freebies such as lockers, coffee, tea and breakfast. Musicians and performers get a free night's stay in exchange for an hour's performance for fellow guests.

🍴 Eating

You'll have to love Croatian and Italian food to enjoy Zagreb's restaurants, but new places are branching out to include cuisines from around the world, as well as some vegetarian options. The city centre's main streets are lined with fast-food joints, bakeries and snack bars. Many restaurants close in August for their summer holiday, which lasts anywhere from two weeks to a month.

🍴 Lower Town

Bistro 75   BISTRO €
(📞01-48 40 545; Preradovićeva 34; mains 36-42KN; ⏰11am-11pm Mon-Thu, to 1am Fri & Sat) Tasty bites like oxtail sandwiches and falafel wraps, a set of daily specials, twisted cocktails and a great range of local craft beers (like Zmajska and Varionica) are all reasons to check out this sleek little bistro. It has a colourful wall mural and a banquette inside, plus tables on a streetside deck.

Zrno   VEGETARIAN €
(www.zrnobiobistro.hr; Medulićeva 20; mains 47-65KN; ⏰noon-9.30pm Mon-Sat; 🍴) This contemporary 'bio-bistro' (as it dubs itself) is tucked away in a courtyard a 10-minute walk from the main square and serves tasty options with ingredients from their own farm, from brown-rice gomoku to a daily 'makroplata' meal (macrobiotic platter of the day) and desserts like *crostata* (baked tart) with seasonal fruit.

Bistro Divas BISTRO €
(☑01-45 79 390; www.facebook.com/divasbistro; Martićeva 14f; mains 45-70KN; ⊙noon-6pm Mon-Sat) Light and bright, artsy and airy, this recent addition to the up-and-coming Martićeva neighbourhood offers a different take on lunch, featuring food with an international touch. Think wok dishes, Moroccan chicken salad and Vietnamese rolls, depending on what's market fresh and listed on the small menu that day.

Torte i To Atrij CAFE €
(Teslina 7; biscuits & cakes 3-19KN; ⊙8am-11pm Mon-Sat, 9am-11pm Sun) An airy cafe in an atrium off Teslina, with a light-flooded section that has a small vertical garden and tables outside. They are known for their great cakes, particularly their signature cheesecake. The flagship is on the 2nd floor of Kaptol Centar.

Pingvin SANDWICHES €
(Teslina 7; sandwiches 15-35KN; ⊙10am-4am Mon-Sat, 6pm-2am Sun) This quick-bite institution, around since 1987, offers tasty designer sandwiches and salads, which locals savour on a couple of bar stools.

Vincek BAKERY €
(Ilica 18; pastries 7-18KN; ⊙8.30am-11pm Mon-Sat) This institution of a *slastičarna* (pastry shop) serves some of Zagreb's creamiest cakes. They have several locations around town, including at Zvonimirova 7 and Kvaternikov Trg. Their newest Vis a Vis offshoot around the corner in Tomićeva serves gluten- and sugar-free ice creams and cakes.

Burgeraj BURGERS €
(Preradovićeva 13; burgers 35-47KN; ⊙11am-11pm Mon-Thu, to midnight Fri & Sat) American-style burger bar that whips up tasty double and triple burgers, and serves good craft beers (like the local Zmajska). Chow down at the counter or grab one of the few tables.

Mak Na Konac BAKERY €
(Dukljaninova 1; cakes 16-22KN; ⊙9am-9pm Mon-Sat) At this storefront cake shop just east of the main square, the signature poppy-seed cake filled with raspberry jam is divine, as are the other sweet treats.

Karijola PIZZA €
(☑01-55 31 016; www.pizzeria-karijola.com; Vlaška 63; pizzas 46-70KN; ⊙11am-midnight Mon-Sat, to 11pm Sun) Locals swear by the crispy, thin-crust pizza churned out of a clay oven at this central location of Zagreb's best pizza joint. Pizzas come with high-quality ingredients, such as smoked ham, olive oil, rich mozzarella, cherry tomatoes, rocket and shiitake mushrooms. They close for two weeks in August.

Dinara BAKERY €
(Gajeva 8; pastries 3.50-20KN; ⊙5.30am-10.30pm) The best bakery in town churns out an impressive variety of baked goodies. Try the *bučnica* (filo pie with pumpkin). Also has branches at **Ilica 71** (pastries 3.50-20KN; ⊙5.30am-10.30pm) and **Preradovićeva 1** (pastries 3.50-20KN; ⊙5.30am-10.30pm).

Tip Top SEAFOOD €
(Gundulićeva 18; mains 40-90KN; ⊙11am-11pm Mon-Sat) How we love Tip Top and its wait staff, who still sport old socialist uniforms and scowling faces that eventually turn to smiles. But we mostly love the excellent Dalmatian food. Every day has a different set menu. Their octopus goulash on Thursdays is a hit.

Nishta VEGETARIAN €
(www.nishtarestaurant.com; Masarykova 11/1; mains 57-69KN; ⊙noon-11pm Mon-Sun; 🖉) This offshoot of its Dubrovnik namesake serves imaginative, globally inspired dishes in a chintzy, artsy space. The menu ranges from *ćevapovrćići* (a veggie version of the spicy sausage dish *ćevapčići*) to Mexican burritos, with many vegan and gluten-free options.

Bistro Fotić CROATIAN €
(☑01-48 10 476; www.bistrofotic.com; Gajeva 25; mains 55-70KN; ⊙8am-11pm Mon-Sat) Popular for its hearty lunch menu, this family-run bistro doubles as a photo gallery. The cosy interiors display old cameras, and there's a proper studio on site where you can get your travel photos printed as you chow down on tiramola pizza with prosciutto slices pegged on a rope above the plate. Don't miss their homemade desserts, which change daily.

Green Point VEGETARIAN €
(Varšavska 10; dishes 25-31KN; ⊙9am-10pm Mon-Sat; 🖉) For a quick, healthy bite on the go, grab a burger (take your pick from seitan, hemp or tofu) or one of the wok dishes or salads at this vegetarian storefront with just a couple of tables, smack in the centre of town.

Vallis Aurea CROATIAN €
(☑01-48 31 305; www.vallis-aurea.com; Tomićeva 4; mains 35-77KN; ⊙9am-11pm Mon-Sat) This

true local eatery has some of the best home cooking you'll find in town, so it's no wonder that it's chock-a-block at lunchtime for its *gableci* (traditional lunches). Located right by the lower end of the funicular.

★Vinodol CROATIAN €€

(☑ 01-48 11 427; www.vinodol-zg.hr; Teslina 10; mains 48-160KN; ⊙ 10am-midnight) The well-prepared central-European fare here is much-loved by local and overseas patrons. On warm days, eat on the covered patio (entered through an ivy-clad passageway off Teslina); the cold-weather alternative is the dining hall with vaulted stone ceilings. Highlights include the succulent lamb or veal and potatoes cooked under *peka* (a domed baking lid), as well as *bukovače* (local mushrooms).

★Mundoaka Street Food INTERNATIONAL €€

(☑ 01-78 88 777; Petrinjska 2; mains 65-85KN; ⊙ 9am-midnight Mon-Sat) This tiny eatery clad in light wood, with tables outside, serves up American classics – think chicken wings and pork ribs – and a global spectrum of dishes, from Spanish tortillas to *shakshuka* eggs. Great breakfasts, muffins and cakes, all prepared by one of Zagreb's best-known chefs. Reserve ahead.

Mali Bar TAPAS €€

(☑ 01-55 31 014; Vlaška 63; dishes 45-120KN; ⊙ 12.30pm-midnight Mon-Sat) This spot by star chef Ana Ugarković shares the terraced space with Karijola (p61), hidden away in a *veža* (alleyway). The interior is cosy and earth-tone colourful, and the food is focused on globally inspired tapas-style dishes.

Boban ITALIAN €€

(☑ 01-48 11 549; www.boban.hr; Gajeva 9; mains 60-138KN; ⊙ 11am-11pm Mon-Thu, 11am-midnight Fri & Sat, noon-11pm Sun) Italian is the name of the game in this cellar restaurant that's owned by the Croatian football star Zvonimir Boban. The menu features a robust range of pasta, risotto, gnocchi and meat dishes.

Lari & Penati MODERN CROATIAN €€

(☑ 01-46 55 776; www.laripenati.hr; Petrinjska 42a; mains 40-90KN; ⊙ noon-11pm Mon-Sat) Small stylish bistro that serves up innovative lunch and dinner specials – they change daily according to what's market-fresh. The food is fab, the music cool and the few sidewalk tables lovely in warm weather. Closes for two weeks in August.

Bistroteka BISTRO €€

(☑ 01-48 37 711; Teslina 14; mains 52-120KN; ⊙ 8am-midnight Mon-Thu, to 1am Fri & Sat) Riding the recent wave of bistro openings in Zagreb, this chic small eatery dishes out breakfasts (till 11am on weekdays and 12.30pm on weekends), sandwiches and daily specials that include dishes such as duck confit, homemade lasagne and tuna ragout. It can get busy at lunchtime.

Ribice i Tri Točkice SEAFOOD €€

(☑ 01-56 35 479; www.ribiceitritockice.hr; Preradovićeva 7/1; mains 40-85KN; ⊙ 9am-11pm) Funky and fun seafood spot offering simple but good Dalmatian mainstays, with daily specials announcing what's freshest. Sit inside in the colourful upstairs or at the sidewalk tables on Teslina.

Zinfandel's INTERNATIONAL €€€

(☑ 01-45 66 644; www.zinfandels.hr; Mihanovićeva 1; mains 150-295KN; ⊙ 6am-11pm Mon-Sat, 6.30am-11pm Sun) Some of the tastiest, most creative dishes in town are conjured up by chef Ana Grgić and served with flair here in the dining room of the Esplanade Zagreb Hotel (p59).

Le Bistro FRENCH €€€

(www.lebistro.hr; Mihanovićeva 1; mains 145-185KN; ⊙ 9am-11pm) The casual chic restaurant at Esplanade Zagreb Hotel (p59) serves the city's best *štrukli* (cottage-cheese-filled dumplings).

Upper Town

Otto & Frank INTERNATIONAL €

(www.otto-frank.com; Tkalčićeva 20; mains 35-95KN; ⊙ 8am-midnight Mon-Thu, to 1am Fri & Sat, 9am-11pm Sun) One of Tkalča's cooler spots, this small bistro has a gorgeously sleek interior with two small rooms and a streetside terrace. They serve all-day breakfasts, weekly board specials and signature dishes like their spicy lamb burger. There's good craft beer and a nice wine selection, too.

Amfora SEAFOOD €

(☑ 01-48 16 455; www.restoran-amfora.com; Dolac 2; mains 40-70KN; ⊙ 6am-5pm) This locals' lunch favourite serves fresh seafood straight from the market next door, paired with off-the-stalls veggies. This hole in the wall has a few tables outside and an upstairs gallery with a nice market view.

Agava INTERNATIONAL €€

(www.restaurant-agava.hr; Tkalčićeva 39; mains 60-180KN; ⊙ 9am-11pm) The best thing about this smart spot on the main strip is its terrace. Food ranges from starters such as swordfish carpaccio to mains of steak and truffle. The wine list features plenty of Istrian and Slavonian choices.

Trilogija MEDITERRANEAN €€
(☑ 01-48 51 394; www.trilogija.com; Kamenita 5; mains 70-140KN; ☺11am-midnight Mon-Thu, to 10am Fri & Sat, to 4pm Sun) Right by the Stone Gate, in a location that has seen many a restaurant open and close – though this one seems to be here to stay. The secret lies in the quality of its fresh Croatian-Mediterranean food, friendly staff and friendly prices.

Didov San DALMATIAN €€
(☑ 01-48 51 154; www.konoba-didovsan.com; Mletačka 11; mains 40-130KN; ☺10am-midnight) This Upper Town tavern features a rustic wooden interior with ceiling beams, and tables on a streetside deck. The food is based on traditional cuisine from the Neretva River delta in Dalmatia's hinterland, such as grilled frogs wrapped in prosciutto. Reservations recommended.

Kaptolska Klet CROATIAN €€
(☑ 01-48 76 502; www.kaptolska-klet.eu; Kaptol 5; mains 40-145KN; ☺11am-midnight) This friendly restaurant has a huge outdoor terrace and a brightly lit, beer-hall-style interior. Although famous for its Zagreb specialities, such as grilled meats, lamb and veal under *peka,* and homemade sausages, it also turns out a nice vegetable loaf.

Baltazar CROATIAN €€
(www.restoran-baltazar.hr; Nova Ves 4; mains 90-200KN; ☺noon-midnight Mon-Sat, to 5pm Sun) All kinds of meat – duck, lamb, pork, beef and turkey – are grilled and prepared the Zagorje and Slavonian way at this upmarket old-timer. There's a good choice of Mediterranean dishes and local wines. The summer terrace is a great place for dining under the stars.

Stari Fijaker 900 CROATIAN €€
(☑ 01-48 33 829; www.starifijaker.hr; Mesnička 6; mains 50-190KN; ☺11am-11pm Mon-Sat, to 10pm Sun) This restaurant and beer hall was once the height of dining out in Zagreb, and its decor of banquettes and white linen still has a staid sobriety. Tradition reigns in the kitchen, so try the homemade sausages and *štrukli,* or one of the cheaper daily dishes.

Bistro Apetit GASTRONOMY €€€
(☑ 01-46 77 335; www.bistroapetit.com; Jurjevska 65a; mains 145-175KN; ☺10am-midnight Tue-Sun)

COFFEE BREAK

Rumours of Croatia's first Starbucks died a quick death. That's because Starbucks would never stand a chance at competing with *špica,* the very local Zagreb tradition of sipping coffee in the town centre between 11am and 2pm on Saturday, before or after a run at the Dolac Market (p54). This showdown of latest fashions, mobile phones and gossip has people rushing for prime sidewalk tables along Bogovićeva, Preradovićeva and Tkalčićeva. It's a great way to experience Zagreb in its liveliest incarnation.

Touted as the place with the best terrace in town – high up on villa-lined Jurjevska street – this popular top-end restaurant uses fresh seasonal ingredients in amazingly bold combinations. Think octopus with sausage or strawberry soup with cucumber and frozen yoghurt.

Mano INTERNATIONAL €€€
(☑ 01-46 69 432; www.mano.hr; Medvedgradska 2; mains 110-240KN; ☺noon-1am Mon-Sat) Swish steakhouse in a beautiful brick building steps from the Kaptol Centar, with an airy interior featuring exposed stone walls, steel pillars and a glass-enclosed kitchen. The lighting is moody and the mains innovative. Their Mano2 offshoot in Green Gold Centar has become a culinary hot spot.

Western Zagreb

Lauba Bistro BISTRO €€
(☑ 01-63 02 140; www.lauba.hr; Baruna Filipovića 23a; mains 50-150KN; ☺9am-11pm Mon-Fri, 11am-11pm Sat) This chic bistro in the lobby of one of Zagreb's coolest art spaces serves delicious miniloaves of bread as their signature – think quinoa and beer bread – with tasty spreads, if you want a small bite. Their more substantial dishes include lovely stews and daily changing mains.

Drinking & Nightlife

In the Upper Town, the chic Tkalčićeva is throbbing with bars and cafes. With half a dozen bars and sidewalk cafes between Trg Petra Preradovića (known locally as Cvjetni trg) and Bogovićeva in the Lower Town, the scene on summer nights resembles a vast outdoor party. Things wind down by midnight though, and get quieter from mid-July through late August.

🍷 Lower Town

Cogito Coffee Shop   CAFE
(www.cogitocoffee.com; Varšavska 11; ⊘ 8am-9pm Mon-Fri, 9am-7pm Sat) This tiny ultra-cool Berlin-style cafe tucked away in a hidden passageway serves the city's best coffee, all roasted by the local Cogito Coffee Roasters at Cafe u Dvorištu (p65). They serve coffee with almond milk (not easy to find in Zagreb) and sell delicious Medenko ice cream. Shorter hours in August.

Johann Franck   CAFE
(www.johannfranck.hr; Trg Bana Jelačića 9; ⊘ 8am-2am Mon-Thu & Sun, 8am-4am Fri & Sat) When it reopened in 2015, this Bauhaus-style palace was dubbed the 21st-century coffee house. Named after Croatia's pioneer coffee roaster and the namesake coffee brand, the venue transformed from a Vienna-type cafe to an all-day fun hub. The ballroom-like ground floor serves speciality coffee brews.

Kino Europa   BAR
(www.kinoeuropa.hr; Varšavska 3; ⊘ 8.30am-midnight Mon-Thu, to 4am Fri & Sat, 11am-11pm Sun; ☎) Zagreb's oldest cinema, from the 1920s, now houses a splendid cafe, wine bar and *grapperia*. At this glass-enclosed space with an outdoor terrace you can enjoy great coffee, over 30 types of grappa and free wi-fi. The cinema hosts film screenings and occasional dance parties.

Peper   CLUB
(www.peper-zagreb.com; Ilica 5; ⊘ 8am-midnight Sun-Tue, to 4am Wed & Thu, to 6am Fri & Sat) A city-centre club that caters to a well-to-do older crowd and doubles as a cafe during the day. Programs (Wednesday to Saturday only) change weekly, ranging from disco and swing to soul and house.

Vinyl   BAR
(www.vinylzagreb.com; Bogovićeva 3; ⊘ 8am-midnight Sun-Tue, 8am-2am Wed & Thu, 8am-4am Fri & Sat) Much beloved by the locals, this all-day lounge on a popular stretch is split into cafe and club areas. It delivers fun both day and night, including live-music events, readings and exhibitions of books and vinyl, such as Masters of Memories on Monday evenings. Don't miss their vinyl-only DJ sets on weekends and the superb range of whiskies.

Express   CAFE
(Petrinjska 4; ⊘ 7am-9pm Mon-Thu, 7am-11pm Fri & Sat, 11am-7pm Sun) A tiny little cafe with tables outside, serving some of Zagreb's best coffee and tea. They close on Sundays in August.

Divas   CAFE
(Martićeva 17; ⊘ 7am-11pm Mon-Sat, 9am-5pm Sun) Great for daytime hanging out in the chintzy-chic interior or the sidewalk tables, this boho little cafe is on up-and-coming Martićeva street. It closes earlier (at 3pm) on Sundays in summer.

Eliscaffe   CAFE
(Ilica 63; ⊘ 8am-7pm Mon-Sat, 9am-2pm Sun) The award-winning coffee from 100% arabica beans here is tops. Try the smooth *triestino*. The recently opened Eliscaffe II, a couple of doors down (at Ilica 65, in the courtyard), is a swankier and larger affair, with longer hours (open till 10pm), small bites, great cakes and a wine list.

Mojo   BAR
(www.facebook.com/MojoBar; Martićeva 5; ⊘ 7am-2am Mon-Sat, 8am-midnight Sun) Smoky basement hang-out where live music and DJ-spun tunes happen every night. On warm nights, take your pick from 70 *rakijas* and liqueurs and sample them on the sidewalk tables out front.

Bacchus   BAR
(Trg Kralja Tomislava 16; ⊘ 11am-midnight Mon-Fri, noon-midnight Sat) You'll be lucky if you score a table at Zagreb's funkiest courtyard garden, lush and hidden in a passageway. After 10pm the action moves inside the artsy subterranean space, which hosts poetry readings and classic-rock nights. Things get quiet in the summer.

Old Pharmacy Pub   PUB
(www.pub.pondi.hr; Andrije Hebranga 11; ⊘ 8am-midnight Sun-Thu, 8am-1am Fri & Sat) This traditional English pub hides inside an Austro-Hungarian town house, but once you walk in, all the elements are there: a mirror behind the bar, pharmacy-related paraphernalia, washed-out photos, all set up among the wood and leather decor.

The non-smoking back room, decked out with comfy armchairs, makes a perfect chummy corner. For a cool start of the evening, add a drop of whisky, scotch or bourbon from the extensive drinks menu.

MK Krolo
BAR

(Radićeva 7; ⊙9am-1am Mon-Sat, to 11pm Sun) This darling of Zagreb's dive bars is the gathering spot for the city's artists, bohos, media types and local drunks. Socialist chic at its best.

Sherry's Wines & Bites
WINE BAR

(☑091 25 07 712; www.sherrys.eu; Ilica 73; ⊙10am-midnight Tue-Sun) Cool little wine bar-bistro, in a courtyard off Britanac, that serves more than 100 wine varieties, and bites to pair your tipple with. The terrace is one of Zagreb's best-kept secrets, with frequent live-music events.

Booksa
CAFE

(www.booksa.hr; Martićeva 14d; ⊙10am-9pm Tue-Sun; ☜) Bookworms and poets, writers and performers, oddballs and artists...basically anyone creative in Zagreb comes here to chat and drink coffee, browse the library, surf with free wi-fi and hear readings at this lovely, book-themed cafe. There are English-language readings here, too. Closes for a month from mid-July. Note that you'll need to pay a one-time membership fee of 10KN.

Cafe u Dvorištu
CAFE

(Jurja Žerjavića 7/2; ⊙9am-midnight Mon-Sat, 11am-7pm Sun) A sweet little cafe-bar tucked away inside a courtyard, serving excellent organic and fair-trade coffee (roasted on-site) and tea. There are occasional readings and art exhibitions. It closes on Sundays during late July and August.

Time
BAR

(www.facebook.com/time.zagreb; Petrinjska 7; ⊙7am-2am Mon-Thu, to 3am Fri, 9am-3am Sat) This cavernous former ironmonger's store is now a swish coffee-drinking hang-out during the day and a buzzing American-style bar with DJ music come nightfall, catering to a young, moneyed crowd. The adjacent restaurant serves Asian fusion fare.

Sedmica
BAR

(Kačićeva 7a; ⊙8am-1am Mon-Thu, to 2am Fri & Sat, 5pm-1am Sun) This low-key bar is hidden in an alleyway off Kačićeva, with a big Guinness sign marking the entrance. A gathering point for Zagreb's boho-intellectual crowd, it has a poky interior with a mezzanine and an outside patio that buzzes in warmer months.

Bulldog
PUB

(www.bulldog-pub-zagreb.com; Bogovićeva 6; ⊙8am-2am) The sidewalk tables here are prime for people-watching on this busy pedestrian street. At night it's a good place to meet for drinks.

Basement
WINE BAR

(www.basement-bar.net; Tomićeva 5; ⊙noon-2am Mon-Fri, 10am-2am Sat, 4pm-midnight Sun) A city-centre hot spot for sampling Croatian wines by the glass, this basement bar (with a few sidewalk tables) sits right by the funicular. Pair the tipple with meat and cheese platters.

Pivnica Medvedgrad
BREWERY

(www.pivnica-medvedgrad.hr; Ilica 49; ⊙10am-midnight Mon-Sat, noon-midnight Sun) Sip on one of five house-brewed beers at this beer hall, which offers up reliably cheap and tasty grub and a bustling atmosphere. It's accessed through a shopping passageway off Ilica, with a large, chestnut-tree-shaded courtyard.

VIP Club
CLUB

(www.vip-club.hr; Trg Bana Jelačića 9; ⊙8pm-5am Tue-Sat) A swank basement place on the main square, it offers a varied line-up, from jazz to Balkan beats.

Art Kino Grič
BAR

(www.artkinogric.hr; Jurišićeva 6; ⊙8am-11pm) This old-school cinema has been revamped into a colourful, two-floor bar and a small basement club (weekends only). It has since become a locals' favourite, with art exhibits and film screenings in the cosy projection room.

⬤ Upper Town

Stross
BAR

(Strossmayerovo Šetalište; ⊙9.30pm-late Jun-Sep) A makeshift bar is set up most nights in summer at the Strossmayer promenade in the Upper Town, with cheap drinks and live music. The mixed-bag crowd, great city views and leafy ambience make it a great spot to while away your evenings.

Dežman Bar
BAR

(www.dezman.hr; Dežmanova 3; ⊙8am-midnight Mon-Thu, 8am-1am Fri & Sat) Shielded from traffic inside the cosy passage leading to the semi-wild Tuškanac forest, this cafe-cum-bistro excels in pretty much any drink or simple food you can imagine. Chef Christian Cabalier's savvy touch makes a simple sandwich or a cake an artsy affair, boldly concocted from exquisite ingredients, such as tuna prosciutto or gluten-free bread.

Velvet CAFE
(Dežmanova 9; ⊙8am-10pm Mon-Fri, to 3pm Sat, to 2pm Sun) Stylish spot for a good (but pricey) cup of java and a quick bite amid the minimalist-chic interior decked out by owner Saša Šekoranja, Zagreb's hippest florist. The Velvet Gallery bar next door, known as 'Black Velvet', stays open till 11pm (except on Sunday).

Booze and Blues CLUB
(www.booze-and-blues.com; Tkalčićeva 84; ⊙8am-midnight Sun-Tue, 8am-2am Wed-Sat) Perched at the top of the buzzy Tkalča strip, this haven of jazz, blues and soul rhythms stands out with its weekend live-music line-up. The interior is designed in the tradition of American blues and jazz clubs, with music-history memorabilia, and Heineken on tap flowing from a functioning saxophone.

Kava Tava CAFE
(www.kavatava.com; Britanski trg bb; ⊙7am-midnight) It's hard to miss this delightful cafe, set up in a black-and-red wooden hut among the stalls of the farmers' market. Don't skip the signature all-day breakfast: American-style pancakes oozing with fillings of every kind imaginable or the super-layered toasties.

Funk BAR
(www.facebook.com/funkklub; Tkalčićeva 52; ⊙11am-2am) Sip coffee and watch people during the day, and at night go down the spiral staircase and you'll see why this cult spot has locals at its beck and call. In a small basement with stone vaulted ceilings, DJs spin house, jazz, funk and broken beats for a boogie-happy crowd.

Palainovka CAFE
(Ilirski trg 1; ⊙8am-midnight Mon-Thu, to 2am Fri & Sat, 9am-11pm Sun) Claiming to be the old-est cafe in Zagreb (dating from 1846), this Viennese-style place serves delicious coffee, tea and cakes under pretty frescoed ceilings.

🍸 Peščenica – Žitnjak

Garden Brewery BREWERY
(www.thegarden.hr/the-garden-brewery; Slavonska avenija 22f; ⊙noon-8pm Mon-Thu & Sun, noon-2am Fri & Sat) A new craft brewery in the industrial east of Zagreb, inside an old redbrick factory turned an all-day hang-out, with club nights on Saturdays featuring live and unplugged music. They offer craft beer made on site (try the Session Ale with floral overtones or the Kettle Sour full of fruity flavours), brewery tours and tastings, artisanal burgers and family-friendly Sunday Sessions.

🍸 Western Zagreb

Das Haus CLUB
(Samoborska cesta 215; ⊙hours vary Fri & Sat) Zagreb's most underground club, on the western outskirts of the city, has a really mixed crowd and is the only one that opens extra late, after other clubs close. See its Facebook page for details.

☆ Entertainment

Zagreb's theatres and concert halls present a great variety of programs throughout the year. Many are listed in the monthly brochure *Zagreb Events & Performances*, available from the main tourist office. Also check out the free *Zagreb 4 You* monthly; it lists cool Zagreb events.

Croatian National Theatre THEATRE
(📞01-48 88 415; www.hnk.hr; Trg Maršala Tita 15; ⊙box office 10am-7pm Mon-Fri, to 1pm Sat & 1hr

---

GAY & LESBIAN ZAGREB

The gay and lesbian scene in Zagreb is finally becoming more open than it has previously been – although free-wheeling it isn't. For more information, browse www.friendlycroatia.com. Also look out for performances by Le Zbor (www.lezbor.com), Croatia's lesbian and feminist choir with an activist edge.

Hotpot (Petrinjska 31; ⊙11pm-5am Fri & Sat) A small gay bar with cheap booze, and one of the city's favourites.

Kolaž (Amruševa 11; ⊙7pm-2am Jun-Sep, noon-2am Mon-Fri, 6pm-2am Sat & Sun Oct-May) This basement speakeasy-style bar behind an unmarked door caters to a primarily gay crowd.

Vimpi (Prolaz Sestara Baković 3; ⊙8am-1am) Gathering spot for Zagreb's lady-loving ladies.

Rush Club (Amruševa 10; ⊙11pm-5am Thu, Fri & Sat) A younger gay and lesbian crowd mixes at this fun club in the city centre, with themed nights such as karaoke.

before the show) This neo-baroque theatre, established in 1895, stages opera and ballet performances. Check out Ivan Meštrović's sculpture *The Well of Life* (1905) standing out front.

Zagrebačko Kazalište Mladih · THEATRE
(☑ 01-48 72 554; www.zekaem.hr; Teslina 7; ☉ box office 10am-8pm Mon-Fri, to 2pm Sat, plus 1hr before the show) The Zagreb Youth Theatre, better known as ZKM, is considered the cradle of Croatia's contemporary theatre. It hosts several festivals and many visiting troupes from around the world.

Vatroslav Lisinski Concert Hall · CONCERT VENUE
(☑ 01-61 21 166; www.lisinski.hr; Trg Stjepana Radića 4; ☉ box office 10am-8pm Mon-Fri, 10am-2pm & 6-8pm Sat & Sun) This is the city's most prestigious venue in which to hear symphony concerts, jazz and world-music performances; it also stages theatrical productions.

Pogon Jedinstvo · ARTS CENTRE
(www.upogoni.org; Kneza Mislava 11) At Pogon – Zagreb Center for Independent Culture and Youth, you can catch contemporary dance and theatre, concerts, parties, public lectures, exhibitions and festivals.

Tvornica · LIVE MUSIC
(www.tvornicakulture.com; Šubićeva 2; ☉ cafe 7am-11pm Mon-Fri, 4-11pm Sat & Sun, club 8pm-2am Sun-Thu, to 4am Fri & Sat) Excellent multimedia venue showcasing a variety of live-music performances, from Bosnian *sevdah* to alternative punk rock. Check out the website to see what's on.

Cibona Tower · BASKETBALL
(☑ 01-48 43 333; www.cibona.com; Savska 30; tickets 10-150KN) Basketball is popular in Zagreb, and the city is home to the Cibona basketball team. This tower is the team's base.

Stadion Maksimir · FOOTBALL
(☑ 01-23 86 111; www.gnkdinamo.hr; Maksimirska 128; tickets 250-550KN) Dinamo is Zagreb's most popular football team; it plays matches at Stadion Maksimir, on the eastern side of Zagreb. Take trams 4, 7, 11 or 12 to Maksimirska.

🛍 Shopping

Ilica is Zagreb's main shopping street, with fashionable international brands peeking out from the staid buildings. Most stores are closed on Sunday.

Cool stores have popped up all over the city, including design stores, shoemakers and handmade-bag boutiques.

🏠 Lower Town

Croatian Design Superstore · DESIGN
(www.croatiandesignsuperstore.com; Martićeva 4; ☉ 9am-9pm Mon-Sat) This one-stop shop for the best of Croatian design stocks more than 130 curated items by 150 different creators. Clad in all red, the store showcases the cream of Croatia's homegrown design, from accessories and gifts to wine and lighting. It doubles as a platform for promoting Croatian design and also has a sweet little cafe serving healthy bites.

Vintesa · WINE
(www.vintesa.hr; Vlaška 63; ☉ 9am-9pm Mon-Fri, 9am-8pm Sat) Hidden inside a courtyard, this pioneer wine shop is a treasure trove of local wines charmingly lined up on brick and wood shelves. The extra-friendly staff will not only suggest a bottle that suits everyone's taste but will unravel a story behind each grape variety, batch and bottle.

Zvonimir · SHOES
(www.facebook.com/balerinke; Dalmatinska 12; ☉ 9am-1pm & 5-8pm Mon-Fri, 9am-3pm Sat) Nataša Trinajstić is a third-generation shoemaker from this well-known Zagreb family. Visit her small shop and studio where she craftily blends the tradition of artisanship with modern signature touches. Go for ready-made shoes (Oxfords, ballerinas, pumps, Mary Janes, stilettos), sandals or boots or get Nataša to whip up some custom-made footwear.

Cerovečki Umbrellas · FASHION & ACCESSORIES
(www.kisobrani-cerovecki.hr; Ilica 49; ☉ 8.30am-8pm Mon-Fri, to 2.30pm Sat) Quality, design and a brand story safeguard this umbrella artisan from the onslaught of global products. Visit their shop – a wormhole to a different era – showcasing a distinctive award-winning range of umbrellas, used by people worldwide. The red-patterned Šestine umbrella has become the epitome of Zagreb. To show off, choose one of the ladies' parasols with rich intricate lace.

Salon Croata · CLOTHING
(www.croata.hr; Ilica 5, Oktogon Passage; ☉ 8am-8pm Mon-Fri, to 3pm Sat) Since the necktie originated in Croatia, nothing could make a more authentic gift – and this is the place to get one. The locally made silk neckties are priced from 400KN to 2000KN.

68

MARKET DAYS

Zagreb doesn't have many markets but those it does have are stellar. The weekend **antiques market** (Britanski trg; ⊘7am-2pm Sat, 7.30am-2.30pm Sun) on Britanski trg, for example, is one of central Zagreb's joys.

But to see a flea market that's unmatched in the whole of Croatia, you have to make it to Hrelić (p69). This humongous space is chock-full of eclectic items and quirky bric-a-brac. Don't miss it.

If you're into food, don't miss **Mali Plac s Tavana** (Little Market from the Attic; www.mali-plac.org; ⊘hours vary), a weekly gathering of small producers who hawk their wares in various locations around the city (see the website for the current schedule); you'll find anything from organic citrus fruits and sage honey to hemp oil and hummus, plus handcrafted natural cosmetics.

Profil Megastore　　　　BOOKS
(Bogovićeva 7; ⊘8am-9pm Mon-Sat) Inside an entryway, this most atmospheric of Zagreb bookstores has a great selection of books (including a whole section of titles in English) and a nice cafe.

Vilma Natura Croatica　　　　FOOD
(www.naturacroatica.com; Preradovićeva 8; ⊘9am-9pm Mon-Fri, 10am-4pm Sat) Over 300 Croatian products and souvenirs are sold at this shop, from *rakija,* wines and chocolates to jams, spices and truffle spreads. A perfect pit stop for gifts.

Upper Town

Koza　　　　FASHION & ACCESSORIES
(Basaričekova 18; ⊘11am-7pm Mon-Sat) This tiny studio-shop on a quiet Upper Town street turns out gorgeous handmade leather bags and accessories like wallets, belts and even flip-flops. The elegant, chic yet quirky bags are crafted with all-Croatian materials, including high-quality leather.

Take Me Home　　　　GIFTS & SOUVENIRS
(www.takemehome.hr; Tomićeva 4; ⊘9.30am-8pm Mon-Fri, 10am-3pm Sat) Great choice of cool souvenirs, all by Croatian designers.

Aromatica　　　　COSMETICS
(www.aromatica.hr; Vlaška 7; ⊘8am-8pm Mon-Fri, to 3pm Sat) Flagship store of a small chain showcasing all-natural skincare products, from handcrafted soaps to fragrant oils, with a focus on local herbs. Great gift baskets, too.

Bornstein　　　　WINE
(www.bornstein.hr; Kaptol 19; ⊘9am-8pm Mon-Fri, to 4.30pm Sat) If Croatia's wine and spirits have gone to your head, get your fix here. Stocks an astonishing collection of brandy, wine and gourmet products. There's also a wine bar on site.

Notes of Zagreb　　　　PERFUME
(www.notesofzagreb.com; Skalinska 2; ⊘10am-8pm Mon-Fri, 10am-3pm Sat) This tiny storefront carries home fragrances inspired by different scents of Zagreb, such as chestnut and plane trees in autumn. Think room sprays, incense sticks, textile sprays and scented candles, with fun names like The Witch of Grich, Secret of the Bloody Bridge and the Well of Life.

Love, Ana　　　　DESIGN
(www.loveanadesign.com; Dežmanova 4; ⊘2-8pm Mon-Fri, noon-2pm Sat) Internationally acclaimed product designer Ana Tevšić sells her signature products at her all-white studio-store, including portable lamps, bucket bags and beach towels.

Boudoir　　　　FASHION & ACCESSORIES
(www.boudoirzagreb.com; Radićeva 22; ⊘11am-7pm Mon-Fri, 10am-2pm Sat) When you walk up cobbled Radićeva street, stop by the buzzer that says 'press for champagne' and let yourself into an otherworldly designer shop where silk, satin and lace dresses are handmade on site. The owners, sisters Morana and Martina, create outfits that are a unique mixture of elegance and funkiness with an added spice of Moulin Rouge.

Cahun　　　　HATS
(www.cahun.hr; Podzidom 8; ⊘9am-7pm Mon-Fri, 9am-2pm Sat) This 80-year-old family-run hat shop oozes the old Zagreb charms. Their headgear is meticulously handcrafted following a traditional approach, but infused with modern designer touches. Take your pick from hats galore, for both ladies and gents, and for all seasons: cloche, fedora, panama and trilby hats; beret, newsboy and flat caps, and many more. Discounts available for cash payments.

I-GLE FASHION & ACCESSORIES
(www.i-gle.com; Dežmanova 4; ⊙10am-8pm Mon-Fri, to 3pm Sat) Get one of the almost sculptural yet wearable creations by Nataša Mihaljčišin and Martina Vrdoljak-Ranilović, the movers and shakers of Croatia's fashion industry since the 1990s.

Novi Zagreb

Hrelić MARKET
(⊙7am-3pm Wed, Sat & Sun) Croatia's largest and most colourful flea market, a huge space packed with everything from car parts and antique furniture to clothes, records and kitchenware. All goods are secondhand, of course, and bargaining is the norm.

It's a great experience in itself and is a side of Zagreb you probably won't see anywhere else – expect lots of Roma people, music, general liveliness and grilled meat smoking in the food section. If you're going in the summer months, bring a hat and wear sunscreen, as there's no shade.

Take bus 295 (15KN, 20 minutes, Sundays only) to Sajam Jakuševac from behind the railway station. By tram, take number 6 in the direction of Sopot, get off near the bridge and walk 15 minutes along the Sava to get to Hrelić; or take tram 14, get off at the last stop in Zaprude and begin the 15-minute walk from there.

Western Zagreb

Grga Čvarak FOOD
(☑01-88 95 036; www.facebook.com/Grga-Čvarak-510825808976258; Kutnjački Put 9; ⊙7.30am-9pm Mon-Sat, 8am-2pm Sun) Food connoisseurs won't regret tracking down this leading speciality food shop in the Jarun neighbourhood, with the best choice of exclusive artisan products available. Get your organic fruit and veg here or indulge your sweet tooth with homemade strudel, raw desserts or organic ice cream.

ⓘ Information

MEDICAL SERVICES

Dental Emergency (☑01-48 97 688; Perkovčeva 3; ⊙10pm-6am)

Emergency Health Clinic (☑01-63 02 911; Heinzelova 87; ⊙24hr)

KBC Rebro (☑01-23 88 888; Kišpatićeva 12; ⊙24hr) East of the city; provides emergency aid.

Pharmacy (☑01-48 16 198; Trg Bana Jelačića 3; ⊙24hr)

POST

Main Post Office (☑01-72 303 304; Branimirova 4; ⊙7am-midnight) Holds poste restante mail. Right by the train station.

Post Office (☑072 303 304; Jurišićeva 13; ⊙7am-8pm Mon-Fri, to 2pm Sat) Has a telephone centre.

TOURIST INFORMATION

Main Tourist Information Centre (☑information 0800 53 53, office 01-48 14 051; www.infozagreb.hr; Trg Bana Jelačića 11; ⊙8.30am-9pm Mon-Fri, 9am-6pm Sat & Sun Jun-Sep, 8.30am-8pm Mon-Fri, 9am-6pm Sat, 10am-4pm Sun Oct-May) Distributes free city maps and leaflets. There are also tourist information centres at Lotrščak Tower (☑01-48 51 510; ⊙9am-9pm Mon-Fri, 10am-9pm Sat & Sun Jun-Sep, 9am-5pm Mon-Fri, 10am-5pm Sat & Sun Oct-May); the main railway station (⊙9am-9pm Mon-Fri, 10am-5pm Sat & Sun); the main bus station (☑01-61 15 507; ⊙9am-9pm Mon-Fri, 10am-5pm Sat & Sun); and Zagreb Airport (☑01-62 65 091; ⊙9am-9pm Mon-Fri, 10am-5pm Sat & Sun).

Zagreb County Tourist Association (☑01-48 73 665; www.tzzz.hr; Preradovićeva 42; ⊙8am-4pm Mon-Fri) Has information and materials about attractions in Zagreb's surroundings, including wine roads and bike trails.

TRAVEL AGENCIES

Atlas Travel Agency (☑01-48 07 300; www.atlas-croatia.com; Zrinjevac 17; ⊙8am-8pm Mon-Fri, 9am-2pm Sat) Offers tours around Croatia.

Croatia Express (☑01-49 22 224; www.croatia-express.com; Trg Kralja Tomislava 17; ⊙8am-6.30pm Mon-Fri, 9am-1pm Sat) Train reservations, car rental, air and ferry tickets, hotels around the country and a daily trip to the beach from June to September.

Zdenac Života (☑01-48 16 200; Tkalčićeva 5; ⊙9am-5pm Mon-Fri) In addition to thematic sightseeing tours of Zagreb, this small agency does active day trips from the capital and multiday adventures around Croatia.

ⓘ Getting There & Away

AIR

Croatia Airlines (☑01-48 19 633; www.croatiaairlines.com; Zrinjevac 17; ⊙8am-6pm Mon-Fri, 9am-3pm Sat & Sun) The country's national carrier operates international and domestic flights to and from Zagreb.

Zagreb Airport (☑01-45 62 170; www.zagreb-airport.hr) Located 17km southeast of Zagreb, this is Croatia's major airport, offering a range of international and domestic services.

BUS

Zagreb's **bus station** (🖉 060 313 333; www. akz.hr; Avenija M Držića 4) is 1km east of the train station. If you need to store bags, there's a **garderoba** (🖉 01-60 08 649; per hour 5KN; ⏲ 24hr). Trams 2 and 6 run from the bus station to the train station. Tram 6 goes to Trg Bana Jelačića.

Before buying your ticket, ask about the arrival time – some of the buses take local roads and stop in every town en route.

Bus line 106 goes from Kaptol to Mirogoj.

TRAIN

The **train station** (🖉 060 333 444; www.hzpp. hr; Trg Kralja Tomislava 12) is in the southern part of the city centre. As you come out of it, you'll see a series of parks and pavilions directly in front of you that lead into the town centre.

Seating is limited so it's advisable to book train tickets in advance. The station also has a **garderoba** (locker per 24hr 15KN; ⏲ 24hr) if you need to store bags.

🛈 Getting Around

TO/FROM THE AIRPORT

The Croatia Airlines bus to the airport (30KN) leaves from the bus station every half-hour or hour from about 4.30am to 8pm, and returns from the airport on the same schedule.

Taxis cost between 110KN and 200KN to the city centre.

BICYCLE

Zagreb has a bike-sharing system called Next-Bike (www.nextbike.hr), with several stations around the city centre. You can register at the station directly, via the website or with their app.

CAR

Zagreb is a fairly easy city to navigate by car (main streets are wide, and parking in the city centre, although scarce, only costs 6KN per hour). Watch out for trams buzzing around.

A number of international car-hire companies, such as **Hertz** (🖉 01-72 72 7277; www.hertz.hr;

BUSES FROM ZAGREB

Note that listed schedules are somewhat reduced outside high season.

DOMESTIC DESTINATION	COST (KN)	DURATION (HR)	DAILY SERVICES
Dubrovnik	191-231	9½-11	9-12
Korčula	261	11	1
Krk	111	3-4½	10-13
Makarska	175-230	6½	12-15
Mali Lošinj	149-189	5-6	5
Osijek	131-144	4	10-12
Plitvice	85-93	2-3	15
Poreč	156-232	4-4½	11
Pula	105-196	3½-5½	20
Rab	207-219	4-5	5
Rijeka	49-106	2½-4	20-25
Rovinj	100-195	4-6	20
Šibenik	151-165	4½-7	20-22
Split	115-205	5-8½	32-34
Varaždin	65-87	1-2	19-23
Zadar	90-135	3½-5	31

INTERNATIONAL DESTINATION	COST (KN)	DURATION (HR)	DAILY SERVICES
Belgrade	230	6	6
Ljubljana	40-129	2½-3	20
Milan	290-410	9	3
Munich	149-379	7-8	19
Paris	703	23	1
Sarajevo	198	7-8	4-5
Vienna	160-247	5	10

TRAINS FROM ZAGREB

DOMESTIC DESTINATION	COST (KN)	DURATION (HR)	DAILY SERVICES
Osijek	132-150	4½-5½	4
Rijeka	111-118	4-5	3
Šibenik	176-194	8	13-18
Split	190-208	5-7	3-4
Varaždin	64-71	2-3	6-14
Zadar	184-202	12	12-18

INTERNATIONAL DESTINATION	COST (KN)	DURATION (HR)	DAILY SERVICES
Banja Luka	78	4½-5	1
Belgrade	184	6½	2
Budapest	246	6-7	2
Ljubljana	68	2½	5
Mostar	207 (via Sarajevo)	11½	1
Munich	817	8-9	2
Sarajevo	165	8-9½	1
Venice	497 (via Villach)	8-9	3
Vienna	549	6-7	1

Grada Vukovara 274; ⊙7am-6pm Mon-Fri, 8am-6pm Sat, 8am-noon Sun), are represented in Zagreb. Bear in mind that local companies will usually have lower rates.

H&M (⏀01-37 04 535; www.hm-rentacar.hr; Grahorova 11) Local car-rental company; also at the airport.

Hrvatski Autoklub (HAK; Croatian Auto Club; ⏀0800 99 87; www.hak.hr) Motorists can call 1987 for help on the road. For traffic information, call ⏀072 777 777.

Oryx (⏀01-62 60 800; www.oryx-rent.hr; Grada Vukovara 74; ⊙reservation office 7am-7pm Mon-Fri, 8am-4pm Sat & Sun) Local car-rental company; also at the airport.

PUBLIC TRANSPORT

Zagreb's public transport (www.zet.hr) is based on an efficient network of trams, although the city centre is compact enough to make them almost unnecessary. Tram maps are posted at most stations, making the system easy to navigate.

Buy tickets at newspaper kiosks or from the driver for 10KN (15KN at night). You can use your ticket for transfers within 90 minutes, but only in one direction. A *dnevna karta* (day ticket) is valid on all public transport until 4am the next morning; it's available for 30KN at most newspaper kiosks.

Make sure you validate your ticket when you get on the tram by pressing it on the yellow box.

TAXI

Radio Taxi (⏀1717) charges 10KN to start, then 5KN per kilometre; waiting time is 40KN per hour. **Ekotaxi** (⏀1414, 060 77 77; www.ekotaxi.hr) charges similar rates.

You'll have no trouble finding idle taxis, usually at blue-marked taxi signs; note that these are Radio Taxi stands.

For short city rides, **Taxi Cammeo** (⏀1212, 01-62 88 926) is typically the cheapest, as the 15KN initial fare includes the first two kilometres (it's 6KN for every subsequent kilometre).

Zagreb also has Uber.

Inland Croatia

Why Go?

In addition to Zagreb, the country's burgeoning capital, inland Croatia offers diverse landscapes featuring a mix of small-town highlights, countryside delights and natural marvels.

To the east of Zagreb, towards Hungary and Serbia, stretch Pannonian plains and the flat farmlands of Slavonia. Here you'll find the watery wonderland of Kopački Rit Nature Park, as well as wine roads with historic cellars, scenic cycling routes, delightful rural B&Bs, and the riverside city of Osijek with its ancient quarter set in a baroque citadel.

The bucolic northern region of Zagorje showcases fairy-tale medieval castles, vineyard-speckled hills, towns built around thermal springs, and the baroque beauty of Varaždin, one of Croatia's prettiest small towns. Other highlights include Lonjsko Polje Nature Park, southeast of Zagreb, with its historic timber villages and great birdwatching, and the undulating landscapes, wine cellars, country restaurants and thermal spas of Međimurje, northeast of Varaždin.

Best Places to Eat

➡ Kod Ruže (p91)
➡ Josić (p95)
➡ Grešna Gorica (p83)
➡ Klet Kozjak (p79)

Best Places to Sleep

➡ Maksimilian (p89)
➡ Vuglec Breg (p78)
➡ Park Boutique Hotel (p84)
➡ Hiže na Bregu (p79)

When to Go
Osijek

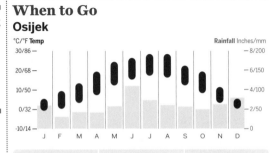

°C/°F Temp   Rainfall Inches/mm
30/86 —   — 8/200
20/68 —   — 6/150
10/50 —   — 4/100
0/32 —   — 2/50
-10/14 —   — 0
        J F M A M J J A S O N D

Apr & May Nature wakes up after winter hibernation and inland areas become lovely to explore.

Jul & Aug Most people head to the coast and it's a blissfully crowd-free time, though hot.

Sep & Oct Join the wine harvest and sample great local offerings.

AROUND ZAGREB

The area around Zagreb is rich with quick getaway options, from picturesque towns with great food to peaceful hikes and nature reserves.

Samobor

☑ 01 / POP 19,000

Samobor is where stressed-out city dwellers come to wind down and get their fix of hearty food, creamy cakes and pretty scenery. A shallow stream of the Gradna curves through the town centre, which is composed of trim pastel houses and several old churches.

The main focus of the town's economic activities are tourism and bolstering small family businesses, including restaurants and those involved in handicrafts and the production of mustard, wine and spirits. The town's literary and musical traditions are reflected in a number of annual festivals, most famously the Fašnik (Samobor Carnival) in January and February, and the Samobor Autumn Music Festival in September and October.

🏃 Activities

Samobor is a good jumping-off point for hiking into the Samoborsko Gorje, a mountain system (part of the Žumberak Range) that links the high peaks of the Alps with the karstic caves and abysses of the Dinaric Range; carpeted with meadows and forests, it's the region's most popular hiking destination, and has been the cradle of organised mountaineering activity in Croatia since 1875. Most of the hikes are easy and there are well-marked trails and nine mountain huts that make pleasant rest stops. Many are open weekends only (except in high season); more information is available through the **Croatian Mountaineering Association** (www.hps.hr; Kozarčeva 22; ⊙ 8am-4pm Mon-Fri). In 1999 the whole area, covering 333 sq km, was proclaimed a nature park, Žumberak and Samobor Hills (www.park-zumberak. hr), because of its biodiversity, forests, karst caves, river canyons and four waterfalls.

The range is divided into three sections: the Oštrc group in the centre, the Japetić group to the west and the Plešivica group to the east. Both the Oštrc and Japetić groups are accessible from the Šoićeva Kuća mountain hut and restaurant, 10km west of Samobor, reachable by bus 144 (direction Lipovec). From there it's a rather steep 30-minute climb to the medieval hill fort of Lipovec and an hour's hike to the peak of Oštrc (752m), with another mountain hut.

Another popular hike is the 1½-hour climb from Šoićeva Kuća to Japetić (879m), the highest peak of Samobor Hills and a famous paragliding spot (see www.parafreek. hr for information). You can also follow a path from Oštrc to Japetić (two hours). The Plešivica group has ruins of a medieval fort and a protected park forest area, and it's also a famous rock-climbing spot; you can access it from the village of Rude (bus 143 services Rude and Braslovje). From Rude, head east to the hunting cabin Srndać on the mountain saddle of Poljanice (12km), from where it's a 40-minute, rather steep hike to the peak of Plešivica (779m).

🛏 Sleeping & Eating

Most people come to Samobor on a day trip from Zagreb, but there are a couple of sleeping options should you wish to stay, including a family-run hotel right in the town centre and a hostel.

Samobor is mostly known for its famous custard pies *(kremšnite)* but it's also home to one of Croatia's best ice-cream shops and a fantastic classic restaurant.

U Prolazu   DESSERTS €
(Trg Kralja Tomislava 5; ⊙ 7am-11pm) The best *kremšnite* (7KN to 18KN) in town.

Slatka Tvornica Medenko   ICE CREAM €
(Mirka Kleščića 1; ⊙ 9am-9pm) Don't miss this amazing ice-cream shop, which has quickly become one of Croatia's best. Their ice cream is made in a traditional way, with no artificial aromas, colourings or preservatives, and the flavours are unique – pumpkin oil, spinach, blue cheese and carrot. They recently opened a shop in Zagreb too (next door to Cafe u Dvorištu; p65).

Gabreku 1929   CROATIAN €€
(www.gabrek.hr; Starogradska 46; mains 55-150KN; ⊙ noon-midnight) This classic restaurant, a short walk from the town centre, has been run by the same family since the 1920s. It's known for its 40 types of sweet and savoury *palačinke* (crêpes).

ℹ Information

Tourist Office (☑ 01-33 60 044; www.tz-samobor.hr; Trg Kralja Tomislava 5; ⊙ 8am-4pm Mon-Fri, 9am-5pm Sat & Sun) In the town centre. Has plentiful brochures and maps of

Inland Croatia Highlights

1 **Varaždin** (p81) Admiring its immaculately preserved baroque architecture.

2 **Baranja** (p94) Exploring the region's wine roads and historic cellars.

3 **Kopački Rit Nature Park** (p93) Taking a boat tour through the vast wetlands.

4 **Vučedol Culture Museum** (p96) Learning about a fascinating ancient

civilisation at this significant archaeological site at Vukovar.

5 **Museum of the Krapina Neanderthal** (p80) Learning about our distant ancestors in Krapina.

6 **Tvrđa** (p91) Feasting on Slavonian specialities in Osijek's fortress quarter.

7 **Vuglec Breg** (p78) Sampling Zagorje cuisine near Krapinske Toplice.

8 **Samobor** (p73) Tasting this lovely town's famous *kremšnite* (custard pies).

9 **Kumrovec Staro Selo Museum** (p77) Getting an insight into traditional village life at Kumrovec's open-air ethnographic museum.

10 **Lonjsko Polje Nature Park** (p86) Checking out the traditional villages, white storks and swamplands.

Samobor, as well as maps and hiking information for Samoborsko Gorje and Žumberačko Gorje.

ℹ Getting There & Away

Samobor is easy to reach by public transport. Get a Samoborček or Autoturist Samobor bus from the main bus station in Zagreb (28KN, 40 minutes, half-hourly). Samobor's bus station (no left-luggage office) is on Ulica 151 Samoborske Brigade HV 1, about 20 minutes on foot from the main square.

Mt Medvednica

The mountain of Medvednica perches proudly above Zagreb, its verdant slopes offering an easy escape for Zagreb locals. The city's most popular spot for outdoor activities – with skiing in wintertime and hiking the rest of the year – the mountain showcases some superb scenery and a handful of appealing sights. From a medieval fort and humongous cave to mountain huts that serve local specialities, Medvednica Nature Park features enough to keep visitors happily entertained for a day or two.

◎ Sights

Medvedgrad   FORTRESS
(🖉 01-45 86 317; www.pp-medvednica.hr; 15KN; ⏰ 11am-7pm Tue-Sun Apr-Sep, 10am-6pm Tue-Sun Oct, 10am-7pm Sat & Sun Nov) The medieval fortress of Medvedgrad, just above the city on the southern side of Mt Medvednica, is Zagreb's most important medieval monument. Built from 1249 to 1254, it was erected to protect the city from Tartar invasions. Today you can see the rebuilt thick walls and towers, a small chapel with frescoes and the Shrine of the Homeland, which pays homage to those who died for a free Croatia. On a clear day it offers beautiful views of Zagreb and surrounds.

In July it hosts Medvedgrad Music Evenings, concerts under starry skies with amazing vistas of the twinkling lights below. To get here, take bus 102 from Britanski Trg and get off at the church in Šestine; continue on foot following hiking trail #12 (from Lagvić to Medvedgrad)

Veternica Cave   CAVE
(www.pp-medvednica.hr/en/turisticka-ponuda/spilja-veternica/; adult/student/child 40/25/20KN; ⏰ 8am-4pm Mon-Fri, 10am-4pm Sat & Sun Apr-Oct) The sixth-largest cave in Croatia, Veternica is open for visitors. You can explore the first

380m of the cave on a guided tour that takes about an hour. It's located in the western part of Medvednica, which is also home to Glavica Mountain Hut.

To reach the cave from Zagreb, take city bus 124 from Črnomerec to Gornji Stenjevec (the ride takes about 15 minutes). Then walk by the Dubravica stream uphill to Veternica for about 20 minutes on the trail marked 3 (it's another 15 minutes on to Glavica).

🏃 Activities

Medvednica Nature Park, just to the north of Zagreb, offers excellent hiking opportunities. There are several popular and well-marked routes. Allow about three hours' return for any of the hikes – and remember that this is a heavily wooded mountain with ample opportunities to get lost. Maps are available at the Croatian Mountaineering Association (p73) and at the head office of Medvednica Nature Park. Take water and warm clothes, and make sure you return before sundown. There is also a danger of disease-carrying ticks in spring, so wear trousers and long sleeves, and examine your body after hiking. For more information, contact the Medvednica Nature Park (p77).

One of the popular routes is the easy Leustekov trail (marked 14), which ends at Sljeme, the top of Mt Medvednica. Along the way you can stop at one of Sljeme's oldest huts, **Runolist** (🖉 01-45 57 519; mains 35-65KN; ⏰ 8am-8pm), which offers beautiful views of the city and traditional food and drink.

Alternatively you can hike in the direction of the Puntijarka (p77) and Hunjka mountain huts. There is also the shorter but steeper and more intense Bikčevićeva path (marked 18), which starts at the Bliznec entrance to Medvednica Nature Park.

To visit the attractive eastern side of the Medvednica mountain, take bus 205 or 208 from Dubrava bus terminal in Zagreb to Bidrovec or Vidovec villages. From there, take marked mountain trails 24 or 25/25a to Gorščica mountain hut; the walk takes approximately two hours.

Ski Resort Sljeme   SKIING
(🖉 01-45 53 382; www.sljeme.hr; day lift ticket adult/child weekdays 70/40KN, weekends 100/50KN) Although Zagreb is not normally associated with winter sports, you can ski right outside town at Sljeme, the main peak of Mt Medvednica. It has five ski runs, two ski lifts and a triple chairlift. There's night skiing on the Red Slope and the White Meadow.

Passes are available at the bottom of the Red Slope.

Check the website for information on snow conditions. During winter months, Sljeme hosts a number of skiing competitions, such as the FIS World Ski Cup.

🛏 Sleeping & Eating

It's unlikely you'll want to sleep on Medvednica with Zagreb so close, though several mountain huts are available, should you wish to overnight.

Puntijarka   CROATIAN €
(☑ 01-45 80 384; mains 35-60KN; ☺ 9am-9pm Mon-Fri, 7am-9pm Sat & Sun) This mountain hut is very popular on weekends for its home-cooked traditional Croatian dishes served in a rustic setting.

Grafičar   CROATIAN €
(☑ 01-45 55 844; mains 30-60KN; ☺ 9am-9pm Tue-Fri, 8am-9pm Sat & Sun) On the western side of Medvednica, this beloved mountain hut at 864m has great basic lodgings and serves hearty food.

❶ Information

Medvednica Nature Park Info Point (☑ 01-45 86 317; www.pp-medvednica.hr; Bliznec 70)

❶ Getting There & Away

Mt Medvednica can be accessed easily from Zagreb. You can take tram 14 to the last stop and then change to tram 15 and take it to its last stop. Walk straight through the tunnel, which takes you directly to Dolje park entrance.

You can also take bus 102 from Britanski trg in Zagreb, west of the centre on Ilica, to the church in Šestine, and take the easy hiking route from there.

Alternatively, if you are driving, any of the nature-park entrances have car parking available.

ZAGORJE

Despite its proximity to Zagreb, the bucolic northern region of Zagorje receives few tourists, even at the height of summer – especially surprising given the delightful villages, medieval castles, endless vineyards and thermal springs that speckle its rolling hills. These leafy landscapes, with Austrian-influenced food and architecture (and the same prices year-round), present a nice alternative to the busy Mediterranean south and a good escape from the summer heat. You'll find it blissfully crowd-free, although slightly less so on weekends, when day-tripping families from Zagreb storm the area.

The Zagorje region begins north of Mt Medvednica (1035m), near Zagreb, and extends west to the Slovenian border, and as far north as Varaždin, a showcase of baroque architecture. Whether you want to feast on hearty cuisine at rustic restaurants, dip into the hot springs, get a taste of village life or tour ancient castles, with Zagorje you're in for an offbeat treat.

INLAND CROATIA ZAGORJE

WORTH A TRIP

KUMROVEC

Nestled in the Sutla River valley near the Slovenian border, the pretty village of Kumrovec has been transformed into an open-air ethnographic museum. A re-creation of a 19th-century village, the **Kumrovec Staro Selo Museum** (Kumrovec bb; adult/concession 20/10KN; ☺ 9am-7pm Apr-Sep, to 4pm Nov-Feb, to 4pm Mon-Fri, to 6pm Sat & Sun Mar & Oct) features 40 restored houses and barns made of pressed earth and wood. The village was also the birthplace of Josip Broz Tito, the former President of Yugoslavia. His house has been made into a museum containing original furniture, letters from foreign leaders and memorabilia, with a life-sized bronze sculpture outside.

With a stream bubbling through the idyllic setting, the museum presents a vivid glimpse of peasant traditions and village life. These *hiže* (traditional Zagorje huts) are now filled with furniture, mannequins, toys, wine presses and baker's tools (all accompanied by English captions) in order to evoke the region's traditional arts, crafts and customs. On some weekends (April to September) the museum hosts demonstrations of blacksmithing, candlemaking, pottery making and flax weaving. For Tito's birthday, on 25 May, the village comes alive with devotees from all over former Yugoslavia.

There are two daily buses running between Zagreb and Kumrovec (52KN, 1¼ hours) on weekdays only.

Marija Bistrica

☑ 049 / POP 6600

Croatia's largest pilgrimage centre is in Zagorje at Marija Bistrica, a village 37km north of Zagreb on the slopes of Mt Medvednica. What steals the show here is the Marija Bistrica Church, with its Black Madonna statue, and the Way of the Cross path up Calvary Hill. For the most popular pilgrimage, Velika Gospa, visit on 15 August.

🛏 Sleeping

Bluesun Hotel Kaj HOTEL €€
(☑ 049-326 600; www.hotelkaj.hr; Zagrebačka bb; s/d 510/720KN; P❄🖦🛉🖦) One of Zagorje's most luxurious hotels, Hotel Kaj offers well-appointed rooms, two excellent restaurants and an extensive spa and wellness area with a whirlpool, saunas and beauty treatments. The Academia restaurant has an impressive wine list with over 200 wines from Croatia and beyond.

ℹ Getting There & Away

There are up to 20 buses a day from Zagreb to Marija Bistrica on weekdays (36KN to 44KN, one hour), with fewer on weekends.

Klanjec

☑ 049 / POP 3200

The pleasant town of Klanjec is a nice pit-stop to catch some fantastic sculpture art: it's the birthplace of a notable Croat, sculptor Antun Augustinčić (1900–79), who created the *Monument to Peace* in front of the UN building in New York, and the town is home to the Antun Augustinčić Gallery. Also here is a 17th-century baroque church and Franciscan monastery.

◉ Sights

**Baroque Church
and Franciscan Monastery** CHURCH
(Mihanovićev Trg 11; 10KN) This 17th-century baroque church at the heart of town was built in 1630 by the noble Erdödy brothers. The adjacent Franciscan monastery has two recently restored sarcophagi of the Erdödy family, elaborate findings from the baroque era, hidden in the crypt. Make arrangements to see them through the tourist office.

Antun Augustinčić Gallery GALLERY
(Trg Antuna Mihanovića 10; adult/concession 20/10KN; ☺ 9am-5pm Apr-Sep, to 3pm Tue-Sun Oct-Mar)

The Antun Augustinčić Gallery is devoted to his opus, plus there's lots of headless bronze torsos and a huge replica of his *Monument to Peace*. There's a small sculpture garden outside and the sculptor's memorial to fallen Partisans nearby.

ℹ Information

Tourist Office (☑ 049-550 235; www.klanjec.hr; Trg A Mihanovića 3; ☺ 8am-4pm Mon-Fri, to 1pm Sat) Though it has sporadic hours, it can arrange visits to the church and monastery.

ℹ Getting There & Away

The two daily buses running from Zagreb to Kumrovec stop in Klanjec on weekdays (51KN, one to 1½ hours). There are no buses on weekends.

Krapinske Toplice

☑ 049 / POP 5700

The spa town of Krapinske Toplice, about 17km southwest of Krapina, is located amid the rolling hills of the Zagorje countryside. The showpieces are the four thermal springs, rich in magnesium and calcium and never below a temperature of 39°C. The town itself isn't particularly attractive nor is its atmosphere upbeat, as the visitor pool mainly has elderly patients in various rehabilitation programs. However, the recent unveiling of the swank thermal spa centre, Aquae Vivae, has injected new energy into the town.

🏊 Activities

Aquae Vivae SPA
(☑ 049-501 999; www.aquae-vivae.hr; Ulica Antuna Mihanovića 1a; adult/concession weekdays 70/50KN, weekends 90/60KN; ☺ 9am-9pm) This swank new spa centre has brought a breath of fresh air to Krapinske Toplice. The biggest and most modern complex of indoor pools in Croatia, spanning 18,000 sq metres, it also has an outdoor pool with underwater features like massages, spouts and cascades, a large terrace with a view of the valley, and even a pool for scuba diving.

🛏 Sleeping

★**Vuglec Breg** INN €€
(☑ 049-345 015; www.vuglec-breg.hr; Škarićevo 151, Škarićevo; s/d 390/540KN; P@🛉🖦) This delightful rural inn has a scenic location in the village of Škarićevo, 4km from Krapinske Toplice. The five traditional cottages

RURAL ESCAPES

Rural retreats that offer food and accommodation have been mushrooming around Zagorje in the last few years. Weekends at these hideaways are typically packed with Zagreb day trippers, but come on a weekday and you'll have them practically to yourself. All of the following are best reached with your own wheels.

Tuheljske Toplice (www.terme-tuhelj.hr; hot springs per day adult/child 65/35KN Mon-Fri, 75/45KN Sat & Sun; ⊙24hr) The spa of Tuheljske Toplice, a short drive from Zagreb in the pretty village of Tuhelj, en route to Kumrovec, has been a long-standing favourite for urbanites. There are several accommodation options here, including the four-star Hotel Well, as well as the recently opened Hostel Villa and a seasonal campsite.

Bolfan Vinski Vrh (www.bolfanvinskivrh.hr; Hraščina) For tastings of award-winning wines, head to Bolfan Vinski Vrh in the village of Hraščina, near the town of Zlatar. Inside this beautiful hilltop *klet* (typical Zagorje cottage), with sloping vineyards and some of Zagorje's best views, there's also a great restaurant (open Wednesday to Sunday).

Hiže na Bregu (☑098 92 90 881; www.hizenabregu.com; Hižakovec 2/1, Donja Stubica; s/cottages 100/690KN; ℙ) Hiže na Bregu, in the village of Hižakovec (near Donja Stubica), is an adorable hideaway in the northern foothills of Mt Medvednica. The traditional Zagorje cottage, clad in wood, has three sweet rooms – two doubles in the main house and a single in a separate cottage – and lovely surroundings that include an orchard and garden for guest use.

Majsecov Mlin (☑049-288 092; www.majsecov-mlin.com; Obrtnička 47, Donja Stubica; mains 55-80KN; ⊙9am-11pm; ℙ🍴) Housed in two traditional cottages near the village of Donja Stubica, Majsecov Mlin serves local mainstays, seasonally inspired and cooked up by one of Zagorje's best chefs. Try the delicious steak with nettle chips and Zagorje-style pesto. On site is an old mill, which to this day grinds maize for use in corn flour. In summer months, small producers sell their edible wares at the little market here. You can also spend the night in one of five rooms (singles/doubles 180/360KN).

Klet Kozjak (☑049-228 800; www.klet-kozjak.hr; Kozjak 18a, Sveti Križ Začretje; mains 55-110KN; ⊙8am-10pm) Klet Kozjak in Sveti Križ Začretje, southeast of Krapina, is an adorable little cottage that serves traditional food from the region – such as homemade nettle pasta with cheese and vegetable sauce – and pairs it with sweeping views of the hills and valleys from the terrace. Run by a local family that has been in the goat-breeding business for generations, it is known for its excellent goat cheese and oven-baked kid goat. If you also want to stay, there are a few rooms here (singles/doubles 315/475KN).

(featuring rooms and suites) sit amid hills, vineyards and forests. The restaurant (mains 95 to 120KN) serves fantastic Zagorje specialities, such as *purica s mlincima* (slow-roasted turkey with baked noodles) and *štrukli* (baked cheese dumplings), on a terrace with panoramic vistas.

Villa Magdalena   HOTEL €€€
(☑049-233 333; www.villa-magdalena.net; Mirna Ulica 1; s/d 700/1010KN; ℙ🕙@🛜) This small hotel up the hill from Hotel Toplice is a pink-themed lap of luxury, featuring swank and spacious (mostly) suites and an à la carte restaurant that serves healthy fare. Most of the units have jacuzzis with thermal water, terraces, teak-wood floors and kitchenettes. Check out their website for online specials and packages.

ⓘ Getting There & Away

The bus station is in the centre of town, a stone's throw from most facilities and the tourist office. The spa, 46km northwest of Zagreb, is well connected to the capital (52KN, 1¼ hours, six to 10 buses daily), making it an easy day-trip option.

Krapina

☑049 / POP 12,900

Krapina is a busy provincial town at the heart of a pretty rural region. The main reason to visit is one of Europe's largest Neanderthal excavation sites, now a high-tech museum.

In 1899 an archaeological dig on the Hušnjakovo hill unearthed findings of human and animal bones from a Neanderthal tribe that lived in the cave from 100,000 BC to 35,000

DON'T MISS

ZAGORJE'S GRAND CASTLES

A distinctive feature of the Zagorje region is its medieval castles, built to protect the Croatian heartland from invaders from the east and north. Both Varaždin and Varaždinske Toplice have their own castles, but it's the rural setting of Veliki Tabor and Trakošćan that makes them the region's most impressive fortresses.

Veliki Tabor Castle (www.veliki-tabor.hr; Košnički Hum 1, Desinić; adult/concession 20/10KN; ☺9am-5pm Tue-Fri, to 7pm Sat & Sun Apr-Sep, 9am-4pm Tue-Sun Nov-Feb, 9am-4pm Tue-Fri, to 7pm Sat & Sun Oct & Mar) As you approach the hilltop castle of Veliki Tabor, 57km northwest of Zagreb, what unfolds is a pleasing panorama of hills, corn fields, vineyards and forests. The Croatian aristocracy began building fortified castles in the region – to stave off the Turkish threat – at the end of the 16th century. The pentagonal Veliki Tabor Castle (recently renovated and now housing a museum) was built on the grounds of an earlier medieval structure in the early 16th century, with the four semicircular towers added later.

Strategically perched on top of a hill, the golden-yellow castle-fortress has everything a medieval master could want: towers, turrets and holes in the walls for pouring tar and hot oil on the enemy. It even houses the skull of Veronika Desinić, a poor village girl who, according to local lore, was punished for her romance with the castle owner's son and bricked up in the walls.

The castle also hosts the **Tabor Film Festival** (www.taborfilmfestival.com; ☺Jun or Jul) in June or July. There are eight daily buses from Zagreb to Desinić (58KN to 70KN, 1½ to two hours) from Monday to Saturday, and four on Sunday. You will have to walk 3km northwest to Veliki Tabor.

To admire the castle from a distance, lunch or dine alfresco at the rustic eatery **Grešna Gorica** (☎049-343 001; www.gresna-gorica.hr; Taborgradska Klet 3, Desinić; mains 40-80KN; ☺9am-9pm; 🖳). Often overtaken by day-tripping families from Zagreb on weekends, this restaurant is a tad gimmicky but great for kids, with farm animals roaming around, a playground and lots of open space. Adults will appreciate the countryside views and the well-prepared Zagorje staples, such as štrukli (dumplings with cottage cheese) and srneći gulaš (venison goulash). It's located about 2km east of Veliki Tabor; a marked trail leads from the back of the castle to the restaurant (40 minutes on foot).

Trakošćan Castle (☎042-796 281; www.trakoscan.hr; Trakošćan 1; adult/concession 30/15KN; ☺9am-6pm Apr-Oct, to 4pm Nov-Mar) This castle, 80km northwest of Zagreb, is worth a visit for its well-presented museum and attractive grounds. The exact origin of its construction is unknown, but the first official mention dates to 1334. Not many of the castle's original Romanesque features were retained when it was restored in neo-Gothic style in the mid-19th century; the 215-acre castle grounds were landscaped into a romantic English-style park with exotic trees and an artificial lake.

Occupied by the aristocratic Drašković family until 1944, the castle features three floors of exhibits that display the family's original furniture, a plethora of portraits, an armament's collection of swords, and a period kitchen in the basement. The rooms range in style from neo-Renaissance to Gothic and baroque.

After soaking up the history, wander along the verdant paths down to the wooden jetty at the lake, where you can rent a two-person paddleboat (30KN for 30 minutes).

No buses operate between Zagreb and Trakošćan, but there are connections from Varaždin daily except for Sunday, making a day trip here possible.

BC. Alongside stone tools and weapons from the Palaeolithic Age, the remains of 876 humans were found, including 196 single teeth belonging to several dozen individuals. Once you've connected with our long-gone ancestors and briefly meandered around town, though, Krapina offers little to keep you entertained.

⊙ Sights

Museum of the Krapina Neanderthal MUSEUM
(www.mkn.mhz.hr; Šetalište Vilibalda Sluge bb; adult/concession 50/25KN; ☺9am-7pm Tue-Sun Apr-Jun & Sep, 9am-6pm Tue-Fri, to 7pm Sat & Sun Jul & Aug, 9am-4pm Tue-Fri, to 5pm Sat & Sun Nov-Feb, 9am-6pm Tue-Sun Mar & Oct) This is Krapina's

highlight, just west of the centre. Built into a vertical rock and fronted with a glass wall, this cavernous two-floor space has high-tech exhibits tracing the region's history and geology. After an introductory video in the main hall, the walk through the museum is designed to emulate a journey of discovery back to the Neanderthals' origins, with subterranean chambers, hyper-realistic dioramas and interactive games. Don't miss the entrance to the 2nd floor, set in a dark passageway with funky lights.

The outdoor part of the museum, the leafy hill where the remains were found, contains a display of sculpted life-sized models of Neanderthals engaged in everyday activities, such as wielding clubs and throwing stones.

Last admission for the day is one hour before the official closing time.

Franciscan Monastery MONASTERY
(Samostanska 3) Peek into this baroque monastery just west of the centre, which once housed a philosophy and theology school. The adjoining church has evocative frescoes by the Pauline monk Ivan Ranger in the sacristy.

❶ Information

Tourist Office (☑ 049-371 330; www.tzg-krapina.hr; Magistratska 28; ☺ 8am-3pm Mon-Fri, to noon Sat) Not particularly helpful but does offer some brochures and scant information.

❶ Getting There & Away

Several daily buses run from Monday to Saturday from Zagreb to Krapina (36KN to 42KN, one hour); on Sundays there is only an evening bus. There are up to 11 trains from Zagreb (40KN, 1½ hours), with a change at Zabok.

The train station is about 300m to the south, on Frana Galovića 8. The bus terminal is another 600m away along the same street, at number 15.

Varaždinske Toplice

☑ 042 / POP 6980

Sulphurous thermal springs at a steaming temperature of 58°C have been attracting weary visitors to Varaždinske Toplice since the Romans first established a health settlement here in the 1st century AD. Gentle, wooded hills surround this appealing spa town, which has an assortment of churches and historic buildings, including the baroque castle. Adjacent is the city museum, with its sculpture of Minerva from the 3rd century AD. Aqua

Iasae is the remains of the Roman spa built between the 1st and 4th centuries AD.

✖ Eating

Zlatne Gorice EUROPEAN €€
(☑ 042-666 054; www.zlatne-gorice.eu; Banjščina 104, Varaždin Breg; mains 60-130KN; ☺ noon-10pm Tue-Thu, to 11pm Fri & Sat, to 8pm Sun) If you have your own wheels, stop for lunch at this sparkling restored mansion, set 3km from Toplice along the old road to Varaždin. Surrounded by vineyards, it serves central European fare (think schnitzels, stews and veal medallions) in the four interior salons, or on a terrace with pastoral views.

There's a wine trail, a garden labyrinth and three cosy doubles (300KN) upstairs. Reserve ahead on weekends.

❶ Information

Tourist Office (☑ 042-633 133; www.toplice-vz.hr; Trg Slobode 16; ☺ 8am-4pm Mon-Fri) Hiding behind the neo-Gothic facade of the baroque castle, it distributes brochures and info about relaxing health therapies and can help you find private accommodation.

❶ Getting There & Away

There are approximately 20 buses per day from Varaždin on weekdays and the trip takes about 30 to 45 minutes; a one-way ticket costs 21KN. Note that fewer buses run on weekends.

Varaždin

☑ 042 / POP 47,000

Varaždin, 81km north of Zagreb, is a largely overlooked destination that's often used as a mere transit point on the way to or from Hungary. Yet the town is worth a visit in its own right – its centre is a showcase of scrupulously restored baroque architecture and well-tended gardens and parks. It was once Croatia's capital and its most prosperous city, which explains the extraordinary refinement of its buildings. Topping off the symphony is the gleaming-white and turreted Stari Grad (Old Town), which contains a city museum.

The pedestrian zone of attractive 18th-century buildings centres on Trg Kralja Tomislava, with old streets radiating from this square.

History

The town of Garestin (now Varaždin) played an important role in Croatia's history. It first became a local administrative centre in

1181 under King Bela III, and in 1209 it was raised to the status of a free royal borough by King Andrew II, receiving its own seal and coat of arms.

When Croatia was under siege by the Turks, Varaždin was the most powerful stronghold and the residence of choice for generals. Once the Ottoman threat receded, Varaždin prospered as the cultural, political and commercial centre of Croatia. Its proximity to northern Europe facilitated the boom of baroque architecture, which flourished in Europe during this period. Top artisans and builders flocked to Varaždin, designing mansions, churches and public buildings.

The town was made the capital of Croatia in 1767, a position it held until a disastrous fire in 1776, when the Croatian *ban* (viceroy) packed up and moved his administration to Zagreb. The still-thriving town was quickly rebuilt in the baroque style, which is still visible today.

The town is a centre for textiles, shoes, furniture and agricultural products. It's also an increasingly popular day-trip destination, with a recently spruced-up historic core.

◉ Sights

Varaždin's town centre offers a fine ensemble of baroque buildings, a number of which have been turned into museums. Many of its aristocratic mansions and elegant churches are being restored as part of the town's bid to be included in Unesco's list of World Heritage Sites. Conveniently, most buildings have plaques with architectural and historical explanations in English, German and Croatian.

Varaždin Cemetery CEMETERY
(Hallerova Aleja 8; ⊙7am-9pm May-Sep, to 8pm Mar, Apr & Oct, to 5pm Jan, Feb, Nov & Dec) A 10-minute stroll west of Stari Grad takes you to this serene horticultural masterpiece, designed in 1905 by Viennese architect Hermann Helmer. Meander amid tombstones, avenues, promenades and over 7000 trees, including magnolia, beech and birch.

Town Museum MUSEUM
(Gradski Muzej; www.gmv.hr; Strossmayerovo Šetalište 3; adult/concession 20/15KN; ⊙9am-5pm Tue-Fri, to 1pm Sat & Sun) This whitewashed fortress, a gem of medieval defensive architecture housed inside Stari Grad (Old Town), is surrounded by a manicured park. Construction began in the 14th century, with the present Gothic-Renaissance structure

dating back to the 16th century, when it was the regional fortification against the Turks.

The building was in private hands until 1925; today, as a museum, it houses furniture, paintings, watches, ceramics, decorative objects, insignia and weapons, amassed over centuries and displayed throughout 30 exhibition rooms. Even more interesting than the historic collections is the architecture: enter via a drawbridge and wander around to view the archways, courtyards and chapels of this sprawling castle-fortress.

Traditional Crafts Square SQUARE
(Trg Tradicijskih Obrta; ⊙10am-6pm Tue-Sat Apr-Oct) Demonstrations of pottery, weaving, beekeeping and hat-making re-create the olden times here.

Gallery of Old & Modern Masters GALLERY
(Galerija Starih i Novih Majstora; Trg Miljenka Stančića 3; adult/concession 25/15KN; ⊙9am-5pm Tue-Fri, to 1pm Sat & Sun) The rococo-style Sermage Palace, which houses the gallery, was built in 1759. Note the carved medallions on the facade and pay a quick visit to the museum, which displays portraits and landscapes from Croatian, Italian, Dutch, German and Flemish schools. The permanent exhibition occasionally shuts down in favour of temporary shows.

Franciscan Church & Monastery of St John the Baptist CHURCH
(Crkva Svetog Ivana Krstitelja; Franjevački Trg 8; ⊙6.30am-noon & 5.30-7.30pm) Built in 1650 in baroque style on the site of an earlier structure, this church contains the town's tallest tower (54.5m) and houses an ancient pharmacy ornamented with 18th-century ceiling frescoes. Next door is a copy of the bronze statue of Bishop Grgur Ninski that Ivan Meštrović created for Split. Touch the statue's big toe and good luck will come your way (so the story goes).

Town Hall HISTORIC BUILDING
(Gradska Vijećnica; Trg Kralja Tomislava 1) This striking Romanesque-Gothic structure has been the town hall since the 16th century. Notice the town's coat of arms at the foot of the tower and the carved portal dating from 1792. There's a guard-changing ceremony every Saturday at 11am from mid-May to mid-October.

Cathedral of the Assumption CATHEDRAL
(Katedrala Uznesenja Marijina; Pavlinska 4; ⊙7am-12.30pm & 3.30-7.30pm) This former Jesuit church, located southeast of Trg Kralja

Varaždin

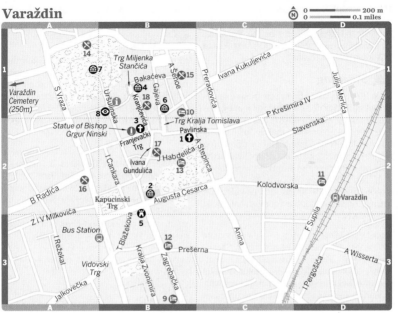

Varaždin

◉ Sights

1 Cathedral of the Assumption	B2
2 Croatian National Theatre	B2
3 Franciscan Church & Monastery of St John the Baptist	B2
4 Gallery of Old & Modern Masters	B1
5 Patačić-Puttar Palace	B2
6 Town Hall	B1
7 Town Museum	A1
8 Traditional Crafts Square	B1

🛏 Sleeping

9 Garestin	B3
10 Hotel Istra	B1
11 Hotel Varaždin	D2
12 Maltar	B3
13 Park Boutique Hotel	B2

🍴 Eating

14 Bedem	A1
15 Market	B1
16 Palatin	A2
17 Restoran Raj	B2
18 Verglec	B1

Tomislava, was built in 1646. The facade is distinguished by an early baroque portal bearing the coat of arms of the noble Drašković family. Occupying the central nave is the altar, which has elaborate engravings and a gilded painting of the Assumption of the Virgin Mary. Famous for its great acoustics, the cathedral is the site of concerts during the Varaždin Baroque Evenings festival.

Drava River Waterfront WATERFRONT

A 15-minute walk northeast of the town centre takes you to this verdant, tranquil riverfront, bordered by footpaths and several outdoor cafes where you can kick back.

✨ Festivals & Events

Špancirfest CULTURAL

(www.spancirfest.com) In late August, the eclectic Špancirfest enlivens the town's parks, streets and squares with world music, street performances, theatre, creative workshops, traditional crafts and contemporary arts.

Varaždin Baroque Evenings MUSIC

(www.vbv.hr) Varaždin is famous for its baroque music festival, Varaždin Baroque Evenings, which takes place over two weeks each September. Local and international orchestras play in the cathedral, churches and theatres around town. Tickets range from

75KN to 250KN (depending on the event), and become available one hour before the concert at travel agencies or the **Varaždin Concert Bureau** (☑ 042-212 907; Auga Cesarca 1, Croatian National Theatre).

Sleeping

Most hotels in Varaždin are clean, well maintained and offer decent value for money, and are generally less expensive than in Zagreb. The clientele consists mostly of visiting businessfolk from Zagreb and neighbouring countries, which means hotels are likely to be busy on weekdays and empty on weekends.

If you're looking for private accommodation, turn to the tourist office, which has listings of single/double rooms from about 150/400KN.

Hotel Varaždin HOTEL **€€**
(☑ 042-290 720; www.hotelvarazdin.com; Kolodvorska 19; s/d 388/576KN; P ✳ @ ☎) Contemporary rooms at this well-appointed hotel opposite the train station are jam-packed with amenities such as minibars. On the premises is a restaurant with a bar and terrace.

Maltar GUESTHOUSE **€€**
(☑ 042-311 100; www.maltar.hr; Prešerna 1; s/d 255/498KN, ste 465-595KN; P ✳ @) Good value for money can be had at this cheerful little family-run guesthouse near the centre. Rooms, with TV, are well kept. Four suites (which sleep two or three people) have kitchenettes.

Garestin PENSION **€€**
(☑ 042-214 314; Zagrebačka; s/d 308/466KN; P ✳) Locals frequent the popular restaurant of this establishment located a stone's throw from the centre, while visitors kick back in 13 comfy rooms upstairs, each outfitted with a minibar.

Park Boutique Hotel BOUTIQUE HOTEL **€€€**
(☑ 042-420 300; www.park-boutique-hotel.eu; Jurja Habdelića 6; s/d 610/810KN; P ✳ ☎) This new city-centre boutique is by far Varaždin's swankiest hotel. With only 19 rooms, which come in three styles – contemporary (called Park), retro and split-level (so-called Gallery rooms) – it has a lovely intimate vibe and all the four-star perks.

Hotel Istra HOTEL **€€€**
(☑ 042-659 659; www.istra-hotel.hr; Ivana Kukuljevića 6; s/d from 497/630KN; P ✳ @ ☎) The standard facilities, an unbeatable location and in-room perks are all in place at this

11-room property, Varaždin's oldest four-star hotel (though wowed you won't be).

Eating

While it doesn't stand out as a gourmet destination, Varaždin offers plentiful opportunities to try Croatia's continental cuisine, suitable for all budgets. There is a daily **market** (Auga Šenoe 12; ☺ 7am-1pm), and many bakeries sell Varaždin's savoury, finger-shaped bread, *klipić*.

Restoran Raj CROATIAN **€**
(☑ 042-213 146; Ivana Gundulića 11; mains 25-55KN; ☺ 9am-10pm Mon-Fri & Sun, 9am-2am Sat) This cavernous restaurant, with lots of wood accents, serves great weekly lunches (till 1.30pm), and features a meat-heavy menu (particularly pork). Food choices are varied though, as is the drinks menu, with lots of beers and *rakija* (grappa) varieties. During warm weather, sit on the wisteria-covered back terrace.

Verglec CROATIAN **€**
(☑ 042-211 131; www.verglec.com; Kranjčevića 12; mains 25-50KN; ☺ 9am-11pm Mon-Thu, 9am-midnight Fri & Sat, 10am-11pm Sun) No-frills but great-value *gableci* (cheap, filling lunches, served on weekdays) are popular with locals at this eatery in the town centre, known for its wide range of traditional dishes and family weekend lunches from 50KN.

Bedem CROATIAN **€€**
(☑ 042-557 545; www.bedem-varazdin.com; Vladimira Nazora 9; mains 18-100KN; ☺ 10am-10pm Mon-Thu & Sun, to 11pm Fri & Sat) The most exciting culinary experience in town, Bedem is a venture by two local chefs experimenting with regional cuisine using local ingredients – think foie-gras-filled puff pastry and pork belly rolled in pumpkin seeds. The downstairs covered terrace, overlooking grassy expanses and the Old Town ramparts, is lovely on warm days; the vaulted-ceiling interiors are cosy, if a little dark.

The weekday *gableci* served till 3pm are excellent value at just 27KN for a fish, meat or veggie plate.

Palatin CROATIAN **€€**
(☑ 042-398 300; www.palatin.hr; Braće Radića 1; mains 35-140KN; ☺ 7.30am-11pm Mon-Sat, 7.30am-10pm Sun) An ambitious menu, a great wine list of over 50 wines and great lunch specials daily, plus homemade ice cream. Sit in the vaulted basement or on the covered terrace outside.

ℹ Information

Horizont Travel (☑ 042-395 111; www.horizont-travel.hr; Kralja Zvonimira 1) Located inside Hotel Turist, this agency offers tours around the city and Zagorje region, as well as northern Croatia.

Tourist Office (☑ 042-210 987; www.tourism-varazdin.hr; Ivana Padovca 3; ⊙ 8am-6pm Mon-Fri, 10am-5pm Sat May-Oct, 8am-4pm Mon-Fri, 10am-1pm Sat Nov-Apr) A wealth of information and plenty of colourful brochures are available here.

ℹ Getting There & Away

Varaždin is a major transport hub in north Croatia, with bus and train lines running in all directions. About 1km apart, the bus and train stations are linked by minibuses (5KN to 15KN) that serve the town and nearby villages from Monday to Saturday.

TRAIN

The **train station** (Kolodvorska 17) is to the east, at the opposite end of town to the bus station. Leave luggage at the train station's **garderoba** (per day 15KN; ⊙ 6.25am-6.25pm).

There are 12 daily trains to Zagreb (65KN, 2½ hours); connect in Zagreb for trains to the coast. Two trains run daily to Budapest, Hungary (222KN, 6½ hours), with a change in Koprivnica.

BUS

The **bus station** (Zrinskih i Frankopana bb) lies just to the southwest of the town centre. You can leave your luggage at the **garderoba** (per bag 7KN; ⊙ 4.30am-8.30pm Mon-Fri, 6.30am-8.30pm Sat & Sun).

Northbound buses originate in Zagreb and make a stop at Varaždin, but they cost the same whether you buy the ticket in Zagreb or Varaždin. Most buses to the coast go through Zagreb. Note that service to Trakošćan Castle and Varaždinske Toplice is greatly reduced on weekends.

Buses from Varaždin include the following:

DESTINATION	COST	TIME	SERVICES
Berlin (Germany)	825KN	15hr	2 weekly
Munich (Germany)	262KN	8hr	2 daily
Trakošćan Castle	36KN	1¾hr	9 daily
Varaždinske Toplice	21KN	30min	hourly
Vienna (Austria)	219KN	5hr	1 daily
Zagreb	81KN	1¾hr	hourly

MEĐIMURJE

The undulating landscapes of Međimurje stretch northeast of Varaždin, towards the borders with Hungary and Slovenia. Fertile, scenic and packed with vineyards, orchards, wheat fields and gardens, this area sees few tourists. That is slowly changing, however, as its attractions, such as up-and-coming wine cellars and the spa village of Sveti Martin, become uncovered.

🏃 Activities

From wine tastings and guided tours of family-run cellars to soaking up the thermal waters and indulging in spa treatments, Međimurje offers a variety of options for both

CROATIAN NAIVE ART

Croatia is the birthplace of its own version of naive art, a distinct style of 20th-century painting that features fantastical and colourful depictions of rural life.

It was the painter Krsto Hegedušić (1901–75) who founded the Hlebine School, in the village of the same name in the Podravina region, 13km east of the provincial centre of Koprivnica. Upon his return from studying in Paris in the 1930s, he gathered a group of artists – all self-taught, with no formal art education – and gave them a chance to shine. This first generation of Croatian naive painters included Ivan Generalić (1914–92), now the most internationally acclaimed; Franjo Mraz (1910–81); and Mirko Virius (1889–1943). All were amateur artists portraying vibrantly coloured and vividly narrated scenes of village life.

Today, a clutch of painters and sculptors still work in Hlebine. Their work can be seen on display in **Hlebine Gallery** (Trg Ivana Generalića 15, Hlebine; adult/concession 10/5KN; ⊙ 10am-4pm Tue-Fri, to 2pm Sat & Sun). Also in Hlebine is **Galerija Josip Generalić** (☑ 048-836 430; Gajeva 75, Hlebine; adult/concession 10/5KN; ⊙ 9.30am-4.30pm Mon-Fri, by appointment Sat & Sun); named after Josip (son of Ivan), also a renowned painter, it is located in the Generalić family home. Call ahead to check that it's open.

Other places to see naive art in Croatia are the Croatian Museum of Naïve Art (p52) in Zagreb and the **Koprivnica Gallery** (Zrinski trg 9, Koprivnica; ⊙ 8am-4pm Mon-Fri, to 1pm Sat & Sun) FREE, which has a small applied-arts section.

active types and those in search of some leisure time.

Lovrec Vineyard   WINE
(☑040-830 171; www.vino-lovrec.hr; Sveti Urban 133, Štrigova; tour & tasting 80KN; ⊙ by appointment) To sample the region's top wines in an authentic family environment, head to Lovrec Vineyard in the village of Sveti Urban, 20km northwest of Čakovec, the region's capital. The guided tour (available in English, French and German) of this country estate tells you about the boutique wine production and its fascinating history, which spans six generations of winemakers.

You'll peek into the 300-year-old wine cellar, with its old wine presses and barrels, rest in the shade of two towering plane trees, take in the vistas of the 6-hectare vineyards, and top it off with tasting around 10 wine varieties, from chardonnay to local *graševina*. For 20KN extra you can have some snacks, like cheese, salami and bread sticks, and a bottle of wine to take home.

Cmrečnjak   WINE
(☑098-295 206; www.cmrecnjak.hr; Sveti Urban 273, Štrigova; ⊙ 8am-4pm Mon-Sat) One of the area's best family-run cellars, where the wine production dates back to 1884. The winery offers tours, and tastings in a rustic room with a panoramic terrace. By appointment only.

Klet Sveti Martin na Muri   FISHING
(☑040-868 288; www.klet-svetimartin.com; Dunajska 26) At this lakeside farm about 4km from Sveti Martin, you can try fishing, hiking, boating in wooden boats and fishing (30KN per day). They also rent bungalows for 100KN per person per day.

🛏 Sleeping & Eating

Međimurje has an assortment of family-run guesthouses scattered around the region,

WORTH A TRIP

LONJSKO POLJE NATURE PARK

Nominated for World Heritage Site status, **Lonjsko Polje Nature Park** (☑044-672 080; www.pp-lonjsko-polje.hr; Krapje 18, Čigoč 26; adult/concession 40/35KN; ⊙ 9am-5pm Apr-Oct) is a 506-sq-km stretch of swampland (*polje* means 'field') in the Posavina region, between the Sava River and Mt Moslavačka Gora. Situated along Lonja River, a Sava tributary that gives the park its name, this huge retention basin is famed for the diversity of its flora and fauna. It's packed with 19th-century wooden architecture, and birdwatchers (well, stork lovers) can have a field day here, as can those who appreciate all things equestrian.

The area is divided into several villages. Čigoč is a world-famous 'stork meeting point' – the white storks nest on top of Čigoč's lovely wooden houses. The birds flock here in late March and early April, hanging around and munching on the swampland insects up until late August, when they start their two- to three-month flight back towards southern Africa. Čigoč is home to the park's information point and ticket office, and a small ethnographic collection owned by the Sučić family (10KN).

The heritage village of **Krapje** is known for its well-preserved traditional wooden houses and rich fishing and hunting areas. Check out the covered external staircases, porches and pillars, and various farm buildings with their barns, drying sheds, pigsties and hen houses. The Palaić family has a small ethnographic collection you should see (and a couple of apartments to boot). From April through October an information centre in one of the wooden houses has a guide who will be happy to enlighten you about the cultural heritage of the area. Look out for the *posavski* horse, a local breed that grazes in the oak forests of Lonjsko Polje. Also worth a visit is the village of **Mužilovčica**, known for its swallows. Don't miss a meal at the Ravlić family farm here.

There are three entrances to the park: at Krapje, Čigoč and Repušnica. The visitor centres at Krapje and Repušnica offer bike and canoe rentals (80KN per day for bikes, 60KN per canoe for up to three hours).

Lonjsko Polje is 50km southeast of Zagreb. The best way to visit is with your own transport or on a tour, as public transport is poor and makes moving around the park quite difficult. Private accommodation is available in various wooden houses inside the park; more information is available on the website. Our recommendations for hideaways that feature both lodging and food include Tradicije Čigoč, Etno Selo Stara Lonja and Ekoetno Selo Strug.

but the best of its lodging options focus on the village of Sveti Martin Na Muri, with its spa resort.

LifeClass Terme Sveti Martin RESORT €€€
(☑040-371 111; www.spa-sport.hr; Grkaveščak bb; s/d 600/826KN; P❄️📶🏊💪) The pleasant village of Sveti Martin Na Muri showcases the four-star LifeClass Terme Sveti Martin. It has a series of outdoor, indoor and thermal pools, a water park, tennis courts, forest trails, shops, restaurants and a golf course. Adjacent to the resort are swanky apartment-style units (from 300KN), each with living room, kitchen and balcony. The on-site restaurants serve good-quality local food.

For nonguests, day tickets to the pools start at 57KN (67KN on weekends); the price drops by 10KN after 2pm. Other facilities include a fitness room (30KN per hour), a sauna complex (105KN for three hours) and various body therapies, including mud wraps (320KN per hour) and Vichy massages (310KN for 40 minutes).

Potrti Kotač CROATIAN €
(☑040-868 318; www.potrti-kotac.com; Jurovčak 79; mains 45-80KN; ⊘9am-midnight Mon-Fri & Sun, to 2am Sat) Potrti Kotač, 1km uphill from LifeClass Terme Sveti Martin, serves good local food. It also has an apartment for rent (250KN).

Mala Hiža CROATIAN €€
(☑040-341 101; www.mala-hiza.hr; Balogovec 1, Mačkovec; mains 65-135KN; ⊘10am-10pm Sun-Thu, to 11pm Fri & Sat) Foodies from Zagreb travel to Mala Hiža in the village of Mačkovec, 4km north of Čakovec, for their lauded and awarded seasonal cuisine done up with flair. Served in an old wooden Međimurje cottage, it features creative local mainstays plus over 150 wine labels, at least 30 of which are from Međimurje. Don't miss *međimurska gibanica,* the local dessert.

❶ Getting There & Away

To explore this area you'll need to have your own car; public transport is virtually nonexistent.

SLAVONIA

Pancake-flat, river-rich Slavonia is all but untouched by tourism, with unique natural wonders and delicious regional cuisine. The wetlands of Kopački Rit are one of Europe's finest ornithological reserves, perfect for boat tours, biking and hiking. Osijek, Slavonia's largest town, has a lovely riverfront setting and fortress quarter, while the Baranja region is renowned for its wineries.

The impact of the war hit hardest in southeast Slavonia, where historic Vukovar is slowly regaining its role as an important regional city and Ilok, on the Serbian border, is again attracting visitors to its fine wine cellars and historic old town.

Bordered by three major rivers (Sava, Drava and Danube), this fascinating region has long held strong connections with Hungary, Serbia and Germany. Slavonia's key appeal lies in this culturally intriguing mix that makes it closer to central Europe than coastal Croatia.

History

Before the 1991 war displaced tens of thousands of inhabitants, Slavonia contained one of the most ethnically diverse populations in Europe. Settled by Slavic tribes in the 7th century, the region was conquered by the Turks in the 16th century. Catholic residents fled, and Serbian Orthodox settlers, who were better received by the Turks, arrived en masse.

In 1690 Serb supporters of Vienna, in their battles with the Turks, left Kosovo and settled in the Srijem region around Vukovar. The Turks ceded the land to Austria in 1699 and the Habsburgs turned a large part of the region into a Vojna Krajina (military frontier).

The Muslim population left but more Serbs arrived, joined by German merchants; Hungarian, Slovak and Ukrainian peasants; Catholic Albanians and Jews. Much land was sold to German and Hungarian aristocrats who built huge baroque and classical mansions around the towns of Osijek, Vukovar and Ilok.

The large Serbian community prompted Slobodan Milošević to attempt to incorporate the region into a 'Greater Serbia'. This assault began with the destruction of Vukovar and the shelling of Osijek in 1991. A ceasefire prevailed in 1992, but it wasn't until January 1998 that the region was returned to Croatia as part of the Dayton peace agreement.

The fighting may be over but the war's impact remains profound. In towns such as Vukovar, Serbs and Croats lead almost totally separate lives. Efforts are being made to bring the communities together, but with limited success so far.

INLAND CROATIA SLAVONIA

Đakovo

📍 031 / POP 27,700

The peaceful provincial town of Đakovo, just 35km to the south of Osijek, makes an easy day trip. There are three major reasons to visit: its impressive neo-Romanesque cathedral, the famous Lipizzaner horses at Ergela stable, and a wonderful folk festival every summer.

◉ Sights

Ergela   FARM
(☎ 031-822 535; www.ergela-djakovo.hr; Auga Še-noe 45; adult/concession 20/10KN; ☉ 7am-5pm Mon-Fri, 9am-1pm Sat & Sun Mar-Oct, 7am-3pm Mon-Fri Nov-Feb) Đakovo is famous for its Lipizzaner horses, a noble purebred with a lineage that can be traced back to the 16th century. They're bred on a farm outside town and trained here at Ergela, a short walk from the cathedral. Around 30 horses undergo daily training for their eventual work as high-class carriage and riding horses.

Guided tours that go for 30 minutes are available (adult/concession 30/20KN), as are rides in an old-fashioned carriage for 150KN (15 minutes).

Đakovo Cathedral of St Peter   CATHEDRAL
(☎ 031-802 306; Strossmayerov Trg 6; ☉ 6.30am-noon & 3-7.30pm) The town's pride and glory is this red-brick cathedral, which dominates the town centre with its two 84m-high belfries. Commissioned by Bishop Strossmayer in 1862, this neo-Romanesque structure features a three-nave interior colourfully painted with biblical scenes.

✪ Festivals & Events

Đakovački Vezovi   CULTURAL
(Đakovo Embroidery) Đakovački Vezovi features a display by the Lipizzaner horses and a folklore show on the first weekend in July each year, complete with dancing and traditional songs.

❶ Getting There & Away

Đakovo is well connected to Osijek by bus so it's pretty easy to do as a day trip. There are up to 16 buses daily (34KN, 40 minutes).

Osijek

📍 031 / POP 107,800

A historic, leafy university town with a stunning waterfront promenade along the broad Drava River and an imposing 18th-century fortress, Osijek is well worth a visit.

The city suffered terribly in the 1990s from Serb shelling and pock-marks still scar some structures, but most of Osijek's grand buildings (including some fine 19th-century Secessionist mansions) have been renovated.

This elegant regional capital has steadily regained its poise, boosted by the booming student numbers, new hotels and restaurants and a flow of tourists. You'll find Osijek perfect as an intriguing, cosmopolitan and enjoyable base for day trips to Slavonia's countryside and the wonderful Kopački Rit Nature Park.

History

Osijek's location on the Drava River, near its junction with the Danube (Dunav in Croatian), has made it strategically important for more than two millennia. It was the Slavic settlers that gave Osijek its name; by the 12th century it was a thriving market town. In 1526 the Turks destroyed Osijek, rebuilt it in Ottoman style and made it into an administrative centre.

Austrians chased the Turks out in 1687, the Muslims fled into Bosnia, and the city was repopulated with Serbs, Croats, Germans and Hungarians. Still wary of Turkish attacks, the Austrians built Tvrđa, the fortress that still stands today, in the early 18th century.

Until the recent 1990s war, Osijek was a powerful industrial centre of former Yugoslavia. When the war broke out in 1991, the federal Yugoslav army and Serbian paramilitary units overran the Baranja region north of Osijek. The first shells were dropped in July 1991 from Serbian positions across the Drava River. When Vukovar fell in November of that year, federal and Serbian forces made Osijek the object of their undivided attention, pounding it with artillery as thousands of residents poured out of the city. This devastating shelling continued until May 1992, but the city never fell.

◉ Sights

Tvrđa   HISTORIC SITE
Built under Habsburg rule as a defence against Turkish attacks, the 18th-century citadel was relatively undamaged during the recent war. This baroque complex of cobblestone streets, spacious squares and stately mansions reveals a remarkable architectural unity, lending it the feel of an open-air museum.

➡ Gloria Maris

(www.gloria-maris.hr; Svodovi bb; adult/concession 20/10KN; ⏱10am-4pm Tue, Wed & Fri, to 8pm Thu, to 1pm Sat & Sun) Housed inside vaults of the old citadel, this museum is dedicated to seashells and marine and freshwater life. It's the labour of love of Vladimir Filipović, who has amassed around one million shells in his 48 years of collecting, from all corners of the globe. Enter through the street to the right side of the church.

➡ Museum of Slavonia

(Muzej Slavonije Osijek; www.mso.hr; Trg Svetog Trojstva 2 & 6; adult/concession 20/10KN; ⏱10am-6pm Tue-Sat) Housed in two separate buildings on Trg Svetog Trojstva, this museum has an exceptionally well-curated collection of findings. The renovated city guard structure at number 2, with a lovely oak-block floor and glass dome over an arcaded patio, showcases finds from Roman stones to Celtic helmets, with explanations also in English.

Across the square is the huge collection of treasures and artefacts relating to Slavonian history, including Bronze Age implements, Roman artefacts from the colony of Mursa, beautiful textiles, weavings, jewellery and fine furniture. Exhibits rotate every few months.

Museum of Fine Arts　　　　GALLERY

(Muzej Likovnih Umjetnosti; www.mlu.hr; Europska Avenija 9; adult/concession 15/5KN; ⏱10am-6pm Tue, Wed & Fri, to 8pm Thu, to 1pm Sat & Sun) Housed in an elegant neoclassical mansion, the Museum of Fine Arts contains a collection of paintings and sculptures by Slavonian artists from the 18th century onwards.

Church of St Peter & Paul　　　CHURCH

(☎031-310 020; Pavla Pejačevića 1; ⏱1-7pm Mon, 7am-7pm Tue-Sun) FREE Looming over Trg Ante Starčevića, this church's 90m-high tower is surpassed in height only by the cathedral in Zagreb. Built in the 1890s, this red-brick, neo-Gothic structure features an interior with 40 elaborate stained-glass windows in Viennese style and vividly coloured frescoes by Croatian painter Mirko Rački.

Watermill　　　　LANDMARK

(entry by donation; ⏱9am-1pm & 4-8pm Wed-Sun) Osijek's newest attraction is this replica of a watermill, a wooden construction anchored on the Drava River. This EU-backed project, part of the Miller's Route that crosses through Hungary as well, makes for a lovely pit stop on the riverfront walk.

It has a little cottage, used to demonstrate how the grain is ground. In the mid-19th century, Osijek had 60 watermills, the last one of which closed in 1944.

Zoo Osijek　　　　ZOO

(www.zoo-osijek.hr; Sjevernodravska Obala 1; adult/concession 20/10KN; ⏱9am-8pm) As an escape from the museums and churches, take a free ride on the emblematic *kompa* (a wooden pedestrian ferry propelled by the water current) from the shore of Gornji Grad to Zoo Osijek, on the other side of the Drava. Croatia's largest zoo spreads over 11 verdant riverside hectares, with 80 animal species and a reptile-filled aquarium.

The *kompa* operates from 9am to 7pm April to October.

🛏 Sleeping

⭐**Maksimilian**　　　　GUESTHOUSE €

(☎031-497 567; www.maksimilian.hr; Franjevačka 12; s 230-320KN, d 330-420KN; ❋@🅐) In the heart of the old town, this superb guesthouse is run by a hospitable, English-speaking team. All 14 rooms in the historic 1860 building come with satellite TV, high ceilings and good fittings (most also have air-con).

Hostel Street Osijek　　　　HOSTEL €

(☎031-327 743; www.hostel-street-osijek.com; Ivana Gundulića 5; dm/r 130/312KN; ❋🅐) This chic and charming brand-new hostel in the heart of town has seven bright, light and nicely decked-out rooms. All are triples and some have skylights. There's a shared common space, and the bus and train stations are both only a walk away.

Hotel Drava　　　　HOTEL €€

(☎031-250 500; www.hotel-drava.com; Ivana Gundulića 25a; s/d 390/582KN; 🅿❋🅐) An inviting hotel close to the train and bus stations that has 11 colourful, well-appointed rooms with a little kitsch thrown in. There are discounts if you pay in cash. Weekend rates are 100KN per night lower.

Hotel Osijek　　　　HOTEL €€€

(☎031-230 333; www.hotelosijek.hr; Šamačka 4; s/d 840/955KN; 🅿❋@🅐) Right on the river, this towering concrete landmark is the town's most luxurious hotel, drawing business travellers in droves. The 147 rooms and suites are city-slicker smart, with a nod to modernist style; most have spectacular views. The wellness centre on the 14th floor has a Turkish bath, jacuzzi and sauna.

Osijek

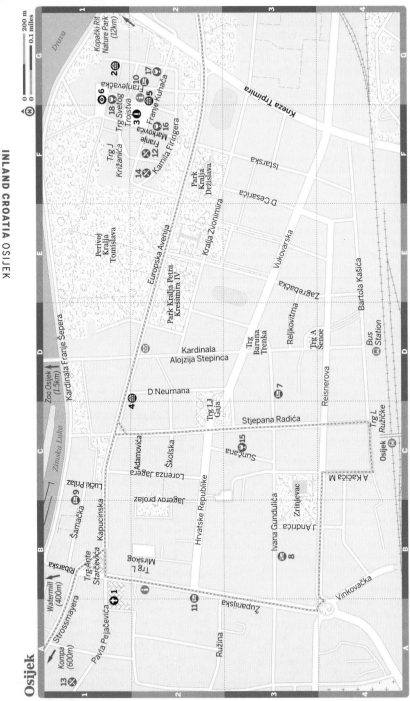

Drava

Kopački Rit
Nature Park
(12km)

Kneza Trpimira

Zoo Osijek
(1.5km)

Zimska Luka

Watermill
(400m)

Kompa
(600m)

Perivoj
Kralja
Tomislava

Park
Kralja
Držislava

Park Kralja Petra
Krešimira IV

Europska Avenija

Kralja Zvonimira

Trg J
Križanica

Trg Svetog
Trojstva

Trg
Franje
Markovića

Franje Kuhača

Kamila Firingera

Kardinala
Alojzija Stepinca

Kardinala Franje Šepera

Istarska

D Cesarica

Vukovarska

Zagrebačka

Bartola Kašića

Reljkovitma

Trg A
Šenoe

Trg
Baruna
Trenka

Reisnerova

Bus
Station

D Neumana

Trg LJ
Gaja

Stjepana Radića

Trg L
Ružičke

Osijek

Sunčana

Adamovića

Školska

Lorenza Jägera

Jägerov prolaz

Hrvatske Republike

Kapucinska

Trg L
Mirskog

Trg Ante
Starčevića

Pavla Pejačevića

Strossmayera

Ribarska

Šamačka

Lučki Prilaz

A Kačića M

Ivana Gundulića

J Andrića

Zrinjevac

Vinkovačka

Ružina

Županijska

Trajnevačka

Osijek

◉ Sights

🛌 Sleeping

🍴 Eating

🍷 Drinking & Nightlife

INLAND CROATIA OSIJEK

Waldinger
HOTEL €€€

(☎031-250 450; www.waldinger.hr; Županijska 8; pension s/d 290/440KN; hotel s/d 650/950KN; P ❄ @ 🛜) This is a grand little hotel of two halves. The bedrooms in the main building offer lashings of old-school charm, with plush furnishings and thick carpets. The pension in the back is a humbler abode, with functional rooms. The hotel offers discounts for midsummer stays; rates drop by 25% on weekends.

🍴 Eating

Osijek is the place to sample hearty and spicy Slavonian cuisine. The local food is strongly influenced by neighbouring Hungary, with paprika sprinkled on almost every dish. There are several excellent restaurants inside the Tvrđa fortress quarter – these are great places to try specialities like *fiš paprikaš*, river-fish stew in a paprika sauce, served with noodles.

Slavonska Kuća
SLAVONIAN €

(☎031-369 955; www.slavonskakuca.com; Kamila Firingera 26; mains 45-70KN; ⊙10am-11pm Mon-Sat, 11am-5pm Sun) This is a great choice for authentic Slavonian food, with lots of *pečena riba* (baked fish), including delicious catfish. Prices are moderate and portions hearty. Wash your meal down with *graševina*, a fruity white wine.

Kompa
SLAVONIAN €

(☎031-375 755; www.restorankompa.hr; Splavarska 1; mains 40-70KN; ⊙10am-11pm) The locals' favourite joint on the riverfront, across from the zoo, this is a no-frills spot with a tiny interior and tables right on the river. Good for mainstays and low prices – although there's no menu in English, nor is English spoken here.

★ Kod Ruže
SLAVONIAN €€

(☎031-206 066; Kuhačeva 25a; mains 35-100KN; ⊙10am-11pm) The rustic paraphernalia is laid on pretty thick here (think taxidermy galore) but this is certainly a highly atmospheric place for a Slavonian meal, especially at weekends, when a live band plays gypsy music. Try the *čobanac* (traditional meat stew) or one of the substantial salads, such as the *alas salata* with river fish.

Rustika
PIZZA €€

(☎031-369 400; www.rustika.hr; Pavla Pejačevića 32; mains 35-100KN; ⊙9am-11pm) A popular spot steps from the cathedral – pizzas and grilled meats are the order of the day, dished out in a rustic interior with a contemporary touch, or on the terrace in the back.

🍷 Drinking & Nightlife

Merlon
BAR

(Franje Markovića 3; ⊙8am-midnight Mon-Wed, to 2am Thu-Sat, 9am-11pm Sun) This swank new bar with a beer theme serves tasty bites (think burgers, wraps, ribs and chicken wings for 28N to 34KN) and a good range of beers, including some local ones such as Staropramen. It has a sidewalk terrace on a cobblestone street.

Outside
CLUB

(Trg Vatroslava Lisinskog bb; ⊙10pm-5am Thu-Sat) This chic new club in Tvrđa has a gorgeous terrace space and a rich repertoire of themed events.

Gajba
BEER GARDEN

(Sunčana 3; ⊙noon-11pm Mon-Sat) Great little spot for beer lovers, with a small terrace on an off-the-radar pedestrian strip. Try some local craft beers, like Black Hat from Osijek.

Old Bridge Pub PUB

(☑ 031-211 611; Franje Kuhača 4; ☺ 7am-1am Mon-Wed, to 4am Thu & Fri, 10am-4.30am Sat, 5pm-1am Sun) A dead ringer for a London boozer, the Old Bridge has three levels and a slim outdoor terrace – the top floor is a classy space with elegant Chesterfield sofas. There's live music on weekend nights.

ⓘ Information

Hospital (☑ 031-511 511; Josipa Huttlera 4)

Panturist (☑ 031-214 388; www.panturist.hr; Kapucinska 19; ☺ 8am-8pm Mon-Fri, to 1pm Sat) Slavonia's largest travel agency. Runs buses to the coast as well as to international destinations.

Post Office (Kardinala Alojzija Stepinca 17; ☺ 7am-8pm Mon-Sat) Also for phone calls and cash advances on MasterCard.

Tourist Information Centre (☑ 031-210 120; www.tzosijek.hr; Trg Svetog Trojstva 5; ☺ 10am-4pm Mon-Fri, 9am-1pm Sat) Friendly info point in the same building as the Museum of Slavonia.

Tourist Office (☑ 031-203 755; www.tzosijek. hr; Županijska 2; ☺ 8am-8pm Mon-Fri, to noon Sat mid-Jun–mid-Sep, 8am-4pm Mon-Fri, to noon Sat mid-Sep–mid-Jun) A well-briefed office with plentiful brochures, booklets and maps.

ⓘ Getting There & Away

AIR

Osijek Airport (☑ 060 339 339; www.osijek-airport.hr) is 20km from Osijek on the road to Vukovar; it's a very minor airport with only a few Croatia Airlines flights to Dubrovnik and Zagreb.

BUS

International buses can be found at the **bus station** (☑ 060 353 353; Bartola Kašića 70), located on Bartola Kašića.

TRAIN

Osijek's train station is located on Trg Lavoslava Ružičke, just south of the centre. Trains run to Rijeka (232KN, 8½ hours, once daily) and Zagreb (132KN to 150KN, four to 4½ hours, four daily on weekdays, three on weekends).

ⓘ Getting Around

A shuttle bus meets arrivals at the airport and heads to the city centre. It departs from the bus station 2½ hours before scheduled flights and costs 30KN. The taxi company Sunce departs from the same spot and charges 50KN per ride.

There's an excellent, very affordable taxi service in the city. **Cammeo** (☑ 1212; www.taxi-cammeo.hr) has modern cars with meters; most rides in town cost just 20KN.

Osijek has two tram lines. Line 2 connects the train and bus station with Trg Ante Starčevića in the centre (but in a roundabout way, which takes you to the outer edge of town first), and line 1 goes to Tvrđa. The fare is 10KN, which you pay to the driver.

Buses connect Osijek to nearby Bilje; from the bus station take the Panturist bus heading to Beli Manastir and get off in Bilje (16KN, 20 minutes).

BUSES FROM OSIJEK

DOMESTIC DESTINATIONS	COST (KN)	DURATION	DAILY SERVICES
Đakovo	34	40 minutes	16
Dubrovnik	340	14 hours	1
Ilok	61	1½ hours	1 (none on weekends)
Rijeka	265	7 hours	1
Slavonski Brod	62	1¾ hours	10
Split	290	11 hours	1
Vukovar	34	45 minutes	8
Zagreb	119	4 hours	15
INTERNATIONAL DESTINATIONS	COST (KN)	DURATION	DAILY SERVICES
Belgrade	128	3½ hours	4
Vienna	224	10 hours	1 (none on Sunday)
Zürich	490	19 hours	3 weekly

Kopački Rit Nature Park

Situated 12km northeast of Osijek, **Kopački Rit Nature Park** (Park Prirode Kopački Rit; www.pp-kopacki-rit.hr; adult 10KN, under 2yr free; ⊙9am-5pm Apr-Oct, 8am-4pm Nov-Mar) is one of Europe's largest wetlands, home to more than 290 bird species and rich aquatic and grassland flora showcasing water lilies, irises, duckweeds and ryegrass, as well as oak and poplar forests. Comprised of a series of ponds, backwaters and two main lakes, Sakadaško and Kopačevo, this massive floodplain was created by the meeting of the Drava and Danube Rivers. These two rivers, together with the Mura, are a Unesco biosphere reserve.

⦿ Sights

Beneath the waters lie 44 species of fish, including carp, bream, pike, catfish and perch. Above the water buzz 21 kinds of mosquito (bring a tonne of repellent!) and on land roam red deer, wild boar, beaver, pine marten and foxes. But it's really about the birds here – look for the rare black storks, white-tailed eagles, great crested grebes, purple herons, spoonbills and wild geese. The best time to come is during the spring and autumn migrations.

The park was heavily mined during the war and closed for many years as a result. Most mines have now been cleared: safe trails have been marked. The park has a **visitor centre** (☎031-445 445; www.pp-kopacki-rit.hr; ⊙9am-5pm Apr-Oct, 8am-4pm Nov-Mar) located at the main entrance, along the Bilje–Kopačevo road, featuring a lovely new interpretation centre in a string of straw-roofed wooden huts that house interactive exhibits and a cafe. You can walk the new series of wooden boardwalks and the educational trails nearby. There are also various guided tours offered, including a **zoological reserve tour** (adults/concession 80KN/60KN) by boat, taking in a castle complex; a **wildlife tour** (per hr 100KN; max 4 people) in a small boat; and a **canoe tour** (per hr 80KN). Tours depart from an embarkation point about 1km from the visitor centre. Book in advance, especially during spring and autumn.

At the northern end of the park, 12km from the visitor centre, is an Austro-Hungarian castle complex and bio-ecological research station, Dvorac Tikveš. Once used by Tito as a hunting lodge, the castle was occupied by Serbs during the 1990s and forests around the complex are still mined, so don't wander off by yourself.

🏃 Activities

Cycling is an increasingly popular activity in the region, and a cycle path connects Bilje with Osijek. The Pannonian Peace Route is an 80km ride from Osijek to the Serbian city of Sombor, along the Danube and through Kopački Rit. For more info and a map, browse www.zeleni-osijek.hr, the website of a local association for environmental protection. Also popular is the 138km-long Danube Route, which traces easternmost Croatia along its borders with Hungary and Serbia.

Kopački Rit Nature Park also rents bikes at its visitor centre, for 20KN per hour or 100KN for a whole day.

Zlatna Greda   ADVENTURE SPORTS
(☎031-565 181; www.zlatna-greda.org; adrenaline park for two hours 50KN, zipline 30KN; ⊙by appointment) Zlatna Greda runs superb tours of Kopački Rit and has its own ecocentre in a deserted village – now a protected cultural heritage site – on the border of the park, 28km north of Osijek. Hikes, birdwatching trips, horseback riding and canoe adventures begin here, and the recently unveiled adrenaline park has a zipline.

🛏 Sleeping & Eating

Bilje, 5km north of Osijek, is a dormitory suburb for the city, with a clutch of accommodation options. It makes an alternative base for exploring Kopački Rit. Family-run B&B **Mazur** (☎031-750 294; www.mazur.hr; Kneza Branimira 2, Bilje; s/d 175/310KN; P☀🛜) is a good bet here, and **Crvendać** (☎091-55 15 711; www.crvendac.com; Biljske satnije ZNG RH 5, Bilje; r per person 155KN) is another great B&B in Bilje. **Zlatna Greda** (☎031-565 181; www.zlatna-greda.org; dm per person 100KN, r 120-180KN; P) is also a fantastic alternative on the park's edge, with hostel-type accommodation.

Kopački Rit Nature Park and the immediate area around it have a clutch of excellent country restaurants that serve regional specialities, such as river fish and game-meat stews.

Krcma Dárócz   SLAVONIAN €
(☎031-753 113; Šandora Petefija 39, Vardarac; mains 35-80KN; ⊙9am-11pm Mon-Thu, to 1am Fri & Sat, to 10am Sun) This great roadside restaurant in the village of Vardarac is worth the drive from Kopački Rit, which is only about 10 minutes away. Packed with

rustic knick-knacks, old furniture and ceiling lamps made of carriage wheels, it serves traditional specialities like rooster *perkelt*, venison with gnocchi, fish meatballs and carp cracklings, and has live music on weekend nights.

Didin Konak
SLAVONIAN €

(📞031-752 100; www.didinkonak.hr; Petefi Šandora 93, Kopačevo; mains 40-80KN; ☺8am-10pm) The quiet village of **Kopačevo**, on the edge of Kopački Rit, is home to this outstanding regional restaurant. The vibe is rustic and real, and the food delicious. Don't miss the fish skewers of catfish and perch. Some of the dishes, like the venison stew and meats under the *peka* (domed baking lid) require advance booking.

Kormoran
SLAVONIAN €

(📞031-753 099; Podunavlje bb; mains 40-95KN; ☺11am-10pm Mon-Sat, 10am-10pm Sun) With a full roster of local dishes, this is a reliable restaurant run by Vina Belje. Located on the very edge of Kopački Rit Nature Park.

❶ Getting There & Away

There's no public transport to the park, but you can take a local Osijek bus to Bilje and walk the remaining 3km. Alternatively, you can rent a bike in Osijek at **Šport za Sve** (📞031-208 135; Istarska 1; bicycle hire per day 40KN; ☺9am-1pm Mon-Fri).

Northern Baranja

The northern stretch of Baranja is a land of gently rolling hills, pretty roadside villages and *surduci*, as the traditional wine roads are called. Several of the villages in northern Baranja have excellent wine cellars and regional restaurants, including Karanac, Suza, Zmajevac and Kneževi Vinogradi.

◉ Sights & Activities

Located 8km east of Beli Manastir, the ethno-village and farming community of **Karanac** provides an authentic slice of Slavonian village life and is well set up to welcome visitors. Lined with cherry trees and lovingly tended gardens, it is home to three churches (Reformist, Catholic and Orthodox) and some well-preserved Pannonian architecture.

Batina
MONUMENT

Right on the tripartite border where Croatia touches Serbia and Hungary is this striking communist-era memorial by well-known Croatian sculptor Antun Augustinčić; it commemorates a key victory by Soviet-led forces over the Nazis in WWII. A colossal female statue sits on high ground, and offers spectacular views over the Danube. The wine bar near the monument serves a good choice of local wines.

Tri Mudraca
OUTDOORS

(📞091 21 01 212; www.trimudraca.com; Ive Ribara 27, Karanac) The family who runs Tri Mudraca in Karanac offer adventure tours on request (starting at 100KN), including ATV riding, geocaching, off-road 4WD jaunts, archery and expeditions to an old abandoned basalt mine. They are also behind the recent unveiling of Šećeransko Jezero, a lake near Beli Manastir that is open on weekends and offers canoeing (15KN).

🛏 Sleeping

Kolar
B&B €

(📞031-733 006; www.camping.suzabaranje.com; Maršala Tita 94b, Suza; s/d 195/350KN, campsite per adult/child/site 38/19/38KN; 🅿❄🛜) In addition to its great wine cellar, Kolar offers three well-equipped rooms that each have a private bathroom. There's a lovely shared terrace and a homemade breakfast with locally sourced ingredients. Across the road, on a leafy patch of land, is a campsite often used by cyclists on the Pannonian route.

Ivica i Marica
FARMSTAY €

(📞091 13 73 793; www.ivica-marica.com; Ivo Lola Ribara 8a, Karanac; s/d 350/450KN; 🅿🛜🎏) An excellent choice on the edge of Karanac village, this upmarket working farm is run by a friendly couple and offers delightful pine-trimmed rooms and suites, as well as bike rental (100KN per day), good kids' facilities, and farm fun such as horse-drawn carriage rides (350KN per hour).

🍴 Eating

Tri Mudraca
SLAVONIAN €

(📞091 21 01 212; www.trimudraca.com; Ive Lole Ribara 27, Karanac; mains 40-90KN; ☺10am-11pm Thu-Sun) A traditional Slavonian farm, known as *salaš*, this lovely spot does elaborate dishes, if you call ahead, such as duck glazed with honey, and pork neck in a sauce of reduced merlot and root veggies. Or else just show up and eat whatever the cook has whipped up that day. Sit in the back garden for a view of rolling fields and vineyards.

WINE TASTING IN SLAVONIA

Vines have been cultivated in Slavonia for millennia – it's thought that the name Baranja is derived from the Hungarian for 'wine mother' – and after a period of stagnation the region is undergoing a serious renaissance. White wines with local grapes, including *graševina*, are justifiably renowned, and earthy reds are also produced, primarily from *frankovka* (*blaufränkisch*), merlot and cabernet sauvignon. You should call ahead at all these cellars to make sure somebody is there to show you around.

Kutjevo (☑034-255 075; www.kutjevo.com; Kralja Tomislava 1, Kutjevo; guided tour & tasting 30KN; ☺ by appointment), in the town of the same name, is home to a medieval wine cellar dating from 1232, formerly of the Cistercian Abbey. You can visit on a guided tour and sample their wines.

Nearby are two of Slavonia's top wineries: **Krauthaker** (☑034-315 000; www.krauthaker.hr; Ivana Jambrovića 6, Kutjevo; tasting 40KN; ☺ by appointment), whose *graševina* and sweet wines regularly win top awards, and **Enjingi** (☑034-267 200; www.enjingi.hr; Hrnjevac 87, Vetovo; tasting & tour 50KN; ☺ by appointment), one of Croatia's leading ecological producers, with winemaking experience dating back to 1890; try the award-winning Venje white blend. For a complete selection of Kutjevo's wines, visit **Vina Čamak – Kolijevka Graševine** (☑034-255 689; Republike Hrvatske 56, Kutjevo; ☺ by appointment), a wine shop and tasting room in the town centre.

In Baranja, grape cultivation has been revived on the gentle hills around Kneževi Vinogradi. Up-and-coming winegrowers, mainly in the villages of Zmajevac and Suza, work along well-marked wine trails. Traditionalist in its approach to winemaking, **Gerstmajer** (☑091 35 15 586; www.vina-gerstmajer.weebly.com; Petefi Šandora 31, Zmajevac; ☺ by appointment) offers tasting tours of its 11 hectares of vineyard and cellar. Just down the hill is the area's biggest producer, **Josić** (☑031-734 410; www.josic.hr; Planina 194, Zmajevac; ☺ by appointment), which also has a fine restaurant. **Kolar** (☑031-733 006; Maršala Tita 94, Suza; three-wine tasting 24KN; ☺ by appointment) offers a restaurant, shop and wine tastings in its 100-year-old cellar, located on the main road in nearby Suza. Don't miss a visit to **Vina Belje** (☑091 17 90 118; www.vinabelje.hr; Šandora Petefija 2, Kneževi Vinogradi; tour & tasting 15KN, tour & tasting of 3-4 wines 45-90KN; ☺10am-5pm), with its ancient cellars and gorgeous viewpoint amid vineyards.

Slavonia also boasts ancient cellars in Ilok at **Ilocki Podrumi** (p98), as well as wineries in Dalj and Erdut north of Vukovar, the best of which is **Vina Antunović** (☑031-590 350; www.vina-antunovic.hr; Braće Radić 17; ☺ by appointment), which has a lovely tasting room where you can savour their white-wine varieties.

INLAND CROATIA NORTHERN BARANJA

Kovač Čarda
SLAVONIAN €

(Maršala Tita 215, Suza; mains 40-60KN; ☺10am-11pm) In the small village of Suza, the Hungarian-run Kovač Čarda is a no-frills roadside eatery known for Baranja's best *fiš paprikaš*. They make it spicy, so ask for the paprika on the side.

★ Josić
SLAVONIAN €€

(☑031-734 410; www.josic.hr; Planina 194, Zmajevac; mains 29-90KN; ☺1-10pm Tue-Thu & Sun, to midnight Fri & Sat) Josić, in the village of Zmajevac, is on a historic *surduk* (wine road) that leads up a steep hill. It's an upmarket restaurant with tables set in vaulted cellars; meat is the strong suit here. Try the duck *perkelt* stew and be sure to visit the wine cellar for tastings of local *graševina*. Reserve ahead in September and October.

Piroš Čizma
SLAVONIAN €€

(☑031-733 806; Maršala Tita 101, Suza; mains 35-80KN; ☺7am-10pm Mon-Thu & Sun, 1pm-midnight Fri & Sat) Located on the roadside when you enter Suza, this restaurant serves up Slavonian dishes prepared with a twist – think marinated catfish on an endive base with lemon, honey and mustard emulsion, and beef steak in a sauce of grapes with *frankovka* wine reduction.

It doubles as a hotel, with 25 pleasant rooms (singles/doubles 250/360KN) in two buildings, all well equipped and featuring breakfasts of local fresh cheeses, jams and cold cuts such as *kulen*.

Baranjska Kuća
SLAVONIAN €€

(☑031-720 180; www.baranjska-kuca.com; Kolodvorska 99, Karanac; mains 35-90KN; ☺11am-10pm

Mon-Thu, to 1am Fri & Sat, to 5pm Sun) Baranjska Kuća is an excellent restaurant that serves many traditional dishes, such as meat and fish stews. There's a chestnut-tree-shaded backyard with a barn, a blacksmith's workshop and other huts with old-fashioned crafts. On weekend nights there is live gypsy music.

❶ Getting There & Away

The bus connections to northern Baranja and within the region are limited so you'll need to have your own wheels to explore this area.

Vukovar

📞 032 / POP 27,700

When you visit Vukovar today, it's a challenge to visualise this town as it was before the war. A pretty place on the Danube, with roots stretching back to the 10th century and a series of elegant baroque mansions, it once bustled with art galleries and museums. All that changed with the siege of 1991, which destroyed its economy, culture, infrastructure, civic harmony and soul.

Since the return of Vukovar to Croatia in 1998, there has been much progress in repairing the damage. Many pock-marked and blasted facades remain, and the former water tower on the road to Ilok has been left as a testament to destruction.

Serbs and Croats live in parallel and hostile universes, socialising in separate spheres. Children attend separate schools and their parents drink in either Serb or Croat cafes.

International organisations are trying to encourage more integration, but forgiveness comes hard to those who lost family members and livelihoods.

❍ Sights

Vučedol Culture Museum MUSEUM
(📞 032-373 930; www.vucedol.hr; Vučedol 252; adult/concession 30/20KN; ⊙ 10am-6pm Tue-Sun) Located 4km downriver from Vukovar, this newly built museum sits on one of Europe's most significant archaeological sites and in less than a year drew 50,000 visitors. The 19 exhibit rooms on two levels give an insight into the rich, ancient Vučedol culture you've likely never heard of, referred to as the European Troy.

A blue tourist train runs here from the town centre, next to Hotel Dunav, at 3pm on Fridays, Saturdays and Sundays, returning at 4.30pm (tickets cost 10KN).

The gorgeous riverside location was first inhabited by farmers in 6000 BC, while Vučedol culture reached its peak between 3000 BC and 2500 BC. On display are ceramics, replicas of furnaces where copper was cast, skulls and bones found in situ, earthen bowls and trays, wooden canoes and fishbone needles. Check out the cool animation that shows the settlement during its golden age, when it housed some 2000 people. While the exhibits are well marked with bilingual boards, it's worth taking a guided tour; tours in English run every hour and cost 75KN. Ask to be taken to the

---

THE SIEGE OF VUKOVAR

Before the war, Vukovar had a multi-ethnic population of about 44,000, of which Croats comprised 44% and Serbs 37%. As Croatia edged away from the former Yugoslavia in early 1991, tensions mounted between the two groups. In August 1991, the federal Yugoslav force launched a full-scale artillery and infantry assault in an attempt to seize the town.

By the end of August all but 15,000 of Vukovar's original inhabitants had fled. Those who remained cowered in bomb-proof cellars, living on tinned food and rationed water while bodies piled up in the streets above them. For several months of the siege, the city held out as its pitifully outnumbered defenders warded off the attacks.

After weeks of hand-to-hand fighting, Vukovar surrendered on 18 November. On 20 November Serb-Yugoslav soldiers entered Vukovar's hospital and removed 400 patients, staff and their families, 194 of whom were massacred near the village of Ovčara, their bodies dumped in a mass grave nearby. In 2007 at the War Tribunal in the Hague, two Yugoslav army officers, Mile Mrkšić and Veselin Šljivančanin, were sentenced to 20 and 10 years in prison, respectively, for their role in this massacre.

In all, it's estimated that 2000 people – including 1100 civilians – were killed in the defence of Vukovar. There were 4000 wounded, several thousand who disappeared (presumably into mass graves), and 22,000 who were forced into exile.

Megaron a five-minute walk away from the museum – a bunker-like building with skylights that houses skeletons in a sand pit, including a grave of a deer that was used on shamanic journeys. The Megaron's rooftop has lovely views out to the river and the leafy surroundings.

Castle Eltz MUSEUM
(Županijska 2; adult/concession 25/15KN, Wed 2-4pm free; ◷10am-6pm Tue-Sun) Closed for several years following the war, the 18th-century Eltz Palace reopened its doors after renovations in 2014. It now showcases four levels of exhibits, many with interactive multimedia features and all marked in English. Don't miss the moving 3rd-floor exhibit about the siege of Vukovar. You can take a guided tour in English (100KN).

Place of Memory:
Vukovar Hospital 1991 MUSEUM
(☑091 45 21 222; Županijska 37; adult/concession 15/7KN; ◷8am-3pm Mon-Fri, or by appointment) This multimedia museum recounts the tragic events that took place in the hospital during the 1991 siege. The stirring tour takes you through a series of sandbag-protected corridors, with video projections of war footage, bomb holes and the claustrophobic atomic shelter where newborn babies and the nurses' children were kept.

There are small cubicles where you can listen to interviews and speeches by the victims and survivors.

Ada BEACH
Head out to this sandy island in the Danube, where on a summer weekend you'll find lots of locals swimming, lounging on the beaches and hanging out at the cafe. Boats (free) depart from the restaurant **Vrške** (www.restoran-vrske.hr; Parobrodarska 3; ◷8am-10pm Mon-Fri, to 11pm Sat & Sun).

Ovčara Memorial MEMORIAL
(5KN; ◷10am-5pm) Around 6km out of town, en route to Ilok, there's a turn-off to the Ovčara Memorial, another 4km down the road. This is the hangar where 194 victims from Vukovar's hospital were beaten and tortured after the town's surrender in November 1991. Inside the dark room are projections of victims' photos, with a single candle burning in the middle. The victims met their deaths in a cornfield another 1.5km down the road, now marked with a black marble gravestone covered with candles and flowers.

⛴ Tours

Vukovar Waterbus Bajadera BOATING
(☑098-344 741; www.danubiumtours.hr/redplov idbe; adult/concession/family 45/40/90KN) Run by Danubium Tours, a glass-topped boat plies the Danube every evening at 6pm for a scenic 45-minute trip. You'll need to reserve on weekends.

✦✦ Festivals & Events

Vukovar Film Festival FILM
(www.vukovarfilmfestival.com) The annual Vukovar Film Festival in late August shows features, documentaries and shorts, mainly from Danubian countries.

🛏 Sleeping & Eating

Hostel 101 Dalmatinac HOSTEL €
(☑032-616 109; www.101dalmatinac.com; Europ-ske Unije 11; dm from 135KN, d 400KN; ❀🐾🛜) A sweet new hostel behind a bank building a short walk from the riverside, this place has nine dorms (sleeping up to seven) and one double in two separate buildings. Rooms are minimalist, with a black-and-white theme (think Dalmatians). There's not much shared space, and breakfast is served (25KN) at Dunavska Golubica. Call ahead if you're arriving after 10pm.

Hotel Lav HOTEL €€€
(☑032-445 100; www.hotel-lav.hr; JJ Strossmayera 18; s/d 490/780KN; 🅿❀🛜) A modern, well-run, four-star hotel. Rooms and suites are spacious and well equipped; many have lovely river views. There's a good bar, coffee room, restaurant, small fitness room and terrace.

Dunavska Golubica SLAVONIAN €€
(Dunavska Šetnica 1; mains 50-100KN; ◷7am-11pm) A pleasant restaurant by the riverside, with an excellent reputation for Slavonian specialities (it does great boneless *fiš papri-kaš*) and live music on summer weekends.

ⓘ Information

Tourist Office (☑032-442 889; www.turizam-vukovar.hr; JJ Strossmayera 15; ◷7am-3pm Mon-Fri, 8am-1pm Sat)

ⓘ Getting There & Away

The town has good bus connections to Osijek (35KN, one hour, 10 daily), Ilok (35KN, one hour, 12 daily) and Zagreb (166KN, five hours, five daily). There are also regular services to Belgrade (99KN, 2½ hours, four daily) in Serbia.

Ilok

✍ 032 / POP 7000

The easternmost town in Croatia, 37km from Vukovar, Ilok sits perched on a hill overlooking the Danube and the Serbian region of Vojvodina, across the river. It's part of the Srijem region of Croatia, together with Vukovar. Surrounded by the wine-growing hills of Fruška Gora, famous for viniculture since Roman times, this well-preserved medieval town has a landmark castle that's now one of Slavonia's best museums.

Occupied by Serbia in the early 1990s, Ilok was reintegrated into Croatia in 1998. Wine production has since been revived – the area now has 20 wineries you can tour – and the fortified town centre is being renovated following recent archaeological excavations.

◉ Sights & Activities

The **medieval town** is a leafy place surrounded by the remains of huge city walls. It has two rare specimens of Ottoman heritage: a 16th-century **hammam** and a **turbe**, the grave of a Turkish nobleman.

City Museum   MUSEUM
(Muzej Grada Iloka; www.mgi.hr; Šetalište Oca Mladena Barbarića 5; adult/concession 20/10KN; ⊙ 9am-3pm Tue-Thu, to 6pm Fri, 11am-6pm Sat) Ilok's principal attraction is this excellent municipal museum located in the Odescalchi palace high above the Danube with spectacular river views. The castle was built on the foundations of a 15th-century structure, which the Italian family Odescalchi later rebuilt in today's baroque-classicist style.

The museum's displays are very well presented, with illustrated information panels in English and Croatian. Sabres and muskets represent the town's Turkish period, there's fine 19th-century furniture and art, and a tombstone and tapestry from an ancient synagogue.

Ilocki Podrumi   WINE
(✍ 032-590 088; www.ilocki-podrumi.hr; Šetalište OM Barbarića 4; tours 30KN; ⊙ 7am-11pm) The old wine cellars adjacent to the castle are well worth a look. Be sure to taste the *traminac,*

a dry white wine served at the coronation of Queen Elizabeth II. A 30-minute tour takes you to the atmospheric underground cellar with its oak barrels. There's also a terrific wine store. Tours in English need to be arranged in advance.

🛏 Sleeping

Stari Podrum   HOTEL €
(✍ 032-590 088; www.ilocki-podrumi.hr; s/d 250/430KN; P ❋ @ 🛜) The motel-style accommodation block in the back has 18 large, modern rooms, all with Danube views and plush decor. Located inside the castle's old wine cellars are banqueting rooms lined with wood panelling and giant oak barrels – a splendid setting for a hearty meal of Ilok pork sausages and shepherd's stew with dumplings (mains are 30KN to 95KN). The wine list is superb.

Old Town Hostel   HOSTEL €
(✍ 098 92 22 512; www.cinema.com.hr/old-town-hostel; Julija Benešića 42; dm/s/d 100/250/400KN; P ❋ @ 🛜) Inside a restored old cinema, this hostel just below the old town has four colourful dorms upstairs, a funky bar with vinyl-plastered walls and a disco on weekend nights.

Hotel Dunav   HOTEL €€
(✍ 032-596 500; www.hoteldunavilok.com; Julija Benešića 62; s/d 300/500KN; P ❋ @ 🛜) Right on the Danube, this fine hotel has 16 attractive rooms with verdant views, some with balconies overlooking the river, and a lovely terrace cafe on the riverfront.

ℹ Information

Tourist Office (✍ 032-590 020; www.turizam-ilok.hr; Trg Sv Ivana Kapistrana 5; ⊙ 8am-4pm Mon-Fri) Can recommend rural hotels and walking routes around Ilok and has a lot of local information. Call ahead, as opening hours are sporadic.

ℹ Transport

The bus arrives in the town centre just steps from the medieval town. Ilok is connected to Osijek by four daily buses (60KN, 1¾ hours), all passing through Vukovar.

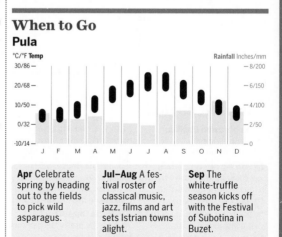

Istria

📞 052

Best Places to Eat

➜ Male Madlene (p115)

➜ Marina (p122)

➜ Toklarija (p129)

➜ Barba Danilo (p116)

Best Places to Sleep

➜ Villa Meneghetti (p111)

➜ Hotel Mauro (p120)

➜ Hotel Kaštel (p127)

➜ Vela Vrata (p128)

➜ Pula Art Hostel (p103)

Why Go?

Continental Croatia meets the Adriatic in Istria (Istra to Croats), the heart-shaped, 3600-sq-km peninsula just south of Trieste in Italy. The bucolic interior of rolling hills and fertile plains attracts artsy visitors to Istria's hilltop villages, rural hotels and farmhouse restaurants, while the verdant indented coastline is enormously popular with the sun-and-sea set. While vast hotel complexes line much of the coast and the rocky beaches are not Croatia's best, facilities are wide-ranging, the sea is clean and secluded spots are still plentiful.

Istria's madly popular coast gets flooded with Central European tourists in summer, but you can still feel alone and undisturbed in the peninsula's interior, even in mid-August. Add acclaimed gastronomy (starring fresh seafood, prime white truffles, wild asparagus, top-rated olive oils and award-winning wines), sprinkle it with historical charm and you have a little slice of heaven.

When to Go

Pula

Apr Celebrate spring by heading out to the fields to pick wild asparagus.

Jul–Aug A festival roster of classical music, jazz, films and art sets Istrian towns alight.

Sep The white-truffle season kicks off with the Festival of Subotina in Buzet.

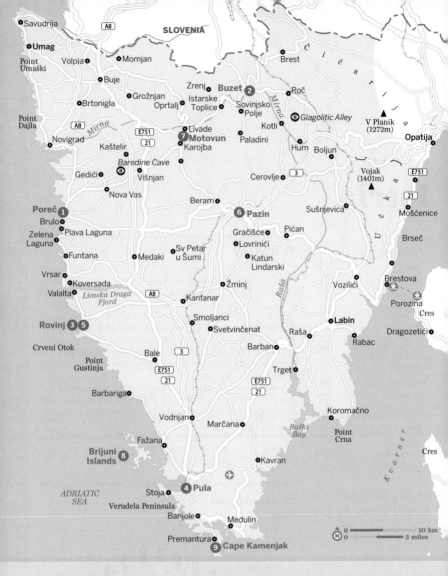

Istria Highlights

1 Euphrasian Basilica
(p118) Admiring the
mosaics of Poreč's top temple.

2 Truffle hunting (p129)
Searching for the elusive truffle
in the forests around Buzet.

3 Rovinj (p111) Getting
the perfect holiday snap of this
west-coast gem's old town.

4 Roman Amphitheatre
(p102) Scrambling around
northern Croatia's most
famous Roman ruin in Pula.

5 Batana House (p113)
Taking in Rovinj's fishing history
at this fascinating museum
celebrating this local industry.

6 Pazin Chasm (p131)
Walking the pretty trails of this
legendary cave.

7 Motovun (p127)
Catching alfresco screenings
during Motovun's summer film
festival.

8 Brijuni (p109) Soaking
up the communist chic at
Tito's island playground.

9 Cape Kamenjak (p108)
Exploring the wild landscapes
near Pula.

History

Towards the end of the 2nd millennium BC, the Illyrian Histrian tribe settled the region and built fortified villages on top of the coastal and interior hills. The Romans swept into Istria in the 3rd century BC and began building roads and more hill forts as strategic strongholds.

From AD 539 to 751, Istria was under Byzantine rule, the most impressive remnant of which is the Euphrasian Basilica in Poreč. In the period that followed, power switched between Slavic tribes, the Franks and German rulers until an increasingly powerful Venice wrestled control of the Istrian coast in the early 13th century.

With the fall of Venice in 1797, Istria came under Austrian rule, followed by the French (1809–13) and then the Austrians. During the 19th and early 20th centuries, most of Istria was little more than a neglected outpost of the Austro-Hungarian Empire.

When the empire disintegrated at the end of WWI, Italy moved quickly to secure Istria. Italian troops occupied Pula in November 1918 and, in the 1922 Treaty of Rapallo, the Kingdom of Serbs, Croats and Slovenes ceded Istria along with Zadar and several islands to Italy, as a reward for joining the Allied powers in WWI.

A massive population shift followed as 30,000 to 40,000 Italians arrived from Mussolini's Italy and many Croats left, fearing fascism. Their fears were not misplaced, as Istria's Italian masters attempted to consolidate their hold by banning Slavic speech, education and cultural activities.

Italy retained the region until its defeat in WWII when Istria became part of Yugoslavia, causing another mass exodus, as Italians and many Croats fled Tito's communists. Trieste and the peninsula's northwestern tip were points of contention between Italy and Yugoslavia until 1954, when the region was finally awarded to Italy. As a result of Tito's reorganisation of Yugoslavia, the northern part of the peninsula was incorporated into Slovenia, where it remains.

ISTRIA'S WEST COAST

The west coast of Istria is the tourist showcase. At the tip of the peninsula is Pula, the coast's largest city. The Brijuni Islands, Tito's former playground, are an easy day trip from here. Rovinj is the most enchanting town and Poreč the easiest – and cheaper – holiday choice, with lodging and entertainment options aplenty. Just across the water is Italy, and the pervasive Italian influence makes it seem even closer. Italian is a second language in Istria, many Istrians have Italian passports and each town name has an Italian counterpart.

Pula

POP 57,460

The wealth of Roman architecture makes otherwise workaday Pula (ancient Polensium) a standout among Croatia's larger cities. The star of the show is the remarkably well-preserved Roman amphitheatre, smack in the heart of the city, which dominates the streetscape and doubles as a venue for summer concerts and festivals.

Historical attractions aside, Pula is a busy commercial city on the sea that has managed to retain a friendly small-town appeal. Just a short bus ride away, a series of beaches awaits at the resorts that occupy the Verudela Peninsula to the south. Although marred with residential and holiday developments, the coast is dotted with fragrant pine groves, seaside cafes and a clutch of good restaurants. Further south along the indented shoreline, the Premantura Peninsula hides a spectacular nature park, the protected cape of Kamenjak.

History

In 1853, during Austro-Hungarian rule, the monarchy chose Pula as the empire's main naval centre. The construction of the port and the opening of its large shipyard in 1886 unleashed a demographic and economic expansion that transformed Pula into a military and industrial powerhouse.

The city fell into decline once again under Italian fascist rule, which lasted from 1918 to 1943, when it was occupied by the Germans. At the end of WWII, Pula was administered by Anglo-American forces until it became part of postwar Yugoslavia in 1947. Pula's industrial base weathered the Balkan wars relatively well and the city remains an important centre for shipbuilding, textiles, metals and glass.

⊙ Sights

The oldest part of the city follows the ancient Roman plan of streets circling the central citadel, while the city's newer portions follow a

ISTRIA PULA

rectangular grid pattern. Most shops, agencies and businesses are clustered in and around the old town as well as on Giardini, Carrarina, Istarska and Riva, which runs along the brand-new harbour. The beaches are 4km to the south on the Verudela Peninsula.

★ **Roman Amphitheatre**   HISTORIC BUILDING
(Arena; Flavijevska bb; adult/concession 50/25KN; ⊘8am-midnight Jul & Aug, to 9pm May-Jun & Sep, to 7pm Oct-Apr) Pula's most famous and imposing sight is this 1st-century oval amphitheatre, overlooking the harbour northeast of the old town. It's a huge and truly magnificent structure, slotted together entirely from local limestone and known locally as the Arena. Designed to host gladiatorial contests and seating up to 20,000 spectators, it's now Istria's stellar tourist attraction but still serves the mass entertainment needs of the local populace in the shape of concerts, some by big-name acts.

When you emerge from the ticket office on to the floor of the amphitheatre, there are a few features you should look out for. On the top of the walls is a gutter that collected rainwater – you can still see the slabs used to secure the fabric canopy, which protected spectators from the sun. You can clamber round the stones, take a seat and imagine the scenes that were played out here 2000 years ago, or hire some Roman garb and have your photo taken.

In the chambers next to the ticket office there is a small, gravel-floored museum with displays on the Roman olive-oil industry and Roman life in Istria.

Check out the weekly Spectacvla Antiqva, an evening summer event that recreates gladiator fights, workshops featuring ancient Roman clothing and hairstyles, and tasting of Roman food and drinks. It costs 70KN for adults, 30KN for children.

**Museum of
Contemporary Art of Istria**   MUSEUM
(Ivana 1; 10KN; ⊘11am-9pm Jul & Aug, to 9pm rest of the year) Pop in to Pula's contemporary-art museum, inside the old printing house off the harbour, to see Istrian art from the second half of the 20th century until today. Rotating exhibits change frequently.

Cathedral   CATHEDRAL
(Katedrala; Trg Sv Tome 2; ⊘10am-6pm Jul & Aug, shorter hours rest of the year) The main altar of Pula's 5th-century cathedral is a Roman sarcophagus holding relics of saints from the

3rd century. The floor reveals fragments of 5th- and 6th-century mosaics. Stones from the amphitheatre were used to build the bell tower in the 17th century.

**Historical & Maritime
Museum of Istria**   MUSEUM
(Gradinski Uspon 6; adult/concession 20/10KN; ⊘8am-9pm Apr-Sep, 9am-5pm Oct-Mar) Housed in a 17th-century Venetian hilltop fortress in the old town's centre, the meagre exhibits here deal mostly with the maritime history of Pula. However, the views from the citadel walls are worth a stop, though perhaps not the climb!

Temple of Augustus   HISTORIC BUILDING
(Forum; adult/concession 10/5KN; ⊘9am-9pm Mon-Fri, to 3pm Sat & Sun) This is the only visible remnant from the Roman era on the Forum, Pula's central meeting place from antiquity through the Middle Ages. It used to contain temples and public buildings, but today this temple, erected from 2 BC to AD 14, is the showcase. When the Romans left, it became a church and then a grain warehouse. Reconstructed after a bomb hit it in 1944, it now houses a small **museum** of Roman sculpture with the occasional temporary show.

Roman Floor Mosaic   HISTORIC SITE
(Sergijevaca) `FREE` This well-preserved mosaic dates from the 3rd century and is a must-see for fans of things Roman. In the midst of remarkably well-preserved geometric motifs is the central panel, which depicts bad girl Dirce from Greek mythology being punished for the attempted murder of her cousin. It's tricky to find – follow the brown signs from the car park on Flaciusova.

Lighting Giants   PUBLIC ART
(Pula harbour; ⊘dusk-10pm) Don't miss Pula's star evening attraction, a gobsmacking lighting display at the city's 19th-century Uljanik shipyard, one of the world's oldest working docks. Renowned lighting designer Dean Skira has lit up the shipyard's iconic cranes in 16,000 different colour schemes, which come alive four times every evening on the hour for 15 minutes.

Triumphal Arch of Sergius   RUINS
(Sergijevaca) Along Carrarina are Roman walls, which mark the eastern boundary of old Pula. Follow these walls south and continue down Giardini to this majestic arch, erected in 27 BC to commemorate three

members of the Sergius family who achieved distinction in Pula.

Zerostrasse   HISTORIC SITE
(☑052-211 566; Gradinski uspon 6; adult/concession 15/5KN; ☺10am-10pm mid-Jun–mid-Sep) This underground system of tunnels was built before and during WWI to shelter the city's population and serve as storage for ammunition. Now you can walk through several of its sections, which all lead to the middle, where a photo exhibit shows early aviation in Pula. There are three entrances – one by the Forum (in a tiny unmarked street off Kandlerova), another by the Archaeological Museum and the third by the taxi stand on Giardini.

🏃 Activities & Tours

An easy 41km cycling trail from Pula to Medulin follows the path of Roman gladiators. The tourist centre (p107) can provide information on the trail, including a map.

If you're interested in cycling, check out Istria Bike (www.istria-bike.com). This website run by the tourist board outlines trails, packages and agencies that offer cycling trips.

Orca Diving Center   DIVING
(☑099 83 10 867; www.orcadiving.hr; Verudela bb, Hotel Histria) Arranges boat and wreck dives at this centre on the Verudela Peninsula.

White Dust Sailing   BOATING
(☑091 60 17 268; www.whitedust-sailing.com) For a unique sailing experience, charter a boat through White Dust Sailing, which runs excellent daily tours as well as thematic week-long sails (adventure, family, gastronomy) to undiscovered nautical routes and off-the-radar beaches; high-season sails start at €500.

Martinabela   BOATING
(☑098 99 75 875; www.martinabela.hr) This one-boat company operates twice daily in summer to Brijuni.

🎉 Festivals & Events

Pula Film Festival   FILM
(www.pulafilmfestival.hr) Running for more than six decades, this July film festival is the town's most important event, with screenings of mainly Croatian and some international films in the Roman Amphitheatre (p102) and other locations around town.

Seasplash Festival   MUSIC
(www.seasplash.net) In the last week in July, this hopping music fest, featuring wide-ranging

BEACHES

Pula is surrounded by a half-circle of rocky beaches, each one with its own fan club. Like bars or nightclubs, beaches go in and out of style. The most tourist-packed are undoubtedly those surrounding the hotel complex on the **Verudela Peninsula**, although some locals will dare to be seen at the small turquoise-coloured **Hawaii Beach** near the Hotel Park.

live performances – from reggae and ska to dancehall and hip hop – alights Štinjan's Punta Christo Fort, just northwest of Pula.

Outlook Festival   MUSIC
(www.outlookfestival.com; ☺Sep) Europe's largest bass music and sound-system culture festival takes place in early September in Punta Christo Fort in Štinjan. The opening event takes place in the 'Arena' Roman Amphitheatre (p102).

🛏 Sleeping

★Pula Art Hostel   HOSTEL €
(☑098 874 078; www.pulaarthostel.com; Marulićeva 41; dm/d 120/330KN; 🖥) Intimate hostel run by a friendly family with a love of imaginative tiling (check out the roof terrace and common-room floors as well as many of the bathrooms and dorms). Facilities are simple but clean and well-maintained, and it has an old-school backpacker-hostel atmosphere. The only slight downside is the location just south of the city centre.

Camping Stoja   CAMPGROUND €
(☑052-387 144; www.arenacamps.com; Stoja 37; campsites per person/pitch 63/126KN; ☺Apr-Oct) This is the closest campground to Pula, 3km southwest of the centre. It has lots of space on the shady promontory, with a restaurant, a diving centre and swimming off the rocks. Take bus 1 to Stoja.

Youth Hostel   HOSTEL €
(☑052-391 133; www.hfhs.hr; Valsaline 4; dm 135KN, caravan 155KN, campsite per person/tent 80/15KN; 🖥) Overlooking a beach in Valsaline Bay, 3km south of central Pula, this hostel has dorms, caravans split into two tiny four-bed units and campsites. To get here, take bus 2A or 3A to the 'Veruda 2' stop, walk back towards the city to the

Pula

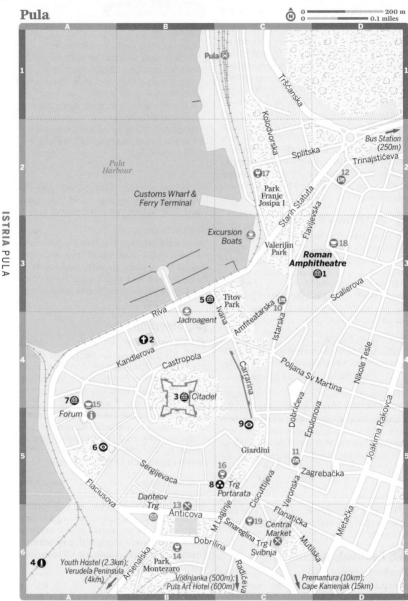

Pula Harbour

Customs Wharf & Ferry Terminal

Excursion Boats

Roman Amphitheatre

Park Franje Josipa I

Valerijin Park

Titov Park

Jadroagent

Kandlerova

Castropola

Citadel

Forum

Sergijevaca

Flaciusova

Danteov Trg

Anticova

Dobrilina

Park Montezaro

Giardini

Zagrebačka

Trg Portarata

Central Market

Trg I Svibnja

Bus Station (250m)

Youth Hostel (2.3km);
Verudela Peninsula (4km)

Vodnjanka (500m);
Pula Art Hotel (600m)

Premantura (10km);
Cape Kamenjak (15km)

first street, then turn left and look for the hostel sign.

Hotel Scaletta
HOTEL €€

(☎052-541 025; www.hotel-scaletta.com; Flavijevska 26; s/d 498/718KN; Ⓟ❄🕾) There's a friendly family vibe at this cosy hotel. The rooms have tasteful decor and a bagful of trimmings (such as minibars). Plus it's just a hop and a skip from town, and a short walk from the amphitheatre and the waterfront. Rates include a buffet breakfast.

Pula

ISTRIA PULA

Hotel Galija   HOTEL €€€

(☑ 052-383 802; www.hotelgalija.hr; Epulonova 3; s/d 608/836KN; P ✳ 🛜) This well-maintained, two-part hotel sits a stone's throw from the central market. Standard rooms are in the building above the restaurant, while the newer, more modern rooms are in the building that houses the reception.

Hotel Amfiteatar   HOTEL €€€

(☑ 052-375 600; www.hotelamfiteatar.com; Amfiteatarska 6; r from 833KN; P ✳ 🛜) The swankiest spot in town, right by the amphitheatre, this post-millennial hotel has contemporary rooms with upscale trimmings such as mini-bars and very flat TVs. Rooms range in size and view. The **restaurant** is one of Pula's smartest.

Park Plaza Histria Pula   HOTEL €€€

(☑ 052-590 000; www.arenaturist.hr; Verudella 17; s/d 950/1400KN; P ✳ @ 🛜 ☒) Extensive four-star facilities, competently maintained rooms with balconies and easy beach access make up for the lack of character at this concrete behemoth on the Verudela Peninsula. There are indoor and outdoor swimming pools and a spa. Reserve online for the best prices.

🍴 Eating

The centre of Pula is full of tourist traps, so for the best food and good value you'll have to head out of town. To grab a cheap quick bite, browse around the central market.

Fish-Food More   SEAFOOD €

(Rizzijeva 47; mains 5100KN; ◷ 8am-11pm Mon-Sat Jun-Jul & Sep, also Sun in Aug) This simple seafood joint in a residential area is some 15 minutes' walk from the central market (part of it uphill). It buzzes with locals at

lunchtime, who come for fresh fish dishes. The marinated sardines are to die for. Walk south on Radićeva to Rizzijeva.

Fresh   SANDWICHES €

(Anticova 5; snacks 16-20KN; ◷ 9am-4.30pm Mon-Fri) Best for a quick and wholesome bite, this tiny sandwich-and-salad bar serves a mean ham-and-cheese toast plus tasty vegetarian/vegan dishes (think spinach and chicory quiche), traditional Croatian savoury pies such as *zlevanka,* plus wraps, pastas and tortillas.

★Konoba Batelina   SEAFOOD €€

(☑ 052-573 767; Čimulje 25, Banjole; mains 75-155KN; ◷ 5-11pm Mon-Sat) The superb food that awaits at this family-run tavern is worth a trek to Banjole village, 3km southeast of Pula. The owner, fisherman and chef David Skoko, dishes out seafood that's some of the best, most creative and lovingly prepared you'll find in Istria. Reserve ahead.

Medeja   CROATIAN €€

(Šijanska cesta 24; mains 45-120KN; ◷ noon-11pm) Around 3km northeast of the centre, near the motorway junction, this small restaurant promises little from the outside, but once ensconced at one of its hefty timer tables, the food is a real treat. The Croatian dishes have copious amounts of cream, pasta, truffles and bacon like grandmother used to make, but the desserts go way beyond her culinary expertise.

Farabuto   MEDITERRANEAN €€

(www.farabuto.hr; Sisplac 15; mains 70-140KN; ◷ 11am-midnight Jun-Sep, closed Sun Oct-May) It's worth a trek to this nondescript residential area, about 1.5km southwest of the centre, for stylish decor, but more importantly, finely executed Mediterranean fare with a creative touch. There are daily specials and a well-curated wine list; try the house wine from Piquentum winery.

Vodnjanka   ISTRIAN €€
(Vitezića 4; mains 40-100KN; ☺noon-10pm Mon-Sat) Locals swear by the real-deal home cooking at this no-frills spot. It's cheap, casual and cash-only, and there's a reassuringly brief menu that focuses on simple Istrian cuisine. It's a bit of trek out of town – to get here, walk south on Radićeva to Vitezića.

Milan   MEDITERRANEAN €€
(www.milanpula.com; Stoja 4; mains 80-180KN; ☺noon-11pm) An exclusive vibe, seasonal specialities, four sommeliers and an olive-oil expert on staff all create one of the city's best fine-dining experiences. The five-course fish menu is well worth it should you have a few hundred kunas spare.

Gina   ISTRIAN €€
(Stoja 23; mains 50-130KN; ☺noon-11pm) This low-key eatery near Camping Stoja (p103) draws in a local crowd for its well-prepared Istrian mainstays, cosy decor and lovely sea views. Try the cream fish soup with *malvazija* wine and the lavender semifreddo with a hot sauce of figs and pine nuts.

🍷 Drinking & Nightlife

Most of the nightlife is out of the town centre, but in mild weather the cafes on the Forum and along the pedestrian streets Kandlerova, Flanatička and Sergijevaca are lively people-watching spots. To mix with Pula's young crowd, grab some beers and head to the Lungomare coastal strip, where music blasts out of parked cars. For beach-bar action, head to Verudela or Medulin.

★Cvajner   CAFE
(Forum 2; ☺7.30am-2am Mon-Fri, from 8am Sat, from 8.30am Sun) Housed in a former bank on the Forum (the huge safe is used as a storeroom), this is Pula's hippest cafe, scattered with random Tito-era furniture, art by up-and-coming local artists and chilled staff. In the warmer months most miss the joys of the interior by plumping for an alfresco seat out front.

★Cabahia   BAR
(Širolina 4; ☺8am-midnight Mon-Sat, 10am-midnight Sun) This artsy hideaway, 2km south of the centre in Veruda, has a cosy wood-beamed interior, eclectic old objects, dim lighting, South American flair and a great garden terrace out the back. It hosts concerts and gets packed on weekends.

Club Uljanik   CLUB
(www.clubuljanik.hr; Dobrilina 2; ☺8am-5am Thu-Sat) Going strong since the 1960s, the legendary Pula club these days caters to a young party crowd who come for its range of themed weekend parties.

Pietas Julia   BAR
(Riva 20; ☺8am-midnight Mon-Thu & Sun, to 4am Sat; 🛜) This trendy bar on the harbour, next to the rowing club, really comes into its own late on weekends, as it stays open till 4am. During the day, there are breakfasts and snacks. The seats on the roadside are a nice spot for a sundowner.

Scandal Express   BAR
(Ciscuttijeva 15; ☺7am-midnight Mon-Fri, 7am-2pm & 6pm-midnight Sat & Sun; 🛜) Mingle with a mixed-bag crowd of locals at this popular gathering spot with a vague train-carriage theme and lots of posters. Try *pašareta,* a local Istrian soda.

Scala   CAFE
(Ozad Arene; ☺8am-9pm Mon-Fri, from 9am Sat) Stop at this humble cafe-bar for outdoor seating with an unrivalled view down into the amphitheatre. The view and the cheapish drinks make it a good place to take a sightseeing break.

James Joyce   BAR
(Trg Portarata 1; ☺7am-10pm Mon-Sat) A statue of James Joyce greets you at the entrance to this colourful bar, which occupies the ground floor of a building where he taught English. Inside, an unexpected sight meets the eyes: all brass, Tiffany lamps, art-nouveau stained glass and maritime knick-knacks. However, if you don't like secondhand nicotine vapour, it's not a great place in which to tarry.

Zeppelin   BEACH BAR
(Saccorgiana Bay; ☺10am-2am Mon-Thu & Sun, to 4am Fri & Sat) Après-beach fun is on the menu at this beach bar in Saccorgiana Bay on Verudela. It also does night parties ranging in theme from vodka to reggae and karaoke to martini.

Bass   BAR
(Širolina 3; ☺8am-midnight Mon-Sat, from 10am Sun) Characterful bar in Veruda with a long cocktail menu and a laid-back clientele.

TAKING IT OFF IN ISTRIA

Naturism in Croatia enjoys a long and venerable history that began on Rab Island around the turn of the 20th century. It quickly became a fad among Austrians influenced by the growing German *freikörperkultur* movement, which loosely translates as 'free body culture'. Later, Austrian Richard Ehrmann opened the first naturist camp on Paradise Beach in Lopar (on Rab), but the real founders of Adriatic naturism were Edward VIII and Wallis Simpson, who popularised it by going skinny-dipping along the Rab coast in 1936.

The coast of Istria now has many of Croatia's largest and most well-developed naturist resorts. Naturist campgrounds are marked as FKK, an abbreviation of *freikörperkultur*.

Start in the north at **Camp Kanegra** (☑052-700 700; www.istracamping.com; Umag; per person/unit 48/107KN), north of Umag, a relatively small site on a long pebbly beach. Continuing south along the coast, you'll come to **Naturist Centre Ulika** (☑052-410 102; www.plavalaguna.hr; Červar; per person/unit 55/130KN) in Červar, just outside Poreč, which has 559 pitches, as well as caravans and mobile homes available for rent. For those who prefer to stay in an apartment, **Naturist Resort Solaris** (www.valamar.hr; Tar; r from 587KN; ✤ ☎) is the ideal choice. Only 12km north of Poreč, on the wooded Lanterna Peninsula, the complex also includes a naturist campground. South of Poreč, next to the fishing village of Funtana, is the larger **Naturist Camping Istra** (www.valamar.hr; Grgeti 35, Funtana; per person/unit 60/130KN), which sleeps up to 3000 people. Continue south past Vrsar and you come to the mother ship of naturist resorts, **Koversada** (www.camp ingrovinjvrsar.com; Koversada 1, Vrsar; per person/unit 55/130KN). In 1961 Koversada islet went totally nude and the colony soon spread to the nearby coast. Now this behemoth can accommodate up to 8000 people in campsites, villas and apartments. If that seems a little overwhelming, keep going south to **Valalta Naturist Camp** (☑052-804 800; www.valalta.hr; Lim 7; per person/pitch 85/208KN), on the other side of the Lim Channel north of Rovinj. It has a manageable number of apartments, bungalows, caravans, mobile homes and campsites. If you prefer to be within easy reach of Pula, travel down the coast to Medulin and **Camp Kažela** (www.arenacamps.com; Kapovica 350, Medulin; per person/unit 61/131KN), which has mobile homes for rent, plus campsites right by the sea.

☆ Entertainment

You should definitely try to catch a concert in the spectacular amphitheatre. The tourist office has schedules and there are posters around Pula advertising live performances.

Rojc CULTURAL CENTRE
(www.rojcnet.pula.org; Gajeva 3) For an arty underground experience, check out the program at Rojc, a converted army barracks that houses a multimedia arts centre and studios with occasional concerts, exhibitions and other events. Head south of Park Montezaro, just below the centre of Pula, and follow Gajeva to reach Rojc.

❶ Information

Active Travel Istra (☑052-215 497; www.activa-istra.com; Scalierova 1) Agency specialising in excursions around Istria, adventure trips and concert tickets.

Arenaturist (☑052-529 400; www.arenaturist.hr; Riviera Guest House, Splitska 1a) Arenaturist manages a network of hotels. It can help

you book rooms and offers guide services and excursions.

Hospital (☑052-376 500; Zagrebačka 30; ☺24hr)

IstrAction (☑095 70 07 822; www.istraction.com; Kolodvorska 5) Offers fun half-day tours to Cape Kamenjak and around Pula's fortifications, as well as medieval-themed full-day excursions around Istria.

Main Post Office (Danteov trg 4; ☺7am-8pm Mon-Fri, to 2pm Sat) Housed in a magnificent Functionalist building from the 1930s – the spiralling red staircase inside is an architectural masterpiece.

Maremonti Travel Agency (☑052-384 000; www.maremonti-istra.hr; Zadarska 5) It can help you book accommodation, and rent cars and scooters (from 150KN to 300KN per day). It also rents bikes from 90KN per day and offers a guided cycling tour around Pula for 300KN.

Tourist Information Centre (☑052-219 197; www.pulainfo.hr; Forum 3; ☺9am-9pm) Knowledgeable and friendly staff provide maps, brochures and schedules of events in Pula and around Istria. Pick up two useful booklets: *Domus Bonus*, which lists the best-quality private accommodation in Istria, and *Istra Gourmet*, with a list of all restaurants.

If you plan on taking in all the sights, it's worth buying the Pula Card for 120KN (70KN for children over seven), which allows you free entry to many sights.

❶ Getting There & Away

AIR

Pula Airport (☑ 060 308 308; www.airport-pula. hr) is located 6km northeast of town. There four daily flights to Zagreb. In summer, there are low-cost and charter flights from major European cities, such as with Ryanair and Germanwings. **Croatia Airlines** (☑ 072 500 505; www.croatia airlines.hr) has an office at the airport.

BOAT

Pula's harbour is located just west of the amphitheatre and a handy 500m southwest of the bus station. **Jadroagent** (☑ 052-210 431; www. jadroagent.hr; Riva 14; ⊘ 7am-3pm Mon-Fri) has schedules and tickets for Jadrolinija boats connecting Istria with the islands and south of Croatia.

BUS

The Pula **bus station** (Šijanska 4) is 500m northeast of the town centre. Scheduled connections include:

Dubrovnik 383KN, 15 hours, one daily
Labin 48KN, one hour, eight daily
Poreč 60KN, 1½ hours, seven daily
Rijeka 90KN, 2½ hours, 18 daily
Rovinj 33KN, 40 minutes, at least hourly
Zadar 176KN, seven hours, daily
Zagreb 140KN, 5½ hours, seven daily

Brioni Pula (☑ 052-544 537; www.brioni. hr) Based in Pula. Connections to Istria, Split, Zagreb, Padua and Trieste.

TRAIN

Less than 1km north of town, the train station is near the sea along Kolodvorska. Connections from Pula:

Buzet 57KN, two hours, eight daily
Pazin 36KN, one hour, eight daily
Zagreb 154KN, nine hours, eight daily

Cape Kamenjak

For seclusion, head out to the wild Cape Kamenjak on the **Premantura Peninsula**, 10km south of Pula. Istria's southernmost point, this gorgeous, entirely uninhabited cape has lovely rolling hills, wild flowers (including 30 species of orchid), low Mediterranean shrubs, fruit trees and medicinal herbs, and around 30km of virgin beaches

ISTRIAN CUISINE

Istria's food is one of the main reasons you might want to visit this region of Croatia. Local truffles, seafood, pasta, game and wine are the highlights of menus in Istria and standards are high almost everywhere you go. There's also a heavy Italian influence in Istria's cuisine with some claiming the local pizza is better than in most of Italy.

Istria-based **Eat Istria** (☑ 095 85 51 962; www.eatistria.com; Kapovica 322, Medulin) offers cooking classes and wine tours around the peninsula.

and coves. It's criss-crossed with a maze of gravel roads and paths, making it nice and easy to get around on foot or by bike. The views to the island of Cres and the peaks of Velebit are extraordinary. Leave no trace – take all your rubbish out with you at the end of the day. Watch out for strong currents if swimming off the southern cape.

⊙ Sights & Activities

Kolombarica Beach   BEACH
Kolombarica Beach, on the southern end of the peninsula, is popular with daring young men who dive from the high cliffs and swim through the shallow caves at the water's edge. Just above it is a delightful beach bar, half-hidden in the bushes near the beach, about 3.5km from the entrance to the park. A shady place with lush alcoves, lots of driftwood, found objects and a bar that serves tasty snacks, it's a great place to while away an afternoon.

Gornji Kamenjak   AREA
For the wildest and least-discovered stretch of Cape Kamenjak, head to Gornji Kamenjak, which lies between the village of Volme and Premantura.

Windsurf Bar   WATER SPORTS, CYCLING
(☑ 091 51 23 646; www.windsurfing.hr; windsurfing equipment/courses per hr from 80/200KN) In addition to windsurfing, this Premantura outfit offers cycling (250KN) and kayaking (300KN) excursions, and rents bikes (30/100KN per hour/day).

🛏 Sleeping

All visitors must leave the cape by 10pm and camping is prohibited. Nearby Pula has plenty of accommodation.

ℹ Information

Visitors Centre (☑ 052-575 287; www.kamen jak.hr; Selo 120, Premantura) Deals with all aspects of visiting Cape Kamenjak.

ℹ Getting There & Away

Getting to Cape Kamenjak by car is the easiest option, but drive slowly in order not to generate too much dust, which is detrimental to the environment. You'll be charged 40KN for bringing a car on to the cape – this can be paid from 7am at the entrance. A more ecofriendly option is taking city bus 28 from Pula to Premantura (20KN), then renting a bike to get inside the park.

Brijuni Islands

The Brijuni (Brioni in Italian) archipelago consists of two main pine-covered islands and 12 islets off the coast of Istria, just northwest of Pula across the 3km-wide Fažana Channel. Only the largest island, Veli Brijun, can be visited, usually on an organised trip. Covered by meadows, parks and oak and laurel forests – and some rare plants such as wild cucumber and marine poppy – the islands were pronounced a national park in 1983. A visit makes a fascinating and eclectically themed day trip from Pula or Rovinj.

◉ Sights

As you arrive on Veli Brijun, after a 15-minute boat ride from Fažana, you'll dock in front of the Hotel Neptun-Istra, where Tito's illustrious guests once stayed. A guide will take you on a four-hour island tour on a miniature **Tourist Train**, beginning with a visit to the 9-hectare **Safari Park** containing animals given to Tito by various famous individuals. Other stops on the tour include the ruins of a

Roman Country House, dating from the 1st century BC, an **Archaeological Museum** inside a 16th-century citadel, and **St Germain Church**, now a gallery displaying copies of medieval frescoes in Istrian churches.

Most interesting is the **Tito on Brijuni Exhibit** in a building behind Hotel Karmen. A collection of stuffed animals occupies the ground floor. Upstairs are photos of Tito with film stars such as Josephine Baker, Sophia Loren, Elizabeth Taylor and Richard Burton, and world leaders including Indira Gandhi and Fidel Castro. Outside is a 1953 Cadillac that Tito used to show the island to his eminent guests.

⮕ Sleeping

There is no private accommodation on Veli Brijun but there are three luxurious villas (from 7500KN per day for the smallest one, which sleeps four) available for rent through the national-park office. Boat transport to and from the mainland is included in some hotel rates.

Hotel Neptun-Istra   HISTORIC HOTEL €€€
(☑ 052-525 807; www.np-brijuni.hr; s/d 840/1430KN; 🖨) This is the ultimate in communist chic. Even though it's spruced up and comfy, rooms retain their plain utilitarian look. Each comes with a balcony; some have forest views, too. You can just imagine Tito's famous guests lounging here.

Hotel Karmen   HISTORIC HOTEL €€€
(☑ 052-525807; www.np-brijuni.hr; s/d 600/1000KN; 🖨) Designers and architects from Zagreb flock to this 54-room spot on the harbour for its authentic communist-era design – it's trashy, real and feels as if it's still in the 1950s. Let's just hope they don't renovate.

ISTRIA BRIJUNI ISLANDS

TITO & THE BRIJUNI ISLANDS

Even though traces of habitation go back to Roman times, the islands really owe their fame to Tito, the extravagant Yugoslav leader who turned them into his private retreat.

Each year from 1947 until just before his death in 1980, Tito spent six months in Brijuni at his hideaway. To create a lush comfort zone, he introduced subtropical plant species and created a safari park to house the exotic animals gifted to him by world leaders. The Somali sheep you'll see roaming around came from Ethiopia, while a Zambian leader gave a gift of waterbuck.

At his summer playground, Tito received 90 heads of state and a bevy of movie stars in lavish style. Bijela Vila on Veli Brijun was Tito's 'White House': the place for issuing edicts and declarations as well as entertaining. The islands are still used for official state visits, but are increasingly a favourite on the international yachting circuit. They're also a holiday spot of choice for royalty from obscure kingdoms and random billionaires who love its bygone aura of glamour.

☆ Entertainment

Ulysses Theatre   THEATRE
(☑052-525 829; www.ulysses.hr) Come summer, theatre aficionados make their way across the channel to the Minor Fort on Mali Brijun for performances by Ulysses Theatre. You can buy tickets online or at the **National Park Office** (☑052-525 888; www.np-brijuni.hr; Brionska 10, Fažana) in Fažana.

ℹ Getting There & Away

A number of excursion boats leave from the Pula waterfront for the islands. Instead of booking an excursion with one of the travel agencies in Pula, Rovinj or Poreč, you could take public bus 21 from Pula to Fažana (15KN), 8km away, then sign up for a tour at the National Park Office, near the wharf. In July and August, tours cost 210KN per person (children 105KN). It's best to book in advance, especially in summer, and request an English-speaking tour guide.

Check along the Pula waterfront for excursion boats to Brijuni. Note that many of the two-hour 'panorama' trips from Pula to Brijuni (150KN) don't actually stop at the islands; make sure yours does.

ℹ Getting Around

The only ways to get around the island are by bike (35KN per hour or 110KN per day) and electric cart (300KN per hour).

Vodnjan

POP 6100

Connoisseurs of the macabre shouldn't miss Vodnjan (Dignano in Italian), 10km north of Pula. Lying inside a sober church in this sleepy town are the mummies that constitute Vodnjan's primary tourist attraction. These desiccated remains of centuries-old saints, whose bodies mysteriously failed to decompose, are considered to have magical powers.

There's not much going on in the rest of the town, which has Istria's largest Roma population. The centre is Narodni trg, composed of several neo-Gothic palaces in varying stages of decay and restoration.

⊙ Sights

St Blaise's Church   CHURCH
(Crkva Sv Blaža; Župni trg 1; Collection of Sacral Art incl mummies 75KN, mummies only 55KN, Collection of Sacral Art only 55KN, church only 15KN; ⊙9.30am-7pm Mon-Sat, noon-5pm Sun) A few steps from Narodni trg, this handsome neo-baroque church was built at the turn of the 19th cen-

tury, when Venice was the style-setter for the Istrian coast. With its 63m-high **bell tower** as high as St Mark's in Venice, it's the largest parish church in Istria, and worth a visit for its magnificent altars alone. The **mummies** are in a curtained-off area behind the main altar.

In the dim lighting, the complete bodies of Nikolosa Bursa, Giovanni Olini and Leon Bembo resemble wooden dolls in their glass cases. Assorted body parts of three other saints complete the display. As you examine the skin, hair and fingernails of these long-dead people, a tape in English narrates their life stories. Considered to be Europe's best-preserved mummy, the body of St Nikolosa is said to emit a 32m bioenergy circle that has caused 50 miraculous healings.

If the mummies have whetted your appetite for saintly relics, head to the **Collection of Sacral Art** (Zbirka Sakralne Umjetnosti) in the sacristy. Here there are hundreds of relics belonging to 150 different saints, including the casket with St Mary of Egypt's tongue.

✗ Eating & Drinking

Vodnjanka   ISTRIAN €€
(Istarska bb; mains 60-120KN; ⊙11am-midnight Mon-Sat, from 5pm Sun, closed winter) This excellent regional restaurant has several rustic rooms, lots of style and personal service. Specialities include *fuži* (homemade egg pasta twisted into a unique shape) topped with truffles, beefsteak with porcini and truffles, and various kinds of *fritaja* (omelette). The terrace has pretty views of the old-town rooftops and the church spire.

Lighthouse Music Club   CLUB
(www.lighthouseclub.com; Krnjaloža 1; ⊙midnight-6am Fri & Sat, to 2am Sun) On the road between Bale and Vodnjan, this club is one of Istria's best places to party, with big-name DJs and jazz concerts. In fact it claims to be Istria's biggest outdoor club.

ℹ Information

The **tourist office** (☑052-511 700; www.istra.hr/vodnjan; Narodni trg 10; ⊙8am-8pm Mon-Fri, 9am-1pm & 6-8pm Sat, 9am-1pm Sun) is located on the main square.

ℹ Getting There & Away

By bus, Vodnjan is well connected with Pula (20KN, 10 minutes, 13 Monday to Saturday) and Rovinj (29KN, 30 minutes, 14 daily); there are only four buses in either direction on Sunday.

Bale

POP 1130

In the southwestern reaches of Istria, between Rovinj and Vodnjan, the medieval town of Bale is one of Istria's best-kept secrets. Only 7km from the sea, it boasts a maze of narrow cobblestone streets and ancient town houses that developed around a Gothic-Renaissance castle belonging to the Bembo family. Dominated by the 36m-high belfry of the baroque St Julian church, it also has several old churches and a town hall with a 14th-century loggia. The 9km stretch of shoreline nearby is the most pristine in Istria, with delightful beaches and shallow water.

Bale draws a spiritually minded and bohemian crowd for its apparently very powerful energy – a fact you won't find in the tourist brochures. Come here to meet kindred spirits and spend endless hours talking, drinking, dreaming and scribbling.

★ Festivals & Events

Last Minute Open Jazz Festival   MUSIC
(www.kameneprice.com; ☻early Aug) The small but excellent Last Minute Open Jazz Festival takes place in the heat of summer at Kamene priče and features mostly Croatian artists plus the odd overseas guest.

🛏 Sleeping & Eating

La Grisa Hotel   BOUTIQUE HOTEL €€
(☑052-824 501; www.la-grisa.com; La Grisa 23; r 571-954KN; P❄🛜) The boutique La Grisa Hotel has 22 tasteful rooms and suites in eight interconnected buildings on the edge of the old town of Bale, with an ambitious restaurant (try the dishes with *boškarin;* Istrian ox) and a small spa with a sauna (160KN per hour), Jacuzzi and massages (from 290KN).

Villa Meneghetti   HOTEL €€€
(☑091 24 31 600; www.meneghetti.info; Stancija Meneghetti 1; r from 1500KN; P❄🛜≋) For a splurge, book one of four rooms at the exclusive Villa Meneghetti in the secluded countryside near Bale, known for its olive oil, wines and renowned food served at the on-site restaurant. Though pricey, the rooms are exquisitely made up and have heavy beams, real fires and crisp linens.

Kamene Priče   MEDITERRANEAN €€
(Stone Tales; ☑052-824 235; www.kameneprice. com; Castel 57; mains 110-140KN) Kamene Priče is an artsy oasis amid the ancient stone. Enjoy the whimsical decor, a plethora of bizarre objects and two terraces out the back, before tucking into local favourites which always contain seasonal and local ingredients. If you are lucky you may stumble upon a poetry reading, theatre performance or stand-up comedy...there's always something happening here.

ⓘ Getting There & Away

You'll need your own car to reach Bale.

Rovinj

POP 14,300

Rovinj (Rovigno in Italian) is coastal Istria's star attraction. While it can get overrun with tourists in summer, and residents have developed a sharp eye for maximising profits by upgrading hotels and restaurants to four-star status, it remains one of the last true Mediterranean fishing ports. Wooded hills and low-rise hotels surround the old town, which is webbed with steep cobbled streets and piazzas. The 14 islands of the Rovinj archipelago make for a pleasant afternoon away; the most popular are Sveta Katarina and Crveni Otok (Red Island), also known as Sveti Andrija.

The old town is contained within an egg-shaped peninsula. About 1.5km south is the Punta Corrente Forest Park and the wooded cape of Zlatni Rt (Golden Cape), with its age-old oak and pine trees and several large hotels.

History

Originally an island, Rovinj was settled by Slavs in the 7th century and began to develop a strong fishing and maritime industry. In 1199 Rovinj signed an important pact with Dubrovnik to protect its maritime trade, but in the 13th century the threat of piracy forced it to turn to Venice for protection.

From the 16th to 18th centuries, its population expanded dramatically with an influx of immigrants fleeing Turkish invasions of Bosnia and continental Croatia. The town began to develop outside the walls put up by the Venetians, and in 1763 the islet was connected to the mainland and Rovinj became a peninsula.

Although the town's maritime industry thrived in the 17th century, Austria's 1719 decision to make Trieste and Rijeka free ports

Rovinj

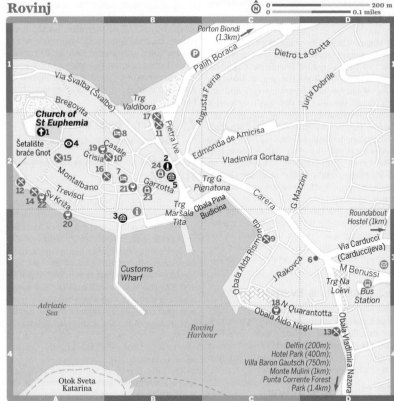

Rovinj

dealt Rovinj a blow. The decline of sailing ships further damaged its shipbuilding industry, and in the middle of the 19th century it was supplanted by the shipyard in Pula. Like the rest of Istria, Rovinj bounced from Austrian to French to Austrian to Italian rule before finally becoming part of postwar Yugoslavia. There's still a considerable Italian community here, who speak a particular dialect.

⊙ Sights

★ Church of St Euphemia   CHURCH
(Sveta Eufemija; Petra Stankovića; ⊙10am-6pm Jun-Sep, to 4pm May, to 2pm Apr) **FREE** The town's showcase, this imposing church dominates the old town from its hilltop location in the middle of the peninsula. Built in 1736, it's the largest baroque building in Istria, reflecting the period during the 18th century when Rovinj was its most populous town. Inside, look for the marble **tomb of St Euphemia** behind the right-hand altar.

Rovinj's patron saint was tortured for her Christian faith by Emperor Diocletian before being thrown to the lions in AD 304. According to legend, the body disappeared one dark, stormy night only to appear off the coast of Rovinj in a spectral boat. The townspeople were unable to budge the heavy sarcophagus until a small boy appeared with two calves and moved it to the top of the hill, where it still stands in the present-day church. On the anniversary of her martyrdom (16 September), devotees congregate here.

Modelled on the belfry of St Mark's in Venice, the 60m bell tower is topped by a copper statue of St Euphemia, which shows the direction of the wind by turning on a spindle. You can climb the tower (to the left of the altar) for 15KN.

Grisia   STREET
Lined with galleries where local artists sell their work, this cobbled street leads uphill from behind the Balbi Arch to St Euphemia. The winding narrow backstreets that spread around Grisia are an attraction in themselves. Windows, balconies, portals and squares are a pleasant confusion of styles – Gothic, Renaissance, baroque and neoclassical. Notice the unique *fumaioli* (exterior chimneys), built during the population boom when entire families lived in a single room with a fireplace.

Batana House   MUSEUM
(www.batana.org; Pina Budicina 2; adult/concession 10/5KN; ⊙10am-2pm & 7-11pm) On the harbour, Batana House is a museum dedicated to the *batana*, a flat-bottomed fishing boat that stands as a symbol of Rovinj's seafaring and fishing traditions. The multi-media exhibits inside the 17th-century town house have interactive displays, excellent captions and audio with *bitinada*, which are typical fishers' songs. Check out the *spacio*, the ground-floor cellar where wine was kept, tasted and sold amid much socialising (open evenings on Tuesday and Thursday).

Balbi Arch   MONUMENT
The elaborate Balbi Arch was built in 1679 on the location of the former town gate. The top of the arch is ornamented with a Turkish head on the outside and a Venetian head on the inside.

Heritage Museum   MUSEUM
(www.muzej-rovinj.com; Trg Maršala Tita 11; adult/concession 15/10KN; ⊙10am-2pm & 6-10pm Tue-Sun Jun-Sep, closed Sun Oct-May) This museum in a baroque palace contains a collection of contemporary art and old masters from Rovinj and elsewhere in Croatia, plus archaeological finds, a maritime section and occasional special exhibits.

Punta Corrente Forest Park   PARK
(Zlatni Rt) Follow the waterfront on foot or by bike past Hotel Park to this verdant area, locally known as Zlatni Rt, about 1.5km south. Covered in oak and pine groves and boasting 10 species of cypress, the park was established in 1890 by Baron Hütterott, an Austrian admiral who kept a villa on Crveni Otok. You can swim off the rocks or just sit and admire the offshore islands.

✦ Activities

Most people hop aboard a boat for **swimming**, **snorkelling** and **sunbathing**; boat trips across to Crveni Otok or Sveta Katarina are easily arranged through operators along the waterfront. The main diving attraction is the **Baron Gautsch wreck**, an Austrian passenger steamer sunk in 1914 by a sea mine in 40m of water.

There are 80 **rock-climbing routes** in a former Venetian stone quarry at Punta Corrente Forest Park (Zlatni Rt), many suitable for beginners. Birdwatchers can bike to the **ornithological reserve** at Palud Marsh, 8km southwest of Rovinj.

Cycling around Rovinj and the Punta Corrente Forest Park is a superb way to spend an afternoon.

Adistra   KAYAKING
(☑095 83 83 797; www.adistra.hr; Carera 69) Adistra runs kayaking tours, including 9km

ISTRIA ROVINJ

jaunts around the Rovinj archipelago and a 14km outing to the Lim fjord; both cost 280KN and include picnic lunch and snorkelling gear. It also offers a sunset paddle (190KN) with wine, cheese and olives.

Rovinj Sub DIVING
(⌨ 052-821 202; www.rovinj-sub.hr; Braće Brajkovića bb) Professional diving outfit running boat dives down to the many wrecks that lie just offshore. Prices range from 112KN for a shore dive to around 400KN for some of the trickier wrecks. Prices include equipment hire.

Petra DIVING
(⌨ 052-812 880; www.divingpetra.hr) Tiny operation offering boat dives to some of the offshore wrecks.

Tours

Most travel agencies in Rovinj sell day trips to Venice (around 500KN), Plitvice (500KN to 600KN) and Brijuni (around 400KN). There are also fish picnics (250KN), panoramic cruises (120KN) and boat outings to Limska Draga Fjord (180KN). These can be slightly cheaper if booked through one of the independent operators that line the waterfront.

Delfin TOURS
(⌨ 091 51 42 169; www.excursion-delfin.com) A reliable independent tour operator on the waterfront. Runs boat trips to Lim Fjord, Poreč and the Rovinj archipelago.

Festivals & Events

Rovinj Jazz Festival MUSIC
(⊙ Jul) Rovinj's annual jazz festival attracts big names from Croatia and across the globe. Concerts are held at the former Rovinj Tobacco Factory.

Summer Festival of
Music & Traditions MUSIC
(Ljetni Ugodaj uz Glazbu i Tradiciju; ⊙ Jul & Aug) Rovinj Summer Festival is a series of classical and folk concerts plus other events that take place at various venues around town.

Grisia Art Show CULTURAL
The second Sunday in August sees the town's most renowned event, when narrow Grisia becomes an open-air art exhibition. Anyone from children to professional painters displays their work in churches, studios and on the street.

Sleeping

Rovinj has become Istria's destination of choice for summertime tourists, so reserving in advance is strongly recommended. Prices have risen steadily since Croatia joined the EU and many now feel the town is overpriced.

If you stay less than three nights you may be charged a surcharge of up to 50%, or 100% if you stay only one night. Outside summer, you should be able to bargain the surcharge away. You can book through one of the travel agencies.

Roundabout Hostel HOSTEL €
(⌨ 052-817 387; www.roundabouthostel.com; Trg na Križu 6; dm from 135KN; P ❄ @ 🛜) This brand-new hostel, Rovinj's only real budget option, has smart, crisp rooms, bunks with individual reading lights and lockers. Reception is open 24 hours but there's no kitchen – however, the hostel does have its own cafe. It's located on the main roundabout as you come into Rovinj, hence the only downside – the distance into the old town (1.3km).

Polari Camping CAMPGROUND €
(⌨ 052-801 501; www.campingrovinjvrsar.com; Polari bb; campsites per person/tent 85/165KN; ⊙ Apr-Sep; 🛜 ⛱ �) This campsite enjoys a superb beach location around 3km southeast of town. Facilities include swimming pools, restaurants and playgrounds, and it is chockablock with Czech and German tourists in the hot months.

Porton Biondi CAMPGROUND €
(⌨ 052-813 557; www.portonbiondirovinj.com; Aleja Porton Biondi 1; campsites per person/tent 57/50KN; ⊙ Apr-Oct; 🚗) This beachside camping ground, which sleeps 1200, is about 700m north of the old town. It has a restaurant, snack bar and, oddly enough, a massage service.

Villa Baron Gautsch GUESTHOUSE €€
(⌨ 052-840 538; www.baron-gautsch.com; IM Ronjgova 7; s/d 293/586KN; ❄ 🛜) This German-owned *pansion* (guesthouse), on the leafy street leading up from Hotel Park, has 17 spick-and-span rooms, some with terraces and views of the sea and the old town. Breakfast is served on the small terrace out the back. It's cash (kuna) only and prices almost halve in low season.

Hotel Lone DESIGN HOTEL €€€
(⌨ 052-800 250; www.lonehotel.com; Luje Adamovića 31; s/d 1900/2400KN; P ❄ 🛜) Croatia's

first design hotel, this 248-room powerhouse of style is a creation of Croatia's starchitects 3LHD. It rises over Lone Bay like a ship dropped in the forest. Light-flooded rooms come with private terraces, all with Adriatic views, and five-star trimmings. Top-notch facilities include a couple of restaurants, an extensive spa and a beach club.

Villa Valdibora HOTEL €€

(☑ 052-845 040; www.valdibora.com; Silvano Chiurco 8; s/d 1970/2645KN, apt from 2350KN; ❄ 🤖) The 11 rooms, suites and apartments in this old-town building come with cool stone floors and upscale trimmings such as hydromassage sauna showers. There's a fitness room, massage and bikes for guest use.

Casa Garzotto GUESTHOUSE €€€

(☑ 052-811 884; www.casa-garzotto.com; Via Garzotto 8; s/d 1050/1350KN; P🤖) Rooms and apartments in this historic town house have original details such as fireplaces and wooden beams, an antique touch and up-to-the-minute facilities. The use of bikes is complimentary. The complex has three other buildings nearby, one with slightly more basic rooms.

Monte Mulini HOTEL €€€

(☑ 052-636 000; www.montemulinihotel.com; A Smareglia bb; d from 3500KN; P❄🤖) This swanky and extremely pricey hotel slopes down towards Lone Bay, a 10-minute stroll from the old town along the Lungomare. Balconied rooms all have sea views and upscale trimmings. The spa and Wine Vault restaurant are both tops. There are three outdoor pools, and the design is bold and bright, but you'll need a fat wallet to enjoy it.

Hotel Park HOTEL €€€

(☑ 052-800 250; www.maistra.com; IM Ronjgova 11; d from 1350KN; P❄🤖) Hotel Park is conveniently close to the ferry dock for Crveni Otok and has crowd-pleasing amenities such as two outdoor pools, a fitness room with a range of classes and a sauna. Most rooms have vista-rich balconies, but you'll find an old-fashioned bathroom and TV popping up here and there.

🍴 Eating

Picnickers can get supplies at the supermarket next to the bus station or at one of the Konzum stores around town. For a cheap bite, grab a *burek* (heavy pastry stuffed with meat or cheese) from a kiosk near the vegetable market.

Most restaurants lining the harbour offer the standard fish and meat mainstays at similar prices. For a more gourmet experience, you'll need to bypass the water vistas. Many restaurants close between lunch and dinner.

🍴 Old Town

★Male Madlene TAPAS €

(☑ 052-815 905; Sv Križa 28; snacks 35-100KN; ☺ 11am-2pm & 7-11pm May-Sep) This adorable and popular spot is in the owner's tiny jumble sale of a living room hanging over the sea, where she serves creative finger food with market-fresh ingredients, based on old Italian recipes. Think tuna-filled zucchini, goat's-cheese-stuffed peppers and bite-size savoury pies and cakes. A 12-snack plate for two is 100KN. It has great Istrian wines by the glass. Many consider this a candidate for a Michelin star. Reserve ahead, especially for evenings.

Da Sergio PIZZA €€

(Grisia 11; pizzas 40-115KN; ☺ 11am-11pm) It's worth waiting in line to get a table at this old-fashioned two-floor pizzeria. It dishes out Rovinj's best thin-crust pizza, and locals swear by it. It also serves decent house wine.

Monte MEDITERRANEAN €€€

(☑ 052-830 203; www.monte.hr; Montalbano 75; mains 150-260KN; ☺ 6.30-11pm Mon-Fri, noon-2pm & 6.30-11pm Sat & Sun) Rovinj's top restaurant, right below St Euphemia Church, is worth the hefty bill at the end. Sample expertly presented dishes on the elegant glassed-in terrace. If you don't want to splurge too much have a pasta or risotto (from 150KN). Try the fennel ice cream. Reserve ahead in high season.

Ulika MEDITERRANEAN €€€

(Porečka 6; mains 90-200KN; ☺ 12.30-3pm & 6pm-midnight) Tucked away in an alleyway, this small, pretty tavern with street-side seating excludes staples of Adriatic food kitsch (pizza, calamari, *čevapčići* – a spicy sausage dish) and instead features well-prepared if pricey Mediterranean fare. If it isn't in season, you probably won't find it on the menu. Service here is several notches above Croatia's normal standard.

Puntulina MEDITERRANEAN €€€

(☑ 052-813 186; Sv Križa 38; mains 80-180KN; ☺ noon-10pm) Sample creative Med cuisine on one of the three alfresco terraces. The pasta dishes are more affordable (from

ISTRIA ROVINJ

70KN). At night grab a cushion and sip a cocktail on the rocks below this converted town house – it's especially romantic at sunset. Reservations are recommended.

✕ Surrounds

Grota CROATIAN €
(Valdibora bb; snacks 40-80KN; ⊙ 7am-7pm) Right by the city market, this tiny barrel-lined spot serves daytime snacks such as local cheese and prosciutto, paired with carefully curated wines from the region (the owner is a winemaker). It gets busy with foodies who flock here for après-beach bites.

Vegetable Market MARKET €
(Trg Maršala Tita; ⊙ 7am-6pm) For a cheap bite, pick up a *burek* (heavy pastry stuffed with meat or cheese) from one of the kiosks near the vegetable market.

Konoba Bruna ISTRIAN €€
(📞 098 95 67 836; Monsena 7a; mains 50-130KN; ⊙ 5-11pm May-Sep) A five-minute taxi ride out of town, this family-run, summer-only *agroturizam* (rural farmstay) serves seasonal dishes using its own veggies and fish and meat under *peka* (a domed baking lid; from 110KN). The tables are scattered interestingly around an olive-tree orchard. Reserve ahead.

Kantinon SEAFOOD €€
(Alda Rismonda bb; mains 70-165KN; ⊙ noon-11pm) Located right on the harbourside, this excellent eating choice is headed up by a stellar team – one of Croatia's best chefs and an equally amazing sommelier. The food is 100% Croatian, with ingredients as local and fresh as they get, plus lots of seafood based on old-fashioned fishers' recipes. The seafood stew with polenta is a real treat.

Maestral MEDITERRANEAN €€
(Vladimira Nazora bb; mains from 50-155KN; ⊙ 11am-midnight) Grab an alfresco table at this tavern on the sea edge for great views of the old town and well-prepared simple food that's priced just right. Its *ribarska pogača* (pizza-like pie with salted fish and veggies) is a winner. It's in an old stone house away from the tourist buzz – a wonderful place to watch the Adriatic sunset.

★ Barba Danilo MEDITERRANEAN €€€
(📞 052-830 002; www.barbadanilo.com; Polari 5; mains 90-280KN; ⊙ 6-11.30pm) The last place you might expect to find one of Rovinj's best restaurants is on a campsite 3km from the centre, but that's where you'll find Barba Danilo. With just 45 seats in summer, booking several days ahead is essential. Dishes by head chef Goran Glavan are modern takes on traditional Mediterranean fare with net-fresh seafood taking a star turn. Decor is very 21st-century metropolitan; an odd experience in this busy Adriatic holiday resort.

🍷 Drinking & Nightlife

Piassa Granda WINE BAR
(Veli trg 1; ⊙ 10am-1am) One of Istria's best wine bars, this stylish little joint with red walls and wood-beamed ceilings stocks 150 wine labels, mainly Istrian, 20 *rakija* (Croatian grappa) varieties and delicious thirst-inducing snacks.

Limbo BAR
(Casale 22b; ⊙ 10am-midnight) Cosy cafe-bar with small candlelit tables and cushions laid out on the stairs leading to the old town's hilltop. It serves tasty snacks and good Prosecco.

Havana COCKTAIL BAR
(Aldo Negri bb; ⊙ 10am-2am) Tropical cocktails, Cuban cigars, straw parasols and the shade of tall pine trees make this open-air bar a popular spot.

Monte Carlo COCKTAIL BAR
(Sv Križa 21; ⊙ 10am-1am) Perched right on the water's edge, this low-key cafe-bar has unsurpassed views of the Adriatic and Sveta Katarina across the briny.

Valentino COCKTAIL BAR
(www.valentino-rovinj.com; Sv Križa 28; ⊙ 6pm-midnight) Premium cocktail prices at this high-end spot include fantastic sunset views from cushions scattered on the water's edge.

🛍 Shopping

Zdenac 13 CERAMICS
(Zdenac 13) Zdenac 13 sells beautiful ceramic pieces from the ground floor of a gorgeous old town house.

Galerija Brek ARTS
(Fontica 2; ⊙ 10am-midnight daily) Galerija Brek sells great photos of Rovinj and Istria and a small selection of diverse works by local artists.

ℹ Information

Globtour (📞 052-814 130; www.globtour-turizam.hr; Alda Rismonda 2) The agency to turn to for private accommodation and excursions.

Main Post Office (Matteo Benussi 4; ⊘7am-8pm Mon-Sat)

Medical Centre (☑052-840 702; Istarska bb; ⊘24hr)

Planet (☑052-840 494; www.planetrovinj.com; Sv Križa 1) This local tour operator offers reasonably priced private accommodation. Staff are more than willing to print out those pesky budget-airline boarding passes.

Tourist Office (☑052-811 566; www.tzgrovinj.hr; Pina Budicina 12; ⊘8am-10pm Jun-Sep, to 8pm Apr-May & Oct-Nov) Just off Trg Maršala Tita.

🛈 Getting There & Away

The **bus station** (Mattea Benussi) is just to the southeast of the old town. Buses from Rovinj:

Dubrovnik 402KN, 16 hours, one daily (overnight)

Labin 82KN, 1½ to two hours, two daily

Poreč 36KN to 47KN, 35 minutes to one hour, eight daily

Pula 33KN, 40 minutes, at least hourly

Rijeka 94KN, two hours 20 minutes, five daily

Split 285KN, 11 hours, one daily (overnight)

Zagreb 109KN to 150KN, 3¼ to 5½ hours, nine daily

Crveni Otok & Sveta Katarina

A popular day trip from Rovinj is a boat ride to lovely Crveni Otok (Red Island) 2km from the harbour. Only 1.9km long, the island includes two islets, **Sveti Andrija** and **Maškin**, connected by a causeway. In the 19th century, Sveti Andrija became the property of Baron Hütterott, who transformed it into a luxuriantly wooded park. The Hotel Istra complex now dominates Sveti Andrija, where small gravel beaches and a playground make it popular with families. Maškin is quieter, more wooded and has plenty of secluded coves. Bring a mask for snorkelling around the rocks.

Nearer to Rovinj, just outside the harbour, lies Sveta Katarina, a small island forested by a Polish count in 1905 and now home to Hotel Katarina.

🛏 Sleeping

Hotel Istra   RESORT €€€
(☑052-800 250; www.maistra.com; Crveni Otok 1; d from 1500KN; ✹🌐⌨♿) Dominating the islet of Sveti Andrija, this upmarket resort ho-

tel is a self-sufficient hideaway from which holidaymakers need never emerge. The 326 rooms and 32 luxury suites are comfort havens and there are several bars and restaurants, two beaches nearby and myriad activities and facilities. The regular boat to Rovinj means you can get to dry land any time you like.

Hotel Katarina   HOTEL €€€
(☑052-800 250; www.maistra.com; Otok Sv Katarina; d from 1445KN; ✹🌐⌨♿) Located on the island of Sveta Katarina, this smart hotel is a wonderful getaway, far from the tourist crowds of nearby Rovinj. Rooms are pleasantly done up, though they do have some dated features, there are two eateries and a bar, and a whole range of facilities and activities at your disposal.

🛈 Getting There & Away

In summer, there are hourly boats from Rovinj from 5.30am till midnight to Sveta Katarina (return 25KN, 10 minutes) and to Crveni Otok (return 40KN, 20 minutes). They leave from just opposite Hotel Adriatic and also from the Delfin ferry dock near Hotel Park.

Limska Draga Fjord

About 10km long, 600m wide and with steep valley walls that rise to a height of 100m, the Limska Draga Fjord (Limski Kanal) is the most dramatic sight in Istria. The inlet was formed when the Istrian coastline sank during the last Ice Age, allowing the sea to rush in and fill the Draga Valley. The deep-green bay has a hillside cave on the southern side where the 11th-century hermit priest Romualdo lived and held ceremonies. Fishing, oyster and mussel farming and excursion boating are the only activities found here.

Small excursion boats will take you on a one-hour boat ride for 75KN per person (negotiable); these run frequently in July and August, and sporadically in June and September.

🍴 Eating

Viking   SEAFOOD €€
(Limski Kanal 1; mains 60-90KN; ⊘11am-11pm) This waterside restaurant serves up superbly fresh shells, right from the source. Enjoy oysters (15KN per piece), great scallops (25KN per piece) and mussels, or fish (priced by the kilogram) on a terrace overlooking the fjord.

ISTRIA CRVENI OTOK & SVETA KATARINA

❶ Getting There & Away

To get to the fjord, you can take an excursion from Rovinj, Pula or Poreč, or follow the signs to Limski Kanal past the village of Sveti Lovreč.

Poreč

POP 16,700

The ancient Roman town of Poreč (Parenzo in Italian; Parentium in Roman times) and the surrounding region are entirely devoted to summer tourism. Poreč is the centrepiece of a vast system of tourist resorts that stretches north and south along the west coast of Istria, attracting holidaymakers in their tens of thousands from June to September.

Mass tourism means this is definitely not the place for a quiet getaway (unless you come out of season). However there's a World Heritage–listed basilica, a medley of Gothic, Romanesque and baroque buildings and a well-developed tourist infrastructure, and the pristine Istrian interior is within easy reach. It's also become the party hub of Istria in the last couple of years, drawing in young party-goers from all corners of Europe and beyond.

History

The coast of Poreč measures 37km, islands included, but the ancient town is confined to a peninsula 400m long and 200m wide. The Romans conquered the region in the 2nd century BC and made Poreč an important administrative centre, from where they were able to control a sweep of land from the Limska Draga Fjord to the Mirna River. Poreč's street plan was laid out by the Romans, who divided the town into rectangular parcels marked by the longitudinal Decumanus and the latitudinal Cardo.

With the collapse of the Western Roman Empire, Poreč came under Byzantine rule between the 6th and 8th centuries. It was during this time that the Euphrasian Basilica, with its magnificent frescoes, was erected. In 1267 Poreč was forced to submit to Venetian rule.

With the decline of Venice, the town oscillated between Austrian and French dominance before the Italian occupation that lasted from 1918 to 1943. Upon the capitulation of Italy, Poreč was occupied by the Germans and damaged by Allied bombing in 1944 before becoming part of postwar Yugoslavia and, more recently, Croatia.

◉ Sights

The compact old town is squeezed on to the peninsula and packed with hundreds of shops and agencies. The ancient Roman Decumanus, with its polished stones, is still the main street running through the peninsula's middle. Hotels, travel agencies and excursion boats are on the quayside Maršala Tita, which runs from the small-boat harbour to the tip of the peninsula.

Venetian Towers   LANDMARK
Poreč has three 15th-century towers that date from the time of the Venetian rule and once formed the city walls: the gothic **Pentagonal Tower** (Decumanus) at the beginning of Decumanus; the **Round Tower** on Narodni trg; and the **Northern Tower** on Peškera Bay.

★**Euphrasian Basilica**   BASILICA
(Eufrazijeva bb; adult/concession 40/20KN; ⊙9am-4pm Mon-Sat Nov-Mar, to 6pm Apr-Jun, Sep & Oct, to 9pm Jul & Aug) Top billing in Poreč goes to the 6th-century Euphrasian Basilica, a World Heritage Site and one of Europe's finest intact examples of Byzantine art. Built on the site of a 4th-century oratory, the complex includes a church, an atrium and a baptistery. The glittering wall **mosaics** in the apse – 6th-century masterpieces featuring biblical scenes, archangels and Istrian martyrs – are the highlights.

Notice the group to the left, which shows Bishop Euphrasius, who commissioned the basilica, with a model of the church in his hand. The belfry, accessed through the octagonal baptistery, affords an invigorating view of the old town. Make sure to pop into the adjacent Bishop's Palace, which contains a display of ancient stone sculptures, religious paintings and 4th-century mosaics from the original oratory.

Trg Marafor   SQUARE
The Roman Forum, where public gatherings took place, once stood on the site of the present-day Trg Marafor. The original pavement has been preserved along the northern row of houses on the square. West of this rectangular square, inside a small park, are the ruins of the 1st-century **Temple of Neptune** FREE, dedicated to the god of the sea.

Sveti Nikola   ISLAND
The island of Sveti Nikola lies just short of half a kilometre south of the peninsula. From May to October small passenger boats

Poreč

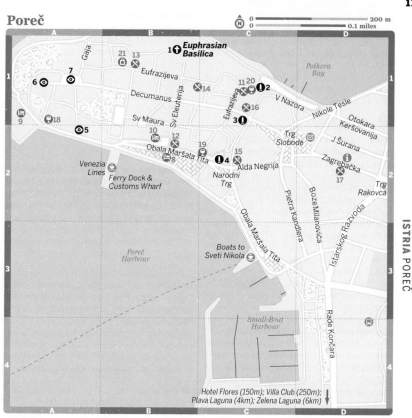

Poreč

⊙ Top Sights

⊙ Sights

⊟ Sleeping

⊗ Eating

☕ Drinking & Nightlife

⊙ Shopping

(adult/concession 25/15KN) make the crossing, departing every 30 minutes or so from the wharf on Maršala Tita. Once there, pebble and concrete beaches, rocky breakwaters, shady pine forests and great views of the town across the way await.

Baredine Cave
CAVE
(www.baredine.com; Nova Vas; adult/concession/child aged 5-15 70/60/45KN; ⊙10am-6pm Jul & Aug, to 5pm May, Jun & Sep, to 4pm Oct & Apr) Within easy reach of Poreč, Baredine Cave has subterranean chambers replete with stalagmites and stalactites; various agencies offer excursions.

🏃 Activities

Nearly every activity you might want to enjoy is on offer outside the town in either Plava Laguna or Zelena Laguna. Most of the sports and recreational centres (there are 20) are affiliated with hotels and have tennis, basketball and volleyball courts, windsurfing, rowing, bungee jumping, paintball, golf, water-skiing, parasailing, boat rentals, go-karting and canoeing. If the weather turns bad, you can always work out in a fitness centre or get a massage at one of the spas. For details, pick up the annual *Poreč Info and Events* booklet, which lists all the recreational facilities in the area, from the tourist office (p122).

The gentle rolling hills of the interior and the well-marked paths make **cycling** and **hiking** prime ways to explore the region. The tourist office issues a free map of roads and trails stemming from Poreč, along with suggested routes. You can rent a bike at many agencies around town.

Diving Centre Poreč
DIVING
(☑052-433 606; www.divingcenter-porec.com; Brulo 4) At Diving Centre Poreč, boat dives start at 150KN (more for caves or wrecks); 400KN with full equipment rental.

Cossetto
WINE
(☑052-455 204; www.cossetto.net; Roškići 10, Kaštelir) This winery 9km northeast of Poreč produces some of Istria's finest reds and whites. Its *malvazija* grapes are of particularly high quality. Call ahead for a tasting session.

✿ Festivals & Events

Poreč Summer
MUSIC
(⊙Jul & Aug) Free concerts take place on Trg Slobode as part of Poreč Summer.

Classical Music Concerts
MUSIC
(www.culture-vision.com; ⊙Jul & Aug) Classical-music concerts take place at the Euphrasian Basilica (p118) several times a week during summer; tickets can be purchased one hour before the concert at the venue.

Jazz Concerts
MUSIC
(⊙mid-Jul–Aug) There are jazz concerts between mid-July and late August, held once a week in the courtyard of the regional museum, beside Lapidarium.

Poreč Annale
CULTURAL
One of the oldest Croatian contemporary-art exhibitions takes place at the Istrian Parliament in early August and is curated around a single theme.

🛏 Sleeping

Accommodation in Poreč is plentiful but gets booked in advance; reservations are essential in July or August. The old town has a handful of hotels, though most campgrounds, hotels, apartment complexes and resorts are spread along the coast north and south of Poreč. Some impose a 20% surcharge if you stay less than three nights.

Camping Zelena Laguna
CAMPGROUND €
(☑052-410 147; www.lagunaporec.com; Zelena Laguna; campsite per adult/site 67/124KN; ⊙mid-Apr–Sep; ❋@🐾🛏) Well equipped for sports, this campground 5km from the old town can accommodate up to 2700 people. It has access to many beaches, including a naturist one. Despite its size, booking ahead between mid-July and the end of August is advised.

★ Hotel Mauro
BOUTIQUE HOTEL €€€
(☑052-219 500; www.hotelmauro.com; Obala Maršala Tita 15; s/d 865/1300KN; ❋🐾) With its epicentral location, tasteful and ever-so-slightly retro 21st-century rooms, cool marble bathrooms and balconies with Adriatic views, there's no more stylish a place to lay your head in Poreč, should you have the cash. The Mauro also has a pricey gourmet restaurant and a lobby bar, and staff can help out with anything from transfers to sports activities.

Hotel Palazzo
HOTEL €€€
(☑052-858 800; www.hotel-palazzo.hr; Obala Maršala Tita 24; r 1600KN; P❋@🐾🛏) Housed in a 1910 building on the seafront, this smart hotel boasts 70 elegant, dark-wood rooms and four suites plus a spa, restaurants and bars. The style is swish historic, blending modern design with classical beauty. Rooms 120 to 126 have open sea and lighthouse views – and higher prices.

Valamar Riviera Hotel
HOTEL €€€
(☑052-465 000; www.valamar.com; Maršala Tita 15; d 1300KN; P❋🐾♿) This rather swanky

four-star incarnation right on the harbour-front has some rooms with seafront balconies if you're willing to pay considerably more for the pleasure. There's also a gourmet restaurant and two bars plus a long list of guest facilities. The resort has a private beach on Sveti Nikola that you can reach by a free boat every 30 minutes.

Hotel Flores HOTEL €€€
(☎052-408 800; www.hostin.hr; Rade Končara 4; r 1300KN; P☀@🛜🏊) This unassuming hideaway in verdant parkland just steps from the bus station has 39 well-equipped rooms, each with a balcony. An indoor swimming pool, a fitness room, a Turkish bath and a sauna are nice perks but the main draw is the pebble beach only 70m away.

🍴 Eating

Buffet Horizont FAST FOOD €
(Eufrazijeva 8; mains 40-70KN; ⊙11am-midnight) For cheap and tasty seafood snacks such as sardines, shrimp and calamari, look out for this yellow house with wooden benches outside.

Dva Ferala ISTRIAN €
(Obala Maršala Tita 13; mains 65-120KN; ⊙noon-midnight) Try well-prepared Istrian specialities, such as istarski tris (a copious trio of homemade pastas) for two, on the terrace of this pleasant, rustically themed konoba (tavern). Food can be hit and miss but is generally good.

⭐Konoba Daniela ISTRIAN €€
(☎052-460 519; www.konobadaniela.com; Veleniki 15a; mains 70-135KN; ⊙noon-11pm) In the sweet little village of Veleniki 4.5km northeast of town, this family-run tavern in an 1880s house with rustic decor and a big terrace is known for its steak tartare and seasonal Istrian mainstays. It also rents rooms for around 400KN.

Konoba Aba MEDITERRANEAN €€
(Matka Vlačića 2; mains 75-185KN; ⊙noon-midnight) For the best seafood in Poreč, head down the narrow alleyway off Matka Vlačića 2 to find this small eatery that specialises in local seafood, risottos and truffle dishes. The food is delicious, the staff polite but the portion sizes of some mains are on the miserly side.

Nono PIZZA €€
(Zagrebačka 4; pizzas 35-100KN; ⊙noon-midnight) Be warned – the wheels of pizza here are supersized and one is enough for two. Some

of their creations are topped with truffle shavings, but all are scrumptious, no matter what has been scattered on top.

Konoba Ćakula ISTRIAN €€
(www.konobacakula.com; Vladimira Nazora 7; mains 70-150KN; ⊙10am-11pm) This tavern with a subtly hipster vibe does interesting cold appetisers and solid mains. Try the pasta with truffles as a starter, then perhaps the fish platter for two, which contains only freshly caught ingredients. It's also a great spot to come for tapas, paired with a glass of wine.

Konoba Ulixes MEDITERRANEAN €€
(Decumanus 2; mains 85-165KN; ⊙noon-4pm & 6pm-midnight) Lost in the backstreets of Poreč, this lovely tavern serves great fish and shellfish dishes in a cosy setting. The food is usually spot on but some complain of lazy service here. However, there's a good selection of Istrian wines to take your mind off it.

Gourmet ITALIAN €€
(Eufrazijeva 26; mains 70-150KN; ⊙11am-1am) Comforting Italian concoctions come in all shapes and forms here – penne, tagliatelle, fusilli, gnocchi and so on. There are also pizzas from a wood-fired oven as well as meat and seafood dishes. On a summer's eve there's a superb atmosphere with tables spilling out on to the piazza, but some may wish they would lose the faux gourmet touches.

🍷 Drinking & Nightlife

Byblos CLUB
(www.byblos.hr; Zelena Laguna 1; ⊙11pm-6am) On weekends, celeb guest DJs such as David Morales crank out electro house tunes at this humongous open-air club, one of Croatia's hottest places to party, 2.5km south of town.

ISTRIA POREČ

WORTH A TRIP

NOVIGRAD SEAFOOD STOPS

Halfway between Poreč and Umag, the little seaside town of Novigrad has a busy marina and a couple of excellent seafood restaurants.

Marina (Antona 38; mains from 80KN; ⊕9am-11pm Mon-Sat, from 10am Sun) This Novigrad hotel restaurant is headed up by one of Croatia's best chefs, Marina Gaši, who whips up playful versions of Croatia's mainstays in this contemporary space right by the marina. The six-course tasting menu (370KN) is worth the splurge.

Damir & Ornella (☑052-758 134; www.damirornella.com; Zidine 5; mains from 70KN; ⊕12.30-3.30pm & 7.30-11.30pm) One of Istria's best restaurants, this 28-seat tavern is famous for its twitchingly fresh, raw-fish specialities. The Mediterranean-style sashimi is to die for. Be sure to reserve ahead in summer.

Villa Club   BEACH CLUB
(www.villa-club.net; Rade Končara 4a; ⊕9am-6am) Popular beach bar and club that draws in a party crowd for a boogie to DJ-spun tunes each night in summertime.

Vinoteka Bacchus   WINE BAR
(Eufrazijeva 10; ⊕10am-1am Mon-Sat, to midnight Sun) Sweet little wine shop with a clutch of tables outside, where you can try local wines on tap. Try the *malvazija* and the *refošk*.

Epoca   BAR
(Maršala Tita 24; ⊕8am-2am) Kick back by the water and watch the sun go down, grab a quick espresso or have a leisurely nightcap cocktail at this low-key cafe-bar.

Saint & Sinner   BAR
(www.saint-sinner.net; Maršala Tita 12; ⊕8pm-4am) A black-and-white plastic theme runs throughout this beach hang-out, where the young and beautiful sip caffeine-based beverages by day, and ethanol concoctions late into the night. It has sister establishments in Umag and Rovinj.

Torre Rotonda   BAR
(www.torrerotonda.com; Narodni trg 3a; ⊕10am-2am) Take the steep stairs to the top of the historic Round Tower to find this odd, circular, open-air cafe from where there are

action-packed views of the quays. Definitely not a spot to head to in bad weather!

🔒 Shopping

Koza   ARTISANAL
(Eufrazijeva 28; ⊕10am-10pm) Don't miss the great leather items designed and handmade by a brother-and-sister team at this tiny storefront with cool bags, flip-flops, briefcases and wallets.

ℹ️ Information

Fiore Tours (☑052-431 397; www.fiore.hr; Mate Vlašića 6) Handles private accommodation and adventure travel across the former Yugoslavia.

Main Post Office (Trg Slobode 14; ⊕8am-9pm Mon-Sat) Has a telephone centre.

Poreč Medical Centre (☑052-451 611; Maura Gioseffija 2)

Sunny Way (☑052-452 021; www.sunnyway.hr; Alda Negrija 1) Specialises in boat tickets and excursions to Italy and around Croatia.

Tourist Office (☑052-451 293; www.to-porec.com; Zagrebačka 9; ⊕8am-9pm Mon & Thu-Sun, to 6pm Tue-Wed) Very knowledgeable office with one of the best city tourism websites in the country.

ℹ️ Getting There & Away

BOAT

Between May and September there's a daily fast catamaran to Venice (two hours) operated by **Venezia Lines** (www.venezialines.com; one way 480KN, return 1060KN). All services leave from the Ferry Dock & Customs Wharf.

BUS

The **bus station** (K Huguesa 2) is just outside the old town, behind Rade Končara. There's a left-luggage facility at the station.

Between Poreč and Rovinj, the bus runs along the Limska Draga Fjord. To see it clearly, sit on the right-hand side if you're travelling south, or on the left if you're northbound.

Connections from Poreč:

Pula 60KN, one to 1½ hours, seven daily

Rijeka 70KN to 90KN, 1½ hours, 11 daily

Rovinj 36KN to 47KN, 35 minutes to one hour, eight daily

Zagreb 134KN to 183KN, 3¾ to 4½ hours, eight daily

Umag

POP 13,500

Tight by the border with Slovenia, and Croatia's most westerly point, Umag (Umago in Italian) is a minor hidden gem. Its old town protruding out into the Adriatic is pleasant to explore, its restaurants offer authentic net-fresh seafood and tight rocky coves north and south of the town boast some secluded pebble beaches. Though far from one of the highlights of the Istrian peninsula, this slightly quieter feel makes it a refreshing place to end a tour of the Croatian coast before entering Slovenia just 6km to the northeast.

Umag has been around since Roman times and has pretty much gone with the Istrian flow since, passing through the hands of several European empires (Genoa, Venice, Austria) before finally ending up in Yugoslavia in 1954. Before WWI Italians made up the majority of the town's population, but today this figure is now down to just over 18%.

◉ Sights & Activities

Umag Municipal Museum   MUSEUM
(Muzej grada Umaga; ☑ 052-720 386; www.mgumcu.hr; Trg Sv Martina 1; 15KN; ☉ 10am-1pm & 6-9pm Tue-Sat, 10am-1pm Sun Jun-Sep, shorter hours rest of the year) Located almost at the tip of the old-town peninsula, Umag's small but well-curated museum displays archaeological finds from the wider area dating from Roman times to the 17th century. There are also old photographs of the Umago of yesteryear and a sculpture collection.

Degrassi   WINE
(☑ 052-759 250; www.degrassi.hr; Bašanija – Podrumarska 3, Savudrija) The Degrassi winery, 6km north of Umag, is a fairly recent affair having only really begun to produce quality wines in the mid-1990s. Call ahead for tasting sessions.

🛏 Sleeping

Umag has lots of accommodation though there's very little in the old town – most stay in the big resorts up and down the coast. A bed is easier to find without reservations than in other parts of Istria, even at the height of summer. The only exception is during the Croatia Open tennis tournament, held for 10 days from mid-July, when the town and surrounding areas get fully booked.

Villa La Rossa   B&B €€
(☑ 052-720 626; www.villalarossa.com; Istarska cesta 19; r from 500KN; ⓟ❋⌗) This Italian villa just north of the old town, near a beach and the town centre, is the antidote to the huge resort hotels that line the coast. It

boasts comfortable rooms, big balconies and friendly staff. The buffet breakfast could do with an upgrade but is always included.

Villa Badi   HOTEL €€€
(☑ 052-756 402; www.badi.hr; Umaška ulica 1, Lovrečica; r 1120KN; ⓟ⌗❋) This intimate family-run hotel in the fishing village of Lovrečica, around 5km south of Umag, has immaculate 21st-century rooms, an illuminated outdoor seawater pool, a small wellness area and buffet breakfasts. It's just 200m from the sea and the same distance from the centre of the village.

✖ Eating

Umag has plenty of excellent taverns, restaurants and cafes, many specialising in Mediterranean fish and seafood, though the best of the bunch are a short car ride away in the town's hinterland.

Konoba Da Lorenzo   MEDITERRANEAN €€
(☑ 095 90 74 762; www.konoba-dalorenzo.com; Šetalište Vladimira Gortana 72; mains 45-150KN; ☉ noon-11pm daily) Situated just back from the marina opposite the old-town peninsula, this is probably the best dining option in the area not requiring a taxi ride out of town. The vaguely oriental interior sets the scene for perfectly crafted, almost gourmet creations using local ingredients wherever possible. Adriatic fish sashimi and truffle ice cream are real treats.

Konoba Rustica   MEDITERRANEAN €€
(☑ 052-732 053; www.konoba-rustica.com; Sv Marija na Krasu 41; mains 35-120KN; ☉ noon-11pm daily) Located 4km out of town on the road towards the Slovenian border, this much-lauded tavern serves the best thin-crust pizza, pastas and steaks in the area. As the name suggests, the interior is done out in faux-rustic style and the location is quite bucolic.

ℹ Information

Tourist Office (☑ 052-741 363; www.colours ofistria.com; Trgovačka 6; ☉ 8am-8pm daily May-Sep, shorter hours rest of the year)

ℹ Getting There & Away

Umag has the following bus connections:
Poreč 42KN, 50 minutes, eight daily
Pula 86KN, two hours 40 minutes, four daily
Rijeka 98KN, 2½ hours, six daily
Rovinj 74KN, 1¾ hours, four daily
Zagreb 225KN, five hours, four daily

CENTRAL & EASTERN ISTRIA

Head inland from the Istrian coast and you'll notice that crowds dissipate, hotel complexes disappear and what emerges is an unspoiled countryside of medieval hilltop towns, pine forests, fertile valleys and vineyard-dotted hills. The pace slows down considerably, defined less by the needs of tourists and more by the demands of harvesting grapes, hunting for truffles, picking wild asparagus and cultivating olive groves. Farmhouses open their doors to visitors looking for authentic holiday experiences, remote rustic taverns serve up slow-food delights and Croatia's top winemakers provide tastings in their cellars. Hilltop villages that once seemed doomed to ruin are attracting colonies of artists and artisans as well as well-heeled foreigners. While many compare the region to Tuscany – and the Italian influence can't be denied – it's a world all of its own: unique, magnetic and wholesome.

Momjan
POP 283

The oft-skipped-over town of Momjan in northwestern Istria, just south of the Slovenian border, is situated on a hilltop commanding incredible vistas of Istria's interior and the sea. A 15th-century church and the ruins of a clifftop castle from the 13th century offer mild historical interest – otherwise it's worth a quick stop-off for a spot of aimless wandering on the way elsewhere.

🛏 Sleeping & Eating

B&B Tinka   B&B €
(☎ 098 17 58 279; www.bb-tinka.com; Dolinja Vas 23; s/d 380/600KN; ❋ 🤶) Filling a modern villa in the centre of town, these 21st-century digs are pretty good value with immaculate, imaginatively decorated rooms and a friendly staff. There's a handy restaurant on the premises and pretty views from some windows.

Konoba Rino   ISTRIAN €
(Dolinja Vas 23; mains 60-130KN; ⊙ noon-10pm Wed-Mon) This rustic tavern in the B&B Tinka serves local specialities, such as pastas with *boškarin* and *pulic* (young donkey), and truffle gnocchi under heavy beams and stone archways.

Stari Podrum   ISTRIAN €€
(www.staripodrum.info; Most 52; mains 75-200KN; ⊙ noon-10pm Thu-Tue) Stari Podrum, a

---

ISTRIA BY BIKE
....
Cyclists shouldn't miss the **Parenzana Bike Trail** (☎ 052-351 603; www.parenzana.net), which runs along a defunct gauge railway that operated from 1902 to 1935 between Trieste and Poreč. Today, it traverses three countries, Italy, Slovenia and Croatia (the Croatian stretch is 78km), and has become a quite popular way to take in the highlights of Istria, especially in spring and autumn.

---

five-minute drive out of Momjan, is where Istrian mainstays are served with a creative touch, and at slightly higher prices; hence the flashier-than-usual cars parked outside. Try their renowned tenderloin steak; truffles feature heavily on the menu when in season.

Konoba Morgan   ISTRIAN €€
(www.konobamorgan.eu; Bracanija 1; mains 70-150KN; ⊙ noon-10pm Wed-Mon) For a fine gastronomic experience, head to Konoba Morgan, 2km northeast of Brtonigla on the road to Buje. It has a lovely terrace on a hill, with sweeping views of the countryside and in winter a stone dining room warmed by a real fire. The daily-changing menu focuses on game meat and seasonal ingredients such as truffles and asparagus.

ℹ Getting There & Away

To reach Momjan, you must get behind the wheel, as bus connections are practically nonexistent.

Grožnjan
POP 740

Until the mid-1960s, tiny Grožnjan, 27km northeast of Poreč, was slipping towards oblivion. First mentioned in 1102, this hilltop town was a strategically important fortress for the 14th-century Venetians. They created a system of ramparts and gates, and built a loggia, a granary and several fine churches. With the collapse of the Venetian empire in the 18th century, Grožnjan suffered a decline in its importance and population.

In 1965, sculptor Aleksandar Rukavina and a small group of artists 'discovered' the crumbling medieval appeal of Grožnjan and began setting up studios in the abandoned buildings. As the town crawled back to life, it attracted the attention of Jeunesses Musicales International, an international training program for young musicians. In 1969 a summer school for musicians was established here and it has been going strong ever since with annual summer music, orchestra and ballet courses, recitals and concerts taking place in the local castle and the leafy squares.

◎ Sights

Church of St Vitus, St Modest & St Crescentia   CHURCH
(Trg Ruggera Paladina) The town's skyline is dominated by the yellow sandstone bell tower of the Church of St Vitus, St Modest and St Crescentia, which was built in the 14th century and renovated in baroque style in 1770. Inside look for the altar, donated by pope Pius VII in 1800 and believed to have special powers.

Fonticus Gallery   ART GALLERY
(Gradska Galerija Fonticus; Trg Lođe 3; ⊗10am-1pm & 5-8pm Tue-Sun) There are more than 30 galleries and studios scattered around town; Fonticus Gallery promotes recent works of mainly Croatian artists. Though it doesn't have a permanent collection it does host a small display of heraldic paraphernalia that includes helmets, insignia and escutcheon.

✯✯ Festivals & Events

Summer music concerts are organised by the International Cultural Centre of Jeunesses Musicales Croatia (www.hgm.hr). The concerts are free and no reservations are necessary. They are usually held in the church, the main square, the loggia or the castle.

✗ Eating

Konoba Pintur   ISTRIAN €
(Mate Gorjana 9; mains 45-120KN; ⊗8am-11pm) On the main square, this family-run place has tables outside and acceptable, affordable food and cheap beer. It also rents rooms upstairs.

Bastia   ISTRIAN €€
(1 Svibnja 1; mains 70-160KN; ⊗8am-midnight) A bit hit and miss, the town's oldest restaurant sits on the verdant main square. The decor is bright and cheerful, and the menu extensive and heavy on truffles.

▼ Drinking & Nightlife

Kaya Energy Bar & Design   BAR
(Vincenta iz Kastva 2; ⊗9am-11pm) This family-run hideaway at the entrance to town has many faces – it's a cafe, a bar, a shop, a showroom and a gallery, with a stylish stone interior, tables on the square and a lovely little terrace off to the side with fantastic valley views. It serves freshly squeezed juices, smoothies, breakfasts, all-day snacks and good local *malvazija* wine.

Cafe Vero   BAR
(Trg Cornera 3; ⊗8am-10pm) The marvellous valley views below are the main draw of this cafe-bar at the end of the village, with wooden tables gracing its terrace.

🛍 Shopping

Zigante Tartufi   FOOD
(www.zigantetartufi.com; Umberta Gorjana 5; ⊗9am-10pm) The best place in town to buy Istrian truffles.

ⓘ Information

Tourist Office (☑052-776 131; www.tz-groznjan.hr; Umberta Gorjana 3; ⊗10am-1pm & 5-8pm Tue-Sun)

Motovun

POP 500

Motovun is a captivating little town perched on a 277m hill in the Mirna River valley, about 25km northeast of Poreč. It was the Venetians who decided to fortify the town in the 14th century, building two sets of thick walls.

There are a number of galleries and shops before you enter the old town and between the town gates, including a wine-tasting shop and a Zigante food store. Within the walls, an atmospheric cluster of Romanesque and Gothic buildings houses a smattering of artist studios. Newer houses have sprung up on the slopes leading to the old town, where the popular film festival takes place every summer – the very film fest that has, in recent years, made Motovun the most touristy of Istria's hilltop towns.

◎ Sights

Ramparts   CITY WALLS
Be sure to walk on the outer walls of the ramparts for memorable vistas over vineyards, fields and oak woods below. Take a break in the hidden cafe on the city walls, by the post office.

Church of St Stephen   CHURCH
(Svetog Stjepana; Trg Andrea Antico) The town's highlight is the Renaissance Church of St Stephen, designed by Venetian artist Andrea Palladio. The interior is a restrained affair,

typical of churches of the period. Along the inner wall that encloses the old town rises a 16th-century bell tower.

🏃 Activities

Paragliding PARAGLIDING
(📞098 92 28 081; www.istraparagliding.com; per person 600KN) Jump off Motovun's hilltop for a tandem glide (with an instructor) with stunning vistas over Istria's hills. Book ahead.

Parenzana Train TOURIST TRAIN
(www.parenzana.hr; per person 160KN, child aged 2-12 80KN) This tourist train takes visitors along the old Parenzana train line from Motovun to the scenic hill town of Vižinada above the Mirna River valley. The ride stops in the village of Ratokule, where you can taste homemade Istrian treats from a local farm. There are five daily departures; the trip lasts one hour and 40 minutes; with free return. The trip can also be done from Vižinada to Motovun.

Geržinić WINE
(📞052-446 285; www.gerzinic.com; Vižinada) This award-winning winery in the village of Vižinada, 16km west of Motovun, has been in the same family for a century. It cultivates 10 hectares of vineyards growing the Cro-

CENTRAL ISTRIA'S RURAL RETREATS

Agritourism is an increasingly popular accommodation option in Istria's interior. Some of these residences are working farms engaged in producing wine, vegetables and poultry; some are country houses with apartments to let; while others are plush modern villas with swimming pools. Whatever you choose, the highlights are hiking and cycling opportunities and, in some, wholesome food.

The **Istrian tourist office** (📞052-452 797; www.istra.hr) has a brochure with photos and information about rural holidays throughout Istria. You'll need your own car to reach most of these lodgings, as many are located in the middle of nowhere. There's often a supplement for stays of less than three nights.

Agroturizam San Mauro (📞052-779 033; www.sinkovic.hr; San Mauro 157, Momjan; per person incl breakfast 214KN; 🛜) Near the hilltop town of Momjan, Agroturizam San Mauro specialises in tastings of its award-winning wines, truffle dishes and homemade jams, honeys and juices that you get to sample for breakfast. Some of the apartments, each with a kitchenette, have terraces and sea vistas. There's a small surcharge for one-night stays, and payments are cash only.

Agroturizam Ograde (📞052-693 035; www.agroturizam-ograde.hr; Katun Lindarski 60, Katun Lindarski; per person incl breakfast 280KN; 🅿🛜⊠🏠) At leafy Agroturizam Ograde, in the village of Katun Lindarski, 10km south of Pazin, you'll hang out with horses, sheep, chickens, pigs and geese. The food, served in a dark and cool *konoba* (tavern), is a real-deal affair: veggies from the garden, home-cured meats and wine from the cellar. Accommodation is in two separate houses, one with a pool.

Pruga (📞091 78 17 263; www.apartments-pruga.com; Lovrinići 14, Lovrinići; Jul & Aug 750KN, Jun & Sep 610KN; 🛜) In the village of Lovrinići, 9.5km from Pazin, this is a lovely choice for a quiet getaway. Choose one of two beautifully renovated apartments in an original limestone Istrian house, each showcasing rustic chic, original details and fully equipped kitchens. Breakfast of local cheese, homemade jams and cakes is served outside among fruit trees and forests.

La Parenzana (📞052-777 460; www.parenzana.com.hr; Volpia 3, Volpia, Buje; s/d 290/580KN; 🅿@🛜) La Parenzana is a notable rural inn, 3km from Buje in the village of Volpia. It features 16 rooms with rustic wood-and-stone decor, and a *konoba* popular for its Istrian food, such as *čripnja* (roast meat or fish cooked with potatoes in a cast-iron pot over an open fire).

San Rocco (📞052-725 000; www.san-rocco.hr; Srednja Ulica 2, Brtonigla; r from 1460KN; 🅿✳@🛜⊠) This family-run, award-winning boutique hotel in the village of Brtonigla, near Buje, is a rural hideaway with 14 stylish rooms – no two are alike, but all are equipped with modern conveniences and graced with original detail. There's an outdoor swimming pool, a top-rated restaurant and a small spa.

atian *malvazija* that goes into their superb whites. It's a great place to stop off for a tasting though you might want to call ahead.

✪ Festivals & Events

Motovun Film Festival   FILM
(www.motovunfilmfestival.com) The Motovun Film Festival presents a roster of independent and avant-garde films in late July. Since its inception in 1999, this small event has grown pretty popular and now attracts quite a crowd, with nonstop outdoor and indoor screenings, concerts and parties.

🛌 Sleeping

Motovun Camping   CAMPGROUND €
(☑ 052-681 557; www.motovun-camping.com; 2-person site for 1 night 200KN, subsequent nights 120KN) Small campground with 12 pitches right below town, run by Hotel Kaštel. Campers get free use of the hotel's swimming pool and a 10% discount at the restaurant.

Villa Borgo   B&B €€
(☑ 052-681 708; www.villaborgo.com; Borgo 4; s/d 413/550KN; 🛜) Gorgeous spot at the top of the old town, with 10 rooms of different styles and configurations – some with shared baths, some with panoramic views, others overlooking the street. The decor is clean-lined and minimalist, breakfast is always included, and there's a lovely shared terrace with sweeping valley views, a gallery shop downstairs plus a ground-floor apartment that sleeps four.

Hotel Kaštel   HOTEL €€€
(☑ 052-681 607; www.hotel-kastel-motovun.hr; Trg Andrea Antico 7; s/d 500/860KN; 🅿@🛜🏊) The town's only real hotel is an utterly charming little place in a restored 17th-century palazzo, with 33 simply furnished rooms. There's a good restaurant offering truffles and Istrian wines and bike rental (110KN per day) but many come here for the wellness centre, which offers a wide range of spa procedures and pampering.

🍴 Eating

Pod Napun   ISTRIAN €€
(www.antique-motovun.com.hr; Gradizol 33; mains 70-120KN; ⊙noon-10pm) A great choice at the beginning of the old town as you walk uphill, this intimate and friendly restaurant has a terrace with sweeping valley views. It whips up well-prepared traditional dishes from the area. The owners also rent out rooms and houses around the town.

❶ PARKING IN MOTOVUN

There are three parking areas in town. The first is at the foot of the village, from where it's a steep 2km hike up to the city gates. Another is 300m below the old town. The last one is for residents and hotel guests. Unless you're staying at the hotel, there's a 20KN charge per day from April to October at the other two parking lots.

Konoba Dolina   ISTRIAN €€
(www.konobadolina.hr; Gradinje 59/1; mains 50-100KN; ⊙noon-9pm Wed-Mon) If you have wheels, this low-key locals' favourite is worth the drive for its unassuming vibe and honest, simple fare featuring Istrian dishes, many with truffles. Wash it down with local Favorit beer. From Motovun, turn right towards Buzet, continuing till the left turn-off for Gradinje; it's 2.5km from here.

Pod Voltom   ISTRIAN €€
(Trg Josefa Ressela 6; mains 70-130KN; ⊙noon-10pm daily) In a vaulted space within the town gates, this wood-beamed place serves simple down-home Istrian cuisine and pricier truffle dishes (for dessert go for the amazing truffle panna cotta). From June to September, grab a seat in the loggia with great valley views.

Mondo   ISTRIAN €€
(Barbacan 1; mains 75-150KN; ⊙noon-3.30pm & 6-10pm) Just before the outer town gate, this little tavern with a small side terrace serves up imaginatively conceived and poshly presented Istrian mainstays, many featuring truffles. Wash it all down with wines from the Tomaz winery.

★ Restaurant Zigante   GASTRONOMIC €€€
(☑ 052-664 302; www.zigantetartufi.com; Livade 7, Livade; mains 185-350KN; ⊙noon-10pm) Gourmets from afar come to this destination restaurant belonging to Istria's top truffle company and located a few kilometres below Motovun in the village of Livade. Expect five-star fancy dining, with truffles as the showcase in a reassuringly brief, seasonally evolving menu.

❶ Information

The town's **tourist office** (☑ 052-681 726; www.tz-motovun.hr; Trg Andrea Antico 1;

⊘ 10am-6pm) is located on the main square, right below Hotel Kaštel.

Montana Tours (☑ 052-681 970; www.mon tonatours.com) is another great source of info; it can help with accommodation in central Istria, rural stays and private apartments and rents bikes for 110KN per day.

❶ Getting There & Away

It's not easy to visit Motovun without your own car. There are bus connections from Pazin (35KN, 40 minutes, three daily) and Poreč (35KN, 45 minutes, one daily), but only on week-days during school-term time.

Buzet

POP 6100

It may not be Istria's most fascinating town, but sleepy Buzet, 39km northeast of Poreč over the Mirna River, offers a hint of the timeless grace of old Istria. First settled by the Romans, Buzet achieved real promi-nence under the Venetians, who endowed it with walls, gates and churches. With grey-stone buildings in various stages of decay and restoration, and cobblestone streets nearly deserted (most of Buzet's residents resettled at the foot of the hill in the unbe-coming new part of town long ago), the old town is quiet but charming.

Enjoy a wander around the maze of nar-row streets and squares, with sights all well signposted in English. And don't miss the glorious truffles. Self-dubbed the city of truf-fles, Buzet is at the epicentre of the truffle-growing region. Sample Istria's favourite fungus at the old town's restaurant or par-take in truffle-related activities, including the Festival of Subotina.

◉ Sights

Most commerce is in the new Fontana sec-tion of town at the foot of the hilltop old town. If you have wheels, you must park your car by the cemetery on the hill and make the five-minute walk up to the old town.

Regional Museum   MUSEUM
(Zavičajni Muzej Buzet; Ulica Rašporskih Kapetana 5; adult/concession 15/10KN; ⊘9am-3pm Mon-Fri) Housed in the grand 17th-century Bigatto Palace, Buzet's main sight displays an inter-esting collection of prehistoric and Roman artefacts as well as some ethnological items such as field tools and folk costumes. One

room is also given over to temporary shows of local art.

Baroque Well   LANDMARK
On a square a few metres north of the Re-gional Museum is this exquisite well, which was restored in 1789 and sports a Venetian lion relief.

🏃 Activities

Pick up a guide from the tourist office to wine, olive-oil and truffle routes throughout the region, as well as various activities such as hiking (check out the seven trails in the area), cycling (there are 14 trails around town), free climbing, hot-air ballooning and paragliding.

Istriana Travel (☑ 091 54 12 099; www. istrianatravel.hr; Vrh 28) offers truffle-hunting excursions, workshops, wine and olive-oil tours, bike jaunts, hiking, caving, paraglid-ing and more.

⭐ Festivals & Events

Festival of Subotina   FOOD & DRINK
Buzet's top truffle event is on the second Sat-urday in September, marking the start of the white-truffle season (which lasts through December). The pinnacle of it all is the preparation of a giant truffle omelette – with more than 2000 eggs and 10kg of truffles – in a 1000kg pan.

🛏 Sleeping & Eating

A number of farmhouses in the surround-ing area have rooms and apartments to rent (from 100KN to 150KN per person). The tourist office has details.

Truffles are the menu item to seek out in Buzet, though they add tens of kuna to the price of your meal. Buzet doesn't have many restaurants but those that are here are of high quality.

Vela Vrata   BOUTIQUE HOTEL **€€**
(☑052-494 750; www.velavrata.net; Šetalište Vladi-mira Gortana 7; s/d 593/810KN; ❄@🛜) This lovely boutique hotel on the edge of the old town, with panoramic views of the surrounding hills, has revitalised Buzet's hilltop. Twenty rooms in five interconnected buildings are tasteful and well-equipped. Room 11 has a gorgeous vista from its balcony. The hotel has a **restaurant** (mains from 50KN; ⊘ 1-11pm) that serves great homemade pastas, good meat and mean crêpes with *skuta* (ricotta) and honey, paired with leafy views.

There's also a cafe on-site and a small spa.

IDYLLIC INDULGENCE

They may be less than 20km apart, but the blissful countryside between Motovun and Buzet offers an extraordinary range of opportunities for self-indulgence, including delicious food, fine wine and a venerable spa resort.

Istarske Toplice (☑ 052-603 000; www.istarske-toplice.hr; Sv Stjepana 60, Livade) Dating from the Roman era, Istarske Toplice is one of Croatia's oldest, most scenic thermal spas. Beneath an 85m-high cliff and surrounded by greenery, the complex features a concrete-box-style hotel, a wellness centre and, like most spas in Croatia, a slightly geriatric touch. The rotten-egg smell is from the high sulphur content of the large pool, where temperatures reach 34°C.

It's not worth spending the night (unless you love spas), but come for a few hours to indulge. The treatments menu is wide and varied, and includes anything from hot stone to signature body treatments with wine, honey and lavender. Or simply spend time paddling around in the thermal pool (40KN for three hours) or sweating it all away in the sauna (170KN for three hours). The thermal waters are said to help rheumatism, skin diseases and respiratory tract disorders.

There's no public transport, but the spa is easily accessible by road, 10km north of Motovun and 11km south of Buzet on the main road that connects the two towns.

Ipša Estate (☑ 052-664 010; www.ipsa-maslinovaulja.hr) Four kilometres to the southeast of Oprtalj, amid scenic hills, is the gorgeous Ipša Estate, worth a visit for the taste of its award-winning olive oils; call ahead.

Truffle Hunting (☑ 052-667 304; www.karlictartufi.hr; Paladini 14, Paladini; tour per person 260-965KN) If you want to experience truffle hunting, the friendly Karlić family, who live in the village of Paladini 12km from Buzet, run tours in English though you should ideally contact them well ahead. The tour includes cheese and truffle tasting, many a truffly tale and a hopeful hunt in the forest that lasts up to two hours.

Agroturizam Tončić (☑ 052-644 146; www.agroturizam-toncic.com; Čabarnica 42, Zrenj; mains from 50KN; ☺ weekends only) For a solid meal featuring the best lamb and potatoes under *peka* (a domed baking lid), head to Agroturizam Tončić at the end of Zrenj village, where tasty food is dished out in the rustic interior or on the terrace with stunning views of Čićarija mountains. Try their cumin *rakija* (grappa) and ask to see the farm animals.

Reserve ahead, as it's hugely popular and sometimes receives big groups.

Agroturizam Nežić (☑ 052-644 285; Zrenj 11, Zrenj; mains from 50KN; ☺ Sun only) For a light meal of truffle-infused antipastos served with homemade bread, such as cheese drowned in olive oil, truffles and butter, Istrian prosciutto and truffle *fritaja* (scrambled eggs), look no further than Agroturizam Nežić. The farm owners Paolo and Nadia serve up these lovingly prepared snacks on weekends in their traditional stone tavern; be sure to reserve ahead.

Toklarija (☑ 091 92 66 769; Sovinjsko Polje 11, Sovinjsko Polje; 6-course meal incl wine 400-500KN; ☺ 1-10pm Wed-Mon) The reason to come to Sovinjsko Polje is to enjoy one of Istria's finest dining experiences. At this beautifully converted 600-year-old olive mill (bought by his grandfather in the 1950s), eccentric owner Nevio Sirotić serves delectable, homemade Istrian slow food. A meal can take up to four hours in a well-timed string of delicate courses.

Stara Oštarija   ISTRIAN €€
(☑ 052-694 003; Petra Flega 5; mains 90-350KN; ☺ noon-10pm daily) Truffles, truffles and more truffles are the inevitable speciality here. They even find their way into the local dessert – panna cotta with truffle honey – a real treat for the taste buds. For a splurge, order a slow-food truffle menu of six courses (800KN for two) and enjoy views of the valley below. Reserve ahead.

🛍 Shopping

Zigante Tartufi   FOOD
(www.zigantetartufi.com; Trg Fontana; ☺ 9am-8pm) Stock up on truffles in various shapes and forms – whole, hand-sliced, puréed, and with

MAGIC MUSHROOMS

The truffle trade is less like a business than a highly profitable cult. It revolves around an expensive subterranean fungus allegedly endowed with semimagical powers, which is picked in dark woods and then sent across borders to be sold for a small fortune. Devotees claim that once you've tasted this small, nut-shaped delicacy, all other flavours seem insipid.

There are 70 sorts of truffle in the world, of which 34 come from Europe. The traditional truffle-producing countries are Italy, France and Spain, but Istrian forests boast three sorts of black truffles as well as the big white truffle – one of the most prized in the world, at around 35,000KN per kilogram. Croatia's largest exporter of Istrian truffles is Zigante Tartufi (p129), with its share of the overall Croatian export market being about 90%. In 1999 the company's owner, Giancarlo Zigante, along with his dog Diana, found the world's largest truffle in Istria, weighing 1.31kg and making it into *Guinness World Records*.

The Istrian truffle business is relatively young. In 1932, when Istria was occupied by Italy, an Italian soldier from the truffle capital of Alba allegedly noticed similarities in vegetation between his region and Istria. He returned after his military service with specially trained dogs, which, after enough sniffing and digging, eventually uncovered the precious commodity.

Because no sign of the truffle appears above ground, no human can spot it, so dogs (or, traditionally, pigs) are the key to a successful truffle hunt. Istrian *breks* (dogs) may be mongrels, but they are highly trained. Puppies begin their training at two months, but only about 20% of them go on to have fully fledged careers as truffle trackers.

The truffle-hunting season starts in early October and continues for three months, during which time at least 3000 people and 9000 to 12,000 dogs wander around the damp Motovun forests. The epicentre of the truffle-growing region is the town of Buzet.

Some people believe truffles are an aphrodisiac, though scientific research has failed to prove this. Conduct your own experiment!

olives or mushrooms. Zigante stores are ubiquitous in Istria.

ℹ️ Information

Tourist Office (📞 052-662 343; www.tz-buzet. hr; Šetalište Vladimira Gortana 9; ⏰ 8am-3pm Mon-Fri, 9am-2pm Sat) In a swanky space next to Vela Vrata, with info about accommodation and plentiful maps and brochures about regional activities.

ℹ️ Getting There & Away

Connections from Buzet's **bus station** (Riječka bb) include the following:
Poreč 50KN, one hour, three daily
Pula 65KN, 1½ hours, one daily
Rijeka 60KN, one hour, five daily

Roč

POP 153

Small and sleepy Roč, 8km southeast of Buzet, is snug within its 15th-century walls. A meander will reveal the Romanesque **Church of St Anthony**, a 15th-century **Renaissance house** in the square next to the church, and a **Roman lapidarium** within the town gate. The tourist office (p131) has keys to all the

town's churches, so ask here if you want to see the interiors. It also has information about the fresco workshop that's on offer in town.

✨ Festivals & Events

Roč Accordion Festival   MUSIC
Roč slumbers most of the year, roused only by the annual Accordion Festival on the second Sunday in May, which gathers accordion players from Croatia, Italy and Slovenia.

🍴 Eating

Ročka Konoba   ISTRIAN €€
(mains 40-100KN; ⏰ noon-10pm Tue-Sun) One of the town's stone buildings houses this worthwhile regional restaurant, which has outdoor tables and a fireplace indoors. It's a great place to discover Istrian specialities such as *fuži,* homemade sausages and *maneštra* (vegetable stew).

🔒 Shopping

Biskoteka   SPIRITS
(Roč 14; ⏰ 9.30am-6.30pm daily) At the Biskoteka shop you can try about 30 *rakija* varieties, including seven brands of *biska* (white mistletoe grappa).

ℹ️ Information

Tourist Office (☎ 092 16 94 598; Roč bb;
⊙ 9am-5pm)

ℹ️ Getting There & Away

You'll need your own car to get to Roč as virtually
no public transport heads this way.

Hum

POP 30

Reached by road from Roč, Hum is a beautifully preserved place that bills itself as the
world's smallest town, with a permanent
population of around 30. Legend has it
that the giants who built Istria had only a
few stones left over and they used them to
build Hum.

When you are finished in Hum, don't
miss the abandoned ancient village of **Kotli**,
just 2.5km off the main road between Roč
and Hum. Set on the Mirna River, this protected rural complex has preserved courtyards, outer staircases, arched passages and
picturesque chimneys.

◉ Sights

It takes just 30 minutes to see the town on
a self-guided tour, as each church and building is marked with informative multilingual
plaques.

Glagolitic Alley   LANDMARK
(Aleja Glagoljaša) On the way from Roč you'll
pass Glagolitic Alley, a series of 11 outdoor
sculptures placed along the road commem-
orating the area's importance as a centre of
the Glagolitic alphabet.

Chapel of St Jerome   CHURCH
(Crkvica Svetog Jerolima) Don't miss the 12th-
century frescoes in this Romanesque chapel
which depict the life of Jesus in unusually
vivid colours.

✪ Festivals & Events

On the last Sunday of October, about 4000 visitors pour into Hum for **Dan Rakije** (Day of
Grappa). During this fun event, you get a tasting glass and sip on different-flavoured grappas produced in the area, till they run out.

🍴 Eating

Humska Konoba   ISTRIAN €€
(☎ 052-660 005; www.hum.hr; Hum 2; mains
45-190KN; ⊙ 11am-10pm) The town's tavern
serves first-rate Istrian mainstays on a lovely

outdoor terrace offering panoramic views.
Start with a shot of sweet *biska* (made according to an ancient Celtic recipe). Next try
maneštra s kukuruzom (bean and fresh-
maize soup), continue with truffle-topped
fuži and end with *kroštuli* (fried crispy
dough covered in sugar).

🛍️ Shopping

Aura   GIFTS & SOUVENIRS
(⊙ 10am-7pm) In summer, this tiny and adorable town gets a steady stream of visitors
who come to meander around the narrow
lanes and to visit Aura, which displays some
old village tools but serves mostly as a souvenir shop selling wine, grappa and truffles.

ℹ️ Getting There & Away

You'll need your own car to reach Hum as no
public transport passes this way.

Pazin

POP 4400

Most famous for the gaping chasm that
inspired Jules Verne, and for its medieval
castle, Pazin is a workaday provincial town
slap bang in the middle of Istria. It deserves
a stop mainly for the chasm and the castle,
but part of the appeal is its small-town feel
and the lack of international tourists stomping its streets. Most of the town centre is
given over to pedestrian-only areas, while
rolling Istrian countryside surrounds the
slightly unsightly outskirts.

Lying at the geographic heart of Istria,
Pazin is the region's administrative seat and
is well connected by road and rail to virtually
every other destination on the peninsula.
However, hotel and restaurant pickings are
skimpy, meaning you're better off visiting on
a day trip – Pazin is within an hour of most
other Istrian towns by car. The countryside
around Pazin offers plentiful activities, such
as hiking, free climbing, zip-lining, cycling
and visiting local honey-makers.

◉ Sights & Activities

The Pazin tourist office distributes a map of
hiking trails and honey spots (you can visit
beekeepers and taste their delicious acacia
honey), and a brochure about wine cellars
around Pazin.

Pazin Chasm   CAVE
(www.pazinska-jama.com; adult/concession 30/15KN;
⊙ 10am-7pm Jun-Aug) Pazin's most renowned

site is undoubtedly this 100m-deep abyss, through which the Pazinčica River sinks into subterranean passages forming three underground lakes. Its shadowy depths inspired the imagination of Jules Verne, as well as numerous Croatian writers. Visitors can walk the 1.3km **marked path** inside the natural canyon, which takes about 45 minutes and involves a gentle winding climb.

There are two entrances, one by Hotel Lovac and one by the footbridge that spans the abyss, 100m from the castle. You can enter the cave with an expert speleologist (150KN), if arranged in advance through the tourist office, and even zipline across it. If the trip into the abyss doesn't appeal, there's a viewing point just outside the castle.

Castle   CASTLE
(Trg Istarskog Razvoda 1) Looming over the chasm, Pazin's Kaštel is the largest and best-preserved medieval structure in all of Istria. First mentioned in AD 983, it is a medley of Romanesque, Gothic and Renaissance architecture and inside you will find two **museums** – the town museum and the Istrian Ethnographic Museum (one ticket gets you into both).

Istrian Ethnographic Museum   MUSEUM
(www.emi.hr; Trg Istarskog Razvoda 1275; 25KN; ⊙10am-6pm Tue-Sun) Housed in Pazin's impressive castle, this Ethnographic Museum covering all of Istria possesses around 4000 artefacts which give an idea of traditional Istrian village life through the ages. Collections include furniture, national dress, agricultural tools and pottery, and there are sections on Slavic festivals and migration.

Town Museum   MUSEUM
(www.muzej-pazin.hr; Trg Istarskog Razvoda 1; 25KN; ⊙10am-6pm Tue-Sun) The town museum inside Pazin's castle has a collection of medieval Istrian church bells, an exhibition about slave revolts, and torture instruments in the dungeon.

★ Festivals & Events

Days of Jules Verne   CULTURAL
(⊙early Jun) This festival is Pazin's way of honouring the writer who somewhat inadvertently put the town on the cultural map. There are races, re-enactments from the novel and journeys retracing the footsteps of Verne's hero Mathias Sandorf.

🛏 Sleeping & Eating

Hotel Lovac   HOTEL €€
(☑052-624 324; www.hotel-lovac.com.hr; Šime Kurelića 4; s/d 280/560KN; P❋🎧) The late-1960s architecture of Pazin's only hotel could be a hit, if only the rooms were done up right. Request one of the spruced-up rooms with a chasm view. On the western edge of town.

Lovac   ISTRIAN €€
(☑098 421 317; Šime Kurelića 4; mains 70-135KN; ⊙7am-11pm daily) The restaurant at the Hotel Lovac rustles up decent local mains such as pastas, venison and truffle dishes. The place to consume is definitely the terrace, which has chasm views.

Konoba Vela Vrata   ISTRIAN €€
(Beram 41; mains 60-150KN; ⊙noon-11.30pm Tue-Sun) Located 5km northwest of Pazin, in the village of **Beram**, this rural tavern serves

---

MATHIAS SANDORF & THE PAZIN CHASM

The writer best known for going around the world in 80 days, into the centre of the earth and 20,000 leagues under the sea found inspiration in the centre of Istria. The French futurist-fantasist Jules Verne (1828–1905) set *Mathias Sandorf* (1885), one of his 27 books in the series Voyages Extraordinaires, in the castle and chasm of Pazin.

In the novel, later made into a movie, Count Mathias Sandorf and two cohorts are arrested by Austrian police for revolutionary activity and imprisoned in Pazin's castle. Sandorf escapes by climbing down a lightning rod but, struck by lightning, he tumbles down into the roaring Pazinčica River. He's carried along into the murky depths of the chasm, but our plucky hero holds on fast to a tree trunk and (phew!) six hours later the churning river deposits him at the tranquil entrance to the Limska Draga Fjord. He walks to Rovinj and is last seen jumping from a cliff into the sea amid a hail of bullets.

Verne never actually visited Pazin – he spun Sandorf's adventure from photos and travellers' accounts – but that hasn't stopped Pazin from celebrating it at every opportunity. There's a street named after Jules Verne as well as special Jules Verne days.

some of the best *pršut* (prosciutto), handmade pasta, gnocchi and truffle dishes you'll taste in Istria. In winter the interior is a cosy affair; in summer head for the terrace with amazing views of the central Istrian countryside.

ℹ Information

Tourist Office (☑ 052-622 460; www.central-istria.com; Franine i Jurine 14; ⏱10am-5pm Mon-Fri, to 1pm Sat)

ℹ Getting There & Away

BUS

Services from the main **bus station** (Miroslava Bulešića 2) include the following:

Motovun 30KN, 30 minutes, two daily
Poreč 42KN, 35 minutes, six daily
Pula 50KN, 50 minutes, three daily
Rijeka 45KN, one hour, six daily
Rovinj 47KN, one hour, eight daily
Zagreb 123KN, three to four hours, eight daily

TRAIN

The **train station** (Stareh Kostanji 1) is east of the town centre. Connections from Pazin:

Buzet 25KN, 50 minutes, seven daily
Pula 36KN, one hour, six daily
Zagreb 136KN, five to 8½ hours, seven daily

Gračišće

POP 1400

Gračišće, 7km southeast of Pazin, is a sleepy medieval town surrounded by rolling hills, and is one of Istria's well-kept secrets. Its collection of ancient buildings includes the 15th-century Venetian-Gothic **Salamon Palace**, the Romanesque **Church of St Euphemia**, and the **Church of St Mary** from 1425.

Most of these buildings are unrestored (although some work is being done). You won't need more than 30 minutes to circle the tiny town, but the ambience is truly lovely. There's an 11.5km circular **hiking trail** that leads from here, which is well marked with signs.

✕ Eating

Konoba Marino   ISTRIAN €
(☑ 052-687 081; www.konoba-marino-gracisce.hr; Gračišće 75; 40-150KN; ⏱2-11pm Thu-Tue) Istrian specialities are served at Konoba Marino, a cosy tavern that dishes out copious portions

of *fuži* with game and *ombolo* (boneless pork loin) with cabbage.

ℹ Getting There & Away

Buses heading between Pazin and Rijeka or Zagreb stop in Gračišće, but naturally the best way to reach the town is with your own hire car.

Svetvinčenat

POP 200

Situated around halfway between Pazin and Pula in southern Istria, Svetvinčenat (also known as Savičenta) is a pretty little town with enough to keep most interested for half a day or so. First settled by Benedictines, it centres on a Renaissance town square. With its surrounding cypress trees, harmoniously positioned buildings and laid-back ambience, it's a delightful place for an aimless wander en route to somewhere else.

⊙ Sights

Morosini-Grimani Castle   CASTLE
(Gradski trg) The northern part of the main square is occupied by this beautifully preserved 13th-century palace. A Venetian makeover in the 16th century added towers that served as a residence and a prison. It now hosts various festivals and events but you can wander the grounds anytime you like.

The castle is home to a seasonal **medieval park** (adult/under 15yr 20KN/free; ⏱11am-2pm & 6-9pm Mon-Fri, 11am-3pm Sun Jul & Aug); on weekends, visitors can roam around the castle on their own.

Church of Mary's Annunciation   CHURCH
(Gradski trg) This parish church on the east side of the main square has a trefoil Renaissance facade made of local cut stone, and five elaborate Venetian marble altars inside.

✷ Festivals & Events

Dance & Nonverbal Theatre Festival   DANCE
(www.svetvincenatfestival.com; ⏱late Jul) The time to be in Svetvinčenat is late July, during the village's annual festival. It features contemporary dance pieces, street theatre, circus and mime acts, and various other nonverbal forms of expression. This international event hosts performers from Croatia and Europe, its acts ranging from Finnish hip hop to Brazilian capoeira.

🛏 Sleeping & Eating

The only accommodation in town comes in the form of private rooms. Ask at the tourist office or consult popular booking websites.

Stancija 1904　　　　　　　　INN €€€
(📱 098 738 974; www.stancija.com; Smoljanci 2-3; d from 940KN; 🅿) In the village of Smoljanci, just 3km from Svetvinčenat on the road to Bale, this traditional stone Istrian house has been stylishly converted by a Swiss-Croatian family. Surrounded by fragrant herb gardens and shaded by tall old-growth trees, it offers elaborate breakfasts. The owner is the Swiss honorary consul in Istria.

Konoba Puli Pineta　　　　　　ISTRIAN €
(📱 098 99 11 795; Karlov Vrt 1, Žminj; mains from 60KN; ⊙ 5-10pm) Don't miss Konoba Puli Pineta in the town of Žminj, 7km north of Svetvinčenat. The tavern is known around Istria for its superb homemade pastas and great grilled meats. The location may not be the best in Istria but the food is top-notch.

Konoba Klarići　　　　　　　　ISTRIAN €€
(Klarići 83; mains 60-135KN; ⊙ 11am-11pm Tue-Sun) This delightful stone tavern in the south of the village serves up superb home-made Istrian pastas and its own exquisite wines. The roaring fire in winter can be a very welcoming sight.

ℹ Information

The **tourist office** (📱 052-560 349; www.tz-svetvincenat.hr; Svetvinčenat 20; ⊙ 8am-7pm Mon-Fri, 11am-6pm Sat & Sun) opposite the main square has information about private accommodation in and around town (from 150KN per person), brochures and a map of a bike path that takes you on a 35km circuit from Svetvinčenat, with information boards explaining the local history, flora and fauna in English.

ℹ Getting There & Away

Svetvinčenat is barely served by public transport so you'll need your own car to get there.

Labin & Rabac

Perched on a hilltop just above the coast, Labin is the undisputed highlight of eastern Istria, as well as its historical and administrative centre. The showcase here is the labyrinthine old town, a beguiling potpourri of steep streets, cobbled alleys and pastel houses festooned with stone ornamentation.

Surrounding it below is a grubby new town that has sprouted as a result of the coal-mining industry. Labin was the mining capital of Istria until the 1970s, its hill mined so extensively that the town began to collapse. Mining stopped in 1999, the necessary repairs were undertaken and the town surfaced with a new sense of itself as a tourist destination.

Labin's coastal resort is Rabac, a former fishing village hugging a shallow cove hemmed with pebble beaches.

⦿ Sights

Wandering the medieval streets of Labin is the highlight of any visit. Labin is divided into two parts: the hilltop old town with most of the sights and attractions; and Podlabin, a much newer section below the hill, with most of the town's shops and services.

Loggia　　　　　　　HISTORIC BUILDING
(Titov trg) This 1550 loggia served as the community centre of Labin in the 16th century. News and court verdicts were announced here, fairs were held and wayward people were punished on the pillar of shame.

Town Gallery　　　　　　　　MUSEUM
(Gradska Galerija; 1 Maja 6; adult/concession 15/10KN; ⊙ 10am-1pm & 5-10pm Mon-Sat) The ground floor of this museum, housed in the baroque 18th-century Battiala-Lazzarini Palace, is devoted to archaeological finds. Upstairs is a collection of musical instruments with some fun interactive features, and the top floor has a contemporary art gallery. The museum is over a coal pit that has been turned into a realistic recreation of an actual coal mine.

Fortress　　　　　　　　　FORTRESS
This fortress at the western edge of town is the highest point in Labin. To get there, either walk along Ulica 1 Maja or take the long way around by following Šetalište San Marco along the town walls. What unfolds below you is a sweeping view of the coast, the Učka mountain range and Cres island.

✨ Festivals & Events

Labin Art Republic　　　　　　　ART
(Labin Art Republika; www.labin-art-republika.com; ⊙ Jun-Sep) Labin Art Republic completely takes over this artsy town in summer – there are more than 30 artists living and working here. During the festival, the town comes

alive with street theatre, concerts, plays, clown performances and open studios. Every Tuesday at 9.30pm, free guided tours (in various languages) depart from the tourist office in the old town.

🛏 Sleeping

There are no hotels in Labin itself but choices abound just below in Rabac. Most of the lodging is of the large hotel-resort kind, with a few smaller properties. There are also plenty of private rooms in the area – contact the tourist office for these.

Stari Hrast Hostel　　　　　　　HOSTEL €
(☑ 098 17 55 763; Obala Maršala Tita 33, Rabac; dm €17; 🛜) This bare-bones hostel right in the centre of Rabac offers 12 basic dorms with bunks and a table or two. Facilities are new, the owners friendly enough and the location handy for everything in town.

Villa Annette　　　　　　　　　HOTEL €€€
(☑ 052-884 222; www.villa-annette.com; Raška 24; s/d 1120/1400KN; 🅿❄🛜🏊) This posh, family-run hideaway up on a hill slope has 12 suites and a wonderful outdoor pool providing dramatic bay views. Half board is an extra €30 and meals are taken in the hotel restaurant.

Hotel Amfora　　　　　　　　　HOTEL €€€
(☑ 052-872 202; www.hotel-amfora.com; Rabac bb; s/d 670/1200KN; 🅿❄🛜🏊) Right in the heart of Rabac, this large, slightly dated but unusually intimate resort hotel has two swimming pools and a fitness centre. All rooms boast baths and rates include half board.

🍴 Eating

Labin is known for its *krafi,* ravioli-like pasta which is served either sweet or savoury. Rabac has plenty of restaurants serving seafood standards, but most cater to the unfussy tourist crowds.

WORTH A TRIP

DON'T FORGET TRGET FISH
....
In the fishing village of Trget, wrapped around a small bay, **Martin Pescador** (Trget 11a; mains from 50KN; ⊙ noon-11pm) is a fine and very authentic seafood restaurant that has a boat-shaped bar inside and a lovely terrace right on the seafront. It serves a mean fish soup and boat-fresh seafood.

Velo Kafe　　　　　　　　　　　CAFE €€
(Titov trg 12; 45-130KN; ⊙ 11am-11pm daily) Dominating Titov trg, this popular, vine-shaded, multitasking spot serves everything from beefsteaks, local pasta and truffle-infused dishes to coffee, cakes and ice creams. There's plenty of outdoor seating and a real fire when things get chilly in winter.

Restaurant Kvarner　　　　　ISTRIAN €€
(Šetalište San Marco bb; mains 70-230KN; ⊙ 10am-midnight Jun-Sep) Steps from Titov trg, this restaurant has a terrace overlooking the sea, a menu of authentic Istrian fare and a loyal local following. Handmade *fuži* is the main speciality here but almost anything you order is guaranteed to be packed with local flavour. Also has **rooms** to rent.

ℹ Information

Tourist Office (☑ 052-852 399; www.rabac-labin.com; Titov trg 2/1; ⊙ 8am-9pm Mon-Fri, 10am-2pm & 6-9pm Sat & Sun) At the entrance to the old town, this helpful office can point those looking for private rooms in the right direction.

ℹ Getting There & Around

Labin is well connected by bus with Pula (48KN, one hour, eight daily). In summer, the bus to Rabac (12KN), via the old town, departs 13 times daily.

Kvarner

Why Go?

Sheltered by soaring mountains, the Kvarner Gulf has long been loved by visitors attracted by the mild climate and cobalt waters, and those in search of more than just beach appeal. In the days of the Austro-Hungarian Empire, the wealthy built holiday homes here, bestowing places like Rijeka and Opatija with a rich legacy of stately Habsburg-era architecture. From both of these neighbouring towns you can easily connect to hiking trails inside the protected forests of Učka Nature Park and Risnjak National Park.

The islands of Cres, Lošinj, Krk and Rab all have highly atmospheric old port towns and stretches of unspoiled coastline dotted with remote coves for superb swimming. Wildlife puts in an appearance too: Cres has an important griffon vulture population and Lošinj has a marine centre devoted to preserving the Adriatic's dolphins and turtles.

Best Places to Eat

➜ Bistro Bukarica (p159)
➜ Kukuriku (p145)
➜ Konoba Valle Losca (p147)
➜ Bora Bar (p157)
➜ Mlinar (p142)

Best Places to Sleep

➜ Mare Mare Suites (p155)
➜ Hotel Miramar (p146)
➜ Carnevale (p141)
➜ Hostel Dharma (p141)
➜ Hotel Manora (p153)

When to Go

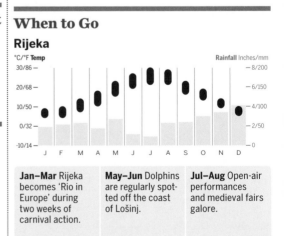

Rijeka

Jan–Mar Rijeka becomes 'Rio in Europe' during two weeks of carnival action.

May–Jun Dolphins are regularly spotted off the coast of Lošinj.

Jul–Aug Open-air performances and medieval fairs galore.

Kvarner Highlights

1 **Opatija** (p144)
Adopting a Habsburg swagger as you stroll along the promenade in Opatija.

2 **Rab Town** (p166)
Wandering the cobbled, streets of this ancient town.

3 **Volosko** (p145)
Sampling Croatian specialities in this former village.

4 **Trsat Castle** (p139)
Admiring the panoramic views from Rijeka's castle.

5 **Kukuriku** (p145)
Heading to the hills for a memorable meal in Kastav.

6 **Lopar** (p170) Seeking out the gently shelving and wonderfully remote beaches of the Lopar Peninsula.

7 **Mali Lošinj** (p154)
Soaking up the buzzy summertime vibe of the Mali Lošinj waterfront.

8 **Krk Town** (p160) Losing yourself in history in the sloping streets of Krk Town.

9 **Osor** (p153) Exploring the hidden corners of this tiny walled town.

RIJEKA

📱 051 / POP 129,000

Croatia's third-largest city, Rijeka is a bustling blend of gritty 20th-century port and Italianate Habsburg grandeur. Most people speed through en route to the islands or Dalmatia, but those who pause will discover charm, culture, good nightlife, intriguing festivals and Croatia's most colourful carnival.

Despite some regrettable architectural ventures in the outskirts, much of the centre is replete with ornate Austro-Hungarian–style buildings. It's a surprisingly verdant city once you've left its concrete core, which contains Croatia's largest port, with ships, cargo and cranes lining the waterfront.

Rijeka is a vital transport hub, but as there's no real beach in the city most people base themselves in nearby Opatija.

History

Following their successful conquest of the indigenous Illyrian Liburnians, the Romans established a port here called Tarsaticae. Slavic tribes migrated to the region in the 7th century and built a new settlement within the old Roman town.

The town changed feudal masters – from German nobility to the Frankopan dukes of Krk – before becoming part of the Austrian empire in the late 15th century. Rijeka was an important outlet to the sea for the Austrians and a new road was built in 1725 connecting Vienna with the Kvarner coast. This spurred economic development, especially shipbuilding, the industry that has remained the centrepiece of Rijeka's economy ever since.

In 1750 Rijeka was hit by a devastating earthquake which destroyed much of its medieval heart. Thirty years later the old-town walls were removed to allow for the construction of a more modern commercial centre. Korzo, Rijeka's main pedestrian strip, was built as a grand avenue on the site of the demolished walls.

With the birth of the Austro-Hungarian Dual Monarchy in 1867, Rijeka was given over to the jurisdiction of the Hungarian government. Imposing municipal buildings were constructed and a new railway linked the city to Zagreb, Budapest and Vienna, bringing the first tourists to the Kvarner Gulf.

Between 1918, when Italian troops seized Rijeka and Istria, and 1945, when Rijeka became part of postwar Yugoslavia, it changed hands several times, with sporadic periods as a free city (known under its Italian name,

Fiume). In 1991 Rijeka became part of independent Croatia but still retains a sizeable, well-organised Italian minority who have their own newspaper, *La Voce del Popolo*.

◉ Sights

The maze of streets and squares in the ancient core of Rijeka have excellent multilingual plaques explaining the history of each sight.

◎ City Centre

Our Lady of Lourdes
Capuchin Church   CHURCH
(Kapucinska Crkva Gospe Lurdske; Kapucinske Stube 5; ☺8am-noon & 4-8pm) If you're arriving by bus, you won't help but notice this imposing church towering over the station. Dating from 1904, its ornate neo-Gothic facade stands above an elaborate Italianate double staircase.

Museum of Modern
& Contemporary Art   GALLERY
(Muzej Moderne i Suvremene Umjetnosti; www.mmsu.hr; Dolac 1; adult/concession 20/10KN; ☺11am-8pm Tue-Fri, 11am-2pm & 6-9pm Sat & Sun) On the 2nd floor of the university library, this small museum puts on high-quality rotating shows, from street photography to contemporary drawings and sculptures.

City Tower   TOWER
(Gradski Toranj; Korzo) One of the few buildings to have survived the 1750 earthquake, the distinctive yellow City Tower was originally a gate from the waterfront to the old town centre. The Habsburgs added the baroque decorations after the disaster, including the portal with coats of arms and busts of emperors. The still-functioning clock was mounted in 1873.

Roman Arch   GATE
(Rimski Luk; Stara Vrata) This plain archway marks the former entrance to the Praetorium, an ancient military complex. Other Roman remains can be seen in a small excavation site nearby.

St Vitus' Cathedral   CATHEDRAL
(Katedrala Sv Vida; Trg Grivica 11; ☺6am-5pm Mon-Fri, 6am-noon Sat, 9am-1pm Sun) FREE North of the Roman Gate is this unusual round cathedral, built by the Jesuit order in 1638 on the site of an older church and dedicated to Rijeka's patron saint. If it looks familiar, it's probably because it features on the reverse of the 100KN note. Massive marble pillars

support the central dome under which are housed baroque altars and a 13th-century Gothic crucifix.

Rijeka City Museum   MUSEUM
(Muzej Grada Rijeke; www.muzej-rijeka.hr; Muzejski trg 1; adult/concession 15/10KN; ⊙10am-8pm Mon-Sat, to 3pm Sun) Housed in a boxy 1970s structure, this small museum houses ever-changing themed exhibitions, ranging from art to aspects of local history.

Maritime & History Museum   MUSEUM
(Pomorski i Povijesni Muzej; www.ppmhp.hr; Muzejski trg 1; adult/concession 15/10KN; ⊙9am-4pm Mon, 9am-8pm Tue-Sat, 4-8pm Sun) The star of this museum is the building itself, the former palace of the Austro-Hungarian governor. It's a splendid showcase of Hungarian architecture, with grand staircases, glittering chandeliers and many sumptuously restored rooms. The maritime collection includes Roman amphorae, model ships, sea charts, navigation instruments and portraits of captains; little of it is captioned in English.

Natural History Museum   MUSEUM
(Prirodoslovni Muzej; www.prirodoslovni.com; Lorenzov Prolaz 1; adult/concession 10/5KN; ⊙9am-7pm Mon-Sat, to 3pm Sun) 🖉 Located in a very grand 19th-century villa, this museum is devoted to the geology, botany and sea life of the Adriatic area. There's a small aquarium, exhibits on sharks, taxidermic animals and lots of bugs. Don't miss the adjacent botanical garden, with more than 2000 native plant species.

⊙ Surrounding Hills

★ **Trsat Castle**   CASTLE
(Trsatska Gradina; Petra Zrinskoga bb; adult/concession 15/5KN; ⊙9am-8pm Jun-Oct, to 5pm Nov-May) High on a hill above the city, this semiruined 13th-century fortress offers magnificent vistas from its bastions and ramparts, looking down the Rječina River valley to the docks, the Adriatic and the distant island of Krk. The present structure was built by the Frankopan dukes of Krk, but its latest facelift was in 1824 when Irish-born count Laval Nugent, a commander in the Austrian army, bought the castle and had it restored in a romantic neoclassical Biedermeier design.

Guarded by basilisks, the ancient Greek–style Nugent family mausoleum houses a gallery, while underground a former dungeon hosts occasional exhibits. During summer, the fortress features concerts, theatre

performances and fashion shows. The open-air cafe-bar (open until midnight in summer) is a wonderful spot to take in the views.

Our Lady of Trsat Church   CHURCH
(Crkva Gospe Trsatske; www.trsat-svetiste.com; Frankopanski trg; ⊙8am-5pm) According to legend, the angels carrying the house of Jesus' mother from Nazareth rested here in the late 13th century before moving it to Loreto across the Adriatic in Le Marche. Pilgrims started trickling into the chapel erected on the site, and then pouring in when the Pope donated an icon of St Mary in 1367 (located on the main altar, behind a magnificent wrought-iron gate). The church still attracts thousands of pilgrims each year.

View offerings of votive gifts in the baroque cloister and make an appointment to see the valuable sacral-art collection in the treasury, where you can watch a 15-minute film about the church.

To follow in the pilgrims' steps, climb the **Petar Kružić Stairway** from Titov trg. It was built in 1531 for the faithful to use on their way to the church, and it's lined with chapels once used as rest stops for the pilgrims. Alternatively, take a quick ride on city bus 2 to Trsat.

Astronomical Centre   OBSERVATORY
(Astronomski Centar; ☎051-455 700; www.rijeka sport.hr; Sv Križ 33; adult/child 20/10KN; ⊙8am-10pm Tue-Sat) High on a hill in the east of the city, Croatia's first astronomical centre is a striking modern complex encompassing an observatory, planetarium and study centre. Check the website for details of evening presentations, some of which are held in English, Italian, French, German, Russian and Spanish. To get here, catch bus 7A from the centre.

🏃 Activities

Yacht Rent   BOATING
(☎098 726 065; www.yacht-rent.com) With nearly 4000 boats on their books, this outfit can sort you out with a yacht, launch or catamaran, with or without a skipper and/or crew (you'll need a valid skipper's licence if you choose the 'bareboat' option). Expect to pay upwards of €1300 per week.

Paragliding Kvarner   PARAGLIDING
(☎095 85 49 995; www.paragliding-kvarner.com) Based in **Crikvenica**, 30km down the coast, this crew offers tandem flights taking off from 770m above the Kvarner Gulf. Choose between a 20-minute panoramic flight (€80) and 40 minutes riding the thermals (€130).

Rijeka

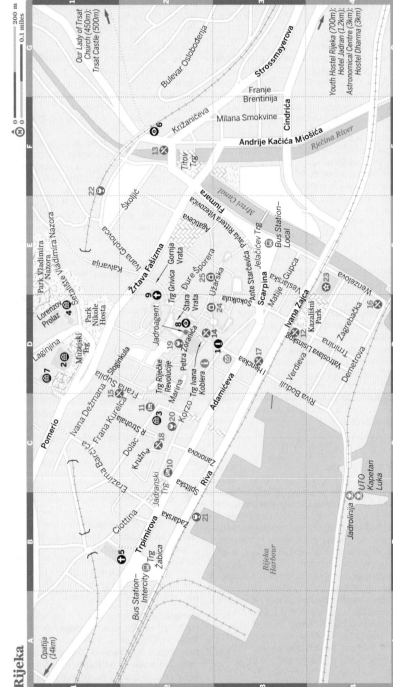

Rijeka

✿ Festivals & Events

Rijeka Carnival   CARNIVAL
(Riječki Karneval; www.rijecki-karneval.hr; ☺mid-Jan–early Mar) Rio or Funchal it isn't, but the largest carnival in Croatia provides a good excuse to tarry in Rijeka between mid-January and Ash Wednesday. The festivities include pageants, street dances, concerts, masked balls, exhibitions and a parade. Check out the *zvončari,* masked men clad in animal skins who dance and ring loud bells to frighten off evil spirits.

Rijeka Summer Nights   THEATRE
(Riječke Ljetne Noći; ☺Jun–Jul) Theatre performances and concerts are held at the Croatian National Theatre (p143) and on outdoor stages set up on the Korso and the beaches.

🛏 Sleeping

Unlike the rest of the Croatian coast, prices at the few hotels in Rijeka are quite consistent year-round except at Carnival time, when you can expect to pay a surcharge and you'll need to book well in advance. There are few private rooms in Rijeka itself; the tourist office lists these on its website. Nearby Opatija has a lot more accommodation, but it tends to be much pricier.

★**Hostel Dharma**   HOSTEL €
(📞051-562 108; www.dharmahostels.com; Spinčićeva 2; dm/s/tw 135/270/370KN; P❄🌐) A clever conversion of what was once an iron smelter on the eastern edge of town has produced this highly recommendable hostel, with a yoga studio and vegetarian restaurant attached. Start your day with a free yoga class and tuck into a substantial vegetarian breakfast, before chilling out in the large verdant garden.

★**Carnevale**   HOSTEL €
(📞051-410 555; www.hostelcarnevale.com; Jadranski trg 1; dm/r 200/413KN; ❄🌐) With metallic paint on the walls, billowing fabric on the ceilings, animal-print bed linen and art scattered everywhere, this supercentral hostel should put you in a festive mood. Towels are provided (and changed regularly) and there are big suitcase-size lockers. The only downside is there's no kitchen.

Hostel Česká Beseda   HOSTEL €
(📞098 709 676; www.ceskabesedarijeka.hr; Ćićarijska 20; dm 120KN; P❄🌐) The hostel at the Czech cultural centre, around 4.5km northwest of the city centre, is a cheap option, albeit one a fair way from the waterfront and attractions. Rooms and facilities are kept almost obsessively clean and the staff are very helpful. If you are lucky you might catch a Czech cultural event such as folk dancing or puppet theatre.

Grand Hotel Bonavia   HOTEL €€
(📞051-357 100; www.bonavia.hr; Dolac 4; r from 700KN; P❄🌐) Around for almost 140 years, this striking glass-fronted box of a hotel right in the heart of town offers well-equipped, comfortable, 21st-century rooms that are much more stylish than you might expect. There's also a restaurant, a spa and a small gym.

Hotel Jadran   HOTEL €€€
(📞051-216 600; www.jadran-hoteli.hr; Šetalište XIII Divizije 46; s/d from 600/730KN; P❄@🌐)

KVARNER RIJEKA

Located 2km east of the centre, this immaculate four-star hotel clings to a cliff above the Adriatic: book a sea-view room and revel in the tremendous vistas from your balcony right above the water. There's a concrete-edged beach below too.

✗ Eating

There's very little choice on Sundays, when most eateries are closed. Many cafes on the Korzo serve light meals. Foodies should consider heading to nearby Volosko where there's a strip of high-quality restaurants.

★ Mlinar   BAKERY €
(Frana Supila; items from 8KN; ⊘ 5.30am-8pm Mon-Fri, 6.30am-3pm Sat) The best bakery in town, with delicious filled baguettes, wholemeal bread, croissants and *burek* (pastry stuffed with meat, spinach or cheese). There are several branches around town and across Croatia.

Maslina Na Zelenom Trgu   ITALIAN €
(www.pizzeria-maslina.hr; Koblerov trg bb; mains 26-80KN; ⊘ 11am-midnight Mon-Sat) For the best pizza in the city centre head to this small Italian place with wobbly art-nouveau decor and tiled tables. The wheels of pizza here are popular among Rijeka's (or should we say Fiume's) Italian population, with only the tastiest toppings making it onto the stretchy dough.

City Market   MARKET €
(Tržnica; Ivana Zajca 3; ⊘ 7am-2pm Mon-Sat, to noon Sun) This local market is one of the best places in town for seasonal fruit and vegetables.

★ Konoba Nebuloza   CROATIAN €€
(⊘ 051-374 501; www.konobanebuloza.com; Titov trg 2b; mains 45-110KN; ⊘ 11am-midnight Mon-Fri, from noon Sat) Straddling the line between modern and traditional Croatian fare, this slightly upmarket riverside restaurant serves lots of seafood along with selected beef and turkey dishes. Specialities include *sous vide* swordfish and baby rump steak with prosciutto and cheese. The chef seems to have a thing about mangel-wurzel, a vegetable you may never have eaten (or heard of).

Na Kantunu   CROATIAN, SEAFOOD €€
(Demetrova 2; mains 50-100KN; ⊘ 8am-midnight) Fresh fish and seafood are the stars of the show at this bright and breezy restaurant in a somewhat grimy location by the port. It's a good place to try traditional fish or octopus stews, followed by crispy fruit pastries.

Ristorante Spagho   ITALIAN €€
(⊘ 051-311 122; www.ristorantespagho.fullbusiness.com; Ivana Zajca 24; mains 35-160KN; ⊘ 12.30-9.30pm Mon-Fri, to 11pm Sat, to 9pm Sun; ❀ 🖘) A stylish, contemporary Italian job with exposed brickwork, art and hip seating that offers delicious and filling portions of pasta, pizza, salads and meat dishes. But the real deal here is the whole section of the menu devoted to truffles!

Zlatna Školjka   SEAFOOD, ITALIAN €€
(⊘ 051-213 782; www.zlatna-skoljka.hr; Kružna 12; mains 50-150KN; ⊘ 11am-11pm Mon-Sat) Savour the superbly prepared seafood, Italian pasta and risottos, and choice Croatian wines at this formal though oddly done-out restaurant (Gaudí-esque columns and stones implanted into the walls). Daily specials such as *pečena hobotnica* (roast octopus) are chalked up on a board.

🍷 Drinking & Entertainment

CukariKafe   BAR
(Trg Jurja Klovica 2; ⊘ 7am-midnight Mon-Thu, 7am-2am Fri & Sat, 10am-10pm Sun) Tucked into a tiny lane in the old part of town, this is Rijeka's coolest cafe-bar. Grab a seat on the oversized white wooden furniture on the covered deck or head inside to admire the oddball art-nouveau-style knick-knacks. Enjoy great coffee and cakes to a soothing soundtrack.

Život   CLUB
(Ružićeva 2; ⊘ 10pm-5am Fri & Sat) Funky, retro weekend-only nightclub for the over 25s playing '80s and '90s hits and much more. The decor is an eclectic mix of grandmother's antiques and hipster junk.

Tunel   BAR, CLUB
(Školjić 12; ⊘ 9am-midnight Tue & Wed, 9am-2am Thu, 9am-3am Fri, 7pm-3am Sat; 🖘) Tucked beneath the railway tracks in an actual tunnel, this popular place morphs from a daytime cafe, to a comedy and live-music venue, to a late-night club. It gets rammed on the weekends.

Nina 2   BAR, CLUB
(Adamićev Gat; ⊘ 8am-4am Mon-Thu, 8am-5am Fri, 10am-5am Sat; 🖘) This boat moored on the harbour-front offers daytime drinking and lots of night-time action, including DJs and live bands.

Filodrammatica Bookshop Cafe   BAR
(Korzo 28; ⊘ 7am-11pm) A cafe-bar with luxurious decor, comfy sofas and a VBZ (Croatia's

WORTH A TRIP

RISNJAK NATIONAL PARK

Just 32km northeast of Rijeka, the **Risnjak National Park** (Nacionalni Park Risnjak; www. risnjak.hr; adult/concession 45/25KN) occupies 63 sq km of thickly forested mountainscape, the highest peak being Veliki Risnjak at 1528m. Linking the Alps and the Balkan mountains, these cool peaks provide respite from the sweltering heat, humidity and crowds of the coast. There are only a few villages within the park, which means limited accommodation and food. Those who do make it to these parts often visit on day trips from Rijeka.

The starting point for the **Leska Path**, an easy and shady 4.2km trail, is at the Park Information Office. The route is punctuated by several dozen explanatory panels (with English translations) telling you all about the park's history, topography, geology, flora and fauna. Allow around two hours to complete the route.

You'll pass crystal-clear streams, forests of tall fir trees, bizarre rock formations, a feeding station for the deer and a mountain hut with a picnic table.

For accommodation, **Hotel Risnjak** (⬛051-508 160; www.hotel-risnjak.hr; Lujzinska 36; s/d 350/596KN; 🅿🛜) is a three-storey, yellow building that has its charm, with 21 rooms, a restaurant (known for its game dishes), a cafe-bar and a gym. The hotel also organises activities for groups of 10 or more (paragliding, rafting, canoeing, paintball, archery, skiing, canyon visits); ask if there are any you can join.

The **Park Information Office** (⬛051-836 133; www.np-risnjak.hr; Bijela Vodica 48; s/d 300/480KN; ⊙9am-5pm; 🛜) is just west of the village of Crni Lug. There's a restaurant attached and five simple, clean B&B rooms above (also available for half or full board).

There's no public transport to the park but there are trains to **Delnice** from Rijeka (43KN, one hour 10 minutes, six daily) and buses from Opatija (60KN, one hour 10 minutes, two daily), Pula (139KN, 3½ hours, two daily), Rijeka (48KN, 45 minutes, roughly hourly) and Zagreb (99KN, two hours, nine daily). To access the park by car, exit the main Zagreb–Rijeka motorway at Delnice and follow the signs.

KVARNER RIJEKA

biggest publisher) bookshop at the back, Filodrammatica prides itself on specialist coffees and fresh, single-source beans. It also serves sandwiches and snacks.

**Croatian National
Theatre Ivan Zajc**   THEATRE
(Hrvatsko Narodnog Kažalište Ivana pl Zajca; ⬛051-337 114; www.hnk-zajc.hr; Verdijeva 5a) In 1885 the inaugural performance at this imposing theatre was lit by the city's first light bulb. These days you can catch dramas in Croatian and Italian, as well as opera and ballet. Gustav Klimt painted some of the ceiling frescoes.

🛍 Shopping

Šta Da?   GIFTS & SOUVENIRS
(Užarska 14; ⊙9am-8pm Mon-Fri, to 1pm Sat) Literally translating as 'what yes?', '*šta da*' is an idiom peculiar to Rijeka meaning something like 'you what!?' or 'really, you don't say!'. This cool little store stocks T-shirts, jewellery and clocks, including many emblazoned with images of its logo and of the distinctive orange local buses.

VBZ   BOOKS
(www.vbz.hr; Korzo 32; ⊙7.30am-8.30pm Mon-Fri, to 5pm Sat) Large bookshop on the Korzo

selling maps and guides and much more, though mostly in Croatian.

Mala Galerija   ARTS & CRAFTS
(www.mala-galerija.hr; Užarska 25; ⊙8am-8pm Mon-Fri, 9am-2pm Sat) This small art shop stocks the traditional Rijeka design known as *morčići*, a ceramic jewellery piece depicting a Moor wearing a turban.

ℹ Information

Clinical Hospital Center Rijeka (Klinički Bolnički Centar Rijeka; ⬛051-658 111; www. kbc-rijeka.hr; Krešimirova 42)

Post Office (Korzo 13; ⊙7am-8pm Mon-Fri, to 2pm Sat) Has a telephone centre and an exchange office.

Tourist Office (⬛051-335 882; www.visitrijeka. hr; Korzo 14; ⊙8am-8pm Mon-Sat, to 2pm Sun)

ℹ Getting There & Away

AIR

Rijeka Airport (Zračna Luka Rijeka; ⬛051-841 222; www.rijeka-airport.hr; Hamec 1, Omišalj), located 30km from town on the island of Krk, is only used for seasonal flights from April to October. There are international flights to London, Oslo, Warsaw and more. The only domestic routes are **Trade Air** (☑ 091 62 65 111; www.trade-air.com) services to Dubrovnik, Split and Osijek.

BOAT

Jadroagent (☑ 051-212 466; www.jadroagent. hr; Trg Ivana Koblera 2; 🚭) Has information on all boats around Croatia.

Jadrolinija (☑ 051-211 444; www.jadrolinija.hr; Riječki Lukobran bb) A daily catamaran connects Rijeka to Rab Town (80KN, 1¾ hours) and Novalja on Pag (80KN, 2¾ hours).

UTO Kapetan Luka (☑ 021-645 476; www. krilo.hr) Has daily passenger-only ferries to/from Cres (45KN, 1¼ hours) and Mali Lošinj (60KN, three to 4½ hours) year-round, some of which also stop at Martinšćica (50KN, two hours), Unije (55KN, 2½ hours), Susak (60KN, three hours) and Ilovik (60KN, 3½ hours).

BUS

The **intercity bus station** (☑ 051-660 300; Trg Žabica 1) is in the town centre. Buses for Opatija leave from the local bus station on Jelačićev trg.

Cres 105KN, two hours 20 minutes, four daily

Dubrovnik 331KN to 411KN, 12½ hours, two daily

Krk 64KN, one hour 20 minutes, hourly

Pula 90KN, 2½ hours, 18 daily

Rovinj 94KN, two hours 20 minutes, five daily

Split 174KN to 209KN, eight hours, seven daily

Zadar 109KN to 130KN, four hours, nine daily

Zagreb 69KN to 120KN, 2½ hours, at least hourly

Autotrans (☑ 051-660 660; www.autotrans.hr) Based in Rijeka. Connections to Istria, Zagreb, Varaždin and Kvarner.

TRAIN

The **train station** (Željeznički Kolodvor; www. hzpp.hr; Trg Kralja Tomislava 1) is a 10-minute walk east of the city centre. Direct services include:

Ljubljana 129KN, three hours, two daily

Osijek 232KN, nine hours, daily

Pazin 40KN, 40 minutes, four daily

Zagreb 119KN, 3¾ hours, three daily

🛈 Getting Around

TO/FROM THE AIRPORT

An airport bus meets all flights for the 30-minute ride to the intercity bus station; it leaves for the airport two hours and 20 minutes before flight times. You can buy a ticket (50KN) on the bus.

Taxis from the airport charge up to 350KN to the centre.

PUBLIC TRANSPORT

Rijeka has an extensive network of orange city buses run by **Autotrolej** (☑ 051-311 400; www. autotrolej.hr), operating from the local **bus station** (Jelačićev trg). Buy two-trip tickets for 15.50KN from any *tisak* (news stand). A single ticket from the driver costs 10KN.

The same company also operates a 24-hour, colourful, open-topped, double-decker, hop-on, hop-off sightseeing bus (adult/child 50/35KN) that runs between central Rijeka, Trsat and Opatija. The ticket is also valid for travel on all city buses.

TAXI

Taxis are very reasonable in Rijeka (if you use the right firm). **Cammeo** (☑ 051-313 313; www. taxi-cammeo.hr) cabs are modern, inexpensive, have meters and are highly recommended; a ride in the central area costs 20KN.

OPATIJA

☑ 051 / POP 6660

Genteel Opatija, 13km to the west of Rijeka, was the most chic seaside resort for the Austro-Hungarian elite during the days of the Austro-Hungarian Empire – as evidenced by the many handsome belle-époque villas that the period bequeathed. Although it lost a lot of its sheen during the Yugoslav period, the town has spruced itself up in the last decade and once again attracts a mainly mature crowd, drawn to its grand spa hotels, spectacular location and agreeable year-round climate. Some excellent restaurants have sprung up to cater to them, with a particularly good cluster in the pretty Volosko neighbourhood.

The town sprawls along the coast between forested hills and the sparkling Adriatic, and the whole waterfront is connected by a promenade. Don't expect great beaches (there aren't any), but there's still excellent swimming in the sheltered bays.

History

Until the 1840s Opatija was a minuscule fishing village with 35 houses and a church, but the arrival of wealthy Iginio Scarpa from Rijeka turned things around. He built Villa Angiolina (named after his wife) and surrounded it with exotic subtropical plants. The villa hosted European aristocrats aplenty (including the Austrian queen Maria Anna, wife of emperor Ferdinand I) and Opatija's classy reputation was sealed.

Opatija's development was also assisted by the completion of a direct rail link to Vienna which opened in 1873. Construction of Opatija's first hotel, the Quarnero (today the Hotel Kvarner), began and wealthy visitors arrived en masse. It seemed everyone who was anyone was compelled to visit Opatija, including kings from Romania and Sweden, Russian tsars and celebrities of the day.

Today Opatija remains a refined (some would say conservative) resort, very popular with German and Austrian senior citizens. It's not the place for wild nights or round-the-clock clubbing, and that's just how the regulars like it.

◎ Sights

Croatian Museum of Tourism   MUSEUM
(Hrvatski Muzej Turizma; www.hrmt.hr; Park Angiolina 1; adult/concession 15/7KN; ⊙10am-8pm Apr-Jun, to 10pm Jul-Sep, shorter hours rest of the year) Spread between three historic buildings, this excellent museum houses a permanent collection of old photographs, postcards, brochures and posters tracing the history of tourism, and there's always a well-presented travel-themed exhibition as well. But really, it's the buildings themselves that are the main attraction. The restored **Villa Angiolina** is one of Opatija's grandest structures – a marvel of trompe l'œil frescoes, Corinthian capitals, gilded mirrors and geometric floor mosaics – though the addition of modern windows is a crime against architecture.

Verdant gardens surround the villa, replete with ginkgo trees, sequoias, holm oaks, Japanese camellia (Opatija's symbol) and even a little open-air theatre where costumed recitals are held. Neighbouring **Swiss House** (1875) was an outbuilding of the main villa, used partly as a buttery. Further west, past St James' Church, the **Juraj Šporer Artistic Pavillion** (1900) was originally built as a patisserie.

Lungomare   PROMENADE
Lined with majestic villas and ample gardens, this wonderful path (more formally known as the Franz Joseph I Promenade) is a people-watcher's dream and stroller's delight. It winds along the coast, past villa after villa, for 12km from Volosko to Lovran via the villages of Ičići and Ika. Along the way you can peer into the homes of the wealthy and marvel at their seafront palaces.

The path weaves through exotic bushes, thickets of bamboo, a marina and rocky bays where you can throw down a towel and jump into the sea – a better option than Opatija's concrete beach.

Volosko   VILLAGE
The former village of Volosko on the northern edge of Opatija is one of the prettiest places on this coastline and still maintains a local ambience. It's very scenic indeed – men repair fishing nets in the tiny harbour, while stone houses with flower-laden balconies rise up from the coast via a warren of narrow alleyways. From central Opatija it's best reached by a 2km, 30-minute stroll along Lungomare, past laurels, palms, fig trees, oaks and magnificent villas.

🎊 Festivals & Events

Festival Opatija   CULTURAL
(☑051-271 377; www.festivalopatija.hr; ⊙Jun-Sep) In the warmer months Opatija's open-air theatre by the waterfront plays host to live music (including classical, jazz and international pop acts), theatre, ballet and cinema.

🛏 Sleeping

There are few good budget or midrange hotels in Opatija and everything gets booked

KVARNER OPATIJA

WORTH A TRIP

GOING KUKURIKU IN KASTAV

Filled with stone churches and squares, Kastav is an atmospheric fortified hilltop town 10km from Rijeka and 7km from Opatija.

At slow-food pioneer Nenad Kukurin's wonderful hotel-restaurant **Kukuriku** (☑051-691 519; www.kukuriku.hr; Trg Lokvina 3; 6-course meal 400-580KN; ⊙7am-midnight; ℗✳🛜) there's no menu, so you need to be prepared to place your trust in the staff. Tell them whether you prefer meat, fish or vegetarian, and whether you have any particular dislikes or dietary requirements (or budget constraints). Then prepare for course after course of delicious, beautifully presented, innovative, local cuisine.

To top it all off there are 15 extremely chic rooms here – handy if you're planning to partake in the recommended matches from the excellent wine list. And if you're wondering about the rooster-themed paraphernalia scattered about, *kukuriku* is the Croatian take on 'cock-a-doodle-doo'.

up over summer and at Christmas, so reserve ahead. Private rooms are abundant but a touch pricier than in other seaside regions.

Autocamp Medveja   CAMPGROUND €

(☑ 051-710 444; www.remisens.com; Medveja bb; pitch for 3 people 400KN, unit 1050KN; ⊙ Easter– mid-Oct; P ✳ @) Given the lack of affordable hotels in Opatija, the new mobile homes and simple en suite rooms at this peaceful campground are worth considering. It's set in a cleft in the mountains in a leafy valley leading to a pretty pebbly cove, 10km south of Opatija. You can pay for full and half board and facilities are well maintained.

Borka   B&B €€

(☑ 051-712 118; Maršala Tita 192; s/d 420/525KN; 🖭) Just about the only cheapish formal accommodation provider in Opatija, this old B&B in a pink villa has basic rooms, brown-tiled bathrooms and a flower-filled garden. The owner's dog might annoy some.

★ Hotel Miramar   HOTEL €€€

(☑ 051-280 000; www.hotel-miramar.info; Ive Kaline 11; r from 1900KN; P ✳ @ 🖭 ☀) Marketed primarily to a German-speaking clientele, the Miramar is glam almost to the point of kitsch but fabulous nonetheless. The space-rich rooms are spread between five pastel buildings, set among lovely gardens, and there's a rocky little beach, indoor and outdoor pools, a spa centre and a surfeit of chandeliers.

Villa Ariston   HOTEL €€€

(☑ 051-271 379; www.villa-ariston.hr; Ulica Maršala Tita 179; s/d/ste 480/850/1300KN; P ✳ 🖭) With a gorgeous location beside a rocky cove, this historic hotel has celebrity cachet in spades (Coco Chanel and the Kennedys were former guests). The interior remains grand and impressive, with a sweeping staircase, chandeliers and plenty of period charm. Many have sea views, though the mansard rooms are a bit poky for these prices.

Hotel Mozart   HOTEL €€€

(☑ 051-718 260; www.hotel-mozart.hr; Obala Maršala Tita 138; s/d from 1100/1330KN; P ✳ 🖭 🎮 ☀) The beautifully decorated, classic rooms harmonise perfectly with the Secession-style halls, dining room and rosy facade in this centrally located vintage hotel. It has its own spa centre and fitness room, but some guests complain about the breakfast.

Villa Kapetanović   HOTEL €€€

(☑ 051-741 355; www.villa-kapetanovic.hr; Nova cesta 12a; r from 863KN; P ✳ 🖭 ☀) High on the hill above Volosko, this modern block offers 27 stylish rooms, extraordinary sea views, a fish restaurant and a particularly inviting outdoor pool area. A free shuttle takes the sting out of the walk from Opatija.

Hotel Ambasador   HOTEL €€€

(☑ 051-710 444; www.remisens.com; Feliksa Perišića 1; s/d 795/1245KN; P ✳ 🖭 ☀) A 10-storey tower, this one-time Yugoslav-era lumpen hotel is now a smart residence with 200 spacious rooms offering easy living and distracting views. The complex includes a spa centre, swimming pool, small beach terrace, bars and restaurants.

Design Hotel Astoria   HOTEL €€€

(☑ 051-706 350; www.hotel-astoria.hr; Ulica Maršala Tita 174; s/d 803/870KN; P ✳ 🖭) Bored with all that fussy Habsburg style? Then the 50 sleek, understated, subtly hued rooms here should fit the bill nicely. The balconies offer magnificent views of the Kvarner coast, there's a glass lobby bar and staff are as professional as you'll find in Croatia.

CYCLING THE KVARNER

The Kvarner region offers a variety of options for biking enthusiasts, from gentle rides to heart-pumping climbs on steep island roads. There are several trails around Opatija; two easier paths depart from Mt Kastav (360m), while a challenging 4½-hour adventure goes from Lovran to Učka Nature Park. Lošinj offers a moderately difficult 2½-hour route that starts and ends in Mali Lošinj. On Krk, a leisurely two-hour ride from Krk Town shows you meadows, fields and hamlets of the island's little-visited interior. A biking route from Rab Town explores the virgin forests of the Kalifront Peninsula. On Cres, a 50km trail takes you from the marina at Cres Town past the medieval hilltop village of Lubenice and the seaside gem of Valun.

For details of these itineraries, ask at any tourist office for the **Kvarner by Bicycle** brochure, which outlines 19 routes across the region. The websites www.kvarner.hr and www.pedala.hr both have details of rides in this region.

✗ Eating

Maršala Tita is lined with serviceable restaurants that offer pizza, grilled meat and fish, but don't expect anything particularly outstanding. Head to Volosko for fine dining and regional specialities.

✗ Central Opatija

Pizzeria Roko   PIZZA €€
(Maršala Tita 114; mains 35-90KN; ☺ 11am-midnight) Not just great wheels of heavily laden pizza, but risottos, salads, seafood and cakes are on offer at this rare treat of an affordable Opatija eatery. The food is imaginatively served, portions are large and the service superb. The dining room is simple whitewashed brick and the kitchen is open for anyone to view the food being prepared.

Istranka   ISTRIAN €€
(☎ 051-271 835; www.istranka.net; Bože Milanovića 2; mains 35-130KN) This atmospheric little family-run eatery specialises in Istrian cuisine such as maneštra (vegetable and bean soup) and, of course, you'll find plenty of truffles infusing the menu. There's a shady side terrace and live traditional folk music some evenings.

Kaneta   ISTRIAN €€
(☎ 051-291 643; www.kaneta.fullbusiness.com; Nova cesta 80; mains 50-100KN; ☺ 10am-11pm Mon-Sat, noon-7pm Sun) This unassuming family-run restaurant specialises in big flavours and generous portions: feast on roast veal shanks, roast octopus, game stew, turkey, homemade pasta and risotto. The wine list is well chosen.

Bevanda   MODERN EUROPEAN €€€
(☎ 051-493 888; www.bevanda.hr; Zert 8; mains 130-320KN) A marble pathway leads to this amazing-looking restaurant, which enjoys a huge ocean-facing terrace complete with Grecian columns and hip monochrome seating. The contemporary menu features terrific fresh fish and meat dishes, including lots of indulgences (lobster etc).

✗ Volosko

Konoba Ribarnica Volosko   SEAFOOD €
(☎ 051-701 483; Andrije Štangera 5; mains 45-90KN; ☺ 9am-9pm Mon-Sat, 11am-5pm Sun) If you're a hard-up seafood fan, this tiny, unpretentious shopfront has Volosko's cheapest fresh fish. Point to your desired sea creature – whatever is in season – and enjoy the superbly prepared dish in a small downstairs dining

room around the corner. It's located on the main village road, up from the harbour.

★ Konoba Valle Losca   CROATIAN €€
(☎ 095 58 03 757; Andrije Štangera 2; mains 60-100KN; ☺ 11.30am-2pm & 5pm-midnight) The word konoba usually denotes a little family-run eatery – most of which have identikit menus. Here, French and Italian techniques combine with top-notch local ingredients to take things to another level entirely. But don't come here if you're in a hurry – it takes time to fully savour the deliciously rustic dishes, served by multilingual staff in the stone-walled dining room.

Skalinada   CROATIAN €€
(☎ 051-701 109; www.skalinada.org; Put Uz Dol 17; snacks & mains from 25-130KN; ☺ 1pm-midnight Sun, Mon, Wed & Thu, 3pm-2am Fri & Sat) An intimate, highly atmospheric, wholly unpretentious little eatery/bar with sensitive lighting, exposed stone walls and a creative menu of Croatian food (small dishes or mains) using seasonal and local ingredients. Many local wines are available by the glass.

Tramerka   CROATIAN €€
(☎ 051-701 707; Andrije Mohorovičića 15; mains 50-120KN; ☺ 1pm-midnight Mon-Sat) Hidden away off the seafront, this wonderful tavern doesn't enjoy sea views but does score on every other level. Actually, the setting is tremendous; a cave-like restaurant that occupies the cool interior of an ancient town house. Staff will expertly guide you through the short menu, chosen from the freshest available seafood and locally sourced meats.

🍷 Drinking & Nightlife

Hemingway   COCKTAIL BAR
(www.hemingway.hr/opatija; Zert 2) A very sleek bar ideal for a cocktail session with cool seating and distant views of the Rijeka skyline. It's the original venue of what's now a nationwide chain; there's an adjoining restaurant too.

Caffe Bar Surf   BAR
(Supilova Obala bb; ☺ 8am-midnight) This scruffy but friendly little waterfront bar in Volosko has a shady sea-facing terrace and a good mix of Rijeka trendies and fishing folk.

ℹ Information

Da Riva (☎ 051-272 990; www.da-riva.hr; Nova cesta 10) A good source of private accommodation and excursions around Croatia.

Kvarner Touristik (☑ 051-703 723; www.
kvarner-touristik.com; Maršala Tita 162) Books
accommodation in Opatija and northern Croatia
as well as offering a range of activities and hire
services.

Post Office (Eugena Kumičića 4; ☺7am-8pm
Mon-Fri, to 2pm Sat mid-Sep–mid-Jun, to 8pm
Sat mid-Jun–mid-Sep) Behind the market.

Tourist Office (☑ 051-271 310; www.opatija-
tourism.hr; Maršala Tita 128; ☺8am-8pm
Mon-Sat, 11am-7pm Sun) This office has
knowledgeable staff and lots of maps, leaflets
and brochures.

ⓘ Getting There & Away

Bus 32 runs roughly every half-hour from Rijeka
to Opatija (16KN, 30 minutes) and as far as
Lovran; some continue further south along the
coast.

Other destinations include the following:

Pula 90KN, two hours, six daily

Rovinj 124KN, three hours, two daily

Zadar 135KN, five hours, daily

Zagreb 100KN, 3¼ hours, four daily

UČKA NATURE PARK

One of Croatia's best-kept natural secrets,
this 160-sq-km rarely visited park lies just
30 minutes from the Opatija Riviera. Comprised of the Učka mountain massif and the
adjacent Ćićarija plateau, it's officially split
between Kvarner and Istria. On clear days
Vojak (1401m), its highest peak, affords sublime views of the Italian Alps and the Bay
of Trieste.

Much of the area is covered by beech forest but there are also sweet chestnut trees,
oaks and hornbeams. Sheep graze the alpine
meadows, golden eagles fly overhead, brown
bears roam and endemic bellflowers blossom.

The main access point to the park is the
Poklon pass.

⊙ Sights

Vela Draga   CANYON

The spectacular canyon of Vela Draga on
the eastern side of the park is an astound-
ing sight, its valley floor scattered with limestone pillars or 'fairy chimneys'. Raptors,
including kestrels and peregrine falcons,
can be seen cruising the thermals here, and
eagle owls and wallcreepers are also present.
From the highway, it's a lovely 15-minute descent along an interpretive trail to a viewpoint over the canyon.

Mala Učka   VILLAGE

This half-abandoned village at over 995m
above sea level is an intriguing place. A few
shepherds live here from May to October and
you can buy delicious sheep's cheese from
the house with green windows by the stream
at the village's end. Just ask for *sir* (cheese).

🛏 Sleeping & Eating

There are seven guesthouses and weekend-
only mountain refuges within the park boundaries. See the park website (www.pp-ucka.hr)
for details.

Dopolavoro   CROATIAN €€

(☑ 051-299 641; www.dopolavoro.hr; Učka 9; mains
55-135KN; ☺noon-11pm) For country cooking,
Dopolavoro offers excellent game – deer
steak with blueberries, wild boar with forest
mushrooms, venison stew – as well as homemade pasta and delicious sweet platters.

ⓘ Information

Staff at the **park office** (☑ 051-293 753; www.
pp-ucka.hr; Liganj 42, Lovran; ☺8am-4.30pm
Mon-Fri) will help plan a trip. There are also two
seasonal info points, one at **Poklon** (☑ 051-299
643; ☺9am-6pm mid-Jun–mid-Sep) and another at **Vojak** (☑ 091 89 59 669; ☺9am-6pm
mid-Jun–mid-Sep).

ⓘ Getting There & Away

Two buses a day leave Opatija for Poklon
(9.30am and 2.05pm, returning 10.30am and
3.45pm). Lovran, on the eastern edge of the
park, is served by bus from Rijeka (32KN, 30
minutes, nine daily). There's a car park at the
Poklon pass information centre.

CRES & LOŠINJ ISLANDS

Separated only by an 11m-wide canal and
joined by a bridge, these two sparsely populated and highly scenic islands in the Kvarner archipelago are often treated as a single
entity. Although their topography is different, the islands' identities are blurred by a
shared history.

Nature lovers will be in heaven here. Both
islands are criss-crossed by hiking and biking trails, and the surrounding waters are
home to the only known resident population of dolphins in the Adriatic. Much of the
sea off the eastern coast is protected by the
Lošinj Dolphin Reserve, the first of its kind
in the entire Mediterranean.

THE HUNTERS & THE HUNTED

Cres' semiwild Tramuntana sheep are unique to the island and perfectly adapted to the karst pastures that were first developed by the Illyrians more than 1000 years ago. But now the island's culture of free-range sheep farming is on the slide. A couple of decades ago Cres had 100,000 Tramuntana sheep; now it's around 15,000. One of the main factors in this decline has been the introduction of wild boar by Croatia's powerful hunting lobby. Boar numbers have grown exponentially (they have even spread as far as the campsites in Mali Lošinj). Wild boar prey on sheep and lambs.

Declining sheep numbers have an impact on the environment in many ways. Griffon vultures now don't have enough sheep carrion to survive upon, and have to be fed at feeding sites by volunteers. As pastureland has dwindled, juniper and thornbush have replaced native grasses and wildflowers with a resulting drop in plant biodiversity. Low stone walls used by sheep farmers called *gromače* used to criss-cross Cres, acting as windbreaks and preventing soil erosion, but these are no longer maintained and many are crumbling away.

Wilder, greener Cres (Cherso in Italian) has remote camping grounds, pristine beaches, a handful of medieval villages and a real off-the-beaten-track feel. The 31km-long Lošinj (Lussino in Italian) is more populated, touristy and offers more lush vegetation.

History

Excavations indicate that a prehistoric culture spread out over both Lošinj Island and Cres Island from the Stone Age to the Bronze Age. The ancient Greeks called the islands the Apsyrtides. They were in turn conquered by the Romans, then put under Byzantine rule and settled by Slavic tribes in the 6th and 7th centuries.

The islands subsequently came under Venetian rule, followed by that of the Croatian-Hungarian kings, then back to the Venetians. By the time Venice fell in 1797, Veli Lošinj and Mali Lošinj had become important maritime centres, while Cres devoted itself to wine and olive production.

During the 19th century shipbuilding flourished in Lošinj, but with the advent of steamships it was replaced by health tourism as the major industry. Meanwhile, Cres had its own problems in the form of a phylloxera epidemic that wiped out its vineyards. Both islands were poor when they were annexed to Italy as part of the 1922 Treaty of Rapallo. They became part of Yugoslavia in 1945 and, most recently, Croatia in 1991.

Today, apart from a small shipyard in Nerezine in north Lošinj and some olive cultivation, sheep farming and fishing on Cres, the main source of income on both islands is tourism. Until very recently one of Cres' main income sources was rearing sheep (the island's lamb is famed for its flavour) but the introduction of wild boar for hunting has upset the unique environment and an age-old culture is now waning.

❶ Getting There & Away

BOAT

The main maritime port of entry for the islands is Mali Lošinj, which is connected to Rijeka, Pula, Zadar, Venice and Koper in summer.

Jadrolinija (☑ 051-231 765; www.jadrolinija. hr; Riva Lošinjskih Kapetana 22, Mali Lošinj) runs the main car ferries between Brestova (on the mainland, 29km south of Opatija) and Porozina on Cres (adult/child/car 18/9/115KN, 20 minutes, seven to 13 daily); and between Valbiska on Krk and Merag on Cres (adult/child/car 18/9/115KN, 25 minutes, nine to 13 daily).

A weekly (daily in July and August) car ferry runs between Mali Lošinj and Zadar (adult/child/car 59/30/271KN, seven hours), stopping at some of the smaller islands en route.

There's also a passenger-only ferry which loops from Mali Lošinj to the islands of Unije (1½ hours) and Susak (one hour) twice daily.

UTO Kapetan Luka (☑ 021-645 476; www. krilo.hr) has daily passenger-only ferries from Rijeka to Cres Town (45KN, 1¼ hours) and Mali Lošinj (60KN, three to 4½ hours) year-round, some of which also stop at Martinšćica (50KN, two hours). Some of these boats also stop at the islands of Unije, Susak and Ilovik.

BUS

Most bus services in the islands begin (or end) in Veli Lošinj and stop in Mali Lošinj and Cres. Off-island destinations include Malinska on Krk (126KN, 2½ hours, four daily), Opatija (142KN, 3¾ hours, two daily), Rijeka (149KN, four hours, four daily) and Zagreb (183KN, six hours, four daily).

Beli

🎵 051 / POP 35

Clinging to a 130m hill above a lovely pebbly beach, Beli is one of Cres' oldest settlements. Its 4000-year history can be felt in its twisting lanes and austere stone town houses overgrown with plants. You can walk a loop around this evocative but diminutive settlement in five minutes or so, stopping at a viewpoint to take in incredible vistas over the Adriatic to the mainland mountains.

Even with its tiny population, Beli is the main settlement in the Tramuntana region, which covers the island's northern tip. It's a place that time forgot, with ancient virgin forests, abandoned villages, lone chapels and myths of good elves. Much of it is covered with dense oak, hornbeam and chestnut forest and it's prime cruising terrain for the protected griffon vulture.

🏃 Activities

Diving Beli   DIVING

(📞 051-840 519; www.diving-beli.com; beach/boat dives 110/190KN) Based at the beach below Beli, this tiny local outfit offers boat- and beach-based dive trips; nondivers can come along too.

🛌 Sleeping & Eating

Autokamp Brajdi   CAMPGROUND €

(📞 051-840532; www.perica666.wix.com/autokamp-brajdi; Beli bb; per adult/child 75/40KN; ⊙May-Sep; 🅿🐾) Situated in an olive grove right by the beach, this is a pretty spot to pitch a tent but the facilities are fairly basic. There's a summertime snack bar nearby.

Pansion Tramontana   B&B €€

(📞 051-840 519; www.beli-tramontana.com; s/d 342/600KN; ⊙Mar-Dec; 🅿✳@📶) On the approach to Beli, this attractive place has 12 comfortable rooms upstairs and a fine rustic restaurant (mains 55KN to 120KN) below, where great chunks of meat are barbecued. Fish, pasta, risotto and superb organic salads are available too. Staff can also organise various adventure activities, from griffon watching to mountain climbing.

Konoba Beli   CROATIAN €€

(www.beli-cres.com; Beli 6; mains 45-120KN; ⊙10am-10pm) The stone dining room bedecked with the agricultural implements of yesteryear creates a suitably rustic setting in which to enjoy locally flavoured grilled fish and meat dishes.

When the mercury pushes north, take a seat on the large terrace.

ⓘ Getting There & Away

You'll need a car to reach Beli.

Cres Town

🎵 051 / POP 2960

Pastel-hued terrace houses and Venetian mansions embrace the medieval harbour of Cres Town, a beautiful sheltered bay wrapped in vivid green hills of pine and Adriatic scrubs. As you amble along the seaside promenade and explore the atmospheric maze of old-town streets, you cannot fail to notice reminders of Italian rule, including coats of arms of powerful Venetian families and Renaissance loggias.

The town's strong Italian influence dates to the 15th century when Venetians relocated here after Osor fell victim to plague and pestilence. Public buildings and patricians' palaces were built along the harbour and a town wall was added in the 16th century.

⊙ Sights

Trg Frane Petrića   SQUARE

Right by the harbour, the main town square was the scene of public announcements, financial transactions and festivals under Venetian rule. It's now the site of a morning fruit-and-vegetable market. Look for the graceful 16th-century **gate**, topped by a blue-faced clock and coats of arms.

St Mary of the Snow Church   CHURCH

(Sv Marije Snježne; Trg Frane Petrića; ⊙Mass only) Just inside the main harbour gate, this church's facade is notable for the Renaissance portal with a relief of the Virgin and Child. A glassed-in foyer allows you to peer inside but the church is only open during Mass. If you do find it open, look for the carved wooden pietà from the 15th century (now under protective glass) at the left altar.

Cres Museum   MUSEUM

(Creski Muzej; Ribarska 7; 10KN; ⊙9am-1pm & 7-11pm Tue-Sun mid-Jun–mid-Sep, 9am-noon Tue-Sat Apr–mid-Jun & mid-Sep–mid-Oct) Housed in the Arsan Renaissance palace just off the harbour front, this local museum is worth the modest entry fee for its 16th-century Venetian architecture and its displays on various aspects of local life.

🏃 Activities

There's an attractive promenade on the west side of the bay with sunbathing zones and good swimming, plus good beaches around Hotel Kimen. Drop by the tourist office for a map of walking and cycling trails around Cres.

Diving Cres   DIVING
(☑ 051-571 706; www.divingcres.de; Melin 1/20; boat dive incl equipment €49) Based in Kamp Kovačine, this German crew offers PADI and SSI courses and wreck dives.

🛏 Sleeping

For the cheapest accommodation, contact travel agencies for private room rentals. Single rooms in Cres Town start at around 250KN, doubles cost from 300KN.

Kamp Kovačine   CAMPGROUND €
(☑ 051-573 150; www.camp-kovacine.com; Melin 1/20; camping per adult/site 104/100KN, s/d 405/743KN, cabin 690KN; ☺ Easter–mid-Oct; 🅿@🛜) With a fine location on the tip of a little wooded peninsula about 1km southwest of town, this large campsite offers excellent shower blocks, beachside bathing platforms, a restaurant and activities galore. A quarter of the area is reserved for naturists, including some of the beach. Private rooms are available in Tamaris, a small guesthouse near the water.

Villa Neho   B&B €€
(☑ 051-571 868; www.villaneho.com; Zazid 5; r 675KN; ❄🛜) This guesthouse just back from the harbour front offers smart, crisp but smallish rooms with trendy features. Though it lacks any local colour, the standards are a cut above the normal Croatian B&B niveau, breakfast is a substantial affair and half board is available for a reasonable 110KN a day. Cash only.

Hotel Kimen   HOTEL €€€
(☑ 051-573 305; www.hotel-kimen.com; Melin 1/16; s/d from 650/945KN; 🅿❄🛜♿) With a prime spot by a beach and grounds pleasantly shaded by pine trees, this large Yugoslav-era 128-room slab was comprehensively renovated a decade or so ago and offers fresh-looking rooms with balconies. Rooms in the neighbouring 'Depandance' are cheaper, but the main hotel is much nicer.

🍴 Eating

Gostionica Belona   CROATIAN €€
(Šetalište 23, Travnja 24; mains 55-150KN; ☺ 11am-11pm) This excellent local tavern plates up Cres

A VILLAGE FEAST

Cres lamb gets the top billing at **Konoba Bukaleta** (☑ 051-571 606; Loznati 99; mains 40-100KN; ☺ noon-11pm Apr-Sep), a down-to-earth village restaurant, which has been run by the same family for more than three decades. Try it breaded, grilled or roasted on the spit, or tuck into homemade gnocchi and pasta instead. Bukaleta is in Loznati, 5km south of Cres Town, and signposted from the highway. It also rents rooms.

seafood, lamb dishes, grilled meat and salads. The roadside terrace isn't in the prettiest location, so try instead for a seat indoors. It has excellent service, a good Croatian wine card and it's just a short walk from the harbour.

Riva   SEAFOOD €€
(☑ 051-571 107; Riva Creskih Kapetana 13; mains 60-110KN; ☺ 11am-midnight) This well-established place spills onto the harbourside promenade and is the local choice for fish and seafood: scampi, squid and prawns.

ℹ Information

Cresanka (☑ 051-750 600; www.cresanka.hr; Varozina 25) This local travel agency books private rooms, apartments, campsites and hotels.

Post Office (Cons 3; ☺ 7.30am-9pm Mon-Sat Jun-Sep, 7am-8pm Mon-Fri, to 2pm Sat Sep-May)

Tourist Agency Croatia (☑ 051-573 053; www.cres-travel.com; Cons 10; ☺ 8am-1pm & 4-7pm Mon-Sat, 10am-1pm Sun) This travel agency arranges private accommodation, offers internet access and hires boats, bikes, cars and scooters.

Tourist Office (☑ 051-571 535; www.tzg-cres.hr; Cons 11; ☺ 8am-noon & 3.30-8pm Mon-Sat, 9am-1pm Sun Jun-Aug, 8am-2pm Mon-Fri Sep-May) Well stocked with maps and brochures, including accommodation listings with photographs.

ℹ Getting There & Away

Cres has the following bus connections:
Mali Lošinj 60KN, 1¼ hours, six daily
Osor 42KN, 45 minutes, six daily
Rijeka 105KN, two hours 20 minutes, four daily
Valun 30KN, 22 minutes, daily
Veli Lošinj 65KN, 1½ hours, six daily

ℹ Getting Around

Gonzo Bikes (☑ 051-573 107; Turion 8; per hr/day 25/100KN; ☺ Mar-Dec) Rents out good-quality bikes and camping equipment from its Cres base, as well as bikes from Hotel Kimen (p151) and various campgrounds.

Valun

⬛ 051 / POP 65

The pretty seaside hamlet of Valun, 14km southwest of Cres Town, is secluded at the foot of cliffs and surrounded by pebbly beaches. Its appeal lies in its tranquillity: its restaurants are rarely crowded, and there's a refreshing lack of souvenir stalls or touristy tack.

Park in the lot above the village and take the steep steps down. To the right of the harbour, a path leads to a beach and camping ground. About 700m in the other direction there's another lovely pebble beach bordered by pines.

⊙ Sights

St Mary's Church CHURCH
(Crkva Sv Marije; ⊙varies) The parish church houses the village's main sight, the 11th-century Valun Tablet. Inscribed in both Glagolitic and Latin, this tombstone reflects the ethnic composition of the island, which was inhabited by Roman descendants and newcomers who spoke Croatian. Sadly, the church's opening hours are erratic.

🛏 Sleeping & Eating

Camping Zdovice CAMPGROUND €
(⬛ 051-571 161; per adult/child 110/50KN; ⊙May-Sep; 🏊) This idyllic campsite is a small affair with pitches occupying old terraced fields right by a great swimming beach. There's also a volleyball court and a clean toilet block.

BEACHSIDE CAMPING

Tucked away on the west coast of Cres near a nondescript fishing village called Martinšćica, **Campsite Slatina** (⬛051-661 124; www.camps-cres-losinj.com; camping per adult/site from €67/63, unit from 850KN; ⊙May-Sep) offers access to two lovely pebbly beaches. The complex includes restaurants, a pizzeria, cafes, a grocery shop, a dive school, and boat and bike hire. Despite its large size (500 sites), it's well spaced out and doesn't feel too cramped.

There's a minimum seven-night stay in July and August.

The Cresanka (p151) agency in Cres Town deals with bookings.

Konoba Toš-Juna SEAFOOD €€
(mains 45-100KN; ⊙10am-11pm) Of Valun's half a dozen restaurants, this one stands out for its seafood and attractive terrace emblazoned with Glagolitic writing. It's inside a converted olive mill with exposed stone walls, right by the harbour and the church.

ⓘ Getting There & Away

Valun is not well served by public transport. Buses head to and from Cres Town (30KN, 20 minutes) on Monday, Wednesday and Friday in summer, with even fewer services in winter.

Lubenice

⬛ 051 / POP 24

Perched on an exposed rocky ridge, 378m above the western shore of the island, this medieval hilltop hamlet is one of the most evocative places on Cres Island. Semi-abandoned, Lubenice's maze of ancient austere, stone-built houses and churches seems fused to the very bedrock of the island itself.

It sits above one of Kvarner's most remote and beautiful beaches, a secluded cove accessible by a steep path through the bush. The 45-minute descent is a breeze, but coming up is more of a challenge (you might want to take a taxi boat from Valun or Cres).

🎉 Festivals & Events

Lubenice Musical Evenings MUSIC
(Lubeničke Glazbene Večeri; ⊙Jul-Aug) Atmospheric alfresco concerts of classical music are held every Friday night in July and August.

🍴 Eating

Konoba Hibernicia CROATIAN €
(Lubenice 17; mains 45-100KN; ⊙noon-10pm) Extremely rustic, with stone walls and an outdoor terrace popular with the village cats, this humble eatery is notable for its lamb dishes and local ham.

ⓘ Getting There & Away

If you have the time and the inclination, the best way to get here is on foot: it's a one-hour hike from Valun.

If you're driving up, note that the road is narrow and winding.

In summer, two daily buses connect Lubenice with Cres Town (34KN, 30 minutes), but not on Sundays.

Osor

📖 051 / POP 60

The tiny walled town of Osor is one of the most peaceful places you could imagine, despite its grand and troubled past. The village sits on the narrow channel dividing Cres and Lošinj, which is thought to have been dug by the Romans. Because of it, Osor was able to control a key navigational route.

In the 6th century a bishopric was established here, with authority over both islands throughout the Middle Ages. Until the 15th century Osor was a strong commercial, religious and political presence in the region, but a combination of plague, malaria and new sea routes devastated the town's economy and it slowly decayed.

Today it's becoming a kind of museum-town of churches, open-air sculptures and lanes that meander from its 15th-century town centre. Look out for the Ivan Meštrović statue *Daleki Akordi* (Distant Chords), one of the town's many modern sculptures on a musical theme.

⊙ Sights

Entering through the gate on the canal, you pass old city walls and the remains of a castle before you hit the centre of town.

Church of the Assumption　　CHURCH
(Crkva Uznešenja; ⊙10am-noon & 7-9pm Jun-Sep) Completed in 1498, this large church's rich Renaissance portal faces on to the main square. The baroque altar inside has relics of St Gaudentius, Osor's patron saint.

Osor
Archaeological Collection　　MUSEUM
(Arheološka Zbirka Osor; www.muzej.losinj.hr; Gradska vijećnica; adult/child 35/25KN; ⊙10am-1pm & 7-10pm Tue-Sun mid-Jun–mid Sep, 9am-2pm Tue-Sat Easter–mid-Jun & mid-Sep–Oct) On the main square in the 15th-century town hall, this outpost of the Lošinj Museum contains a collection of stone fragments, reliefs, ceramics and sculptures from the Roman, early Christian and medieval periods.

✰ Festivals & Events

Osor Musical Evenings　　MUSIC
(Osorske Glazbene Večeri; www.osorfestival.eu; ⊙mid-Jul–mid-Aug) Well into its fifth decade, this festival sees high-calibre Croatian artists perform classical music in the cathedral and on the main square.

🍴 Sleeping & Eating

The tourist office (p156) in Mali Lošinj has listings of private rooms and apartments.

Camping Bijar　　CAMPGROUND €
(📞051-237 147; www.camps-cres-losinj.com; per adult/site 67/79KN; ⊙May-Sep; 🅿🛜) Set among the pines on a lovely pebbly cove 500m from Osor, this attractive campground offers fabulous swimming as well as table tennis, volleyball and basketball. There's also a restaurant and wi-fi at reception.

Konoba Bonifačić　　CROATIAN €€
(Osor 64; mains 50-110KN; ⊙noon-11pm) Tuck into home-cooking – such as dependable risottos, grilled meat and fish, and traditional pork with sage – in a particularly lovely garden setting. Have a shot of elderflower grappa while you're at it.

❶ Getting There & Away

Depending on the time of the year and the day of the week, between two and eight buses a day pass through Osor en route to Cres Town (42KN, 45 minutes), Nerezine (19KN, five minutes), Mali Lošinj (35KN, 30 minutes) and Veli Lošinj (38KN, 45 minutes).

When crossing from Lošinj to Osor by car you may have to wait at the drawbridge spanning the Kavuada Canal – the bridge is raised twice a day (at 9am and 5pm) to allow boats to pass.

Nerezine

📖 051 / POP 400

The first town on the Lošinj side of the bridge, little Nerezine has a pretty harbour lined with pastel houses and a few cafe-bars. It's Lošinj's third-biggest settlement, with a whopping great population of 400. All buses heading along the main highway stop here, and if you are travelling by car it makes a relaxing halt between Rijeka, Cres and all points south. There's little to actually do here other than grab a coffee or lunch and watch the Adriatic world go by.

🍴 Sleeping & Eating

Hotel Manora　　HOTEL €€€
(📞051-237 460; www.manora-losinj.hr; Magdalenska 26b; s/d 615/1290KN; 🅿❄🛜🏊👶) Hidden in the outskirts of Nerezine, cheerful Hotel Manora is brightly painted inside and out, and well set up for families. There's a beautiful swimming pool, a sauna, an outdoor playground and even an indoor playroom for

KVARNER OSOR

when the weather turns bad. Rooms have attractive parquet floors and stylish lighting.

Konoba Bonaparte CROATIAN €€
(Trg Studenac 1; mains 40-140KN; ⊙ 11am-11pm) The best place to eat during a stopover in Nerezine is this cosy, rustically themed tavern on the town's main square. If you don't fancy the net-fresh fish and seafood dishes, the steaks and schnitzel are superb. Bookings may be necessary for dinner in July and August.

❶ Getting There & Away

Nerezine has the following bus connections:
Cres 44KN, one hour, seven daily
Mali Lošinj 32KN, 30 minutes, eight daily
Rijeka 149KN, three to 3½ hours, four daily
Veli Lošinj 35KN, 40 minutes, eight daily

Mali Lošinj

📋 051 / POP 8116

Mali Lošinj is a stunner: a natural harbour ringed by graceful, gently weathered Mediterranean town houses and green surrounding hills. The town straddles both coasts on the narrowest section of the island, at the apex of a long protected harbour. A string of imposing 19th-century sea captains' houses lines the seafront, and even with the summer tourist commotion, this historic quarter still retains its charm and atmosphere.

You'll find the resort hotels just out of town by the pebbly beaches **Sunčana Uvala** (meaning 'Sunny Bay') and **Čikat**. This leafy area started to flourish in the late 19th century, when the wealthy Vienna and Budapest elite, who gravitated to the 'healthy air' of Mali Lošinj, started building villas and luxurious hotels around Čikat. Some of these grand residences remain, but most of the current hotels are modern developments surrounded by pine forests.

◉ Sights

Fritzy Palace MUSEUM
(Palača Fritzy; www.muzej.losinj.hr; Vladimira Gortana 35; adult/concession 35/25KN; ⊙ 10am-1pm & 4-10pm Tue-Sun Jul & Aug, shorter hours rest of the year) The largest branch of the three-headed Lošinj Museum (the others are in Osor, p153 and Veli Lošinj, p157), this grand mansion houses a trio of distinct collections: a moderately interesting set of mainly 17th- and 18th-century paintings; a more interesting array of early-20th-century

photographs; and a fascinating display of 20th-century art.

The most intriguing exhibit is one of the smallest: a 10cm-high, possibly Etruscan, clay statue dating from the 7th century BC, known as the 'Lady of Čikat'. In the modern section, look out for works by Croatia's three most important 20th-century sculptors: Ivan Meštrović, Frano Kršinić and Antun Augustinčić.

Church of the Nativity CHURCH
(Župna Crkva Male Gospe; Sv Marije bb) The parish church (built 1696–1775) towers over the town from the ridge. Inside are some notable artworks, including a painting of the Nativity by an 18th-century Venetian artist, and relics of St Romulus. It's usually only open during Mass.

Garden of Fine Scents GARDENS
(Miomirisni Otočki Vrt; www.miomirisni-vrt.hr; Bukovica 6; ⊙ 8.30am-12.30pm & 6-9pm Jul & Aug, 8am-3pm Mar-Jun & Sep-Dec) **FREE** This fragrant paradise on the southern edge of town has more than 250 native plant varieties plus 100 exotic species, all framed with *gromače* (traditional stone fences). Natural fragrances, salts and liquors are sold too.

Sea Turtle Rescue Centre WILDLIFE CENTRE
(Oporavilište za Morske Kornjače; www.blue-world.org; Sunčana Uvala bb; ⊙ 10am-2pm Mon-Fri Jun-Sep) 🅿 **FREE** Small but extremely interesting, this centre is dedicated to rehabilitating injured sea turtles, most of which have been entangled in plastic or fishing nets. There aren't a lot of displays but the staff on hand will talk you through their work. You might even get to see some of the patients. It's located between the Adriatic and Vespera hotels, just up from the promenade.

🏃 Activities

Cycling and **hiking** have become increasingly popular on Lošinj. The tourist office (p156) has an excellent brochure, *Promenades and Footpaths,* with maps of 250km of trails and accurate walking times. All five islands of the archipelago (Lošinj, Cres, Ilovik, Susak and Unije) are covered. Climb the highest peak of Televrina (589m) for great views, hike to the remote coves south of Mali Lošinj, or access secret bays on Susak.

Diver Sport Center DIVING
(📋 051-233 900; www.diver.hr) Lošinj has good diving with excellent visibility and good sea life. There's a wreck dating from 1917, a large, relatively shallow cave suitable for begin-

ners, and the wonderful Margarita Reef off the island of Susak. Based by the water at Čikat, this centre offers a 'Discovery' course and the SSI Open Water certification.

Sunbird WINDSURFING, SAILING
(🖉 095 83 77 142; www.sunbird.de) Čikat is a good spot for windsurfing, with its narrow shingle beach and great wind exposure. This German outfit, based on the beach near the Hotel Bellevue, offers courses in windsurfing (from 970KN) and sailing catamarans (from 675KN). It also rents windsurfers (from 60KN per hour), kayaks (per hour/day 35/150KN) and bikes (20/95KN).

🛏 Sleeping

Camping Village Poljana CAMPGROUND €
(🖉 051-231 726; www.campingpoljana.com; Rujnica 9a; camping per pitch 160KN, units from 550KN; 🅿 ❄ 🛜) Surrounded by mature trees, this complex on the northern approach to Mali Lošinj has power-fitted pitches, good air-conditioned units, a restaurant and a supermarket. There is also a small pebble beach and a rocky area for nude bathers.

Alaburić B&B €
(🖉 051-231 343; Stjepana Radića 17; r from 430KN; 🅿 🛜 🍽) This welcoming family-run guesthouse has simple, well-equipped rooms and

apartments, all with bathrooms – two have distant sea views. It's in a suburban street just below the Garden of Fine Scents (p154). Breakfast is 50KN extra.

★ Mare Mare Suites HOTEL €€€
(🖉 051-232 010; www.mare-mare.com; Riva Lošinjskih Kapetana 36; s/d/apt 900/950/1350KN; 🅿 ❄ @ 🛜) Enjoying a prime position towards the northern end of the harbour, this historic town house has been converted into immaculately presented, individually styled rooms and an apartment with a private terrace. There's a rooftop spa pool and free use of kayaks and bikes.

Hotel Aurora RESORT €€€
(🖉 051-667 200; www.losinj-hotels.com; Sunčana Uvala bb; s/d from 950/1260KN; 🅿 ❄ @ 🛜 ⛱ ♿) 🏊 This former state-owned behemoth is now the very model of a modern-day resort hotel. Rooms are decorated in sunny shades and each has its own balcony. If you're not tempted by the brilliant blue waters of the beach below, there are indoor and outdoor pools, and a popular spa centre with wellness procedures on offer.

Hotel Vespera RESORT €€€
(🖉 051-667 300; www.losinj-hotels.com; Sunčana Uvala bb; s/d from 1000/1300KN; 🅿 ❄ 🛜 ⛱ ♿)

KVARNER MALI LOŠINJ

WORTH A TRIP

ISLANDS AROUND LOŠINJ

The nearby car-free islands of Susak, Ilovik and Unije are the most popular day trips from Mali Lošinj. Tiny **Susak** (population 151, area 3.8 sq km) is unique for the thick layer of fine sand that blankets the underlying limestone and creates excellent beaches. It's the island's unusual culture that makes it particularly interesting. Islanders speak their own dialect, which is nearly incomprehensible to other Croats. On feast days and at weddings you can see the local women outfitted in traditional multicoloured skirts (a little like tutus) and red leggings. When you see the old stone houses on the island, consider that each stone had to be brought over from Mali Lošinj and carried by hand to its destination. The island has steadily lost its population in the last few decades (it was more than 1600 in 1948), with many of its citizens settling in Hoboken, New Jersey.

In contrast to flat Susak, **Ilovik** (population 85, area 5.8 sq km) is a hilly island known for its profusion of flowers. Overgrown with oleanders, roses and eucalyptus trees, it's popular with boaters and has some secluded swimming coves.

The largest of the islands, **Unije** (population 88, area 18 sq km) has an undulating landscape that abounds with Mediterranean shrubs, pebble beaches and numerous coves and inlets. The island's only settlement is a picturesque fishing village of gabled stone houses.

Travel agencies in Mali Lošinj sell excursions to the islands or you can peruse the boats moored along the harbour and see which deal takes your fancy.

Otherwise, Jadrolinija has a passenger-only ferry which loops from Mali Lošinj to Unije (1½ hours) and Susak (one hour) twice daily. Most of UTO Kapetan Luka's daily Rijeka/Cres Town/Martinšćica/Mali Lošinj ferries also service the islands, stopping at Unije and Susak five days a week and at Ilovik on two.

Very much a family-friendly resort, this huge hotel offers excellent facilities including tennis courts, a large resort-style pool and two smaller kids' pools, plus the beach is right at its doorstep. Recently renovated rooms have bright colour schemes and contemporary lighting.

✕ Eating & Drinking

Konoba Dišpet
CROATIAN €€

(☑091 56 91 955; Sv Martin 10; mains 45-160KN; ⊙11am-2pm & 6pm-midnight daily) Regaled in rural knick-knackery, the Dišpet specialises in all kinds of barbecued meat and fish, stews and traditional Croatian pastas. If you are really hungry, go for the seafood platter for two, a veritable 3D encyclopedia of local sea life.

Baracuda
CROATIAN, SEAFOOD €€

(☑051-233 309; Priko 31; mains 60-140KN; ⊙noon-midnight) The cosy and elegant Baracuda is highly rated for the freshness of its fish, the skill of its chefs and the cheeky charm of the waiting staff. There's a large terrace and usually a daily special or two chalked up on the blackboard. Much of the fish is priced per kilo.

Porto
CROATIAN, SEAFOOD €€

(Sv Martin 33; mains 45-120KN; ⊙8am-11pm) Up over the hill on the east side of town, this fine, family-run seafood buffet enjoys a pretty bay location next to a church. Fish fillet with sea urchins is the signature dish, but all seafood is expertly prepared and presented.

WORTH A TRIP

A COVE OF YOUR OWN

South of Mali Lošinj the island forms a glorious, barely inhabited, thumb-shaped peninsula that's blessed with exquisite natural bays and is perfect for hiking; pick up a map from the **tourist office**. One lonely road snakes down the spine of this hilly, wooded land mass, eventually fizzling out at Mrtvaška, Lošinj's land's end. You can circumnavigate the entire peninsula on foot in a full day, stopping to swim at deserted coves. If you only want to hit one beach, drive 5km to the turn-off for **Krivica**. It's a 30-minute descent from the parking area to this idyllic, sheltered bay, which is ringed by pine trees. The water is emerald-tinged and superb for swimming.

Konoba Cigale
CROATIAN €€

(☑051-238 583; Sabina Hausknecht bb; mains 70-140KN; ⊙9am-10pm) With a large terrace overlooking the briny at Čikat, this laid-back eatery makes a good job of the usual selection of grilled meat, seafood, pasta and salads. The homemade pasta with truffles is excellent, and if there's a group of you and you call ahead, it will cook lamb under a *peka* (traditional domed baking lid).

Priko
BAR

(Priko 2; ⊙11am-11pm Mon-Thu, to late Fri & Sat; ☎) On summer evenings the terrace of this harbourside bar is the place to be, with live music on most nights.

❶ Information

Cappelli (☑051-231 582; www.cappelli-tourist. hr; Lošinjskih Brodograditelja 57) Travel agency that books private accommodation on Cres and Lošinj, and offers cruises and excursions.

Manora (☑051-520 100; www.manora-losinj. hr; Priko 29) Friendly agency associated with Nerezine's Hotel Manora, which hires scooters and mountain bikes.

Post Office (Vladimira Gortana 4; ⊙7.30am-9pm Mon-Sat Jun-Aug, 7am-8pm Mon-Fri, to 2pm Sat Sep-May)

Sanmar (☑051-238 293; Priko 24) Travel agency which rents private accommodation, mountain bikes (per day 70KN), mopeds (250KN) and boats (from 1000KN; licence required). It also exchanges foreign currencies.

Tourist Office (☑051-231 884; www.visitlosinj. hr; Priko 42) ⊙8am-8pm Mon-Sat, 9am-1pm Sun Jun-Sep, 8am-3pm Mon-Fri Oct-May) A very useful office, with knowledgeable staff and tonnes of (practical and glossy) leaflets and maps, plus a comprehensive accommodation list with owners' emails and websites.

❶ Getting There & Away

Island buses head to/from Veli Lošinj (12KN, 12 minutes, at least hourly), Nerezine (32KN, 30 minutes, two to nine daily), Osor (32KN, 20 to 30 minutes, eight daily) and Cres Town (60KN, 1¼ hours, seven daily).

UTO Kapetan Luka has daily passenger-only ferries to/from Cres Town (45KN, three hours) and Rijeka (60KN, four hours).

❶ Getting Around

Between late April and mid-October there's an hourly shuttle bus (10KN) that runs from the town centre to the hotel district in Sunčana Uvala and Čikat.

Note that you have to pay to enter the centre of Mali Lošinj in a car (two hours 20KN).

KVARNER MALI LOŠINJ

Veli Lošinj

⏺ 051 / POP 900

Despite the name (in Croatian, *veli* means big and *mali* means small), Veli Lošinj is much smaller, more languid and somewhat less crowded than Mali Lošinj, only 4km to the northwest. It's an exceptionally scenic place, really nothing more than a huddle of pastel-coloured houses, cafes, hotels and stores around a tiny harbour. Dolphins sometimes enter the narrow mouth of the bay in April and May. Don't miss a walk to Rovenska, another idyllic little bay, a 10-minute stroll along a coastal path to the southeast.

Like its neighbour, Veli Lošinj had its share of rich sea captains who built villas and surrounded them with gardens of exotic plants they brought back from afar. You can glimpse these villas on a walk up the steep streets from the harbour.

◉ Sights

Church of St Anthony the Hermit   CHURCH
(Obala Maršala Tita) Built in baroque style in 1774 and funded by local seafarers, this pretty pink church is elaborately decked out with marble altars, a rich collection of Italian paintings (including on the ceiling), a pipe organ and relics of St Gregory. It's normally only open for Sunday Mass but you can catch a glimpse of the interior through its metal gate.

Tower Museum   MUSEUM
(Kula-Lošinjski Muzej; adult/concession 35/25KN; ⏺10am-1pm & 4-10pm Tue-Sun Jul & Aug, 10am-1pm Tue-Sat Easter-Jun & Sep) This striking defence tower, in the maze of streets set back from the harbour, was built by the Venetians in 1455 to defend the town from pirates. It now contains a branch of the Lošinj Museum (the other being in Mali Lošinj; p154), dedicated to the island's maritime history. Browse the Roman ceramic fragments, sabres and old postcards before climbing up to the battlements for unrivalled views of the old town.

**Lošinj Marine
Education Centre**   WILDLIFE CENTRE
(⏺051-604 666; www.blue-world.org; Kaštel 24; adult/concession 15/10KN; ⏺10am-9pm Jul & Aug, 10am-4pm Mon-Fri, to 2pm Sat May, Jun & Sep, 10am-2pm Mon-Fri Oct-Mar) 🐟 A companion piece to Blue World's practical conservation work, this enlightening attraction aims to educate locals and visitors about the marine environment and the threats it's facing. Inside its swanky modern centre there's

a highly informative video (in a variety of languages), the vertebra of an 11m fin whale (a baby) and some multimedia displays, including an acoustic room where you can hear dolphin click communications.

🛏 Sleeping

Youth Hostel Veli Lošinj   HOSTEL €
(⏺051-236 234; www.hfhs.hr; Kaciol 4; dm 129KN; ⏺May-Oct; 🛜) One of Croatia's best YHA-associated hostels, this converted town house has a friendly vibe and hospitable management. Dorms (all with lockers) are spacious, the pine-trimmed private rooms are quite classy and the front terrace is a great place to meet up for an evening beer.

Pansion Saturn   B&B €€
(⏺051-236 102; www.val-losinj.hr; Obala Maršala Tita bb; r 550KN; ❄🛜) A recent renovation has left some rather odd bubbly gold walls (a space theme, perhaps?) but Saturn's eight rooms are spacious and the bathrooms are modern. It's above a popular terrace bar, so pack earplugs if you don't want to join the party. There's a hefty 100KN supplement for one-nighters in July and August, but breakfast is included in rates.

Villa Mozart   B&B €€
(⏺051-236 262; Kaciol 3; r 650KN; ❄🛜) The 18 character-packed rooms at this attractive guesthouse may all be smallish but they have TVs and tiny bathrooms, and some have harbour views. The breakfast terrace overlooks the shimmering harbour waters and the church. There's a 120KN surcharge for one-night stays in July and August.

🍴 Eating

★ Bora Bar   ITALIAN €€
(⏺051-867 544; www.borabar.net; Rovenska Bay 3; mains 60-160KN; ⏺noon-10pm Mar-Oct) Truffle heaven, this casual-chic restaurant, Veli Lošinj's best, has a Tuscan chef and a passion for the mysterious fungi. Feast on delicious homemade pasta with a generous shaving of truffle, and finish with panna cotta with truffle honey. Istrian wines put in a strong appearance.

Ribarska Koliba   CROATIAN €€
(Obala Maršala Tita 1; mains 45-130KN; ⏺9am-midnight Apr-Oct) Just past the church, this old stone structure has a nice port-side terrace at the entrance to the harbour and serves up flavoursome meat dishes (try the suckling lamb or pig on a spit) as well as fresh seafood.

KVARNER VELI LOŠINJ

BLUE WORLD

The Blue World Institute of Marine Research & Conservation (www.blue-world.org) is a Veli Lošinj–based nongovernmental organisation founded in 1999 to protect the Adriatic's marine environment. As well as hands-on research and conservation work, including running the Sea Turtle Rescue Centre (p154) in Mali Lošinj, it promotes environmental awareness through lectures, media presentations and the organisation of the annual **Dolphin Day**, held in Veli Lošinj on 1 July. It's quite an event, involving photography exhibitions, an ecofair, street performances, water-polo contests, treasure hunts and displays of hundreds of children's drawings and paintings.

As part of the Adriatic Dolphin Project, Blue World studies bottlenose dolphins that frequent the Lošinj-Cres area. Each dolphin is named and catalogued by photos taken of the natural marks that can be seen on its dorsal fin.

Dolphins were hunted here in the 1960s and '70s, when each kill was rewarded by the local government – fishers were paid by the tail. Protection began in 1995, but a steep decline in bottlenose dolphins was recorded between 1995 and 2003. Subsequently, Blue World worked to establish the Lošinj Dolphin Reserve. Numbers are now believed to be stable, though still critically endangered, at around 180 individuals. In August 2009 a pod of 60 dolphins was seen near the island of Trstenik, a record sighting. Occasionally, other dolphin species are seen too, including striped dolphins. The giant basking shark has also been spotted.

The biggest threat to Lošinj's dolphins is boat traffic, which brings noise and disturbance. During July and August dolphins are never seen close to the shore and avoid their main feeding grounds south and east of Cres where hake is common. Overfishing is another big concern, reducing available prey.

You can get involved by adopting a dolphin (from 200KN), which supports the Adriatic Dolphin Project, or volunteering. From May to September it's possible to join a 10-day program which starts at €800 per person (with discounts available for students), and includes food and accommodation.

Seasonal specials complement the standard menu. It's a wonderful place to watch the sunset, a Croatian white in hand.

ℹ Information

Palma Tourist Agency (☑ 051-236 179; www.losinj.com; Vladimira Nazora 22) Offers information, currency exchange, internet access and private accommodation rentals.

Post Office (Obala Maršala Tita 33; ⊘ 8am-5pm Mon, to 3pm Tue-Fri Sep-Jun, 7.30am-9pm Mon-Sat Jul & Aug)

Turist (☑ 051-236 256; www.island-losinj.com; Obala Maršala Tita 17) Private travel agency which runs excursions to Susak and Ilovik (650KN), rents private accommodation, changes money and rents bikes and scooters.

Val Tourist Agency (☑ 051-236 604; www.val-losinj.hr; Vladimira Nazora 29) Books private accommodation, runs excursions, offers internet access and rents bikes and scooters.

ℹ Getting There & Away

If arriving by car you'll have to park up above the bay and walk down the narrow cobblestone streets in summer.

Veli Lošinj has the following bus connections:

Cres Town 65KN, 1½ hours, seven daily
Mali Lošinj 12KN, 12 minutes, 13 daily
Nerezine 35KN, 40 minutes, eight daily
Osor 38KN, 45 minutes, eight daily
Rijeka 149KN, four hours, four daily

KRK ISLAND

Croatia's largest island, connected to the mainland by a toll bridge, Krk (Veglia in Italian) is also one of the busiest – in summer, hundreds of thousands of central Europeans stream to its holiday houses, campsites and hotels. It's not the lushest or most beautiful island, though its landscape is quite varied, ranging from forests in the west to sunburned ridges in the east. The northwestern coast of the island is rocky and steep with few settlements because of the fierce *bura* (cold northeasterly) that whips the coast in winter. The climate is milder in the southwest and can be scorching in the southeast.

You'll find Krk an easy place to visit, with good transport connections and infrastructure. Rijeka Airport is at the northernmost tip of the island, though flights only land here from April to October.

History

The earliest known inhabitants of Krk were the Illyrian Liburnian tribe, followed by the Romans who settled on the northern coast. Krk was later incorporated into the Byzantine Empire, then passed between Venice and the Croatian-Hungarian kings.

In the 11th century Krk became a leading centre for the preservation of the Glagolitic alphabet, the original Slavic script introduced by Sts Cyril and Methodius in the 9th century. When the church in Rome demanded that the Croatian church fall into line and use the Latin script and language for divine services, the clergy in Krk staged a short-lived revolt. However, Rome eventually granted an exemption for some Croatian dioceses to continue using the vernacular (a rarity in the Catholic tradition until the reforms of the 1960s) and the Glagolitic alphabet was used here until the 19th century.

In 1358 Venice granted rule over the island to the Dukes of Krk, later known as the Frankopans, who became one of the richest and most powerful families in Croatia. Although vassals of Venice, they ruled with a measure of independence until 1480, when the last member of the line put the island back under the protection of Venice.

Although tourism is the dominant activity on the island, there are two small shipyards (in Punat and Krk) and some agriculture and fishing.

🛈 Getting There & Away

Buses head across the bridge from Rijeka to Malinska (50KN, one hour, at least hourly), Krk Town (64KN, one hour 20 minutes, hourly), Punat (71KN, 1¾ hours, 11 daily) and Baška (84KN, 2¼ hours, seven daily).

There are also summer services from Zagreb to Malinska (105KN, three hours, 12 daily), Krk Town (105KN, three hours, eight daily), Punat (115KN, 3½ hours, six daily) and Baška (115KN, four hours, six daily).

The main ferry port is at Valbiska, with services to the islands of Cres and Rab.

There are buses from Malinska to both Cres Town (77KN, 1¼ hours, two to three daily) and Mali Lošinj (126KN, 2½ hours, three daily).

Malinska
📞 051 / POP 965

Once the main port for the export of wood on the island, Malinska is now basically a sprawl of colourful holiday apartments grouped around a little marina. Sheltered from the winds and averaging 260 sunny days per year, it became a popular holiday destination with the Viennese aristocracy back in the dying days of the Austro-Hungarian Empire. Now the tidy gardens and well-kept abodes speak to a large population of retirees. The surrounding Dubašnica area is scattered with little lost-in-time villages.

Although it's a little removed from the island's main sights, the location is handy for the Cres–Rijeka buses and for its proximity to the airport.

🛏 Sleeping & Eating

Villa Haya   APARTMENT €€
(📞 051-604 021; www.villahaya.com; Linardići 28/4; apt 410-890KN; 🅿 ❄ 🛜 🏊) Located in a middle-of-nowhere village between Malinska and the ferry port, this block of nine apartments makes a good-value, relaxing base, provided you have your own car. It has its own little blue-tiled pool and there are remote beaches within a 40-minute walk.

Pinia   HOTEL €€€
(📞 051-866 333; www.hotel-pinia.hr; Porat bb; d 1600KN; 🅿 ❄ 🛜 🏊 🍴) This curvy hotel gazes over a dining terrace and lush lawns to the beach, 4km west of the harbour. The rooms are very well fitted out and there's an indoor pool and spa centre to enjoy. All rates are for half board.

★ Bistro Bukarica   MODERN EUROPEAN €€
(📞 051-859 022; www.bistrobukarica.com; Nikole Tesle 61; mains 70-180KN; ⊗ 11am-11pm) Tucked away up the hill in an unlikely residential street, this inventive restaurant is well worth seeking out. Asian flavours make their way on to a solidly European menu, highlighting the best Croatian produce. The desserts are sensational too.

🛈 Information

Post Office (Obala 48; ⊗ 7.30am-9pm Mon-Sat Jun-Aug, 7am-8pm Mon-Fri, to 2pm Sat Sep-May)

Tourist Office (📞 051-859 207; www.tz-malinska.hr; Obala 46; ⊗ 8am-9pm Mon-Sat, 9am-1pm & 5-8pm Sun, reduced hours in winter)

KVARNER MALINSKA

❶ Getting There & Away

Malinska is something of a bus hub for the island. Destinations include the following:

Cres Town 77KN, 1¼ hours, two to three daily
Krk Town 30KN, 24 minutes, hourly in summer
Mali Lošinj 126KN, 2½ hours, three daily
Rijeka 50KN, one hour, six to 15 daily
Zagreb 105KN, 2½ to four hours, 12 daily

Krk Town

☑ 051 / POP 6200

On the island's southern coast, Krk Town clusters around an ancient walled centre. The newer part of town spreads out over the surrounding hills and bays, and includes a port, beaches, camping grounds and hotels. The seafront promenade can get seriously crowded in summer with tourists and weekending Croats, who spill into the narrow cobbled streets that make up the pretty old quarter.

Minus the crowds, this stone labyrinth is the highlight of Krk Town. The former Roman settlement still retains sections of the ancient city walls and gates, as well as a grand Romanesque cathedral and a 12th-century Frankopan castle.

You won't need more than a couple of hours to see the sights, but Krk Town is a good base from which to explore the rest of the island.

◎ Sights & Activities

Cathedral of the Assumption CATHEDRAL
(Katedrala Uznešenja; Trg Sv Kvirina; ☺ from 7.30am Mon-Sat, from 7am Sun) **FREE** This imposing 12th-century Romanesque structure was built on the site of Roman baths and an early Christian basilica. Inside note the rare early Christian carving of two birds eating a fish on the first column next to the apse. The left nave features a Gothic chapel from the 15th century, with the coats of arms of the Frankopan princes who used it as a place of worship. Grafted on to the side is an 18th-century **campanile** with onion dome and angel statue.

Next door the adjoining **St Quirinus' Church** is another Romanesque church built of white stone and dedicated to the island's patron saint. Among the art and vestments stored in its treasury is a silver altarpiece depicting the Madonna dating to 1477.

Kaštel FORTRESS
(Trg Kamplin; 15KN; ☺ 9am-10pm Jun-Aug, to 2pm rest of the year) This crumbling old seafront fortress guarded the old town from pirate attacks. Check out the inscribed Liburnian and Roman stones displayed in the courtyard before scrambling up the newly renovated 12th-century tower that was once used as a Frankopan courtroom – the views from the top are worth the climb.

Fun Diving Krk DIVING
(☑ 051-222 563; www.fun-diving.com; Braće Juras 3; day tour incl 2 dives 400KN; ☺ Easter-Oct) This German crew offers courses and dives around the island. Some of the best dive sites include *Peltastis,* the wreck of a 60m Greek cargo ship, and the Punta Silo and Kamenjak reefs, which are rich with sea life including sea snails and octopuses.

✦ Festivals & Events

Krk Fair CULTURAL
(☺ 8-10 Aug) This Venetian-inspired event takes over the town for three days, with concerts on four stages, people dressed in medieval costumes and around 200 stalls selling traditional food and handicrafts.

⊨ Sleeping

Camping Bor CAMPGROUND €
(☑ 051-221 581; www.camp-bor.hr; Crikvenička 10; per adult/tent 67/36KN; P ⊛ ⊠ ⊕) On a hill covered with olive trees, this tightly packed campground has well-kept shower blocks, a tiny swimming pool, a playground and a restaurant. It's a 10-minute walk west of the seafront.

Hotel Marina HOTEL €€€
(☑ 051-221 128; www.hotelmarina.hr; Obala Hrvatske Mornarice 8; s/d from 800/1340KN; P ⊛ 🛜) Marina is the only hotel in the Old Town, and it's a good one too. The prime waterfront location allows you to gaze out over the yachts from the balconies of all 10 plush units (book a room with a terrace for the best views). All boast stylish but understated contemporary decor and hip bathrooms, plus there's a good restaurant.

✗ Eating

Konoba Nono CROATIAN €€
(☑ 051-222 221; www.nono-krk.com; Krčkih Iseljenika 8; mains 35-150KN; ☺ 11am-late) Just outside the old town, this rustic place is renowned for its Krk cooking and produces its own olive oil, as evidenced by the large traditional press around which tables are arranged. It also hangs its own prosciutto, which goes into some of the dishes. Big por-

tions and incredibly knowledgeable and polite staff make Nono worth seeking out.

There's a smaller branch, Mali Nono, in
the old town.

Galija   CROATIAN, PIZZERIA €€
(☑051-221 250; Frankopanska 38; mains 40-
190KN; ⊙11am-11pm; 🏶) Set well back from
the seafront at the top of the Old Town, this
atmospheric stone building looks slightly
gloomy from the street but the convivial
timber-rich dining room opens out on to a lovely
internal garden. It's part traditional *konoba*
(tavern), part pizzeria serving anything from
a cheap margarita to fish platters for two.

🍷 Drinking & Nightlife

★ **Volsonis**   BAR, CLUB
(Vela Placa 8; ⊙7am-midnight Sun-Thu, to 1am
Fri & Sat) This dark, cool, cave-like place
has an outdoor terrace, a pool table, a delicious secret garden and even a collection
of archaeological relics that were uncovered
during the renovations. Live bands and DJs
do their thing on weekend nights, or you
can just chill on the terrace with a coffee
or cocktail.

Caffettaria XVIII st.   BAR
(Vela Placa 1; ⊙7am-2am May-Sep, to midnight Oct-
Apr; 🛜) Located right on the main square in
the erstwhile entrance of the historic town
hall, this is a characterful place for a bit of
people-watching and a delicious coffee in
the shade. It has good wi-fi and nice sofas
to lounge on.

ⓘ Information

Aurea (☑051-221 777; www.aurea-krk.hr;
Vršanska 26l; ⊙8am-2pm & 3-8pm) A local
agency offering island excursions and private
accommodation bookings.
Hospital (☑051-221 224; Vinogradska bb)
Post Office (Bodulska bb; ⊙7.30am-9pm
Mon-Sat Jun-Aug, 7am-8pm Mon-Fri, to 2pm
Sat Sep-May)
Tourist Office (☑051-220 226; www.tz-krk.hr;
JJ Strossmayera 9; ⊙8am-9pm daily Jun, to
10pm Jul & Aug, reduced hours rest of the year)

ⓘ Getting There & Away

The bus station is near the water, only 350m west
of the old town. Destinations include the following:
Baška 35KN, 40 minutes, 12 daily in summer
Malinska 30KN, 24 minutes, hourly in summer
Punat 26KN, 13 minutes, at least hourly in
summer

Rijeka 64KN, 1½ hours, 12 daily
Zagreb 105KN, three hours, one to eight daily

Punat
☑051 / POP 1800

Six kilometres southeast of Krk, the small
town of Punat has an attractive promenade
lined with gelaterias, a marina much loved
by yachties, and decent beaches on its outskirts. The main attraction here is the monastery islet of **Košljun**, only a 10-minute
boat ride away.

⊙ Sights & Activities

Košljun Franciscan Monastery   MONASTERY
(Franjevački Samostan Košljun; www.kosljun.hr;
20KN; ⊙9.30am-5pm Mon-Sat, 10.30am-12.30pm
Sun) The tiny island of Košljun contains a
16th-century Franciscan monastery built on
the site of a 12th-century Benedictine abbey.
Taxi boats wait on the Punat harbourside,
ready to shuttle people across to the island
(25KN return); in summer there'll be plenty
of interested parties with whom you can
share a ride. Visitors should dress modestly.

Highlights include a large, appropriately
chilling *Last Judgment,* painted in 1653 and
housed in the monastery church. There's
also a small **museum** with religious paintings, an ethnographic collection and a rare
copy of Ptolemy's *Atlas* printed in Venice
in the late 16th century. Allow extra time to
stroll around the forested island and admire
its 400 plant species. There are no beaches
or swimming on the island.

WORTH A TRIP

BEACH PEACE

Many of Krk's best beaches are heavily
developed and crowded in summer.
For more tranquillity, head south of
Punat on the lonely road that heads to
Stara Baška (not southeast to Baška).
It's a superlative drive, through steep
parched hills and lunar scenery. Stara
Baška itself is a run-of-the-mill tourist
sprawl of holiday homes and caravan
parks, but if you pull up 500m before
the first campsite there is a series of
gorgeous pebble-and-sand coves with
wonderful swimming. You'll have to park
on the road, and then walk down one of
the rocky paths for five minutes to get
to the coast.

KVARNER PUNAT

Cable Krk Wakeboard Center WAKEBOARDING
(🖉 091 26 27 303; www.wakeboarder.hr; per hr/day 100/230KN; ☉10am-dark May-Sep) Adrenaline junkies can get their fix at this 650m-long cableway for wakeboarding and waterskiing, running at a speed of 32km per hour. It's located just off the main road at the head of the bay (before the turn-off to Punat). The complex includes a restaurant, bar and board shop.

🛈 Getting There & Away

Bus to/from Punat include the following:
Baška 34KN, 30 minutes, 12 daily in summer
Krk Town 26KN, 13 minutes, at least hourly in summer
Malinska 35KN, 35 minutes, at least hourly in summer
Rijeka 71KN, 1½ hours, four to nine daily
Zagreb 115KN, 3½ hours, one to six daily

Vrbnik
🖉 051 / POP 950

Perched on a 48m cliff overlooking the sea, Vrbnik is a beguiling medieval village of steep, arched streets. It's not a real secret (tour groups pass through from time to time), but most of the year it's a peaceful, unhurried place.

Vrbnik was once the main centre where the Glagolitic script was used and was the repository for many Glagolitic manuscripts. It was kept alive by priests, who were always plentiful in the town since many young men entered the priesthood to avoid serving on Venetian galleys.

Now the town is a terrific place to soak up the vistas and sample the *žlahtina* white wine produced in the surrounding region. After wandering the tightly packed cobbled alleyways, head down to the town beach for a swim.

🏃 Activities

Toljanić-Gospoja WINE
(🖉 051-857 201; www.gospoja.hr; Frankopanska 1) This local winery is the best place in town to sample the crisp local *žlahtina* white.

🍴 Eating

Restaurant Nada CROATIAN €€
(🖉 051-857 065; www.nada-vrbnik.hr; Glavača 22; mains 60-180KN; ☉11am-midnight Apr-Oct) Nada is a great place to sample local favourites such as Krk lamb or *šurlice* (noodles) topped

with meat goulash. There are two attractive dining terraces – one shaded and one overlooking the sea – plus a cellar where you can snack on deli treats surrounded by wine barrels. It also has some classy stone houses for rent.

🛈 Information

Mare Tours (🖉 051-604 400; www.mare-vrbnik.com; Pojana 4; ☉8am-8pm Mon-Sat, 9am-4pm Sun) Travel agency offering tourist information and renting private rooms.

🛈 Getting There & Away

Buses head to/from Krk Town (30KN, 35 minutes, three daily in summer) and Malinska (35KN, 40 minutes, one daily year-round)

Baška
🖉 051 / POP 1674

The drive to the southern end of Krk Island is dramatic, passing through a fertile valley that's bordered by eroded mountains. Eventually the road peters out at Baška, where there's a fine crescent beach set below barren hills. With the peaks of the mainland directly opposite you're effectively enveloped by soaring highlands, giving the sea the impression of being an alpine lake.

However, and this is a considerable caveat, in summer tourists are spread towel-to-towel and what's otherwise a pretty, if slimline, pebble beach turns into a fight for your place in the sun.

The small 16th-century core of Venetian town houses is pleasant enough, but what surrounds it is a bland tourist development of modern apartment blocks and generic restaurants. Facilities are plentiful and there are nice hiking trails into the surrounding mountains, and more secluded beaches to the east of town, reachable on foot or by water taxi.

◉ Sights & Activities

Several popular **trails** begin around Camping Zablaće (p163), including an 8km walk over the stark, salt-washed limestone hills to Stara Baška. Along the way you'll see the flower-shaped stone pens traditionally used for mustering and shearing sheep. There are also two **rock-climbing** sites in the area.

St Lucy's Church CHURCH, MUSEUM
(Crkva Sv Lucija; 25KN; ☉9am-9pm daily Jun-Aug, 10am-5pm Sep-May) More than just a village church, little St Lucy's was the site of one

of the most important cultural discoveries in Croatia – the 11th-century Baška tablet – which was found in the floor of the church in 1851. Written in Glagolitic it contains the earliest reference in the Croatian language to a Croatian king. Visitors are invited to watch a video which tells the fascinating story of the tablet's discovery and eventual translation, before being shown around the church itself.

The squat, early-Romanesque church was built on the foundations of a 4th-century villa and has a Roman column and gravestone built into its porch. The famous stone tablet is now in the Archaeological Museum in Zagreb, but a replica has been positioned in its original place where the rood screen would have once stood. On the feast of St Lucy (13 December), the sun strikes the inscription referring to the saint. Look out for the statue of St Lucy, depicted with an angel holding her gouged-out eyes on a plate – a reference to her gruesome martyrdom.

The church is in the village of Jurandvor and well-signposted from the approach to Baška; it's only 2km from town, so is easily reached on foot.

🛏 Sleeping

Naturist Camp Bunculuka CAMPGROUND €
(☑ 051-656 223; www.hotelbaska.hr; camping per adult/site from 84/195KN, unit from 1600KN; ☉ Apr-Oct; P @ 🛜 🛥) This shady 400-pitch naturist camp is a 15-minute walk over the hill east of the harbour on a lovely beach. It's equipped with good facilities for kids including minigolf and a playground, as well as a restaurant, a fruit-and-veg market, bakery and internet cafe. Minimum five-night stay in summer.

Camping Zablaće CAMPGROUND €
(☑ 051-656 223; www.hotelbaska.hr; camping per adult/site from 60/113KN, mobile homes 950KN; ☉ Apr–mid-Oct; P ❄ 🛜) Voted one of Croatia's best campgrounds in 2015, this well-equipped site extends along the long pebble beach and has excellent showers, laundry facilities and snazzy mobile homes with barbecues.

Atrium Residence Baška HOTEL €€€
(☑ 051-656 111; www.hotelibaska.hr; Emila Geistlicha 39; r/apt from 1600/2300KN; P ❄ 🛜) Sleek and contemporary, this midsized beachside hotel has options ranging from rooms with mountain views to a two-bedroom apartment with a sauna and Jacuzzi on the deck overlooking the sea. Guests have use of the resort-style pool at sister hotel Corinthia-Baška

plus access to a range of high-quality extra services.

Hotel Tamaris HOTEL €€€
(☑ 051-864 200; www.baska-tamaris.com; Emila Geistlicha bb; r from 850KN; ☉ Easter-Sep; P ❄ @ 🛜) Right on the beach on the west side of town this small, well-run hotel started life as an Austro-Hungarian army barracks. The emperor's troops have long since departed and today it's the tourists who enjoy the decent, if smallish, carpeted rooms and apartments. Dinner is a very reasonable extra 90KN and breakfast a less-attractive 60KN.

🍴 Eating

Bistro Forza MEDITERRANEAN €€
(Zvonimirova 98; mains 40-130KN; ☉ 7am-midnight; 🛜) With its funky dining room open to the balmy summer elements, this is as good a place as any in town for a pizza, grilled-meat dish, pasta or salad.

Cicibela CROATIAN €€€
(☑ 051-856 013; www.cicibela.hr; Emila Geistlicha 22a; mains 55-220KN; ☉ 9am-midnight Mar-Oct) At the heart of the beach promenade, this is Baška's top cat, with stylish seating, a maritime theme and a massive and tempting menu of seafood and meat dishes, just steps from the lapping *Jadran* (Adriatic). If you're ordering fish by the kilogram, ask for the price in advance to avoid awkward post-meal situations.

ℹ Information

PDM Guliver (☑ 051-864 007; www.pdm-guliver.hr; Zvonimirova 98) Based within the Hotel Forza, this travel agency lets private rooms and apartments.

Primaturist (☑ 051-856 132; www.primaturist. hr; Zvonimirova 98) Agency dealing in private rooms and apartments.

Tourist Office (☑ 051-856 817; www.tz-baska. hr; Zvonimirova 114; ☉ 8am-9pm Mon-Sat Jun-Aug, to 2pm Mon-Fri Sep-May) Just down the street from the bus station, between the beach and the harbour. Walkers should definitely head here to pick up their hiking-path map. Staff are multilingual.

ℹ Getting There & Away

Buses head to/from Baška:

Krk Town 35KN, 40 minutes, 12 daily in summer
Malinska 42KN, one hour, 10 daily in summer
Punat 34KN, 30 minutes, 12 daily in summer
Rijeka 84KN, two hours, four to seven daily
Zagreb 115KN, four hours, one to six daily

KVARNER BAŠKA

SENJ

053 / POP 7200

The historic walled town of Senj is the largest town on the coast between Rijeka and Zadar. In the 16th century it became a base for the Uskoks, Croats driven from their homes by the Ottoman invasion. They became a feared fighting force, harassing both Turkish and Venetian vessels with their own pirate fleet, painted red and black – the colours of blood and death. Their castle is the main reason to stop here en route to somewhere else.

If you travel along the Dalmatian coast by bus, you're sure to spend at least some time in Senj as it's a popular coffee or *burek* halt.

◉ Sights

Nehaj Castle   CASTLE
(Tvrđava Nehaj; www.muzej-senj.hr; adult/child 20/10KN; ⊙10am-9pm Jul & Aug, to 6pm May-Jun & Sep-Oct) The story of the Uskoks is show-cased in the dramatic setting of Nehaj Castle, a sturdy stone cube that looms above the town from a 62m-high hill to the south. It was completed in 1558 with funds supplied by the Austrian Emperor; the current structure was largely reconstructed in 1970. Head up to the parapets for fine views along the coast and over the island of Krk.

Municipal Museum   MUSEUM
(Milana Ogrizovića 5; adult/child 20/10KN; ⊙7am-3pm & 6-8pm Mon-Fri, 10am-noon & 6-8pm Sat, 10am-noon Sun Jul & Aug, 7am-3pm Mon-Fri rest of the year) The local museum, housed in a Gothic-Renaissance 15th-century palace built by Senj's medieval first family, the Vukasovićs, is a mixed bag of local history from the past 2000 years. The most interesting sections for Slavophiles are the exhibition dealing with the erstwhile printing house that

---

THE THREATENED GRIFFON VULTURE

With a wingspan of almost 3m, measuring about 1m from end to end, and weighing 7kg to 9kg, the Eurasian griffon vulture looks big enough to take passengers. It cruises comfortably at 40km/h to 75km/h, reaching speeds of up to 160km/h. The vulture's powerful beak and long neck are ideally suited to rummaging around the entrails of its prey, which is most likely to be a dead sheep.

Finding precious sheep carcasses is a team effort for griffon vultures. Usually a colony of birds will set out and fly in a comb formation of up to a kilometre apart. When one of the vultures spots a carcass, it circles as a signal for its neighbours to join in the feast. Shepherds don't mind griffons, reasoning that the birds prevent whatever disease or infection killed the sheep from spreading to other livestock.

The total known number of griffon vultures in Croatia is around 280, more than half of them living on the coastal cliffs of Cres, the others in small colonies on Krk and Prvić islands. The birds' dietary preferences mean that griffons tend to follow sheep although they will eat other dead mammals, to their peril: the last remaining birds in Paklenica National Park died after eating poisoned foxes.

The griffon population enjoys legal protection as an endangered species in Croatia. Killing a bird or disturbing it while nesting carries a €5000 fine. Intentional killing is rare but because the young birds cannot fly more than 500m on a windless day, tourists on speedboats who provoke them into flight often end up threatening their lives. The exhausted birds drop into the water and drown.

Breeding habits discourage a large population, as a pair of griffons only produces one fledgling a year and it takes five years for the young bird to reach maturity. During that time the growing griffons travel widely: one tagged in Paklenica National Park was found in Chad, 4000km away. When they're about five, the vultures head home to Cres (sometimes to the same rock where they were born) to find a mate, who will be a partner for life.

Captive vultures can live for more than 55 years, but in the wild 20 to 30 years is more normal. The dangers facing young Cres vultures include the guns of Italian hunters, poison and power lines, but by far the biggest issue is the massive decline in sheep farming in Cres, which is reducing the birds' food source day by day.

If you want to find out more about Croatia's griffon vultures, contact the **Grifon Birds of Prey Conservation Centre** (Grifon Centar za Zaštitu Ptica Grabljivica; ☑ 091 357 123; www.supovi.hr; Obala dr F Tuđmana 2) FREE on the mainland, 14km south of Senj.

produced religious texts in the Glagloitic script, and the ethnographic section with its colourful folk costumes.

ℹ️ Information

Tourist Office (☑ 053-881 068; www.tz-senj. hr; Stara 2; ☉ 8am-9pm daily Jun–mid-Sep, shorter hours & closed Sun rest of the year)

ℹ️ Getting There & Away

Senj is a halt on the Rijeka–Split route, often a long one involving caffeine. Connections from Senj:

Rijeka 73KN, one hour 20 minutes, 13 daily
Split 176KN, 6½ hours, seven daily
Zadar 94KN, 2¾ to 3½ hours, seven daily
Zagreb 123KN, two hours 25 minutes, five daily

RAB ISLAND

Madly popular, Rab (Arbe in Italian) has some of the most diverse landscapes in the Kvarner region, leading to its declaration as a Geopark in 2008. The more densely populated southwest coast has pine forests and beaches, while the northeast coast is a windswept region with few settlements, high cliffs and a barren look. In the interior, fertile land is protected from cold winds by mountains, allowing the cultivation of olives, grapes and vegetables. The Lopar Peninsula offers the best sandy beaches.

The cultural and historical highlight of the island is enchanting Rab Town, characterised by four elegant bell towers rising from the ancient stone streets. Even at the peak of the summer season, when the island is overrun with visitors, you still get a sense of discovery wandering its old quarter and escaping to nearly deserted beaches just a quick boat ride away.

History

Originally settled by the Illyrian Liburnian people in around 360 BC, Rab was declared a city in 10 BC by the Roman Emperor Augustus. It was Augustus who ordered the first walls to be built. The town first made its way into the history books in AD 70 when Pliny the Elder referred to it as Arba (meaning dark, obscure or green). It later became known as Felix Arba, or 'Happy Arba'.

After the Romans, Rab underwent periods of Byzantine and Croatian rule before being sold to Venice, along with Dalmatia, in 1409. Farming, fishing, vineyards and salt production were the economic mainstays, but most income ended up in Venice. Two plague epidemics in the 15th century nearly wiped out the population and brought the economy to a standstill.

When Venice fell in 1797, there was a short period of Austrian rule until the French arrived in 1805. After the fall of Napoleon in 1813, the power went back to the Austrians who favoured the Italianised elite and it was not until 1897 that Croatian was made an official language. The tourism industry began at the turn of the 20th century.

After the fall of the Austro-Hungarian Empire in 1918, Rab eventually became part of the Kingdom of Yugoslavia. Occupied by Italian and then German troops in the early 1940s, it was liberated in 1945. During Tito's rule Goli Otok ('Barren Island'), off the Lopar Peninsula, served as a notorious prison camp for fascists, Stalinists and other political opponents.

These days, tourism is Rab's bread and butter. Even during the 1990s war, Rab managed to hold on to its German and Austrian visitors.

ℹ️ Getting There & Away

BOAT

Jadrolinija (☑ 051-666 111; www.jadrolinija.hr) A daily catamaran stops in Rab Town en route between Rijeka (80KN, 1¾ hours) and Novalja on Pag (45KN, 45 minutes). The company also runs a handy car ferry between Valbiska on Krk and Lopar (adult/child/car 37/19/225KN, 1½ hours) twice daily (October to May) and four times daily in high season.

Rapska Plovidba (☑ 051-724 122; www. rapska-plovidba.hr) A car ferry shuttles back and forth between Mišnjak on the island's southeastern tip and Stinica (adult/child/car 17/7/98KN, 15 minutes) on the mainland; even in winter there are a dozen boats a day, increasing to nearly double that in high season. There's also a passenger boat from Rab Town to Lun on the island of Pag, operating three days a week (daily from June to August).

BUS

Buses head to Rab Town from Rijeka (119KN, three hours, two daily) and Senj (74KN, 1½ hours, five daily); from Zadar you'll need to change at Senj. In the high season there are four direct buses a day from Zagreb to Rab (216KN, four hours); book ahead on this busy route.

ⓘ Getting Around

There are 11 buses a day (nine on Sunday) between Rab Town and Lopar (20KN, 15 minutes); some are timed to meet the Valbiska–Lopar ferry.

Taxi boats will take you to any island beach.

Rab Town

♩ 051 / POP 8070

Walled Rab Town is among the northern Adriatic's most spectacular sights. Crowded on to a narrow peninsula, its four instantly recognisable bell towers rise like exclamation marks from a red-roofed huddle of stone buildings. A maze of streets leads to the upper town, where there are ancient churches and dramatic lookout points. It's quite a scene, the glinting azure waters of Rab's pocket-sized harbour set against the island's backbone of hills that shelter the bay from cool *bura* (cold northeasterly) winds. Once you've soaked up the town vibe, there are excursion and taxi boats waiting to whisk you off to lovely beaches scattered around the island.

A five-minute walk north of the Old Town is the ageing, down-at-heel commercial centre, with stores and the bus station. Built-up suburbs sprawl along the coast, including Banjol and Barbat in the south and Palit and Kampor in the north.

◯ Sights

It's a pure delight to meander through the narrow old alleys of Rab and explore the harbour, upper town and parks. Rab's principal sights are its historic churches and towers, which are clustered together on the narrow lane of Ulica Gornja (Upper St), which runs parallel to Srednja (Central) and Donja (Lower) streets. Most of the churches are usually only open for morning and evening Mass, but even when they're closed you can often peer through metal railings to view their interiors.

Komrčar Park   PARK

(Banjol/Obala Petra Krešimira) This 8.3-hectare park abuts the Old Town and stretches along the coast to the marina at Palit. It was originally used as a place to graze cattle, but was planted in forest in the 19th century, much to the consternation of the townsfolk. It's leafy and deliciously cool on a summer's day – pack a picnic from the supermarket at the harbour and enjoy a couple of hours chilling on the grass. There's a good children's playground at the harbour end.

Viewpoint   VIEWPOINT

For a great view over the rooftops including all four bell towers, head to the northwesternmost corner of the Old Town and look for a small courtyard containing fragments of old monuments. Stone stairs lead up from here on to the walls and a lookout – take care with children here as the drops are steep and the railings past their best.

St John the Evangelist's Church   RUINS

(Crkva Sv Ivana Evanđelista; Gornja bb) It's thought that parts of this atmospherically ruined Romanesque basilica date as far back as the 5th century. Today, amid assorted rubble, only a handful of columns are still standing, along with the restored 12th-century bell tower.

Holy Cross Church   CHURCH

(Crkva Sv Križa; Gornja bb) This 13th-century church takes its present name from a crucifix upon which, in 1556, the image of Christ was said to have wept due to the immoral conduct of the people of Rab. Sadly, the miraculous cross was lost in the early 20th century. Today the church is the venue for summer concerts during Rab Musical Evenings (p167).

St Justine's Church   CHURCH

(Crkva Sv Justine; Gornja bb) This semiderelict church has a bell tower dating from 1672. It's located beside pretty **Trg Slobode**, which has a holm oak tree and sea vistas. Below is an easily accessible stretch of shingle/concrete beach for foot-soothing, mid-sightseeing paddles.

St Andrew's Monastery   CHURCH

(Samostan Sv Andrije; Ivana Rabljanina bb) Founded in 1018, this Benedictine monastery has Rab's oldest bell tower (1181) and a still-functioning bell dating from 1396. Peer through the railings at the church's triple nave; some of the plasterwork has been uncovered to reveal the original stonework. Nearby, the monks run a monastery shop selling oils and honey.

St Mary's Campanile   TOWER

(Toranj Sv Marije; Ivana Rabljanina bb; 15KN; ⊙9.30am-1pm & 7-9pm May-Sep) Dating from the 12th century, this is Rab's tallest bell tower and one of the most beautiful on the entire Croatian coast. The 26m edifice is topped with an octagonal pyramid surrounded by a Romanesque balustrade, and features a cross with five small globes and reliquaries of several saints. Climb up the very steep wooden staircase for glorious views over the Old

Town rooftops and sea. You'll emerge right by the chiming mechanism itself.

Church of the Assumption   CHURCH
(Crkva Uznesenjca; Ivana Rabljanina bb) It hasn't been a cathedral since 1828 when the diocese was dissolved, but locals still refer to this, their grandest church, as the *katedrala*. Its striking facade has stripes of pink and cream stone, and a Gothic-style pietà over the door. Inside, key features include 15th-century choir stalls and weathered pillars. It's been remodelled a lot over the years but mosaics found here indicate that this has been a Christian place of worship since the 4th or 5th century.

St Anthony the Abbot's Church   CHURCH
(Crkva Sv Antuna Opata; Ivana Rabljanina bb) At the eastern tip of the Old Town, this church attached to a still-operating Franciscan convent has lots of inlaid marble and a carving of a seated St Anthony decorating the altar. It's the final resting place of St Marin of Rab whose statue graces a beautifully landscaped park below, a relaxing halt during a sightseeing tour.

🏃 Activities

Rab is criss-crossed with 100km of marked **hiking trails** and 80km of **biking trails**, several of which can be accessed from Rab Town. Pick up the excellent *Biking and Trekking* map from the tourist office (p170) or call into the Geopark Visitor Centre (p169) for information on the new 'geotrails'. Bikes can be rented from several travel agencies.

From Rab Town there's a trail that leads northeast to the mountain peak of Sveti Ilija. It only takes about 30 minutes on foot and the view is great.

A long pebbly beach stretches all around Rab Town, so take a towel and freshen up after sightseeing – just mind those sea urchins!

Mirko Diving Centre   DIVING
(📞 051-721 154; www.mirkodivingcenter.com; Barbat 710) Mirko Diving Centre, based in nearby Barbat, offers courses and fun dives as well as trips to well-known dive sites such as the wreck of the Rosa and a protected amphora field off the cape of Sorinj.

☞ Tours

Day tours of the island by boat, including swim stops and visits to nearby islands such as Sveti Grgur and the infamous Goli Otok, are offered by many travel agents; expect

WORTH A TRIP

A HEAVENLY DESTINATION

A 2.5km walk heading north along the seaside promenade from Rab's Old Town will bring you to the **Monastery of St Euphemia** (Samostan Sv Eufemije; Kampor; adult/child 20/10KN; ⊙10am-noon & 4-6pm Mon-Sat), a peaceful Franciscan Monastery dating from the 13th century. The monks have a small museum here with old manuscripts and religious paintings. Check out the pleasant cloister and, inside the baroque church of St Bernardine, the ethereal painted ceiling – a stark contrast to the visceral agony depicted on the late-Gothic wooden crucifix in the side chapel. Note also the 15th-century polyptych by the Vivarini brothers.

to pay about 200KN to 250KN, including lunch. You can also chat directly with skippers about trips: in the evening the main harbour-front is lined with excursion boats. Trips to the islands of Lošinj and Krk are also possible.

🎉 Festivals & Events

Rab Musical Evenings   MUSIC
(Rapske Glazbene Večeri; ⊙mid-Jun–mid-Sep) This top-notch classical-music festival revolves around Thursday-night concerts at venues including Holy Cross Church (p166).

Rab Fair   FIESTA
(Rapska Fjera; ⊙Jul) Witness Rab transporting itself back to the Middle Ages. Residents dress in period garb and there are drummers, processions, fireworks, medieval dancing and crossbow competitions.

Summer Festival   MUSIC
In early August, Croatian pop stars and international DJs perform in the Old Town.

🛏 Sleeping

Camping Padova III   CAMPGROUND €
(📞 051-724 355; www.rab-camping.com; Banjol 496; camping per adult/site 60/131KN, unit from 600KN; ⊙Apr-Oct; @) About 2km east of town, this tightly packed campsite sits right on a sandy beach – perfect for toddlers, painfully shallow for adults. The facilities were in the process of being updated at the time of research and included a restaurant, cafe, supermarket and kids' playgrounds.

Rab Town

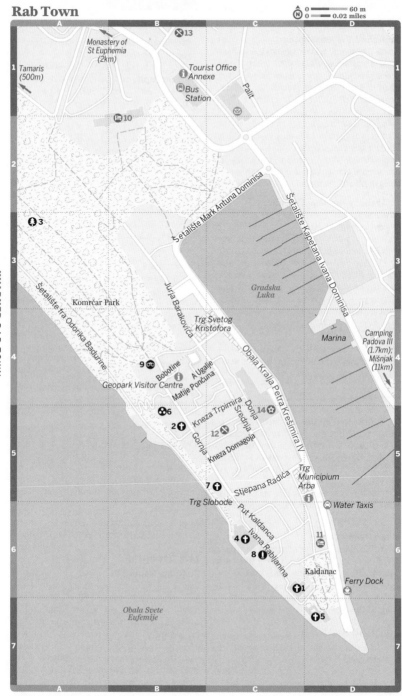

0 — 60 m
0 — 0.02 miles

Monastery of St Euphemia (2km)

Tamaris (500m)

13

Tourist Office Annexe

Bus Station

Palit

10

Šetalište Mark Antuna Dominisa

Šetalište Kapetana Ivana Dominisa

3

Gradska Luka

Šetalište fra Odorika Badurine

Komrčar Park

Jurja Barakovića

Trg Svetog Kristofora

Obala Kralja Petra Krešimira IV

Marina

Camping Padova III (1.7km); Mišnjak (11km)

9

Bobotine

Geopark Visitor Centre

A Ugalje

Matije Ponćuna

6

2

Kneza Trpimira

Donja

Srednja

14

12

Gornja

Kneza Domagoja

7

Stjepana Radića

Trg Municipium Arba

Trg Slobode

Put Kaldanca

Water Taxis

11

4

Ivana Rabljanina

8

Kaldanac

Ferry Dock

1

Obala Svete Eufemije

5

Rab Town

Tamaris HOTEL €€
(☎051-724 925; www.tamaris-rab.com; Palit 285; s/d 564/806KN; P❄🛜) About a 10-minute walk north of town, this is a well-run little hotel, with attentive staff and a peaceful location near the sea. Rooms are simple but quite stylish with laminate floors and soft linen. Most have sea views from their balconies.

Hotel Arbiana HOTEL €€€
(☎051-725 563; www.arbianahotel.com; Obala Kralja Petra Krešimira IV 12; s/d 750/1500KN; P❄🛜) The classiest address in Rab, this historic hotel dates to 1924 and retains plenty of period character and formal elegance. All 27 rooms are perfectly maintained and come with 21st-century TVs, sturdy desks and good-quality repro furniture. Most have balconies. The hotel **restaurant** is also worth a shot, even if you're not staying here.

Grand Hotel Imperial HOTEL €€€
(☎051-667 788; www.imperial.hr; Šetalište Markantuna Dominisa 9; s/d from 555/1110KN; P❄🛜🏊) Pleasantly old-fashioned, this place is not as grand as the name would have you believe. Nonetheless this large hotel enjoys a pretty location amid the trees of Komrčar Park. Facilities include tennis courts, a gym, a spa and a very appealing outdoor swimming pool. Rooms have warm colour schemes.

✖ Eating

Konoba Rab CROATIAN €€
(Kneza Branimira 3; mains 75-130KN; ⊙10am-2pm & 5-11pm Mon-Sat, 5-11pm Sun) For real country cooking – albeit in a multilevel, faux-rural setting – this place excels. Find one of the many nooks and crannies containing tables and order mains of grilled meat and fish staples or the lamb baked under *peka* in advance. Fish is priced by the kilo.

Ristorante Ana MEDITERRANEAN €€
(☎051-724 376; Palit 80; mains 70-160KN; ⊙11am-3pm & 5pm-midnight) In the newer part of town, just around the corner from the bus station, this apricot-hued restaurant has a quiet internal terrace overlooking a garden. The cook plates up a better-than-usual lineup of pasta, pizza, risotto and grilled meat and fish; the spaghetti with scampi is particularly good.

☆ Entertainment

Santos Beach Club CLUB
(www.sanantonio-club.com; Pudarica Beach; ⊙10am-dawn late Jun-early Sep) This summer-only beach club is about 10km from Rab Town, far away from any complaining neighbours in a remote spot near the Mišnjak car ferry (shuttle boats run at night). DJs spin to a lively party crowd and there are live concerts and fashion shows. It also doubles as a daytime beach hang-out, with loungers and volleyball.

Dock 69 BAR, CLUB
(Obala Kralja Petra Krešimira IV; ⊙8am-3pm & 7pm-midnight Sun-Thu, to 3am Fri & Sat) This slick lounge bar has a harbour-facing cafe terrace and clubby interior where DJs ramp up the volume on the weekends.

ⓘ Information

Geopark Visitor Centre (Bobotine bb; ⊙10am-5pm Mon, Tue & Thu-Sat, 3-8pm Sun) Call in for information on 'geotrail' paths, exploring the island's unique geology. There are also interactive information screens and samples of local rocks.

Katurbo (☎051-724 495; www.katurbo.hr; Šetalište Markantuna Dominisa 5) Organises private accommodation, money exchange, bike rental, boat excursions and even tours to distant places such as the Plitvice Lakes National Park.

Numero Uno (☎098 329 897; www.numero-uno.hr; Banjol 30) Books private accommodation, rents bicycles and offers trekking trips, and kayak and bike tours.

Post Office (Mali Palit 67; ☺7.30am-9pm Mon-Sat Jun-Aug, 7am-8pm Mon-Fri, to 2pm Sat Sep-May)

Tourist Office (✎ 051-724 064; www.rab-visit. com; Trg Municipium Arba 8; ☺8am-9pm Mon-Sat, to 1pm Sun Easter-Oct, 8am-3pm Mon-Fri Nov-Easter) A well-organised office with helpful staff and loads of useful maps, brochures and leaflets. In summer, it operates a second **branch** (☺8am-3pm Jun-Sep) around the corner from the bus station.

Lopar

✎ 051 / POP 1260

At the northern tip of the island, the beach town of Lopar is still semirural around the edges, with garden plots and roses growing in front gardens. Even in early June it's a sleepy place, but in the school holidays Central European families flock here, as the sea is very shallow and perfect for small children. This is particularly so on 1500m-long Paradise Beach on Crnika Bay, right in the centre of town, where you can almost wade right across to a little offshore island.

There are 22 sandy beaches bordered by shady pine groves scattered around the peninsula, including nearby **Livačina Beach**. If you wish to shed your Speedos, **Sahara Beach** is a popular nudist spot in a gorgeous but shallow bay. Look for the signpost pointing off the main road before you reach Paradise Beach; it's a 1.8km (half-hour) walk from here, or you can drive along the narrow lane and walk for 15 minutes from the parking area.

◉ Sights

★ Paradise Beach   BEACH
(Rajska Plaža) One of Croatia's finest beaches, this sickle of fine sand hems Lopar's southern flank and is the biggest attraction in these parts. Backed by all sorts of attractions – from minigolf to ice-cream parlours – this is the ideal spot for a family holiday with the kids. The beach hardly shelves as it goes out

into the warm Adriatic and a small offshore island makes for a great swimming or kayaking destination.

🛏 Sleeping & Eating

Hotel Epario   HOTEL €€
(✎051-777 500; www.epario.net; Lopar 456a; r 450KN; P ❀ 🛜) Just about the only real hotel in Lopar, the laid-back Epario is a modern block facing the fields on the main road leading towards Paradise Beach. The rooms all have desks, balconies and good bathrooms. It's a short walk to the beach and to the large Konzum supermarket at the nearby crossroads.

Gostionica Laguna   MEDITERRANEAN €€
(✎051-775 177; www.laguna-lopar.com; Lopar 547; mains 40-180KN; ☺noon-10pm; P ❀ 🛜) The greenery-trimmed wooden-roofed terrace at this friendly tavern is by far the nicest place to eat up this end of the island. House specialities include spit-roast or *peka*-cooked lamb, but there's also a large menu of pasta, monster pizzas and grilled meat and fish. Inside there's a soft playroom where kiddies can make international friends as you kick back.

🍷 Drinking & Nightlife

Bamboocho   BAR
(Rajska Plaža; ☺noon-late) Among the pine trees lining the eastern end of Paradise Beach, this open-air beach bar has been quirkily sculpted from bits of scrap metal and chunky bamboo. It's a wonderful spot for a sundowner.

❶ Information

Sahara Tours (✎ 051-775 633; www.sahara-lopar.com; Lopar bb, opposite the tennis courts) Has dozens of private rooms, houses and apartments on its books.

Tourist Office (✎051-775 508; www.lopar. com; Lopar 248, next to Konzum; ☺8am-10pm Mon-Sat, to 2pm Sun Jul & Aug, to 11am Mon-Fri Sep-Jun)

KVARNER LOPAR

Northern Dalmatia

Why Go?

Serving that classic Dalmatian cocktail of historic towns, jewel-like waters, rugged limestone mountains, sun-kissed islands, gorgeous climate and Mediterranean cuisine, this region is a holidaymaker's paradise. Yet it's the cities and islands further south that hog all the limelight, leaving Northern Dalmatia, if not quite undiscovered, then certainly less overrun. Yachties can sail between unpopulated islands without a shred of development, lost in dreams of the Mediterranean of old, while hikers can wander lonely trails where bears and wolves still dwell, and explore three of Croatia's most impressive national parks, which shelter in the hinterland.

By contrast, Zadar is a cultured city rich with museums, Roman ruins, restaurants and hip bars. Meanwhile summertime clubbers gravitate to Zrće Beach and Tisno, which together form the nucleus of Croatia's premier clubbing scene.

Best Places to Eat
➜ Pelegrini (p197)
➜ Mediteran (p198)
➜ Kaštel (p186)
➜ Pet Bunara (p186)
➜ Konoba Figurica (p181)

Best Places to Sleep
➜ Art Hotel Kalelarga (p185)
➜ Boškinac (p180)
➜ House Župan (p175)
➜ Drunken Monkey (p185)
➜ Indigo (p196)

When to Go
Zadar

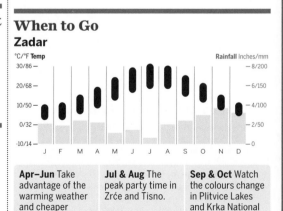

Apr–Jun Take advantage of the warming weather and cheaper prices.	**Jul & Aug** The peak party time in Zrće and Tisno.	**Sep & Oct** Watch the colours change in Plitvice Lakes and Krka National Parks.

Northern Dalmatia Highlights

1 Plitvice Lakes National Park (p173) Marvelling at the otherworldly turquoise lakes and dramatic waterfalls.

2 Krka National Park (p192) Strolling alongside gurgling crystalline streams, swimming in a waterfall-fed lake and exploring historic monasteries.

3 Zadar (p181) Exploring Roman ruins, intriguing museums, local eateries and hip bars within the marbled streets of the old town.

4 Šibenik (p193) Stopping to admire the celebrated architecture of St James' Cathedral while wandering the medieval streets.

5 Pag Island (p178) Enjoying the sensory delights of sun-scorched scenery, fine wine, rustic cooking, pungent cheese and partying in the sun.

6 Kornati National Park (p190) Seeing the Mediterranean as it looked to the ancients while boating between its unpopulated islands.

LIKA

Covering a large swath of the interior between the coastal mountains and the Bosnian border, this lightly populated region has blissful scenery ranging from bucolic farmland to dense forest and craggy uplands. In parts, the karstic nature of the underlying limestone has bequeathed a wonderland of caves, canyons, lakes and waterfalls. The most dramatic of these natural attractions is the Plitvice Lakes National Park, one of Croatia's unmissable experiences.

History

Part of the Croatian heartland since the early 7th century, Lika was attacked by the Ottomans in the 16th century and was incorporated into the military frontier *(vojna krajina)*. Vlach and Serb refugees, driven from Bosnia by the encroaching Ottomans, settled in the region with the blessing of the Habsburg monarchy, on the condition that they were prepared to fight. By the 1910 census the population was almost evenly split between the Orthodox and Catholic faiths, with many districts in the east having an outright Serbian majority.

During WWII, Lika's Serbian population suffered greatly at the hands of the Ustaše regime. In 1991, following Croatia's declaration of independence, the Serbs of the Krajina declared themselves an autonomous republic and it was in Lika that the first shots of the war rang out. Much of the local Croatian population was forced to abandon their homes and flee. When Croatian forces regained the area in 1995, most of the Serb population fled – leaving in their wake the many abandoned homes and villages that can still be seen today. Some, however, chose to return, and today the ethnic make-up of the region is 86% Croat and 12% Serb.

Plitvice Lakes & Around

☑ 053

By far Croatia's top natural attraction and the absolute highlight of Croatia's Adriatic hinterland, this glorious expanse of forested hills and turquoise lakes is excruciatingly scenic – so much so that in 1979 Unesco proclaimed it a World Heritage Site. The name is, however, slightly misleading as it's not so much the lakes that are the attraction here but the hundreds of waterfalls that link them. It's as if Croatia has decided to gather all its waterfalls in one place and charge admission to view them.

The extraordinary natural beauty of the park merits a full day's exploration, but you can still experience a lot on a half-day trip from Zadar or Zagreb. You must be able to walk a fair distance to get the most out of the place.

History

A preservation society was founded in 1893 to ensure the protection of the lakes, and the first hotel was built here in 1896. The boundaries of the national park were set in 1951 and the lakes became a major tourist attraction until the civil war (which actually began in Plitvice on 31 March 1991, when rebel Serbs took control of the park headquarters). Croatian police officer Josip Jović became the war's first victim when he was killed here in the park. The Serbs held the area for the war's duration, turning the hotels into barracks. The Croatian army retook the park in August 1995, and subsequently the park's facilities have been fully restored.

◉ Sights

★ **Plitvice Lakes National Park** NATIONAL PARK
(☑ 053-751 015; www.np-plitvicka-jezera.hr; adult/child 180/80KN Jul & Aug, 110/55KN Apr-Jun, Sep & Oct, 55/35KN Nov-Mar; ☺ 7am-8pm) Within the boundaries of this heavily forested national park, 16 crystalline lakes tumble into each other via a series of waterfalls and cascades. The mineral-rich waters carve through the rock, depositing tufa in continually changing formations. Clouds of butterflies drift above the 18km of wooden footbridges and pathways that snake around the edges and across the rumbling water.

It takes upwards of six hours to explore the lakes on foot, or you can slice two hours off by taking advantage of the park's free boats and buses (departing every 30 minutes from April to October). From Entrance 2, catch the bus to the top of the upper lakes and wander back down to the shore of **Kozjak**, the park's largest lake (about 4km in length). A boat will whisk you from here to the lower lakes, where the circuit culminates in the aptly named **Veliki Slap**, the tallest waterfall in Croatia (78m). The path then climbs steeply (offering great views and photo opportunities) to a bus stop, where you can grab a lift back to Entrance 2.

If you've got limited time, the upper lake section can be completed in two hours. The lower section takes about three, although we recommend that you start with the bus ride and end with the boat to save yourself a climb.

Note that swimming is not permitted in any of the lakes.

Barać's Caves
CAVE

(Baraćeve špilje; ☑047-782 007; www.baraceve-spilje.hr; Nova Kršlja bb; adult/child Mar-May 50/25KN, Jun-Oct 60/30KN; ⏰10am-5pm Fri-Sun Mar, to 6pm daily Apr-Jun & Sep, 9am-7pm daily Jul & Aug, 10am-5pm daily Oct) The same karstic limestone that created the Plitvice Lakes is responsible for these vast caverns hidden beneath verdant farmland 15km northeast of the national park (it's well signposted from the main road). Visits are by way of 45-minute guided tours (minimum two people) through chambers with cheery names such as 'Drag-on's Gorge' and 'Hall of Lost Souls'. Wear warm clothes and sensible shoes.

🛏 Sleeping

The four hotels operated by the national park are relatively charmless institutions but they're conveniently positioned right on the park's borders (see the park's website for details). Otherwise, there are excellent guesthouses within walking distance in sur-rounding villages. For a particularly atmospheric alternative, hunt for private rooms in tiny Korana, an idyllic village set by a gurgling stream, reached by a narrow road north of the Korana bridge.

🛏 Mukinje & Jezerce

Plitvice Backpackers
HOSTEL €

(☑053-774 777; www.plitvicebackpackers.com; Jezerce 62; d/tw 143/315KN; ☎) Located in the village of Jezerce, the nearest village to the lakes just 3km from Entrance 2, this well-run hostel occupies a large house on the main highway. Rooms are clean, lockers are big and there's a fully equipped kitchen. The owners really look after their guests, even shuttling them to and from the park and local supermarket.

Plitvice Mirić Inn
GUESTHOUSE €€

(☑098 93 06 508; www.plitvice-croatia.com; Jezerce 18/1; s/d 500/710KN; ⏰Apr-Oct; P❄☎) Run by a delightful family, this flower-strewn guesthouse has 13 well-cared-for rooms divided between neighbouring buildings, conveniently located a mere 1.5km from Entrance 2. Rooms boast slightly more floor space in the newer annex but they're all very comfortable. Try the home baking if you get a chance.

THE NATURE OF PLITVICE LAKES

The Plitvice lake system is divided into upper and lower sections. The upper lakes, lying in a dolomite valley, are surrounded by dense forests and are linked by several gushing waterfalls. The lower lakes are smaller and shallower. Most of the water comes from the Bijela and Crna (White and Black) Rivers, which join south of Prošćansko Lake, but the lakes are also fed by underground springs. In turn, water disappears into the porous limestone at some points only to re-emerge in other places. All the water empties into the Korana River near Sastavci Falls.

The upper lakes are separated by dolomite barriers, which expand with the mosses and algae that absorb calcium carbonate as river water rushes through the karst. The en-crusted plants grow on top of each other, forming travertine barriers and creating water-falls. The lower lakes were formed by cavities created by the water of the upper lakes. They undergo a similar process, as travertine is constantly forming and reforming itself into new combinations so that the landscape is ever changing. This unique interaction of water, rock and plant life has continued more or less undisturbed since the last ice age.

The lakes' colours also change constantly. Most of the time they're a surreal shade of turquoise, but hues shift with the quantity of minerals and organisms in the water, rainfall and the angle of sunlight. On some days the lakes can appear more jade green or steely grey.

The luxuriant vegetation of the national park includes beech, fir, spruce and white pine forests, dotted with patches of whitebeam, hornbeam and flowering ash, which change colour in autumn.

The mammalian stars of the park are bears and wolves, but there are also deer, boar, rabbits, foxes and badgers. Look out for bird species including hawks, owls, cuckoos, kingfishers, wild ducks and herons, and occasionally black storks and ospreys.

Plitvice Etno-House GUESTHOUSE €€

(☏ 053-774 760; www.plitviceetnohouse.com; Jezerce 21; d 750KN; P 🖥 ☲) Consisting of two large stone-and-wood houses hung with flowerboxes, this attractive complex has just eight pine-trimmed rooms with real character and comfort. There's also a pool outside, with a little paddling area for children.

Villa Lika GUESTHOUSE €€€

(☏ 053-774 302; www.villa-lika.com; Mukinje 63; r 1000KN; ☺ Apr-Oct; P 🌢 🖥 ☲) Right by the bus stop in Mukinje, these two large houses have shiny white rooms offset with brightly coloured curtains and tiles. There are 15 in total, all set around a beautifully landscaped pool, and a recently opened restaurant offering international and Croatian dishes (portion sizes are small).

Selište Drežničko

Kamp Korana CAMPGROUND €

(☏ 053-751 888; www.np-plitvicka-jezera.hr; Rakovica; site per adult/child/tent/car 67/47/15/22KN, bungalow s/d 148/252KN; ☺ Apr-Oct; P) Spread over 35 hectares flanking the Korana River, this huge national-park-run campground is about 6km north of Entrance 1, on the road to Zagreb. Facilities include a restaurant, a cafe-bar and a shop.

Hotel Degenija HOTEL €€€

(☏ 047-782 143; www.hotel-degenija.com; Selište Drežničko 57a; s/d from 675/960KN; P 🌢 🖥) With a crisp, newish feel, this 20-room roadside hotel, 4km north of Plitvice Lakes National Park's Entrance 1, has smart international-standard rooms and an attractive cafe, grafted onto the side in its own wooden pavilion, offering grilled meats and pizza.

Grabovac & Rakovica

★**House Župan** GUESTHOUSE €€

(☏ 047-784 057; www.sobe-zupan.com; Rakovica 35; s/d 224/329KN; P 🌢 🖥) With an exceptionally welcoming hostess and clean, contemporary and reasonably priced rooms, this is a superb choice. There's even a guest kitchen and plenty of other diversions when you want to relax after a hike. It's set back from the highway in the small town of Rakovica, 11km north of the park.

House Tina GUESTHOUSE €€

(☏ 047-784 197; www.housetina.com; Grabovac 175; d/bungalow 523/838KN; P 🌢 🖥 🅿) Smart

and modern but with a rural ambience, this large family-run guesthouse offers first-rate family-friendly accommodation both in the main house and in two rustic wooden bungalows in the yard. It's 9km from the park's Entrance 1, but the owners can organise transport for a relatively small cost.

✗ Eating

Eating options are limited in the national park itself, with a handful of options scattered about the entrances and the bus and boat stops.

Vila Velebita CROATIAN €€

(☏ 053-755 040; www.vila-velebita.com; Rudanovac 12a; mains 50-90KN; ☺ 7am-11pm) Traditional meat grills are the speciality here, especially spit-roast lamb and suckling pig. If you've got your own transport, it's well worth the 14km trip south along the highway from Entrance 2.

Restaurant Degenija EUROPEAN €€

(☏ 047-782 060; www.hotel-degenija.com; Selište Drežničko 57a; mains 45-125KN; ☺ 7am-11pm; 🖥) The menu of this upmarket restaurant covers a lot of bases (pasta, pizza, fish) but meat is the star player. Traditional treats include turkey on gnocchi-like dumplings and, in summer, veal and potatoes slow-cooked under a *peka* (a dome-shaped cooking 'bell').

ⓘ Information

Both of the park's two main entrances have parking (per hour/day 7/70KN) and an information office stocking brochures and maps.

ℹ Getting There & Away

Buses stop at both park entrances and there's a small ticket office at the stop near Entrance 2. Destinations include:

Šibenik 110KN, four hours, three daily

Split 166KN, 4½ hours, six daily

Zadar 90KN, 2½ hours, seven daily

Zagreb 85KN, two hours, many daily

Paklenica National Park

📷 023

Stretching for 145km and creating a natural barrier between inland and coastal Croatia, the rugged peaks of the Velebit Massif are an impressive sight. The **Paklenica National Park** (www.paklenica.hr; adult/child Jun-Sep 50/30KN, Oct-May 40/20KN; ⊙ entrance booths 6am-8.30pm Jun-Sep, 7am-3pm Oct-May) takes up 95 sq km of these limestone mountains and boasts some of Croatia's most dramatic alpine vistas. It's a superb place to cast off the swimwear and instead trek gorges, do a bit of climbing or just amble along one of the many streams that score the land.

The two biggest attractions in the park are the gorges of Velika Paklenica (Great Paklenica) and Mala Paklenica (Small Paklenica), where cliffs rise 400m into the azure skies. Animals you might spot along the way include golden eagles, striped eagles, peregrine falcons, lynx, bears and chamois – the last of these gather near the park entrances.

◎ Sights & Activities

Most hikes in the park are one-day affairs from either of the two main park entrances (accessed from Starigrad-Paklenica on the coast), or from one of the mountain huts. Given the nature of the terrain, most of them are reasonably challenging, although there are shorter routes suitable for novices. It's a good idea to ask at the national park office about walks that will suit your level of ability.

Landmines left over from the 1990s are still a risk in some of the higher zones of the park. Follow only clearly marked paths and check with the park office before attempting any unusual routes.

Paklenica has rock-climbing routes ranging from beginner level to borderline suicidal. The firm, occasionally sharp limestone offers graded climbs, including 72 short sports routes and 250 longer routes.

Manita Peć   CAVE

(adult/child 20/10KN; ⊙ 10am-1pm Jul-Sep, reduced days Apr-Jun & Oct) The only cave in the park that's open to the public, Manita Peć has a wealth of stalagmites and stalactites enhanced by strategically placed lighting in the main chamber (40m long and 32m high). Entry is by way of a 30-minute tour.

The cave is about 90 minutes' walk from the Entrance 1 car park. The path heads right up and into the Velika Paklenica gorge. When you pass a rocky waterfall with a stream on your right, you'll be at Anića Luka, a green, semicircular plateau. After another kilometre a steep trail leads up to the cave.

Anića Kuk   CLIMBING

Climbing is a popular activity in Paklenica National Park. You'll see the beginners' routes at the entrance to the park, with cliffs reaching about 40m, but the best and most advanced climbing is on Anića Kuk, which offers over 100 routes up to a maximum of 350m. Most of the routes are bolted.

The most popular climbs here are Mosoraški (350m), Velebitaški (350m) and Klin (300m).

Spring is the best climbing season as summers can be hot and winters too windy. A rescue service is also available. Consult Boris Čulić's *Paklenica* climber's guide for the complete rundown; it's available from the park office.

🛏 Sleeping

Within the park's boundaries there's some rustic accommodation for hikers and climbers, but most people prefer to base themselves in the relative comfort of Starigrad-Paklenica, the small settlement that sprawls along the coastal road near the entrances to the park. It's neither particularly *stari* (old) or much of a *grad* (town) but it does have access to the sea for a cooling dip after a day's exertions.

🛏 National Park

Rugged types can avail themselves of three basic free-of-charge mountain shelters: Ivine Vodice, Struge and Vlaški Grad. There's no electricity and you'll need your own sleeping bag, but each has a spring that is a reliable source of water in all but the height of summer; check with the park office or at Planinarski Dom Paklenica before setting out.

Planinarski Dom Paklenica   HUT **€**

(📷 023-301 636; www.pdpaklenica.hr; dm 90KN; ⊙ Sat & Sun year-round, daily mid-Jun–mid-Sep) Offering such luxuries as running water, a toilet and electricity, this lodge crams 50 beds into

LIKA'S HIDDEN GEMS

The administrative capital of Lika-Senj county, **Gospić**, is a sleepy kind of place, but there are a couple of sights in the vicinity that are well worth seeking out. You'll need your own wheels though.

Nikola Tesla Memorial Centre (☑ 053-746 530; www.mcnikolatesla.hr; Smiljan; adult/child 50/20KN; ⊗ 8am-8pm Tue-Sun Apr-Oct, 9am-3pm Tue-Sun Nov-Mar) It's extraordinary to think that one of the greatest minds of the modern world originated from such a peaceful and obscure place as the tiny village of **Smiljan**, 5km west of Gospić. Yet it was here that Nikola Tesla – the man responsible for bringing electricity into our homes and inventing wireless technology – was born. This fascinating museum includes displays about his life and working replicas of some of his most famous inventions.

Tesla's father was a Serbian Orthodox priest and, sadly, the family house, barn and church on this site were torched during the 1990s war. What stands here today is a re-construction, financed by the Croatian government.

Grabovača Cave Park (Pećinski Park Grabovača; ☑ 053-679 233; www.pp-grabovaca.hr; Perušić; tours adult/child 45/35KN; ⊗ 9am-8pm Jun-Aug, to 5pm Apr, May, Sep & Oct) The small town of **Perušić**, 12km north of Gospić, is notable for its pretty onion-domed church and its perfect chess-piece Turkish castle. However, the main attraction is this extraordinary cave complex on the edge of town. The largest cave, Samograd, has four beautiful chambers – the biggest of which is large enough to host a concert every Easter Monday. Tours depart on the hour, descending 480 handmade stairs into the depths (not suitable for small children). Wear warm clothes and sensible footwear.

Kuterevo Refuge (www.kuterevo-medvjedi.org; ⊗ hours vary) In the village of **Kuterevo** in the northern Velebit Range lies the Kuterevo Refuge for young bears. Founded in 2002 by Velebit Association Kuterevo (Velebitska Udruga Kuterevo; VUK), it works together with villagers to protect orphaned bears that are endangered due to traffic, hunting and poaching. From spring to late autumn, it's possible to visit the baby bears at the refuge, which attracts some 10,000 visitors per year. The website is in Croatian, but emails will be answered in English.

Linden Tree Retreat & Ranch (☑ 053-685 616; www.lindenretreat.com; Velika Plana 3; s/d 410/820KN) Nestled within the wild reaches of the Velebit mountains, 27km northwest of Gospić, this remote dude ranch offers atmospheric accommodation in tepees or wooden chalets. The highlight here is horse riding (646KN for a two-hour jaunt, 1026KN for a day trip), but you can also partake in wagon rides, guided hikes to nearby caves, mountain biking and mountain climbing.

four rooms; bring a sleeping bag. There's also a kitchen and dining room. The hut is a two-hour walk up from the Velika Paklenica gorge. Reservations are recommended on summer weekends.

🏠 Starigrad-Paklenica

Camp 'National Park'   CAMPGROUND **€**
(☑ 023-369 155; www.paklenica.hr; Starigrad-Paklenica; adult/pitch 40/35KN; ⊗ mid-Mar–mid-Nov) On a bit of gravelly Adriatic beach next to the park's admin building, this basic 100-person campground is a favourite among climbers and other adventurers heading into the limestone canyons of the Paklenica National Park. The swimming is great. No reservations are taken.

Pansion Kiko   GUESTHOUSE **€€€**
(☑ 023-369 784; www.pansion-kiko.com; Ante Starčevića bb, Seline; s/d 1120/1350KN; P ❋ 🛜) Just outside of Starigrad, in the coastal village of Seline, this superb guesthouse offers 12 balconied rooms as well as access to a private beach and a decent restaurant. The friendly family owners will go out of their way to make sure your stay is as comfortable as possible, and this is a great base for exploring the Paklenica National Park.

🍴 Eating

Taverna-Konoba Marasović   CROATIAN **€€**
(Marasovići bb; mains 60-140KN; ⊗ 1-10pm May-Oct) 🍴 A kilometre inland from Entrance 1, this eatery occupies a fantastic old village house with a terrace at the front and chunky

tables in the dining room. All the food is locally sourced and, with advance notice, can be cooked in a traditional *peka*. The national park owns the property and usually has interesting displays upstairs.

Buffet Dinko   CROATIAN **€€**
(☑ 091 51 29 445; www.dinko-paklenica.com; Paklenička 1; mains 50-110KN; ◑ 7am-11pm) At the junction of the coastal highway and the access road to Entrance 1 in Starigrad, this popular restaurant has a shady terrace and a hefty menu of grilled meat and seafood. Helpings are normally huge. The owners also have rooms to rent.

ⓘ Information

Paklenica National Park Office (☑ 023-369 155; www.paklenica.hr; Dr Franje Tuđmana 14a; ◑ 7am-3pm Mon-Fri) Sells booklets and maps. The *Paklenica National Park* guide gives an excellent overview of the park and details on walks. Rock-climbing permits cost 60KN to 80KN depending on the season; climbers should talk to guides at the park office for advice.

Starigrad Tourist Office (☑ 023-369 245; www.rivijera-paklenica.hr; Trg Tome Marasovića 1; ◑ 8am-9.30pm Jul & Aug, to 8pm Jun & Sep, to 2pm Mon-Fri Oct-May) In the Starigrad town centre, across from the small marina.

Croatian Mountaineering Association (Hrvatski planinarski savez; ☑ 01-48 23 624; www.hps.hr) Has up-to-date information and publishes a useful map of the park. Or consult Boris Čulić's *Paklenica* climber's guide for the complete rundown.

ⓘ Getting There & Away

Most buses travelling along the coastal highway stop at Starigrad-Paklenica. Destinations include Rijeka (110KN, 3½ hours, five daily), Zadar (26KN, 50 minutes, five daily), Split (102KN, four hours, five daily), Dubrovnik (from 200KN, nine hours, three daily) and Zagreb (127KN, 3¾ hours, daily).

There are generally no taxis in Starigrad. Some hotels will drop off and pick up guests at the park's entrance gates.

PAG ISLAND

Pag is like something you'd find in a 1950s Italian film, perfect for a broody black-and-white Antonioni set – it's barren, rocky, and sepia coloured, with vast empty landscapes. The Adriatic is a steely blue around it and,

when the sky is stormy, the island is the most dramatic-looking place in the whole of Croatia. Its karstic rock forms a moonscape defined by two mountain ridges, patches of shrubs and a dozen or so villages and hamlets.

Nowadays it's connected to the mainland by a bridge – but in terms of culture it's very independent and distinct. Islanders farm the miserly soil and produce some excellent wine. Tough local sheep graze on herbs and salty grasses, lending their meat and milk a distinctive flavour and producing *paški sir* (Pag cheese). Intricate Pag lace is famed and framed on many a Croat's wall.

Pag is now an unlikely clubbing mecca with Zrće Beach a summer nightlife hot spot.

History

The island was inhabited by the Illyrians before falling to Rome in the 1st century BC. Slavs settled around Novalja in the 7th century AD. In the 11th century, salt production began to take off, resulting in conflicts with Zadar and Rab over the salt trade. In 1409 Pag was sold to Venice along with Zadar and the rest of Dalmatia. Subsequent squabbles saw the island invaded by Venetians, Austrians, French (and Austrians again), then a German-Italian occupation during WWII.

ⓘ Getting There & Away

BOAT

A daily catamaran with Jadrolinija (www.jadrolinija.hr) connects Novalja to Rab (45KN, 55 minutes) and Rijeka (80KN, 2¾ hours).

Regular Jadrolinija car ferries also link Žigljen on Pag's northeast coast to Prizna on the mainland (per adult/child/car 17/8.50/96KN, 15 minutes); these run roughly every 90 minutes, increasing to hourly in July and August. If you're coming from the north, this will save you at least 1½ hours driving time as opposed to taking the bridge.

BUS

Buses head to Zadar year-round (52KN, two hours, three to five daily), and to Šibenik (124KN, 2½ hours, two daily), Split (204KN, five hours, two daily), Rijeka (152KN, four hours, two daily) and Zagreb (205KN, 4½ to six hours, three daily) in summer.

ⓘ Getting Around

Three to 11 buses a day make the 30-minute trip between Pag Town and Novalja (from 30KN).

Pag Town

📞 023 / POP 3120

Historic Pag Town enjoys a spectacular setting, fringing a narrow spit of land between sun-scorched hills, with an azure bay on its eastern flank and shimmering salt pans to its west. It's an intimate grid of narrow lanes and bleak-looking stone houses with pebble beaches close by.

In the early 15th century the prosperous salt business (Pag sea salt can still be bought in any supermarket) prompted the construction of Pag Town when adjacent Stari Grad could no longer meet the demands of its burgeoning population. Venetian rulers engaged the finest builder of the time, Juraj Dalmatinac, to design a new city – the first cornerstone was laid in 1443. In the centre, there's a square with a cathedral, a ducal palace and an unfinished bishop's palace. In 1499 Dalmatinac began working on the city walls, but only the northern corner, with parts of a castle, remains.

⊙ Sights

Pag Lace Gallery   MUSEUM
(Galerija paške čipke; Trg Kralja Krešimira IV; 10KN; ⊙9am-noon & 7-10pm Jul & Aug, 9am-noon Jun & Sep, call tourist office for access Oct-May) Housed in the spectacular restored Ducal Palace (Kneževa Palača), designed by Juraj Dalmatinac, this museum showcases some remarkably intricate designs. The history of lacemaking in Pag and its importance to the community is skilfully illustrated with photographs and information panels.

**Collegiate Church
of the Assumption**   CHURCH
(Zborna Crkva Marijinog Uznesenja; Trg Kralja Krešimira IV; ⊙9am-noon & 5-7pm May-Sep, Mass only Oct-Apr) Dalmatinac's Gothic church sits in perfect harmony with the modest structures surrounding it on the pretty main square. The lunette over the portal shows the Virgin with women of Pag in medieval blouses and headdresses, and there are two rows of unfinished sculptures of saints. Completed in the 16th century, the interior was renovated with baroque stucco ceiling decorations in the 18th century.

✦ Festivals & Events

Pag Carnival   CULTURAL
(⊙last weekend in Jul) The Pag Carnival is a tradition that's been 80 years in the making.

Watch the *kolo* (a lively Slavic circle dance) and appreciate the elaborate traditional dress of Pag. The main square fills with dancers and musicians, and a theatre troupe presents the folk play *Paška Robinja* (The Slave Girl of Pag).

🛏 Sleeping & Eating

While Pag Town is an interesting place to visit, there are better places to stay. There are a few hotels scattered around the bay immediately north of the old town and plenty of private accommodation on offer; enquire at a travel agency or look for signs advertising '*sobe*' (rooms available).

Konoba Barcarola   SEAFOOD €
(Golija 41; mains 55-70KN; ⊙11am-midnight) A simple seafood restaurant near a pebbly beach a short walk north of the old town, with a fishing-paraphernalia-bedecked dining room and a terrace shaded by pungent jasmine trees. Fish is sold by the kilo and there's plenty of meat for those who don't like their dinner plucked from the briny. Full marks to this place for staying open even in winter.

Bistro Na Tale   CROATIAN €€
(Radićeva 2; mains 40-180KN; ⊙9am-11pm Tue-Sun) This dependable, casual and highly popular place has a little front terrace facing the salt flats and another with plenty of shade. Pag lamb is a real speciality, or opt for the fresh fish of the day cooked in wine and herbs. Open year-round.

🛍 Shopping

It would be a shame to leave the island without buying lace, since the prices are relatively cheap and buying a piece helps keep the tradition alive. A small circle or star about 10cm in diameter takes a good 24 hours to make. If you walk down Kralja Tomislava or Kralja Dmitra Zvonimira you

---

BEACH CAMPING

On a gorgeous cove with a shingle beach, about 12km from Pag Town in the direction of Novalja, **Camping Šimuni** (📞023-697 441; www.camping-simuni.hr; Šimuni bb; per adult/child/site 87/61/205KN, unit from 874KN; 🅿❄🛜) is a large complex that has a good vibe and lots of activities on offer. All local buses stop here.

can buy directly from the lace makers, virtually all of whom have fixed prices.

Siroteka CHEESE
(Vela 12; ⊙ 10am-5pm Tue-Sat, 9am-2pm Sun) Near the tourist office, this tiny shop sells a range of reeking, locally produced cheeses and is open year-round.

ℹ️ Information

Mediteran Pag (📞 023-611 238; www.mediteranpag.com; Zrinsko-frankopanska 8; ⊙ hours vary) Agency with a very wide selection of private accommodation and excursions.

Meridian 15 (📞 023-612 162; www.meridijan15.hr; Ante Starčevića 1; ⊙ hours vary) Travel agency that runs island excursions and trips to national parks including Paklenica. Also has a long list of apartments on its books.

Post Office (Golija bb; ⊙ 7.30am-9pm Mon-Fri, 8am-noon Sat mid-Jun–mid-Sep, 8am-5pm Mon-Fri, 8am-noon Sat rest of the year)

Tourist Office (📞 023-611 286; www.tzgpag.hr; Vela bb; ⊙ 8am-10pm Jul & Aug, 8am-8pm Mon-Fri, 8am-1pm Sat & Sun Jun & Sep, 8am-3pm Mon-Fri Oct-May)

Novalja & Around

📞 053 / POP 3670

In a nation of sedate resorts, Novalja bucks the trend big time. Its thumping bars and clubs offer nightlife as raucous as you'll find in Croatia and as a consequence it attracts a noticeably younger crowd. Depending on which side of 35 you sit on, this could be heaven or it could be hell. Cultural interest is confined to the incendiary club scene based on nearby Zrće Beach; there are no historic sights. That said, the promenade has an appealing buzz, and there are fine beaches close by. In winter it reverts to being a cold, virtually uninhabited, sleepy backwater.

🎉 Festivals & Events

Hideout MUSIC
(www.hideoutfestival.com; ⊙ late Jun-early Jul) The festival that put Zrće on the EDM (electronic dance music) map takes over the beach bars and clubs in summer. Expect big-name DJs and multiple nights of mayhem.

Fresh Island MUSIC
(www.fresh-island.org; ⊙ mid-Jul) Fresh Island comes to Zrće's Papaya and Aquarius clubs for three nights in mid-July. Past headliners have included the likes of Rick Ross, Method Man and Redman.

Sonus MUSIC
(www.sonus-festival.com; ⊙ mid-Aug) Five days and nights of EDM on Zrće. In previous years it's featured the likes of John Digweed and Laurent Garnier.

🛏️ Sleeping

Most of the best places to stay are a little out of the town centre. Accommodation is incredibly hard to find during the summer party season, especially during the big events, so make sure you book ahead.

Big Yellow Hostel HOSTEL €
(📞 053-663 539; www.bigyellowhostel.com; Lokunje 1; dm/r from 210/500KN; P@🛜) The best of a gaggle of hostels catering to the young party crowd, Big Yella offers a laid-back, post-club vibe, free breakfast and basic four- to eight-bed dorms, some of which have balconies and terrific sea views. Near the bus stop for Zrće Beach. It's not flash but it hits the spot.

Barbati HOTEL €€
(📞 091 12 11 233; www.barbati.hr; Vidalići 39; r/apt from 750/1870KN; P✱@🛜🏊) Located across the bay from Zrće (you'll hear it in the distance) within a scrappy development of beach apartments 6km from Novalja, this chic little hotel has well-designed rooms, a tiny covered pool and an attractive waterside bar/restaurant.

★ Boškinac HOTEL €€€
(📞 053-663 500; www.boskinac.com; Škopaljska 120; r 1800KN; P✱🛜🏊) Hands down the most sophisticated place to stay, eat and drink on Pag, this wonderful little winery hotel offers eight huge rooms and three suites in a blissful rural location surrounded by vines. Even if you're not staying here you should make the pilgrimage to sample the wine (cellar hours are noon to 1am) and to dine at the acclaimed restaurant (mains 70KN to 160KN).

Their cabernet merlot blend is excellent and they're the only place in the world growing and making wine from Gegić, a grape endemic to Pag (producing an elegant white). It's about 3km north of Novalja; follow the signs towards Stara Novalja.

Luna HOTEL €€€
(📞 053-654 700; www.lunaislandhotel.com; Jakišnica bb; r from 930KN; P✱🛜🏊) Up the northern end of the island, 14km from Novalja, this big modern hotel is a good option for a poolside holiday. Rooms are spacious, and fa-

CULINARY KOLAN

The agricultural village of Kolan sits on Pag Island's sunburnt central ridge, on the main road between Pag Town and Novalja. It's a great place to shop for Pag cheese.

Just below the lower road running through Kolan sits **Konoba Figurica** (Figurica 11, Kolan; mains 50-160KN; ⊘noon-10pm Jun-Oct), a rustic restaurant that occupies a covered terrace surrounded by olive trees. Share a Pag cheese platter and then tuck into delicious grilled squid or *peka*-roasted Pag lamb.

cilities include pools and a spa centre. You'll need your own transport to reach it.

✗ Eating

Within Novalja itself there are plenty of eateries catering to the foreign backpacker/clubber crowd, including an American burger bar, a Mexican joint and loads of places selling pizza slices. For a more memorable meal you're better off jumping in the car (if you've got one) and heading to Kolan or the acclaimed restaurant at the Boškinac hotel.

Starac i More   SEAFOOD **€€**
(⊘053-662 423; Braće Radić bb; mains 40-115KN; ⊘noon-11.30pm) For a bit of sober Croatian authenticity in clubbing Novalja, head to this characterful tavern (the name translates as 'the old man and the sea') set just back from the seafront and bedecked in fishing paraphernalia (and the odd giant fish). The seafood here is the best in town and waiters will recommend wine to go with your meal.

🍷 Drinking & Nightlife

About 3km southeast of Novalja, **Zrće Beach** is staking its claim as the Ibiza of Croatia. Unlike Ibiza, the clubs and bars are right on the beach – but in terms of scale, it's got a long way to go. Basically there are three main clubs and a scattering of bars in between, all of which open in late June and close by mid-September. Entrance prices very much depend on the event: nights are usually free at the beginning of the season but cost as much as €35 for big-name DJs in mid-August.

The beach itself is a picturesque 1km-long treeless crescent of pebbles overlooking a parched strip of eastern Pag, with the mountains of the mainland rearing up on the horizon – rent an umbrella for shade. Out of season you'll have this otherwise lonely place to yourself.

★**Papaya**   CLUB
(www.papaya.com.hr; ⊘10am-6am) Rated one of the best clubs in the world, Papaya is the kingpin of the Zrće scene, complete with palm trees, waterfalls and a shell-like roof over the dancefloor. On big nights it can cram 5000 people onto its terraces.

Kalypso   CLUB
(www.kalypso-zrce.com; ⊘10am-6am) Kalypso is the coolest-looking club on the strip, built into a cove at the north end of the beach with myriad cabana-like bars surrounded by palm trees. While the sun shines you can chill out on day beds by a small pool; after dark, DJs spin deep house mixes to a sophisticated crowd.

Aquarius   CLUB
(www.aquarius.hr; ⊘hours vary) Repeatedly voted one of the top 100 clubs in the world, Aquarius is a huge space with stylish alcoves, great views and a glassed-off area.

ℹ Information

Aurora (⊘053-663 493; www.aurora-novalja. com; Slatinska 9; ⊘9am-8pm) Well-organised agency with rental apartments and rooms on its books. Can arrange excursions too.
Sunturist (⊘053-661 211; www.sunturist.hr; Silvija Strahimira Kranjčevićeva bb; ⊘hours vary) Books private accommodation and trips.
Tourist Office (⊘053-661 404; www.tz-novalja.hr; Trg Brišćić 1; ⊘8am-8pm Jun-Sep, to 3pm Mon-Fri Oct-May) Stocks free town maps and timetables for boats and buses.

ℹ Getting Around

In summer shuttle buses run from Novalja to Zrće Beach (10KN). If you fancy the walk or bike ride, it's 4.1km from Novalja's centre.

ZADAR

⊘023 / POP 75,100

Boasting a historic old town of Roman ruins, medieval churches, cosmopolitan cafes and quality museums set on a small peninsula, Zadar is an intriguing city. It's not too crowded, it's not overrun with tourists and its two unique attractions – the sound-and-light spectacle of the *Sea Organ* and the *Sun Salutation* – need to be seen and heard to be believed.

While it's not a picture-postcard kind of place, the mix of ancient relics, Habsburg elegance, coastal setting and unsightly tower blocks is what gives Zadar so much character. It's no Dubrovnik, but it's not a museum town either – this is a living, vibrant city, enjoyed by residents and visitors alike.

Zadar is also a key transport hub with superb ferry connections to the surrounding islands.

History

Zadar was inhabited by the Illyrian Liburnian tribe as early as the 9th century BC. By the 1st century BC, it had become a minor Roman colony. Slavs settled here in the 6th and 7th centuries AD, and Zadar eventually fell under the authority of Croatian-Hungarian kings.

The rise of Venetian power in the mid-12th century was bitterly contested – there was a succession of citizens' uprisings over the next 200 years – but the city was finally acquired by Venice in 1409, along with the rest of Dalmatia.

Frequent Veneto-Turkish wars resulted in the building of Zadar's famous city walls in the 16th century, partly on the remains of the earlier Roman fortifications. With the fall of Venice in 1797, the city passed to Austrian rulers, who administered the city with the assistance of its Italianised ruling aristocracy. Italian influence endured well into the 20th century, with Zadar (or Zara as the Italians call it) captured by Italy at the end of WWI and officially ceded to Italy with the Treaty of Rapallo in 1922.

When Italy capitulated to the Allies in 1943, the city was occupied by the Germans and then bombed to smithereens by the Allies, with almost 60% of the old town destroyed. The city was rebuilt following the original street plan.

History repeated itself in November 1991 when Yugoslav rockets kept Zadar under siege for three months. Few war wounds are now visible, however, and Zadar has re-emerged as one of Croatia's most dynamic towns.

⊙ Sights

Land Gate
GATE

(Kopnena vrata; Ante Kuzmanića bb) The most elaborate of the city gates also has the prettiest setting, facing a sheltered little marina.

Dating from 1543, its Renaissance-style decorations include St Chrysogonus (Zadar's patron saint) on horseback and the Venetian winged lion. The gate is still used by traffic.

Five Wells Square
SQUARE

(Trg Pet Bunara) Built in 1574 on the site of a former moat, this square takes its name from the five wells that supplied Zadar with water until 1838. Set into the neighbouring bastion is **Queen Jelena Madijevka Park**, a lovely little garden with shady paths, a cafe and views from the ramparts.

St Simeon's Church
CHURCH

(Crkva Sv Šime; Poljana Šime Budinića bb; ⊙ 8.30am-noon & 5-7pm Mon-Fri, 8.30am-noon Sat May-Oct) While this 17th-century baroque church is pretty enough, it's what lies inside that makes it truly noteworthy. Taking pride of place above the main altar, the sarcophagus of St Simeon is a masterpiece of medieval goldsmithery. Commissioned in 1377, the coffin is made of cedar and covered inside and out with finely executed gold-plated silver reliefs.

The middle relief showing the Presentation of Jesus to Simeon at the Temple is a copy of Giotto's fresco from Cappella dell'Arena in Padua, Italy. Other reliefs depict scenes from the lives of the saints and King Ludovic's visit to Zadar. The lid shows a reclining St Simeon.

Museum of Ancient Glass
MUSEUM

(Muzej antičkog stakla; www.mas-zadar.hr; Poljana Zemaljskog Odbora 1; adult/concession 30/10KN; ⊙ 9am-9pm Mon-Sat May-Sep, to 4pm Oct-Apr) It's baffling that a medium as delicate as glass could survive the earthquakes and wars that have plagued this region over the millennia, but this impressive museum has thousands of objects on display: goblets, jars, vials, jewellery and amulets. Many of the larger glass urns were removed from the local Roman necropolis (cemetery) where they held cremated remains. The layout is superb, with large light boxes and ethereal music to heighten the experience.

There are daily demonstrations of glassblowing, beadmaking and miniature bottle production, usually between 10am and 2pm.

People's Square
SQUARE

(Narodni trg) Traditionally the centre of public life, this pretty little square is constantly abuzz with the chatter from its many cafebars. The western side is dominated by the late-Renaissance **City Guard** building, dating from 1562; the clock tower was added under the Austrian administration in 1798. Public proclamations and judgments were announced from the **loggia** opposite (1565), which is now an art-exhibition space.

Archaeological Museum
MUSEUM
(Arheološki Muzej; www.amzd.hr; Trg Opatice Čike 1; adult/concession 30/15KN; ⊙ 9am-9pm Jun & Sep, to 10pm Jul & Aug, to 3pm Apr, May & Oct, to 2pm Mon-Fri, to 1pm Sat Nov-Mar) A wealth of pre-historic, ancient and medieval relics, mainly from Zadar and its surrounds, awaits at this fascinating museum. Highlights include a 2.5m-high marble statue of Augustus from the 1st century AD, and a model of the Forum as it once looked.

Museum of Religious Art
MUSEUM
(Trg Opatice Čike bb; adult/concession 30/10KN; ⊙ 10am-1pm & 5-7pm Mon-Sat, 10am-1pm Sun) This impressive museum in the Benedictine convent boasts a fine collection of reliquaries, sculpture, embroidery and paintings. Of particular note are works by Venetian masters Paolo Veneziano and Vittore Carpaccio.

Roman Forum
RUINS
(Zeleni trg) One of the most intriguing things about Zadar is the way Roman ruins seem to sprout randomly from the city's streets. Nowhere is this more evident than at the site of the ancient forum, constructed between the 1st century BC and the 3rd century AD. As in Roman times it's still the centre of civic and religious life, with St Donatus' Church dominating one side of it.

Among the ruins of temples and colonnades stands one intact Roman column, which in the Middle Ages served as a shame post where wrongdoers were chained and publicly humiliated. Nearby are more Roman remains, including altars with reliefs of the mythical figures Jupiter Ammon and Medusa. On the top you can see the hollows used in blood sacrifices. It is believed that this area was a temple dedicated to Jupiter, Juno and Minerva dating from the 1st century BC.

St Donatus' Church
CHURCH
(Crkva Sv Donata; Šimuna Kožičića Benje bb; 20KN; ⊙ 9am-9pm May-Sep, to 4pm Oct-Apr) Dating from the beginning of the 9th century, this unusual circular Byzantine-style church was named after the bishop who commissioned it. As one of only a handful of buildings from the early Croatian kingdom to have survived the Mongol invasion of the 13th century, it's a particularly important cultural relic. The simple and unadorned interior includes two complete Roman columns, recycled from the Forum. Also from the Forum are the paving slabs that were revealed after the original floor was removed.

The church hasn't been used for services for around 200 years and these days it often serves as a concert hall.

St Anastasia's Cathedral
CATHEDRAL
(Katedrala Sv Stošije; Trg Sv Stošije; ⊙ 6.30-7pm Mon-Fri, 8-9am Sat, 8-9am & 6-7pm Sun) Built in the 12th and 13th centuries, Zadar's cathedral has a richly decorated facade and an impressive three-nave interior with the remains of frescoes in the side apses. The cathedral was badly bombed during WWII and has since been reconstructed. On the altar in the left apse is a marble sarcophagus containing the relics of St Anastasia, while the choir contains lavishly carved stalls. A glass vestibule allows you to peer inside when the cathedral's closed.

Climb the **bell tower** (Široka; 15KN; ⊙ 9am-10pm Mon-Sat) for old-town views.

Franciscan Monastery
MONASTERY
(Franjevački Samostan; www.svetifrane.org; Trg Sv Frane 1; adult/child 10/5KN; ⊙ 9am-6pm) Entry to this historic monastery includes access to a lovely Renaissance cloister, the Gothic church (the oldest of its kind in Dalmatia, consecrated in 1280), the sacristy (where the 1358 treaty under which Venice relinquished its rights to Dalmatia in favour of the Croatian-Hungarian king Ludovic was signed) and a small treasury. Highlights of the last include a large 12th-century painted wooden crucifix, a 15th-century polyptych from the island of Ugljan and a 16th-century painting of the dead Christ by Jacopo Bassano.

★ Sea Organ
MONUMENT
(Morske orgulje; Istarska Obala) FREE Zadar's incredible *Sea Organ,* designed by local architect Nikola Bašić, is unique. Set within the perforated stone stairs that descend into the sea is a system of pipes and whistles that exudes wistful sighs when the movement of the sea pushes air through it. The effect is hypnotic, the mellifluous tones increasing in volume when a boat or ferry passes by. You can swim from the steps off the promenade while listening to the sounds. This is a superb spot to peacefully watch the sun go down to the mesmerising tones of Zadar's most popular attraction.

NORTHERN DALMATIA ZADAR

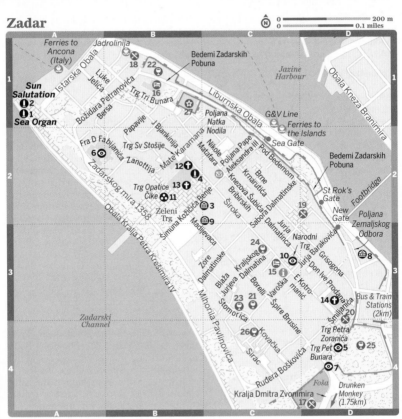

Zadar

NORTHERN DALMATIA ZADAR

Zadar

★ Sun Salutation — MONUMENT

(Pozdrav Suncu; Istarska Obala) Another wacky and wonderful creation by Nikola Bašić (along with the nearby Sea Organ; p183), this 22m-wide circle set into the pavement is filled with 300 multilayered glass plates that collect the sun's energy during the day. Together with the wave energy that makes the *Sea Organ's* sound, it produces a trippy light show from sunset to sunrise that's meant to simulate the solar system. It also collects enough energy to power the entire harbour-front lighting system.

The place is packed with tourists, excited children and locals every night, especially at sunset, when the gorgeous sea views and the illuminated pavement make for a spectacular sight.

★ Activities

There's a **swimming area** with diving boards, a park and cafe on the coastal promenade south of the old town; from the Land Gate, follow the road as it curves to the right and continue on Kralja Dmitra Zvonimira. The promenade takes you to a beach in front of Hotel Kolovare and then winds on for about 1km along the coast.

☞ Tours

Local travel agencies offer **boat cruises** to Telašćica Bay and the beautiful Kornati Islands; tours generally include lunch and a swim in the sea or a salt lake. Ask around on Liburnska Obala (where the excursion boats are moored) or contact Aquarius Travel Agency (p187). Organised trips to the national parks of Paklenica, Krka and Plitvice Lakes are also very popular, making it easy for visitors to access the parks without having to worry about organising transport.

★☆ Festivals & Events

Full Moon Festival — CULTURAL

(Noć Punog Miseca; ☉ Jul) During this festival (held on the night of the full moon in July), Zadar's quays are lit with torches and candles, stalls sell local delicacies and boats lining the quays become floating fish markets.

St Donatus Musical Evenings — MUSIC

(Glazbene večeri u Sv Donatu; www.donat-festival. com; ☉ late Jul-early Aug) Classical-music performances featuring prominent artists from across the globe, held in St Donatus' Church.

Zadar Dreams — THEATRE

(Zadar Snova; www.zadarsnova.hr; ☉ early-Aug) International festival of contemporary theatre, held over a week.

🛏 Sleeping

There's little accommodation in the old town itself, but plenty in the surrounding city.

Most visitors stay in the 'tourist settlement' of Borik, 4km north of the old town. Although a 40-minute walk away, it has good swimming, a nice promenade and lots of greenery.

There are many private rooms and apartments in Zadar and the surrounding satellite communities, most notably in Bibinje, a handy stopover for the airport.

★ Drunken Monkey — HOSTEL €

(☎ 023-314 406; www.drunkenmonkeyhostel.com; Jure Kastriotica Skenderbega 21; dm/r from 165/424KN; ※ @ 🛜 ≋) Snuck away in a suburban neighbourhood, this friendly little hostel has brightly coloured rooms, a small pool, a guest barbecue and an all-round funky vibe. Staff can arrange trips to the Plitvice Lakes and the Krka National Park. When full, the Drunken Monkey has a nearby sister – the Lazy Monkey, with similar standards and rates.

Windward Hostel — HOSTEL €

(☎ 091 62 19 197; www.windwardhostelzadar.com; Put Gazica 12; dm/d 112/450KN; ※ 🛜) Just 1.5km from the old town, this 20-bed, yachting-themed hostel is run by a passionate sailor. Rooms are immaculate, with big lockers, electric window blinds and private reading lights. There's a supermarket and bakery nearby and staff can organise sailing tours and lessons.

Apartmani Petra — APARTMENT €€

(☎ 023-331 113; www.apartman-petra.com; Roberta Frangeša Mihanovića 63; apt 420-595KN; P ※ 🛜) Hidden in a scrappy cluster of holiday homes up on the hill (not too far from the beach but a fair hike from the old town), this tidy apartment block boasts clean, quiet and secure units, and the hostess couldn't be more welcoming.

★ Art Hotel Kalelarga — HOTEL €€€

(☎ 023-233 000; www.arthotel-kalelarga.com; Majke Margarite 3; s/d 1340/1640KN; ※ 🛜) Built and designed under strict conservation rules due to its old-town location, this 10-room boutique hotel is an understated and luxurious beauty. Exposed stonework and mushroom hues imbue the spacious rooms with plenty of style and character. The gourmet breakfast is served in the hotel's own stylish restaurant.

Club Funimation Borik
RESORT €€€

(☑ 023-555 600; www.borik.falkensteiner.com; Majstora Radovana 7; r 2000KN all-inclusive; P ❄ @ 🛜 ♨ 👪) Families are well catered for in this huge, 258-room beachfront hotel, with an impressive indoor-outdoor pool complex and all-inclusive rates. Kids can explore their own 'Falky Land', while mum and dad avail themselves of the outstanding spa and gym. Rooms are very spacious and suites are palatial.

Hotel Niko
HOTEL €€€

(☑ 023-337 888; www.hotel-niko.hr; Obala Kneza Domagoja 9; s/d 780/1090KN; P ❄ 🛜) The spacious rooms in this small, elegant, family-run hotel are kitted out with richly coloured carpets and good-quality reproduction furniture. All have balconies and some have lovely views over the Adriatic towards the old town. It's around 4.5km north of the old town near the Borik Marina.

Hotel Bastion
HOTEL €€€

(☑ 023-494 950; www.hotel-bastion.hr; Bedemi Zadarskih Pobuna 13; s/d/ste from 1560/1900/2490KN; P ❄ 🛜) Built over the remains of a Venetian fortress, Bastion radiates character and sophistication. The 23 rooms and five suites successfully combine a classic early-20th-century feel with a contemporary sensibility. It also boasts a top-drawer restaurant and a basement spa.

Hotel Adriana
HOTEL €€€

(☑ 023-555 600; www.adriana.falkensteiner.com; Majstora Radovana 7; r from 1800KN; ⊗ mid-May–Oct; P ❄ @ 🛜 ♨) Aimed at grown-ups (as opposed to its neighbouring sister establishment), this 48-room upmarket hotel is centred on a handsome 19th-century villa with lovely shady grounds that extend down to the Adriatic and a Blue Flag beach. The rooms, in a 1960s extension, are suitably well appointed. Rates include half board.

✗ Eating

Market
MARKET €

(Zlatarska; ⊗ 7am-1pm) One of Croatia's best traditional markets, with seasonal, local produce at cheap prices: juicy watermelons and oranges, cured ham and Pag cheese.

★ Kaštel
MEDITERRANEAN €€

(☑ 023-494 950; www.hotel-bastion.hr; Bedemi Zadarskih Pobuna 13; mains 80-170KN; ⊗ 7am-11pm) Hotel Bastion's fine-dining restaurant offers contemporary takes on classic Croatian cuisine (octopus stew, stuffed squid, Pag cheese). France and Italy also make their presence felt, particularly in the delectable dessert list. Opt for the white-linen experience inside or dine on the battlements overlooking the harbour for a memorable evening's dining.

★ Pet Bunara
DALMATIAN €€

(☑ 023-224 010; www.petbunara.com; Stratico 1; mains 60-165KN; ⊗ 11am-11pm) With exposed stone walls inside and a pretty terrace lined with olive trees, this is an atmospheric place to tuck into Dalmatian soups and stews, homemade pasta and local faves such as octopus and turkey. Save room for a traditional Zadar fig cake or cherry torte.

Kornat
MEDITERRANEAN €€

(☑ 023-254 501; www.restaurant-kornat.hr; Liburnska Obala 6; mains 48-140KN; ⊗ noon-midnight Mon-Sat) Sitting pretty in a prime harbourfront spot with lots of polished wood and a slim covered terrace, this elegant place is one of Zadar's best restaurants. The cooking marries fresh Croatian produce, rich French-style sauces and plenty of Italian touches. The seafood, however, is a touch on the pricey side for what you get.

Gourmet Kalelarga
CAFE €€

(Široka 23; breakfast 25-60KN, mains 60-140KN; ⊗ 7am-10pm) Beneath the Art Hotel Kalelarga (p185), this chic little beige cafe is your best option for a cooked breakfast or a decadent cake. As the day progresses, the focus shifts towards more substantial Dalmatian fare. Service is very good here.

Foša
SEAFOOD €€€

(☑ 023-314 421; www.fosa.hr; Kralja Dmitra Zvonimira 2; mains 95-225KN; ⊗ noon-1am) With a gorgeous terrace that juts out into the harbour and a sleek interior that combines ancient stone walls with 21st-century style, Foša is a very classy place. The main focus of chef Damir Tomljanović is fresh fish, plucked from the Adriatic and served grilled or salt-baked.

🍷 Drinking & Entertainment

Zadar has a lively and diverse bar scene, buoyed by a large student population. Head to the Varoš neighbourhood, on the southwest side of the old town, for interesting little cafe-bars popular with arty types.

★ **La Bodega**   WINE BAR
(www.labodega.hr; Široka 3; ⊘ 7am-1am Sun-Thu, to 1.30am Fri & Sat) With its slick, eccentric, semi-industrial decor, a bar with a line of hams and garlic hanging above, Portuguese-style tiles and welcoming, open-to-the-street approach, this is one of Zadar's hippest bars. There's a good range of Croatian wines by the glass and an extraordinary selection by the bottle – to be enjoyed with a variety of cheese and prosciutto.

Ledana   BAR, CLUB
(www.ledana.hr; Perivoj kraljice Jelene Madijevke; ⊘ 8am-4am Jun-Sep) Ledana's gorgeous garden setting and cheesy music choices make it a good place for a trashy night out. Party nights see guest DJs, dancers and (occasionally) live bands entertaining the troops. If it's chilly outside, grab a seat in the circular 19th-century *ledana* (icehouse).

Galerija Đina   BAR
(Varoška 2; ⊘ 7am-midnight) A lively hole-in-the-wall bar that spills out into a narrow lane in the heart of the Varoš action. It gets infectiously raucous at weekends.

Kult Caffe   BAR
(Stomorića 4; ⊘ 7.30am-midnight Sun-Thu, to 1.30am Fri & Sat) Kult's huge umbrella-shaded terrace is one of the old town's key meeting points. It's great for a quiet afternoon coffee or the start of a raucous night out.

Garden   BAR
(www.watchthegardengrow.eu; Bedemi Zadarskih Pobuna bb; ⊘ 10am-1am late May-Oct) Perched on top of the old city walls, this exceedingly cool bar-club-garden is very Ibiza-esque, with harbour views, day beds, secluded alcoves, billowing fabric and contemporary electronic music. The same crew runs the Garden Tisno.

Zodiac   BAR
(Simana Ljubavca 2; ⊘ 8am-1.30am Mon-Sat, 6pm-1.30am Sun) Zadar HQ for artists and writers, daydreamers and doers, Zodiac's backstreet seats are full of interesting characters. The music's usually excellent too: indie, rock, ska, reggae etc, but even the streetside seats exist in a cloud of smoke.

Arsenal   CONCERT VENUE
(www.arsenalzadar.com; Trg Tri Bunara 1) This huge former shipping warehouse, complete with bars and a restaurant, is now mainly used for concerts, art exhibitions and private functions. Check its website to see what's on when you are in town.

ⓘ Information

Aquarius Travel Agency (☏ 023-212 919; www.aquariuszadar.com; Nova Vrata bb; ⊘ hours vary) Books private accommodation and runs tours to the Plitvice Lakes National Park, as well as the Kornati Islands (300KN including food and drink).

Post Office (Šimuna Kožičića Benje 1; ⊘ 7.30am-9pm Mon-Fri, to 8pm Sat Jun-Sep, 7am-8pm Mon-Fri, to 1pm Sat Oct-May)

Tourist Office (☏ 023-316 166; www.zadar.travel; Mihe Klaića 5; ⊘ 8am-11pm May-Jul & Sep, to midnight Aug, 8am-8pm Mon-Fri, 9am-2pm Sat & Sun Oct-Apr; ☏) Publishes a good colour map and rents audioguides (35KN) for a self-guided tour around the town. Also offers free wi-fi.

Zadar General Hospital (Opća Bolnica Zadar; ☏ 023-505 505; www.bolnica-zadar.hr; Bože Peričića 5)

ⓘ Getting There & Away

AIR
Zadar Airport (☏ 023-205 800; www.zadar-airport.hr) is 12km east of the town centre. Croatia Airlines flies to Zadar from Zagreb. There are international flights to Brussels, Dublin, London, Munich, Paris, Warsaw and many more destinations, often with budget airlines.

BOAT
G&V Line (www.gv-zadar.hr) has three daily passenger ferries to Dugi Otok, stopping at both Sali (50 minutes) and Zaglav (one hour).

Jadrolinija (☏ 023-254 800; www.jadrolinija.hr; Liburnska Obala 7) ferries pull right up to the old town, with the large international boats mooring on Istarska Obala and the smaller boats on Liburnska Obala (where you'll also find the ticket office). Six ferries per week head to/from the Italian port of Ancona from June to September, increasing to 14 in July and August (per passenger/car from 480/1060KN).

Local ferries sail to destinations including Mali Lošinj (per adult/child/car 59/30/271KN, 6¾ hours, daily July and August), Brbinj on Dugi Otok (30/15/176KN, 1¼ hours, two to three daily) and Preko on Ugljan (18/9/103KN, 25 minutes, 11 to 17 daily). Passenger-only catamarans also head to Božava on Dugi Otok (40KN, 1¼ hours, three daily).

BUS
The **bus station** (☏ 060 305 305; www.liburnija-zadar.hr; Ante Starčevića 1) is about 1km southeast of the old town.

Domestic destinations include the following:

Dubrovnik 173KN, eight hours, six daily
Pula 176KN, seven hours, two daily
Rijeka 130KN, four hours, 12 daily
Split 80KN, three hours, hourly
Zagreb 110KN, 3½ hours, hourly

❶ Getting Around

TO/FROM THE AIRPORT
Buses are timed around all Croatia Airlines flights, departing from outside the main terminal, and from the old town (Liburnska Obala) and the bus station one hour prior to flights (25KN).

A taxi will cost around 140KN to the old town and 170KN to Borik.

PUBLIC TRANSPORT
Liburnija (www.liburnija-zadar.hr) runs buses on 10 routes, which all loop through the bus station. Tickets cost 10KN on board – or 16KN for two from a *tisak* (news-stand). Buses 5 and 8 (usually marked 'Puntamika') head to/from Borik regularly.

DUGI OTOK
☑ 023 / POP 1700
The largest island in the Zadar area, Dugi Otok has a lost-in-time feel, with plenty of relatively untouched natural beauty to enjoy. The name means 'long island': stretching from northwest to southeast it's 43km long and just 4km wide. The southeastern coast is marked by steep hills and cliffs, while the northern half is cultivated with vineyards, orchards and sheep pastures. In between is a series of karstic hills rising to 338m at Vela Straža, the island's highest point.

History
Ruins on the island reveal early settlement by Illyrians, Romans and then early Christians, but the island wasn't documented until the mid-10th century. It later became the property of the monasteries of Zadar. Settlement expanded with the 16th-century Turkish invasions, which prompted immigration from elsewhere along the coast.

Dugi Otok's fortunes have largely been linked with Zadar as it changed hands between Venetians, Austrians and the French, but when Northern Dalmatia was handed over to Mussolini the island stayed within Croatia. Old-timers still recall the hardships they endured when the nearest medical and administrative centre was Šibenik, a long, hard boat ride along the coast.

Economic development has always been hampered by the lack of any freshwater supply – drinking water must be collected from rainwater or brought over by boat from Zadar. The population has drifted away over the last few decades, leaving only the hardiest souls to brave the dry summers and *bura*-chilled winters.

❶ Getting There & Away
G&V Line (www.gv-zadar.com) runs three daily passenger ferries from Zadar, stopping at both Sali (25KN, 50 minutes) and Zaglav (25KN, one hour).

Jadrolinija (www.jadrolinija.hr) has daily catamarans from Zadar to Božava (40KN, 1¼ hours) and Brbinj (40KN, 1¾ hours). The company also runs a car ferry to Brbinj (per adult/child/car 30/15/176KN) three times a day in summer.

❶ Getting Around
The only bus services in Dugi Otok are timed to coincide with boat connections, running between Božava and Brbinj in the north. You can rent scooters in both Sali and Božava. Having your own wheels, be that a bike or hire car, is essential if you want to explore the island.

Veli Rat
POP 60
Veli Rat is a pretty village with a marina on a sheltered bay close to the northwestern point of the island. Aside from a solitary store-cum-bar, there's not a lot here. However, if you continue for 3km towards the tip of the island you'll reach the striking **Punta Bjanca lighthouse** (built 1849). At 42m, it's the largest such beacon on the Adriatic. A small chapel dedicated to St Nicholas, patron saint of sailors, is positioned nearby. Facing nearly due west, it's hard to imagine a more sublime spot to watch the sunset.

🛏 Sleeping
Camp Kargita   CAMPGROUND €
(☑ 098 532 333; www.camp-kargita.hr; adult/child/site 68/40/140KN; ☺ Apr-Oct) Virtually in the shadow of the Punta Bjanca lighthouse, this friendly little campground has a terrifically remote feel to it and a rocky beach nearby. It's of fairly recent vintage so the facilities are in good shape.

Božava

POP 120

Božava is a peaceful little place huddled around a lovely natural harbour that's mutated from fishing village to holiday resort in a couple of generations. The village is overgrown with lush, flowering trees and there are lovely shady paths along the coast. Tourism now totally dominates the local economy in the shape of the four hotels of the Božava 'tourist village' and a couple of harbourside restaurants.

During the summer season a little land 'train' (10KN) tootles between the hotels and Sakarun Bay. Mainly pebbly with a small strip of sand, this is one of the island's prettiest beaches – although there's not much shade and the water's painfully shallow (but great for families with small children). If you're driving, turn right onto the main island road and look for the turn-off on the left after 3km.

🛏 Sleeping

Hotel Maxim   HOTEL €€€
(📞 023-291 291; www.hoteli-bozava.hr; s/d from 740/1480KN; P ❋ @ 🏊) The four-star Maxim is Božava's most upmarket option. The smart rooms and apartments all have satellite TV, fridges, and balconies overlooking the sea. Plus there's an appealing little pool terrace and access to floodlit tennis courts and a small spa centre.

ℹ Information

Tourist Office (📞 023-377 607; www.dugiotok. hr; ⏰ 9am-1pm & 5-8pm Mon-Fri, to 2pm Sat Jun-Sep) Just above the tiny harbour; can help with bike, scooter and car rental, and with finding private accommodation.

Sali

POP 740

As the largest town on Dugi Otok, Sali is a positive metropolis when compared with the rest of the settlements scattered around the island. Named after a now-defunct salt works, the town has a rumpled, lived-in look. Its little harbour is a working fishing port and in summer it fills up with the small passenger boats and yachts that dock here on their way to and from Telašćica Bay and the Kornati Islands.

🏃 Activities

Kornati Diver   DIVING
(📞 098 16 93 107; www.kornati-diver.com; per 1/5/10 dives 200/930/1700KN) Based in the village of Zaglav, 3km to the north of Sali, this operator leads expeditions to caves, drop-offs and a wreck off the western coast of Dugi Otok.

Tome   BOATING
(📞 023-377 489; www.tome.hr) Offers a full-day cruise to Telašćica Bay and the Kornati Islands (2200KN; maximum of six people), including food and entry fees, or you can hire a boat and skipper and set your own itinerary (1500KN). Fishing trips (from 2200KN) can also be arranged.

✴ Festivals & Events

Sali Fiesta   CULTURAL
(Saljske Užance; ⏰ early Aug) The weekend before the Assumption, this celebration draws visitors from the entire region with donkey races and a candlelight procession of boats around the harbour. Men and women don traditional costumes, play instruments fashioned from cow horns and perform traditional village dances.

🍴 Eating & Drinking

Spageritimo   CROATIAN €€
(📞 023-377 227; Sali bb; mains 45-120KN; ⏰ 11am-10pm) Sali's best place to eat is this harbourside tavern specialising in local seafood fresh off the boat. The service is excellent and the owners produce their own olive oil, but some moan about small portion sizes.

Maritimo   BAR
(Obala Petra Lorinija bb; ⏰ 11am-1am) The heart and soul of Sali, this bar has a vibrant buzz about it, rain or shine. It's got plenty of character, with a long wooden bar and photographs of yesteryear decorating the walls, plus a popular terrace that's good for a cocktail, coffee or draught beer.

ℹ Information

Adamo Travel (📞 023-377 208; www.adamo. hr; Obala Kralja Tomislava bb; ⏰ 8am-6pm Mon-Sat) Sharing space with the tourist office, this very helpful agency rents a good range of private rooms and apartments, and sells tickets for car and boat excursions to Telašćica Bay.

NORTHERN DALMATIA BOŽAVA

Post Office (Obala Petra Lorinija bb; ☺8am-noon & 6-9pm Mon-Fri, 8am-noon Sat Jun-Sep, 8am-5pm Mon, to 2pm Tue-Fri Oct-May)

Tourist Office (☑023-377 094; www.dugiotok.hr; Obala Kralja Tomislava bb; ☺8am-8pm Mon-Sat, 11am-1pm Sun Jul & Aug, 8am-3pm Mon-Fri Sep-Jun) On the harbour front.

ℹ Getting Around

Louvre (☑098 650 026; Obala Kralja Tomislava bb) Hires out scooters and mountain bikes.

Telašćica Bay

The southeastern tip of Dugi Otok is split in two by the deeply indented **Telašćica Bay** (Park prirode Telašćica; www.telascica.hr; 25KN), dotted with five small islands and five even tinier islets. With superb sheltered azure waters, it's one of the largest, most beautiful and least spoilt natural harbours in the Adriatic. Consequently, it's very popular with yachties.

The Kornati Islands extend nearly to the edge of Telašćica Bay and the topography of the two island groups is identical – stark white limestone with patches of brush. The tip of the western side of the island faces the sea where the wind and waves have carved out sheer cliffs dropping 166m. There are no towns, settlements or roads on this part of Dugi Otok.

◉ Sights

Mir Lake   LAKE

Saltwater Mir Lake is fed by underground channels that run through limestone to the sea. The lake, which is clear but has a muddy bottom, is surrounded by pine forests and its water is much warmer than the sea. Like most mud in unusual places, it's supposed to be very good for your skin.

ℹ Getting There & Away

The only ways to reach Telašćica Bay are by boat or on foot from Sali, a hike of around 3km. Adamo Travel in Sali runs trips here.

ŠIBENIK-KNIN REGION

Wedged between the bigger, more attention-grabbing cities of Zadar and Split, this slice of Croatia is often unfairly overlooked. Yet it's loaded with interesting attractions, including the incredible medieval heart of Šibenik and two national parks – the pris-tine Kornati Islands and the inland watery wonderland of Krka.

Kornati Islands

🎵 022 / POP 20

Composed of 140 uninhabited islands, islets and reefs covering 300 sq km, the Kornatis are the largest and densest archipelago in the Adriatic. Due to the typically karstic terrain, the islands are riddled with cracks, caves, grottoes and rugged cliffs. Since there are no sources of fresh water they are mostly barren. The evergreens and holm oaks that used to be found here were long ago burned down. Far from stripping the islands of their beauty, the deforestation has highlighted startling rock formations, whose stark whiteness against the deep-blue Adriatic is an eerie and wonderful sight.

The Kornati Islands form four groups running northwest to southeast. The first two groups of islands lie closer to the mainland and are known locally as Gornji Kornat. The largest of these islands is **Žut**.

There are about 300 buildings on the Kornati Islands, mostly clustered on the southwestern coast of Kornat.

◉ Sights

Kornati National Park   NATIONAL PARK

(www.np-kornati.hr) The two series of islands facing the open sea comprise Kornati National Park and have the most dramatically rugged coastline. **Kornat** is by far the largest island in the park, extending 25km in length but only 2.5km in width. Both the land and surrounding sea are protected. Fishing is strictly limited in order to allow the regeneration of fish shoals. The island of **Piškera**, also within the park, was inhabited during the Middle Ages and served as a fishing collection and storage point.

🛏 Sleeping & Eating

If you'd like to stay on a Kornati island, Adamo Travel (p189) in Sali and Kornat-Turist (p192) in Murter both have private houses on their books. Small cottages start at around 4500KN per week including a boat transfer, gas for cooking and lighting, and the national park admission fee.

There are a surprising number of eateries on the islands catering for yachties and day trippers, many within the national park on the main Kornat island and on Piškera.

ⓘ Information

Entrance fees are priced by boat; a small vessel costs 180KN per day if the ticket is bought in advance. Scuba-diving permits cost 100KN per person per day.

The Kornati National Park Office (p192) is located in Murter, and is well stocked with information.

ⓘ Getting There & Away

There is no ferry transport between the Kornatis and other islands or the mainland. Unless you have your own boat, you'll have to book an excursion from Zadar, Sali, Šibenik, Split or another coastal city, or arrange private accommodation from Sali or Murter.

The largest marina is on the island of Piškera, on the southern part of the strait between Piškera and Lavsa. There's another large marina on Žut and a number of small coves throughout the islands where boaters can dock.

Tisno & Murter Island

☑ 022 / POP 5140

Tisno is a cute little town, straddling the bridge that connects the island of Murter to the mainland. Its relatively newfound fame as host to a series of high-profile music festivals is totally out of keeping with its otherwise sleepy appeal.

On the island proper, the main settlement is Murter village, which although unremarkable in itself is an excellent base from which to explore the Kornati Islands. Murter's steep southwestern coast is indented by small coves, most notably Slanica, which is great for swimming.

✯ Festivals & Events

Between July and August, Tisno is imbued with some of the globe's most celebrated electronic music. Styles are myriad and music is eclectic: cosmic disco, soul and funk, folk-tinged electronica, deep house and jazzy lounge. The ringmaster for all of these festivals is the Zadar-based Garden bar.

The festival site is a grand affair, only 1km from town, with a private sandy beach, 80 apartments and a luxury campsite – with 30-sq-metre Indian Shikar cotton tents that have electric fans and lighting, real beds and mosquito nets, and even a separate dressing room and porch area. These are all for the revellers to stay in and make as much noise as they like without annoying the locals. There are shady chill-out zones and three

different music areas, including the open-air Barbarella's club, a short bus or water-taxi ride away. Chuck in the infamous Argo-naughty boat parties on the sparkling Adriatic sea and you have yourself quite a scene.

Electric Elephant   MUSIC
(www.electricelephant.co.uk; ☉ early Jul) Five days and nights of DJ-driven lunacy. In 2016 it featured the likes of Andrew Weatherall, Boo Williams and Psychemagik.

SUNćeBeat   MUSIC
(www.suncebeat.com; ☉ late July) Spreading musical sunshine over eight days, with a solid line-up of legendary DJs (the likes of Black Coffee, Louie Vega and Derrick Carter).

Soundwave   MUSIC
(www.soundwavecroatia.com; ☉ early Aug) Kicking off over five nights in the heat of midsummer, Soundwave has a focus on live acts from the alternative, dub and world-music end of the dance-music spectrum.

Stop Making Sense   MUSIC
(www.stopmakingsense.eu) Four days of dancing in the sun to underground DJs in early August.

⮒ Sleeping

Hotel Tisno   HOTEL €€€
(☑ 022-438 182; www.hoteltisno.com; Zapadna Gomilica 8, Tisno; r 900-1400KN; ❋ ☎ ❂) Creating a rather grand impression on the Tisno waterfront, this late-19th-century house has been converted into a stylish little hotel. The rooms are in keeping with the era, with gathered crimson curtains and lots of polished wood, but the ambience isn't even remotely stuffy.

Hotel Murter   HOTEL €€€
(☑ 022-434 500; www.hotelmurter.com; Nerezine bb, Murter; tw 1275KN; P ❋ ☎ ☀) Recently renovated, this well-kept hotel a five-minute walk from Slanica Beach offers decently furnished if not luxurious rooms, a range of facilities including a small pool and some of the most gobsmacking views you'll see from any Dalmatian hotel. Breakfast is an ample affair and the staff are very accommodating.

ⓘ Information

Coronata (☑ 022-435 447; www.coronata.hr; Rudina 17, Murter; ☉ 9am-6pm Mon-Fri, to 1pm Sat) One of several agencies that rents private apartments and runs full-day excursions to the Kornati Islands from Murter.

Kornati National Park Office (☎ 022-435 740; www.kornati.hr; Butina 2, Murter; ⊗ 8.30am-5pm Mon-Fri) The Kornati National Park Office is well stocked with information and can advise on tours and tickets.

KornatTurist (☎ 022-435 855; www.murter-active.holiday; Hrvatskih Vladara 2, Murter; ⊗ hours vary) Rents private accommodation and organises a range of mostly water-based activities.

Tourist Office (☎ 022-434 995; www.tzo-murter.hr; Rudina bb, Murter; ⊗ 8am-10pm Jun-Aug, 8am-3pm Sep-May)

ℹ Getting There & Around

Buses on the coastal highway stop at the Tisno turn-off, 6km from the centre.

Krka National Park

☎ 022

Extending along the 73km River Krka, the **Krka National Park** (☎ 022-201 777; www.np krka.hr; adult/child 150/90KN Jul & Aug, 110/80KN Apr-Jun, Sep & Oct, 30/20KN Nov-Mar) runs from the Adriatic near Šibenik inland to the mountains of the Croatian interior. It's a magical place of waterfalls and gorges, with the river gushing through a karstic canyon 200m deep. Sights built by humans are also a major draw of the region, the area's remoteness attracting monks who constructed their monasteries here.

The park has five main entrances, at Skradin, Lozovac, Roški Slap, Krka Monastery and Burnum – all are accessible by car.

◎ Sights

Skradin   VILLAGE
Skradin is a pretty little riverside town with a combination of brightly painted and bare stone houses on its main street and a ruined fortress towering above. Apart from the opportunity to see the town itself, the advantage to starting your visit to the Krka National Park in Skradin is that the park admission includes a boat ride through the canyon to Skradinski Buk. The disadvantage is that there can be queues for the boats in summer.

Skradinski Buk   WATERFALL
The highlight of Krka, an hour-long loop follows boardwalks, connects little islands in the emerald-green, fish-filled river and terminates at the park's largest waterfall. Skra-

dinski Buk's 800m-long cascade descends by almost 46m before crashing into the lower lake, which is a popular swimming spot. Nearby, a cluster of historic mill cottages have been converted into craft workshops, souvenir stores and eateries. The whole area gets insanely busy in summer.

From the Lozovac entrance, buses (free with park admission) shuttle visitors from the large car park (also free) down a serpentine road to Skradinski Buk. Neither the free boats or buses operate from November to February, but in these months you're able to drive right down to the falls.

Mother of Mercy
Franciscan Monastery   MONASTERY
(Franjevački samostan Majke od Milosti; ☎ 022-775 730; www.visovac.hr) Upstream of Skradinski Buk the river broadens out into Lake Viskovac, bordered by reeds and bulrushes sheltering marsh birds. At its centre is an idyllic, tree-fringed island, the perfect place for a monastery. Founded in the 14th century by Augustinian hermits it was expanded in 1445 by Franciscans escaping the Ottoman invasion of Bosnia. The church was extensively remodelled in the 17th century and the bell tower added in 1728. Boat trips head here from Skradinski Buk and include 30 minutes on the island.

Roški Slap   WATERFALL
(adult/child 60/40KN, incl in park entry; ⊗ 9am-8pm Jul & Aug, shorter hours rest of the year) Beginning with shallow steps and continuing in a series of branches and islets to become 23m-high cascades, this 650m-long stretch is another flamboyantly pretty part of the river. On the eastern side you can visit the water mills that used to grind wheat. Boats leave from Skradinski Buk (adult/child 130/90KN, 3½ hours).

Krka Monastery   MONASTERY
(Manastir Krka; ⊗ 10am-6pm) Not only is this the most important Serbian Orthodox monastery in Croatia, it ranks as one of that faith's most important sites full stop. Featuring a unique combination of Byzantine and Mediterranean architecture, it occupies a peaceful position above the river and a small lake. From mid-June to mid-October a national park guide is at hand to tour you around. At other times you're welcome to visit the church and wander the lakeside path.

Dedicated to the Archangel Michael, the monastery was founded in 1345 by Jelena Šubić, the wife of a local Croatian noble

KNIN

Located in a historical hot seat on the borders of Dalmatia and Bosnia, Knin was an important trading centre in the Middle Ages, becoming the capital of the Croatian Kingdom in the 11th century. However, the huge Croatian flag flying from the top of the fortress is more to do with recent events than medieval history.

Ethnic Serbs made up 86% of the population when in 1991 Knin declared itself the capital of the breakaway Republic of Serbian Krajina. Most of the Serbs fled before Croatia recaptured the town in 1995 and it was subsequently repopulated with Croatian refugees from Bosnia. Knin's economy evaporated along with the Serbs and there's still a somewhat grim feel to the town today.

The **Knin Fortress** (Kninski Tvrđava; 10KN; ☉ 7am-7pm mid-Mar–Nov) looms over the town from steep Spas hill. Commenced from the 9th century and reaching its peak as a royal residence in the 11th century, its strategic importance is well demonstrated by the extraordinary views it offers over the valley to the mountains of Bosnia and Hercegovina.

When the Croatian kings fell, Knin was battered by a series of invaders until the Ottomans snatched it in 1522. Later, Venice swept in (note the republic's winged lion emblem over the main gate), followed by Austria, France and then Austria again. Much of the present structure dates from the 17th and 18th centuries.

Knin is accessible by train from Split (82KN, 1½ hours, three daily) and Šibenik (50KN, 1¾ hours, four daily). There are also five buses a day from Split (67KN, 2½ hours, five daily).

and half-sister to Emperor Dušan of Serbia. However, its Christian origins are much older than that. Beneath the complex in a natural cave system are catacombs bearing early Christian graffiti, possibly from the 1st century. Local lore has it that this hidden church was visited by St Titus and possibly even St Paul. The guided tours only visit a small section of cave, where the graffiti and human bones can be seen; the cave system continues for at least 100m and possibly for a couple of kilometres.

During the war of the 1990s, the monastery's substantial treasury – including priceless manuscripts and religious paraphernalia – was moved to Belgrade for safekeeping. A new museum has been constructed to display the items. The monastery itself was protected during the fighting by the UN. The complex is also home to the Serbian Orthodox church's oldest seminary. It reopened in 2001 and now has 50 theological students.

From Roški Slap, boats to Krka Monastery leave by arrangement (2½ hours, April to October only).

❶ Information

There are information offices at each of the park entrances.

Krka National Park Office (☑ 022-771 688; www.npkrka.hr; Skradin; ☉ 8am-8pm) Near the harbour in Skradin; provides good maps and information, and can arrange excursions.

Skradin Tourist Office (☑ 022-771 329; www. skradin.hr; Trg Male Gospe 3; ☉ 9am-5pm Mon-Fri) The main tourist office is in the town hall but from Easter to October it also staffs a kiosk by the national park office.

❶ Getting There & Away

Numerous agencies sell excursions to Krka from Šibenik, Zadar and other coastal cities, but it's not difficult to visit independently. In summer, seven daily buses (three on Sunday) with Autotransport Šibenik (www.atpsi.hr) depart from Šibenik for Lozovac and Skradin (25KN, 25 minutes). In winter the only buses are timed around the school run.

Šibenik

☑ 022 / POP 46,300

Driving through the somewhat shabby outskirts of Šibenik you might find yourself questioning your choice of destination. However, that is guaranteed to change as soon as you reach the city's magnficent medieval heart, gleaming white against the placid waters of the bay. The stone labyrinth of steep backstreets and alleys are a joy to explore. Šibenik is also an important access point for Krka National Park and the Kornati Islands.

History

Unlike many other Dalmatian coastal communities, Šibenik was founded not by Illyrians,

Šibenik

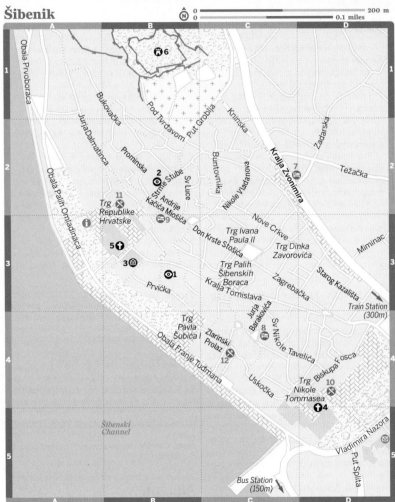

NORTHERN DALMATIA ŠIBENIK

Šibenik

Greeks or Romans but by the Croatian king Petar Krešimir IV in the 11th century. The city was conquered by Venice in 1116, and tossed around between Venice, Hungary, Byzantium and Bosnia until Venice ultimately seized control in 1412. Ottomans periodically attacked the town, disrupting trade and agriculture in the 16th and 17th centuries.

Venetian control was usurped in 1797 by Austrian rule, which continued until 1918. Following on from the discoveries of compatriot Nikola Tesla, local engineer and inventor (and later mayor) Ante Šupak built one of the world's first hydroelectric plants on the Krka River in 1895, and Šibenik became only the third city in the world with an alternating current (AC) street-lighting system.

Šibenik fell under attack in 1991 from Yugoslav federal forces and was subject to shelling until its liberation as part of 'Operation Storm' by the Croatian army in 1995. Little physical damage is evident, but the city's aluminium industry was shattered and unemployment grew to over 50%. But Šibenik has made a serious comeback in the past few years, and tourism has slowly become a vital part of the local economy.

◎ Sights

Many of Šibenik's beautiful smaller churches are only open around Mass times.

St James' Cathedral   CATHEDRAL
(Katedrala Svetog Jakova; Trg Republike Hrvatske; adult/child 15KN/free; ⊗9.30am-6.30pm) The crowning architectural glory of the Dalmatian coast and the undisputed masterpiece of its principal designer Juraj Dalmatinac, this World Heritage Site is worth a detour to see. It was constructed entirely of stone quarried from the islands of Brač, Korčula, Rab and Krk, and is reputed to be the world's largest church built completely of stone without brick or wooden supports. The structure is also unique in that the interior shape corresponds exactly to the exterior.

Dalmatinac was not the first (nor the last) architect to work on the cathedral. Construction began in 1431 but, after 10 years of toying with various Venetian builders, the city appointed Dalmatinac, a Zadar native, who increased the size and transformed the conception of the church into a transitional Gothic-Renaissance style. The unusual domed-roof complex was completed after Dalmatinac's death by Nikola Firentinac, who continued the facade in a pure Renaissance style. It was all finally completed in 1536.

The cathedral's most unusual feature is the **frieze** of 71 heads on the exterior walls at the rear of the building. These portraits – placid, annoyed, comical, proud and fearful –

ISLAND OF CULTURE

A new destination, the tiny car-free island of **Obonjan Island** (☑in UK +44 203 808 7333; www.obonjan-island.com; ⊗late Jul–early Sep) around 10km off Šibenik, has been transformed into a holiday resort, but one with a twist. Accommodation is in safari-type tent lodges, some with views straight out across the Adriatic, but the main attraction here is the month-long cultural program packed with DJs, film screenings, talks, workshops, art events and sport. There are also four restaurants, three bars, free yoga classes, and boat trips around the region.

Three boats leave Šibenik daily when the resort is open. The fare is 105KN each way. Obonjan is expected to be pretty popular so booking ahead is absolutely essential.

almost appear like caricatures, but are depictions of ordinary 15th-century citizens. The building cost a great deal of cash to construct, and it's said that the stingier the individual, the grosser the caricature.

Note also the **Lion's Portal** on the northern side, created by Dalmatinac and Bonino da Milano, in which two lions support columns containing the figures of Adam and Eve, who appear to be excruciatingly embarrassed by their nakedness.

Pick up the excellent brochure (available in various languages) as you enter the church, which provides a self-guided circuit of the many artworks and architectural features inside. A highlight is Dalmatinac's extraordinary **baptistery** in the rear corner, with its exquisitely carved ceiling and font supported by three angels.

Other interior artworks worth noting are the tomb of Bishop Šižigorić (by Dalmatinac), who supported the building of the cathedral; the altar painting of St Fabian and St Sebastian (by Filippo Zaniberti); and a particularly gruesome 15th-century Gothic crucifix (by Juraj Petrović).

Šibenik City Museum   MUSEUM
(Muzej grada Šibenika; www.muzej-sibenik.hr; Gradska Vrata 3; adult/child 30/10KN; ⊗10am-9pm Tue-Sat) Housed in the 17th-century Rector's Palace, this well-curated museum focuses on the city and its surrounds. The permanent collection of artefacts dating from prehistory

WORTH A TRIP

RAPTOR RESCUE

Dedicated to protecting birds of prey in Croatia, the **Sokolarski Centre** (☎091 50 67 610; www.sokolarskicentar.com; Škugori bb; adult/concession 45/35KN; ☉9am-7pm Apr-Nov) performs a kind of rescue and rehab service for around 150 injured raptors each year. Visitors are treated to a highly entertaining and educational presentation from centre director Emilo Mendušić, who uses a tame eagle owl and Harris hawks to demonstrate these birds' agility and skills. Rescued native birds aren't used for these shows; they're only kept at the centre until they're healthy enough to be released back into the wild.

Most of the patients at the centre have been involved in a collision on Croatian roads. Other threats to the birds include illegal poisoning, shooting and the use of pesticides.

The Sokolarski Centre is about 7km from Šibenik and is not served by public transport. It's a little tricky to find: to get here take the road to Krka National Park, turn east at Bilice and look for the signs.

to the end of the Venetian period is split into four clear periods. There are English translations throughout and the odd bit of video to spice things up.

Aquarium Terrarium Šibenik AQUARIUM
(www.aquariumsibenik.com; Kralja Tomislava 15a; adult/child 37/27KN; ☉10am-9pm) A useful rainy day diversion for the kids, this little aquarium has a display of local and tropical fish, along with crabs, lobsters, rays, small sharks and the odd octopus.

**Medieval Monastery
Mediterranean Garden** GARDENS
(Srednjevjekovni samostanski Mediteranski vrt; www.spg.hr; Strme Stube 1; group tours adult/child 15/10KN; ☉9am-11pm May-Oct, reduced hours Nov-Apr) Designed and completed by Dragutin Kiš (an award-winning landscape artist), this tiny recreated medieval garden has a formal layout, with herbs and medicinal plants in neat borders between pathways in the shape of a cross. The attached cafe is a pleasant spot to stop for an ice-cream sundae or coffee and cake before you continue your ascent to the fortress.

St Michael's Fortress FORTRESS
(Tvrđava Sv Mihovila; adult/child 35/20KN; ☉8am-10pm) Clamber up to this large medieval fort for magnificent views over Šibenik, the Krk River and the Adriatic islands from its battlements (they're particularly impressive at sunset). Parts of it date to the 13th century but the surviving shell has been shored up with a polished concrete understructure and converted into a summer stage.

St Francis' Church CHURCH
(Crkva Sv Frane; Trg Nikole Tommasea 1; ☉7.30am-7.30pm) The Franciscan monastery's mammoth church dates from the end of the 14th century. It has fine frescoes and an array of Venetian baroque paintings but the highlight is the painted wooden ceiling, dating from 1674. It's the principal shrine of St Nikola Tavilić, a Franciscan missionary who became the first Croatian saint when he was martyred in Jerusalem in 1391. In the adjacent courtyard you'll find an exhibition on the church's history.

★☆ Festivals & Events

International Children's Festival CULTURAL
(www.mdf-sibenik.com; ☉mid-Jun–early Jul) Šibenik hosts a renowned international children's festival, starting from the third Saturday in June and lasting for three weeks. There are craft workshops, along with music, dance, children's film and theatre, puppets and parades.

Terraneo MUSIC
(☉Jun-Aug) Terraneo is a series of individual concerts by big international pop-music acts, held at St Michael's Fortress.

🛏 Sleeping

Apart from a couple of hostels, there's very little accommodation actually in Šibenik, so you might like to consider basing yourself along the coast and heading to town on day trips. Tribunj, Vodice, Primošten and Rogoznica are all good options. Contact travel agencies for private digs.

★Indigo HOSTEL €
(☎022-200 159; www.hostel-indigo.com; Jurja Barakovića 3; dm 129KN; 🕸🛜) Much lauded by all who stay the night and longer, this friendly little hostel has a four-bed dorm with pine bunks and lockable drawers on each of its

four floors. At the very top, the terrace has views over the rooftops to the sea. Blue jeans provide a kooky decoration throughout. Sadly, there's no kitchen.

Hostel Mare   HOSTEL €
(☑ 022-215 269; www.hostel-mare.com; Kralja Zvonimira 40; dm 139-159KN, r 450KN; ❄ 🛜) Pass through the heavy door that opens from the busy road onto a cobbled courtyard and behind lies this breezy hostel. The decor is fresh, bright and IKEA-style modern, the dorms have backpack-sized lockers and there's one double room with its own bathroom. Breakfast is extra and there's bike storage available.

Pansion Šibenik   GUESTHOUSE €€
(☑ 098 98 01 862; Andrije Kačića Miošića 5; r 450KN; 🛜) Epicentrally located just a leisurely stroll from the cathedral and at the heart of everything Šibenik has to offer, this reasonably priced set of old-fashioned digs occupies an old-town stone house with many of its original features still in place. The five small rooms are simply furnished and rather spartan. Staff are helpful.

✖ Eating

★ Pelegrini   MEDITERRANEAN €€
(☑ 022-213 701; www.pelegrini.hr; Jurja Dalmatinca 1; mains 70-185KN; ⊙ noon-midnight) Responsible for upping the culinary ante in Šibenik, this wonderful restaurant raids the globe for flavours, with influences from Japan and France, but its heart is in the Mediterranean. Dalmatian offerings are very well represented on the wine list. Call ahead to bag one of the outside tables.

Nostalgija   EUROPEAN €€
(www.nostalgija-sibenik.com; Biskupa Fosca 11; mains 60-80KN; ⊙ 8am-2pm & 6-10pm; 🛜) With a pleasant covered terrace right by the Franciscan monastery, this is an unpretentious option for breakfast (cereal, omelettes, pancakes), light lunches (soup, sandwiches) and simple, rustic Croatian cuisine (local fish, grilled meat, pasta). The waiters are very knowledgable about the food they bang down and will happily recommend wines to go with dishes.

SHE Bistro   BISTRO €€
(www.shebenik.com; Zlarinski Prolaz 2; mains 73-115KN; ⊙ 9am-midnight; ☑) 🌿 A sleek new bistro serving organic, locally sourced vegetarian and vegan food, it also doubles as a hub for ecology. The gorgeous interior of the

1920s building has an open kitchen and a raw industrial look with a living-room vibe – think lots of books, plants and wood. SHE serves breakfasts and snacks, with more substantial dishes at dinner (such as red-lentil burgers and raw courgette linguini).

ℹ Information

General Hospital Šibenik (Opća bolnica Šibenik; ☑ 022-641 641; www.bolnica-sibenik. hr; Stjepana Radića 83)

NIK Travel Agency (☑ 022-338 550; www.nik. hr; Ante Šupuka 5; ⊙ 8am-8pm) Large agency offering excursions to Kornati and Krka, private accommodation and international bus and air tickets.

Post Office (Vladimira Nazora 1; ⊙ 7am-2pm Mon-Fri)

Tourist Office (☑ 022-214 441; www.sibenik-tourism.hr; Obala Palih Omladinaca 3; ⊙ 8am-9pm May-Oct, to 4pm Mon-Fri Nov-Apr)

ℹ Getting There & Away

BUS

Šibenik's **bus station** (☑ 060 368 368; Draga 14) has plenty of regular services and is only a short walk from the old town.

Destinations include the following:

Dubrovnik 139KN, 6½ hours, at least three daily

Rijeka 166KN, 6½ hours, at least six daily

Split 45KN, 1½ hours, 12 daily

Zadar 40KN, 1½ hours, at least hourly

Zagreb from 130KN, five to seven hours, at least hourly

TRAIN

The only place you can go from Šibenik's **train station** (☑ 022-333 696; Fr Jerolima Milete bb) is Knin (50KN, 1¾ hours, four daily).

Primošten

☑ 022 / POP 3000

Pretty little Primošten occupies what was once a little islet just off the coast, 28km south of Šibenik. During the Turkish threat of the 16th century it was fortified – and when the Turks disappeared, the drawbridge connecting it to the mainland was replaced by a causeway.

Sleepy to the point of inertia in winter, in the summer it comes alive, with bands playing in the main square, interesting gift shops selling their wares and excited kids racing around the cobbled streets. Romantics stroll up the hill to St George's Church to watch the sunset, and loop around the peninsula's perimeter after dark.

Sleeping & Eating

Hotel Zora   HOTEL €€€

(📞 022-581 111; www.hotelzora-adriatiq.com; Raduča 11; r from 1250KN; ⊙ Mar-Nov; 🅿 ❄ 🛜 🏊) One of the few hotels in Primošten itself, this 324-room complex, almost lost amid the trees of a small promontory a short walk from town, has direct access to a marvellous pebble beach. Rooms are a little in need of updating, but almost all have balconies, and facilities are well maintained.

⭐**Mediteran**   MEDITERRANEAN €€€

(📞 022-571 780; www.mediteran-primosten.hr; Put Briga 13; mains 70-240KN; ⊙ 1pm-midnight) Mediteran centres on a lovely old stone building, although in summer the action moves into the courtyard and up to the little 1st-floor terrace. Chef Pero Savanović's dishes offer a modern take on Dalmatian traditions and highlight delicious local produce. Visit when Istrian truffles are in season and you'll be in for a treat.

❶ Information

Tourist Office (📞 022-571 111; www.tz-primosten. hr; Trg biskupa Josipa Arnerića 2; ⊙ 8am-9pm Jul & Aug, shorter hours rest of the year)

❶ Getting There & Away

Buses run at least hourly to Primošten from Šibenik (23KN, 30 minutes), normally continuing on to Split (36KN, one hour).

Rogoznica

📞 022 / POP 2400

A well-protected harbour on a peninsula 38km by road south of Šibenik, laid-back Rogoznica is popular with Adriatic yachts-people in the know and tourists looking for a quiet hideaway. With its pebbly beaches, tranquilly historic streets and some good eating options, the town makes a pleasant base for exploring the Šibenik area. It also has one of the best climates in Croatia, with more sunny days per year than most other coastal communities.

Sleeping & Eating

Hotel Life   HOTEL €€€

(📞 022-558 128; www.hotel-life.hr; Rtić 12e; s/d 1040/1500KN; 🅿 ❄ 🛜 🏊) Located in Zečevo Bay between Rogoznica and Primošten, this small, family-run hotel offers quite minimalist-chic accommodation near a quiet pebble beach. Rooms are studies in grey and white 21st-century styling, there's a restaurant on-site and the small indoor pool is lovely for an early morning wallow.

Konoba Mario   CROATIAN €€

(📞 022-558 508; www.mario-konoba.hr; Hrvatske Mornarice 1; mains 55-160KN; ⊙ 11am-10.30pm) Housed in a typical limestone town house and with a great sea-view terrace, this long-established tavern serves up a wide range of Adriatic fish and seafood plus a few meat dishes. Black risotto, grilled squid, clams in white-wine sauce and cuttlefish with lentil sauce are some of the dishes to look forward to, all plonked on your table by knowledgable waiters.

❶ Information

Tourist Office (📞 022-559 253; www.loverogoz nica.eu; Obala kneza Domagoja 56) Helpful office with one of the most informative websites in Dalmatia. Also serves the surrounding villages.

❶ Getting There & Away

Buses link Rogoznica to Šibenik (30KN, 45 minutes, at least hourly) and Split (31KN, one hour, at least hourly).

Split & Central Dalmatia

Includes ➜

Best Places to Eat

➡ Konoba & Bar Lola (p250)

➡ Konoba Trs (p222)

➡ Konoba Matejuška (p214)

➡ Zinfandel (p213)

➡ Konoba Kalalarga (p227)

Best Places to Sleep

➡ Antique Split Luxury Rooms (p212)

➡ Villa Skansi (p243)

➡ Apartments Magdalena (p212)

➡ Villa Split (p212)

➡ Hostel Emanuel (p213)

Why Go?

Central Dalmatia is the most action-packed, sight-rich and diverse part of Croatia, with pretty islands, quiet ports, rugged mountains, dozens of castles and an emerging culinary scene, as well as two Unesco World Heritage sites: Diocletian's Palace in Split and the medieval walled town of Trogir. Throughout it all, the rugged 1500m-high Dinaric Range provides a dramatic background.

Hot spots include the buzzing Mediterranean-flavoured city of Split and gorgeous little Hvar Town, where the cashed meet the trashed on the Adriatic's most glamorous party island. But if it's peace and quiet you're after, there are seductive sandy beaches and secluded pebbly coves scattered about islands near and far.

Best of all: Dalmatia is always warmer than Istria or the Kvarner Gulf. You can plunge into the crystalline Adriatic from the middle of May right up until the end of September.

When to Go
Split

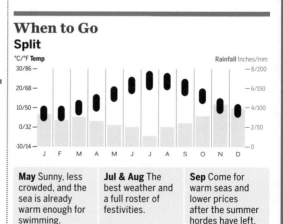

May Sunny, less crowded, and the sea is already warm enough for swimming.

Jul & Aug The best weather and a full roster of festivities.

Sep Come for warm seas and lower prices after the summer hordes have left.

Split & Central Dalmatia Highlights

❶ Diocletian's Palace (p202) Discovering Split's ancient heart in Diocletian's Palace, a quarter that buzzes day and night.

❷ Vis (p248) Savouring the food and beaches of one of Croatia's remotest islands.

❸ Zlatni Rat (p236) Stretching out on Zlatni Rat, Croatia's most photogenic beach, in Bol.

❹ Hvar Town (p239) Capping off endless beach days with sunset cocktails and back-lane boogie sessions.

❺ Biokovo Nature Park (p232) Hiking up dramatic peaks and enjoying views right across the Adriatic to far-off Italy.

❻ Trogir (p219) Taking in the remarkably preserved ancient architecture of the tiny World Heritage star of Central Dalmatia.

❼ Brač (p233) Exploring the historic hamlets of the interior and the sleepy little towns scattered around the coast.

SPLIT

POP 178,000

Croatia's second-largest city, Split (*Spalato* in Italian) is a great place to see Dalmatian life as it's really lived. Always buzzing, this exuberant city has just the right balance of tradition and modernity. Step inside Diocletian's Palace (a Unesco World Heritage site and one of the world's most impressive Roman monuments) and you'll see dozens of bars, restaurants and shops thriving amid the atmospheric old walls where Split life has been humming along for thousands of years.

To top it off, Split has a unique setting. Its dramatic coastal mountains act as the perfect backdrop to the turquoise waters of the Adriatic and help divert attention from the dozens of shabby high-rise apartment blocks that fill its suburbs. It's this thoroughly lived-in aspect of Split that means it will never be a fantasy land like Dubrovnik, but you could argue that it's all the better for that.

History

Split achieved fame when the Roman emperor Diocletian (AD 245–313), noted for his restructure of the empire and persecution of early Christians, had his retirement palace built here between 295 and 305. After his death the great stone palace continued to be used as a retreat by Roman rulers. When the nearby colony of Salona (now Solin) was abandoned in the 7th century, many of the Romanised inhabitants fled to Split and barricaded themselves behind the high palace walls, where their descendants live to this day.

First the Byzantine Empire and then Croatia controlled the area, but from the 12th to the 14th centuries medieval Split enjoyed a large measure of autonomy, which favoured its development. The western part of the old town around Narodni trg, which dates from this time, became the focus of municipal life, while the area within the palace walls remained the ecclesiastical centre.

In 1420 the Venetian conquest of Split led to its slow decline. During the 17th century, strong walls were built around the city as a defence against the Ottomans. In 1797 the Austrians arrived and remained until 1918.

◎ Sights

The ever-frenetic waterfront promenade – officially called Obala hrvatskog narodnog preporoda (Croatian National Revival waterfront) but more commonly known as the Riva – is your best central reference point in Split. East of here, past the wharf, are the buzzy beaches of Bačvice, Firule, Zenta and Trstenik bays. The wooded Marjan Hill dominates the western tip of the city and has even better beaches at its base.

★ **Diocletian's Palace**   HISTORIC SITE
(Map p208) Facing the harbour, Diocletian's Palace is one of the most imposing Roman ruins in existence and where you'll spend most of your time while in Split. Don't expect a palace though, nor a museum – this is the city's living heart, its labyrinthine streets packed with people, bars, shops and restaurants. Built as a military fortress, imperial residence and fortified town, the palace measures 215m from north to south and 180m east to west, altogether covering 38,700 sq metres.

Although the original structure has been added to continuously over the millennia, the alterations have only served to increase the allure of this fascinating site. The palace was built in the 4th century from lustrous white stone transported from the island of Brač, and construction lasted 10 years. Diocletian spared no expense, importing marble from Italy and Greece, and columns and sphinxes from Egypt.

Each wall has a gate at its centre, named after a metal: the **Golden Gate** (Zlatna Vrata; Dioklecijanova bb) on the north, **Bronze Gate** (Brončana Vrata; Obala hrvatskog narodnog preporoda bb) on the south, **Silver Gate** (Srebrna Vrata) on the east and **Iron Gate** (Željezna Vrata) on the west. Between the eastern and western gates there's a straight road (Krešimirova; also known as Decumanus), which separates the imperial residence on the southern side, with its state rooms and temples, from the northern side, once used by soldiers and servants.

There are 220 buildings within the palace boundaries, home to about 3000 people. The narrow streets hide passageways and courtyards, some deserted and eerie, others thumping with music from bars and cafes, while the local residents hang out their washing overhead, kids play football amid the ancient walls, and grannies sit in their windows watching the action below.

➡ Diocletian's Palace Substructures
(Supstrukcije Dioklecijanove Palače; www.mgst.net; Obala hrvatskog narodnog preporoda bb; adult/concession 40/20KN; ⊘8.30am-9pm May-Sep, 8.30am-9pm Mon-Sat, 9am-5pm Sun Oct, 9am-5pm Mon-Sat, to 2pm Sun Nov-Apr) The Bronze Gate of Diocletian's Palace once opened straight

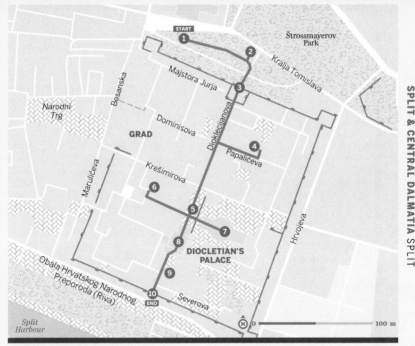

🏃 Walking Tour
Diocletian's Palace

START ST BENEDICT'S CHURCH
END BASEMENT HALLS
LENGTH 500M; TWO HOURS

Begin outside the well-preserved northwestern corner tower of the palace at the remains of the pre-Romanesque church of St Benedict, with the 15th-century **1 Chapel of Arnir**. Through the protective glass you'll see the altar slab and sarcophagus carved by the early Renaissance master Juraj Dalmatinac.

Head in the direction of the imposing statue of **2 Gregorius of Nin** (p207), and stop to rub his toe for good luck. The statue is outside the palace's **3 Golden Gate** (p202), which features fragments of the statues, columns and arches that once decorated it. Enter the palace and walk along its main north–south street, Dioklecijanova. Turn left at Papalićeva to admire the Papalić Palace, housing the worthwhile **4 City Museum** (p207).

Return to Dioklecijanova and continue on to the **5 Peristil** (p205), the entrance court, three steps below street level. The longer side is lined with six granite columns, linked by arches and decorated with a stone frieze. The southern side is enclosed by the Protiron, the entrance to the imperial quarters.

Turn right (west) on to the narrow Sv Ivana, which leads to the palace's former ceremonial and devotional quarter. You can still see parts of columns and a few fragments of the two temples that once flanked these streets. At the end of the street is the **6 Temple of Jupiter** (p207), notable for its vaulted roof.

Returning to the Peristil, directly opposite is the **7 Cathedral of St Domnius** (p206). Immediately west of the cathedral are steps leading up through the Protiron into the well-preserved **8 Vestibule** (p206). The story goes that Diocletian was so paranoid someone would kill him that he slept in different rooms. To get to the sleeping quarters you had to pass through this space and the echo would warn the emperor if anyone was coming.

Below the vestibule is the entrance to the palace's **9 substructures** (p202), which are now lined with market stalls. Head through the **10 Bronze Gate** (p202), at the far end, and let your eyes adjust to the light of the Riva.

Split

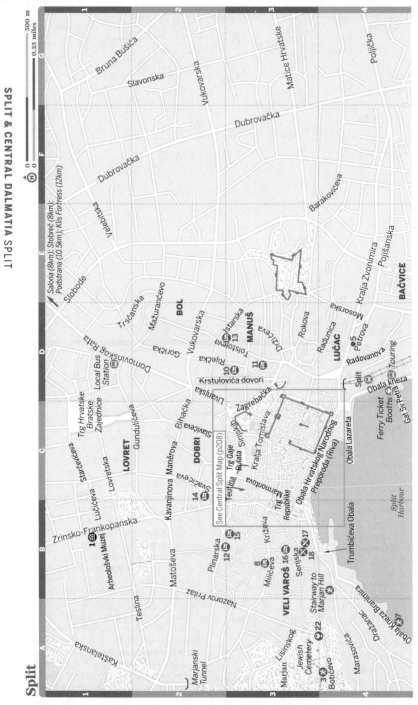

0
0.25 miles
0
500 m

Salona (8km); Stobreč (8km); Podstrana (10.5km); Klis Fortress (12km)

Kaštelanska
Teslina
Zrinsko-Frankopanska
Arheološki Muzej **1**
Matoševa
Nazorov Prilaz
Lučićeva
Starčevićeva
Lovretska
Plinarska
Milićeva **8**
Seniska
Stairway to Marjan Hill
Marjan Tunnel
Lisinskog
Jewish Cemetery
Botićevo **3**
Marasovića
Marjanski
Trg Hrvatske Bratske Zajednice
Gundulićeva
Kavanjinova
Manđerova
Svačićeva **14**
Bihaćeva
Slavićeva
Križeva
VELI VAROŠ **16**
22
Lučac
Zagrebačka
Livanjska
Krstulovića dovori
Sinjskih
Trg Gaje Bulata
Teutina
Marmontova
Kralja Tomislava
Trg Republike
Obala Hrvatskog Narodnog Preporoda (Riva)
Obala Lazareta
Trumbićeva Obala
Split Harbour
Dražanac
Obala Kneza Branimira **37**
12 15
17
18
See Central Split Map (p208)
Trsćanska
Mažuranićevo
Goricka
Vukovarska
Rijecka
Domovinskog Rata
Local Bus Station
LOVRET
DOBRI
BOL
MANUŠ
Istarska
Toltstojeva **13**
Držićeva
Rokova
Radunica
Petrova
Radovanova
10 11
Bruna Bušica
Slavonska
Dubrovačka
Vukovarska
Matice Hrvatske
Poljička
Velebitska
Dubrovačka
Barakovićeva
Kralja Zvonimira
Poljišanska
Mosorska
BAČVICE
5
Split
Obala kneza
Ferry Ticket Booths
Gat Sv Petra
Touring

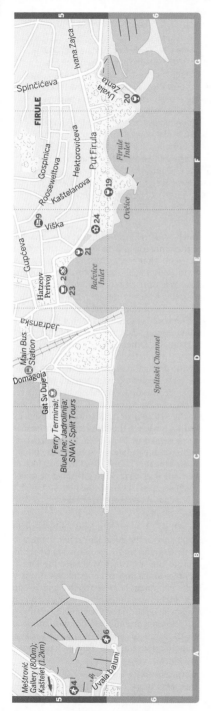

Split

from the water into the palace basements, enabling goods to be unloaded and stored here. Now this former tradesman's entrance is the main way into the palace from the Riva. While the central part of the substructure is now a major thoroughfare lined with souvenir stalls, entry to the chambers on either side is ticketed.

Although mostly empty save the odd sarcophagus or bit of column, the basement rooms and corridors exude a haunting timelessness that is well worth the price of admission. For fans of *Game of Thrones,* here be dragons – Daenerys Targaryen keeps her scaly brood here when she's in Meereen.

➡ Peristil

This picturesque colonnaded ancient Roman courtyard (or peristyle) lies at the very heart of Diocletian's Palace. In summer you can almost be guaranteed a pair of strapping local lads dressed as legionaries adding to

WORTH A TRIP

CHASING DRAGONS

Controlling the valley leading into Split, the imposing **Klis Fortress** (Tvrđava Klis; ☑021-240 292; www.tvrdavaklis.com; Klis bb; adult/child 40/15KN; ◷9am-7pm Tue-Sun) spreads along a limestone bluff, reaching 385m at its highest point. Its long and narrow form (304m by 53m) derives from constant extensions over the course of millennia. Inside, you can clamber all over the fortifications and visit the small museum, which has displays of swords and costumes and detailed information on the castle's brutal past.

Klis' real history (in a nutshell) goes like this: founded by the Illyrians in the 2nd century BC; taken by the Romans; became a stronghold of medieval Croatian duke Trpimir; resisted attacks for 25 years before falling to the Turks in 1537; briefly retaken in 1596; finally fell to the Venetians in 1648. However, let's face it, the only history that most visitors to the site these days are interested in is courtesy of *Game of Thrones* – this is Meereen, where Daenerys Targaryen had all those nasty slave-masters crucified in season four.

Klis is located 12km northeast of the city centre, and can be reached by city bus 22 (13KN) from Trg Gaje Bulata or Split's local bus station.

the scene. Notice the black-granite sphinx sitting between the columns near the cathedral; dating from the 15th century BC, it was one of several imported from Egypt when the palace was constructed.

➤ ★ Cathedral of St Domnius

(Katedrala Sv Duje; Map p208; Peristil; cathedral/belfry 35/20KN; ◷8am-7pm Mon-Sat, 12.30-6.30pm Sun) **FREE** Split's octagonal cathedral is one of the best-preserved ancient Roman buildings standing today. It was built as a mausoleum for Diocletian, the last famous persecutor of the Christians, who was interred here in 311 AD. The Christians got the last laugh, destroying the emperor's sarcophagus and converting his tomb into a church in the 5th century, dedicated to one of his victims. Note that a ticket for the cathedral includes admission to its crypt, treasury and baptistery (Temple of Jupiter).

The exterior of the building is still encircled by an original colonnade of 24 columns. A much later addition, the tall Romanesque belfry, was constructed between the 12th and 16th centuries and reconstructed in 1908 after it collapsed. Notice the two lion figures at its base. Tickets are sold separately for those eager to climb up the belfry for views over the old town's rooftops.

Visitor access to the cathedral is via the sacristy, situated in an annex around the right-hand side of the building. This structure also houses the cathedral's treasury, which is rich in reliquaries, icons, church robes, illuminated manuscripts and documents in Glagolitic script.

Inside the cathedral itself, the domed interior has two rows of Corinthian columns and a frieze running high up on the walls

which, surprisingly, still includes images of the emperor and his wife. To the left of the main altar is the altar of St Anastasius (Sveti Staš; 1448), carved by Juraj Dalmatinac. It features a relief of *The Flagellation of Christ*, which is considered one of the finest sculptural works of its time in Dalmatia.

The choir is furnished with 13th-century Romanesque seats, the oldest of their kind in Dalmatia. Other highlights include a 13th-century pulpit, the right-hand altar carved by Bonino da Milano in 1427, and the vault above the altar decorated with murals by Dujam Vušković. As you leave, take a look at the remarkable scenes from the life of Christ carved on the wooden entrance doors. Carved by Andrija Buvina in the 13th century, the scenes are presented in 28 squares, 14 on each side, and recall the fashion of Romanesque miniatures of the time. Don't forget to take a look in the Cathedral crypt, an eerily quiet chamber which stays cool even on the hottest days. It's now a chapel dedicated to St Lucy.

➤ Vestibule

(Peristil) **FREE** At the southern end of Peristil (p205), above the basement stairs, is the vestibule, a grand and cavernous domed room, open to the sky, which was once the formal entrance to the imperial apartments. If you're lucky, you might come across a *klapa* group here, taking advantage of the acoustics for an a cappella performance. Beyond the vestibule and curving around behind the cathedral are the ruins of various Roman structures, including the imperial dining hall and a bathhouse.

➤ Ethnographic Museum

(Etnografski Muzej; ☑021-344 161; www.etnografski-muzej-split.hr; Severova 1; adult/concession 15/

10KN; ⊘9.30am-8pm Mon-Sat, to 1pm Sun Jun-Sep, 9am-4pm Mon-Fri, to 1pm Sat Oct-May) This mildly interesting museum has a collection of traditional costumes, jewellery, musical instruments, toys and tools. The ground floor hosts temporary exhibits. Make sure you climb the reconstructed Roman staircase that leads to the Renaissance terrace encircling the top of the vestibule. The views from up there are reason enough to visit the museum.

➡ Temple of Jupiter

(Jupiterov Hram; 10KN; ⊘8am-7pm Mon-Sat, 12.30-6.30pm Sun) Although it's now the cathedral's baptistery, this wonderfully intact building was originally an ancient Roman temple, dedicated to the king of the gods. It still has its original barrel-vaulted ceiling and a decorative frieze on the walls, although a striking bronze statue of St John the Baptist by Ivan Meštrović now fills the spot where the god once stood. Of the columns that once supported a porch, only one remains.

The black granite sphinx guarding the entrance was already ancient when the Romans dragged it from Egypt in the 3rd century. It was literally defaced by the Christians, who considered it a pagan icon.

➡ Split City Museum

(Muzej Grada Splita; ☑021-360 171; www.mgst.net; Papalićeva 1; adult/child 20/10KN; ⊘8.30am-9pm) Built by Juraj Dalmatinac in the 15th century for one of the many noblemen who lived within the old town, Papalić Palace is considered a fine example of late Gothic style, with an elaborately carved entrance gate that proclaimed the importance of its original inhabitants. The interior has been thoroughly restored to house this museum, which has interesting displays on Diocletian's Palace and on the development of the city.

Captions are in Croatian, but wall panels in a variety of languages provide a historical framework for the displays of medieval sculpture, 17th-century weapons, fine furniture, coins, documents and drawings.

Gregorius of Nin statue   STATUE

(Grgur Ninski; Map p208; Kralja Tomislava bb) Sculpted by Ivan Meštrović, this gargantuan statue is one of the defining images of Split. The 10th-century Croatian bishop Gregorius of Nin fought for the right to use old Croatian in liturgical services. Notice that his left big toe has been polished to a shine – it's said that rubbing the toe brings good luck and guarantees that you'll come back to Split.

Gallery of Fine Arts   GALLERY

(Galerija Umjetnina Split; Map p208; ☑021-350 110; www.galum.hr; Kralja Tomislava 15; adult/concession 40/20KN; ⊘10am-6pm Tue-Fri, to 2pm Sat & Sun) In the building that once housed the city's first hospital, this gallery exhibits nearly 400 works of art spanning almost 700 years. Upstairs is the permanent collection of mainly paintings and some sculpture, a chronological journey that starts with the old masters and continues with works of modern Croatian art by the likes of Vlaho Bukovac and Ignjat Job. Temporary exhibits downstairs change every few months. The pleasant cafe has a terrace overlooking the palace.

Archaeological Museum   MUSEUM

(Arheološki Muzej; Map p204; ☑021-329 340; www.armus.hr; Zrinsko-Frankopanska 25; adult/concession 30/15KN; ⊘9am-2pm & 4-8pm Mon-Sat) A treasure trove of classical sculpture and mosaic is displayed at this excellent museum, a short walk north of the town centre. Most of the vast collection originated from the ancient Roman settlements of Split and neighbouring Salona (Solin), and there's also some Greek pottery from the island of Vis. There are displays of jewellery and coins, and a room filled with artefacts dating from the Paleolithic to the Iron Age.

LOCAL KNOWLEDGE

PICIGIN

For a bit of fun, join the locals at the beach and play the very Dalmatian sport of *picigin*. The rules are simple: stand in the water up to your knees or waist and pass a small ball (the size of a squash ball) to other players at a rather high speed by whacking it with the palm of your hand. The idea is to keep the ball from falling and touching the water's surface. It is imperative that you throw yourself about and into the water as much as possible. It's also advised to splash all the people standing around you and freely display your sporting vigour.

Check out the *picigin* 'headquarters' page at www.picigin.org or the several YouTube videos demonstrating *picigin* techniques (which vary between Split, Krk and other parts of the coast). Have a go at the special New Year's Eve *picigin* game if you think you're tough enough.

SPLIT & CENTRAL DALMATIA SPLIT

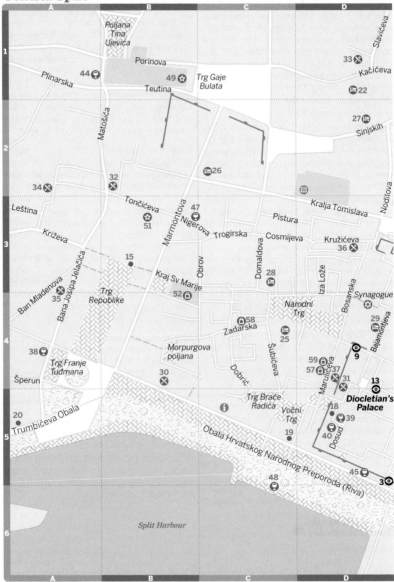

Meštrović Gallery   GALLERY
(Galerija Meštrović; ☎ 021-340 800; www.mestro
vic.hr; Šetalište Ivana Meštrovića 46; adult/child
40/20KN; ⊙ 9am-7pm Tue-Sun May-Sep, to 4pm
Tue-Sun Oct-Apr) At this stellar art museum,
you'll see a comprehensive, well-arranged
collection of works by Ivan Meštrović, Croatia's premier modern sculptor, who built the
gallery as a personal residence in the 1930s.
Although Meštrović intended to retire here,
he emigrated to the USA soon after WWII. Admission includes entry to the nearby Kaštelet,
a fortress housing other Meštrović works.

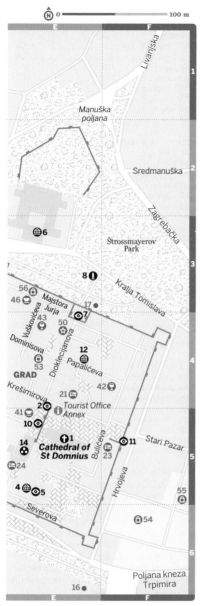

cycle of wood reliefs in the chapel. At the centre of the complex, a large stone sculpture titled *Author of the Apocalypse* looks over a lovely quadrangle.

🏃 Activities

Marjan Forest Park WALKING

(Park šuma Marjan; Map p204) Considered the lungs of the city, this hilly nature reserve offers trails through fragrant pine forests to scenic lookouts, medieval chapels and cave dwellings once inhabited by Christian hermits. For an afternoon away from the city buzz, consider taking a long walk through the park and descending to Kašjuni beach to cool off before catching the bus back. Climbers take to the cliffs near the end of the peninsula.

Zapadna Obala WALKING

(Map p204) The shiny new 'west coast promenade' connects the Riva to the bays below the Marjan Forest Park. This particularly lovely walk heads past the ACI Marina at the southwestern point of Split's harbour, passes by the Jadran swimming-pool complex, then Zvončac and Ježinac bays, and on to Kaštelet.

From Kaštelet, you can head up to the main road (Šetalište Ivana Meštrovića) and either continue west for another 20 minutes to Kašjuni beach or catch the bus back.

Bačvice SWIMMING

(Map p204) A flourishing beach life gives Split its aura of insouciance in summer, and sandy Bačvice is Split's most popular beach. Locals come here during the day to swim, sunbathe, drink coffee and play *picigin* (p207); a younger crowd returns in the evening for the bars and clubs. There are showers and changing rooms at both ends of the beach.

👉 Tours

Red Adventures ADVENTURE

(Map p204; ☎ 091 79 03 747; www.red-adventures. com; Kralja Zvonimira 8) Specialising in active excursions, this crew offers sea kayaking (from €38), rock climbing (from €50), hiking (from €30) and bike tours (from €45) around Split. It also rents bikes, kayaks and cars, charters yachts, provides transfers and arranges private accommodation.

Portal TOURS

(Map p208; ☎ 021-360 061; www.split-excursions. com; Trg Republike 1; ⊙ 8am-8pm) A one-stop shop for booking excursions, cruises and activities, this local agency can arrange rafting (320KN), canyoning (350KN), quad biking

Kaštelet MUSEUM

(☎ 021-358 185; www.mestrovic.hr; Šetalište Ivana Meštrovića 39; admission by Meštrović Gallery ticket; ⊙ 9am-7pm Tue-Sun May-Sep) This 16th-century fortified home near the Meštrović Gallery was bought by Ivan Meštrović in 1939 and restored to house his powerful *Life of Christ*

Central Split

(350KN) and diving (300KN). Boats head to Hvar and the Pakleni Islands (600KN), with some continuing on to the Blue Grotto (800KN). Coach destinations include Šibenik and Krka (420KN), Dubrovnik (500KN), Mostar and Međugorje (500KN) and Plitvice Lakes National Park (600KN).

Split Walking Tours TOURS
(Map p208; ☑ 099 82 15 383; www.splitwalking tour.com; Golden Gate; ⊙ Apr-Oct) Leads walking tours in English, Italian, German, Spanish and French, departing from the Golden Gate at set times during the day (check its website). Options include the 75-minute Diocletian's Palace Tour (100KN) and the two-hour Split Walking Tour (160KN), which includes the palace and the medieval part of town. It also offers kayaking, diving, cycling tours, boat trips and excursions.

Connecto Tours TOURS
(☑ 021-312 594; www.connectotours.com) Private tours plus scheduled day trips to Bol on Brač (€49 including picnic), Krka National Park and Šibenik (€58), Dubrovnik (€67), the Kornati Islands (€69), Mostar and Međugorje (€69), Plitvice Lakes National Park (€79) and Trogir and Zadar (€79). It also offers rafting on the Cetina River (€45), wine tasting on the Pelješac Peninsula and quad biking on Čiovo Island (€69).

Šugaman Tours CRUISE
(Map p208; ☑ 021-344 085; www.sugamantours. com; Dosud 4; ⊙ 8am-10pm) Operates a series of day trips by speedboat to Hvar and the Pakleni Islands (€90), and on to Vis (€116 to €160). It also offers day sails in the bay (€90) and road excursions to Krka National Park

(€58), Dubrovnik (€72) and Plitvice Lakes National Park (€86).

Summer Blues BOATING
(Map p208; ☑ 021-332 500; www.summer-blues.com; Obala hrvatskog narodnog preporoda 12; half/full day from €58/65) Sailing trips to Hvar, Brač and Šolta on board a luxurious catamaran, with dance music, cocktails and lunch included.

Toto Travel TOURS
(Map p208; ☑ 021-887 055; www.totosplit.com; Trumbićeva obala 2; ⊘ 7.30am-11pm mid-Jun–mid-Sep, 8am-5pm mid-Sep–mid-Jun) Offers excursions to the waterfalls at Krka (440KN) and Plitvice Lakes (640KN) National Parks, as well as daytime or sunset sailing trips (both 456KN), and cruises to Hvar (610KN) and to Vis Island and the Blue Grotto (836KN including lunch).

Ultra Sailing BOATING
(Map p204; ☑ 021-398 578; www.ultra-sailing.hr; ACI Marina Split, Uvala Baluni 6a) Among the best and most reliable Croatian sailing charter companies, with a popular sailing school. It also has bases in Dubrovnik, Kaštela and Trogir.

Nautical Centre Nava BOATING
(Map p204; ☑ 021-407 700; www.navaboats.com; Uvala baluni 1) Locally owned charter that has an impressive fleet of luxury catamarans, yachts and launches.

★ Festivals & Events

The tourist office can give you information about all the festivals. From June through to September a variety of free evening entertainment is presented in the old town and along the Riva.

Carnival CARNIVAL
(⊘ Feb) This traditional pre-Lent event sees locals dressing up in masks and costumes, and dancing in the streets for two very fun days.

Sudamja RELIGIOUS, CULTURAL
(⊘ early May) Festivities celebrating Split's patron saint, St Domnius (Sv Duje), start at the beginning of May and stretch out for two weeks. They include concerts, poetry readings, exhibitions and a rowing regatta. On the actual 7 May feast day (aka Split Day) there's a religious procession, Mass is held on the Riva and fireworks fill the skies.

Picigin World Championship SPORTS
(Prvenstvo Svita u Piciginu; ⊘ early Jun) Locals show off their *picigin* (a beach-ball sport of Dalmatia) skills at this fun event at Bačvice beach.

Split Mediterranean Film Festival FILM
(Festival Mediteranskog Filma Split; www.fmfs.hr; ⊘ Jun) Week-long festival screening films from the Mediterranean region, spiced up with exhibitions and parties.

Summer Colours of Split MUSIC
(Splitski Litnji Koluri; ⊘ mid-Jun–mid-Sep) Live music nightly on the Riva, concerts below Diocletian's Palace, a rock weekend, a techno weekend, and the Days of Diocletian: three days of tunics, togas, legionaries and barely dressed gladiators.

Splitski Festival MUSIC
(www.splitskifestival.hr; ⊘ late Jun or early Jul) Four days of pop music, that culminates in a song contest.

Ultra Europe MUSIC
(www.ultraeurope.com; 1-/2-/3-day ticket €99/149/199; ⊘ Jul) One of the world's largest electronic-music festivals takes over the city's Poljud stadium for three days in July before heading to the islands for the rest of Destination Ultra Croatia Music Week. People from across the world swarm to rave to the tunes of celebrity DJs.

Split Summer Festival PERFORMING ARTS
(Splitsko Ljeto; www.splitsko-ljeto.hr; ⊘ Jul & Aug) From 15 July to 15 August, this festival features opera, drama, ballet and concerts on open-air stages.

Split Film Festival FILM
(www.splitfilmfestival.hr; ⊘ mid-Sep) Focuses on new international films and screens lots of art-house movies; held over nine days.

🛏 Sleeping

As you'd expect in a big city that is also a tourist hub, prices in Split tend to be higher than the average – but not as high as the likes of Dubrovnik or Hvar. That said, Split has a good range of hostels and some excellent apartment-style providers catering to the midrange market.

🛏 Old Town

Split Hostel Booze & Snooze HOSTEL **€**
(Map p208; ☑ 021-342 787; www.splithostel.com; Narodni trg 8; dm 210-230KN; ✳🛜) This little party place at the heart of town has four simple dorms, each with its own bathroom and lockers. There's a terrace but no kitchen.

Silver Central Hostel　　HOSTEL €
(Map p208;　☑ 021-490 805;　www.silvercentral
hostel.com; Kralja Tomislava 1; dm 190KN; ❄ ☎) In
an upstairs apartment, this yellow-painted
hostel has four dorm rooms gathered around
a central lounge. There's no proper kitchen
but there is a microwave, toaster and kettle
in the lounge.

★Antique Split Luxury Rooms　　HOTEL €€€
(Map p208;　☑ 021-785 208;　www.antique-split.
com; Poljana Grgura Ninskog 1; r 2690-3845KN;
❄ ☎) Palace living at its most palatial, this
boutique complex has eight chic rooms with
stone walls and impressive bathrooms. In
some you'll wake up to incredible views over
the cathedral.

★Villa Split　　B&B €€€
(Map p208;　☑ 091 40 34 403; www.villasplitluxury.
com; Bajamontijeva 5; r from €207; P ❄ ☎) Built
into the Roman-built wall of Diocletian's
Palace, this wonderful boutique B&B has
only three rooms – the best of which is the
slightly larger one in the attic. If you're happy
to swap the ancient for the merely medieval,
there are six larger rooms in a 10th-century
building on the main square.

Palača Judita　　HOTEL €€€
(Map p208;　☑ 021-420 220; www.juditapalace.com;
Narodni trg 4; r €350-390; ❄ ☎) Occupying a
historic palazzo right on Split's main square,
this boutique hotel has plenty of old-world
charm, abetted by medieval stone walls and
antique-style furniture. Some have old-town
views and one has a balcony.

Hotel Peristil　　HOTEL €€€
(Map p208;　☑ 021-329 070;　www.hotelperistil.
com; Poljana Kraljice Jelene 5; s/d €135/162; ❄ ☎)
This lovely hotel is in the very heart of Diocletian's Palace. Service is warm and the
12 rooms are gorgeous – all have hardwood
floors, antique details and good views, but
smallish bathrooms. Rooms 204 and 304
have small alcoves with a bit of the palace's
ancient wall exposed *and* they overlook the
Peristil (p205).

Hotel Vestibul Palace　　HOTEL €€€
(Map p208;　☑ 021-329 329;　www.vestibulpalace.
com; Iza Vestibula 4a; s/d/ste from 2815/3565/
4950KN; P ❄ ☎) The poshest in the palace,
this boutique hideaway occupies the site
where the emperor's own apartments once
stood. It has seven stylish rooms and suites,
all with exposed ancient walls and the full
spectrum of upscale amenities.

Veli Varoš

★Apartments Magdalena　　APARTMENT €€
(Map p204;　☑ 098 423 087;　www.magdalena-
apartments.com; Milićeva 18; 450-580KN; ❄ ☎)
You may never want to leave Magdalena's
top-floor apartment once you see the old-
town view from the dormer window. The
three apartments are nicely furnished and
the hospitality offered by the off-site owners is
exceptional: chocolates on arrival, beer in the
fridge, a back-up toothbrush in the cupboard
and even a mobile phone with credit on it.

Villa Varoš　　GUESTHOUSE €€
(Map p204;　☑ 021-483 469; www.villavaros.hr; Miljenka Smoje 1; r/apt from €80/121; ❄ ☎) Owned by
a New Yorker Croat, Villa Varoš offers simple,
clean rooms with wooden furniture, en suite
bathrooms and TVs in a quiet but central
location.

Vila Baguc　　B&B €€€
(Map p204;　☑ 021-770 456; www.baguc.com; Plinarska 29/2; r from €140; ❄ ☎) Oozing character, this restored 150-year-old family house
in Veli Varoš has four guest rooms on four
floors, with modern fittings combined with
original details such as exposed stone walls.
The villa is tucked back from the street, only
a five-minute walk from the town centre.

Divota Apartment Hotel　　HOTEL €€€
(Map p204;　☑ 021-782 700;　www.divota.hr; Plinarska 75; s/d from €109/159; ❄ ☎) Owned by
an artsy Swiss-Croatian, Divota (meaning
'splendour') provides a luxurious retreat
from the nearby palace buzz. The six contemporary rooms and nine apartments are
scattered across the Veli Varoš neighbourhood in eight restored stone houses. Best of
all is the three-bedroom villa with a Jacuzzi
in its own courtyard. All come with upscale
amenities and original details.

Dobri

Tchaikovsky Hostel　　HOSTEL €
(Map p204;　☑ 021-317 124; www.tchaikovskyhostel.
com; Čajkovskoga 4; dm 180-200KN; ❄ @ ☎) This
four-dorm hostel in an apartment block in the
neighbourhood of Špinut is run by a German-
born Croat. Rooms are neat and tidy, with
bunks featuring built-in shelves. Freebies include cereal, espresso and tea.

Sleep Split　　GUESTHOUSE €€€
(Map p208;　☑ 091 32 38 302; www.sleepsplit.com;
Sinjska 5; s/d/ste €120/175/200; ❄ ☎) Decked

out in black, white, grey and splashes of colourful fabric, this stylish set of five rooms occupies the 3rd floor of an apartment block on the edge of the old town. It's so popular, it's thinking of expanding downstairs.

Azur Palace　　　　　　　　　　HOTEL €€€
(Map p208; ☎021-785 185; www.azurpalace.com; Kačićeva 2; r €179-229; P❄️🛜) Stepping off an insalubrious lane into an old distillery building, the luxuriousness of this little hotel comes as a complete surprise. There are just 18 rooms and all are stylishly fitted out, with exposed stone, time-worn beams and large bathrooms.

🛏 Manuš

Hostel Emanuel　　　　　　　　HOSTEL €
(Map p204; ☎021-786 533; hostelemanuel@gmail.com; Tolstojeva 20; dm €29; ❄️@🛜) Run by a friendly couple, this hip little hostel in a suburban apartment block has colourful contemporary interiors and a relaxed vibe. In the two dorms (one sleeping five, the other 10), each bunk has a large locker, curtains, a reading light and a power outlet.

CroParadise Green Hostel　　　HOSTEL €€
(Map p204; ☎091 44 44 194; www.croparadise.com; Čulića Dvori 29; dm/s 200/240KN, d with/without bathroom 480/440KN; ❄️@🛜) This crowd-pleasing hostel (winner of Hostelworld's 'most popular' award in 2016) offers a range of brightly coloured dorm rooms and small apartments, spread between three apartment buildings in the central neighbourhood of Manuš. Each dorm has access to lockers and a small kitchen; other facilities include laundry, bike and scooter rental.

CroParadise Blue & Pink Hostels　HOSTEL €€
(Map p204; ☎091 44 44 755; www.croparadise.com; Riječka 3; dm 200KN, d with/without bathroom 480/440KN; ❄️@🛜) Sisters to the Green Hostel, Blue and Pink face off against each other in apartment buildings on opposite sides of the road. Blue handles the reception for both hostels, although we slightly prefer Pink, as it feels a little more spacious.

🛏 Bačvice

Beach Hostel Split　　　　　　HOSTEL €
(Map p204; ☎098 94 50 998; www.facebook.com/splitbeachhostel; Viška 9; dm/tw 200/400KN; ⏱Apr-Oct; @🛜) A hop and a skip from Bačvice beach, this cosy hostel is managed by a friendly Norwegian called Ladybird, who

imbues the place with a chilled-out vibe. There's free coffee and tea, colourful cartoons on the walls and a terrace with a guitar ready.

🍴 Eating

Split is big enough to have an interesting dining scene which isn't limited to the cookie-cutter *konobas* (taverns) and pizzerias that are the norm in Dalmatia. Some upmarket places have embraced modern European trends, and there's even a dedicated vegetarian restaurant. Dozens of restaurants are clustered around the Riva, Diocletian's Palace and the area directly to its west.

🍴 Old Town

Galija　　　　　　　　　　　　PIZZA €
(Map p208; ☎021-347 932; Tončićeva 12; mains 45-100KN; ⏱9am-midnight Mon-Sat, noon-midnight Sun) The go-to place for pizza, Galija is the sort of joint where locals take you for a good, simple meal, where everyone relaxes on the wooden benches with the leftovers of a *quattro stagioni* in front of them. It also serves pasta and Dalmatian-style grills.

★Zinfandel　　　　　　　　EUROPEAN €€
(Map p208; ☎021-355 135; www.zinfandelfoodand winebar.com; Marulićeva 2; mains 90-145KN; ⏱8am-1am) The vibe might be more like an upmarket wine bar, but the food is top-notch here too. The menu includes delicious risotto, homemade pasta, veal cheek *pašticada* (traditional Dalmatian stew), burgers, steaks and fish, and there's a huge choice of local wine by-the-glass to wash it down. The beer selection is good too.

Brasserie on 7　　　MODERN EUROPEAN €€
(Map p208; ☎021-278 233; www.brasserieon7.com; Obala hrvatskog narodnog preporoda 7; mains breakfast 52-88KN, lunch 87-140KN, dinner 130-160KN; ⏱7.30am-11.30pm Jun-Sep, 8am-4pm Oct-May) The best of the Riva eateries, this waterfront brasserie's outdoor tables are the perfect vantage point for the passing parade. Start the day with a cooked breakfast, end it with a cocktail, and fill the hours in between with a light lunch, more substantial dinner, or wine and a cheese platter. The service is excellent too.

Figa　　　　　　　　MEDITERRANEAN €€
(Map p208; ☎021-274 491; Buvinina 1; mains 80-135KN; ⏱8am-1am, closed Sun Oct-Apr) A cool little restaurant and bar, with a funky interior and tables on the stairs outside, Figa serves nice breakfasts, seafood dishes and a wide range of salads. There's live music some

nights and the kitchen stays open late. Service can be slow but comes with smiles and jokes.

Villa Spiza   DALMATIAN €€
(Map p208; Kružićeva 3; mains 60-120KN; ☺9am-midnight Mon-Sat) A locals' favourite, just outside the palace walls, this low-key joint offers great-quality Dalmatian mainstays that change daily – think calamari, risotto, stuffed peppers – at reasonable prices. Service is slow, but the fresh home-cooked food is prepared with care.

🍴 Veli Varoš

Makrovega   VEGETARIAN €
(Map p208; ☑021-394 440; www.makrovega.hr; Leština 2; mains 50-75KN; ☺9am-9.30pm Mon-Fri, to 5pm Sat) Hidden away down a lane and behind a courtyard, this meat-free haven serves macrobiotic, vegetarian and some raw food. Think lots of seitan, tofu and tempeh, and excellent cakes.

★Konoba Matejuška   DALMATIAN €€
(Map p204; ☑021-355 152; www.konobamatejuska. hr; Tomića Stine 3; mains 85-160KN; ☺noon-11pm) This cosy, rustic tavern in an alleyway minutes from the seafront specialises in well-prepared seafood – as epitomised in its perfectly cooked fish platter for two. There are only four small tables outside and a couple of larger ones inside, so book ahead.

Konoba Marjan   DALMATIAN €€
(Map p204; ☑098 93 46 848; www.facebook.com/ konobamarjan; Senjska 1; mains 78-139KN; ☺noon-11pm; 🔊) Offering great-quality Dalmatian fare, this friendly little Veli Varoš tavern features daily specials such as cuttlefish *brujet* (fish stew), goulash and prawn pasta. The wine list is excellent, showcasing some local

---

KLAPA YOUR HANDS!

Few visitors to Dalmatia will leave without at some point being mesmerised by the dulcet tones of a *klapa* song. This a cappella tradition involves a bunch of burly men in a circle, singing tearjerkers about love, betrayal, patriotism, death, beauty and other life-affirming subjects in honeyed multitonal harmonies. In Split, the best place to catch a *klapa* group doing its thing is the Vestibule (p206), the emperor's circular foyer on the south side of the Peristil square within the palace walls.

---

boutique wineries, and there are a few seats outside on the street leading up to Marjan Hill.

Paradigma   MEDITERRANEAN €€€
(Map p208; ☑021-645 103; www.restoranpara digma.hr; Bana Josipa Jelačića 3; mains 100-175KN; ☺11am-midnight Jun-Sep, 11.30am-10.30pm Mon-Sat, to 4.30pm Sun Oct-May) Bringing culinary innovation to Split, this restaurant sports modern interiors with colourful paintings and a rooftop terrace with sea glimpses in an old building resembling a ship's bow. Dishes are presented like mini works of art – and while not everything tastes as exquisite as it looks, most of the dishes are sublime.

🍴 Dobri

Gušt   PIZZA €
(Map p208; ☑021-486 333; www.pizzeria-gust.hr; Slavićeva 1; pizzas 34-53KN; ☺9am-11pm Mon-Sat, 6-11pm Sun, closed Sun Jun-Sep) Split's diehard pizza fans swear by this joint – it's cheap and very local.

🍸 Drinking & Nightlife

Split is great for nightlife, especially in spring and summer. The palace walls are generally throbbing with loud music on Friday and Saturday nights, and you can spend the night wandering the maze-like streets, discovering new places. After the palace bars go quiet at 1am (as people live within the palace walls), the beaches to the east have open-air bars and clubs that stay open till the wee hours.

Ziggy Star   PUB CRAWL
(Map p208; ☑099 54 97 385; www.pubcrawl split.net; crawl 150KN; ☺from 10pm) Named, presumably, after the mythical rocker who took it all too far, Ziggy Star offers an opportunity to push your limits in a guided all-night bender. Starting with a 100-minute 'power hour' of cocktails and shooters, the trail leads to a bar on the Riva, then a club in Bačvice, then breakfast.

🍷 Old Town

Ghetto Club   BAR
(Map p208; www.facebook.com/clubghetto; Dosud 10; ☺9am-1am Mon-Sat, 5pm-1am Sun) Split's most bohemian and gay-friendly bar has ancient Roman walls, a large courtyard with a trickling fountain, a chandelier-festooned piano lounge and a small red-walled club space with poetry on the walls. The music is great and the atmosphere is friendly.

Marcvs Marvlvs Spalatensis WINE BAR
(Map p208; www.facebook.com/marvlvs; Papalićeva 4; ⊙5pm-midnight; 🔊) Fittingly, the
15th-century Gothic home of the 'Dante of
Croatia', Marko Marulić, now houses this
wonderful little 'library jazz bar' – two small
rooms crammed with books and frequented
by ageless bohemians, tortured poets and
wistful academics. Cheese, chess, cards and
cigars are all on offer, and there's often live
music.

To Je To BAR
(Map p208; www.tojetosplit.com; Nigerova 2;
⊙8.30am-1am; 🔊) If you're up for loud rock
and hip hop, Croatian craft beer and Mexican food, this effortlessly hip little bar is the
place to come. The chilled-out Honduran/US
owners engender a feel-good Latin American
party vibe, and there's live music most nights
and a crazy karaoke session on Fridays.

St Riva BAR
(Map p208; Obala hrvatskog narodnog preporoda
19; ⊙7am-1am; 🔊) Bad techno and tacky-
looking cocktails don't stop St Riva being a
great place to hang out. Grab a perch on the
narrow terrace built into the palace walls
and watch the mayhem on the Riva below.
Later in the night, a fair bit of booty-shaking
happens in the small clubby space inside.

Fabrique BAR
(Map p208; 🖉098 17 51 271; www.fgroup.hr; Trg
Frane Tuđmana 3; ⊙8am-1am) Big, bright and
brash, this large industrial-style bar has offset its brick arches with kooky light fixtures
and elegant little tables where the Splitćani
glitterati hold court over beer and barbecue.

Luxor CAFE
(Map p208; www.lvxor.hr; Peristil; ⊙8am-1am;
🔊) Touristy, yes, but this cafe-bar is a great
place to have coffee and cake right in the ceremonial heart of Diocletian's Palace. Cushions are laid out on the steps and there's live
music nightly.

Mosquito BAR
(Map p208; Majstora Jurja 4; ⊙7am-1am) Sit on
the big terrace, grab a cocktail or coffee, listen to music and hang out with the locals.

Fluid BAR
(Map p208; 🖉095 67 00 002; www.facebook.
com/fluid.split; Dosud 1; ⊙9am-midnight Mon-Sat,
5pm-midnight Sun) This chic little place, with
cushions on the lane, is great for a cocktail
and a spot of people watching.

Porta BAR
(Map p208; Majstora Jurja 4; ⊙8am-midnight)
Come here for cocktails or a quiet beer. On
the same square are a couple of other bars,
all of which end up merging into one when
the night gets busy, so remember your waiter!

Teak CAFE, BAR
(Map p208; Majstora Jurja 11; ⊙8am-midnight
Mon-Sat) Located on a busy square, Teak's terrace is superpopular for coffee and chats during the day, and gets busy in the evenings, too.

🍷 **Veli Varoš**

Paradox WINE BAR
(Map p208; Poljana Tina Ujevića 2; ⊙9am-1am Mon-
Sat, 4pm-1am Sun) This stylish wine and cheese
bar has cool wine-glass chandeliers inside,
alfresco tables and a massive selection of Croatian wines (more than 120, including 40 by-
the-glass) and local cheeses to go with them.
The clued-up staff really know their stuff.

Vidilica BAR
(Map p204; Nazorov Prilaz 1; ⊙8am-midnight) It's
worth the climb up the stone stairs through
the ancient Veli Varoš quarter for a sunset
drink at this hilltop cafe with glorious city
and harbour views.

🍹 **Bačvice**

Žbirac CAFE
(Map p204; www.zbirac.hr; Šetalište Petra Preradovića 1b; ⊙7am-midnight) This beachfront cafe
is like the locals' open-air living room, a cult
hang-out with great views of the swimmers
and *picigin* players, and occasional concerts.

Tropic Club CLUB
(Map p204; 🖉099 20 39 222; www.facebook.com/
tropic.club.split; Bačvice bb; ⊙10pm-5am) A 1st-
floor beachfront disco with a curved glass
frontage, and house, pop or Croatian music,
depending on the night.

Euphoria CLUB
(Map p204; www.facebook.com/euphoriasplit; Put
Firula 6; ⊙8am-2am Mon-Thu, to 4am Fri-Sun)
Among pine trees just above Ovčice beach,
with a large terrace overlooking the Adriatic,
this spot draws a young moneyed crowd to
its purple-velvet interior, where DJs spin
smooth tunes every night in summer.

O'Hara CLUB
(Map p204; 🖉095 50 49 909; www.ohara.hr;
Uvala Zenta 3; ⊙9pm-6am Fri-Wed) For alfresco
clubbing on a waterfront terrace, head to

this fun Zenta hang-out. On Wednesdays there's live music but mostly DJs spin dance, R&B and boogie tunes on nights with names like Monday Trash and Double Trash.

☆ Entertainment

Croatian National Theatre Split THEATRE
(Hrvatsko Narodno Kazalište Split; Map p208; ☑ 021-306 908; www.hnk-split.hr; Trg Gaje Bulata 1) Opera, ballet and music performances are presented here year-round. Tickets can be bought at the box office or online. Built in 1891, the theatre was fully restored in 1979 in the original style; it's worth attending a performance for the architecture alone.

Split City Puppet Theatre THEATRE
(Gradsko Kazalište Lutaka Split; Map p208; ☑ 021-395 958; www.gkl-split.hr; Tončićeva 1) Although shows are mainly in Croatian, there's a fair chance your toddlers can speak fluent puppet.

Kinoteka Zlatna Vrata CINEMA
(Map p208; www.zlatnavrata.hr; Dioklecijanova 7) Classic films, art flicks and retrospectives are screened at this university-affiliated cinema. It has few screenings during July and August.

Kino Bačvice CINEMA
(Map p204; Put Firula 2) The after-dark entertainment zone of Bačvice is a perfect venue for the open-air cinema that runs nightly from July to September.

🛍 Shopping

Studio Naranča ART, DESIGN
(Map p208; ☑ 021-344 118; www.studionaranca. com; Majstora Jurja 5; ⏰ 9am-midnight Mon-Sat, 10am-2pm Sun) Showcasing the work of local artist Pavo Majić, this little store sells original art and very cool T-shirts, tote bags and postcards featuring his designs.

Diocletian's Cellars MARKET
(Map p208; Obala hrvatskog narodnog preporoda bb; ⏰ 9am-9pm) The main passage through the basement of Diocletian's Palace is lined with stalls selling jewellery, gifts made from Brač stone, scarves, T-shirts, handmade soap and prints. For a touristy souvenir strip, the quality's actually pretty good.

Uje FOOD & DRINKS
(Map p208; ☑ 021-342 719; www.uje.hr; Marulićeva 1; ⏰ 8am-8.30pm Mon-Fri, to 2pm Sat) For a little place Uje stocks a large range of top-quality Croatian olive oil, along with locally made jam, pasta sauce, *rakija* (grappa), wine, soap and wooden products.

Think Pink FASHION & ACCESSORIES
(Map p208; Zadarska 4; ⏰ 8.30am-10pm) Boho women's clothing and jewellery made by home-grown designers. There's a second store (Map p208; Marulićeva 1; ⏰ 8.30am-10pm) around the corner.

GetGetGet DESIGN
(Map p208; ☑ 021-341 015; www.getgetget.com. hr; Dominisova 16; ⏰ 10am-8pm Mon-Fri, to 4pm Sat) A concept store touting offbeat Croatian design items such as jewellery, clothing, lamps and various cool knick-knacks.

Fish Market MARKET
(Ribarnica; Map p208; Obrov 5; ⏰ 6.30am-2pm) As stinky and chaotic a scene as you could possibly imagine, Split's indoor/outdoor fish market is a spectacle to behold. Locals head here on a daily basis to haggle for all their scaly and slimy requirements from their favourite chain-smoking vendors. It's all over by about 11am, bar the dregs.

Old Market MARKET
(Map p208; Stari Pazar) Split's main outdoor market spreads throughout the streets immediately east of Diocletian's Palace. Unlike the neighbouring Green Market, the bulk of the stalls sell durable goods such as clothes, beach towels, snorkelling masks, Croatian football shirts and a fair bit of tourist tat.

Green Market MARKET
(Map p208; Hrvojeva bb; ⏰ 6.30am-2pm) This open-air market is the place to come to stock up on fruit, vegetables and cut flowers. While it's busiest in the mornings, a few stallholders stay open to sell cherries and strawberries to tourists throughout the afternoon in summer.

ℹ Information

Daluma Travel (☑ 021-338 424; www.daluma-travel.hr; Obala kneza Domagoja 1) Books excursions and boat trips, and arranges private accommodation and car rental.

Main Post Office (Map p208; Kralja Tomislava 9; ⏰ 7am-9pm Mon-Fri, 7.30am-2pm Sat)

Tourist Office (Map p208; ☑ 021-360 066; www.visitsplit.com; Obala hrvatskog narodnog preporoda 9; ⏰ 8am-9pm Mon-Sat, to 7pm Sun Jun-Sep, 8am-8pm Mon-Sat, to 5pm Sun Apr, May & Oct, 9am-4pm Mon-Fri, to 1pm Sat Nov-Mar) Has info on Split and sells the Split Card (70KN), which offers free and reduced prices to Split attractions, plus discounts on car rental, restaurants, shops and theatres. You get the card for free if you're staying in Split more than three nights from October to May.

Tourist Office Annex (Map p208; ☑ 021-345 606; www.visitsplit.com; Peristil bb; ⊙ 8am-9pm Mon-Sat, to 7pm Sun Jun-Sep, 9am-4pm Mon-Fri, to 1pm Sat Oct-May)

Turistički Biro (☑ 021-347 100; www. turistbiro-split.hr; Obala hrvatskog narodnog preporoda 12) This travel agency's forte is excursions and private accommodation.

University Hospital Split (Klinički Bolnički Centar (KBC) Split; ☑ 021-556 111; www. kbsplit.hr; Spinčićeva 1)

❶ Getting There & Away

The bus, train and ferry terminals are clustered on the eastern side of the harbour, a short walk from the old town.

AIR
Airport
Split Airport (Zračna Luka Split; ☑ 021-203 507; www.split-airport.hr; Cesta dr Franje Tuđmana 1270, Kaštel Štafilić, Kaštela) is in Kaštela, 24km northwest of central Split. In summer, dozens of airlines fly here from all over Europe (including Austrian Airlines, British Airways, easyJet, Norwegian Air Shuttle and Scandinavian Airlines). The following airlines operate all year round.

Croatia Airlines (☑ 072 500 505; www.croatia airlines.com) The national carrier has flights to Zagreb, Rome, Munich and Frankfurt year-round. In summer there are also domestic flights to Dubrovnik and Osijek, and international flights to London (Gatwick and Heathrow), Paris, Lyon, Berlin, Düsseldorf, Zurich, Skopje and Athens.

Germanwings (www.germanwings.com) Year-round flights to Cologne/Bonn and Stuttgart, and seasonal flights to Berlin, Dortmund, Düsseldorf, Hamburg and Hanover.

Lufthansa CityLine (www.lufthansacityline. com) Flies to/from Munich.

Seaplane Terminal
European Coastal Airlines (☑ 021-444 813; www.ec-air.eu) From May to October, seaplanes dock near the international ferries in Split Harbour. Destinations include Ancona (Italy), Pula, Rijeka, Rab, Mali Lošinj, Novalja (Pag), Jelsa (Hvar), Lumbarda (Korčula), Vela Luka (Korčula), Lastovo and Dubrovnik.

BOAT
Split's ferry harbour is extremely busy and can be hard to negotiate, so you're best to arrive early. Most domestic ferries depart from Gat Sv Petra, the first of the three major piers, which has ticket booths (Map p204) for both Jadrolinija and

---

JADROLINIJA SERVICES FROM SPLIT

Note that the schedules listed for these ferries are for services between June and September. Service is reduced outside these months.

Car Ferries

DESTINATION	COST PER PERSON/CAR	DURATION (HR)	FREQUENCY
Ancona (Italy)	from 300/450KN	11	3-4 weekly
Drvenik Mali	30/160KN	2¼	weekly
Drvenik Veli	30/160KN	2	weekly
Rogač (Šolta)	33/160KN	1	5-6 daily
Stari Grad (Hvar)	47/318KN	2	6-7 daily
Supetar (Brač)	33/160KN	¾	12-14 daily
Ubli (Lastovo)	68/530KN	4½	daily
Vela Luka (Korčula)	60/530KN	2¾	2 daily
Vis	54/370KN	2¼	2-3 daily

Catamarans

DESTINATION	COST	DURATION (HR)	FREQUENCY
Bol (Brač)	55KN	1¼	2 daily
Hvar (Hvar)	55KN	1	2-4 daily
Jelsa (Hvar)	55KN	1¾	daily
Korčula (Korčula)	80KN	3	1-2 daily
Milna (Brač)	40KN	¾	weekly
Ubli (Lastovo)	75KN	3¼	daily
Vela Luka (Korčula)	65KN	2¼	daily

Kapetan Luka. The giant international ferries depart from Gat Sv Duje, the second of the piers, where there's a large ferry terminal (Map p204) with ticketing offices for all the major lines.

For most domestic ferries you can't reserve tickets ahead of time; they're only available for purchase on the day of departure. In July and August it's often necessary to appear hours before departure for a car ferry, and put your car in the line for boarding. There is rarely a problem or a long wait obtaining a space off-season. Ferry services include the following:

BlueLine (Map p204; ☑ 021-223 299; www. blueline-ferries.com; ☒ Apr-Oct) Has overnight car ferries to Ancona, stopping on Hvar on some days; **Split Tours** (Map p204; ☑ 021-352 553; www.splittours.hr; Gat Sv Duje bb; ☒ closed Sat & Sun afternoon) handles its ticketing.

Bura Line (☑ 095 83 74 320; www.buraline. com; Obala kralja Zvonimira bb; to Split 24KN) Heads backwards and forwards to Trogir on a small boat four to six times a day from June to September.

Jadrolinija (Map p204; ☑ 021-338 333; www. jadrolinija.hr; Gat Sv Duje bb) Operates most of the ferries between Split and the islands (p217), as well as overnight ferries to Ancona in Italy.

Kapetan Luka (Krilo; ☑021-645 476; www. krilo.hr) Has a fast catamaran leaving daily for Vis (55KN, 1½ hours), which on some days also stops in Milna on Brač and Hvar Town. From June to September it also has a daily boat to Milna (40KN, 30 minutes), Hvar Town (70KN, 65 minutes), Korčula Town (120KN, 1¾ hours), Pomena on Mljet (130KN, three hours) and Dubrovnik (190KN, 4¼ hours), dropping to four times per week in May and three per week in October.

LNP (Linijska Nacionalna Plovidba; ☑ 021-352 527; www.lnp.hr) Has one or two catamarans a day to Rogač on Šolta (35KN, 35 minutes).

SNAV (Map p204; www.snav.it) Has nightly ferries to/from Ancona (660KN, five hours) from April to October, some of which stop at Stari Grad on Hvar.

BUS

Most intercity and international buses arrive at and depart from the **main bus station** (Autobusni Kolodvor Split; Map p204; ☑ 060 327 777; www.ak-split.hr; Obala kneza Domagoja bb) beside the harbour. In summer, it's best to purchase bus tickets with seat reservations in advance. If you need to store bags, there's a **garderoba** (Obala kneza Domagoja 12; 1st hr 5KN, then 1.50KN per hr; ☒ 6am-10pm) nearby.

Domestic destinations include Zagreb (130KN, five hours, at least hourly), Pula (300KN, 10 hours, three daily), Rijeka (300KN, eight hours, eight daily), Zadar (100KN, 3½ hours, at least hourly) and Dubrovnik (130KN, 4½ hours, 21 daily). Note that Split–Dubrovnik buses pass briefly through Bosnian territory, so keep your passport handy for border-crossing points.

International destinations include Mostar (130KN, seven daily), Sarajevo (220KN, four daily), Ljubljana (236KN, two daily), Vienna (336KN, at least daily) and Belgrade (439KN, at least daily).

Touring (Map p204; ☑ 021-338 503; www. touring.hr; Obala kneza Domagoja 10; ☒ 8am-8pm Mon-Fri, 9am-3pm Sat & Sun), located near the bus station, represents Deutsche Touring and sells bus tickets to German cities.

CAR

Various car-hire companies have desks at the airport, including **Dollar Thrifty** (☑ 021-399 000; www.thrifty.com.hr; Trumbićeva obala 17), which also has a city office. You can also rent cars, scooters and motorbikes through Daluma Travel (p216) and **Split Rent Agency** (Map p208; ☑ 091 59 17 111; www.split-rent.com; Obala Lazareta 3).

TRAIN

Five trains a day head to Split's **train station** (☑ 021-338 525; www.hzpp.hr; Obala kneza Domagoja 9; ☒ 6am-10pm) from Zagreb (112KN, six hours, five daily) and Knin (91KN, 1½ hours, five daily). There's also a direct service to Budapest (492KN) twice a week from June to September.

The train station has lockers (per day 15KN) that will fit suitcases but you can't leave bags overnight. There's another **garderoba** (☑ 098 446 780; Obala kneza Domagoja 6; per day 15KN; ☒ 6am-10pm Jul & Aug, 7.30am-9pm Sep-Jun) nearby, out on the street.

❶ Getting Around

TO/FROM THE AIRPORT

Airport Shuttle Bus (☑ 021-203 119; www. plesoprijevoz.hr; journey 35KN) Makes the 30-minute journey between the airport and Split's main bus station (platform 1) at least 14 times a day.

City Bus 37 & 38 The regular Split–Trogir bus stops near the airport every 20 minutes. The journey takes 50 minutes from the local bus station (Map p204) on Domovinskog Rata, making it a slower option than the shuttle but also cheaper (17KN from Split, 13KN from Trogir).

Taxi A cab to central Split costs between 200KN and 250KN.

Žele Shuttle (Prijevoz Putnika Žele; ☑ 098 286 220; www.split-airport.com.hr; ticket 35KN) Buses travel between Obala Lazareta and the airport 10 times daily from April to October, four times daily in the off season.

PUBLIC TRANSPORT

Promet Split (☑ 021-407 999; www.promet-split.hr) operates local buses on an extensive network throughout Split (per journey 11KN) and as far afield as Klis (13KN), Solin (13KN), Kaštela (17KN), Trogir (21KN) and Omiš (21KN). You can buy tickets on the bus, but if you buy from a kiosk, a two-journey (ie return) central-zone ticket costs only 17KN. Buses run about every 15 minutes from 5.30am to 11.30pm.

AROUND SPLIT

Kaštela

POP 38,700

If you're looking to hunker down in safety, you can't do much better than having the mountains behind you and the sea in front. At least that's what the Dalmatian nobility thought when faced with the threat of Ottoman invasion in the 15th and 16th centuries. One after the other, rich families from Split headed to the 20km stretch of coast between Trogir and Split to build their sturdy mansions, until a total of 17 castles and towers were built, some with fortified villages attached. The Turks never reached them and many of the castles remain today.

Kaštela is now a municipality in its own right, incorporating seven separate little harbour towns, each named after a castle, which together form the second-largest settlement in Split-Dalmatia County. Running from Split to Trogir, they are Kaštel Sućurac, Kaštel Gomilica, Kaštel Kambelovac, Kaštel Lukšić, Kaštel Stari, Kaštel Novi and Kaštel Štafilić.

◉ Sights

The main highway heads through Kaštela's industrial fringes, leaving a less-than-positive impression, but turn off towards the water and a different Kaštela comes into view – one of historic villages clinging to rocky bays. Confusingly, the names of the seven settlements don't always match up with the castles they contain. Some have more than one castle and some don't have any at all.

Kaštel Gomilica was built for a community of Benedictine nuns and is surrounded by shallow, sandy beaches. *Game of Thrones* fans may recognise it as one of the locations used for the town of Braavos. Next up, **Kaštel Kambelovac** has a cylindrically shaped defence tower, built in 1517 by local noblemen and landowners.

If you visit just one part of Kaštela, make it **Kaštel Lukšić**, home to Kaštel Vitturi, the biggest and best preserved of Kaštela's castles, and the only one open to the public. The

village also has a big baroque church and the most un-castle-like Kaštel Rušinac, a private house and garden enclosed by sturdy walls.

Kaštel Stari (literally Old Castle) was the first to be built along this stretch, dating from 1476, while neighbouring **Kaštel Novi** (New Castle) is a relative spring chicken, built in 1512 – although the only fortification that remains here is a single blocky tower.

Just around the next bend is **Kaštel Štafilić**, which contains two freestanding 16th-century towers, the squat Kaštel Štafileo and a large Renaissance church.

Muzej Grada Kaštela   MUSEUM, CASTLE
(☎ 021-260 245; www.muzej-grada-kastela.hr; Brce 1, Kaštel Lukšić; adult/child 15/5KN; ⊙ 9am-8pm Mon-Sat, to 1pm Sun Jun-Sep, 9am-4pm Mon, Wed & Fri, to 7pm Tue & Thu, to 1pm Sat Oct-May) Built in the late 15th and early 16th centuries, Kaštel Vitturi was home to the Vitturi family right up until 1943 when it was converted into a school. It now houses the tourist office and this small museum. Upstairs, one room is devoted to archaeology (containing Roman coins, jewellery and pottery) and another to the lifestyles of the local nobility (with displays of furniture, weapons and clothing).

❶ Information

Tourist Office (☎ 021-227 933; www.kastela-info.hr; Kaštel Vitturi, Brce 1, Kaštel Lukšić; ⊙ 8am-3pm Mon-Fri, to noon Sat)

❶ Getting There & Away

To get to Kaštela, take bus 37 from Split or Trogir, which departs every 20 minutes and stops in all the towns along the bay. It's best to get off at Kaštel Štafilić and walk eastward along the coastal promenade through the towns. Once you've had enough, walk inland to the main road to catch the bus back.

Trogir

POP 13,200

Gorgeous Trogir (called *Trau* by the Venetians) is set within medieval walls on a tiny island, linked by bridges to both the mainland and to the far larger Čiovo Island. On summer nights everyone gravitates to the wide seaside promenade, lined with bars, cafes and yachts – leaving the knotted mazelike marble streets gleaming mysteriously under old-fashioned streetlights.

The old town has retained many intact and beautiful buildings from its age of glory between the 13th and 15th centuries. In 1997 its profuse collection of Romanesque and Renaissance buildings earned it World Heritage status.

While it's easily reached on a day trip from Split, Trogir also makes a good alternative base to the big city and a relaxing place to spend a few days.

History

Backed by high hills in the north, surrounded by water on all sides and snug within its walls, Trogir proved an attractive place to settlers. It was founded in the 3rd century BC by Greek colonists and later became Romanised. Its defensive position allowed Trogir to maintain a degree of autonomy throughout Croatian and Byzantine rule, while trade and nearby mines ensured its economic viability.

In the 13th century sculpture and architecture flourished, reflecting a vibrant, dynamic culture. When Venice bought Dalmatia in 1409, Trogir refused to accept the new ruler and the Venetians bombarded the town into submission. While the rest of Dalmatia stagnated under Venetian rule, Trogir continued to produce great artists who enhanced the beauty of the town.

◉ Sights

★ **St Lawrence's Cathedral**   CATHEDRAL
(Katedrala Svetog Lovre; Trg Ivana Pavla II; 25KN; ⊗8-7pm Mon-Sat, noon-6.30pm Sun) The showcase of Trogir is its three-naved Venetian cathedral, one of the finest architectural works in Croatia, built from the 13th to 15th centuries. Master Radovan carved the grand Romanesque **portal** (1240). Sculptures on either side depict lions (symbolising Venice) with Adam and Eve standing on their backs, the earliest example of the nude in Dalmatian sculpture. At the end of the portico is another fine piece of sculpture – the 1464 cherub-lined **baptistery** sculpted by Andrija Aleši.

To the left as you enter the cathedral is the richly decorated Renaissance **Chapel of St Ivan**, created by the masters Nikola Firentinac and Ivan Duknović from 1461 to 1497. Be sure to take a look at the **treasury**, which contains an ivory triptych and various silver reliquaries. You can also climb the 47m-high cathedral **tower** for views over the old town.

A sign informs that you must be 'decently dressed' to enter the cathedral, which means that men must wear tops (women too, of course) and shorts are a no-go.

Museum of Sacred Art   MUSEUM
(Muzej Sakralne Umjetnosti; Trg Ivana Pavla II; 10KN; ⊗8am-8pm mid-Jun–mid-Sep, 1-7pm mid-Sep–mid-Jun) Highlights of this small museum include illuminated manuscripts, a large painting of St Jerome and St John the Baptist by Bellini, an almost life-size brightly painted *Crucifix with Triumphant Christ* and the darkly lit fragments of a 13th-century icon which once adorned the cathedral's altar.

St Sebastian's Church   CHURCH
(Crkva Sv Sebastijana; Trg Ivana Pavla II) No longer used for services, this 1476 church shelters stone sarcophagi and the photos of locals killed in the 1990s war. It's topped by a large blue-faced Renaissance clock.

Town Loggia   HISTORIC BUILDING
(Gradska Loža; Trg Ivana Pavla II) On the main square, this 13th-century open-sided structure features an interesting relief by famous Croatian sculptor Ivan Meštrović.

Trogir Museum   MUSEUM
(Muzej Grada Trogira; ☑021-881 406; www.muzejgradatrogira.blogspot.com; Gradska vrata 4; adult/concession 20/15KN; ⊗9am-noon & 6-9pm Jul & Aug, 9am-noon & 5-8pm Jun & Sep, 9am-2pm Mon-Fri Oct-May) Housed in the former Garagnin-Fanfogna palace, this museum exhibits books, documents, drawings and period costumes from Trogir's long history.

Kamerlengo Castle   CASTLE
(Kaštel Kamerlengo; Hrvatskog proljeća 1971 bb; adult/child 25/20KN; ⊗9am-7pm) Built around 1420, this fortress was once connected to the city walls. Inside it's basically an empty shell, but you can climb up and circle the walls. Concerts are held here during the Trogir Summer festival (p221).

Okrug Gornji   BEACH
(Šetalište Stjepana Radića bb) Trogir's most popular beach, Okrug Gornji lies 1.7km south of the old town on the island of Čiovo. Known as Copacabana, this 2km-long stretch of pebbles is lined with cafe-bars. It can be reached by road or boat.

Medena Beach   BEACH
On the Seget Riviera, 4km west of the old town, this stretch of beach has a long promenade lined with bars, tennis courts, minigolf, ice-cream parlours and stands renting jet skis, kayaks and windsurfers. While it's in the grounds of the faded Hotel Medena megaresort, it's open to the general public and there's parking on-site.

WORTH A TRIP

SOLIN: ROAMING A ROMAN CITY

The ruins of the ancient city of **Salona** (☎ 021-213 358; Don Frane Bulića bb, Solin; adult/child 30/15KN; ⊙ 9am-7pm Mon-Sat, to 2pm Sun), situated at the foot of the mountains just northeast of Split, are the most archaeologically important in Croatia. Start by paying your admission fee at the **Tusculum Museum**, near the entrance to the reserve, as you'll need the map from its brochure to help you navigate the vast, sprawling site. This small museum has lots of ancient sculpture and interesting displays on the archaeological team that uncovered the site.

Salona was first mentioned as an Illyrian town in 119 BC and it's thought that it already had walls by then. The Romans seized the site in 78 BC and under the rule of Augustus it became the administrative headquarters of the Roman Dalmatian province. When Emperor Diocletian built his palace in Split at the end of the 3rd century AD, it was the proximity to Salona that attracted him. That grand history all came to a crashing halt in the 7th century, when the city was levelled by the invading Avars and then the Slavs. The inhabitants fled to take refuge within Diocletian's old palace walls and in the neighbouring islands, leaving Salona to decay.

While many of Salona's ancient treasures are now on display in Split's Archaeological Museum (p207), there's a surprising amount in situ. Numerous sarcophagi are scattered about the area known as **Manastirine**, between the car park and the museum. This was a burial place for Christian martyrs prior to the legalisation of Christianity and includes the substantial remains of an early basilica.

From the museum, a path bordered by cypresses runs south to the northern city wall. From here you can get an overview of the foundations of buildings that comprise the **Episcopal Centre**, including a three-aisled, 5th-century cathedral with an octagonal baptistery, and the remains of Bishop Honorius' Basilica with a ground plan in the form of a Greek cross. Public **baths** adjoin the cathedral to the east.

Just beyond this complex and slightly to the right is the 1st-century eastern city gate, **Porta Caesarea**, later engulfed by the growth of the city eastward. Grooves in the stone road left by ancient wheels can still be seen here, along with the remains of a covered aqueduct which ran along the top of the wall. It was probably built around the 1st century AD and supplied Salona and Diocletian's Palace with water from the Jadro River. Just through this city gate was the centre of town, the Forum, with temples to Jupiter, Juno and Minerva, none of which are visible today.

The original city spread west from here to the huge 2nd-century **amphitheatre**, destroyed in the 17th century by the Venetians to prevent it from being used as a refuge by Turkish raiders. At one time it could accommodate 18,000 spectators, which gives an idea of the size and importance of this ancient city.

The main path leading to the amphitheatre follows the line of the ancient wall, with the vineyards to your left covering what was once the western end of town. Just to the right of the path (ie outside the wall) you'll pass another early Christian cemetery, where the remains of some of those killed in the amphitheatre were once buried, along with the ruins of the **Five Martyrs Basilica** (Kapljuč Basilica), built in their honour.

Outside the main Salona complex, but situated at what would have been the southeastern corner of the ancient walled city, is the **Gradina** (Kralja Zvonimira bb, Solin), a medieval fortress built around the remains of a rectangular early Christian church.

Salona is easily accessible on Split city bus 1 (13KN), which goes all the way to the parking lot every half-hour, departing from Trg Gaje Bulata.

✯✯ Festivals & Events

Trogir Summer   MUSIC
(Trogirsko Ljeto; ⊙ Jun-Sep) Every year from 21 June through early September, the town hosts Trogir Summer, a music festival with classical and folk concerts presented in churches, squares and the fortress. Posters advertising the concerts are posted all around town.

🛏 Sleeping

Camp Seget   CAMPGROUND €
(☎ 021-880 394; www.kamp-seget.hr; Hrvatskih Žrtava 121, Seget Donji; site per adult/child/tent/car

38/22/28/40KN; ☺ Mar-Oct) Located 2km west of Trogir, this intimate campground has tent sites under the pines, lockers, a good toilet and shower block, a small shingle beach and a cemented diving point.

Villa Tudor
HOTEL €€

(☑ 091 25 26 652; www.villa-tudor.com; Obala kralja Zvonimira 12; s/d from 584/730KN; P ✸ ☎) With exposed stone offset with baby-blue walls in the stylish bedrooms, and the best water-framed views of Trogir's old town that you could imagine, this little family-run hotel is quite exceptional. The double glazing really does its job on what's a busy strip.

Vila Tina
HOTEL €€

(☑ 021-888 305; www.vila-tina.com; Cesta Domovinske Zahvalnosti 63, Arbanija; s/d 610/750KN; P ✸ @ ☎) Out on a limb in a small seaside settlement, 5km east of Trogir, Vila Tina is excellent for those travelling with a car who value having a little concrete-lined swimming spot at their doorstep. Some of the spacious, tidy rooms have big sea-facing balconies. Plus there's a hot tub and infrared sauna.

Concordia
HOTEL €€

(☑ 021-885 400; www.concordia-hotel.htnet. hr/eng; Obala bana Berislavića 22; s/d from 500/690KN; ✸ ☎) The tidy, older-style rooms in this beautiful 300-year-old stone building on the waterfront are clean but basic, although the service and setting are excellent. Request a room with sea views. Boats to the beaches depart right outside.

Hotel Tragos
HOTEL €€€

(☑ 021-884 729; www.tragos.hr; Budislavićeva 3; s/d from 730/1100KN; ✸ ☎) This medieval family house has been well restored, with lots of exposed stone and original details. Its 12 sleek, nicely decorated rooms come with satellite TV and minibars. Even if you don't stay here, come for the wonderful home cooking served in the hotel restaurant (mains from 55KN); try the *trogirska pašticada* (Trogir-style beef stew).

Aparthotel Bellevue
HOTEL €€€

(☑ 021-492 000; www.bellevue.com.hr; Alojzija Stepnica 42; r/apt from 915/990KN; P ✸ ☎) On the landward side of Trogir, this painfully 1990s-looking block has spacious rooms that are simply furnished except for some over-the-top dangly light fixtures. Some have curved balconies overlooking the old town, although the rear rooms are quieter and the

views aren't quite as *belle* from this side of Trogir anyway.

Hotel Pašike
HOTEL €€€

(☑ 021-885 185; www.hotelpasike.com; Sinjska bb; s/d from €98/135; ✸ ☎) This delightful hotel in a 15th-century house showcases 19th-century furniture, dark timber and elaborate beds. The friendly staff wear traditional outfits, adding to the days-gone-by vibe. Head up to the little roof terrace for views over the old town.

✕ Eating

Pizzeria Mirkec
PIZZA, DALMATIAN €€

(☑ 021-883 042; www.pizzeria-mirkec.hr; Budislavićeva 15; mains 40-150KN; ☺ 9am-midnight) With dozens of tables spilling out on to the waterfront promenade and the main restaurant tucked around the corner, this relaxed joint serves tasty wood-fired pizza along with omelettes, steaks, pasta, grilled fish and, if preordered, traditional meals slow-roasted under a *peka* (domed metal lid). There's also a good-value set breakfast option (40KN).

★ Konoba Trs
DALMATIAN €€€

(☑ 021-796 956; www.konoba-trs.com; Matije Gupca 14; mains 75-225KN; ☺ 11am-midnight) As traditional-looking as they come, this rustic little tavern has wooden benches and old stone walls inside, and an inviting courtyard shaded by grapevines. Yet the menu adds clever, contemporary twists to Dalmatian classics, featuring the likes of panko-crumbed octopus tentacles, and the signature dish, nutmeg-spiced lamb *pašticada,* served with savoury pancakes. Book ahead for a memorable meal.

🛍 Shopping

Small Loggia
MARKET

(Mala Loža; Obala bana Berislavića; ☺ 9am-9pm) This small historic open-sided market, pressed up against the town walls, is still used by street traders, although these days they mainly deal in jewellery. It's a good place to buy interesting pieces showcasing local stone and pearls.

ℹ Information

Atlas Trogir (☑ 021-881 374; www.atlas-trogir. hr) This travel agency arranges private accommodation, runs excursions, and rents cars, scooters, bikes and boats.

Portal Trogir (☑ 021-885 016; www.portaltrogir.com; Bana Berislavića 3; ☺ 8am-8pm May-Sep, 9am-1pm Mon-Fri Oct-Apr) Arranges

Trogir

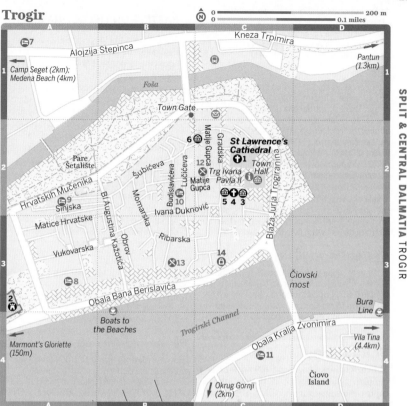

Trogir

◉ Top Sights
1 St Lawrence's Cathedral........................C2

◉ Sights
2 Kamerlengo Castle...............................A3
3 Museum of Sacred Art.........................C2
4 St Sebastian's Church..........................C2
5 Town Loggia..C2
6 Trogir Museum......................................C2

🛏 Sleeping
7 Aparthotel Bellevue...............................A1

8 Concordia..A3
9 Hotel Pašike...A2
10 Hotel Tragos...B2
11 Villa Tudor..C4

🍴 Eating
12 Konoba Trs...C2
13 Pizzeria Mirkec.....................................B3

🛍 Shopping
14 Small Loggia...C3

private accommodation; rents bikes, scooters and kayaks; and books excursions and adventure activities (quad safaris, rafting, diving, canyoning).

Post Office (Blaža Jurjeva Trogiranina 5; ⊙8am-4pm Mon-Fri, 9am-1pm Sat) There's a telephone centre here.

Tourist Office (☑021-885 628; www.tztrogir. hr; Trg Ivana Pavla II 1; ⊙8am-4pm Mon-Fri,

9am-1pm Sat) Inside the town hall; distributes town maps.

ⓘ Getting There & Away

BOAT
Bura Line (p218) has a small boat heading backwards and forwards to Split four to six times a day from June to September.

Jadrolinija (📞 021-338 333; www.jadrolinija. hr) has three daily car ferries (adult/child/car/ motorcycle/bike 16/8/160/70/38KN) heading from Trogir to Drvenik Veli (one hour) and on to Drvenik Mali (a further 20 minutes).

BUS

Intercity buses stop at the **bus station** (📞 021-881 405; Kneza Tripimira bb) near the bridge to Trogir. There's a **garderoba** (Bus Station; per day 15KN; ⏰ 7am-8pm) left-luggage facility, although it's not always staffed. Destinations include Zagreb (from 149KN, 6½ hours, 11 daily), Rijeka (200KN, 7½ hours, three daily), Zadar (80KN, 2½ hours, every half-hour), Split (21KN, 30 minutes, frequent) and Dubrovnik (140KN, 5½ hours, five daily).

Split city bus 37 takes the coastal road through Kaštela to/from Trogir, also stopping at the airport. This is a much slower option than the intercity buses, which take the highway.

ℹ Getting Around

In summer, small passenger **boats** (Obala Bana Berislavića) depart from Obala bana Berislavića, right in front of Hotel Concordia, heading to the beaches of Okrug Gornji (25KN) and Medena (20KN). The journey takes about 45 minutes.

Šolta Island

This lovely, wooded island (59 sq km) is a popular getaway for Split inhabitants escaping the sultry summer heat. The island's main entry point is **Rogač**, where ferries from Split tie up on the edge of a large bay. A shady path leads around the bay to smaller coves with rocky beaches, and a small road leads uphill to the island's administrative centre of **Grohote**, with a market and shops. **Maslinica** is the island's prettiest settlement, with seven islets offshore, a handful of restaurants, a luxurious heritage hotel and a good choice of private accommodation. Another gorgeous village is **Stomorska**, with its pretty sheltered harbour popular with yachters. The island's interior has several worthwhile family-run farm eateries; Kaštelanac in Gornje Selo does tastings of its olive oils, grappas and wines. The tourist office has details of other inland options.

🛏 Sleeping

Martinis Marchi   HOTEL €€€

(📞 021-572 768; www.martinis-marchi.com; Put Sv Nikole 51, Maslinica; ste 2613-4140KN; ❄ ✆) Built in 1703, this seaside castle has been converted into a luxurious heritage hotel, with seven suites, a marina, a restaurant and a spa centre.

RAFTING ON THE CETINA RIVER

The Cetina is the longest river in central Dalmatia, stretching 105km from the eponymous village. It flows through the Dinara mountains, through the fields around Sinj and gathers steam until it pours into a power plant around Omiš. It is an extraordinarily scenic journey as the limpid blue river is bordered by high rocky walls, thick with vegetation. Rafting is possible from spring to autumn, but the rapids can become quite fast after heavy rains. Summer is best for inexperienced rafters.

Rafting operators tout their trips from the riverside on the old town side of the Omiš bridge. The better operators charge upwards of 200KN. Some are cheaper, but not as good.

ℹ Information

Tourist Office (📞 021-654 491; www.visitsolta. com; Obala Sv Terezije 3; ⏰ 10am-5pm Mon & Wed, 8am-8pm Tue & Thu-Sun)

ℹ Getting There & Away

Four to six **Jadrolinija** (📞 021-654 664; www. jadrolinija.hr) car ferries a day run between Split and Rogač (adult/child/car/bicycle 33/17/160/38KN, one hour). Additionally, LNP (p218) has one or two catamarans a day on the same route (35KN, 35 minutes).

Omiš

POP 15,000

The legendary pirates' lair of Omiš has one of the most dramatic locations of any town on the Dalmatian coast. Situated at the mouth of the Cetina River, at the end of a picturesque canyon, it's backed by sheer walls of mottled grey rock topped with craggy peaks.

The coastal highway traffic slows to a crawl as the road narrows into the leafy oak-lined main street. On the landward side is a small but atmospheric maze of old streets capped by a little castle. A sandy-shingly beach stretches out on its other flank, attracting scores of perky families in the summertime.

⊙ Sights

Mirabela Fortress   CASTLE

(Tvrđava Mirabela; 20KN; ⏰ 9am-9pm) Also known as Peovica, this little tower was built in the 13th century on 9th-century Byzantine foundations. It's reached by a steep set of steps, and while there's not a lot inside, it's worth trudging up the internal staircase and taking the final ladder to the top for the views over the town.

🏃 Activities

Omiš' enviable location lends itself to plenty of activities. The most gentle option is a boat cruise up the river canyon to pretty Radmanove Mlinice (Radman's Mills). Small boats line up alongside the bridge and depart when they're full; expect to pay around 100KN.

Hiking is another popular option, with hardy types making the ascent to **Fortica**, a fortress high above the town that blends so well into the mountain's grey hide that's it's hard to discern from below. The track isn't particularly difficult but it is quite a climb.

Zipline   ADVENTURE SPORTS
(☑095 82 22 221; www.zipline-croatia.com; ride 400KN) Blast along a set of eight wires strung high above the Cetina canyon – up to 150m high, to be exact. The longest runs for 700m.

🛏 Sleeping & Eating

Hotel Plaža   HOTEL €€€
(☑021-755 260; www.hotelplaza.hr; Trg kralja Tomislava 6; s/d from 737/988KN; P❋☎) Right by the beach, this large modern hotel has richly coloured rooms, many with balconies and sea views. In winter you can take a spin on the hotel's ice rink then warm up in the spa centre.

Restaurant Bastion   CROATIAN €€
(☑021-757 922; Fošal 9; mains 49-169KN; ☺10am-midnight; ☎) Operating out of an old stone house right on the traffic-choked main street, Bastion serves a tasty selection of grilled meat as well as pizza and lots of seafood. Try the black risotto or call ahead for an octopus to be chucked in the *peka*.

ℹ Information

Tourist Office (☑021-861 350; www.visitomis. hr; Trg kneza Miroslava bb)

ℹ Getting There & Around

Split city bus 60 heads here every half-hour (21KN). Other destinations include Makarska (31KN, 40 minutes, three daily), Dubrovnik (121KN, four hours, three daily), Šibenik (82KN, two hours, two daily) and Zagreb (110KN, six hours, three daily).

MAKARSKA RIVIERA

The Makarska Riviera is a 58km stretch of coast at the foot of the Biokovo Range, where a series of cliffs and ridges forms a dramatic backdrop to a string of beautiful pebble beaches. The foothills are protected from harsh winds and covered with lush Mediterranean greenery, including pine forests, olive groves and fruit trees.

The seaside towns here are orientated towards package tourism; this is one of the most developed stretches of the Dalmatian coast. It is a great place for both families and active types, as facilities are vast. Note that in July and especially August the entire Riviera is jam-packed with holidaymakers, and many hotels impose a seven-night minimum stay.

Brela

POP 1710

The longest and arguably loveliest coastline in Dalmatia stretches through the tiny town of Brela, which has a more chic flavour than neighbouring Makarska, 14km southeast. Six kilometres of pebble beaches curve around coves thickly forested with pine trees, where you can enjoy beautifully clear seas and fantastic sunsets. A shady promenade lined with bars and cafes winds around the coves, which spread out on both sides of the town. The best beach is **Punta Rata**, a gorgeous stretch of pebbles about 300m northwest of the town centre.

🛏 Sleeping & Eating

Hostel Casa Vecchia   HOSTEL €
(☑021-619 014; www.casavecchia.hostel.com; Breljanska cesta 40; dm €17; ☺Jun-Sep; P☎) The most affordable place in Brela is also its most adorable, the funky Hostel Casa Vecchia on the coastal highway (Magistrala). The friendly Aussie owner offers a free shuttle to the beach, and there's a restored wooden boat that does booze cruises for hostel guests.

Konoba Feral   DALMATIAN €€
(☑021-618 909; Obala Domagoja 30; mains 75-150KN; ☺10am-midnight) For well-prepared seafood, head to this friendly tavern on the waterfront; try the squid grilled with garlic and parsley.

ℹ Information

Berulia Travel (☑021-618 519; www.berulia travel-brela.hr; Frankopanska 111) Finds private accommodation, changes money, books excursions and arranges airport transfers.

Tourist Office (☑ 021-618 455; www.brela.hr; Trg Alojzija Stepinca bb; ☺ 8am-8pm) Provides a town map and a regional cycling map.

ⓘ Getting There & Away

Most buses running along the highway stop near the Brela turn-off, 1km above the town centre. Destinations include Zagreb (120KN, 6½ hours), Šibenik (58KN, three hours), Split (35KN, one hour), Makarska (16KN, 20 minutes) and Dubrovnik (100KN, four hours).

Makarska

POP 13,900

Makarska is a port town and beach resort with a spectacular natural setting, backed by the glorious Biokovo mountain range. While the outskirts are a little shabby, there's a lovely long waterfront promenade and a pretty limestone centre that turns peachy orange at sunset. Active types base themselves here to take advantage of the nearby hiking, climbing, paragliding, mountain biking, windsurfing and swimming opportunities, and the good transport connections.

Makarska is favoured by tourists from neighbouring Bosnia, who descend on the town's long pebbly beach in huge numbers during summer. It's also popular with seniors as a 'medical tourism' destination.

The high season is pretty raucous, with many buzzing nightlife spots, but also a lot of fun for those with children. If you're interested in hanging around beach bars and clubs, playing volleyball and generally lounging about, you'll like Makarska. Outside the high season, things are pretty quiet.

◉ Sights

Makarska's harbour and historic centre are located on a large cove bordered by Cape Osejava in the southeast and the Sveti Petar peninsula in the northwest. The long pebble **town beach**, lined with hotels, stretches from the Sveti Petar park at the beginning of Obala kralja Tomislava northwest along the bay. To the southeast are rockier and lovelier beaches, such as **Nugal**, popular with nudists (take the marked trail from the eastern end of the Riva). For a party atmosphere all day long, head past the town beach to **Buba beach**, near the Hotel Rivijera, where music pumps all day during summer.

Municipal Museum MUSEUM
(Gradski Muzej; Obala kralja Tomislava 17/1; 10KN; ☺ 9am-1pm Mon-Sat) Kill time on a rainy day tracing the town's history by checking out this less-than-gripping collection of photos, old stones and nautical relics.

🏃 Activities

Wine Club Croatia WINE
(☑ 091 57 70 053; www.wineclubcroatia.com; workshop 250KN) Enthusiastic and charming wine expert Daniel Čečavac hosts these excellent wine-tasting events in various hotels around Makarska, pairing five top-notch vintages with local food specialities. He also leads private tours to wineries on the Pelješac Peninsula (two to four people, 1500KN) and to a honey maker in Grabovac (per person 300KN).

Biokovo Active Holidays ADVENTURE SPORTS
(☑ 021-679 655; www.biokovo.net; Kralja Petra Krešimira IV 7b) A fount of information on Biokovo, organising hiking, cycling, canyoning, rafting and kayaking trips.

🛏 Sleeping

Hostel Makarska HOSTEL €
(☑ 098 542 785; www.hostelmakarska.com; Prvosvibanjska 15; dm 140KN, r with/without bathroom 350/300KN; ☺ May-Sep; P ❄ 🛜) A friendly old dog will most likely greet you at this basic but friendly place, right in the centre of town. There are six private rooms (two with en suite bathrooms) and a 10-person dorm, plus a shared kitchen and an outdoor area.

Maritimo HOTEL €€€
(☑ 021-679 041; www.hotel-maritimo.hr; Put Cvitačke bb; s/d from 629/838KN; P ❄ 🛜) Right by the beach, this excellent hotel has friendly staff and modern rooms with fridges, safes, good bathrooms and balconies with sea views. Breakfast on the terrace by the water is a blissful way to start the day.

Hotel Osejava HOTEL €€€
(☑ 021-604 300; www.osejava.com; Šetalište fra Jure Radića bb; s & d €109-152; ❄ 🛜 🏊) The sweetest four-star in town, this contemporary property at the southern end of the harbour has whitewashed interiors featuring lots of light wood and black-and-white photos on Dalmatian themes. The complex includes a restaurant, a minispa and an outdoor pool, plus a little beach right in front.

WORTH A TRIP

TASTY TUČEPI

If you have a car, there are also a couple of great options in the hills above the village of Tučepi to the southeast of Makarska.

Konoba Ranč (☑ 021-623 563; www.ranc-tucepi.hr; Kamena 62, Tučepi; mains 80-150KN; ⏱ 6pm-1am) This rustic spot, away from the tourist buzz, is worth the 10-minute drive southeast to the slopes above Tučepi; follow the sign from the highway. Dine on log chairs under olive trees, feasting on grilled meat and fish, a preordered *peka*, house wine and sporadic *klapa* performances.

Jeny Restaurant (☑ 091 58 78 078; www.restaurant-jeny.hr; Čovići 1, Gornji Tučepi; mains from 130KN; ⏱ 6pm-midnight mid-May–Sep) In this fine-dining restaurant on the lower slopes of Biokovo mountain, in the village of Gornji Tučepi, the culinary focus is Mediterranean with a French touch. Splurge on the five-course tasting menu (including wine), for 575KN. The breathtaking riviera views make up for the passable decor.

Hotel Park
HOTEL €€€
(☑ 021-608 200; www.parkhotel.hr; Kralja Petra Krešimira IV 23; s/d from €150/230; P❄️🛜🏊) There's no disguising the ugly 1980s exterior of this hotel but inside the decor is fresh and chic, with colourful carpets in the corridors and soothing tones in the rooms. Most bedrooms have balconies and half of them have sea views. It's the kind of place where you might find yourself mingling with Croatian celebs at the pool or spa.

✖ Eating

There are some excellent restaurants and taverns scattered liberally around Makarska, including in some unlikely back streets.

★ Konoba Kalalarga
DALMATIAN €
(Kalalarga 40; mains from 45KN; ⏱ 9am-2am; 🛜) This traditional Dalmatian tavern has dim lighting, dark wood and alfresco bench seating in an alleyway leading up from Makarska's main square. It serves food the way *baba* (grandma) would make it, and dishes out the best *pašticada* in town. There's no menu – just a daily set of specials.

Riva
DALMATIAN €€€
(☑ 021-616 829; www.vinc-mornar.hr; Obala kralja Tomislava 6; mains 95-190KN; ⏱ 10am-1am) Linger in the quiet leafy courtyard of this classy restaurant just off the main drag, feasting on lamb, steak and fresh fish. There's a good wine list, too.

🍷 Drinking & Nightlife

Grabovac
WINE BAR
(Kačićev trg 11; ⏱ 9am-2am) Right on the main square, in front of the church, this outpost of a famous winery from Imotski (the wine region behind the mountains, right on the Bosnian border) serves its own wine by the glass, plus tasty titbits such as local cheese and *pršut* (proscuitto).

Deep
CLUB
(www.facebook.com/deepmakarska; Šetalište fra Jure Radića 5a; ⏱ 9am-5am mid-Jun–mid-Sep; 🛜) Inside a cave near the Hotel Osejava, Deep attracts a fashionable set who sip cocktails as a DJ spins the latest beats.

Rockatansky
BAR
(www.facebook.com/udrugarockatanskymakarska; Fra Filipa Grabovca 15; ⏱ 6pm-2am) Makarska's most alternative spot, where a diverse crowd gathers to hear live rock, grunge, metal and jazz on a small stage.

Yeti
CAFE, BAR
(☑ 021-278 767; www.facebook.com/hostel.caffe.bar.yeti; Dalmatinska 1; ⏱ 7am-2am) A cosy, much-loved cafe-bar right on the main square. It also has a small hostel up above.

ℹ Information

Atlas Travel Agency (☑ 021-617 038; www.atlas-croatia.com; Obala kralja Tomislava 17; ⏱ 8am-8pm Mon-Sat, 9am-1pm Sun) Excursions and private accommodation.

Marivaturist (☑ 021-615 214; www.marivaturist.hr; Obala kralja Tomislava 15a; ⏱ 8am-3pm Mon-Fri, to noon Sat) Has money-exchange facilities, rents cars, and books excursions and private accommodation along the whole Makarska coast.

Tourist Office (☑ 021-612 002; www.makarska-info.hr; Obala kralja Tomislava 16; ⏱ 8am-8pm) Publishes a useful guide to the city with a map.

Continued on page 232

Croatia's Coast

From the tip of Istria to dazzling Dubrovnik, Croatia is blessed with one of the most unrelentingly gorgeous stretches of coast in the entire Mediterranean region. The crystalline waters provide a constant presence as the backdrop changes from mountains to walled towns to low-slung islands and back again.

Walled Towns

Since ancient times the people of this coast have encased their towns in sturdy walls of stone as a protection against the attacks that came all too frequently. Although the purpose may have been purely defensive, the end result is spectacular; the sight of these stone bastions rising from the sea is one of the most memorable images of the Adriatic coast. Even when the walls themselves have been largely removed, exposing the nest of medieval streets within, they still make for an impressive sight.

Most people know all about Dubrovnik, but there are many mini-Dubrovniks scattered all along the coast. One of the most magical is Trogir, west of Split, occupying a little islet anchored by bridges to the mainland. Split itself has at its heart an ancient fortress growing out of the remains of a Roman imperial palace – although from the water it's hard to distinguish from the sprawl surrounding it. Šibenik's fortified old town arcs up a hill to an imposing castle, while at Ston the fortifications rise up and over the mountainous terminus of the Pelješac Peninsula.

Historic Rovinj was once an island, separated from the mainland by a narrow channel that was subsequently filled in – much like Dubrovnik itself. In Zadar's case the walls enclosed the tip of a peninsula – although these days only about half of them remain. The islands, too, have many such impressive sites; the old towns of Cres, Krk, Rab, Pag and Korčula being principal among them.

Apart from all the well-known places, you might find yourself stumbling on your own little walled treasure. Like sleepy wee Osor, watching over the channel separating the islands of Cres and Lošinj. Or pretty little Primošten, jutting out over a rocky shore south of Šibenik.

Island Life

Croatia's 1244 islands range from little more than rocks poking out of the sea, to large, populated places supporting agriculture and small towns. Two of the biggest, Krk and Pag, are joined to the mainland by bridges, yet they still maintain their own distinct island culture and way of life.

The more popular and populated islands are well served by ferries all year round, although there can be lengthy queues for the car ferries in July and August, and during weekends in June and September. If you're planning on island-hopping at those times, you're better off doing so as a foot passenger and hiring a car or scooter when you arrive. Note: locals only tend to use the term 'ferries' when talking about car ferries; the faster passenger-only boats are generally listed on schedules as 'catamarans'.

1. Fishing boat in the waters off Pag Island (p178)
2. Enjoying coastal Rovinj (p111)

For the clusters of smaller islands, such as the Kornatis, organised tours are popular; enquire at travel agencies, tourist offices and marinas anywhere along the coast. Yachties will find themselves in sailing heaven, with plenty of deserted bays on unpopulated islets to seek out. If you haven't managed to bring your own yacht with you, it's possible to hire one, either with a skipper or without (provided you have a licence). There are numerous island-hopping package sailing tours available, including some specifically targeted at backpackers.

Beaches

Although it's only about 600km long as the crow flies, Croatia's Adriatic coastline would stretch for 1778km if someone were to iron out all the indentations and unwind the numerous islands. The lure of the clear water and the balmy weather sees literally millions of tourists descend on the beaches each summer, with the peak being during the European school holidays in July and August.

If you're expecting long sandy beaches to compete with Bondi, Malibu or Copacabana, you'll be disappointed. Mostly you'll find pretty little rocky or pebbly coves, edged by pines, olives or low scrub. There are some beautiful sandy beaches – mainly on the islands – but the water is often painfully shallow, requiring a lengthy walk to get even your knees wet. It's partly for this reason that the locals tend to prefer the rocky bays.

What is particularly striking all the way along the coast is the clarity and colour of the water, at times seeming almost unnaturally blue or green. Currently there are 99 Blue Flag–rated beaches in the country (a measure of water quality and environmental standards), with the majority in Istria and the Kvarner region.

Swimmers should watch out for sea urchins, which are common along the coast. The sharp spines are painful to tread on and can break off in your skin and become infected. If you're planning on swimming, you're well advised to wear water shoes, which are easily purchased on urchin-infested beaches.

Croatia is not short of places to let it all hang out, with naturist beaches all along the coast, often accompanied by campsites. Look for the signs reading 'FKK', which stands for *freikörperkultur,* meaning 'free body culture' in German. Just don't forget those water shoes!

Snorkelling & Diving

Do yourself a favour and pack your mask and snorkel – the clear, warm waters and the abundance of small fish make for lots to see. Serious divers will also find plenty to keep them busy, with numerous wrecks (dating from ancient times to WWII), drop-offs and caves. Popular sites include the wreck of the *Taranto* near Dubrovnik, the Margarita Reef off the island of Susak, the wreck of the *Rosa* off Rab and around the islands of Brač, Vis, Dugi Otok and Lošinj.

3. Nugal beach (p226). Makarska 4. Sea urchin 5. Swimming off the coast of Croatia

Continued from page 227

ℹ️ Getting There & Away

Three car ferries a day head between Makarska and Sumartin on Brač (adult/child/car/motorbike/bike 33/17/160/70/38KN, one hour), with four in June and September, and five in July and August. The **Jadrolinija ticket stall** (☑ 021-679 515; www.jadrolinija.hr; Obala kralja Tomislava bb) is near the Hotel Biokovo.

From the **bus station** (☑ 021-612 333; Ante Starčevića 30; ⏱ 5am-10.30pm), 300m uphill from the harbour, there are buses to the following destinations:

Dubrovnik 105KN, three hours, five to seven daily

Međugorje 117KN, three daily

Mostar 100KN, 2¼ hours, four daily

Rijeka 259KN, seven hours, two to three daily

Sarajevo 204KN, four hours, two daily

Split 50KN, 1¼ hours, at least hourly

Zagreb 175KN, six hours, 10 daily

Biokovo Nature Park

The limestone Biokovo massif, which is administered and protected by **Biokovo Nature Park** (Park Prirode Biokovo; www.biokovo. com; 50KN), offers wonderful hiking opportunities. If you're hiking independently, you have to enter the park at the beginning of 'Biokovo Rd' – basically the only road that runs up the mountain – and buy an admission ticket there.

⊙ Sights & Activities

Vošac peak (1422m), only 2.5km from Makarska, is the nearest target for hikers. From St Mark's Church on Kačićev trg, you can walk or drive up Put Makra, following signs to the village of Makar, where a trail leads to Vošac. From Vošac a good marked trail leads to **Sveti Jure** (four hours), the highest peak

THE WHOLE PACKAGE

The best of the package hotels, **Sensimar Adriatic Beach Resort** (☑ 021-681 400; www.sensimaradriaticbeach.com; Porat 136, Zivogosce, Igrane; r from €240 all inclusive; P❄🛜🏊) is a large resort that has a pool overlooking the beach, and multiple bars and restaurants. Most of the rooms have views, many have balconies and there are even 'swim-up rooms' which open on to a pool. The clientele is roughly 90% British and 10% Scandinavian.

at 1762m, from where you can get spectacular views of the Croatian coast and, on a clear day, the coast of Italy on the other side of the Adriatic. Take plenty of water, sunscreen, a hat and waterproof clothes – the weather on top is always a lot colder than it is by the sea.

Biokovo Active Holidays (p226) offers guided walks and drives on Biokovo to suit all levels of physical exertion. You can go part way up the mountain by minibus and then take a short hike to Sveti Jure peak, take a 5½-hour trek through black-pine forests and lush fields, or enjoy an early drive to watch the sun rise over Makarska.

Kotišina Botanical Garden   NATURE RESERVE
(Botanički vrt Kotišina) FREE Just up from the village of Kotišina on Biokovo, this isn't so much a traditional botanical garden – more a fenced-off section of indigenous flora offering spectacular views over the islands of Brač and Hvar. Follow the marked trail under a series of towering peaks.

🛏️ Sleeping

The nature park's website (www.biokovo.com) lists contacts for various mountain huts, mainly used by serious hikers and mountain climbers. Otherwise, base yourself in Makarska for day trips.

ℹ️ Getting There & Away

To get to the park entrance from Makarska, head southeast and branch off the highway on the road leading to Vrgorac. Look for the entrance to the left after 6km.

BRAČ ISLAND

POP 14,500

Brač is famous for two things: its radiant white stone, used to build Diocletian's Palace in Split and the White House in Washington, DC (oh, yes!), and Zlatni Rat, the long pebbly beach at Bol that extends lasciviously into the Adriatic and adorns 90% of Croatia's tourism posters. It's the largest island in central Dalmatia, with several towns, sleepy villages and a dramatic Mediterranean landscape of steep cliffs, inky waters and pine forests. The interior is scattered with rocks – the result of the back-breaking labour of women who, over hundreds of years, gathered the rocks to clear land for vineyards and olive, fig, almond and sour-cherry orchards.

The tough living conditions meant that a lot of people moved to the mainland for work,

BRAČ'S QUIET ESCAPES

Sumartin, the entry point to Brač if you're coming from Makarska, is a sleepy port with a few rocky beaches and little to do, but it makes a nice retreat from the busier tourist centres of Bol and Supetar. If you decide to stay, there's a little **tourist office** (☏021-648 209; www.touristboard-selca.com; Porat 1; ◷9am-3pm Mon, Wed & Fri Jun, 8am-8pm Jul & Aug, 9am-3pm Sep) in the centre of town, next to the ferry and bus stop, which has listings of private accommodation providers.

For a quiet coastal getaway, head to **Pučišća** (try saying that quickly three times after a shot of *rakija!*) on Brač's northern coast. This appealing little town curves around a port lined with blindingly white historic buildings. One of these, the 15th-century **Palača Dešković** (☏021-778 240; www.palaca-deskovic.com; Trg Sv Jeronima 4, Pučišća; s/d from €154/206; P ✳ ☏), has been converted into a particularly atmospheric hotel. Another, nearby, houses the **tourist office** (☏021-633 555; www.tzo-pucisca.hr; Trg Hrvatskog skupa 1; ◷8am-noon Mon-Fri May & Oct, to 2pm Mon-Sat Jun & Sep, to 8pm daily Jul & Aug).

The village of **Dol** in the island's interior is one of the oldest settlements on Brač, a collection of well-preserved stone houses sprouting from barren rock. A visit here offers a glance at Brač as it used to be, away from the tourist hubbub. Drop into family-run **Konoba Toni** (☏091 51 66 532; www.toni-dol.info; Dol; mains 45-120KN; ◷noon-midnight), a rustic tavern in a 300-year-old stone house, for a traditional homemade meal.

One of Brač's more interesting sites is the village of **Škrip**, the oldest settlement on the island, about 8km southeast of Supetar. Formerly a refuge of the ancient Illyrians, the fort was taken over by the Romans in the 2nd century BC, followed by refugees escaping the fall of Salona (Solin, near Split). Roman sarcophagi line the main roads, while **Brač Museum** (Brački Muzej; Škrip; adult/child 20/10KN; ◷8am-8pm) is housed in the Kaštil Radojković, a tower built during the Venetian-Turkish wars that incorporates part of an ancient Illyrian wall and an extraordinarily intact Roman mausoleum.

Donji Humac, 8km south of Supetar, has a stone quarry and an interesting onion-domed church tower. However, the main reason to head here is to enjoy the panoramic valley views at **Konoba Kopačina** (☏021-647 707; www.konoba-kopacina.com; Donji Humac 7; mains 55-130KN; ◷10am-10pm Mon-Thu, to midnight Fri & Sat) while sampling traditional Brač specialities such as *vitalac* (skewered lamb offal wrapped in lamb meat).

The most rewarding short hike is to the extraordinary **Blaca Hermitage**, founded in the 16th century by two Glagolitic monks in the highlands near the southern end of the island. Lots of tours head here, or you can drive yourself to Dragovoda and walk from there (30 minutes).

The port of **Milna**, 20km southwest of Supetar, is the kind of lovely intact fishing village that in any other part of the world would have long ago been commandeered by package tourists but, for now, is mainly visited by luxury yachts. The 17th-century town is set at the edge of a deep natural harbour that was used by Emperor Diocletian for shipping stone to Split for the construction of his palace. Paths and walks take you around the harbour, which is studded with coves containing rocky beaches. Dominating the picture-perfect setting is the tall steeple of the 18th-century **Church of Our Lady of the Annunciation**, with a baroque facade and early-18th-century altar paintings.

leaving the interior almost deserted. Exploring Brač's stone villages is a lovely experience.

The two main centres, Supetar and Bol, are quite different: Supetar is pleasant if unassuming, while Bol revels in its more exclusive appeal.

History

Remnants of a neolithic settlement have been found in Kopačina cave near Supetar, but the first inhabitants to make the historical record were the Illyrians, who built a fort in Škrip to protect against Greek invasion. The Romans arrived in 167 BC and promptly set to work exploiting the stone quarries near Škrip and building summer mansions around the island.

From the 11th century, control of the island was passed between Venice, Byzantium, Hungary, Croatia, Venice again, Byzantium again, Omiš, Venice yet again, Bosnia, Dubrovnik and, finally, Venice, which ruled from 1420 until 1797. During this time, the interior villages were devastated by plague and the inhabitants moved to the 'healthier' settlements along the coast, revitalising the towns of Supetar, Bol, Sumartin and Milna.

After a brief period under Napoleonic rule, the island passed into Austrian hands. Wine cultivation expanded until the phylloxera epidemic at the turn of the 20th century ravaged the island's vines and people began leaving for North and South America, especially Chile. The island endured a reign of terror during WWII when German and Italian troops looted and burned villages, imprisoning and murdering their inhabitants.

Although the tourism business took a hit in the mid-1990s, it has rebounded well and the island is now a busy place in summer.

Getting There & Away

AIR

Brač Airport (📞 021-559 711; www.airport-brac. hr) is 14km northeast of Bol and 38km southeast of Supetar.

Croatia Airlines operates a weekly flight from Zagreb on Saturdays from late May until September. In the summertime, charter flights head here from Austria and Italy.

There's no transport from the airport to Supetar so you'll need to take a taxi, which costs about 300KN (150KN to Bol).

BOAT

Jadrolinija (📞 021-631 357; www.jadrolinija.hr; Hrvatskih Velikana bb, Supetar) car ferries (adult/ child/car/motorbike/bike 33/17/160/70/38KN, 50 minutes) head between Split and Supetar roughly every 90 minutes from June to October (every two hours at other times). The ferry drops you off in the centre of Supetar, only steps from the bus station.

Jadrolinija has five daily car ferries between Makarska and Sumartin (adult/child/car/ motorbike/bike 33/17/160/70/38KN, one hour) in July and August, reduced to four in June and September and three in other months. Note, bus connections from Sumartin are infrequent.

From June to September, two high-speed Jadrolinija catamarans per day stop in Bol en route between Split (55KN, 70 minutes) and Jelsa on Hvar (35KN, 20 minutes), dropping to one per day in other months. Buy your ticket in advance in Bol, as these can sell out fast in high season.

From July to mid-September, there's a daily catamaran to Bol from Hvar (60KN, one hour), Korčula (100KN, 2¾ hours) and Dubrovnik (190KN, 5¼ hours).

On Tuesdays from June to September, a catamaran stops in Milna en route between Split (40KN, 40 minutes) and Hvar Town (50KN, 55 minutes).

On Wednesdays, year-round, Kapetan Luka (p218) has a fast catamaran between Split (40KN, 45 minutes) and Vis (55KN, 55 minutes) which stops in Milna.

From June to September it also has a daily boat between Milna and Split (40KN, 30 minutes), Hvar Town (70KN, 30 minutes), Korčula Town (110KN, 1¾ hours), Pomena on Mljet (130KN, 2½ hours) and Dubrovnik (190KN, 3¾ hours), dropping to four times per week in May and three per week in October.

Getting Around

Supetar is the hub for bus transport around the island. Destinations include Milna (28KN, 30 minutes, seven daily), Škrip (22KN, 15 minutes, three daily), Pučišća (28KN, 35 minutes, six daily), Bol (40KN, one hour, nine daily) and Sumartin (40KN, 1¼ hours, three daily). Note that the bus schedule is reduced on Sundays.

From Bol, bus services are much more limited. Aside from the Supetar buses, there are connections to Pučišća (28KN, 35 minutes, nine daily) and, in July and August only, to Sumartin (28KN, 35 minutes, four daily).

A car is useful for exploring the smaller settlements on the island. If you want to avoid the car-ferry charges, it's easy enough to hire a car or a scooter from travel agencies in Supetar or Bol when you arrive.

Supetar

POP 4080

Although it suffers in comparison to its more glitzy sister, Bol, Supetar is a pleasant little town in its own right, with a historic core of old stone streets fanning out from a little harbour dominated by an imposing church. It's a popular holiday destination for Croatian families, with pebbly beaches within an easy stroll of the town centre. The views back across the water to Split and the mountains beyond are universally wonderful.

Sights

Swimming beaches are scattered along the pebbly coast in both directions. **Vrilo beach** is about 100m east of the town centre. Walking west, you'll come first to **Vlačica** then **Banj** beach, a large eastward-facing curve lined with pine trees and beach bars. Continuing around past the cemetery are **Tri Mosta** and **Bili Rat**. Then, beyond the next bend, is **Vela Luka** beach, set on a peaceful bay.

Supetar Cemetery   CEMETERY
(Groblje Supetar; Banj bb) An unexpected highlight of Supetar is its fascinating cemetery,

full of striking sculptural monuments. Grandest of all is the over-the-top **Petrinović family mausoleum**. Built from white Brač stone between 1924 and 1927, it has a cluster of five Byzantine-style domes, an ornate bronze door and a fine carved relief in the style of the Vienna Succession. A striking crucifix is visible if you peer through the keyhole. Just outside the main entrance are the ruins of a 6th-century Roman *villa rustica* (country house).

🏃 Activities

Rent a Robert's   BOATING
(☑091 53 47 575; www.rentaroberts.com; Petra Jakšića 31; ⊙May-Oct) On the main beach, this friendly and reliable agency rents small boats (from 450KN per day), jet skis (200KN for 12 minutes) and bikes (per hour/day 20/90KN). It also offers a taxi-boat service.

Fun Dive Club   DIVING
(☑098 13 07 384; www.fundiveclub.com; Punta 2; ⊙8-9.30am & 3-6pm Mar-Oct) The best diving on the island is found off the southwestern coast between Bol and Milna, making Bol a better base for divers. Still, you can book dives, take a diving course and rent equipment with this crew.

⭐ Festivals & Events

Supetar Summer   CULTURAL
(Supetarsko Lito; ⊙mid-Jun–mid-Sep) This festival includes folk music, *klapa* (traditional unaccompanied singing), dance and classical concerts performed in public spaces and churches, along with exhibitions, talks and outdoor cinema. Most events are free.

🛌 Sleeping

Pansion Palute   GUESTHOUSE €
(☑021-631 541; palute@st.t-com.hr; Put Pašike 16; s/d 210/380KN; P🌀🌐) This small, family-run *pansion* (guesthouse) has clean and tidy rooms (most with balconies), wooden floors, TVs and a voluble proprietor with a penchant for garden gnomes.

Funky Donkey   HOSTEL €
(☑021-630 937; Polanda 20; dm 110-120KN, r 260KN; ⊙May-Aug; P🌀@🌐) Located off a scrappy empty lot on the edge of town, this friendly hostel is cluttered and crammed but has a good vibe nonetheless. Facilities include a kitchen, lockers, a terrace and a barbecue.

Hotel Osam   HOTEL €€€
(☑021-552 333; www.hotel-osam.com; Vlačica 3; s/d from €116/165; 🌀🌐🌊) Only a few summers old, swanky Osam offers a child-free escape for those wanting to lounge around the terrace pool in relative harmony. The rooftop bar offers unbeatable views back towards Split and the mountains.

Bračka Perla   HOTEL €€€
(☑021-755 530; www.brackaperla.com; Put Vele Luke 53; r/ste from €209/249; P🌀🌐🌊) Down the quiet end of town, this exclusive little 'art hotel' has six suites and five rooms, each painted by renowned artist Srećko Žitnik and themed after a native plant. It's a beautifully designed complex built out of white Brač stone, with a lovely little pool, a small spa centre and direct access to the beach.

🍴 Eating

Punta   DALMATIAN €€
(☑021-631 507; www.vilapunta.com; Punta 1; mains 45-145KN; ⊙8am-midnight) This fabulously located restaurant has a beach terrace overlooking the sea. Choose from fish and seafood, dive into some grilled meat or just have a pizza as you watch the waves and windsurfers.

Konoba Luš   DALMATIAN €€
(☑099 80 33 646; Glavna cesta bb; mains 60-145KN; ⊙5-11.30pm) High above the town on the main road to Mirca, this rustic family-run tavern offers good traditional food, brilliant views and a warm welcome. Grab a seat on the terrace under the shade of the olive trees and tuck into *peka*-cooked meat, fish or octopus, spit-roasted lamb (these all need to be ordered in advance) or grilled squid and fish.

Vinotoka   DALMATIAN €€
(☑021-630 969; Jobova 6; mains 60-130KN; ⊙noon-11pm; 🌐) One of the best places in Supetar, Vinotoka is decorated with marine-inspired pieces and has a glassed-in terrace and a wooden boat in the middle. The seafood is excellent, best accompanied by some local white. With advance notice, they also serve spit-roasted or *peka*-cooked lamb.

🍷 Drinking & Nightlife

Beer Garden   PUB
(www.facebook.com/beergardensupetar; Petra Jakšića 1; ⊙8am-midnight) Head to this stone courtyard, tucked away from the buzz of the coastal promenade, to listen to indie tunes, sample from a big selection of local and imported craft beer, and snack on dude food such as boar and roe-deer burgers.

Day n' Night BAR

(Put Vela Luke 2; ⊙ 9am-8pm Mon-Thu, to 5am Fri & Sat) Occupying a large terrace, this big beach bar transforms into a club on summer weekends. In summer it also hosts gigs by popular local performers.

ℹ Information

Adriatic Experience (www.adriaticexperience. com) This agency offers a range of authentic Brač experiences including sailing, bike trips to stonemasons' workshops, wine jaunts and a tour through the back roads of the island.

Atlas (✆ 021-631 105; www.atlas-supetar.com; Porat 10) Books excursions and private accommodation, and exchanges foreign cash.

Tourist Office (✆ 021-630 551; www.supetar. hr; Porat 1; ⊙ 8am-6pm May–mid-Jun, to 10pm mid-Jun–mid-Sep, 8am-6pm Mon-Sat Apr & mid-Sep–Oct, 8am-3.30pm Mon-Fri Nov-Mar) Near the harbour and ferry terminal; has an array of brochures on activities and sights in Supetar, lengthy lists of private accommodation, and up-to-date bus and ferry timetables.

Bol

POP 1630

Gathered around a compact marina, the old town of Bol is an attractive place made up of small stone houses and winding streets dotted with pink and purple geraniums. While short on actual sights, many of the buildings are marked with interpretative panels explaining their cultural and historical significance.

The town's major attraction is Zlatni Rat, the seductive pebbly beach that 'leaks' into the Adriatic and draws crowds of swimmers and windsurfers in summer. A long coastal promenade, lined with pine trees and gardens, connects the beach with the old town. Bol is a buzzing place in summer – one of Croatia's favourites – and perennially packed with tourists.

◉ Sights

★ Zlatni Rat BEACH

Croatia's most photographed beach extends like a tongue into the sea for about 500m. Despite the hype and constant crowds, the 'golden cape' is a gorgeous place. Made up of smooth white pebbles, its elegant tip is constantly shuffled by the wind and waves. Pine trees provide shade and rocky cliffs rise sharply behind it, making the setting one of the loveliest in Dalmatia. There's a small nudist section immediately west of the cape.

Stina Wines WINERY

(✆ 021-306 220; www.stina-vino.hr; Riva bb; tasting incl 3 wines 76KN; ⊙ 4-9pm) This local winery operates a cellar and tasting room in a historic warehouse, right on the waterfront. Call in for a 30-minute tour and leisurely tasting of their top drops, including *pošip* and *plavac mali*.

Galerija Branislav Dešković GALLERY

(✆ 021-637 092; Trg Sv Petra 1; adult/child 15/5KN; ⊙ 9am-noon & 6-11pm Tue-Sun mid-Jun–mid-Sep, 9am-3pm Tue-Sat mid-Sep–mid-Jun) Housed in a renaissance-baroque town house, right on the seafront, this gallery displays around 300 paintings and sculptures by 20th-century Croatian artists. It's a surprisingly prestigious collection for such a small town, including works by such famous names as Ivan Meštrović and Ivo Dulčić.

⚐ Activities

Bol is a **windsurfing** hot spot, with most of the action taking place at the beaches west of the town centre. Although the *maestral* (strong, steady westerly wind) blows from April to October, the best times to windsurf are at the end of May and the beginning of June, and at the end of July and the beginning of August. The wind generally reaches its peak in the early afternoon and then dies down at the end of the day.

If you fancy hiking, try the two-hour walk up to **Vidova Gora** (778m), the area's highest peak. There are also mountain-biking trails leading up. The local tourist office (p238) can give you advice and basic maps.

Nautic Center Bol BOATING

(✆ 098 361 361; www.nautic-center-bol.com; Put Zlatnog rata bb; boat per day from 600KN) Rents boats from the beach in front of the Bretanide Hotel and offers parasailing and excursions to Hvar (€60), Korčula (€80) and Biševo's Blue Grotto (€80).

Big Blue Diving DIVING

(✆ 098 425 496; www.big-blue-diving.hr; Hotel Borak, Put Zlatnog rata bb; dives with/without equipment 330/220KN; ⊙ mid-Apr–mid-Nov) Offers introductory courses and has daily trips for qualified divers to sites including reefs, caves and the remains of a submerged Roman villa with mosaics. Boats go out twice daily during the high season.

Big Blue Sport WINDSURFING

(✆ 021-635 614; www.bigbluesport.com; Put Zlatnog rata bb; ⊙ 8am-9pm Apr-Oct) This large operation offers beginner's windsurfing courses

DRAGON'S CAVE

It takes about an hour to hike to this strange **cave** (Zmajeva Špilja; ☑ 091 51 49 787; per person 50KN, minimum 4) from Murvica, 5km west of Bol, where an extremely unusual set of reliefs decorates the walls. Believed to have been sculpted by an imaginative 15th-century friar, the carvings include angels, animals and a gaping dragon in a blend of Christian and pagan symbols. The cave can only be accessed on a guided tour; either call tour guide Zoran Kojdić directly or ask at the tourist office. You'll need decent walking shoes.

(990KN) and rents windsurfing boards (per hour/half-day 120/270KN), stand-up paddleboards (per hour/day 100/370KN) and kayaks (per hour/day from 52/187KN) from the beach in front of the Hotel Borak (p238). It also rents mountain bikes (per hour/day from 30/900KN) from a stand a little further down the promenade, in front of the Bretanide Hotel.

Potočine Tennis Centre   TENNIS
(☑ 021-635 222; www.hotelbonacabol.com; Put Zlatnog rata) There are 26 professional-quality clay tennis courts at this large centre attached to the Hotel Bonaca. Racquets and balls can be rented.

✪ Festivals & Events

Bol Summer Festival   CULTURAL
(Bolsko Lito; ⊙ mid-Jun–late-Sep) The Bol Summer Festival includes art exhibitions, food events, and dancers and musicians from around the country performing in churches and open spaces.

Imena Culture Festival   CULTURAL
(Festival Kulture Imena; ⊙ late Jun) An annual event that gathers writers, artists and musicians for a few days of exhibits, readings, concerts and happenings.

Destination Ultra Boat Regatta   MUSIC
(www.ultraeurope.com; ⊙ mid-Jul) The only thing racing at this 'regatta' are the heart rates of the up-for-it electronic-dance-music fans. This beach party is held at Zlatni Rat on the Monday after the big Ultra Europe festival in Split.

Our Lady of Carmel Feast Day   TRADITIONAL
(⊙ 5 Aug) The patron saint of Bol is Our Lady of Carmel. On her feast day there's a procession with residents dressed up in traditional costumes, as well as music and feasting on the streets.

🛏 Sleeping

★**Villa Ana**   APARTMENT €
(☑ 021-635 022; www.villa-ana-bol.com; David cesta 55a; apt from €45; P ❄ ⓢ ⊠) A warm welcome awaits at this friendly family-run set of apartments on the eastern fringes of Bol. The simple but well-equipped units are spread between two modern blocks, with a small swimming pool and hot tub in between.

Kamp Kito   CAMPGROUND €
(☑ 021-635 551; www.camping-brac.com; Bračka cesta bb; site per adult/child/tent/car 60/40/20/20KN, cabin 413KN; P ⓢ ⚿) On the main highway, just on the edge of the town, this chilled-out campground has plots positioned in the shade of an olive grove as well as two little cabins for rent. There's also a little restaurant and a good clean toilet and shower block.

Hostel Bol   HOSTEL €€
(☑ 098 758 595; hostelbol.croatia@gmail.com; Podan glavica 1d; dm/r €30/62; P ❄ ⓢ ⊠) Even the dorms get their own bathrooms in this well-run, custom-built hostel, right in the heart of the old town. Some of the private rooms have wonderful sea views, and there's even a small indoor pool and a terrace with an outdoor kitchen.

Hotel Kaštil   HOTEL €€
(☑ 021-635 995; www.kastil.hr; Frane Radića 1; s/d from €80/104; ❄ ⓢ) Although this little hotel occupies a wonderful 17th-century stone town house, you wouldn't know it from the generic decor inside. Still, the rooms are comfortable and some have balconies, and you can't beat the central waterfront location.

Hotel Bol   HOTEL €€€
(☑ 021-635 660; www.hotel-bol.com; Hrvatskih domobrana 19; r/ste from €154/269; P ❄ ⓢ ⊠) There's an olive theme running through this contemporary boutique hotel – and we're not just talking the colour scheme; potted trees grace the balconies and oversized fruit hang on the walls. It's a very slick set-up, with swish rooms (many with sea views), a sauna and a small gym.

Villa Giardino   GUESTHOUSE €€€
(☑ 021-635 900; www.dalmacija.net/bol/villagiardino; Novi Put 2; s/d 653/876KN; ❄ ⓢ) An iron gate opens onto the luxuriant garden fronting this elegant white villa. Its 10 tastefully

restored and spacious rooms are furnished with antiques; some overlook the garden while others have sea views. It's an oasis of peace, with a secluded garden out the back. It only takes payment in cash.

Bluesun Hotel Elaphusa   HOTEL €€€

(☑ 021-306 200; www.hotelelaphusabrac.com; Put Zlatnog rata 46; s/d from €158/210; P ❄ @ 🗻 🛋) Enormous, low-slung Elaphusa feels like the inside of a cruise ship. It's all smooth interiors, glass partitions, slick rooms and every possible amenity, including a wellness centre and indoor and outdoor pools. Best of all, it's very close to the famous beach at Zlatni Rat. That said, it hasn't completely shaken off the ambience of a former state hotel.

Bluesun Hotel Borak   HOTEL €€€

(☑ 021-306 202; www.brachotelborak.com; Put Zlatnog rata 42; s/d from 1320/1760KN; P ❄ 🗻 🛋) Close to Zlatni Rat beach and a wide range of sporting activities, this large complex lacks character thanks to its size and perfunctory architecture. It is, however, a comfortable spot to relax with an appealing pool.

✗ Eating

Konoba Mali Raj   DALMATIAN €€

(☑ 098 756 922; www.maliraj-bol.com; Put Zlatnog rata; mains 75-200KN; ⊙ noon-11pm) In a lovely spot away from the tourist buzz, above the parking lot for Zlatni Rat, this alfresco tavern has a leafy garden in which to enjoy delicious dishes such as monkfish skewers and grilled squid. Call a day ahead and they'll prepare a lamb, veal or octopus *peka*.

Konoba Dalmatino   DALMATIAN €€

(☑ 095 19 74 457; www.konobadalmatino.com; Frane Radića 14; mains 65-160KN; ⊙ noon-11pm; 🗻 🛋) This tavern offers simple, local food in a venerable stone building decorated with old photos and knick-knacks. While the food isn't exceptional, the prices are reasonable and the ambience is lovely.

Ranč   DALMATIAN €€€

(☑ 021-635 635; Hrvatskih domobrana 6; mains 55-190KN; ⊙ 6pm-1am) The simple things stand out at Ranč, such as the delicious homemade bread and the traditional fish soup. Call ahead to preorder spit-roasted lamb or a *peka* filled with lamb, veal or octopus. And make sure you say hi to the loud-mouthed parrot.

Taverna Riva   DALMATIAN €€€

(☑ 021-635 236; www.tavernariva-bol.com; Frane Radića 5; mains 75-215KN; ⊙ 11am-11pm; 🛋) This

pretty terrace right above the Riva is where locals go for a good traditional meal. If you're feeling adventurous, try the *vitalac* (spit-roasted lamb offal) or call ahead to order the delicious lamb or octopus under *peka*.

🍷 Drinking & Nightlife

Varadero   COCKTAIL BAR

(☑ 091 23 33 471; www.varadero-bol.com; Frane Radića 1; ⊙ 7am-2am May-Nov; 🗻) At this open-air cocktail bar on the seafront you can sip coffee and fresh OJ under straw umbrellas during the day and return in the evening for fab cocktails, DJ music and lounging on sofas and armchairs.

Marinero   BAR

(Rudina 46; ⊙ 9am-2am) A popular gathering spot for Bol locals, up the stairs from the seafront (follow the sign), with a leafy terrace on a square, live music on some nights, football on the TV, Bon Jovi on the stereo and a diverse merry-making crowd.

❶ Information

Adria Bol (☑ 021-635 966; www.adria-bol.hr; Bračka cesta 10; ⊙ 8am-8pm May-Sep, 9am-3pm Mon-Fri Oct-Apr) This agency is a great source of tours, transfers, apartments, and rental boats, bikes, scooters and cars. In high season it has a second office by the bus station.

Bol Tours (☑ 021-635 693; www.boltours.com; Vladimira Nazora 18; ⊙ 10am-1pm & 5-8pm) Books excursions, rents cars, changes money and finds private accommodation.

More (☑ 021-642 050; www.more-bol.com; Vladimira Nazora 28) Bike, scooter and car rental, private accommodation, currency exchange, island tours and excursions.

Tourist Office (☑ 021-635 638; www.bol.hr; Porat Bolskih Pomoraca bb; ⊙ 8.30am-10pm Jul & Aug, 8.30am-2pm & 4-9pm Mon-Sat, 9am-noon Sun Jun & Sep, 8.30am-2pm & 4-9pm Mon-Sat Oct-May) Inside a Gothic 15th-century town house, Bol's helpful tourist office is a good source of information on events and it distributes plenty of brochures.

HVAR ISLAND

POP 11,080

Long, lean Hvar is vaguely shaped like the profile of a holidaymaker reclining on a sun lounger, which is altogether appropriate for the sunniest spot in the country (2724 sunny hours each year) and its most luxurious beach destination.

Hvar Town, the island's capital, offers swanky hotels, elegant restaurants and a general sense that, if you care about seeing and being seen, this is the place to be. Rubbing shoulders with the posh yachties are hundreds of young partygoers, dancing on tables at the town's legendary beach bars. The northern coastal towns of Stari Grad and Jelsa are far more subdued and low-key.

Hvar's interior hides abandoned ancient hamlets, craggy peaks, vineyards and the lavender fields that the island is famous for. It's worth exploring on a day trip, as is the southern end of the island, which has some of Hvar's most beautiful and isolated coves.

ℹ Getting There & Away

Hvar has two main car-ferry ports: one near Stari Grad and the other at Sućuraj on the eastern tip of the island. **Jadrolinija** (☑ 021-773 433; www.jadrolinija.hr) operates from both, with ferries from Split to Stari Grad (per adult/child/car/motorcycle/bike 47/24/318/78/45KN, two hours, six daily June to September, three daily at other times) and from Drvenik to Sućuraj (16/8/108/30/16KN, 34 minutes, 10 daily). Note, bus services to/from Sućuraj are extremely limited.

Jadrolinija also has high-speed catamaran services to Hvar Town from the following:
Korčula Town 70KN, 1½ hours, two daily
Milna on Brač 50KN, 55 minutes, Tuesday only
Split 55KN, 65 minutes, seven daily
Ubli on Lastovo 45KN, two hours, daily
Vela Luka on Korčula 40KN, 55 minutes, daily

Services are less frequent from October to May. From July to mid-September, there's also a daily catamaran to Hvar Town from Bol on Brač (60KN, one hour), Korčula (70KN, 1½ hours) and Dubrovnik (190KN, four hours). A daily catamaran also heads from Jelsa to Bol (35KN, 20 minutes) and then on to Split (55KN, 1¾ hours).

Kapetan Luka (p218) has a fast catamaran to Hvar Town from the following:
Dubrovnik 190KN, three hours
Korčula Town 90KN, 65 minutes
Milna 70KN, 30 minutes
Pomena on Mljet 130KN, 1¾ hours
Split 70KN, 65 minutes

These run daily from June to September, dropping to four times per week in May and three per week in October. On Tuesdays, year-round, Kapetan Luka also stops in Hvar Town en route between Vis (40KN, 50 minutes) and Split. Tickets can be purchased from Pelegrini Tours (p246).

From mid-July to August, limited connections to Italy are available, with some Jadrolinija, BlueLine (p218) and SNAV (p218) car ferries stopping in Stari Grad en route between Ancona and Split.

From late July through August, SNAV also has five fast boats a week from Stari Grad to Hvar Town and on to Pescara in Italy.

ℹ Getting Around

Buses meet most ferries that dock at the ferry port near Stari Grad and go to Hvar Town (27KN, 20 minutes), central Stari Grad (13KN, 10 minutes) and Jelsa (33KN, 40 minutes). Buses also connect Hvar Town with Stari Grad (30KN, 30 minutes, 10 daily) and Jelsa (33KN, 50 minutes, eight daily); and Stari Grad with Jelsa (30KN, 25 minutes, 13 daily). Services are less frequent in the low season.

Hvar Town

POP 4260

The island's hub and busiest destination, Hvar Town is estimated to draw around 20,000 people a day in the high season. It's odd that they can all fit in the small bay town, where 13th-century walls surround beautifully ornamented Gothic palaces and traffic-free marble streets, but fit they do.

Visitors wander along the main square, explore the sights on the winding stone streets, swim at the numerous beaches or pop off to the Pakleni Islands to get into their birthday suits – but most of all they come to party. Hvar's reputation as Croatia's premier party town is well deserved.

There are several good restaurants, bars and hotels here, but thanks to the island's appeal to well-heeled guests, the prices can be seriously inflated. Don't be put off if you're on a lower budget though, as private accommodation and multiple hostels cater to a younger, more diverse crowd.

⦿ Sights

Hvar is such a small, manageable town that it only recently got street names, although nobody really uses them. The historic part of town, centred on St Stephen's Sq, is closed to traffic, which helps preserve the medieval tranquillity of its tiny lanes. A long seaside promenade winds along the coast in both directions, dotted with small, rocky coves, hotels, bars and restaurants.

St Stephen's Cathedral CATHEDRAL
(Katedrala svetog Stjepana; Map p242; Trg Sv Stjepana bb; 10KN; ☉9am-1pm & 5-9pm) Providing a grand backdrop to the main square, this baroque cathedral was built in the 16th and

17th centuries at the height of the Dalmatian Renaissance to replace one destroyed by the Turks. Parts of the older building are visible in the nave and in the carved 15th-century choir stalls. Its most distinctive feature is its tall, rectangular bell tower, which sprouts an additional window at each level, giving it an oddly top-heavy appearance.

Episcopal Museum   MUSEUM
(Biskupski Muzej; Map p242; ☑ 021-743 126; Trg Sv Stjepana bb; 10KN; ☺ 9am-noon & 5-7pm Mon-Fri, 9am-noon Sat mid-Jun–mid-Sep, 4-6pm Mon-Fri mid-Sep–mid-Jun) Adjoining the cathedral (p239), this treasury houses silver vessels, embroidered liturgical robes, numerous Madonnas, a 13th-century icon, an elaborately carved sarcophagus and, intriguingly, a stamp collection. A highlight is the 15th-century golden chalice, which was a gift from the last king of Bosnia.

St Stephen's Square   SQUARE
(Map p242; Trg Sv Stjepana) Stretching from the harbour to the cathedral, this impressive rectangular square was formed by filling in an inlet which once reached out from the bay. At 4500 sq metres, it's one of the largest old squares in Dalmatia. Hvar Town's walled core, established in the 13th century, covers the slopes to the north. The town didn't spread south until the 15th century.

Look for the well, which is hidden among the umbrellas of the restaurants closest to the cathedral. It was built in 1520 and has a wrought-iron grill dating from 1780.

Arsenal   HISTORIC BUILDING
(Map p242; Trg Sv Stjepana) Mentioned in Venetian documents as 'the most beautiful and the most useful building in the whole of Dalmatia', the Arsenal once served as a repair and refitting station for war galleons. Its present incarnation was built in 1611 to replace a building destroyed by the Ottomans. Although you can't enter through the large graceful arch, you can wander up the stairs to the terrace to enjoy the views over Hvar's pretty harbour.

Upstairs is an atmospheric theatre decorated with frescoes and baroque loggias, which opened in 1612 and is said to be the first theatre in Europe to have admitted plebeians and aristocrats alike. It remained a regional cultural centre throughout the centuries and plays were still staged here right up until 2008. It's been closed for restoration for many years now, but hopefully it will eventually reopen its doors.

Benedictine Convent   CONVENT
(Muzej Hanibal Lucić; Map p242; ☑ 021-741 052; Kroz Grodu bb; 10KN; ☺ 10am-noon Mon-Sat) Playwright and poet Hanibal Lucić was born here in 1485, but this stone town house has been home to a community of Benedictine nuns since 1664. Over the centuries the nuns have perfected the art of lacemaking, painstakingly weaving together fibres derived from dried agave leaves. This tradition has now been recognised by Unesco on its Intangible Cultural Heritage of Humanity list. A small museum showcases their handiwork alongside a collection of paintings and liturgical paraphernalia.

Fortica   FORTRESS
(Tvrđava Španjola; Map p242; ☑ 021-742 608; Biskupa Jurja Dubokovica bb; adult/child 30/15KN; ☺ 8am-9pm) Looming high above the town and lit with a golden glow at night, this medieval castle occupies the site of an ancient Illyrian settlement dating from before 500BC. The views looking down over Hvar and the Pakleni Islands are magnificent, and well worth the trudge up through the old-town streets. Once you clear the town walls it's a gently sloping meander up the tree-shaded hillside to the fortress – or you can drive to the very top.

The Byzantines built a citadel here in the 6th century, and construction began on the present fortress in 1282. The Venetians strengthened it in 1557, which may have saved the lives of Hvar's population, who sheltered here in 1571 when the Turks sacked their town. The Austrians renovated it in the 19th century, adding barracks. Inside there's a collection of ancient amphorae recovered from the seabed, and a terrace cafe.

Franciscan Monastery   MONASTERY
(Franjevački samostan; Map p241; Šetaliste put Križa; 30KN; ☺ 9am-3pm & 5-7pm Mon-Sat) Overlooking a shady cove, this 15th-century monastery has an elegant bell tower, built in the 16th century by a well-known family of stonemasons from Korčula. Its Renaissance cloister leads to a refectory containing lace, coins, nautical charts and valuable documents, such as an edition of *Ptolemy's Atlas,* printed in 1524. Inside, your eye will immediately be struck by *The Last Supper,* an 8m by 2.5m work by the Venetian Matteo Ingoli, dating from the end of the 16th century.

The adjoining church, dedicated to Our Lady of Mercy, contains more fine paintings such as the three polyptychs created by Francesco da Santacroce in 1583, which represent the summit of this painter's work.

Hvar Town

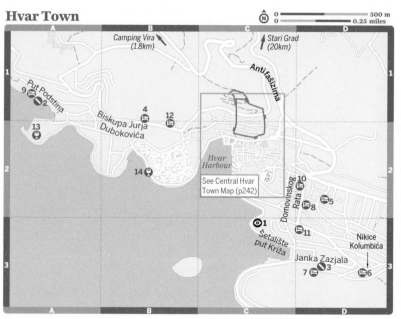

Hvar Town

⦿ Sights
1 Franciscan Monastery C3

✈ Activities, Courses & Tours
2 Diving Centre Viking...............................A1
3 Marinesa Dive Centre............................D3

🛏 Sleeping
4 Apartments Ana Dujmović....................B1
5 Apartments Ivanović.............................D2
6 Apartments Komazin............................D3

7 Earthers Hostel......................................D3
8 Green Lizard..D2
9 Hotel Podstine A1
10 Luka's Lodge...D2
11 Villa Skansi...D3
12 Violeta Hvar...B2

🍷 Drinking & Nightlife
13 Falko...A2
14 Hula-Hula Hvar B2

🏃 Activities & Tours

There are 120km of hiking trails and 96km of marked biking routes within easy access of Hvar Town; ask at the tourist office.

Most of Hvar Town's swimming spots are tiny, rocky bays, some of which have been augmented with concrete sunbathing platforms. Wander along the promenade and take your pick, but check the prices before you settle on a lounger, as some are stupidly expensive (€47 per day at the luxurious Bonj Les Bains beach club, for instance).

Otherwise, grab a taxi boat to the Pakleni Islands or to one of the beaches east along the coast such as **Mekićevica** (where there's a great beachfront restaurant), **Milna** and **Zaraće**. Our favourite is **Dubovica**, a tiny cluster of stone houses and a couple of cafebars set on a gorgeous grin of a beach. The juxtaposition of the white pebbles alongside the brilliant blue-green water is dazzling. If you have your own wheels you can park on the highway, not far from where it turns inland towards the tunnel, and reach Dubovica via a rough stony path.

Hvar Adventure   ADVENTURE SPORTS
(Map p242; ☑ 021-717 813; www.hvar-adventure. com; Obala Riva bb) This agency is a one-stop shop for active travellers, offering sailing, cycling, climbing, hiking, windsurfing, skydiving, jeep safaris, triathlon training and, by way of a breather, wine tours.

Central Hvar Town

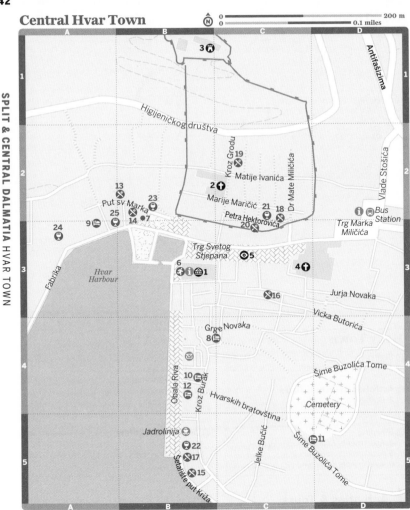

Diving Centre Viking   DIVING
(Map p241; ☎ 091 56 89 443; www.viking-diving.
com; Podstine bb; from €45 incl gear) Offers PADI-
certification courses and boat dives.

Marinesa Dive Centre   DIVING
(Map p241; ☎ 091 51 57 229; www.hvar-vuljan.
com/marinesa-hvar; Janka Zazjala 39; from €35
incl gear) Organises boat dives.

Secret Hvar   TOURS
(Map p242; ☎ 021-717 615; www.secrethvar.com;
Trg Sv Stjepana 49) This great off-road tour
(600KN, with lunch in a traditional tavern)
takes in hidden beauties of the island's interior, including abandoned villages, scenic

canyons, ancient stone huts, endless fields
of lavender and the island's tallest peak,
Sveti Nikola (626m). It also does wine tours
(550KN, with snacks and samplings), walking tours and cycling tours.

✪ Festivals & Events

Hvar Summer Festival   MUSIC
(☺ Jul-Sep) A summer-long music festival,
with concerts held on the square and in the
cloister of the Franciscan Monastery (p240).

Destination Ultra Beach   MUSIC
(www.ultraeurope.com; tickets €99; ☺ mid-Jul) Part
of Destination Ultra Croatia Music Week, this

Central Hvar Town

massive pool party takes place at the Hotel Amfora in the week following the Ultra Europe electronic-dance-music festival in Split.

🛏 Sleeping

As Hvar is one of the Adriatic's most popular destinations, don't expect many bargains. Even the hostels nudge you out of the budget and into the midrange category in summer. Accommodation is extremely tight in July and August, despite there being several large hotels, various hostels and lots of family-run holiday-apartment complexes.

★**Villa Skansi**   HOSTEL €
(Map p241; ☑021-741 426; hostelvillaskansi1@gmail.com; Domovinskog rata 18; dm/r from 250/750KN; ❋@🕏) Hvar's biggest and best hostel has brightly coloured dorms, fancy bathrooms, a great terrace with sea views, a barbecue, a bar, a book exchange and a laundry service, and rents scooters and boats. The private rooms are in a separate newly built block next door, surrounded by citrus trees, pomegranates and bougainvillea. Plus there's a free pub crawl every night.

★**Apartments Ana Dujmović**   APARTMENT €
(Map p241; ☑098 838 434; www.visit-hvar.com/apartments-ana-dujmovic; Biskupa Jurja Dubokovića 36; apt from €55; 🅿❋🕏) This brilliant brace of comfortable holiday apartments are set behind an olive grove, only a 10-minute walk from the centre of town and, crucially, five minutes from the beach and Hula-Hula bar. Call ahead and the delightful owner will pick you up from the town centre.

Hostel Marinero   HOSTEL €
(Map p242; ☑091 41 02 751; hostel.marinero@gmail.com; Put Sv Marka 7; dm 240-320KN; ❋May-Oct; ❋🕏) Located in the heart of Hvar's party precinct, this hostel has six basic but clean dorms with big lockers. There is no shared kitchen but the restaurant downstairs is a good place to mingle. Be ready for some noise, as the Kiva Bar (p245) is right next door.

Jagoda & Ante Bracanović House   GUESTHOUSE €
(Map p242; ☑021-741 416; www.hvar-jagoda.com; Šime Buzolića Tome 21; r/apt 350/525KN) There are three tidy rooms and one apartment for rent in this large private house set on a residential street with very quiet neighbours (it's next to the cemetery). Each has its own fridge, balcony and bathroom, and there's a kitchen for guests to use.

Hvar Out Hostel   HOSTEL €
(Map p242; ☑021-717 375; hvarouthostel@gmail.com; Kroz Burak 32; dm 180-280KN; ❋🕏) Just steps from the harbour, in a maze of old streets, this buzzy backpackers has well-equipped four- to 12-bed dorms with lockers, a small shared kitchen and a terrace on the top floor with views of the harbour.

★**Earthers Hostel**   HOSTEL €€
(Map p241; ☑099 26 79 889; www.earthershostel.com; Martina Vučetića 11; dm/r 250/640KN; ❋Apr-Sep; 🅿❋🕏) The advantages of Earthers' south-end-of-town location are the spacious surrounds and brilliant sunset views. The main hostel occupies a comfortable family home (which in the off-season reverts to being just that), and the well-appointed private

rooms have their own swish house next door. A simple breakfast is included, and the friendly young owners host a barbecue every few days.

Apartments Ivanović
APARTMENT €€

(Map p241; ☑ 021-741 332; www.ivanovic-hvar.com; Ivana Buzolića 9; r from 670KN; P ❈ @ ☎) This large, modern, three-storey house has one double room and five apartments for rent, all with balconies and bathrooms. The hostess speaks English well and welcomes guests with a drink on the large grapevine-shaded terrace.

Luka's Lodge
HOSTEL €€

(Map p241; ☑ 021-742 118; www.lukalodgehvar. hostel.com; Šime Buzolića Tome 75; dm/r/apt 270/620/760KN; P ❈ @ ☎) Friendly owner Luka really takes care of his guests at this homely hostel, a five-minute walk from town. All rooms come with fridges, some with balconies. There's a living room, two terraces, an outdoor kitchen and a laundry service. If he's available, Luka does pick-ups from the ferry dock.

Helvetia Hostel
HOSTEL €€

(Map p242; ☑ 091 34 55 556; hajduk.hvar@gmail. com; Grge Novaka 6; dm/r 210/500KN; ❈ ☎) Run by a friendly islander, this hostel inside his family's old stone house just behind Riva has only a handful of dorms and private rooms. The highlight is the giant rooftop terrace where guests hang out and enjoy undisturbed views of Hvar bay and the Pakleni Islands.

Violeta Hvar
APARTMENT €€

(Map p241; ☑ 099 33 44 779; ursa.lavanda@ gmail.com; Biskupa Jurja Dubokovića 22; r from €100; ❈) White walls are offset with large-scale island images in this schmick apartment block, just above the town. All of the rooms and apartments have large balconies, and the top floor has sea views.

Green Lizard
HOSTEL €€

(Map p241; ☑ 021-742 560; www.greenlizard. hr; Domovinskog Rata 13; dm/r from 220/600KN; ☺ Apr-Oct; ❈ ☎) Chill out in beanbags or hammocks in the garden of this basic but friendly hostel. The dorms are small and cluttered, and there are a couple of private rooms with en suite bathrooms, including a triple with a balcony. Plus there's an outdoor communal kitchen and a laundry service.

Apartments Komazin
APARTMENT €€€

(Map p241; ☑ 091 60 19 712; www.croatia-hvar-apartments.com; Nikice Kolumbića 2; apt from 1025KN; P ❈ @ ☎ ♨) With five bright apartments and one private room to rent, bougainvillea-draped Komazin is an attractive option at the upper end of the private-apartment heap.

Hotel Podstine
HOTEL €€€

(Map p241; ☑ 021-740 400; www.podstine.com; Put Podstina 11; r €242-449; P ❈ @ ☎ ♨) Right by the water at Podstine, 1km southwest of the town centre, this flash-looking hotel has its own beach and a spa and wellness centre. All but the cheapest rooms have sea views.

🍴 Eating

Hvar's eating scene is good and relatively varied although, as with the hotels, many of the restaurants target affluent diners. Make sure you try *hvarska gregada,* the island's traditional fish stew; in some places you'll need to order it in advance.

Nonica
BAKERY €

(Map p242; ☑ 021-718 041; Kroz Burak 23; ☺ 8am-2pm & 5-11pm Mon-Sat, 5-11pm Sun) Savour the best cakes in town at this tiny bakery. Try the old-fashioned local biscuits such as *rafioli* and *forski koloc,* and the Nonica tart with chocolate mousse and orange peel.

★ Fig Cafe Bar
CAFE €€

(Map p242; ☑ 099 42 29 721; www.figcafebar. com; Ivana Frane Biundovića 3; mains 60-100KN; ☺ 9am-10pm mid-Apr–Oct; ☎ ♪) Run by an Aussie-Croat and an American, this great little place serves up delicious stuffed flatbreads (fig and farm cheese, pear and blue cheese, brie and prosciutto), vegetarian curries and, our favourite Hvar breakfast, spiced eggs. There are even some vegan options – a rarity in these parts.

50 Hvar
BURGERS €€

(Map p242; www.50hvar.rocks; burgers 75KN; ☺ 6pm-midnight) Head up to the lovely little rooftop terrace for a selection of juicy gourmet burgers, sandwiches, fries and salads. There's also champagne on offer – it is Hvar after all.

Konoba Menego
DALMATIAN €€

(Map p242; ☑ 021-717 411; www.menego.hr; Kroz Grodu 26; mains 95-110KN; ☺ noon-2.30pm & 6-10.30pm) This rustic old house accessed from a steeply stepped old-town laneway aims to be as simple and authentic as possible. The place is decked out in Hvar antiques, the service is informative, and the marinated meats, cheeses and vegetables are prepared the old-fashioned Dalmatian way.

★ **Dalmatino** DALMATIAN €€€
(Map p242; ☑ 091 52 93 121; www.dalmatino-hvar.
com; Sv Marak 1; mains 70-250KN; ☺ noon-3pm &
5pm-midnight; 🖝) Calling itself a 'steak and
fish house' this place is always popular –
due, in part, to the handsome waiters and
the free-flowing *rakija* (brandy). Thankfully
the food is also excellent; try their *gregada*,
a fish fillet served on potatoes with a thick,
broth-like sauce.

Divino MEDITERRANEAN €€€
(Map p242; ☑ 091 43 77 777; www.divino.com.hr;
Šetalište put Križa 1; mains 125-185KN; ☺ noon-2pm
& 6-10.30pm) The fabulous location and the
island's best wine list are reason enough to
splurge at this swanky restaurant. Add innovative food and dazzling views of the Pakleni Islands and you have a winning formula
for a special night out. Or have some sunset
snacks and wine on the gorgeous terrace.
Book ahead.

Giaxa DALMATIAN €€€
(Map p242; ☑ 021-741 073; www.giaxa.com; Petra
Hektorovića 3; mains 90-220KN; ☺ noon-midnight)
This top-end restaurant inside a 15th-century
palazzo has a reputation as the place to be
seen in Hvar. There is a lovely garden at the
back. The food is excellent, with lobster being
a popular choice, and plenty of traditional
Dalmatian dishes to try.

Zlatna Školjka CROATIAN €€€
(Map p242; ☑ 098 16 88 797; Petra Hektorovića
8; mains 100-230KN; ☺ noon-3pm & 7-11pm) In a
narrow alley packed with restaurants, this
slow-food hideaway stands out for its creative fare conjured up by a local celebrity chef.
A family-run affair, it has a stone interior
and a terrace out back. Innovative dishes include squid in wild-orange sauce and an unbeatable *gregada* with lobster, shellfish and
whatever first-class fish was freshly caught.

Gariful SEAFOOD €€€
(Map p242; ☑ 021-742 999; www.hvar-gariful.hr;
Obala Riva; mains 90-240KN; ☺ noon-11pm) This
is the place to mingle with celebrities coming off their glitzy yachts parked right across
the way over some of Hvar's best-prepared
seafood. Prices match the clientele.

🍷 Drinking & Nightlife

★ **Hula-Hula Hvar** BAR
(Map p241; www.hulahulahvar.com; Šetalište Antuna Tomislava Petrića 10; ☺ 9am-11pm) *The* spot
to catch the sunset to the sound of techno
and house music, Hula-Hula is known for its

après-beach party (4pm to 9pm), where all
of young trendy Hvar seems to descend for
sundowner cocktails. Dancing on tables is
pretty much compulsory.

★ **Kiva Bar** BAR
(Map p242; www.kivabarhvar.com; Fabrika 10;
☺ 9pm-2am) A happening place in an alleyway
just off the Riva, Kiva is packed to the rafters
most nights, with crowds spilling out and filling up the lane. DJs spin a crowd-pleasing
mix of old-school dance, pop and hip-hop
classics to an up-for-it crowd.

3 Pršuta WINE BAR
(Map p242; Petra Hektorovića 5; ☺ 6pm-2am)
Hvar's best wine bar is an unpretentious little place lurking in an alley behind the main
square. Sink into the couch by the bar and
feel as if you're in a local's living room while
sampling some of the best island wines,
paired with Dalmatian snacks.

Carpe Diem COCKTAIL BAR
(Map p242; ☑ 021-742 369; www.carpe-diem-
hvar.com; Obala Riva bb; ☺ 9am-2am) Look no
further – you have arrived at the mother of
Croatia's glitzy coastal bars. From a groggy
breakfast to pricey late-night cocktails, there
is no time of day when this swanky place is
dull. The house music spun by resident DJs
is smooth, the drinks well-mixed, and the
crowd is the well-heeled, jet-setting kind.

Central Park Club BAR
(Map p242; ☑ 021-718 337; www.klubparkhvar.
com; Bankete bb; ☺ 7am-2am) Set behind the
cluster of phoenix palms on the waterfront,
this large terrace bar is Hvar's main locale for
live music. There's something on every night,
ranging from jazz to soul, old-time rock 'n'
roll and funk. The cocktails are good too.

Falko BAR
(Map p241; ☑ 095 23 35 296; Šetalište Antuna
Tomislava Petrića 22; ☺ 8am-9pm mid-May–
mid-Sep; 🖝) Walk almost to the end of the
seaside promenade and you'll reach this
adorable hideaway in a pine forest just
above the beach. A great unpretentious alternative to the flashy spots closer to town, it
serves yummy sandwiches and salads. Think
low-key beach-shack vibe, hammocks and a
chilled-out crowd. Service can be slow.

Nautica BAR
(Map p242; www.nautica-bar.com; Fabrika 8;
☺ 5pm-2am) It starts slowly, with a mixed
crowd enjoying cocktails by the water (there
are more than 100 to choose from on the

DON'T MISS

PAKLENI ISLANDS

Most visitors to Hvar Town visit the crystal-clear waters, hidden beaches and deserted lagoons of the Pakleni Islands (Pakleni Otoci), a gorgeous chain of wooded isles which stretch out immediately in front of the town. Although the name is often translated as 'Hell's Islands', its meaning is thought to derive from *paklina*, a pine resin that was once harvested here to waterproof boats.

The largest of the Pakleni Islands by far is **Sveti Klement**, which supports three villages in its 5 sq km. **Palmižana** village has a marina, accommodation, restaurants and a pebbly beach. Accommodation here includes **Palmižana Meneghello** (☑ 021-717 270; www.palmizana.hr; Palmižana; apt from €120; ❈ ☜), run by the artsy Meneghello family. This beautiful boutique complex of villas and bungalows, scattered among lush tropical gardens, features two restaurants and an art gallery, and often hosts music recitals.

The closest of the islands to Hvar is **Jerolim**, which has a popular naturist beach. Stipanska bay on the nearby island of **Marinkovac** (40KN, 10 to 15 minutes), also has a clothing-optional section, although it's better known for its raucous beach club, **Carpe Diem Beach** (www.carpe-diem-hvar.com; ⊘10am-7pm & 11pm-5am Jun-Sep). This place offers quite the heady Med-glam experience, with daytime beach fun, a restaurant, massage therapies on tap and all-night parties (100KN for boat transfers departing from outside the other **Carpe Diem** (p245) admission is extra and varies depending on the night). Other popular options on Marinkovac include Ždrilca bay and pretty **Mlini beach**.

Taxi boats leave regularly for the islands, departing from in front of the Arsenal (p240) in Hvar. Expect to pay around 50KN for the nearer islands and a little more for further-flung stops.

list), but once Hula-Hula (p245) winds down and **Riva** (Map p242; ☑ 021-750 100; www.sun canihvar.com; Obala Riva 27; ☞ from €172; ❈ ☜) packs out, Nautica comes into its own as an obligatory stop on Hvar's night-crawl circuit. DJs spin everything from techno to hip hop to Euro-disco.

❶ Information

Atlas Hvar (☑ 021-741 911; www.atlas-hvar. com; Fabrika 27) Rents bikes and boats, and books excursions to Vis, Bol and Dubrovnik.

Emergency Clinic (Bolnica; ☑ 021-717 099; Biskupa Jurja Dubokovića bb)

Fontana Tours (☑ 021-742 133; www.happy hvar.com; Obala Riva 18) Finds private accommodation, runs island and wine-tasting tours, books taxi boats, and rents cars, scooters, quad bikes and bicycles. It also has two romantic and isolated apartments in Palmižana.

Garderoba (Trg Sv Stjepana bb; per 3/12/24hr 30/50/60KN; ⊘7am-11pm Jun-Sep) Left-luggage, laundry and toilet facilities are available on the edge of St Stephen's Sq, near the bus station.

Pelegrini Tours (☑ 021-742 743; www. pelegrini-hvar.hr; Obala Riva 20) Private accommodation, boat tickets to Italy with Snav and Blue Line, excursions (including popular daily trips to the Pakleni Islands and Vis' Blue and Green grottoes), and bike, scooter, car and boat rental. It also offers wine-tasting tours (per person 600KN).

Post Office (Map p242; www.posta.hr; Obala Riva 19; ⊘7am-9pm Mon-Sat) You can make international phone calls here.

Tourist Office (Map p242; ☑ 021-741 059; www.tzhvar.hr; Trg Sv Stjepana 42; ⊘8am-9pm Jul & Aug, 8am-8pm Mon-Sat, 8am-1pm & 4-8pm Sun Jun & Sep, 8am-2pm Mon-Fri, to noon Sat Oct-May) In the Arsenal building, right on St Stephen's Sq.

Tourist Office Information Point (Map p242; ☑ 021-718 109; Trg Marka Miličića; ⊘8am-9pm Mon-Sat, 9am-1pm Sun Jun-Sep) A summertime annex of the main tourist office in the bus station.

Stari Grad

POP 2790

Stari Grad, on the island's north coast, is a quieter, more cultured and altogether more sober affair than Hvar Town, its stylish and sybaritic sister. If you're not after pulsating nightlife and thousands of people crushing each other along the streets in the high season, head here and enjoy Hvar at a more leisurely pace. That said, you can easily see all of the little town's sights in half a day.

The name Stari Grad means 'Old Town', a reference to the fact that it was founded in 384 BC by the ancient Greeks, who knew it as Pharos. The surrounding fields are still divided into parcels of land demarcated in antiquity.

The town sits at the end of a deep inlet, with the narrow lanes of the old quarter spreading out on its southern side. The waterfront promenade continues along the northern bank to a small beach.

⊙ Sights

Tvrdalj   GARDENS
(Trg Tvrdalj 11; 15KN; ⊙10am-1pm & 5-9pm) This fortified house was built by artistic aristocrat Petar Hektorović (1487–1572) in the 16th century. At its heart is a lovely, lush Renaissance garden, set around the green waters of a pond stocked with mullet, as it was in Hektorović's day. Its a reflection of his favourite pastime, as recorded in his most famous poetic work, *Fishing and Fishermen's Chat* (1555).

Quotes from the writer's work are inscribed on the walls in Latin and Croatian. Our favourite is the one above the toilet alcove (a rare luxury for the time): 'Know what you are and then you can be proud'. You'll find it tucked away in a corner of the entry hall, which is the only part of the interior of the building that's open to the public.

Dominican Monastery   MONASTERY
(Dominikanski Samostan; Kod Sv Petra 3; 20KN; ⊙9.30am-12.30pm & 4-6.30pm May-Oct) Founded in 1482, this monastery was damaged by the Turks in 1571 and later fortified with a tower. Hydrangeas bloom in the cloister garden and there's an interesting little museum packed with fossils, ancient Greek inscriptions, Greek and Roman coins, and beautiful religious icons dating from the 16th to 18th centuries. The highlight, however, is an engrossing 16th-century painting of the *Lamentation of Christ* by Tintoretto.

🛏 Sleeping & Eating

Apolon   HOTEL €€€
(☑021-778 320; www.apolon.hr; Šetalište Don Šime Ljubića 7; r/ste from €179/249; ⊙May-Oct; P❋🛜) Named after the terracotta statue of Apollo on the roof, this grand old building was built in 1887 for the local luminary who's buried in the lavish domed mausoleum next door. It's now an elegant boutique hotel, with antique-style furniture and a claw-foot bathtub in the spacious suite.

Eremitaž   DALMATIAN €€
(☑091 54 28 395; Obala hrvatskih branitelja 2; mains 50-135KN; ⊙noon-3pm & 6pm-midnight) Housed in a waterfront hermitage, built in 1487 for the monks serving neighbouring St Jerome's Church, this restaurant serves Dalmatian staples in an exposed stone interior and on the shaded terrace.

Antika   DALMATIAN €€
(Duolnja Kola 34; mains 50-95KN; ⊙noon-10pm; 🎵) One of Hvar's best restaurants and bars, Antika has three separate spaces: an ancient, rickety town house; tables lining the alleyway; and a bar on an upstairs terrace. It's *the* place to hang out at night.

🛍 Shopping

Fantazam   JEWELLERY
(☑021-765 070; www.fantazam.com; Ivana Gundulića 6; ⊙11am-3pm & 5pm-1am) Step through the gallery filled with kooky insect sculptures to Zoran Tadić's small and interesting jewellery workshop.

ⓘ Information

Hvar Touristik (☑091 17 17 580; www.hvar-touristik.com; Šiberija 31; ⊙9.30am-2pm & 4-8pm Mon-Sat) Lets private accommodation, arranges transfers (100KN to the ferry; 240KN to Hvar Town) and rents scooters (from 150KN per day), cars (from 400KN per day), boats (from 250KN per day) and bikes (20KN per hour).

Tourist Office (☑021-765 763; www.starigrad-faros.hr; Obala Dr Franje Tuđmana 1; ⊙8am-8pm Jul & Aug, 8am-8pm Mon-Fri, 8am-2pm Sat, 9am-noon & 5-8pm Sun Jun & Sep, 8am-2pm Mon-Fri, 8am-noon Sat Feb-May & Oct, 8am-2pm Mon-Fri Nov-Jan) Distributes a good local map.

Jelsa
POP 3590

Although there's not much to it, the small harbour town of Jelsa is a tidy little place surrounded by thick pine forests and tall poplars. While it lacks the Renaissance buildings of Hvar, its intimate streets, squares and parks are pleasant, and there are some good swimming spots nearby. We wouldn't suggest basing yourself here, but it's a nice spot for a short visit.

✕ Eating

Me & Mrs Jones   DALMATIAN €€
(Mala Banda bb; mains 70-154KN; ⊙noon-midnight Jun-Jul & Sep-Oct, 5pm-midnight Aug) The local couple behind this restaurant offers a creative take on Dalmatian cuisine at the edge of the harbour, merging traditional stone and wood interiors with retro accents. When locals from Hvar Town want to escape for dinner, they come here.

ℹ️ Information

Tourist Office (☎021-761 017; www.tzjelsa.
hr; Strossmayerovo šetalište bb; ☉8am-10pm
Mon-Sat, 10am-noon & 7-9pm Sun Jul & Aug,
8am-1pm & 5.30-8pm Mon-Sat, 9.30am-noon
Sun May-Jun & Sep-Oct) Provides information
on beaches, diving operators, private accommodation and hotels.

VIS ISLAND

POP 3620

Of all the Croatian islands, Vis is the most
mysterious – even to locals. The furthest of
the main Central Dalmatian islands from
the coast, Vis spent much of its recent history serving as a military base for the Yugoslav army, cut off from foreign visitors from
the 1950s right up until 1989. The isolation
preserved the island from development and
drove much of the population to move elsewhere in search of work, leaving it under-
populated for many years.

As has happened with impoverished islands across the Mediterranean, Vis' lack of
development has become its drawcard as a
tourist destination. International and local
travellers alike now flock to Vis, seeking
authenticity, nature, gourmet delights and
peace and quiet.

Vis has its own distinct grape, *vugava,*
a white varietal that's been cultivated here
since ancient times. You'll also taste some
of the freshest seafood here, thanks to a
still-thriving fishing tradition.

History

Inhabited first in neolithic times, Vis Island
was settled by the ancient Illyrians, who
brought the Iron Age to Vis in the 1st millennium BC. In 390 BC a Greek colony was
formed on the island, known then as Issa,
from which the Greek ruler Dionysius the
Elder controlled other Adriatic possessions.
The island eventually became a powerful
city-state and established its own colonies
on Korčula and at Trogir and Stobreč. Ally-
ing itself with Rome during the Illyrian wars,
the island nonetheless lost its autonomy and
became part of the Roman Empire in 47 BC.
By the 10th century Vis had been settled by
Slavic tribes and was sold to Venice along
with other Dalmatian towns in 1420. Fleeing
Dalmatian pirates, the population moved inland from the coast.

With the fall of the Venetian empire in
1797, the island fell under the control of Aus-

tria, France, Great Britain, Austria again
and then Italy during WWII, as the great
powers fought for control of this strategic
Adriatic outpost. During the war, Vis was
an important military base for Josip Broz
Tito's Partisans. Tito established his supreme
headquarters in a cave on Hum Mountain,
from where he coordinated military and diplomatic actions with Allied forces.

ℹ️ Getting There & Away

Two to three large **Jadrolinija** (☎021-711 032;
www.jadrolinija.hr; Šetalište stare Isse 2, Luka)
car ferries head between Vis Town and Split daily
(adult/child/car/bicycle 54/27/370/51KN, 2¼
hours, two to three daily); the ticket office on Vis
only opens 90 minutes before each boat departs.

Kapetan Luka (www.krilo.hr) has a much
faster catamaran heading from Vis Town to Split
(55KN, 1½ hours), which also stops in Hvar Town
on Tuesdays and Milna (Brač) on Wednesdays.

ℹ️ Getting Around

At least six buses a day head between Komiža
and Vis Town (20KN).

Vis Town

POP 1940

The island's original settlement, the ancient
town of Vis stands at the foot of a wide,
horseshoe-shaped bay. Ferry arrivals give
spurts of activity to an otherwise peaceful
town of coastal promenades, crumbling 17th-
century town houses and narrow alleyways
twisting gently uphill from the seafront.

The town is a merger of two settlements:
19th-century Luka (meaning 'port'), where
the ferry docks, and medieval Kut on the
opposite curve of the horseshoe. A harbourside promenade runs scenically between the
two. Vis' long and complicated history has
bequeathed it with the remains of a Greek
cemetery, Roman baths and an English
fortress.

👁️ Sights

Small beaches line the promenade, but the
busiest town beach lies north of the harbour
in front of Hotel Issa. Beyond it are nudist
coves and a series of wild swimming spots.
On the other side, past Kut and the British
Naval Cemetery, is the pretty pebble beach
of **Grandovac**, which has a beach bar (look
out for occasional late-night parties), a small
stretch of pebbles and a string of rocky
beaches on either side.

VIS' BEST BEACHES

Stiniva Tiny Stiniva is Vis' most perfect cove. The high cliffs surrounding it form an almost complete circle, with only a gap of about 10m open to the sea. The beach is lined with large smooth pebbles, which blaze white against the blue waters. Stiniva can be reached by an extremely steep and rough track but it's much more easily accessed by boat. Most excursion boats from Vis Town and Komiža offer Stiniva as an option, but Rukavac is much closer.

Srbrena Near the fishing village of Rukavac, Srbrena is a pretty beach with large white pebbles and clear blue waters, backed with a nature reserve. It has the advantage of being a flat walk from a nearby parking area.

Milna & Zaglav While the rest of the island is rocky or pebbly, Vis' eastern end has a few sandy beaches. Milna sits right beside the main road, a sandy beach with strikingly blue water and several small islands forming an idyllic backdrop. However, you're better off taking a 15-minute walk along the shrub-lined path at the south end of the beach to neighbouring Zaglav, which is even prettier and quieter.

Archaeological Museum MUSEUM
(Arheološkog Muzeja; Šetalište viški boj 12, Kut; adult/child 20/10KN; ⊙9am-1pm & 5-9pm Mon-Sat) Housed in an Austrian fortress built in 1841, this small museum has the largest collection of Hellenistic artefacts in Croatia, including ancient Greek pottery, jewellery and sculpture. The highlight is an exquisite 4th-century BC bronze head of the goddess Artemis. A room on the other side of the courtyard displays relics retrieved from shipwrecks.

Activities

Diving is excellent in the waters around Vis. Fish are plentiful and there are various shipwrecks, an amphorae field and a WWII plane to explore. However, much of the best diving is of a technical nature, requiring a degree of proficiency.

Tours

Most of the travel agencies in town offer a range of tours, which are more or less identical. The most interesting is the tour of the island's **top-secret military sights** abandoned by the Yugoslav National Army in 1992. The trip takes in rocket shelters, bunkers, weapon-storage spaces, submarine 'parking lots', Tito's Cave (which housed partisan leader Josip Broz Tito during WWII) and nuclear shelters that served as communication headquarters for Yugoslavia's secret service. These sites occupy some of the island's most beautiful spots, only recently made accessible to the public.

Other tour options include caving, trekking, food and wine tasting, and boat trips to outer islands that take in the Blue Grotto, the Green Grotto and remote beaches.

Vis Special TOURS
(☑021-711 524; www.vis-special.com; Korzo 33, Luka) Offers a smorgasbord of tours including Wine and Gastro, Military, Top Secret, Trails of Marshall Tito and Queen Teuta Cave. It also arranges boat trips to the Blue Grotto, Green Grotto, Stiniva beach and the outlying islands. On top of that it rents private accommodation, bikes, scooters, cars, boats and kayaks.

Festivals & Events

Resistance MUSIC
(tickets €49; ⊙mid-Jul) The official closing party of Destination Ultra Croatia Music Week is held at Fort George and attracts electronic-dance-music fans from around the world.

Sleeping

There are no camping grounds or hostels in Vis Town and only a few hotels, but you should have no trouble finding private rooms or apartments. Browse www.info-vis.net for the most extensive listings, or refer to the websites of the tourist office (p251), **VisVillas** (☑021-717 786; www.visvillas.com) or any of the local travel agencies. In summer, accommodation needs to be booked in advance, as the capacity is limited.

Apartments Kuljiš APARTMENT €€
(☑098 460 937; www.visapartment.net; Petra Svačića 41, Kut; apt 500KN; 🅿❄🛜) With welcoming hosts and a great location just a short walk from the centre of Kut, this set of four comfortable, reasonably priced apartments is

a smart choice. All have balconies or terraces and a kitchenette.

Pansion Dionis
B&B €€

(☎021-711 963; www.dionis.hr; Matije Gubca 1, Luka; s/d/tr €60/70/90; ❄🛜) Above the pizzeria with the same name, this family-run B&B has eight rooms in an old stone house, just off the seafront. All of them come with a TV and fridge, and some have balconies. The triple room in the attic has a lovely terrace with mountain and town vistas.

Hotel San Giorgio
HOTEL €€€

(☎021-607 630; www.hotelsangiorgiovis.com; Petra Hektorovića 2; s/d from €114/152; ❄🛜) Filled with interesting art, this gorgeous Italian-owned hotel has 10 swish, colourful rooms and suites in two buildings. The rooms have wooden floors, great beds and all sorts of upscale perks. Best of all is room 1, with a large sea-facing terrace and a Jacuzzi.

Villa Vis
GUESTHOUSE €€€

(☎098 94 87 490; www.migration.villaviscroatia.com; Jakšina 11, Kut; s/d 995/1147KN; ❄🛜) This stylish option has four colour-themed rooms (green, cream, chocolate and red) inside a traditional town house with all-modern interiors. The location is great, close to restaurants and bars, and within walking distance of the beach.

OFF THE BEATEN TRACK

TITO'S MOUNTAIN HIDEAWAY

Reaching a height of 587m, **Hum** mountain dominates the western end of Vis. The very top is off limits, but you can drive up and park a little before the end of the road and follow the path marked Panorama Komiža for jaw-dropping views over the town. There's not much to it, but while you're up here you may as well investigate little **St Duh's Chapel**.

Famously, Tito used a cave on the mountain as his headquarters during WWII. The start of the track to **Tito's Cave** is no longer signposted but it's easy to spot, due to the large parking bay under a well-constructed stone wall to the right of the road as you're heading up. A 15-minute walk leads to the partisan leader's refuge – a smallish room enclosed by a stone wall under a limestone overhang.

To reach Hum, turn off the main road at Podšplije and follow the signposts.

✖ Eating

Vis has some wonderful restaurants, scattered around both Luka and Kut. There are a few local specialities to try: *viška pogača*, a flatbread filled with salted fish and onions, and *viški hib*, dried grated figs mixed with aromatic herbs.

Buffet Vis
DALMATIAN, SEAFOOD €

(☎021-711 043; Obala Sv Jurja 35, Luka; mains from 40KN; ⏱6pm-1am) This simple place is tiny and unadorned, with a few tables outside. It's no frills but great value, with a local vibe and delicious seafood.

Kantun
DALMATIAN €€

(☎021-711 306; Biskupa Mihe Pušića 17, Luka; mains 100-130KN; ⏱5pm-midnight) The small menu at this seafront tavern offers flavourful local fare made with top-quality ingredients. The garden area is vine-covered and intimate, while the interior is a tasteful rustic space of exposed stone.

Pojoda
DALMATIAN, SEAFOOD €€

(☎021-711 575; Don Cvjetka Marasovića 40, Kut; mains 85-150KN; ⏱noon-1am) Locals in the know rave about this seafood restaurant with a leafy courtyard dotted with bamboo, orange and lemon trees. Try *orbiko*, its signature dish of orzo, peas and shrimp.

Karijola
PIZZA €€

(☎021-711 358; www.pizzeria-karijola.com; Šetalište viški boj 4, Kut; pizzas 60-81KN; ⏱noon-midnight Jul & Aug, 5-11pm Jun & Sep) Sister to two popular pizzerias of the same name in Zagreb, Karijola's thin-crust concoctions come with high-quality toppings. Try the Karijola (tomato, garlic, mozzarella, rocket and prosciutto) or the surprisingly good sauceless white pizza.

Val
DALMATIAN €€

(☎021-711 763; Trg Eugena Kvaternika 1, Kut; mains 80-140KN; ⏱5pm-midnight) Set in an old stone house, with a palm-shaded terrace overlooking the sea, Val offers a seasonal menu with an Italian twist. Try the offerings of wild asparagus in springtime, wild boar and mushrooms in winter, and lots of fish in summer. Don't miss the *pašta fazol* (Dalmatian bean stew) with fish, and local carob cake for dessert.

★ Konoba & Bar Lola
MEDITERRANEAN €€€

(www.lolavisisland.com; Matije Gupca 12, Luka; mains 115-190KN; ⏱6pm-midnight) Marked by an old-time bicycle on its wall, Lola is tucked away into a beautiful garden courtyard with old stone walls and a Meštrović fountain. The Croatian chef and his Spanish wife pres-

RURAL EATS

Vis' gastronomic offering isn't limited to its main towns. The interior of the island and its isolated coves are becoming a foodie's dream. In recent years a number of rural households have started offering local homemade food worth travelling for.

Konoba Stončica (☑021-711 952; www.konoba-stoncica.com; Stončica 11; mains 60-140KN; ☺1-11pm) Set right by a pretty sandy beach, this relaxed eatery serves excellent grilled squid and fish under the shade of palms, pines and a wooden pergola. Order a side of smashed potatoes with olive oil and garlic – it's a Vis speciality.

Roki's (☑098 303 483; www.rokis.hr; Plisko Polje 17; peka per person 150KN; ☺7pm-midnight) In Plisko Polje, 8km south of Vis Town, this winery restaurant is one of the very best places to try food cooked under a traditional *peka* (metal dome). They'll need four hours' notice, so call ahead to order your choice of lamb, veal, octopus or fish. They also provide free transport for groups of four or more.

Kod Magića (☑091 89 84 859; Stončica 19; entire meal for 230KN; ☺5-11pm) Smack in the middle of fields and vineyards east of Vis Town, this family-run affair serves homemade dishes using fresh local ingredients and great house wine. Don't skip its broad-bean-and-cuttlefish stew and *savur*, a Vis speciality with marinated sardines.

ent a short but highly creative menu with a lot of influence from Spain. The wine list and service are excellent as well.

Vila Kaliopa　　　　　　DALMATIAN **€€€**
(☑091 27 11 755; Vladimira Nazora 34, Kut; mains 150-180KN; ☺1-4pm & 5pm-1am) In the exotic gardens of the 16th-century Gariboldi mansion, Villa Kaliopa is an upmarket restaurant full of yachting enthusiasts. Tall palm trees, bamboo and classical statuary provide the setting for a menu of Dalmatian specialities, which change daily. It hosts occasional concerts and exhibits.

🍸 Drinking & Nightlife

Fort George　　　　　　　　　BAR
(☑091 26 56 041; www.fortgeorgecroatia.com; Utvrda Sv Juraj bb; ☺noon-1am) The service can be offhand, but there's no better place to watch the sunset on a summer night than the terrace of this old fort, built by the British in 1811 (see if you can spot the stone Union Jack above the entrance). Look out for special club nights advertised on posters around town.

Bejbi　　　　　　　　　　　　　BAR
(Pod Ložu 4, Kut; ☺7am-3pm & 5pm-2am; ☜) Head to this cafe-bar to sip coffee between outings to the beach during the day, and return for cocktails at night. If you're peckish, they serve British-style breakfasts, burgers and steak.

Lambik　　　　　　　　　　　　BAR
(Pod Ložu 2, Kut; ☺8am-2am) Kut's best bar has alfresco seating both on the square and in a lovely vine-covered stone passageway under

an ancient colonnade. Acoustic bands and singers perform on some nights.

ℹ️ Information

Ionios Travel Agency (☑021-711 532; ionios@ st.t-com.hr; Sv Jurja 37, Luka & Pod Ložu 5, Kut; ☜) Finds private accommodation; rents cars (from 390KN), bikes (100KN) and scooters (200KN); and runs excursions.

Navigator (☑021-717 786; www.navigator. hr; Šetalište stare Isse 1, Luka; ☺8am-2pm & 4.30-8pm daily) Books tours and diving trips, and rents cars, scooters and boats.

Post Office (Obala Sv Jurja 25, Luka; ☺8am-3pm Mon-Fri, to noon Sat)

Tourist Office (☑021-717 017; www.tz-vis.hr; Šetalište stare Isse 5; ☺8am-2pm & 5-8pm Jun-Sep, 8am-2pm Mon-Sat May & Oct, 8am-2pm Mon-Fri Oct-Apr) Right next to the Jadrolinija ferry dock.

Komiža

POP 1530

With a picturesque setting on a bay at the foot of Hum mountain, this small town has diehard fans among Croats, who swear by its somewhat bohemian ambience. Narrow back streets lined with 17th- and 18th-century stone town houses twist uphill from the port, which has been used by fisherfolk since at least the 12th century.

A friendly rivalry exists between Komiža and Vis Town. The latter was historically associated with the upper-class nobility while Komiža is proud of its working-class fishing heritage and pirate tales.

MAGICAL GROTTOES

Located on the island of Biševo, off Vis' southwestern tip, the coastal **Blue Grotto** (Modra Špilja; Sep-Jun 50KN, Jul & Aug 70KN) is one of the region's most famous natural sights. Between 11am and noon the sun's rays pass through an underwater opening, bathing the interior in an unearthly blue light. Beneath the crystal-blue water, rocks glimmer in silver and pink to a depth of 16m. To get here, the easiest, quickest and best option is to take a tour from Komiža.

When the tourist season is at its peak in July and August, the cave can be woefully crowded and the line of boats waiting to get in discouragingly long. Outside of high season, you may be able to swim here. The only catch is that the water can be too choppy for you to enter the cave outside summer or when the *jugo* (southern wind) is blowing.

Boats head to the cave from all over Vis, the surrounding islands and from as far away as Split. From Komiža, the trips take between an hour and 90 minutes, depending on the waiting time to enter the cave. Expect to pay around 100KN, plus the admission charge.

The **Green Grotto** (Zelena Špilja), located on the tiny uninhabited islet of Ravnik just off the coast from Rukavac, is a much larger sea cave marketed as a less crowded and cheaper option than the more impressive **Blue Grotto**. While it doesn't have the ethereal lighting of its famous sister, it has the advantage of no queues, no admission fee and a chance to get out for a swim. Taxi boats departing from Rukavac charge around 150KN for the trip.

Komiža has its own little sand-and-pebble beaches, but most visitors head here to catch a boat to the Blue Grotto on the nearby island of Biševo. Boat trips can be arranged through any of the local travel agencies, or simply by walking along the harbour.

◎ Sights

At the southern end of the harbour is a blocky Renaissance citadel, built in 1585, known as the **Kaštel**. The large church that you'll pass on the eastern approach to the town dates from the 17th century and is attached to a **Benedictine Monastery**.

Komiža's most popular **beach** is at the northern end of town, right below the Hotel Biševo. It's fringed with pine trees and backed by the triple-naved **Gospa Gusarica Church**.

☞ Tours

Alter Natura   TOURS
(☑ 021-717 239; www.alternatura.hr; Hrvatskih Muče-nika 2) Specialises in adventure tourism, including trekking, kayaking and abseiling. It also offers a military tour and boat trips to the Blue Grotto, the Green Grotto and various hard-to-get-to beaches on Vis and the surrounding islands.

✖ Eating

Slastičarnica Cukar   BAKERY €
(www.facebook.com/cukar.komiza; Hrvatskih Muče-nika 8; cakes 7-15KN; ⊙8am-8pm) Head to this

tiny cake shop for a delicious sweet treat. Sadly, there's no coffee to go with it.

Konoba Jastožera   DALMATIAN, SEAFOOD €€
(☑021-713 253; www.jastozera.eu; Gundulićeva 6; mains from 100KN; ⊙noon-2am) Built in 1883 as a holding facility for live lobsters waiting to be exported to all over Europe, Jastožera has a covered wooden dining terrace jutting out over the water, with lobster pots suspended from the old beams. Obviously, lobster is the speciality (from 950KN per kilogram) – grilled, gratin, boiled...you name it. Call ahead for spit-roasted lamb.

Bako   DALMATIAN, SEAFOOD €€
(☑021-713 742; www.konobabako.hr; Gundulićeva 1; mains 80-140KN; ⊙4pm-2am Jun-Aug, 5pm-midnight Sep-May) Specialising in seafood, Bako has a terrace with water views and a cool stone interior with a fish pond and a collection of Greek and Roman amphorae. It's a good place to try the very localised speciality *komiška pogača*.

❶ Information

Darlić & Darlić (☑021-713 760; www.darlic-travel.hr; Riva Sv Mikule 13) Offers excursions (including to the Blue Grotto; p252), lets private accommodation, and rents cars, scooters and bikes.

Post Office (Hrvatskih Mučenika 8; ⊙8am-5pm Mon, 7.30am-2pm Tue-Fri)

Tourist Office (☑021-713 455; www.tz-komiza. hr; Riva Sv Mikule 1; ⊙9am-1pm Mon-Fri)

Dubrovnik & Southern Dalmatia

🎵 020

Best Places to Eat

➡ Pantarul (p270)

➡ Restaurant 360° (p269)

➡ Konoba Koraćeva Kuća (p276)

➡ Bugenvila (p275)

➡ Konoba Mate (p288)

Best Places to Sleep

➡ Karmen Apartments (p265)

➡ Villa Klaić (p268)

➡ Hotel Kompas (p268)

➡ Hotel Adriatic (p281)

➡ Korčula Royal Apartments (p286)

Why Go?

Dubrovnik is simply unique; its beauty is bewitching, its setting sublime. Not that it's a secret – quite the opposite. Thousands of visitors walk along its marble streets every day of the year, gazing, gasping and happily snapping away.

The remarkable old town, ringed by mighty defensive walls that dip their feet in the cerulean sea, is a highlight of any trip to Croatia, capturing the very essence of a medieval Mediterranean fantasy. It's little wonder that in recent years it's featured so prominently in the *Game of Thrones* TV series.

Dubrovnik is also an ideal launching pad for expeditions throughout southern Dalmatia. From the island of Korčula in the northwest to the dreamy plains of Konavle in the southeast, this is a region to be savoured by beach seekers, wine lovers and history buffs alike.

When to Go
Dubrovnik

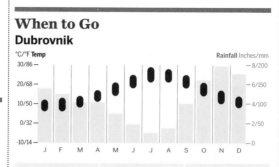

May & Jun Warm sunny days, without the scorching heat or crowds of midsummer.

Jul & Aug Sate your cultural appetite during Dubrovnik's prestigious Summer Festival.

Sep & Oct Still warm enough for swimming and the beaches aren't as crowded.

Dubrovnik & Southern Dalmatia Highlights

1 Dubrovnik (p255)
Circling the historic city's mighty walls and then catching the cable car up Mt Srđ for breathtaking views from above.

2 Korčula (p282) Soaking up the sublime medieval atmosphere of the walled town.

3 Mljet (p276) Seeking out secluded beaches, villages and eateries down the island's east end, before joining summertime throngs at the national park's pretty lakes.

4 Lokrum (p260)
Exploring the gardens, forest and beaches of Dubrovnik's closest island getaway.

5 Pelješac Peninsula (p280) Sampling Croatia's wine direct from the cellar door.

6 Konoba Koračeva Kuća (p276) Watching the sunset shadows dance across the mountains over an evening meal on the terrace of this Konavle restaurant.

7 Ston (p279) Slurping down oysters in the fascinating old port.

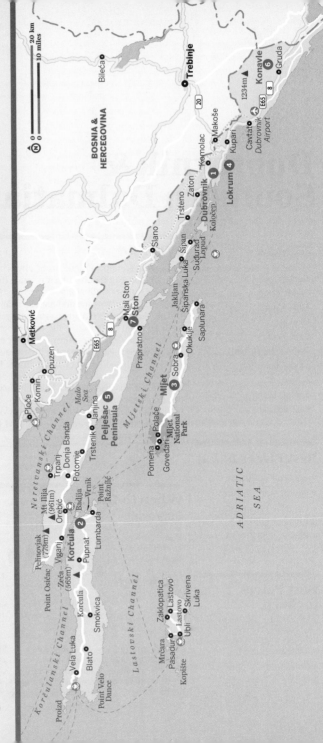

DUBROVNIK

POP 28,500

Regardless of whether you are visiting Dubrovnik for the first time or the hundredth, the sense of awe never fails to descend when you set eyes on the beauty of the old town. Indeed it's hard to imagine anyone becoming jaded by the city's marble streets, baroque buildings and the endless shimmer of the Adriatic, or failing to be inspired by a walk along the ancient city walls that protected a civilised, sophisticated republic for centuries.

Although the shelling of Dubrovnik in 1991 horrified the world, the city has bounced back with vigour to enchant visitors again. Marvel at the interplay of light on the old stone buildings; trace the peaks and troughs of Dubrovnik's past in museums replete with art and artefacts; take the cable car up to Mt Srđ; exhaust yourself climbing up and down narrow lanes – then plunge into the azure sea.

History

The story of Dubrovnik begins with the 7th-century onslaught of the Slavs, which had wiped out the Roman city of Epidaurum (site of present-day Cavtat). Residents fled to the safest place they could find, which was the rocky islet of Ragusa, separated from the mainland by a narrow channel. Building walls was a matter of pressing urgency due to the threat of invasion; the city was well fortified by the 9th century when it resisted a Saracen siege for 15 months.

Meanwhile, another settlement emerged on the mainland, which became known as Dubrovnik, named after the *dubrava* (holm oak) that carpeted the region. The two settlements merged in the 12th century, and the channel that separated them was filled in.

By the end of the 12th century Dubrovnik had become a significant trading centre on the coast, providing an important link between the Mediterranean and Balkan states. Dubrovnik came under Venetian authority in 1205, finally breaking away from its control in 1358.

By the 15th century the Respublica Ragusina (Republic of Ragusa) had extended its borders to include the entire coastal belt from Ston to Cavtat, having previously acquired Lastovo Island, the Pelješac Peninsula and Mljet Island. It was now a force to be reckoned with. The city turned towards sea trade and established a fleet of its own ships, which were dispatched to Egypt, the Levant, Sicily, Spain, France and Istanbul. Through canny diplomacy the city maintained good relations with everyone – even the Ottoman Empire, to which Dubrovnik began paying tribute in the 16th century.

Centuries of peace and prosperity allowed art, science and literature to flourish, but most of the Renaissance art and architecture in Dubrovnik was destroyed in the earthquake of 1667, which killed 5000 people and left the city in ruins. Holy Saviour Church, the Sponza Palace and the Rector's Palace are the only significant buildings remaining from before this time. The earthquake also marked the beginning of the economic decline of the town.

DUBROVNIK IN...

Two Days

Two days is plenty of time to explore the compact old town. Start early and take a walk along the **city walls** (p256) before it gets too hot. Spend the rest of the day wandering the marbled streets and calling into whichever church, palace or museum takes your fancy. Head to **Buža** (p270) for a sunset tipple before dinner.

The next day, start by taking the **cable car** (p261) up Mt Srđ, stopping at the top to visit the exhibition **Dubrovnik During the Homeland War** (p260). Afterwards, pick up where you left off in the old town. When it starts to bake, wander along to **Banje Beach** (p261) for a dip. Spend your last evening splurging on a romantic meal at **Restaurant 360°** (p269), before sampling fine Croatian wines at **D'vino** (p271).

Four Days

With another couple of days up your sleeve you'll have the luxury of confining your old-town explorations to the evenings, when the cruise-ship hordes have returned to their boats. On day three, plan to spend the middle of the day on the island of **Lokrum** (p260). On your final day, jump on a boat to **Cavtat** (p273), allowing a couple of hours to stroll around the historic town before tucking into lunch at **Bugenvila** (p275).

The final coup de grâce was dealt by Napoleon, whose troops entered Dubrovnik in 1808 and announced the end of the republic. The Vienna Congress of 1815 ceded Dubrovnik to Austria; though the city maintained its shipping, it succumbed to social disintegration. It remained a part of the Austro-Hungarian Empire until 1918 and then slowly began to develop its tourism industry.

Caught in the cross-hairs of the war that ravaged the former Yugoslavia, Dubrovnik was pummelled with some 2000 shells in 1991 and 1992, suffering considerable damage. All of the damaged buildings have now been restored.

◉ Sights

Today Dubrovnik is the most prosperous, elegant and expensive city in Croatia. In many ways it still feels like a city state, isolated from the rest of the nation by geography and history. It's become such a tourism magnet that there's even talk of having to limit visitor numbers in the car-free old town – the main thoroughfares can get impossibly crowded, especially when multiple cruise ships disgorge passengers at the same time.

◉ Old Town

★ City Walls & Forts   FORT
(Gradske zidine; Map p262; adult/child 120/30KN; ☺8am-7.30pm Apr-Oct, 9am-3pm Nov-Mar) No visit to Dubrovnik would be complete without a walk around the spectacular city walls, the finest in the world and the city's main claim to fame. From the top, the view over the old town and the shimmering Adriatic is sublime. You can get a good handle on the extent of the shelling damage in the 1990s by gazing over the rooftops: those sporting bright new terracotta suffered damage and had to be replaced.

The first set of walls to enclose the city was built in the 9th century. In the middle of the 14th century the 1.5m-thick defences were fortified with 15 square forts. The threat of attacks from the Turks in the 15th century prompted the city to strengthen the existing forts and add new ones, so that the entire old town was contained within a stone barrier 2km long and up to 25m high. The walls are thicker on the land side – up to 6m – and range from 1.5m to 3m on the sea side.

The round **Minčeta Tower** (Tvrđava Minčeta) protects the landward edge of the city from attack, the **Bokar Tower** (Tvrđava Bokar) and **Fort Lawrence** (Tvrđava Lovrjenac; 30KN; ☺8am-7.30pm) look west and out to sea, while **Fort**

Revelin (Trg Oružja) and **Fort St John** (Tvrđava Sv Ivana) guard the eastern approach and the Old Harbour.

There are entrances to the walls from near the Pile Gate, the Ploče Gate and the Maritime Museum. The Pile Gate entrance tends to be the busiest, and entering from the Ploče side has the added advantage of getting the steepest climbs out of the way first (you're required to walk in an anticlockwise direction). Don't underestimate how strenuous the wall walk can be, especially on a hot day. There's very little shelter and the few vendors selling water on the route tend to be overpriced.

Pile Gate   GATE
(Gradska vrata Pile; Map p262) The natural starting point to any visit to Dubrovnik, this fabulous city gate was built in 1537. While crossing the drawbridge, imagine that this was once lifted every evening, the gate closed and the key handed to the rector. Notice the statue of St Blaise, the city's patron saint, set in a niche over the Renaissance arch.

After passing through the outer gate you'll come to an inner gate dating from 1460, and soon after you'll be struck by the gorgeous view of the main street, Placa, or as it's commonly known, Stradun, Dubrovnik's pedestrian promenade.

Onofrio Fountain   FOUNTAIN
(Velika Onofrijeva fontana; Map p262; Placa bb) One of Dubrovnik's most famous landmarks, this large fountain was built in 1438 as part of a water-supply system that involved bringing water from a well 12km away. Originally the fountain was adorned with sculpture, but it was heavily damaged in the 1667 earthquake and only 16 carved masks remain, with water dribbling from their mouths into a drainage pool.

Franciscan Monastery & Museum MONASTERY
(Muzej Franjevačkog samostana; Map p262; Placa 2; adult/child 30/15KN; ☺9am-6pm) Within this monastery's solid stone walls is a gorgeous mid-14th-century **cloister**, a historic **pharmacy** and a small **museum** with a collection of relics and liturgical objects, including chalices, paintings, gold jewellery and pharmacy items such as laboratory gear and medical books. The remains of artillery that pierced the monastery walls during the 1990s war have been saved, too.

Before you head inside, stop to admire the remarkable **pietà** over the door sculpted by the local masters Petar and Leonard Andrijić in 1498. Unfortunately, the portal is all that remains of a richly decorated church that was destroyed in the 1667 earthquake.

The cloister is one of the most beautiful late-Romanesque structures in Dalmatia. Notice how each capital over the incredibly slim dual columns is topped by a different figure, portraying human heads, animals and floral arrangements. At the centre is a small square garden that's shaded by orange and palm trees.

Further inside is the third-oldest functioning pharmacy in Europe, which has been in business since 1391. It may have been the first pharmacy in Europe open to the general public.

★ **War Photo Limited** GALLERY
(Map p262; ☑020-322 166; www.warphotoltd.com; Antuninska 6; adult/child 40/30KN; ◎10am-10pm daily Jun-Sep, 10am-4pm Wed-Mon May & Oct) An immensely powerful experience, this gallery features intensely compelling exhibitions curated by New Zealand photojournalist Wade Goddard, who worked in the Balkans in the 1990s. Its declared intention is to 'expose the myth of war...to let people see war as it is, raw, venal, frightening, by focusing on how war inflicts injustices on innocents and combatants alike'. There's a permanent exhibition on the upper floor devoted to the wars in Yugoslavia, but the changing exhibitions cover a multitude of conflicts.

Synagogue & Jewish Museum SYNAGOGUE
(Sinagoga i Židovski muzej; Map p262; Žudioska 5; 40KN; ◎9am-9pm May-Oct, to 3pm Nov-Apr) Established in 1352, this is said to be the second-oldest still-functioning synagogue in the world, and the oldest Sephardic one. Inside is a museum that exhibits religious relics and documentation on the local Jewish population, including records relating to their persecution during WWII.

Dominican Monastery & Museum MONASTERY
(Muzej Dominikanskog samostana; Map p262; Sv Dominika 4; 30KN; ◎9am-5pm) This imposing structure is an architectural highlight, built in a transitional Gothic-Renaissance style, and containing an impressive art collection. Constructed around the same time as the city walls in the 14th century, the stark exterior resembles a fortress more than a religious complex. The interior contains a graceful 15th-century **cloister** constructed by local artisans after the designs of the Florentine architect Maso di Bartolomeo.

The large, single-naved church features some bright, modern, stained glass and a

ⓘ MUSEUMS OF DUBROVNIK

Perhaps a cunning plan to get you through the doors of some of the town's smaller museums, nine of Dubrovnik's institutions can only be visited by buying a multimuseum pass (adult/child 100/25KN); individual tickets aren't available. Cleverly the Rector's Palace is one of them – one of the city's higher-profile sights.

If you've bought the ticket mainly to visit the Rector's Palace and want to get your money's worth in a limited amount of time, we suggest you prioritise the rest in the following order: Museum of Modern & Contemporary Art, Maritime Museum, Archaeological Museum, Dulčić Masle Pulitika Gallery, Natural History Museum, Ethnographic Museum, Marin Držić House, Pulitika Studio.

painting by Vlaho Bukovac above one of the side altars. Other priceless pieces of art are hung in rooms off the cloister, including 15th- and 16th-century works by Lovro Dobričević, Nikola Božidarević and Titian.

Archaeological Museum MUSEUM
(Arheološke muzej; Map p262; ☑020-324 041; www.dumus.hr; Fort Revelin, Sv Dominika 3; adult/child multimuseum pass 100/25KN; ◎10am-4pm Thu-Tue) Fragments of masonry and sculpture are presented in this small museum under Fort Revelin. There are some good examples of medieval plait-work *(pleter)* – psychedelic squiggles somewhat similar to those associated with Celtic art.

Sponza Palace PALACE
(Palača Sponza; Map p262; Placa bb) This superb 16th-century palace is a mixture of Gothic and Renaissance styles beginning with an exquisite Renaissance portico resting on six Corinthian columns. The 1st floor has late-Gothic windows and the 2nd-floor windows are in a Renaissance style, with an alcove containing a statue of St Blaise. Sponza Palace was originally a customs house, then a mint, a state treasury and a bank.

It now houses the **State Archives** (Državni Arhiv; ☑020-321 031; www.dad.hr; Sponza Palace, Placa; 25KN; ◎10am-7pm Jun-Sep, 8am-3pm Mon-Fri, to 1pm Sat Oct-May), which contain a priceless collection of manuscripts dating back nearly 1000 years. Although there are some English translations, the displays aren't particularly interesting. Just inside the entrance

Dubrovnik

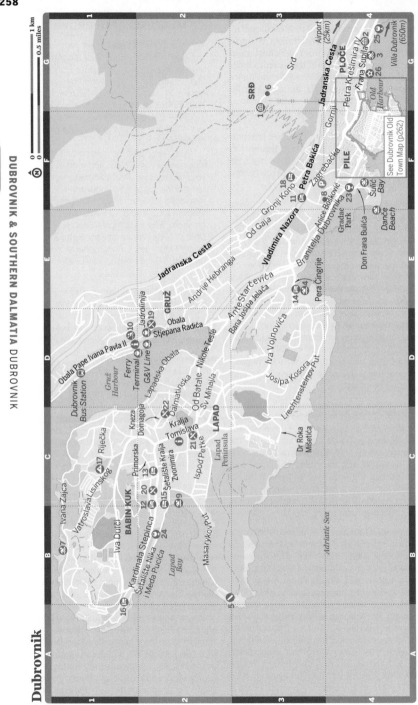

is the **Memorial Room of the Defenders of Dubrovnik** (⊙10am-10pm Mon-Fri, 8am-1pm Sat) **FREE**, a heartbreaking collection of black-and-white photographs of the mainly young men who perished between 1991 and 1995.

Orlando Column MONUMENT
(Orlandov stup; Map p262; Luža Sq) Luža Sq once served as a marketplace, and this stone column – carved in 1417 and featuring the image of a medieval knight – used to be the spot where edicts, festivities and public verdicts were announced. The knight's forearm was the official linear measure of the Republic – the ell of Dubrovnik (51.1cm).

St Blaise's Church CHURCH
(Crkva svetog Vlahe; Map p262; Luža Sq) Dedicated to the city's patron saint, this imposing church was built in 1715 in the ornate baroque style. The interior is notable for its marble altars and a 15th-century silver gilt statue of St Blaise, who is holding a scale model of pre-earthquake Dubrovnik.

★ Rector's Palace PALACE
(Knežev dvor; Map p262; 📞020-321 422; www.dumus.hr; Pred Dvorom 3; adult/child multimuseum pass 100/25KN; ⊙9am-6pm Apr-Oct, to 4pm Nov-Mar) Built in the late 15th century for the elected rector who governed Dubrovnik, this Gothic-Renaissance palace contains the rector's office, his private chambers, public halls, administrative offices and a dungeon. During his one-month term the rector was unable to leave the building without the permission of the senate. Today the palace has been turned into the **Cultural History Museum**, with artfully restored rooms, portraits, coats of arms and coins, evoking the glorious history of Dubrovnik.

The building retains a striking compositional unity despite being rebuilt many times. Notice the finely carved capitals and the ornate staircase in the atrium, which is often used for concerts during the Summer Festival. Also in the atrium is a statue of Miho Pracat, who bequeathed his wealth to the Republic and was the only commoner in the 1000 years of the Republic's existence to be honoured with a statue (1638). We may assume that the bequest was considerable.

Dulčić Masle Pulitika Gallery GALLERY
(Map p262; www.ugdubrovnik.hr; Držićeva poljana 1; adult/child multimuseum pass 100/25KN; ⊙9am-8pm Tue-Sun) This small offshoot of the city's main gallery unites three friends beyond the grave: local artists Ivo Dulčić, Antun Masle

Dubrovnik

and Đuro Pulitika, who all came to the fore in the 1950s and 1960s. There's a permanent collection featuring the trio's work on the lower floor, while the upper gallery is given over to temporary exhibitions by current artists.

Maritime Museum MUSEUM
(Pomorski muzej; Map p262; www.dumus.hr; Tvrđava Sv Ivana; adult/child multimuseum pass 100/25KN; ⊙9am-6pm Tue-Sun Apr-Oct, to 4pm Nov-Mar) Inside the vaulted chambers of Fort St John, this well-presented museum traces the history of navigation in Dubrovnik with ship models, maritime objects and paintings.

Cathedral of the Assumption CATHEDRAL
(Stolna Crkva Velike Gospe; Map p262; Držićeva poljana; ⊙8am-5pm Mon-Sat, 11am-5pm Sun)

DUBROVNIK & SOUTHERN DALMATIA DUBROVNIK

Built on the site of a 7th-century basilica, Dubrovnik's original cathedral was enlarged in the 12th century, supposedly funded by a gift from England's King Richard I, the Lionheart, who was saved from a shipwreck on the nearby island of Lokrum. Soon after the first cathedral was destroyed in the 1667 earthquake, work began on this, its baroque replacement, which was finished in 1713.

The cathedral is notable for its fine altars, especially the altar of St John Nepomuk, made of violet marble. The most striking of its religious paintings is the polyptych of the *Assumption of the Virgin,* hanging behind the main altar, made in the workshop of 16th-century Italian painter Titian.

It's difficult to see the Titian painting without purchasing a ticket to the treasury (20KN), located to the side of the main altar. Dripping in gold and silver, it contains relics of St Blaise as well as 138 other reliquaries largely made in the workshops of Dubrovnik's goldsmiths between the 11th and 17th centuries.

St Ignatius of Loyola Church   CHURCH

(Crkva svetog Ignacija Lojolskoga; Map p262; Uz Jezuite) Dramatically poised at the top of a broad flight of stairs, this Jesuit church was built in the baroque style between 1699 and 1725. Inside, frescoes display scenes from the life of St Ignatius, founder of the Society of Jesus. Abutting the church is the **Jesuit College**.

Ethnographic Museum   MUSEUM

(Etnografski muzej; Map p262; www.dumus.hr; Od Rupa 3; adult/child multimuseum pass 100/25KN; ⊙9am-4pm Wed-Mon) Inhabiting the 16th-century Rupe Granary, this museum contains mildly interesting exhibits relating to agriculture and local customs.

⊙ Surrounds

★ Lokrum   ISLAND

(www.lokrum.hr; adult/child incl boat 100/20KN; ⊙Apr-Nov) Lush Lokrum is a beautiful, forested island full of holm oaks, black ash, pines and olive trees, and an ideal escape from urban Dubrovnik. It's a popular swimming spot, although the beaches are rocky. To reach the nudist beach, head left from the ferry and follow the signs marked FKK; the rocks at the far end are Dubrovnik's de facto gay beach. Also popular is the small saltwater lake known as the **Dead Sea**.

The island's main hub is its large medieval **Benedictine monastery**, which houses a restaurant and a display on the island's history and the TV show *Game of Thrones,* which was partly filmed in Dubrovnik. This is your chance to pose imperiously in a reproduction of the Iron Throne. The monastery has a pretty cloister garden and a significant botanical garden, featuring giant agaves and palms from South Africa and Brazil.

Lokrum is only a 10-minute ferry ride from Dubrovnik's Old Harbour. Boats leave roughly hourly in summer (half-hourly in July and August). Make sure you check what time the last boat to the mainland departs. Note that no one can stay overnight and smoking is not permitted anywhere on the island.

Dubrovnik During the Homeland War   MUSEUM

(Dubrovnik u domovinskom ratu; Map p258; Fort Imperial, Srđ; adult/child 30/15KN; ⊙8am-10pm) Set inside a Napoleonic fort near the cable-car terminus, this permanent exhibition is dedicated to the siege of Dubrovnik during the 'Homeland War', as the 1990s war is dubbed in Croatia. The local defenders stationed inside this fort ensured the city wasn't captured. If the displays are understandably one-sided, they still provide in-depth coverage of the events, including plenty of video footage.

If the cable car's not operating, it's possible to drive up here on a rough narrow road off the main highway (follow the signs to Bosanka).

Museum of Modern & Contemporary Art   MUSEUM

(Umjetnička galerija; Map p258; ☑020-426 590; www.ugdubrovnik.hr; Frana Supila 23; adult/child multimuseum pass 100/25KN; ⊙9am-8pm Tue-Sun) Spread over three floors of a significant modernist building east of the old town, this excellent gallery showcases Croatian artists, particularly painter Vlaho Bukovac from nearby Cavtat. Head up to the sculpture terrace for excellent views.

---

❶ DUBROVNIK CARD

If you want to get through all the essential sights of Dubrovnik in one day, it's well worth buying the **Dubrovnik Card** (150KN). If you were already planning on walking the city walls (admission 120KN) and buying a museum pass (100KN), the Dubrovnik Card card makes a lot of sense. Plus it scores you free rides on buses and discounts at various restaurants and shops. The card is available from tourist offices, hotels and museums.

DUBROVNIK: DESTRUCTION & RECONSTRUCTION

From late 1991 to May 1992, images of the shelling of Dubrovnik dominated the news worldwide. While memories may have faded for those who watched it from afar, those who suffered through it will never forget – and the city of Dubrovnik is determined that visitors don't either. You'll see reminders of it on several plaques throughout the old town, especially at the main gates.

Shells struck 68% of the 824 buildings in the old town, leaving holes in two out of three tiled roofs. Building facades and the paving stones of streets and squares suffered 314 direct hits and there were 111 strikes on the great wall. Nine historic palaces were completely gutted by fire, while the Sponza Palace, Rector's Palace, St Blaise's Church, Franciscan Monastery and the carved fountains Amerling and Onofrio all sustained serious damage. The reconstruction bill was estimated at US$10 million. It was quickly decided that the repairs and rebuilding would be done with traditional techniques, using original materials whenever possible.

Dubrovnik has since regained most of its original grandeur. The town walls are once again intact, the gleaming marble streets are smoothly paved and famous monuments have been lovingly restored, with the help of an international brigade of specially trained stonemasons.

🏃 Activities

Swimming

Banje Beach   SWIMMING
(Map p258; www.banjebeach.eu; Frana Supila 10) Banje Beach is the closest beach to the old town, just beyond the 17th-century Lazareti (a former quarantine station) outside Ploče Gate. Although many people rent lounge chairs and parasols from the beach club, there's no problem with just flinging a towel on the beach if you can find a space.

Bellevue Beach   SWIMMING
(Map p258) The nicest beach within an easy walk of the old town is below the Hotel Bellevue. This pebbly cove is sheltered by high cliffs, which provide a platform for daredevil cliff divers but also cast a shadow over the beach by late afternoon – a boon on a scorching day. Public access is via a steep staircase off Kotorska street.

Lapad Bay   SWIMMING
(Map p258; Masarykov put bb) Dubrovnik's second-most popular (read crowded) beach after Banje sits at the apex of the Lapad horseshoe. There are plenty of diversions here, both in and out of the water, including a floating inflatable playground, slides and lots of cafes and bars.

Copacabana Beach   SWIMMING
(Map p258; Ivana Zajca bb) On the northern coast of Babin Kuk, this pebbly strip has lots of facilities including showers, loungers, an inflatable floating playground, a vine-covered restaurant, masseurs, and kayaks and jet skis for hire.

Porporela   SWIMMING
(Map p262) When Dubrovnik natives need to cool off, they head no further than the rocky stretch by the breakwater of the Old Harbour. People perch either on the pier or on the concrete terraces at the base of the walls.

Kayaking

Adriatic Kayak Tours   KAYAKING, CYCLING
(Map p262; ☑ 020-312 770; www.adriatickayaktours. com; Zrinsko Frankopanska 6; half day from 280KN) Offers sea-kayak excursions (from a half-day paddle to a weeklong trip), hiking and cycling tours, and Montenegro getaways (including rafting).

Outdoor Croatia   KAYAKING
(Map p258; ☑ 020-418 282; www.outdoorcroatia. com; Sv Križa 3; day trip 400KN) Rents kayaks and offers day trips around the Elafiti Islands, along with multiday excursions and kayaking-cycling combos.

Other Activities

★ Cable Car   CABLE CAR
(Žičara; Map p262; ☑ 020-414 355; www. dubrovnikcablecar.com; Petra Krešimira IV bb; return adult/child 120/50KN; ⊙ 9am-5pm Nov-Mar, to 9pm Apr, May, Sep & Oct, to midnight Jun-Aug) Dubrovnik's cable car whisks you from just north of the city walls to Mt Srđ in under four minutes. At the end of the line there's a stupendous perspective of the city from a lofty 405m, taking in the terracotta-tiled rooftops of the old town and the island of Lokrum, with the Adriatic and distant Elafiti Islands filling the horizon. Operations cease if there are high winds or a thunderstorm

Dubrovnik Old Town

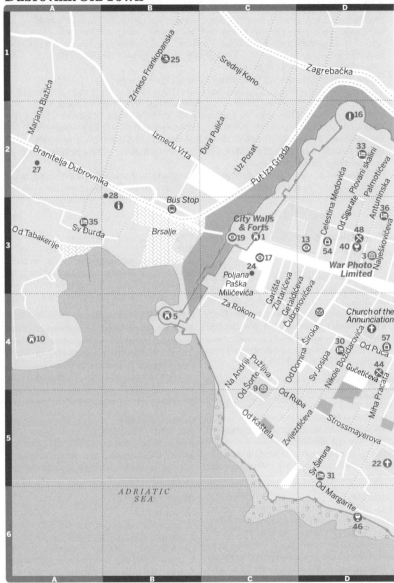

brewing. Telescopes help you pick out details far, far below. There's also a snack bar and a restaurant.

Blue Planet Diving DIVING
(Map p258; ☑091 89 90 973; www.blueplanet-diving.com; Dubrovnik Palace Hotel, Masarykov put

20; introductory dive €65, 2-dive boat trip €65, PADI Open Water course €345) There's some great diving around Dubrovnik, including at the wreck of the *Taranto,* an 1899 Italian merchant ship that hit a mine during WWII. Blue Planet's experienced crew offers recreational dives and courses.

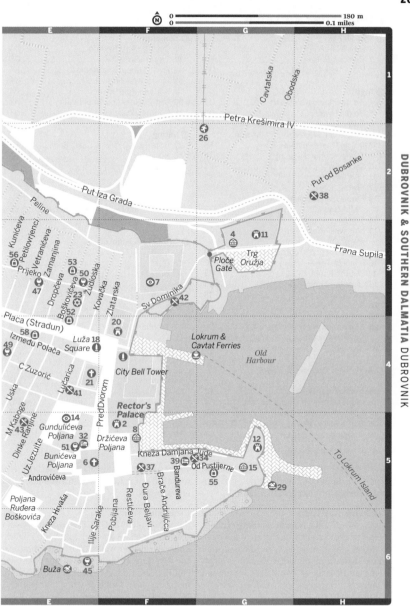

Buggy Safari Dubrovnik ADVENTURE

(Map p258; ☑ 098 16 69 730; www.buggydubrovnik.com; cable-car terminus, Mt Srđ; 45min trip 240KN; ⊙ 9am-7pm) Take a trip in a souped-up quad bike through the mountainous nether regions of Mt Srđ, visiting forts and a farm. Expect to come back caked in mud and dust.

☞ Tours

Dubrovnik Shore Tours TOURS

(Map p262; ☑ 095 80 33 587; www.dubrovnikshoretours.net; Branitelja Dubrovnika 15; prices on application) Offers tailored small-group tours; popular options include a trip to Mt Srđ and

Dubrovnik Old Town

Cavtat followed by a guided walk in the old town (four hours), or to the Pelješac Peninsula for wine and oysters (four hours).

Dubrovnik Day Tours TOURS
(📞091 44 55 846; www.dubrovnikdaytours.net; prices on application) Private day trips led by licensed guides to as far away as Korčula, Split, Kotor, Mostar and Sarajevo, as well as sightseeing and *Game of Thrones* tours around Dubrovnik.

Dubrovnik Boats TOURS
(📞098 757 890; www.dubrovnikboats.com; prices on application) Private speedboat tours to the Elafiti Islands and as far afield as Mljet and Korčula.

Dubrovnik Boat Rentals TOURS
(Map p258; 📞095 90 45 799; www.dubrovnikboatrentals.com; Anice Bošković 6; prices on application)

Offers half- or full-day private speedboat trips to Lokrum, Cavtat, the Elafiti Islands, Mljet and Korčula.

Dubrovnik Walks WALKING
(Map p262; 📞095 80 64 526; www.dubrovnikwalks.com; Brsalje bb; ☺Apr-Nov) Excellent English-language guided walks departing from near the Pile Gate, including 90-minute old-town (100KN) and *Game of Thrones* (150KN) tours, and a two-hour 'Walls & Wars' tour (190KN). No reservations necessary.

Adriatic Explore BUS
(Map p262; 📞020-323 400; www.adriatic-explore.com; Poljana Paska Miličevića 4; day trips 290-400KN; ☺8am-9pm Jun-Aug, to 4pm Sep-May) This travel agency offers day trips to Montenegro (360KN), Mostar (360KN), Korčula and Pelješac (390KN), the Elafiti Islands (290KN) and Mljet (390KN), along with quad-bike

safaris (300KN). They also rent out cars and boats, provide transfers, book private accommodation and arrange private tours.

Sunsail BOATING
(www.sunsail.com; ACI Marina Dubrovnik, Na skali bb, Mokošica; ⊘8am-4pm Mon-Fri, 9am-7pm Sat & Sun) An international operator offering bareboat and skippered charters from Dubrovnik and from Marina Agana, 40km west of Split.

✦✦ Festivals & Events

Feast of St Blaise CULTURAL
(⊘3 Feb) A city-wide bash marked by pageants and processions.

Carnival CARNIVAL
Venetian-style masked high jinks, held in the lead-up to Lent (usually February).

Dubrovnik Summer Festival CULTURAL
(Dubrovačke ljetne Igre; ☑020-326 100; www. dubrovnik-festival.hr; ⊘10 Jul-25 Aug) The most prestigious summer festival in Croatia presents a program of theatre, opera, concerts and dance on open-air stages throughout the city. Tickets are available online, from the festival office on Placa, and on site one hour before the beginning of each performance.

🛏 Sleeping

Dubrovnik is the most expensive city in the country, so expect to pay more for a room here (even hostels fall into our midrange category) and you should book well in advance, especially in summer. There's limited accommodation in the compact old town itself. If you want to combine a beach holiday with your city stay, consider the leafy Lapad peninsula, 4km west of the centre.

Old Town

Hostel Angelina HOSTEL €
(Map p262; ☑091 89 39 089; www.hostelangelina oldtowndubrovnik.com; Plovani skalini 17a; dm 208KN; ❋🛜) Hidden away in a quiet nook of the old town, this cute little hostel offers bunk rooms, a small guest kitchen and a bougainvillea-shaded terrace with memorable views over the rooftops. Plus you'll get a great glute workout every time you walk up the lane.

★ Karmen Apartments APARTMENT €€
(Map p262; ☑098 619 282; www.karmendu. com; Bandureva 1; apt from €95; ❋🛜) These four inviting apartments enjoy a great location a stone's throw from Ploče harbour. All have plenty of character with art, splashes

of colour, tasteful furnishings and books to browse. Apartment 2 has a little balcony while apartment 1 enjoys sublime port views. Book well ahead.

City Walls Hostel HOSTEL €€
(Map p262; ☑091 79 92 086; www.citywallshostel. com; Sv Šimuna 15; dm/r from 303/536KN; ❋@🛜) Tucked away by the city walls, this classic backpackers is warm and welcoming with a lively atmosphere. Downstairs there's a small kitchen and a space for socialising. Upstairs you'll find clean and simple dorms and a cosy double with a sea view.

Rooms Vicelić GUESTHOUSE €€
(Map p262; ☑095 52 78 933; www.rooms-vicelic. com; Antuninska 10; r from €100; ❋🛜) Situated on one of the steeply stepped old-town streets, this friendly, family-run place has four atmospheric stone-walled rooms with private bathrooms. Guests have use of a shared kitchenette with a microwave and a kettle.

Fresh* Sheets Kathedral GUESTHOUSE €€€
(Map p262; ☑091 89 67 509; www.freshsheets kathedral.com; Bunićeva poljana 6; r from €188; ❋🛜) Head up the well-worn stairs past corridors adorned with religious art to this friendly little guesthouse, right in the thick of things. The elegant rooms all have en suites, except for one that has a bathroom just across the corridor. Our favourite is spacious room 9, which looks out on Gundulić Sq. There's also a guest kitchen.

Celenga Apartments APARTMENT €€€
(Map p262; ☑099 80 70 760; www.celengaapart ments.com; Sv Josipa 13; apt from €124; ❋🛜🏊) Located in a historic house in one of the quieter old-town lanes, Celenga has five well-furnished apartments ranging from studios to a two-bedroom penthouse. They also rent a whole three-storey house nearby.

🛏 Viktorija

★ Villa Dubrovnik HOTEL €€€
(☑020-500 300; www.villa-dubrovnik.hr; Vlaha Bukovca 6; r from €581; 🅿❋🛜🏊) Gazing endlessly at the old town and Lokrum from its prime waterfront position, this elegant low-slung boutique hotel gleams white against a backdrop of honey-coloured stone. The windows retract completely to bring the indoor pool into the outdoors, but sunseekers can laze on a lounger by the sea or commandeer a day bed in the rooftop prosciutto-and-wine bar.

Continued on page 268

DUBROVNIK & SOUTHERN DALMATIA DUBROVNIK

Dubrovnik's Old Town

Nothing quite prepares you for your first sight of Dubrovnik's Old Town. From a distance, the compact nest of terracotta roofs enclosed by honey-coloured walls jutting out into the cerulean sea is overwhelmingly picturesque. The effect doesn't diminish as you pass through the ancient gates and stride forth on the marbled lanes.

JASON MAEHL / GETTY IMAGES ©

RASPU / GETTY IMAGES ©

1. Walled City

Enjoy a stroll around the city's historic stone walls and walkways (p256).

2. Views over the Old Town

Take in stellar views of the Old Town and Adriatic Sea from the city's fort lookouts (p256).

3. Old Town Rooftops

Admire the view of the Old Town rooftops, which were replaced with new terracotta after shelling damage in the 1990s (p256).

4. Street Dining

Relax at an outdoor table and enjoy local cuisine at an Old Town restaurant (p268).

JOSEP BERNAT SANCHEZ MONER / GETTY IMAGES ©

Continued from page 265

Pile

Apartments & Rooms Biličić GUESTHOUSE €
(Map p258; ☑098 802 111; www.dubrovnik-online.
net/apartments_bilicic; Priuežna 2; r/apt from €50/
100; ✳ ☎) A highly atmospheric place to stay,
partly due to the green fingers of the friendly
host, whose subtropical garden is a delight.
Rooms are bright, clean and pleasant, though
bathrooms are not en suite. There's a guest
kitchen on the terrace.

★**Villa Klaić** B&B €€
(Map p258; ☑091 73 84 673; www.villaklaic-
dubrovnik.com; Šumetska 9; s/d from €70/90; P ✳
☎ ✖) Just off the main coast road, high above
the old town, this outstanding guesthouse
offers comfortable modern rooms and wonderful hospitality courtesy of the owner,
Milo Klaić. Extras include a small swimming
pool, continental breakfast, free pick-ups and
free beer!

MirÓ Studio Apartments APARTMENT €€€
(Map p262; ☑099 42 42 442; www.mirostudio
apartmentsdubrovnik.com; Sv Đurđa 16; apt €140;
✳ ☎) Located in a quiet residential nook
only metres from the sea, hidden between
the old-town walls and Fort Lawrence, this
schmick complex is an absolute gem. The
decor marries ancient stone walls and whitewashed ceiling beams with design features
such as uplighting, contemporary bathrooms
and sliding glass partitions.

Lapad

Solitudo CAMPGROUND €
(Map p258; ☑020-448 686; www.camping-adriatic.
com; Vatroslava Lisinskog 60; sites per adult/child/
pitch from 81/45/191KN, units from €67; ☺Apr-Nov;
P ☎ ✖ ✤) Solitudo is a strange name for a
giant campground that's full to the gills in
summer, but to its credit it has bright, modern shower blocks, it's close to beaches and
guests have access to a pool at a nearby hotel.
Tenters will find the ground hard and rocky –
or muddy and rocky when it rains.

Apartments Silva GUESTHOUSE €€
(Map p258; ☑098 244 639; silva.dubrovnik@yahoo.
com; Kardinala Stepinca 62; r/apt from €90/120;
P ✳ ☎) Lush Mediterranean foliage lines
the terraces of this lovely hillside complex, a
short hop up from the beach at Lapad. The
rooms are comfortable and well priced, but
best of all is the spacious top-floor apartment
(sleeping five).

Begović Boarding House GUESTHOUSE €€
(Map p258; ☑020-435 191; www.begovic-boarding-
house.com; Primorska 17; dm/r 256/527KN; P ✳
@ ☎) This welcoming long-standing family-
run place has simple, tidy rooms and a communal terrace with amazing views. The
apartments have kitchenettes and the other
rooms have use of a guest kitchen.

★**Hotel Kompas** HOTEL €€€
(Map p258; ☑020-299 000; www.adriaticluxury
hotels.com; Kardinala Stepinca 21; r/ste from
€210/542; P ✳ ☎ ✖) Right by the beach at
Lapad, this big hotel has more personality
that you'd expect for its size, due in large part
to interesting art, slick design and charming
staff. The breakfast buffet is excellent and the
outdoor pool is pleasantly cool on a scorching day (the indoor one's warmer).

Hotel Bellevue HOTEL €€€
(Map p258; ☑020-330 000; www.hotel-bellevue.
hr; Pera Čingrije 7; r from €342; P ✳ @ ☎ ✖) Positioned on a cliff near the very beginning
of the Lapad peninsula (only a 20-minute
walk west of Pile Gate), this classy hotel has
modern decor (despite its dated smoky-glass
facade), excellent facilities and a top-notch
restaurant. Best of all is the direct lift access
to the gem of a cove below.

Royal Princess Hotel HOTEL €€€
(Map p258; ☑020-440 100; www.hotelroyalprin
cess.com; Kardinala Stepinca 31; ste from €450;
P ✳ @ ☎ ✖) The classiest sister in a family
of resort-style hotels grouped on a pretty
stretch of Lapad Bay, the Royal Princess is
deliciously low slung and plush. There's an
old-fashioned luxurious feel to the suites, all
of which have balconies.

✖ Eating

There are some very average restaurants in
Dubrovnik, so choose carefully. Many places
ride on the assumption that you're here just
for a day (as many cruise-ship passengers
are) and that you won't be coming back.
Prices are also the highest in Croatia. That
said there are some great eateries scattered
around the old town, Lapad and Gruž.

✖ Old Town

Oliva Pizzeria PIZZA €
(Map p262; ☑020-324 594; www.pizza-oliva.com;
Lučarica 5; mains 41-86KN; ☺10am-midnight)
There are a few token pasta dishes on the
menu, but this attractive little place is really
all about pizza. And the pizza is worthy of

the attention. Grab a seat on the street and tuck in.

★ Nishta
VEGETARIAN €€

(Map p262; ☑020-322 088; www.nishtarestau rant.com; Prijeko 29; mains 77-85KN; ⊙11.30am-11.30pm; 🛜✍) The popularity of this tiny old-town eatery (expect to queue) is testament not just to the paucity of options for vegetarians and vegans in Croatia but to the excellent, imaginative food produced within. Alongside the expected curries, pastas and vege burgers, the menu delivers more unusual delicious options such as eggplant tartare, 'tempehritos' and pasta-free zucchini 'spaghetti'.

Taj Mahal
BOSNIAN €€

(Map p262; ☑020-323 221; www.tajmahal-dubrov nik.com; Nikole Gučetićeva 2; mains 80-165KN; ⊙10am-2am) This tiny restaurant is like an Aladdin's cave, with an interior loaded with Ottoman decorations. Order the *džingis kan* (dried beef, sausage, peppers and spring onions with curdled milk) and get a taste of everything Bosnian, or feast on spicy *sudžukice* (beef sausage).

Konoba Ribar
DALMATIAN €€

(Map p262; ☑020-323 194; Kneza Damjana Jude bb; mains 77-122KN; ⊙10am-midnight; 🛜) Serving local food the way locals like it, at more or less local prices, this little family-run eatery is a blissfully untouristy choice. They don't attempt anything fancy or clever, just big serves of traditional favourites such as risotto and stuffed squid. It's set in a little lane pressed hard up against the city walls.

Bota Šare Oyster & Sushi Bar
SUSHI €€

(Map p262; ☑020-324 034; www.bota-sare.hr; Od Pustijerne bb; oysters/sushi per piece from 14/15KN; ⊙noon-10pm Tue-Sun) It's fair to say that most Croatians don't have much of an interest in or aptitude for Asian cooking, yet fresh seafood is something that they understand very well, as this little place demonstrates. Grab a terrace table with a view of the cathedral and tuck into Ston oysters (fresh or tempura style) and surprisingly good sushi and sashimi.

★ Restaurant 360°
MODERN EUROPEAN €€€

(Map p262; ☑020-322 222; www.360dubrovnik. com; Sv Dominika bb; mains 240-290KN, 5-course degustation 780KN; ⊙6.30-11pm) Dubrovnik's

---

GAME OF THRONES LOCATIONS

Dubrovnik is like a fantasy world for most people, but fans of *Game of Thrones* have more reason to indulge in flights of fancy than most, as a large chunk of the immensely popular TV series was filmed here. While Split and Šibenik were also used as locations, Dubrovnik has featured the most prominently, standing in for the cities of King's Landing and Qarth. If you fancy taking your own Walk of Shame through the streets of Westeros, here are some key spots:

Fort Lawrence (p256) King's Landing's famous Red Keep. Cersei farewelled her daughter Myrcella from the little harbour beneath it.

City Walls (p256) Tyrion Lannister commanded the defence of King's Landing from the seaward-facing walls during the Battle of the Blackwater.

Minčeta Tower (p256) The exterior of Qarth's House of Undying.

Rector's Palace (p259) The atrium featured as the palace of the Spice King of Qarth – they didn't even bother moving the statue!

Sv Dominika street The street and staircase outside the Dominican Monastery (p257) were used for various King's Landing market scenes.

Uz Jezuite The stairs connecting the St Ignatius of Loyola Church (p260) to **Gundulić Square** (Gundulićeva poljana; Map p262) were the starting point for Cersei Lannister's memorable naked penitential walk. The walk continued down Stradun.

Gradac Park The site of the Purple Wedding feast, where King Joffrey finally got his comeuppance.

Ethnographic Museum (p260) Littlefinger's brothel.

Lokrum (p260) The reception for Daenerys in Qarth was held in the monastery cloister.

Trsteno Arboretum (p275) The Red Keep gardens, where the Tyrells chatted and plotted endlessly during seasons three and four.

glitziest restaurant offers fine dining at its finest, with flavoursome, beautifully presented, creative cuisine, and slick, professional service. The setting is unrivalled, on top of the city walls with tables positioned so you can peer through the battlements over the harbour.

Restaurant Dubrovnik EUROPEAN €€€
(Map p262; ✆020-324 810; www.restorandubrovnik.com; Marojice Kaboge 5; mains 105-210KN; ⊙noon-midnight) One of Dubrovnik's most upmarket restaurants has a wonderfully unstuffy setting, occupying a covered rooftop terrace hidden among the venerable stone buildings of the old town. A strong French influence pervades a menu full of decadent and rich dishes, such as confit duck and plump Adriatic lobster tail served on homemade pasta.

✖ Ploče

Horizont EUROPEAN €€€
(Map p262; ✆099 69 76 729; www.restaurant-horizont.com; Put od Bosanke 8; mains 84-169KN; ⊙noon-2pm & 6-11pm) Seriously fashionable locals rub shoulders with tourists at this chic restaurant, just outside of the old town. The most sought-after tables are out on the lane, although it's pretty smart inside too, with stone walls and a bright turquoise bar. The bistro-style dishes on offer (lamb rack, pork fillet, chicken ballotine, fish of various sorts) are good if not exceptional.

✖ Lapad

★Pantarul MODERN EUROPEAN €€
(Map p258; ✆020-333 486; www.pantarul.com; Kralja Tomislava 1; mains 70-128KN; ⊙noon-4pm & 6pm-midnight) This breezy bistro serves exceptional homemade bread, pasta and risotto, alongside the likes of pork belly, steaks, ox cheeks, burgers and a variety of fish dishes. There's a fresh modern touch to most dishes but chef Ana-Marija Bujić knows her way around traditional Dalmatian cuisine too – she's got her own cookbook to prove it.

★Shizuku JAPANESE €€
(Map p258; ✆020-311 493; www.facebook.com/ShizukuDubrovnik; Kneza Domagoja 1f; mains 65-99KN; ⊙noon-midnight Tue-Sun; ☎) Tucked away in a residential area between the harbour and Lapad Bay, this charming little restaurant has an appealing front terrace and an interior decorated with silky draperies, paper lampshades and colourful umbrellas.

The Japanese owners will be in the kitchen, preparing authentic sushi, sashimi, udon and gyoza. Wash it all down with Japanese beer or sake.

Atlantic Kitchen MEDITERRANEAN €€€
(Map p258; ✆020-435 726; www.atlantic-kitchen.com; Kardinala Stepinca 42; mains 89-159KN; ⊙noon-10pm) With its checked tablecloths and handwritten blackboard menus, there's a distinctly French feel to this breezy bistro – although the food meanders from France to Spain, Italy and Croatia. The seafood is particularly good.

✖ Gruž

★Amfora INTERNATIONAL €€€
(Map p258; ✆020-419 419; www.amforadubrovnik.com; Obala Stjepana Radića 26; mains 145-185KN; ⊙noon-4pm & 7-11pm) From the street, Amfora looks like just another local cafe-bar, but the real magic happens at the six-table restaurant at the rear. Dalmatian favourites such as *pašticada* (stew with gnocchi) and black risotto sit alongside fusion dishes such as swordfish sashimi, veal kofte, and miso fish soup.

⬤ Drinking & Entertainment

You won't go thirsty in Dubrovnik – the city has swanky lounge bars, Irish pubs, bars clinging to cliffs, sophisticated wine bars and lots and lots of Croatian-style cafe-bars. And that's just the old town.

⬤ Old Town

★Bard BAR
(Map p262; off Ilije Sarake; ⊙9am-3am) The more upmarket and slick of two cliff bars pressed up against the seaward side of the city walls, this one is lower on the rocks and has a shaded terrace where you can lose a day quite happily, mesmerised by the Adriatic vistas. At night the surrounding stone is lit in ever-changing colours.

Buža BAR
(Map p262; off Od Margarite; ⊙8am-2am) Finding this ramshackle bar-on-a-cliff feels like a real discovery as you duck and dive around the city walls and finally see the entrance tunnel. However, Buža's no secret – it gets insanely busy, especially around sunset. Wait for a space on one of the concrete platforms, grab a cool drink in a plastic cup and enjoy the vibe and views.

D'vino WINE BAR
(Map p262; ☑020-321 130; www.dvino.net; Pal-motićeva 4a; ☺10am-late; ☎) If you're interested in sampling top-notch Croatian wine, this up-market little bar is the place to go. As well as a large and varied wine list, it offers themed tasting flights (multiple wine tastings; three wines for 50KN) accompanied by a thorough description by the knowledgable staff.

Buzz Bar BAR
(Map p262; ☑020-321 025; www.thebuzzbar.wix site.com/buzz; Prijeko 21; ☺8am-2am) Appropri-ately named, this buzzy little bar is rocky and relaxed, with craft beer and cocktails being the main poisons – aside from those being exhaled by the recalcitrant smokers in the corner.

Matuško WINE BAR
(Map p262; www.facebook.com/WineBarMatusko; Prijeko 6; ☺10am-2am) An outpost of the ac-claimed Pelješac Peninsula winery (p280), this swanky little wine bar offers an oppor-tunity to sample some of Croatia's best reds in an atmospheric, almost cave-like setting.

Troubadour BAR
(Map p262; ☑020-323 796; Bunićeva poljana 2; ☺7.30am-2am; ☎) Tucked into a corner be-hind the cathedral, Troubadour looks pretty nondescript during the day. That all changes on summer nights, when jazz musicians set up outside and quickly draw the crowds.

Gaffe IRISH PUB
(Map p262; www.facebook.com/irishpubthegaffe; Miha Pracata 4; ☺9am-1am; ☎) The busiest place in town when there's rugby on, this Croatian-run Irish joint has a comfortably pub-like interior and a covered side terrace.

Revelin CLUB
(Map p262; www.clubrevelin.com; Sv Dominika 3; ☺11pm-6am daily Jun-Sep, Fri & Sat Oct-May) Housed within the vast vaulted chambers of Fort Revelin, this is Dubrovnik's most impres-sive club space, with famous international DJs dropping in during summer.

Ploče

Banje Beach BAR, CLUB
(Map p258; ☑020-412 220; www.banjebeach.eu; Frana Supila 8; ☺10am-6am May-Sep) By day this upmarket outfit on Banje Beach rents out sun loungers and umbrellas and serves drinks to the bathers who come here to relax and rehy-drate. Later on, it morphs into a cocktail bar and then a club as the night progresses. It can be deathly quiet after the beach-goers depart and before the clubbers descend.

Victoria COCKTAIL BAR
(Map p258; ☑020-440 588; Frana Supila 14; ☺6pm-midnight) Set in blissful gardens with a tinkling fountain, the terrace bar of the Villa Oršula is a wonderful place to dress up, sip cocktails and watch the sun as it sets over the old town. On summer nights there's of-ten live musicians playing smooth jazz.

Lazareti ARTS CENTRE
(Map p258; www.lazareti.com; Frana Supila 8) Housed in a former quarantine centre, Laza-reti hosts cinema nights, club nights, live mu-sic, folk dancing, art exhibitions and pretty much all the best things in town.

Pile

Art BAR
(Map p258; Branitelja Dubrovnika 25; ☺9am-mid-night Mon-Thu, to 2am Fri-Sun) Dubrovnik's most bohemian cafe-bar has seats constructed from bathtubs, tables made from washing-machine agitators, brightly coloured walls, funky mu-sic (James Brown when we last visited) and terraces front and rear.

Lapad

Cave Bar More BAR
(Map p258; www.hotel-more.hr; Hotel More, Šetal-ište Nika i Meda Pucića; ☺10am-midnight) This little beach bar serves coffee, snacks and cocktails to bathers reclining by the daz-zlingly clear waters of Lapad Bay, but that's not the half of it – the main bar is set in an actual cave. Cool off beneath the stalactites in the side chamber, where a glass floor ex-poses a water-filled cavern.

Shopping

Portrait FASHION & ACCESSORIES
(Map p262; www.portrait.hr; Od Puča; ☺10am-10pm) The phrase 'cool souvenir T-shirt' would seem to be an oxymoron, yet this upmar-ket boutique nails it with their range of Dubrovnik-themed tees by Croatian designer Matija Čop, whose work has featured in a Lady Gaga video. They also sell a range of funky jewellery and sunglasses.

Gundulić Square Market MARKET
(Map p262; Gundulićeva poljana; ☺6am-1pm Mon-Sat) Stallholders sell mainly produce, lo-cal artisanal products and craft at this open-air market.

Algoritam
BOOKS

(Map p262; www.algoritam.hr; Placa 8; ⊙9am-9pm Mon-Sat, 10am-1pm Sun) A good bookshop with a wide range of English-language books and a variety of guides on Dubrovnik and Croatia.

Uje
FOOD & DRINKS

(Map p262; www.uje.hr; Placa 5; ⊙9am-11pm) Uje specialises in olive oils – among the best is Brachia, from the island of Brač – along with a wide range of other locally produced epicurean delights, including some excellent jams (the lemon spread is divine), pickled capers, local herbs and spices, honey, figs in honey, chocolate, wine and *rakija* (grappa).

Duchkas
DESIGN

(Map p262; www.duchkas.com; Od Pustijerne 1; ⊙9am-8pm) Everything in this quirky little store is made and designed in Croatia. We particularly like the range of fridge magnets in the shapes of the Dalmatian islands and the T-shirts featuring famous intellectuals, such as Nikola Tesla and Ivo Andrić.

Medusa
GIFTS & SOUVENIRS

(Map p262; ☑020-322 004; www.medusa.hr; Prijeko 18; ⊙9am-9pm) This self-described 'charming shop for charming people' sells locally produced soap, flavoured salt, *rakija*, neckties, objects made from Brač stone, art prints, chocolate and toiletries.

Dubrovnik Treasures
JEWELLERY

(Map p262; ☑020-321 098; Celestina Medovića 2; ⊙9am-10pm Mar-Nov) An Aussie-born, Croatian-bred, locally based brother-and-sister team are behind this treasure trove of very cool, well-crafted, handmade, contemporary jewellery.

Dubrovnik City Shop
GIFTS & SOUVENIRS

(Map p262; www.dubrovnikcityshop.com; Boškovićeva 7; ⊙9am-9pm) Call in for your essential *Game of Thrones* merchandise – or just to pose on the Iron Throne and get a selfie with the Peter Dinklage statue.

❶ Information

Dubrovnik's tourist board has offices in **Pile** (Map p262; ☑020-312 011; www.tzdubrovnik.hr; Brsalje 5; ⊙8am-9pm Jun-Sep, 8am-7pm Mon-Sat, 9am-3pm Sun Oct-May), **Gruž** (Map p258; ☑020-417 983; www.tzdubrovnik.hr; Obala Pape Ivana Pavla II 1; ⊙8am-9pm Jun-Sep, to 3pm Mon-Sat Oct-May) and **Lapad** (Map p258; ☑020-437 460; www.tzdubrovnik.hr; Kralja Tomislava 7; ⊙8am-8pm Mon-Fri, 9am-noon & 5-8pm Sat & Sun Jun-Sep) that dispense maps, information and advice.

Dubrovnik General Hospital (Opća bolnica Dubrovnik; ☑020-431 777; www.bolnica-du.hr; Dr Roka Mišetića 2; ⊙emergency department 24hr) On the southern edge of the Lapad peninsula.

Post Office (Map p262; www.posta.hr; Široka 8; ⊙8am-9pm Mon-Sat May-Oct, 8am-7pm Mon-Fri, to noon Sat Nov-Apr)

Travel Corner (☑020-492 313; Obala Stjepana Radića 40; internet per hr 25KN, left luggage 2hr 10KN then per hr 4KN, per day 40KN; ⊙9am-8pm Mon-Sat, 9am-4.30pm Sun) This handy one-stop shop has a left-luggage service and internet terminals, dispenses tourist information, books excursions and sells Kapetan Luka ferry tickets.

❶ Getting There & Away

AIR

Dubrovnik Airport (DBV, Zračna luka Dubrovnik; ☑020-773 100; www.airport-dubrovnik.hr) is in Čilipi, 19km southeast of Dubrovnik. Both Croatia Airlines and British Airways fly to Dubrovnik all year round. In summer they're joined by dozens of other airlines flying seasonal routes and charter flights.

Croatia Airlines has domestic flights from Zagreb (year round), Split and Osijek (both May to October only). From July to October, European Coastal Air also has seaplane flights to Lumbarda (Korčula) and Split Harbour. Trade Air has seasonal flights to/from Rijeka and Split.

BOAT

The **ferry terminal** (Map p258; Obala Pape Ivana Pavla II 1) is in Gruž, 3km northwest of the old town. Ferries for Lokrum and Cavtat (Map p262) depart from the Old Harbour.

Four catamarans per day with **Jadrolinija** (Map p258; ☑020-418 000; www.jadrolinija.hr; Obala Stjepana Radića 40) head to Koločep (23KN, 30 minutes), Lopud (23KN, 55 minutes) and Suđurađ on Šipan (23KN, 1¼ hours); an additional four to 10 slower car ferries per week also head to Lopud (23KN, one hour) and Suđurađ (23KN, 1½ hours). From July to mid-September, there's also a daily catamaran to Korčula (120KN, 2¼ hours), Hvar (190KN, four hours) and Bol on Brač (190KN, 5¼ hours). From April to October, two to six car ferries per week travel between Dubrovnik and Bari, Italy (passenger/car from €44/59, 10 hours).

G&V Line (Map p258; ☑060 100 000; www.gv-line.hr) has a daily catamaran to Šipanska Luka on Šipan (35KN, 50 minutes) and to Sobra on Mljet (60KN, 1¼ hours). Between June and September a second boat heads directly to Sobra and on to Polače on Mljet (70KN, two hours). In July and August some of these services continue on to Korčula (90KN, 2½ hours) and Ubli on Lastovo (95KN, four hours). Tickets can be purchased from their kiosk by the harbour 30 minutes prior to departure (an hour prior in July and August).

BUSES FROM DUBROVNIK

DESTINATION	COST (KN)	DURATION (HR)	DAILY SERVICES
Kotor (Montenegro)	124	2½	6
Ljubljana (Slovenia)	300	13	2
Mostar (Bosnia & Hercegovina)	107	3½	3
Pula	383	15	1
Rijeka	331-411	12-13¼	4
Sarajevo (Bosnia & Hercegovina)	175	6½	2
Split	130	4½	21
Trieste (Italy)	459	14¾	1
Zadar	213	7½-8½	5
Zagreb	219	9¼-11¾	10

From June to September **Kapetan Luka** (Krilo; ☑ 021-872 877; www.krilo.hr) has a daily fast boat to/from Pomena on Mljet (80KN, 1¼ hours), Korčula (120KN, 1¾ hours), Hvar (190KN, three hours), Milna on Brač (190KN, 3¾ hours) and Split (190KN, 4¼ hours), dropping to four times per week in May and three per week in October.

BUS

Buses from **Dubrovnik Bus Station** (Map p258; ☑ 060 305 070; Obala Pape Ivana Pavla II 44a; ☎) can be crowded, so book tickets in advance in summer. The station has toilets and a *garderoba* for storing luggage (5KN for the first hour then 1.50KN per hour).

Split–Dubrovnik buses pass briefly through Bosnian territory, so keep your passport handy for border-crossing points.

Departure times are detailed at www.libertas dubrovnik.hr.

ⓘ Getting Around

TO/FROM THE AIRPORT

Atlas runs the airport bus service (40KN, 30 minutes), timed to run around flights. Buses to Dubrovnik stop at the Pile Gate and the bus station; buses to the airport pick up from the bus station and from the bus stop near the cable car.

City buses 11, 27 and 38 also stop at the airport but are less frequent and take longer (28KN, four daily, no Sunday service).

Allow up to 280KN for a taxi to Dubrovnik.

CAR

The entire old town is a pedestrian area, public transport is good and parking is expensive, so you're better off not hiring a car until you're ready to leave the city. All of the street parking surrounding the old town is metered from May to October (40KN per hour). Further out it drops to 20KN or 10KN per hour.

It's a short walk down from the covered **Ilijina Glavica Car Park** (Map p258; ☑ 091

23 00 366; Zagrebačka bb; per hr/day/week 35/420/2100KN; ⊘24hr) to the old town, but a hard slog back up. Note that the daily and weekly rates are for prepay only; the machines don't make this clear and we've witnessed people being stung with hefty bills as a result.

All of the usual hire-car companies are represented at the airport and most also have city branches.

PUBLIC TRANSPORT

Dubrovnik has a superb bus service; buses run frequently and generally on time. The key tourist routes run until after 2am in summer, so if you're staying in Lapad, there's no need to rush home. The fare is 15KN if you buy from the driver, and 12KN if you buy a ticket at a *tisak* (news-stand). Timetables are available at www. libertasdubrovnik.hr.

To get to the old town from the bus station, take buses 1a, 1b, 3 or 8. To get to Lapad, take bus 7.

From the main bus stop (Map p262) at Pile Gate, take bus 4, 5, 6 or 9 to get to Lapad.

AROUND DUBROVNIK

Dubrovnik is an excellent base for day trips to the surrounding region – and even in the surrounding countries of Montenegro and Bosnia. You can hop over to the Elafiti Islands for a day of peaceful sunbathing, wander through the gardens at Trsteno or pop down to Cavtat for sights and swimming. Alternatively, Cavtat makes a cheaper and quieter base from which to explore Dubrovnik.

Cavtat

POP 2160

Without Cavtat, there'd be no Dubrovnik, as it was refugees from the original Cavtat who

WORTH A TRIP

CROSS-BORDER JAUNTS

Dubrovnik is an easy bus ride away from **Montenegro** and the towns of Herceg Novi, Kotor and Budva. All three have wonderful historic centres, with curving marble streets and impressive architecture. If you really want to take your time and explore the region, you should hire a car, but you can also get there by public bus or on a tour. The checkpoint can be very slow in summer; allow two hours to get to Herceg Novi by bus and a further hour to reach Kotor. Citizens of most European nations, Australia, New Zealand, Canada and the US don't need a visa to enter Montenegro; other nationalities should check with their embassy.

Buses also go to **Mostar**, giving you a chance to glance at its emblematic bridge and dip your toe into the world of Bosnia and Hercegovina. It's possible to go by public transport, but easier on an organised day excursion in private minibuses (around 380KN); enquire at local travel agencies. These leave around 8am and travel via the incredibly pretty fortified village of Počitelj, arriving in Mostar around 11.30am. After a (typically very brief) guided tour you'll be left to your own devices until 3pm – which doesn't leave a lot of time to have lunch and explore the town. Mostar is still divided along Croat–Bosnian lines (with the river acting as border), but most of the historic sights are on the Bosnian side.

established the city of Dubrovnik in 614. But Cavtat is interesting in itself. A lot more 'local' than Dubrovnik – read, not flooded by tourists on a daily basis – it has its own charm. Wrapped around a very pretty harbour that's bordered by beaches and backed by a curtain of imposing hills, the setting is lovely.

Cavtat's most famous personality is the painter Vlaho Bukovac (1855–1922), one of the foremost exponents of Croatian modernism. His paintings are liberally distributed around the town's main sights.

History

Originally a Greek settlement called Epidaurus, Cavtat became a Roman colony around 228 BC and was later destroyed during the 7th-century Slavic invasions. Throughout most of the Middle Ages it was part of the Republic of Dubrovnik and shared the cultural and economic life of the capital city.

⊙ Sights

Račić Family Mausoleum   MONUMENT
(Mauzolej obitelji Račić; 10KN; ⊙10am-5pm Mon-Sat Apr-Nov) Built in 1921, this beautiful white stone tomb is the handiwork of pre-eminent Croatian sculptor Ivan Meštrović. It's located in the town cemetery, in the wooded area near the tip of the peninsula; take the path leading up from the monastery.

Bukovac House   MUSEUM
(Kuća Bukovac; ☑020-478 646; www.kuca-bukovac.hr; Bukovćeva 5; 20KN; ⊙9am-1pm & 4-8pm Tue-Sat, 4-8pm Sun May-Oct, 9am-5pm Tue-Sat, 2-5pm Sun Nov-Apr) The house where Vlaho Bukovac was born and raised has been converted into

an interesting little museum devoted to his work. The early-19th-century architecture provides a fitting backdrop to his mementoes and paintings. The house itself was actually the artist's first canvas – his earliest painting, a frieze of animals running around the walls, was only uncovered in 1998.

**Our Lady of the
Snow Monastery**   MONASTERY
(Samostan Snježne Gospe; Šetalište Rata bb) The church attached to this Franciscan Monastery (founded 1484) is worth a look for some notable early Renaissance paintings and a wonderful Bukovac work above the entrance to the sanctuary, depicting the Madonna and Child gazing at the Cavtat skyline at sunset.

St Nicholas' Church   CHURCH
(Crkva svetog Nikole; Obala Ante Starčevića bb) Peek inside this 15th-century church to view its wooden altars and Bukovac paintings.

🛏 Sleeping

Castelletto   B&B €€
(☑020-479 547; www.dubrovnikexperience.com; Frana Laureana 22; r 494-722KN; 🅿❄@🛜🏊) This very well-run family-owned place has 13 spacious rooms in a converted villa. All have tea- and coffee-making facilities, a fridge and satellite TV, and some have balconies and sweeping bay views. Airport transfers are free.

Fox Apartments   APARTMENT €€
(☑091 89 50 401; www.dubrovnikfox.com; Stjepana Radića 49; apt €69-105; 🅿❄🛜) Situated in a residential street, this three-storey block has three small apartments and one large unit, all with sea views and balconies. It's owned

by a young Canadian-Croat couple who run an English-language school from the large apartment in winter; the other three are available all year round.

Villa Ivy   APARTMENT €€€
(020-478 328; www.villaivy-croatia.com; SS Kranjčevića 52; apt from 960KN; P ❄ ≋) If the location seems a little odd, tucked away in a scruffy neighbourhood at the top of the town, it all makes sense once you see the sea views from the pool terrace. Plus, it's quiet. The four apartments within the apricot-hued block are modern and very comfortable. They only accept weeklong bookings in July and August.

✕ Eating

Galija   SEAFOOD, DALMATIAN €€
(020-478 566; www.galija.hr; Vuličelićeva 1; mains 70-180KN; ⊙noon-10pm; ✐) This long-established restaurant has a sea-facing terrace shaded by pines and an atmospheric interior of exposed stone walls. The menu majors in seafood – try the excellent platter (with fish, scallops, lobster, shrimps and scampi).

★ Bugenvila   MODERN EUROPEAN €€€
(020-479 949; www.bugenvila.eu; Obala Ante Starčevića 9; mains lunch 80-90KN, dinner 140-270KN; ⊙noon-4pm & 6-10pm; 🛜) The coolest place on Cavtat's seafront strip – with brightly painted signs outside and colourful art on bare stone walls upstairs – Bugenvila is also the town's culinary trendsetter. Local ingredients are showcased in an adventurous and highly delicious menu. Visit at lunchtime to take advantage of the three-course specials (145KN to 165KN).

❶ Information

Post Office (020-362 845; www.posta.hr; Trumbićev put 10; ⊙8am-9pm Mon-Fri, 8am-noon & 6-9pm Sat mid-Jun–mid-Sep, 7am-7pm Mon-Fri, 8am-noon Sat mid-Sep–mid-Jun)

Tourist Office (020-479 025; www.visit.cavtat-konavle.com; Zidine 6; ⊙8am-8pm Mon-Sat, to 2pm Sun Apr-Oct, to 3pm Mon-Fri Nov-Mar) Very well stocked with leaflets and a good colour map.

❶ Getting There & Away

BOAT

From June to September there are 11 sailings a day between Dubrovnik's Old Harbour and Cavtat (one way/return 50/80KN, 45 minutes). For the rest of the year this reduces to three to five a day, weather dependent.

BUS

Bus 10 runs roughly half-hourly to Cavtat (25KN, 25 minutes) from Dubrovnik's bus station; the last buses return at 12.45am.

Konavle

After the dry and rugged coast around Dubrovnik, the lush fields and orderly vineyards of Konavle are quite a surprise. Here, in this hidden nook between the Bosnian and Montenegrin borders, east of Cavtat, the mountains have taken half a step back, providing a dramatic backdrop to the fertile agricultural region. It's best known for *malvasija,* an endemic grape producing a very pleasant white wine.

There's a wonderful restaurant in the village of Gruda, reason alone to make the trip.

WORTH A TRIP

TRSTENO ARBORETUM

The leafy gardens of **Trsteno Arboretum** (020-751 019; adult/child 45/25KN; ⊙8am-7pm Jun-Sep, to 4pm Oct-May), 14km northwest of Dubrovnik, are the oldest of their kind in Croatia and well worth a visit. It was during the 16th century that Dubrovnik's noblesse started to pay extra attention to their gardens. Ivan Gučetić planted the first seeds here and started the trend, and his descendants maintained the garden throughout the centuries. The land was eventually taken over by the (former Yugoslav and now Croatian) Academy of Sciences, which turned it into a public arboretum.

The garden has a Renaissance layout, with a set of geometric shapes made with plants and bushes (lavender, rosemary, fuchsia, bougainvillea), while citrus orchards perfume the air. There's also a maze, a fine palm collection (including Chinese windmill palms) and a gorgeous pond overlooked by a statue of Neptune and rich with white water lilies and dozens of bullfrogs. It's only partially landscaped, though – quite a bit of it is wonderfully wild.

Don't miss the two giant plane trees at the entrance to Trsteno village – each is more than 500 years old and around 50m high. They're among the largest of their kind in Europe.

To get to Trsteno, catch local bus 12, 15, 22 or 35 from Dubrovnik's bus station. Otherwise any intercity bus bound for Split will stop here.

Ljuta village has old mill buildings set on a pretty river, and it's worth following the signs to Sokol Grad, a 14th-century Bosnian-built castle on the edge of the mountains.

✖ Eating

★ Konoba Koraćeva Kuća   DALMATIAN €€
(📱 020-791 557; mmihatovic04@gmail.com; Gruda bb; mains 60-100KN; ⊙6-10pm Mon-Fri, noon-10pm Sat & Sun Apr-Oct) There's no better place to soak up the scenery than the terrace of this exceptional family-run restaurant, specialising in modern takes on Dalmatian traditions. Call ahead for lamb or veal slow-roasted under a *peka* (charcoal-covered metal dome), or just call in to see what's on the menu. We highly recommend the bruschetta, grilled vegetables and wild boar stew with gnocchi.

At the time of research they were putting the finishing touches to five guest bedrooms, upstairs in the 300-year-old house.

❶ Getting There & Away

This region is best explored by car or bike as public transport is limited. City buses 11 and 38 head from Dubrovnik to Gruda (two to five daily), or there's bus 31 from Cavtat (three to five daily).

Elafiti Islands

A day trip to one of the islands in this archipelago northwest of Dubrovnik makes a perfect escape from the summer crowds. Only the three largest – Koločep, Lopud and Šipan – are permanently inhabited. You can see all three in one day on a 'Three Islands & Fish Picnic' tour, which is offered by several operators that have desks at Dubrovnik's Old Harbour (expect to pay about 270KN including drinks and lunch).

◉ Sights

Koločep   ISLAND
The nearest of the Elafitis to Dubrovnik, this sweet little island is inhabited by a mere 163 people and is covered in centuries-old pine forests, olive groves, and orchards filled with orange and lemon trees. A sandy beach stretches out from the main village past a large resort-style hotel. Continue around the corner and you'll reach a pretty but rocky nudist area.

Lopud   ISLAND
Car-free Lopud has interesting churches and monasteries dating from the 16th century, when the inhabitants' seafaring exploits were

legendary. Ruined fortresses overlook Lopud village, an attractive settlement composed of stone houses surrounded by exotic gardens. There's a little beach here, but you're better off walking across the spine of the island to beautiful sandy **Šunj**, where a little bar serves griddled sardines and other types of fish.

Šipan   ISLAND
Šipan is the largest of the Elafiti Islands and was a favourite with the Dubrovnik aristocracy, who built houses here. Most ferries dock in Suđurađ, a little harbour lined with stone houses and the large fortified Skočibuha villa and tower, built in the 16th century. On the other side of the island, the village of Šipanska Luka has the remains of a Roman villa and a 15th-century Gothic duke's palace.

🛏 Sleeping & Eating

Hotel Božica   HOTEL €€€
(📱 020-325 400; www.hotel-bozica.hr; Suđurađ 13; r/ste from €143/390; 🅿 ⚇) If it's peace and quiet you're after, you could do a lot worse than this modern 26-room hotel on Šipan. Shuffle from the pool to the beach terrace and back again before plotting your next move. The restaurant perhaps?

Kod Marka   SEAFOOD €
(📱 020-758 007; Šipanska Luka; mains from 50KN; ⊙noon-10pm May-Oct) This little seaside restaurant serves gloriously prepared seafood – try the Korčula-style fish stew.

❶ Getting There & Away

Aside from the numerous boat tours, there are regular ferries to the Elafitis from Dubrovnik's Gruž Harbour.

Four Jadrolinija (p272) catamarans per day head to Koločep (23KN, 30 minutes), Lopud (23KN, 55 minutes) and Suđurađ on Šipan (23KN, 1¼ hours); a trip between Koločep and Suđurađ costs 14KN (40 minutes). An additional four to 10 slower car ferries per week also head to Lopud (23KN, one hour) and Suđurađ (23KN, 1½ hours).

G&V Line (p272) has a daily catamaran connecting Šipanska Luka (on Šipan) to Dubrovnik (35KN, 50 minutes) and from Šipanska Luka to Sobra on Mljet (30KN, 35 minutes).

MLJET ISLAND
POP 1090

Mljet is one of the most seductive of all the Adriatic islands. Much of the island is covered by forests and the rest is dotted with fields, vineyards and small villages. The western tip contains Mljet National Park, where the lush vegetation, pine forests and spectacular saltwater lakes are exceptionally scenic. It's an unspoilt oasis of tranquillity that, according to legend, captivated Odysseus for seven years. We're sure he didn't regret a moment.

History

Ancient Greeks called the island 'Melita' or 'honey' for the many bees humming in the forests. It appears that Greek sailors came to the island for refuge against storms and to gather fresh water from the springs. At that time the island was populated by Illyrians, who erected hill forts and traded with the mainland. They were conquered by the Romans in 35 BC, who expanded the settlement around Polače by building a palace, baths and servants' quarters.

The island fell under the control of the Byzantine Empire in the 6th century and was later subjected to the 7th-century invasions of Slavs and Avars. After several centuries of regional rule from the mainland, Mljet was given to the Benedictine order in the 13th century. Dubrovnik formally annexed the island in 1410.

Although Mljet's fortunes were thereafter tied to those of Dubrovnik, the inhabitants maintained their traditional activities of farming, viticulture and seafaring. These remain key occupations today. The establishment of the national park in 1960 put Mljet on the tourist map, but the island is anything but overrun and visitors are almost entirely drawn to the tourist enclave around Pomena. If you're searching for tranquillity, you won't have to look hard.

❶ Information

Sobra Tourist Office (☑ 020-746 025; www.mljet.hr; ☺ 9am-2pm & 4-7pm Mon-Sat, 9am-2pm Sun) Tucked away by the Jadrolinija ticket office at the ferry port.

❶ Getting There & Away

The quickest connection from the mainland to Mljet is the car ferry with **Jadrolinija** (☑ 020-746 134; www.jadrolinija.hr) from Prapratno on the Pelješac Peninsula to Sobra (passenger/car 30/140KN, 45 minutes, four to five daily).

G&V Line (p272) has a daily catamaran to Sobra from Šipanska Luka (30KN, 35 minutes) and Dubrovnik (60KN, 1¼ hours). Between June and September a second boat heads to both Sobra and Polače from Dubrovnik (70KN, two hours). In July and August some of these services continue on to Korčula (50KN, 45 minutes) and Ubli on Lastovo (70KN, 2¼ hours).

From June to September Kapetan Luka (p273) has a daily fast boat to Pomena from Dubrovnik (80KN, 1¼ hours), Korčula (80KN, 30 minutes), Hvar (130KN, 1¾ hours), Milna on Brač (130KN, 2½ hours) and Split (130KN, three hours), dropping to four times per week in May and three per week in October.

❶ Getting Around

Mini Brum (☑ 099 61 15 574; www.rent-a-car-scooter-mljet.hr; ☺ 9am-7pm) rents basic cars (five/12/24 hours from 280/320/390KN) and scooters (190/220/250KN) from the ferry port in Sobra and from Polače.

Expect to pay about 300KN for a taxi between Sobra and Polače.

Bus services on the island are limited to a single bus per day departing each end of the island at the crack of dawn and heading to Sopra, returning late in the evening.

Mljet National Park

Although it covers 5400 hectares of land and sea, including the entire westernmost quarter of the island, when most people talk of **Mljet National Park** (Nacionalni park Mljet; ☑ 020-744 041; www.np-mljet.hr; Pristanište 2; adult/child 100/60KN; ☺ 8am-8pm Apr-Oct) they're referring to the small section that's ticketed, taking in the gorgeous saltwater lakes Malo Jezero (Little Lake) and Veliko Jezero (Big Lake). The two are connected to each by a short channel, while the larger one empties into the sea via the much longer Soline Canal, which makes the lakes subject to tidal flows.

The main hubs of the park are the small villages of Pomena and Polače, which are overrun by visitors on summer days but quieten down again once all the boats leave. Kiosks in both villages sell park admission tickets. From Pomena its a 400m walk along a forested path to Malo Jezero; from Polače, your ticket includes a transfer to Pristanište on Veliko Jezero, where there's a park information centre.

◎ Sights

Sveti Marija   ISLAND
Tiny St Mary's Island lies on Veliko Jezero, not far from its southern shore. Boats (included in the park admission price) head here at least hourly during park opening hours from Mali Most, the bridge near the channel between the two lakes, and from Pristanište. The island's **Benedictine monastery** was

founded in 1198 but has been rebuilt several times, adding Renaissance and baroque features to the Romanesque structure.

The monastery was closed in 1809 following the Napoleonic conquest and housed state offices up until 1960. It was then converted into a hotel, which closed in 1991 during the war. It has since been returned to the Catholic Church, which is in the process of restoring it. The complex includes the large St Mary's Church (Crkva Svete Marije), a couple of tiny chapels and the old monks' quarters, which now has a restaurant in its basement. There are also ruins of a Roman building in the island's centre and stables with a donkey.

The original monks were responsible for deepening and widening the passage between the two lakes, building a tidal mill to take advantage of the rush of sea water.

Roman Palace   RUINS
Polače features various remains dating from the 1st to the 6th centuries. Most impressive is this large palace, probably from the 5th century, with a rectangular floor plan and towers on the front corners separated by a pier. It's a vast structure – and the road now passes through the centre of it. Other ancient ruins scattered around the town include a late Antiquity fort, an early Christian basilica and a 5th-century church.

🏃 Activities

Walking & Cycling
There are walking and cycling paths throughout the national park, and bikes and kayaks are available to rent from various locations. Cycling is an excellent way to explore but be aware that Pomena and Polače are separated by a steep hill. The lakeside bike path is an easier and very scenic pedal.

Swimming
The busiest swimming spot is on the little lake, near the bridge – although we suggest that you stroll along the shore until you find a quiet nook of your own. You can walk completely around the little lake, but not the larger one, as there's no bridge over the Soline Channel. If you decide to swim it, keep in mind that the current can be strong.

Diving
Aquatica   DIVING
(☑ 099 81 14 090; www.aquatica-mljet.hr; next to Hotel Odisej, Pomena) Mljet offers some interesting diving opportunities, including a German WWII torpedo boat and several walls.

There's also a 3rd-century Roman wreck in relatively shallow water. The remains of the ship, including amphorae, have calcified over the centuries and this has protected them from pillaging. Aquatica offers boat dives and diving courses.

ℹ Information

Polače Tourist Office (☑ 020-744 186; www. mljet.hr; ⊙ 9am-1pm & 4-7pm Mon-Sat, 9am-1pm Sun Jun-Sep, 8am-1pm Mon-Fri Oct-May)

Okuklje
POP 30

Basically a single row of houses clinging to an almost-circular bay ringed by green hills, Okuklje is the kind of place that's easy to fall in love with at first sight. There's not a lot to do here apart from relax with a book, take a dip in the harbour and walk up to tiny St Nicholas' Church for the views over the bay and back towards the Pelješac Peninsula.

🛏 Sleeping & Eating

Lampalo   APARTMENT €€
(☑ 020-420 059; Okuklje 8; apt €90; P ❄) Despite English not being their strong point, you can expect a warm welcome and maybe even a beer on arrival from the hosts. With a bit of notice they'll fire up the charcoal and throw something under the *peka* for dinner. There are only two apartments for rent: a studio and a spacious two-bedroom apartment.

Konoba Maestral   DALMATIAN €€€
(☑ 098 428 890; www.okukljerestaurantmaestral. com; mains 110-150KN; ⊙ 1pm-midnight mid-Apr–mid-Oct; 🐾) Maestral is an altogether charming family affair, with the owner's young children helping out front of house and the oldest son sweating away shovelling charcoal onto the pre-ordered *pekas*. Make sure you try the octopus carpaccio – we can't recommend it highly enough.

Saplunara
POP 70

At Mljet's very eastern tip, the teensy village of Saplunara feels sublimely isolated – despite the views towards the bright lights of Dubrovnik. The main drawcards are an excellent restaurant and a trio of sandy beaches. If you're tempted to stop at the first or second beach, resist the urge and continue to the third – it's the biggest and the most beautiful.

🛏 Sleeping & Eating

Villa Mirosa   B&B €€
(☑ 099 19 96 270; www.villa-mirosa.com; Saplunara 26; r €96; 🅿 ❄ 🛜 ♨) A gorgeous infinity-lipped rooftop pool is what gives this 12-room guesthouse the edge over similar places on Mljet. The rooms are perfectly pleasant, and there's a grapevine-shrouded terrace restaurant at the front and access to a rocky cove at the rear.

Stermasi   DALMATIAN €€
(☑ 098 93 90 362; www.stermasi.hr; mains 70-190KN; ⊙ 8am-midnight; 🛜) Stermasi's 10 apartments (from €65) are bright and modern, and either have a terrace or private balcony. But the big draw here is the restaurant, serving flavoursome, authentic Dalmatian food prepared with love and skill. House specialities include vegetables, octopus or kid goat cooked under a *peka*, wild boar with gnocchi and Mljet-style *brodet* (fish stew).

PELJEŠAC PENINSULA

The slender fingerlike peninsula of Pelješac is coastal Croatia at its most relaxed. Blessed with craggy mountains, sweeping valleys, idyllic coves and fine wines, it's a gorgeous place to visit. Two historic towns, Ston and Orebić, bookend the peninsula and the slow, winding drive between them is a very pleasant one indeed; allow an hour, or longer if you stop for wine tastings along the way. The peninsula's third-largest settlement is pretty little palm-lined **Trpanj** on the northern coast, where the car ferry leaves for Ploče.

Ston & Mali Ston

POP 690

Ston and its little buddy Mali Ston sit 50km northwest of Dubrovnik on an isthmus that connects the Pelješac Peninsula with the mainland. Formerly part of the Republic of Dubrovnik, Ston was and is an important salt-producing town. Its economic importance to Dubrovnik led, in 1333, to the construction of a 5.5km wall, one of the longest fortifications in Europe. Architects including Juraj Dalmatinac were involved in the design and construction, which included 40 towers and five forts. The walls are still standing, sheltering a cluster of medieval buildings in the town centre.

Mali Ston, a little village and harbour situated 1km northeast of Ston, was built along with the wall as part of the defensive system.

Both towns are major gastronomic destinations, famed for the mussels and large flat oysters that have been farmed here since Roman times.

👁 Sights

Town Walls   FORT
(Gradske zidine; adult/child 40/20KN; ⊙ 8am-7.30pm) The major sight in Ston is the 14th-century wall that stretches from both Ston and Mali Ston far up the hill. Now fully restored, the ramparts can be walked for long stretches, and the clear Pelješac air allows for fine views over the peninsula. You can walk the Ston section in 15 minutes; allow an extra 30 minutes to continue to Mali Ston.

Prapratno   BEACH
The closest beach to Ston, this gem of a bay has a sandy shore and clear, calm waters, making it a hit with local families. It's located 4km southwest of Ston, near the ferry to Mljet.

🛏 Sleeping

Autokamp Prapratno   CAMPGROUND €
(☑ 020-754 000; www.duprimorje.hr; Prapratno; per adult/car/site 56/42/46KN; 🅿 🛜) Sites are arranged under the shade of olive trees at this attractive campground, right by the sparkling beach at Prapratno. It has good facilities including tennis and basketball courts, a shop, an ATM and a restaurant.

Ostrea   HOTEL €€€
(☑ 020-754 555; www.ostrea.hr; Mali Ston; s/d from 690/990KN; 🅿 ❄ 🛜) Behind the stone walls and green shutters of this historic building are elegant rooms with polished timber floors and en suite bathrooms. Staff are welcoming and professional and the hotel is just steps from Mali Ston's pretty harbour.

🍴 Eating

⭐ **Kapetanova Kuća**   DALMATIAN, SEAFOOD €€
(☑ 020-754 264; www.ostrea.hr; Mali Ston; mains 90-140KN; ⊙ 9am-midnight) The 'Captain's House' is one of the most venerable seafood restaurants in the region. Feast on Ston oysters and grilled squid on the shady terrace, but try to leave room for the traditional macaroni pudding – it's unusual but surprisingly delicious.

Stagnum   DALMATIAN €€
(☑ 020-754 158; Imena Isusova 23, Ston; mains 30-120KN; ⊙ 11am-midnight May-Oct) Grab a seat in the lovely garden courtyard where you can watch and smell the fish and meat sizzling on the barbecue. Pizza, fresh mussels and risotto are also served.

PELJEŠAC WINE TRAIL

What travellers might not be aware of as they zip along the winding road through the centre of the Pelješac Peninsula is that they're passing through the realm of the king of Croatian red wines: *plavac mali*.

A descendant of *crljenak kaštelanski* (more commonly known as *zinfandel*) and little-known *dobričić*, this little *(mali)* blue *(plavac)* grape produces big, flavoursome wine (called *primitivo* in Italy). The more inhospitable the terrain, the more flavour-laden the grapes, which is why the very best *plavac mali* is grown on the barren, sunbaked slopes of **Dingač** and **Postup** on the peninsula's southern coast. The vines are so difficult to access that all of the grapes must be harvested by hand. Both of these regions are now recognised appellations, protected by a 'stamp of geographic origin'.

You couldn't hope for a more authentically rustic spot to sample a local drop than **Taverna Domanoeta** (⊘ 9am-1am Jul & Aug), a stone-walled cellar bar in **Janjina**, a small village at the very centre of the peninsula. If it's sunny, grab a table in the garden and order some *plavac mali*, accompanied by local cheese and *pršut* (prosciutto).

A little further on is the turnoff for the village of **Trstenik**, where legendary Napa Valley winemaker Mike Grgich has established **Grgić Vina** (☑ 020-748 090; www.grgic-vina. com; Trstenik; ⊘ 9am-5pm). Call in to the winery to try and buy their award-winning *plavac mali* and *pošip* (a white varietal grown on Korčula).

The main road continues through a valley to **Potomje** village, where a 400m tunnel cuts through the mountain to the famed wine-growing slopes of Dingač. Of the many wineries in Potomje, the best to visit is **Matuško** (☑ 098 428 676; www.matusko-vina.hr; Potomje; ⊘ 8am-8pm), where you can check out their extensive cellars before sitting down to a tasting.

If all this wine tasting is making you thirsty, stop at **Peninsula** (www.peninsula.hr; ⊘ 9am-11pm; 🕿), a roadside wine bar with over 40 high-quality local wines, as well as a selection of *rakija* and liqueurs. It's located in **Donja Banda**, near where the road from Trpanj branches off from the main peninsula road.

ℹ Information

Tourist Office (☑ 020-754 452; www.ston. hr; Pelješki put bb, Ston; ⊘ 8am-2pm & 4-7pm Mon-Fri, 8am-2pm Sat Jun, 8am-7pm Mon-Sat, 8am-noon & 4-7pm Sun Jul-Sep, 8am-2pm Mon-Sat Oct-May) Has brochures and bus timetables and can help you find private accommodation.

ℹ Getting There & Away

The bus stop is in the centre of Ston, near the tourist office and post office. You can walk from here to Mali Ston in 15 minutes.

Bus destinations include Korčula Town (60KN, two hours, four daily), Orebić (48KN, 1¼ hours, five daily), Dubrovnik (52KN, 1¼ hours, four daily), Split (101KN, 3¼ hours, daily) and Zagreb (239KN, 9½ hours, daily).

Orebić

POP 1980

Orebić, on the southern coast of the Pelješac Peninsula, has a strip of lovely little beaches, some sandy and some shingly, bordered by groves of tamarisk and pine. Only 2.5km across the water from Korčula Town,

it makes a perfect day trip or an alternative base.

After lazing on the beach, you can take advantage of some excellent **hiking** up and around Mt Ilija (961m) or poke around a couple of churches and museums. Mt Ilija protects the town from harsh northern winds, allowing vegetation to flourish. The temperature is usually a few degrees warmer than Korčula; spring arrives early and summer leaves late.

◉ Sights & Activities

Trstenica   BEACH

There's a slim beach west of the dock, but the best beach is the long stretch at Trstenica about 700m east of the dock. A beautiful broad crescent of sand and fine shingle, it's fringed by mature trees and its sheltered waters are a near-Caribbean shade of turquoise.

Walks   WALKING

Orebić is great for hiking, so pick up a trail map from the tourist office. A track through the pine trees leads from Hotel Bellevue to a 15th-century **Franciscan monastery** on a ridge 152m above the sea. From this vantage point, Dubrovnik patrols could watch the Venetian ships moored on Korčula and notify the authorities of any suspicious movements.

The village of Karmen near the monastery is the starting point for walks to picturesque upper villages and the more daring climb up **Mt Ilija**, the bare, grey massif that hangs over Orebić. The reward for climbers is a sweeping view of the entire coast. On a hill east of the monastery is **Our Lady of Carmel Church** (Crkva Gospa od Karmena), next to several huge cypresses, as well as a baroque loggia and the ruins of a duke's castle.

🛏 Sleeping

Glavna Plaža   CAMPGROUND €
(☑ 020-713 399; www.glavnaplaza.com; Šetalište kneza Domogoja 49; camping per adult/child/site/car 58/30/50/44KN, apt from €50; ☺ Jun-Oct; 🅿 🤶) This tiny family-run campground is tucked away at the Orebić end of sandy Trstenica beach. As well as sites, there are four simple apartments available (three studios and one that can sleep six).

★**Hotel Adriatic**   HOTEL €€€
(☑ 020-714 488; www.hoteladriaticorebic.com; Šetalište kneza Domogoja 8; s/d from 1000/1254KN; ❄ 🤶) Right by the water, this converted ship-captain's mansion has six luxurious rooms with exposed stone walls, wooden floors, ample bathrooms and sea views. An excellent breakfast is served on the seaside terrace. No children are permitted.

Hotel Indijan   HOTEL €€€
(☑ 020-714 555; www.hotelindijan.hr; Šetalište, Škvar 2; s/d from €109/189; 🅿 ❄ 🤶 🏊 🐕) A contemporary feel pervades this well-designed hotel. Rooms are modern and well equipped, and some have balconies with views to Korčula. The small circular heated pool has a retractable glass roof, so it's usable all year round.

🍴 Eating

Croccantino   CAFE €
(☑ 098 16 50 777; www.facebook.com/Croccantino CRO; Obala Pomoraca 30; snacks 10KN; ☺ 7am-10pm) Satisfy a sweet urge with a strudel or a homemade gelato at this chilled-out little cafe on the promenade.

Konoba Andiamo   DALMATIAN €€
(☑ 098 98 38 614; Šetalište kneza Domogoja 28; mains 50-120KN; ☺ 2pm-midnight; 🎵) A bright mural of a city street provides a cheerfully anachronistic backdrop for this breezy res-

taurant, set in a wooden terrace just metres from the sea. We wholeheartedly endorse the seafood platter for two, packed with prawns, mussels, langoustine and two types of fish. With advance notice they'll also roast lamb, pork, veal or octopus under a *peka*.

ℹ Information

Orebić Tours (☑ 020-713 367; www.orebic-tours.hr; Bana Josipa Jelačića 84a; ☺ 8am-8pm Mon-Sat, 8am-3pm Sun Jun-Sep, 8am-3pm Mon-Fri Oct-May) Rents out private accommodation, changes money and books excursions, including wine tours and boat cruises.

Post Office (☑ 020-362 848; www.posta.hr; Obala Pomoraca 30; ☺ 8am-9pm Mon-Fri, 8am-noon & 6-9pm Sat Jun-Sep, 7.30am-5pm Mon-Fri, 9am-1pm Sat Oct-May)

Tourist Office (☑ 020-713 718; www.visitorebic-croatia.hr; Zrinsko Frankopanska 2; ☺ 8am-10pm Jul & Aug, 8am-8pm May, Jun, Sep & Oct, 8am-4pm Mon-Fri Nov-Apr) Has a good hiking and biking map of the peninsula and plenty of brochures.

ℹ Getting There & Away

Ferries from Korčula tie up just steps from the tourist office and bus stop.

Buses head to/from Ston (48KN, 1¼ hours, five daily), Dubrovnik (86KN, 2½ hours, four daily), Split (117KN, 4½ hours, daily), Mostar (114KN, four hours, daily) and Zagreb (250KN, 10¾ hours, daily).

Viganj

POP 280

If you're into windsurfing, Viganj has some of the best conditions in Croatia. The village is strung out along the coast 7km west of Orebić, near the tip of the Pelješac Peninsula. It's a low-key place, but there are a couple of restaurants, a lively beach bar and a little summertime tourist office.

🛏 Sleeping

Camping Antony-Boy   CAMPGROUND €
(☑ 020-719 077; www.antony-boy.com; per adult/child/tent/car 50/30/40/50KN, apt 530-760KN; 🅿 🤶 🏊) Behind a pebbly beach, this strangely named campsite has good facilities, rents bikes and has a windsurfing school.

ℹ Information

Tourist Office (☑ 020-719 059; www.visitorebic-croatia.hr; ☺ 9am-2pm Mon-Sat mid-Jun–mid-Sep)

KORČULA ISLAND

POP 15,600

Rich in vineyards, olive groves and small villages, and harbouring a glorious old town, the island of Korčula is the sixth-largest Adriatic island, stretching nearly 47km in length. Dense woods led the original Greek settlers to call the island Korkyra Melaina (Black Korčula). Quiet coves and small sandy beaches dot the steep southern coast while the northern shore is flatter and more pebbly.

Tradition is alive and kicking on Korčula, with age-old religious ceremonies, folk music and dances still being performed to the delight of an ever-growing influx of tourists. Oenophiles will adore sampling its wine. Arguably the best of all Croatian whites is produced from *pošip* grapes, which are only grown here and to a lesser extent on the Pelješac Peninsula. The *grk* grape, cultivated around Lumbarda, also produces quality dry white wine.

History

A Neolithic cave (Vela Spila) located near Vela Luka, on the island's western end, points to the existence of a prehistoric settlement, but it was the Greeks who first began spreading over the island somewhere around the 6th century BC. Their most important settlement was in the area of today's Lumbarda around the 3rd century BC.

Rome conquered Korčula in the 1st century, giving way to the Slavs in the 7th century. The island was conquered by Venice in AD 1000 and then passed under Hungarian rule. It was briefly part of the Republic of Dubrovnik before again falling to the Venetians in 1420, who remained until 1797. Under Venetian control the island became known for its stone, which was quarried and cut for export. Shipbuilding also flourished.

After the Napoleonic conquest of Dalmatia in 1797, Korčula's fortunes followed those of the region, changing hands among the French, British, Austro-Hungarians and Italians before becoming a part of the first Yugoslavia in 1921. Today Korčula is one of Croatia's most prosperous islands, its historic capital drawing visitors in increasing numbers.

ℹ️ Getting There & Away

AIR

European Coastal Airlines (☏ 021-444 813; www.ec-air.eu) has seaplane flights to Lumbarda from Split between July and September, and from Dubrovnik in August. From May to October they also fly from Vela Luka to Split and Ubli.

BOAT

The island has three major entry ports: Korčula Town's West Harbour, Dominče (3km east of Korčula Town) and Vela Luka.

Jadrolinija (☏ 020-715 410; www.jadrolinija. hr; Plokata 19 travnja 1921 br 19) has car ferries between Orebić and Dominče (passenger/car 16/76KN, 15 minutes), departing roughly every hour (every 90 minutes from October to May). A daily catamaran heads between Korčula Town and Split (80KN, 2¾ hours), stopping at Hvar (70KN, 1½ hours) on the way. From July to mid-September, there's also a daily catamaran from West Harbour to Dubrovnik (120KN, 2¼ hours), Hvar (70KN, 1½ hours) and Bol on Brač (100KN, 2¾ hours).

From Vela Luka, Jadrolinija has two car ferries a day to Split (passenger/car 60/530KN, 2¾ hours) and up to three a day to Ubli on Lastovo (32/195KN, 1¼ hours). There's also a daily catamaran on this route, stopping in Hvar (40KN, 55 minutes) en route between Split (65KN, 2¼ hours) and Ubli (40KN, 55 minutes).

In July and August, G&V Line (p272) has four catamarans per week to Korčula Town from Dubrovnik (90KN, 2½ hours), Polače on Mljet (50KN, 45 minutes) and Sobra on Mljet (60KN, 1½ hours). Two of these continue on to Ubli (60KN, 1¼ hours).

From June to September, Kapetan Luka (p273) has a daily fast boat between Korčula Town and Dubrovnik (120KN, 1¾ hours), Pomena on Mljet (80KN, 30 minutes), Hvar (190KN, one hour), Milna on Brač (110KN, 1¾ hours) and Split (120KN, 2¼ hours), dropping to four times per week in May and three per week in October.

ℹ️ Getting Around

Buses head from Korčula Town to Lumbarda (single/return 15/25KN, 15 minutes, four to 10 daily) and Vela Luka (40/60KN, one hour, four to six daily).

Korčula Town

POP 2860

Korčula Town is a stunner. Ringed by imposing defences, this coastal citadel is dripping with history, with marble streets rich in Renaissance and Gothic architecture.

Its fascinating fishbone layout was cleverly designed for the comfort and safety of its inhabitants: western streets were built straight in order to open the city to the refreshing summer *maestral* (strong, steady westerly wind), while the eastern streets were curved to minimise the force of the winter *bura* (cold, northeasterly wind).

The town cradles a harbour, overlooked by round defensive towers and a compact

MARCO POLO: ITALY VERSUS CROATIA

In 2011, nearly 700 years after his death, Marco Polo was the subject of a minor diplomatic row between Italy, Croatia and China, when former Croatian president Stjepan Mesić spoke at the opening of a museum dedicated to the explorer in Yangzhou. Mesić described Polo as a 'world explorer, born in Croatia, who opened up China to Europe'. This immediately sent the Italian media into a frenzy, accusing Croatia of the cultural theft of one of their national treasures.

While it's uncertain exactly where Marco Polo was born (both Venice and Korčula claim him), it's generally agreed that it was within the Venetian Republic. It certainly wasn't in Croatia (which was ruled by Hungary at the time and didn't include Korčula) or in Italy (which didn't even exist).

One of Korčula's historic families went by the surname Pilić (meaning 'chicken' in Croatian). It was common at the time for merchants and the aristocracy to use both Croatian and Italian versions of their names; hence Marko Pilić would become Marco Polo (*pollo* meaning 'chicken' in Italian).

Despite the lack of proof one way or another, Korčula trumpets its Marco Polo claim stridently, so much so that there are now two Marco Polo museums in town, neither of which is particularly good.

cluster of red-roofed houses. There are rustling palms all around and several beaches are an easy walk away.

History

Although documents indicate that a walled town existed on this site in the 13th century, it wasn't until the 15th century that the current city was built. Construction coincided with the apogee of stone-carving skills on the island, lending the buildings and streets a distinctive style. In the 16th century masons added decorative flourishes such as ornate columns and coats of arms to building facades, which gave a Renaissance look to the original Gothic core.

People began building houses south of the old town in the 17th and 18th centuries as the threat of invasion diminished and they no longer needed to protect themselves behind walls. The narrow streets and stone houses in the 'new' suburb attracted merchants and artisans, and this is still where you'll find most commercial activity.

◉ Sights & Activities

There are some excellent biking and hiking trails around Korčula; pick up an island map from the tourist office. In the summer, **water taxis** offer trips to **Badija Island**, which has a 15th-century Franciscan monastery and a naturist beach.

City Defences   FORT
Korčula's towers and remaining city walls look particularly striking when approached from the sea, their presence warning pirates

the town would be no pushover. Originally these defences would have been even more foreboding, forming a complete stone barrier against invaders that consisted of 12 towers and 20m-high walls.

On the western side the conical **Large Governor's Tower** (1483; Obala dr Franje Tuđmana bb) and **Small Governor's Tower** (1449) protected the port, shipping and the Governor's Palace, which used to stand next to the town hall. Continuing clockwise around the edge of the old-town peninsula, the small **Sea Gate Tower** (Sv Barbare bb) has an inscription in Latin from 1592 stating that Korčula was founded after the fall of Troy. Next you'll come to the renovated **Kanavelić Tower** (Sv Barbare bb), its semicircular profile topped with battlements, and then the smaller Zakerjan Tower, which now houses the Massimo cocktail bar (p287).

The main entrance to the old city is through the southern land gate in the **Veliki Revelin Tower** (Trg kralja Tomislava). Built in the 14th century and later extended, this fortification is adorned with coats of arms of the Venetian doges and Korčulan governors. There was originally a wooden drawbridge here, but it was replaced in the 18th century by the wide stone steps that give a sense of grandeur to the entrance. The best remaining part of the defensive walls stretches west from here. The upper section of this tower is home to the small **Moreška Museum** (Veliki Revelin Tower; 20KN; ⊙ 9am-3pm May-Oct) dedicated to the Moreška dance tradition; it has some costumes and old photos.

Korčula Town

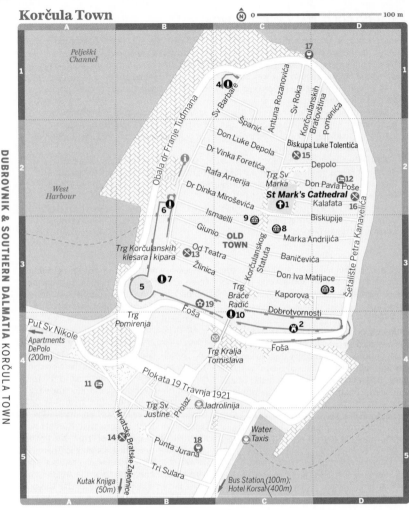

0 100 m

Pelješki Channel

West Harbour

Obala dr Franje Tuđmana

17

Sv Barbare

4

Španić

Don Luke Depola

Dr Vinka Foretića

Rafa Arnerija

Dr Dinka Miroševića

Antuna Rozanovića

Sv Roka

Korčulanskih Bratovština

Pomenića

Biskupa Luke Tolentića

15

Depola

Trg Sv Marka

Don Pavla Poše

12

St Mark's Cathedral

1

Kalafata

16

6

Ismaelli

9

8

Biskupije

Giunio

OLD TOWN

Marka Andrijića

Trg Korčulanskih klesara i kipara

Od Teatra

13

Baničevića

Korčulanskog Statuta

Žlinica

Don Iva Matijace

Šetalište Petra Kanavelića

5

7

Trg Braće Radić

Kaporova

3

Foša

19

10

Dobrotvornosti

2

Put Sv Nikole

Trg Pomirenja

Foša

Apartments DePolo (200m)

Trg Kralja Tomislava

Plokata 19 Travnja 1921

11

Trg Sv Justine

Prolaz

Jadrolinija

Water Taxis

14

Punta Jurana

18

Hrvatske Bratske Zajednice

Tri Sulara

Kutak Knjiga (50m)

Bus Station (100m); Hotel Korsal (400m)

⭐ **St Mark's Cathedral**   CATHEDRAL
(Katedrala svetog Marka; Trg Sv Marka; church 10KN,
bell tower adult/child 20/15KN; ☉9am-9pm Jul &
Aug, Mass only Sep-Jun) Dominating the little
square at Korčula's heart is this magnificent
15th-century cathedral, built from Korčula
limestone in a Gothic-Renaissance style by
Italian and local artisans. The sculptural detail of the facade is intriguing, particularly the
naked squatting figures of Adam and Eve on
the door pillars, and the two-tailed mermaid
and elephant on the triangular gable cornice
at the very top. The **bell tower** is topped by
a balustrade and ornate cupola, beautifully
carved by Korčulan Marko Andrijić.

Inside, the nave soars 30m in height and is
lined with a twin colonnade of exposed limestone pillars. Look out for the ciborium, also
carved by Andrijić, and behind it the altarpiece painting *Three Saints,* by Tintoretto.
Another painting attributed to Tintoretto or
his workshop, *The Annunciation,* is by the
baroque altar of St Anthony.

Other noteworthy artworks include a
bronze statue of St Blaise by Ivan Meštrović
near the altar on the northern aisle, and a
painting by the Venetian artist Jacopo Bassano in the apse of the southern aisle. Check
out the modern sculptures in the **baptistery** too.

Korčula Town

Before leaving the square, notice the elegantly ornamented **Arneri Palace** opposite the cathedral, at the corner of the narrow street of the same name.

St Mark's Abbey Treasury MUSEUM
(Opatska riznica svetog Marka; Trg Sv Marka; 25KN; ☉9am-7pm Mon-Sat May-Nov) The 14th-century Abbey Palace houses a collection of icons and Dalmatian art, with an excellent selection of 15th- and 16th-century paintings. The most outstanding work is the polyptych of *The Virgin* by Blaž Trogiranin. There are also liturgical items, jewellery, furniture and ancient documents relating to the history of Korčula.

Town Museum MUSEUM
(Gradski muzej; ☎020-711 420; www.gm-korcula.com; Trg Sv Marka 20; adult/child 20/6KN; ☉9am-9pm Jul-Sep, 10am-1pm Oct-Jun) Occupying the 16th-century Gabriellis Palace, this museum traces the history and culture of Korčula throughout the ages. It's not that well organised, but there are some interesting curios scattered over its four floors – including a tablet recording the Greek presence on the island in the 3rd century BC. Explanations are in English.

Displays cover stonemasonry, shipbuilding, archaeology, art, furniture, textiles and examples of Korčulan traditional dress.

Icon Museum MUSEUM
(Muzej ikona; Trg Svih Svetih; 15KN; ☉10am-1pm Mon-Sat) This modest museum has a collection of interesting Byzantine icons, painted on gilded wood, and 17th- and 18th-century ritual objects. As a bonus, visitors also have access to the beautiful old **All Saints' Church** (Crkva Svih Svetih) next door. This 18th-century baroque church features a carved and painted 15th-century wooden screen and a late-18th-century pietà, along with a wealth of local religious paintings.

☞ Tours

Local travel agencies can set you up on an island tour or a trip to Mljet, and offer mountain biking, sea kayaking and snorkelling trips.

✲ Festivals & Events

A schedule of events is available at the tourist office. **Holy Week** celebrations are particularly elaborate in Korčula. Beginning on Palm Sunday, the entire week before Easter is devoted to ceremonies and processions organised by the local religious brotherhoods dressed in traditional costumes. The townspeople sing medieval songs and hymns, biblical events are re-enacted and the city gates are blessed. The most solemn processions are on Good Friday evening when members of all brotherhoods parade through the streets.

🛏 Sleeping

Hajduk 1963 GUESTHOUSE €
(☎020-711 267; www.hajduk1963.com; ul 67 br 6; r €40; 🅿❄🛜🏊) Named after Dalmatia's favourite football team, Hajduk offers a warm welcome, well-priced rooms, a good in-house restaurant and even a swimming pool and swings for the kids. It's a couple of kilometres from the centre of town, off the road to the car ferry.

Apartments DePolo GUESTHOUSE €
(☎020-711 621; rezi.depolo@gmail.com; Put Sv Nikole 28; r/apt 330/380KN; 🅿❄🛜) A great budget option, these simple but comfortable

LOCAL KNOWLEDGE

SWORD DANCES

One of the island's most colourful traditions, the Moreška sword dance has been performed in Korčula Town since the 15th century. Although it's probably of Spanish origin, the only place in the world that it's performed now is in Korčula. It tells the story of two kings – the White King (dressed in red) and the Black King – who fight for a princess abducted by the Black King. In the spoken introduction the princess declares her love for the White King, and the Black King refuses to relinquish her. The two armies draw swords and 'fight' in an intricate dance accompanied by a band. Although traditionally performed only on Korčula's town day (29 July), the Moreška Cultural Club (p287) now stages it throughout the summer.

Kumpanija dances in the villages of Pupnat, Smokvica, Blato, Čara and the town of Vela Luka also make for a fun night out, but you'll need your own transport to see them. These dances also involve a 'fight' between rival armies and culminate in the unfurling of a huge flag. They're accompanied by the *mišnice* (similar to a bagpipe) and drums. A variation is the *moštra*, performed in the village of Žrnovo only on the evening of the feast of the Assumption (15 August).

rooms have their own bathrooms and one has a terrace with amazing views. There's a 30% surcharge in the summer for short stays.

★ **Korčula Royal Apartments**   APARTMENT €€
(☑ 098 18 40 444; www.korcularoyalapartments.com; Trg Petra Šegedina 4; apt from €80; ❉ ❀) The setting for these smart, well-equipped apartments couldn't be better, occupying an old stone villa facing a little square by the water, just outside the old town. And the Canadian-Croatian owners couldn't be more welcoming – although the business was for sale last time we visited.

Lešić Dimitri Palace   APARTMENT €€€
(☑ 020-715 560; www.ldpalace.com; Don Pavla Poše 1-6; apt €495-1495; ❉ ❀) In a class of its own, this extraordinary place has five impeccable 'residences' in an 18th-century bishop's palace. All are themed after Marco Polo's journeys – China, India etc – while original features (including exposed beams, stone walls and flagstones) reflect the old-town setting.

Hotel Korsal   HOTEL €€€
(☑ 020-715 722; www.hotel-korsal.com; Šetalište Frana Kršinića 80; s/d from €153/168; ❉ ❀) Near the marina, this newbie has 18 comfortable but unremarkable rooms spread between three buildings. The two older blocks have been fully renovated and have sea views, while the new one is set back behind the others and has only partial views.

✕ Eating

Cukarin   DELI €
(www.cukarin.hr; Hrvatske Bratske Zajednice bb; cakes from 10KN; ◷ 8.30am-noon & 5-7.30pm Mon-Sat) This deli-style place bakes sweet Korčulan creations such as *klašun* (walnut pastry) and *amareta* (a round, rich cake with almonds). It also sells wine, jam and olive oil from the island.

Konoba Adio Mare   DALMATIAN €€
(☑ 020-711 253; www.konobaadiomare.hr; Sv Roka bb; mains 60-180KN; ◷ noon-11pm Mon-Sat, 5-11pm Sun mid-Apr–mid-Oct) Right in the heart of the old town, this popular restaurant's covered rooftop terrace might just be the busiest place in Korčula. The menu focuses on Korčulan specialities such as *brodet, pašticada* and beef with dumplings.

Aterina   SEAFOOD €€€
(☑ 091 98 61 856; www.facebook.com/aterinakorcula; Trg Korčulanskih klesara i kipara 2; mains 75-180KN; ◷ noon-midnight May-Oct) As well as being a brilliant place to watch the sunset, Aterina serves an excellent selection of Italian-influenced seafood dishes. The daily specials are the main show – chalked up on a blackboard to reflect the daily catch. We also love the hipsterish array of knowingly tacky plastic tablecloths.

LD Terrace   MEDITERRANEAN €€€
(☑ 020-715 560; www.lesic-dimitri.com; Šetalište Petra Kanavelića bb; breakfast 42KN, mains 190-240KN; ◷ 8am-midnight; ❀) The LD stands for Lešić Dimitri and it's no surprise that Korčula's most elegant accommodation should also have its finest restaurant. The setting is magnificent, with a chic upstairs dining room as well as romantic tables set right above the water. The modern Mediterranean menu is well matched by a fine wine list, featuring many wonderful Dalmatian choices.

🍷 Drinking & Entertainment

Vinum Bonum WINE BAR
(Punta Jurana 66; ⊙6pm-midnight; 🛜) Tucked away on a little car-free lane just off the harbour, this casual place allows you to sample some of the island's best wine and *rakija*.

Massimo COCKTAIL BAR
(📱098 19 13 538; Šetalište Petra Kanavelića 1; ⊙9am-1am May-Oct) The place to be in Korčula at sunset, this adults-only bar is lodged in the turret of the Zakerjan Tower and is accessible only by ladder; the drinks are brought up by pulley. Visit for the novelty and the views, not for the tacky cocktail list.

Moreška Cultural Club DANCE
(www.moreska.hr; Ljetno kino, Foša 2; 100KN; ⊙shows at 9pm Mon & Thu Jul & Aug, shows at 9pm Thu Jun & Sep) Enthusiastic townspeople perform the traditional Moreška sword dance (p286), accompanied by a brass band, in an hour-long show. The event usually includes unaccompanied singing by a *klapa* group.

🛍 Shopping

Kutak Knjiga BOOKS
(📱020-716 541; http://kutak-knjiga.blogspot.co.nz; Hrvatske Bratske Zajednice 110; ⊙9.30am-8pm Mon-Fri, 10am-3pm Sat) It's a mystery how they cram books written in Croatian, English, French, Spanish, Czech, Italian, German, Polish, Swedish and Mandarin into such a small place. They stock a good selection of Croatian classics translated into English.

ℹ Information

Atlas Travel Agency (📱020-711 060; atlas-korcula@du.htnet.hr; Plokata 19 Travnja 1921 bb; ⊙8am-8pm Mon-Sat, 8am-3pm Sun Jun-Sep, 8am-3pm Mon-Fri Oct-May) Represents American Express, runs excursions and books private accommodation.

Health Centre (Dom zdravlja; 📱020-711 700; www.dom-zdravlja-korcula.hr; ul 57 br 5)

Na 90° (📱099 32 54 448; Obala Korčulanskih brodograditelja bb; ⊙7am-9pm Mon-Sat, 8am-7pm Sun) Laundromat within the bus station offering a left-luggage service.

Post Office (📱020-362 865; www.posta.hr; Trg kralja Tomislava 14; ⊙7am-9pm Mon-Sat Jun-Sep, 7am-8pm Mon-Fri, 8am-1pm Sat Oct-May)

Tourist Office (📱020-715 701; www.visit korcula.eu; Obala dr Franje Tuđmana 6; ⊙8am-8pm Mon-Sat, 8am-3pm Sun Jun, 8am-10pm daily Jul–mid-Sep, 8am-3pm Mon-Fri Oct-May) An excellent source of information, including brochures, maps and ferry times.

Lumbarda

POP 1220
Lumbarda is a laid-back sort of town set around a harbour on the southeastern end of Korčula Island. The sandy soil is perfect for vineyards, and wine from the *grk* grape is Lumbarda's most famous product. In the 16th century, aristocrats from Korčula built summer houses here, and it remains a quieter retreat from the more urbanised Korčula Town. The town beaches are small but sandy.

👁 Sights

Pržina BEACH
Families swarm to this sandy stretch for safe swimming and sandcastle construction, and to hang out in the little cafe-bars. To get here from the main road into town, continue straight ahead on the road past the post office.

ℹ Information

Post Office (www.posta.hr; Lumbarda 546; ⊙8am-noon & 5-8pm Mon-Fri Jul & Aug, 10-10.30am Mon-Fri Sep-Jun)

LASTOVO ISLAND

One of the most remote and undeveloped of Croatia's populated islands, little green Lastovo sits in quiet isolation south of Korčula and west of Mljet. Like similarly far-flung Vis, the island was used as a military base during the Yugoslav era and was closed to foreign visitors.

Now that it's open for business it has become a favourite destination for clued-up yachties, who moor in its blissful wee bays. There's not as much appeal for land-based tourists, though, as there are no decent beaches and there's little to do. The main attraction is Lastovo Town, a striking collection of stone houses and innumerable aged churches clinging to a hillside in the interior.

Lastovo and the dozens of islets that surround it are now protected by the Lastovo Archipelago Nature Park, home to shearwaters, sea corals, sponges, lobsters, rare sea snails, dolphins, and loggerhead and green turtles.

🏃 Activities

The island is criss-crossed with well-marked cycling and hiking trails. Enquire at the

OFF THE BEATEN TRACK

RURAL EATS

Some of Korčula's best eating experiences can be found in its small villages at *konobas* (simple, family-run eateries). If you've got your own transport, it's well worth seeking them out.

Konoba Mate (☑020-717 109; www.konobamate.hr; Pupnat 28; mains 50-80KN; ☺9am-2pm & 7pm-midnight; 🐾) Our favourite place to eat on the entire island has the unlikely setting of the sleepy farming village of Pupnat, 11km west of Korčula Town. The menu is short but universally tempting, offering unusual twists on true-blue traditions, including kid goat cooked under a *peka*. The antipasto platter is sublime. And mate, the name's pronounced *ma*-teh.

Konoba Belin (☑091 50 39 258; www.facebook.com/RestoranBelin; Prvo Selo Žrnovo; mains 50-130KN; ☺10.30am-1.30pm & 6-11.30pm) It's all about the barbecue (which dad is firmly in control of) at this friendly family-run place in the old part of Žrnovo, 2.5km west of Korčula Town. Expect lots of grilled fish and meat; if you call ahead, they'll chuck octopus or lamb under the *peka*.

Konoba Maslina (☑020-711 720; www.konobamaslina.com; Lumbarajska cesta bb; mains 55-130KN; ☺11am-10pm Mon-Sat, to 5pm Sun) With everything you'd want from a rural *konoba*, this traditional place offers rustic character and honest country cooking. Fresh fish, lamb, veal and local cheese feature prominently. It's about 3km out of Korčula on the road to Lumbarda.

tourist office for a route to suit your interests and abilities.

The only place approaching a proper beach is the small pebbly stretch below the Restaurant Porto Rosso in the deeply inset bay of **Skrivena Luka**.

🛏 Sleeping

Perhaps because many visitors stay on their boats, good accommodation is hard to come by. The pretty village of Pasadur, which straddles two islands connected by a little bridge, has Lastovo's only hotel and some basic holiday apartments. Contact the tourist office for details of private accommodation providers.

🍴 Eating

Triton   DALMATIAN, SEAFOOD €€
(☑020-801 161; www.triton.hr; Zaklopatica 15; mains 60-100KN; ☺11am-10pm May-Sep) Positioned at the centre of the lovely horseshoe cove of Zaklopatica, this excellent family-run seafood restaurant serves delicious fresh fish and lobster. Start with the house specialities: fried prawns (eat them shell and all), squid patties and cold tuna with vegetables. They also have rooms to rent upstairs.

ℹ Information

Tourist Office (☑020-801 018; www.tz-lastovo. hr; Pjevor 7, Lastovo Town; ☺8am-2pm & 4-8pm Mon-Sat)

ℹ Getting There & Away

The ferry port is at Ubli, at the western end of the island.

Jadrolinija (☑020-805 175; www.jadrolinija. hr) has up to three car ferries a day to Vela Luka on Korčula (passenger/car 32/195KN, 1¼ hours), with one continuing on to Split (68/530KN, 4½ hours). There's also a daily catamaran on this route, stopping in Vela Luka (40KN, 55 minutes), Hvar (45KN, two hours) and Split (65KN, 2¼ hours).

In July and August G&V Line (p272) has two catamarans a week to Korčula Town (60KN, 1¼ hours), Polače on Mljet (70KN, 2¼ hours), Sobra on Mljet (70KN, three hours) and Dubrovnik (95KN, four hours).

From May to October **European Coastal Airlines** (☑021-444 813; www.ec-air.eu) has seaplane flights from Ubli to downtown Split and Vela Luka.

ℹ Getting Around

The automated bike rental service Next Bike (www.nextbike.hr) has stands near the ferry at Ubli and in Lastovo Town.

Understand
Croatia

Croatia Today

A couple of years since Croatia entered the European Union (EU), tourism is booming, a positive driving force that is helping bolster Croatia's ailing economy. For nigh on a thousand years, Croatia's fortunes were at the mercy of decisions made in Budapest or Venice or Vienna or Belgrade. Now, with control over its own destiny and no one left to blame except its own politicians, the road to recovery is all its own.

Best on Film

You Only Love Once (*Samo jednom se ljubi;* 1981; Rajko Grlić) Considered one of Croatia's best films, this drama was a Cannes contender.

Cyclops (*Kiklop;* 1982; Antun Vrdoljak) Based on the 1965 namesake novel by Ranko Marinković.

How the War Started on My Island (*Kako je počeo rat na mom otoku;* 1996; Vinko Brešan) An acclaimed black comedy.

Number 55 (*Broj 55;* 2014; Kristijan Milić) The action takes place during Croatia's war of independence.

Best in Print

Black Lamb and Grey Falcon (1941; Rebecca West) Recounts the writer's journeys through the Balkans in 1941.

The Fall of Yugoslavia (1992; Misha Glenny) Explains the collapse of Yugoslavia in a remarkably lucid way.

Cafe Europa – Life After Communism (1996; Slavenka Drakulić) Wittily details Western culture's infiltration of Eastern Europe.

Another Fool in the Balkans (2006; Tony White) White retraces Rebecca West's journey, juxtaposing the region's modern life with its political history.

Settling into the EU

Croatia ticked off a major milestone in July 2013, when the country formally joined the EU following a referendum that passed by a margin of two to one. Yet a great deal of scepticism towards the benefits of the move remained, particularly among the younger generation.

Croatia's farmers and manufacturers no longer enjoy the customs exemptions that were in place with their former Yugoslav neighbours, and are facing stiff competition from EU imports. Foreign companies are also having an impact on the traditional southern Mediterranean way of life, with early starts and finishes in time for big family lunches and afternoon siestas slowly but surely fading away.

Despite this there are signs of an uptick in the economy, with GDP, exports and industrial production all growing. In June 2016, the unemployment rate dropped to 13.6%, the lowest it's been since 2008, though the youth unemployment rate stubbornly remains at over 40%.

In September 2015, eastern Croatia began to experience a major influx of refugees. Hungary had erected a fence on its border with Serbia, making Croatia and Slovenia the most direct route from Serbia to Austria. Over 340,000 people passed through a refugee camp created in November 2015 in Slavonski Brod in eastern Croatia before it was dismantled in April 2016. In March 2016 Croatia had started implementing restrictions on its border with Serbia. In July 2016 Croatia received its first group of asylum seekers under the EU quota.

Booming Tourism

Tourism in Croatia continues to boom. In 2015, 14.1 million travellers visited Croatia (an increase of 8.3% compared to the previous year), and the industry now generates up to 20% of the country's GDP, bringing in around €8 billion annually.

The Croatian government hopes to double tourism revenue by 2020 and create 32,000 new jobs in the process. The challenge will be to develop the industry while preserving the natural and cultural assets that make Croatia such an appealing destination. Locals are keen to avoid the overdevelopment so evident in other parts of the Mediterranean, such as Spain's Costa Brava. Development is currently subject to strict regulations, and there are 444 specially protected areas in the country, including eight national parks.

A boom in the number of music festivals is a mixed blessing. The festivals draw a large number of young visitors from Europe and further afield, but they are concentrated mostly in the June–September high season, and held in already popular coastal areas. The Croatian government is attempting to encourage tourists to visit outside the peak season and spread their visits from the coast to the beauty spots of the interior, particularly in Zagorje and Slavonia.

Political Changes

In January 2015, moderate conservative Kolinda Grabar-Kitarović was elected Croatia's first female president. A former foreign minister, ambassador to the United States and NATO assistant secretary general, she narrowly beat social democrat Ivo Josipović in a run-off vote. The general election that followed failed to produce a winner, so the main conservative Croatian Democratic Union (HDZ) and the small populist party Most ('Bridge') formed a coalition.

In January 2016 Tihomir Orešković, a Croatian-Canadian businessman with no political past, was approved by parliament as prime minister. Barely six months later, his government was toppled and for the first time in Croatia's history snap elections were called. They were held in September 2016; only 53% of Croatia's population showed up to vote. The ruling HDZ party, with moderate Andrej Plenković at the helm, fell just short of a majority; a coalition government was formed with the centre-right party MOST. Among the major tasks of the new government will be to ease the fears of rising nationalism and a veer to the right, which have the EU on its toes.

POPULATION: **4.3 MILLION**

GDP PER CAPITA: **US$21,600**

GDP GROWTH: **1.6%**

INFLATION: **-0.5%**

UNEMPLOYMENT: **19.3%**

population per sq km

religious groups
(% of population)

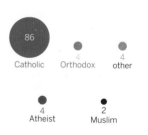

if Croatia were 100 people

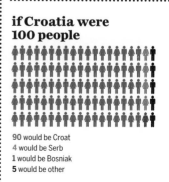

90 would be Croat
4 would be Serb
1 would be Bosniak
5 would be other

History

Trampled over by invading armies, passed back and forth between empires, split up then put back together again in various different shapes: Croatia's history is more convoluted than most. In this part of the world, echoes of the past are ever present, both in the built environment and as the subtext to any serious discussion about the present – not to mention the future.

Early Inhabitants

Around 30,000 years ago, Croatia was the haunt of Neanderthals (an early human species), who roamed through the hills of Slavonia. The Croatian Natural History Museum in Zagreb displays relics of this distant era, and the Museum of the Krapina Neanderthal in Krapina offers a faithful picture of Neanderthal life. By the end of the last ice age (around 18,000 years ago) modern humans were living in places such as the Vela Spila cave on the island of Korčula.

By around 1000 BC, the Illyrians took centre stage in the area now comprised of Slovenia, Croatia, Serbia, Kosovo, Montenegro and Albania. It's thought that the modern Albanian language, a linguistic oddity unrelated to any other language, is derived from ancient Illyrian. The often-warring tribes erected hill forts and created distinctive jewellery made from amber and bronze. In time they established a loose federation of tribes.

The Illyrians had to contend with the Greeks, who established trading colonies on the Adriatic coast at Epidaurus and Korčula in the 6th century BC, and on the islands of Vis and Hvar in the 4th century BC. In the meantime Celts were pushing down from the north.

In the 3rd century BC, Queen Teuta of the Illyrian Ardiaei tribe committed a fatal tactical error in seeking to conquer various Greek colonies. The put-upon Greeks asked the Romans for military support. The Romans pushed their way into the region and by 168 BC they defeated Gentius, the last Illyrian king. And so, gradually, the Illyrians were Latinised.

The word Adriatic is thought to be linked to the ancient Etruscan town of Adria, near Venice, but may also be related to the Illyrian word for water.

TIMELINE	6th century BC	4th century BC	229 BC
	Greek colonies are founded on the island of Korčula and at Epidaurus (modern-day Cavtat, south of Dubrovnik), within an area already populated by people the Greeks refer to as Ilyrians.	Illyrian tribes such as the Histri (the old name of Istria) and the Liburnians achieve supremacy in the Balkans, founding several kingdoms and establishing themselves as maritime powers.	Rome goes to war against Illyrian queen Teuta, at the behest of the Greeks who were being harried by state-sponsored Illyrian pirates. Following her defeat, the Illyrians pay annual tributes to Rome.

When In Rome

Following the fall of Gentius, the southern part of Illyria officially became an independent Roman protectorate known as Illyricum. It later became a Roman province and was enlarged as Rome pushed north in what was known as the Pannonian Wars. In AD 9, Illyricum was split into two separate Roman provinces: Pannonia (present-day Slovenia, northern Croatia and Bosnia, and bits of Austria, Slovakia, Hungary and Serbia) and Dalmatia (the rest of modern-day Croatia and Bosnia, Montenegro, and bits of Albania and Serbia).

Roman rule centred on the administrative headquarters of Salona (now Solin, near Split). It eventually brought peace and prosperity to the region, and cities such as Iader (Zadar), Felix Arba (Rab Town), Curicum (Krk Town), Tarsaticae (Rijeka), Parentium (Poreč), Polensium (Pula) and Siscia (Sisak) gained all the cultural accoutrements of Roman life, such as temples, baths and amphitheatres. The Romans built a series of roads reaching to the Aegean and Black Seas and the Danube, facilitating trade and the expansion of Roman culture. The roads also accelerated the later spread of Christianity.

These provinces even produced important figures in Roman history. Diocletian was born near Salona around AD 244 and distinguished himself as a military commander before becoming emperor in 285. As ruler, Diocletian attempted to simplify the unwieldy empire by dividing it into two administrative halves, thus sowing the seeds for the later division into the Eastern and Western Roman Empires. He is also remembered as a great persecutor of the Christians. In 305 he retired to the grand seaside palace he had built for himself near where he was born. Today, Diocletian's Palace is Croatia's greatest Roman remnant, forming the heart of the old town of Split. The Christians eventually had the last laugh, turfing the deceased emperor out of his mausoleum and converting it into a cathedral.

Christianity reached this region in its very earliest days. In the Bible, St Paul talks of preaching in Illyricum in his letter to the Romans (written in about AD 56), while his second letter to Timothy states that St Titus is in Dalmatia. Early Christian catacombs can be found under the Serbian Orthodox Monastery in Krka National Park, and local lore states that Titus, and possibly even Paul himself, visited the community here. In 313, only two years after Diocletian's death, the Emperor Constantine decriminalised Christianity, and in 380 it became the only tolerated religion under Theodosius the Great.

Theodosius was the last Roman leader to rule a united empire. On his death in AD 395, the empire was formally divided into eastern and western realms. The dividing line fell down the middle of present-day Montenegro, leaving present-day Croatia in the western half and Serbia in the east. The

Best Roman Ruins

Diocletian's Palace in Split, Central Dalmatia

Salona (Solin) on the outskirts of Split

Arena in Pula, Istria

HISTORY WHEN IN ROME

168 BC	27 BC	11 BC	AD 9
The last Illyrian king, Gentius, is defeated by the Romans near his capital Shkodra (present-day Albania), and Rome takes control over all of Dalmatia.	After nearly 500 years, the Roman Republic officially becomes the Roman Empire when Octavian is granted extraordinary powers and takes on the name Augustus.	The Roman province of Illyricum, covering present-day Dalmatia, is extended to the Danube after the defeat of Pannonian tribes. The new province takes in all of modern-day Croatia except Istria.	Illyricum is split into two provinces: Dalmatia to the south and Pannonia to the north. What we now call Croatia is split between the two.

eastern half became the Byzantine Empire, which persisted until 1453. The Western Roman Empire fell in 476, following invasions by various 'barbarian' tribes, such as the Visigoths, Huns and Lombards. The Goths took control of Dalmatia until 535 when the Byzantine Emperor Justinian booted them out.

Salut Slavs, Adios Avars

While the Croats are clearly related to other Slavic nations, the name by which they know themselves – Hrvat – isn't a Slavic word. One theory posits that Hrvat is a Persian word, and the Croats are a Slavic tribe who were briefly ruled – and named – by a ruling cast of Persian-speaking Alans from central Asia.

In the wake of the collapse of the Western Roman Empire, various Slavic tribes headed south from their original territory north of the Carpathians. Around the same time, the Avars (a nomadic Central Asian people known for their brutality) were sallying around the Balkan fringes of the Byzantine Empire. The Avars ravaged the former Roman towns of Salona and Epidaurus, whose inhabitants took refuge in Diocletian's Palace and Ragusa (Dubrovnik), respectively. They then progressed all the way to the mighty Byzantine capital of Constantinople itself (present-day Istanbul), where the Byzantines duly crushed them and they faded into history (to 'die away like Avars' is a common Balkan saying).

Controversy surrounds the role that the Slavs had in the defeat of the Avars. Some claim that Byzantium called on the Slavs to help in the fight against the Avar assault, while others think that they merely filled the void left when the Avars disappeared. Whatever the case, the Slavs spread rapidly through the Balkans, reaching the Adriatic by the early 7th century.

Two closely related Slavic tribes settled along the Adriatic Coast and its hinterland: the Croats and the Serbs. The Croats settled in an area roughly equivalent to present-day Croatia and Bosnia. By the 8th century, they had formed two powerful tribal entities, each led by a *knez* (duke). The Duchy of Croatia included most of present-day Dalmatia, parts of Montenegro and western Bosnia, while the Duchy of Pannonia included present-day Slavonia, Zagorje and the area around Zagreb. The Byzantines maintained control of several coastal cities, including Zadar, Split and Dubrovnik, as well as the islands of Hvar and Krk.

Christianity & the Croat Kings

Charlemagne's Franks gradually encroached on central Europe from the west and in AD 800 they seized Dalmatia, baptising the previously pagan Croats en masse. After Charlemagne's death in AD 814, the Pannonian Croats revolted unsuccessfully against Frankish rule, without the support of the Dalmatian Croats, whose major coastal cities remained under the influence of the Byzantine Empire. The big breakthrough for the Croats happened when Duke Branimir revolted against Byzantine control and won recognition from Pope John VIII. This brought them closer to the Vatican, and Catholicism became a defining feature of Croatian national identity.

257	395	614	800
The city of Salona becomes the first diocese in Roman Dalmatia, thus creating a toehold for Catholicism in the region; within 30 years the Bishop of Salona had become pope.	After Theodosius the Great dies, the Roman Empire is split in two. Slovenia, Croatia and Bosnia fall into the Western Roman Empire, with Serbia, Kosovo and Macedonia in the Byzantine Empire.	Central Asian marauders, the Avars, sack Salona and Epidaurus. Some contend that the Croats followed in their wake; others that they were invited by Emperor Heraclius to fend off the Avars.	The Franks led by their King Charlemagne seize control of Dalmatia and forcibly baptise the pagan Croats. The Byzantines recognise Frankish rule but retain control of several key coastal cities.

Trpimir, who was *knez* from 845 to 864, is widely considered to have founded the first Croatian dynasty, but it was his grandson Tomislav who first crowned himself king *(kralj)* in 925, and united Pannonia and Dalmatia. His kingdom included virtually all of modern Croatia as well as parts of Bosnia and the coast of Montenegro.

But the glory days were not to last. During the 11th century, the Serbs, Byzantines and Venetians imposed themselves on the Dalmatian coast, and new adversaries, the Hungarians, emerged in the north and advanced into Pannonia. Krešimir IV (r 1058–74) turned the tables and regained control of Dalmatia, but Croatia's rebound was only temporary and Krešimir was succeeded by Zvonimir and Stjepan, neither of whom produced an heir. Seeing an opportunity, the Hungarian King Laszlo claimed the throne by virtue of being the brother of Zvonimir's widow, Queen Jelena. He managed to take control of a large area of northern Croatia, but died before he could cement his claims in the south.

> Dalmatian dogs are thought to be one of the oldest breeds, but there's no conclusive evidence that they originated in Dalmatia. Some experts believe the dogs may have been brought to Dalmatia by the Roma.

Covetous Neighbours: Hungary vs Venice

Laszlo's brother Kolman succeeded him to the Hungarian throne and continued in his drive to take the Croatian throne as well. In 1097 he defeated his rival claimant Petar Svačić, thus ending the era of native-born Croat kings. In 1102 he imposed the *Pacta conventa,* ostensibly stating that Hungary and Croatia were separate entities under a single – Hungarian – monarchy. In practice, while Croatia maintained a *ban* (viceroy or governor) and a *sabor* (parliament), the Hungarians steadily marginalised the Croatian nobility. Under Hungarian rule, Pannonia became known as Slavonia, and the interior towns of Zagreb, Vukovar and Varaždin became thriving centres of trade and culture. In 1107, Koloman persuaded the Dalmatian nobility to bring the coast, long coveted by land-locked Hungarian kings, into his realm.

Upon Koloman's death in 1116, Venice launched new assaults on Biograd and the islands of Lošinj, Pag, Rab and Krk. Meanwhile, Zadar had grown to become the largest and most prosperous Dalmatian city and had successfully fended off two Venetian naval expeditions in the 1190s. But a vengeful Venetian doge in 1202 paid the soldiers of the Fourth Crusade to sack Zadar, despite Pope Innocent III specifically banning the crusaders from attacking Christian states. After this they rumbled on to brutally sack Constantinople, the great bastion of Eastern Christianity.

The Mongolian juggernaut ravaged the Croatian interior in 1242, but not before King Bela IV of Hungary fled the onslaught and took refuge in Trogir. The Venetians used the chaos to consolidate their hold on Zadar, and upon the death of King Bela in 1270, added Šibenik and Trogir to their possessions.

Best Gothic Buildings

St James' Cathedral, Šibenik

St Mark's Cathedral, Korčula

St Anastasia's Cathedral, Zadar

Cathedral of the Assumption of the Blessed Virgin Mary, Zagreb

845–64	869	910–28	1000
Trpimir establishes Croatia's first royal line. He fights and defeats the powerful Bulgarian state, and inflicts major defeats on the Byzantines. Croatian territory expands well into what is now Bosnia.	At the behest of Byzantium, Macedonian monks Methodius and Cyril create the Glagolitic alphabet, specifically with a view to speeding the spread of Christianity among the Slavic peoples.	Tomislav proclaims himself king while expanding territory at the expense of the Hungarians and defeating Bulgarian Tsar Simeon in modern Bosnia. Tomislav unites Pannonian and Dalmatian Croats.	Venice capitalises on a lack of stability in Croatia to begin encroaching on the Dalmatian coast. So begins the tussle between Venice and other powers for control of Dalmatia.

THE VENETIAN YOKE

For nearly 800 years the doges of Venice sought to control, colonise and exploit the Croatian coast. Coastal and island towns from Rovinj in the north to Korčula in the south still show a marked Venetian influence in architecture, cuisine and culture. However, as in Venice's other dominions, the period was not a happy time.

Venetian rule in Dalmatia and Istria was a record of virtually unbroken economic exploitation. The Venetians systematically denuded the landscape in order to provide timber for their ships. State monopolies set artificially low prices for olive oil, figs, wine, fish and salt, thus ensuring cheap commodities for Venetian buyers, while local merchants and producers were impoverished. Shipbuilding was effectively banned, since Venice tolerated no competition with its own ships. No roads or schools were built, and no investment was made in local industry.

King Ludovic (Louis) I of Hungary (r 1342–82) re-established control over the country and even persuaded Venice to relinquish Dalmatia. But new conflicts emerged upon his death. The Croatian nobility rallied around Ladislas of Naples, who was crowned king in Zadar in 1403. Short of funds, Ladislas sold Zadar to Venice in 1409 for a paltry 100,000 ducats and renounced his rights to Dalmatia. In the early 15th century, Venice strengthened its grip on the Dalmatian coastline south from Zadar and remained in control until the Napoleonic invasion of 1797. Only the wily citizens of Ragusa managed to retain their independence.

The Ottoman Onslaught

Šibenik-born Faust Vrančić (1551–1617) made the first working parachute.

Croatia had plenty to contend with as Venetians, Hungarians and others picked at the remnants of the original Croatian state, yet another threat loomed from the east. The Ottoman Turks had emerged out of Anatolia in the early 14th century and rapidly swallowed up the Balkans.

The Serbs were rolled at Kosovo Polje in 1389, a hastily choreographed anti-Turkish crusade was garrotted in Hungary in 1396, and Bosnia was despatched in 1463. When the Croatian nobility finally faced up to the Ottomans in 1493 in Krbavsko Polje, they too were pummelled.

Despite a sudden show of unity among the remaining noble families, one city after another fell to the Ottoman sultans. The important bishopric at Zagreb heavily fortified the cathedral in Kaptol, which remained untouched, but the gateway town of Knin fell in 1521. Five years later, the Ottomans engaged the Hungarians in Mohács. Again the Turks won and the Hungarian army was destroyed. The Turks threatened the Adriatic coast, but never actually captured it, while Ragusa maintained its independence throughout the turmoil.

1058–74	1091–1102	1242	1300s
Soon after the 1054 split of the church into Orthodox and Catholic strands, the pope recognises Krešimir IV as king of Dalmatia and Croatia. This places Croatia within the Catholic sphere.	Hungarian King Laszlo, related to the late King Zvonimir, claims the Croatian throne; his successor, Koloman, defeats the last Croatian king and cements Hungarian control of Croatia with the *Pacta conventa*.	The Mongols devastate the royal houses of Hungary and Croatia. The noble Šubić and Frankopan families step in to assume a degree of political and economic power that persists for centuries.	The Hungarian Anjou dynasty under Carl (Charles) and Ludovic (Louis) reasserts royal authority in Croatia and seeks to expel the Venetians who had taken Dalmatian territory.

Turkish assaults on the Balkans caused massive havoc. Cities and towns were destroyed, people were enslaved and commandeered to the Ottoman war machine, and refugees scattered around the region.

Enter the Habsburgs

With the Hungarians out of the picture, the Croats turned to the Austrians for protection. The Habsburg Empire, ruled from Vienna, duly absorbed a narrow strip of territory around Zagreb, Karlovac and Varaždin. The Habsburgs sought to build a buffer against the Ottomans, creating the Vojna Krajina (Military Frontier). In this region composed of a string of forts south of Zagreb, a standing army comprised largely of Vlachs and Serbs faced down the Ottomans.

Exactly a century after their defeat by the Ottomans, the Croats managed to turn the tables on the Turks. At Sisak in 1593 the Habsburg army, including Croat soldiers, finally inflicted a defeat on the Ottomans. In 1699 in Sremski Karlovci the Ottomans sued for peace for the first time, and the Turkish stranglehold on central Europe was loosened. Bosnia remained within the Ottoman Empire but Venice regained the coast, apart from a thin strip of land around Neum that gave the Ottomans' access to the Adriatic and provided a buffer between the territories of Venice and Ragusa.

The Habsburgs reclaimed Slavonia soon after, thus expanding the Krajina. This period saw a return to stability and advances in agricultural production, but Croatian language and culture languished.

The necktie is a descendant of the cravat, which originated in Croatia as part of military attire and was adopted by the French in the 17th century. The name 'cravat' is a corruption of both Croat and Hrvat.

HISTORY ENTER THE HABSBURGS

THE REPUBLIC OF RAGUSA

While most of the Dalmatian coast struggled under Venetian rule, Ragusa (now Dubrovnik) led a charmed life, existing as a republic in its own right. A ruling class, abounding in business acumen and diplomatic skill, ensured that this minuscule city-state punched well above its weight and played a significant role in the immediate region and beyond.

The Ragusans asked the pope for permission to trade with the Turks in 1371 and subsequently established trade centres throughout the Ottoman Empire. Burgeoning trade led to a flowering in the arts and sciences. The Ragusans were extremely liberal for the time, abolishing the slave trade in the 15th century. They were also scientifically advanced, establishing a system of quarantine in 1377.

However, the Ragusans had to maintain a perilous position sandwiched between Ottoman and Venetian interests. An earthquake in 1667 caused a great deal of damage, from which they never fully recovered, and Napoleon finally swallowed up the republic in 1808.

1358	1409	1493	1526–27
Ragusa (modern Dubrovnik) frees itself of Venice and becomes an independent city republic. It grows to become an advanced and liberal society, while cannily fending off Venetians and Ottomans.	Ladislas of Naples assumes the Croatian throne but, scared off by dynastic squabbling, sells Zadar to Venice for 100,000 ducats, renouncing his rights to Dalmatia. Venetian control soon extends from Zadar to Ragusa.	At Krbavsko Polje a joint Croatian-Hungarian army engages the Turks, but is obliterated, leaving Croatia open to Turkish raids. The Turkish advance brings turmoil, as populations flee and famine ensues.	The Battle of Mohács sees the Ottoman Turks annihilate the Hungarian nobility, ending Hungarian control of Croatia. Hungarian King Louis dies heirless, allowing the Austrian Habsburgs control.

Napoleon & the Illyrian Provinces

Habsburg support for the restoration of the French monarchy provoked Napoleon to invade the Italian states in 1796. After conquering Venice in 1797 he agreed to transfer Dalmatia to Austria in the Treaty of Campo Formio in exchange for other concessions. The Croats' secret hopes that Dalmatia would be united with Slavonia were soon dashed, as the Habsburgs made it clear that the two territories would retain separate administrations.

Austrian control of Dalmatia only lasted until Napoleon's 1805 victory over Austrian and Prussian forces at Austerlitz, which forced Austria to cede the Dalmatian coast to France. Ragusa quickly surrendered to French forces, which also swallowed up the Bay of Kotor in present-day Montenegro. Napoleon renamed his conquest the 'Illyrian provinces' and moved swiftly to reform the neglected territory. A tree-planting program was implemented to reforest the barren hills. Roads and hospitals were built and new crops introduced. Since almost the entire population was illiterate, the new government set up primary schools, high schools and a college at Zadar. Yet the French regime remained unpopular.

After Napoleon's Russian campaign and the fall of his empire, the 1815 Congress of Vienna recognised Austria's claims to Dalmatia and placed the rest of Croatia under the jurisdiction of Austria's Hungarian province. For the Dalmatians the new regime meant a return to the status quo, since the Austrians restored the former Italian elite to power, whereas the Hungarians imposed the Hungarian language and culture on the northern Croatian population.

A South Slavic Consciousness

Traditionally, upper-class Dalmatians spoke Italian, and the northern Croatian nobility spoke German or Hungarian, but flush with the Enlightenment fervour, Napoleon had sown the seeds of creating a south Slavic consciousness. This sense of a shared identity eventually manifested itself in an 'Illyrian' movement in the 1830s, which centred on the revival of the Croatian language. Napoleon's grand plan was to foster Serbian culture, too, but Serbia remained under Ottoman occupation.

The establishment of the first Illyrian newspaper in 1834, written in the Zagreb dialect, prompted the Croatian *sabor* to call for the teaching of Slavic languages in schools.

Following the 1848 revolution in Paris, the Hungarians began to press for change within the Habsburg Empire. The Croats saw this as an opportunity to regain some control and unify Dalmatia, the Krajina and Slavonia. The Habsburgs paid lip service to Croatian sentiments and appointed Josip Jelačić *ban* (viceroy or governor) of Croatia. Jelačić promptly called elections, claimed a mandate and declared war on Hungarian agitators

1537–40	1593	1671	1699
The Turks take Klis, the last Croatian bastion in Dalmatia. The Turkish advance continues to Sisak, just south of Zagreb. For reasons unknown, the Turks never push on to Zagreb.	At Sisak, previously the Ottoman high-tide mark, the Habsburgs inflict the first major defeat on the Ottomans, thus prefiguring the long, slow Turkish retreat from central Europe.	A deputation led by Franjo Frankopan and Petar Zrinski, with the aim of ridding Croatia of Hungarian domination, is cut short. Both are hanged, their lands confiscated by the Habsburgs.	At the Treaty of Karlovci, the Ottomans renounce all claims to Croatia. Venice and Hungary reclaim all freed lands over the next 20 years.

in order to curry favour with the Habsburgs, but his demands for autonomy fell on deaf ears. Jelačić is immortalised in a martial pose in the heart of Zagreb.

Disillusionment spread after 1848, and amplified after the birth of the Austro-Hungarian Dual Monarchy in 1867. The monarchy placed northern Croatia and Slavonia within the Hungarian administration, while Dalmatia remained within Austria. Whatever limited form of self-government the Croats enjoyed under the Habsburgs disappeared.

Dreams of Yugoslavia

The river of discontent forked into two streams that dominated the political landscape for the next century. The old 'Illyrian' movement became the National Party, dominated by Bishop Josip Juraj Strossmayer. Strossmayer believed that the Habsburgs and the Hungarians set out to emphasise the differences between Serbs and Croats, and that only through Jugoslavenstvo (literally, 'Southslavism' – or south Slavic unity) could the aspirations of both peoples be realised. Strossmayer supported the independence struggle in Serbia, but favoured a Yugoslav (ie south Slavic) entity within the Austro-Hungarian Empire rather than complete independence.

By contrast, the Party of Rights, led by the militantly anti-Serb Ante Starčević, envisaged an independent Croatia made up of Slavonia, Dalmatia, the Krajina, Slovenia, Istria, and part of Bosnia and Hercegovina. At the same time, the Orthodox Church was encouraging the Serbs to form a national identity based upon their religion. Until the 19th century, Orthodox inhabitants of Croatia identified themselves as Vlachs, Morlachs, Serbs, Orthodox or even Greeks. With the help of Starčević's attacks, the sense of a separate Serbian Orthodox identity within Croatia developed.

Under the 'divide and rule' theory, the Hungarian-appointed *ban* of Croatia blatantly favoured the Serbs and the Orthodox Church, but his strategy backfired. The first organised resistance formed in Dalmatia. Croats in Rijeka and Serbs in Zadar joined together in 1905 to demand the unification of Dalmatia and Slavonia, with a formal guarantee of Serbian equality as a nation. The spirit of unity mushroomed, and by 1906 Croat–Serb coalitions had taken over local government in Dalmatia and Slavonia, forming a serious threat to the Hungarian power structure.

Ivan Vučetić (1858–1925), who developed dactyloscopy (fingerprint identification), was born on the island of Hvar in the Adriatic.

WWI & the First Yugoslavia

With the outbreak of WWI, Croatia's future was again up for grabs. Sensing that they would once again be pawns to the Great Powers, a Croatian delegation called the 'Yugoslav Committee' talked the Serbian government into establishing a parliamentary monarchy that would rule over the two countries. Although many Croats were unclear about Serbian intentions, they were sure about Italian intentions, since Italy lost no time in seizing

1780s	1797–1815	1830–50	1867
The Habsburgs begin a process of Germanisation, ordering all administration be conducted in German. This leads to rising nationalist feelings among the Habsburg's non-German subjects.	Napoleon brings the Venetian Republic to an end; Venetian dominions are initially given to the Habsburgs, but in 1806 Napoleon gains the Adriatic coast, which he dubs the 'Illyrian provinces'.	The south Slavic consciousness is awakened, aiming to reverse the processes of Hungarianisation and Germanisation under the Habsburgs. An offshoot is the Croatian National Revival.	The Habsburg throne devolves to become the Austro-Hungarian Dual Monarchy. Croatian territory is divided between them: Dalmatia is awarded to Austria, and Slavonia is under Hungarian control.

Pula, Rijeka and Zadar after the war. Effectively given a choice between throwing in their lot with Italy or Serbia, the Croats chose Serbia.

The Yugoslav Committee became the National Council of Slovenes, Croats and Serbs after the collapse of the Austro-Hungarian Empire in 1918. The council quickly negotiated the establishment of the Kingdom of Serbs, Croats and Slovenes to be based in Belgrade (the unwieldy name was changed to the Kingdom of Yugoslavia in 1929). The previously independent kingdom of Montenegro was also subsumed into the new entity. Montenegro's King Nikola had escaped to France during the war, and France refused to allow him to leave, thus ending the 300-year-old Petrović dynasty.

Problems with the kingdom began almost immediately. As under the Habsburgs, the Croats enjoyed scant autonomy. Currency reforms benefited Serbs at the expense of the Croats. A treaty between Yugoslavia and Italy gave Istria, Zadar and several islands to Italy. The new constitution abolished Croatia's *sabor* and centralised power in Belgrade, while new electoral districts severely under-represented the Croats.

Opposition to the new regime was led by the Croat Stjepan Radić, who favoured the idea of Yugoslavia, but wished to transform it into a federal democracy. His alliance with the Serb Svetozar Pribićević proved profoundly threatening to the regime and Radić was assassinated in 1928. Exploiting fears of civil war, Yugoslavia's King Aleksandar ended any hope of democratic change by proclaiming a royal dictatorship, abolishing political parties and suspending parliamentary government. Meanwhile, during the 1920s the Yugoslav Communist Party arose; Josip Broz Tito was to become leader in 1937.

The Rise of Ustaše & WWII

Croatia Through History (2007), by Branka Magaš, is a highly detailed doorstop of a history, focusing on pivotal events and clearly delineating the gradual development of Croatian national identity.

One day after the proclamation of the royal dictatorship, a Bosnian Croat, Ante Pavelić, set up the Ustaše Croatian Liberation Movement in Zagreb, inspired by Mussolini. The stated aim was to establish an independent state, by force if necessary. Fearing arrest, he first fled to Sofia in Bulgaria and made contact with anti-Serbian Macedonian revolutionaries. He then moved on to Italy, where he established training camps for his organisation under Mussolini's benevolent eye. In 1934, he and the Macedonians assassinated King Aleksandar in Marseilles. Italy responded by closing down the training camps and imprisoning Pavelić and many of his followers.

When Germany invaded Yugoslavia on 6 April 1941, the exiled Ustaše were quickly installed by the Germans and the Italians, the latter of which hoped to see their own territorial aims in Dalmatia realised. Within days the Independent State of Croatia (NDH; Nezavisna Država Hrvatska), headed by Pavelić, issued a range of decrees designed to persecute and

1905	1908	1918	1920
Burgeoning Croatian national consciousness becomes visible in the Rijeka Resolution, which calls for increased democracy as well as the reunification of Dalmatia and Slavonia.	The Austro-Hungarian Empire takes control of Bosnia and Hercegovina, bringing the Slavic Muslims of the Balkans within its sphere of responsibility, thus creating the nucleus of the future Yugoslav federation.	The Kingdom of Serbs, Croats and Slovenes is created after the dismantling of the Austro-Hungarian Empire following WWI. Serbian Prince Aleksandar Karađorđević assumes the throne.	Stjepan Radić establishes the Croatian Republican Peasant Party, which becomes the primary voice for Croatian interests in the face of Serb domination.

eliminate the regime's 'enemies', a thinly veiled reference to the Jews, Roma and Serbs. The majority of the Jewish population was rounded up and packed off to extermination camps between 1941 and 1945.

Serbs fared little better. The Ustaše program explicitly called for 'one-third of Serbs killed, one-third expelled and one-third converted to Catholicism', an agenda that was carried out with appalling brutality. Villages conducted their own pogroms against Serbs and extermination camps were set up, most notoriously at Jasenovac (south of Zagreb), where Jews, Roma and antifascist Croats were killed. The exact number of Serb victims is uncertain and controversial, although it is likely to have been in the hundreds of thousands.

TITO

Josip Broz was born in Kumrovec in 1892 to a Croat father and a Slovene mother. When WWI broke out, he was drafted into the Austro-Hungarian army and was taken prisoner by the Russians. He escaped just before the 1917 revolution, became a communist and joined the Red Army. He returned to Croatia in 1920 and became a union organiser while working as a metalworker.

As secretary of the Zagreb committee of the outlawed Communist Party, he worked to unify the party and increase its membership. When the Nazis invaded in 1941, he adopted the name Tito and organised small bands of guerrillas, which formed the core of the Partisan movement. His successful campaigns attracted military support from the British and the Americans, but the Soviet Union, despite sharing his communist ideology, repeatedly rebuffed his requests for aid.

In 1945 he became prime minister of a reconstituted Yugoslavia. Although retaining a communist ideology, and remaining nominally loyal to Russia, Tito had an independent streak. In 1948 he fell out with Stalin and adopted a conciliatory policy towards the West.

Yugoslavia's rival nationalities were Tito's biggest headache, which he dealt with by suppressing all dissent and trying to ensure a rough equality of representation at the upper echelons of government. As a committed communist, he viewed ethnic disputes as unwelcome deviations from the pursuit of the common good.

Yet Tito was well aware of the ethnic tensions that simmered just below the surface in Yugoslavia. Preparations for his succession began in the early 1970s as he aimed to create a balance of power among the ethnic groups of Yugoslavia. He set up a collective presidency that was to rotate annually but the system proved unworkable. Later events revealed how dependent Yugoslavia was on its wily, charismatic leader.

When Tito died in May 1980, his body was carried from Ljubljana (Slovenia) to Belgrade (Serbia). Thousands of mourners flocked to the streets to pay respects to the man who had united a difficult country for 35 years. It was the last communal outpouring of emotion that Yugoslavia's fractious nationalities were able to share.

1934	1939	1941	1943
Ustaše and Macedonian revolutionaries conspire to assassinate Yugoslavia's King Aleksandar. He's shot in Marseilles while on a state visit to France. The crown passes to his 11-year-old son Petar.	Nazi Germany invades Poland and WWII begins. Yugoslavia, headed by the regent Prince Paul, attempts to stay neutral. Two years later, when Hitler pressures him to sign a pact, he is deposed in a coup.	Germany invades Yugoslavia. Ante Pavelić proclaims the Independent State of Croatia (NDH; Nezavisna Država Hrvatska), a Nazi puppet state. His Ustaše followers begin exterminating Serbs, Roma and Jews.	Tito's communist Partisans achieve military victories and build a popular antifascist front. They reclaim territory from retreating Italian brigades. The British and the USA lend military support.

Clearly explaining centuries of complicated events, Marcus Tanner's *Croatia: A Nation Forged in War* (3rd edition, 2010) sallies forth from the arrival of the Slavs to the present day, presenting, in a lively, readable style, the trials and tribulations of Croatian history.

Tito & the Partisans

Not all Croats supported these policies, and some spoke out against them. The Ustaše regime drew most of its support from the Lika region, southwest of Zagreb, and western Hercegovina. Pavelić's agreement to cede a good part of Dalmatia to Italy was highly unpopular and the Ustaše had almost no support in that region. Likewise, the Ustaše had little support among Zagreb's intellectuals.

Serbian 'Četnik' formations led by General Draža Mihailović provided armed resistance to the regime. The Četniks began as an antifascist rebellion, but soon retaliated against the Ustaše with in-kind massacres of Croats in eastern Croatia and Bosnia.

The most effective antifascist struggle was conducted by the National Liberation Partisan units lead by Josip Broz, known as Tito. The Partisans, which had their roots in the outlawed Yugoslav Communist Party, attracted long-suffering Yugoslav intellectuals, Croats disgusted with Četnik massacres, Serbs disgusted with Ustaše massacres, and antifascists of all kinds. The Partisans gained wide popular support with their early manifesto, which envisioned a postwar Yugoslavia based on a loose federation.

Although the Allies initially backed the Serbian Četniks, it became apparent that the Partisans were waging a far more focused and determined fight against the Nazis. With the diplomatic and military support of Churchill and other Allied powers, the Partisans controlled much of Croatia by 1943. They established functioning local governments in the territory they seized, which later eased their transition to power. On 20 October 1944, the Partisans entered Belgrade alongside the Red Army. When Germany surrendered in 1945, Pavelić and the Ustaše fled and the Partisans entered Zagreb.

The remnants of the NDH army, desperate to avoid falling into the hands of the Partisans, attempted to cross into Austria. A small British contingent met the 50,000 troops and promised to intern them outside Yugoslavia. It was a trick. The troops were forced into trains that headed back into Yugoslavia, where the Partisans awaited them. The ensuing massacre claimed the lives of at least 30,000 men (although the exact number is in doubt) and left a stain on the Yugoslav government.

The Second Yugoslavia

Tito's attempt to retain control of the Italian city of Trieste and parts of southern Austria faltered in the face of Allied opposition. Dalmatia and most of Istria did, however, become a permanent part of postwar Yugoslavia. In creating the Federal People's Republic of Yugoslavia, Tito was determined to forge a state in which no ethnic group dominated the po-

1945	1948	1960s	1971
Germany surrenders, the Partisans enter Zagreb and the Federal People's Republic of Yugoslavia is founded. Croatia becomes a constituent member of a federation of six republics.	Tito breaks with Stalin and Yugoslavia is expelled from the Cominform, the Soviet-dominated forum of Communist states. Tito begins to steer a careful course between the Eastern and Western blocs.	Croatian unrest about the centralisation of power in Belgrade builds. The use of Croatian money to support poorer provinces is resented, along with the over-representation of Serbs in the public service and military.	In the 'Croatian Spring' Communist Party reformers, intellectuals, students and nationalists call for greater economic and constitutional autonomy for Croatia.

litical landscape. Croatia became one of six republics – along with Macedonia, Serbia, Montenegro, Bosnia and Hercegovina, and Slovenia – in a tightly configured federation. However, Tito effected this delicate balance by creating a one-party state and rigorously stamping out all opposition.

During the 1960s, the concentration of power in Belgrade was an increasingly complicated issue as it became apparent that money from the more prosperous republics of Slovenia and Croatia was being distributed to the poorer autonomous province of Kosovo and the republic of Bosnia and Hercegovina. The problem seemed particularly blatant in Croatia, which saw money from its prosperous tourist business on the Adriatic coast flow into Belgrade. At the same time, Serbs in Croatia were over-represented in the government, armed forces and police.

In Croatia the unrest reached a crescendo in the 'Croatian Spring' of 1971. Led by reformers within the Communist Party of Croatia, intellectuals and students called for a loosening of Croatia's ties to Yugoslavia. In addition to calls for greater economic autonomy and constitutional reform for Croatia, nationalistic elements manifested themselves too. Tito fought back, clamping down on the liberalisation that had gradually been gaining momentum in Yugoslavia. Serbs viewed the movement as the Ustaše reborn; in turn, jailed reformers blamed the Serbs for their troubles. The stage was set for the rise of nationalism and the war of the 1990s.

The Death of Yugoslavia

Tito left a shaky Yugoslavia upon his death in May 1980. With the economy in a parlous state, a presidency that rotated among the six republics could not compensate for the loss of Tito's steadying hand at the helm. The authority of the central government sank along with the economy, and long-suppressed mistrust among Yugoslavia's ethnic groups resurfaced, coinciding with the rise to power of nationalist Slobodan Milošević in Serbia.

In 1989 repression of the Albanian majority in Serbia's Kosovo province sparked renewed fears of Serbian hegemony and precipitated the end of the Yugoslav Federation. With political changes sweeping Eastern Europe and in the face of increasing provocations from Milošević, Slovenia embarked on a course for independence. For Croatia, remaining in a Serb-dominated Yugoslavia without the counterweight of Slovenia would have been untenable.

In the Croatian elections of April 1990, Franjo Tuđman's Croatian Democratic Union (HDZ; Hrvatska Demokratska Zajednica) secured 40% of the vote, to the 30% won by the Communist Party, which retained the loyalty of the Serbian community as well as voters in Istria and Rijeka. On 22 December 1990, a new Croatian constitution changed the status of Serbs in Croatia from that of a 'constituent nation' to a national minority.

The Balkans (2000), by noted historian Mark Mazower, is a highly readable short introduction to the region. It offers clearly discussed overviews of geography, culture and the broad historical sweep of the Balkans.

Misha Glenny's *The Balkans: Nationalism, War & the Great Powers, 1804–1999* (2000) explores the history of outside interference in the Balkans. *The Fall of Yugoslavia* (1992) deciphers the complex politics, history and cultural flare-ups that led to the wars of the 1990s.

1980	1981	1984	1986
President Tito dies. There is a genuine outpouring of grief, and tributes are paid from around the world. Yugoslavia is left beset by inflation, unemployment and foreign debt.	Future president Franjo Tuđman is sentenced to three years in jail following interviews with foreign newspapers about the position of Croats within Yugoslavia.	Yugoslavia hosts a successful Winter Olympic Games in Sarajevo, avoiding the Cold War–inspired boycotts that marred the Summer Olympics of both 1980 and 1984.	Slobodan Milošević becomes the head of the Serbian Communist Party. The following year he comes to public attention following a fiery address to minority Serbs in Kosovo.

The constitution failed to guarantee minority rights and caused mass dismissals of Serbs from the public service. This stimulated Croatia's 600,000-strong ethnic Serb community to demand autonomy. In early 1991, Serb extremists within Croatia staged provocations in order to force federal military intervention. A May 1991 referendum (boycotted by the Serbs) produced a 93% vote in favour of Croatian independence. When Croatia declared independence on 25 June 1991, the Serbian enclave of Krajina proclaimed its independence from Croatia.

The War for Croatia

Dubrovnik: A History (2003), by Robin Harris, is a thoughtful and thorough look at the great city, investigating events, individuals and movements that have contributed to the architectural and cultural fabric of the 'pearl of the Adriatic'.

Under pressure from the EU, Croatia declared a three-month moratorium on its independence, but heavy fighting broke out in Krajina, Baranja and Slavonia. This initiated what Croats refer to as the Homeland War. The Yugoslav People's Army, dominated by Serbs, began to intervene in support of Serbian irregulars under the pretext of halting ethnic violence. When the Croatian government ordered a shutdown of federal military installations in the republic of Croatia, the Yugoslav navy blockaded the Adriatic coast and laid siege to the strategic town of Vukovar on the Danube. During the summer of 1991, a quarter of Croatia fell to Serb militias and the Serb-led Yugoslav People's Army.

In late 1991, the federal army and the Montenegrin militia moved against Dubrovnik, and the presidential palace in Zagreb was hit by rockets from Yugoslav jets in an apparent assassination attempt on President Tuđman. When the three-month moratorium ended, Croatia declared full independence. Soon after, Vukovar finally fell when the Yugoslav army moved in, in one of the more bloodthirsty acts in all of the Yugoslav wars. During six months of fighting in Croatia, 10,000 people died, hundreds of thousands fled and tens of thousands of homes were destroyed.

The United Nations Gets Involved

Beginning on 3 January 1992, a UN-brokered ceasefire generally held. The federal army was allowed to withdraw from its bases inside Croatia and tensions diminished. At the same time, the EU, succumbing to pressure from Germany, recognised Croatia. This was followed by US recognition, and in May 1992 Croatia was admitted to the UN.

The UN peace plan in Krajina was intended to bring about the disarming of local Serb paramilitary formations, the repatriation of refugees and the return of the region to Croatia. Instead, it only froze the existing situation and offered no permanent solution. In January 1993, the Croatian army suddenly launched an offensive in southern Krajina, pushing the Serbs back in some areas and recapturing strategic points. The Krajina Serbs vowed never to accept rule from Zagreb and in June 1993 they voted overwhelmingly to join the Bosnian Serbs (and eventually Greater

1989	1990	1991	1992
The communist system begins to collapse in Eastern Europe; Franjo Tuđman establishes Yugoslavia's first non-communist party, the Croatian Democratic Union (HDZ).	Disagreements between Slovenia and Serbia lead to the disintegration of the Yugoslav Communist Party. The Croatian Communist Party allows multiparty elections, which are won by HDZ.	The Croatian *sabor* (parliament) proclaims the independence of Croatia; Krajina Serbs declare independence from Croatia, with the support of Milošević. War breaks out between Croats and Serbs.	A first UN-brokered ceasefire takes effect temporarily. The EU recognises Croatian independence and Croatia is admitted into the UN. War breaks out in neighbouring Bosnia.

Serbia). A mass expulsion left only about 900 Croats in Krajina out of an original population of 44,000. In early 2004, a comprehensive ceasefire substantially reduced the violence in the region. Demilitarised 'zones of separation' between the parties were established.

Troubles in Bosnia & Hercegovina

Meanwhile, neighbouring Bosnia and Hercegovina had been subjected to similar treatment at the hands of the Yugoslav army and Serbian para-militaries, potentially preparing the ground for the creation of a Greater Serbia including the Serb-controlled parts of Bosnia and Croatia. Initially, in the face of Serbian advances, Bosnia's Croats and Muslims had banded together, but in 1993 the two sides fell out and began fighting each other. The Bosnian Croats, with tacit support from Zagreb, were responsible for several horrific events in Bosnia, including the destruction of the old bridge in Mostar. This conflagration was extinguished when the USA fostered the development of the Muslim–Croatian federation in 1994, as the world looked on in horror at the Serb siege of Sarajevo.

While these grim events unfolded in Bosnia and Hercegovina, the Croatian government quietly began procuring arms from abroad. On 1 May 1995, the Croatian army and police entered occupied western Slavonia, east of Zagreb, and seized control of the region within days. The Krajina Serbs responded by shelling Zagreb in an attack that left seven people dead and 130 wounded. As the Croatian military consolidated its hold in western Slavonia, some 15,000 Serbs fled the region despite assurances from the Croatian government that they were safe from retribution.

Belgrade's silence throughout the campaign showed that the Krajina Serbs had lost the support of their Serbian sponsors, encouraging Croats to forge ahead. On 4 August, the military launched an assault on the rebel Serb capital of Knin. The Serb army fled towards northern Bosnia, along with 150,000 civilians whose roots in the Krajina stretched back centuries. The military operation ended in days, but was followed by months of terror, including widespread looting and burning of Serb villages.

The Dayton Peace Accords signed in Paris in December 1995 recognised Croatia's Yugoslav-era borders and provided for the return of eastern Slavonia. The transition proceeded relatively smoothly, but the two populations still regard each other with suspicion and hostility.

Postwar Croatia

A degree of stability returned to Croatia after the hostilities. A key provision of the peace agreement was the guarantee by the Croatian government to facilitate the return of Serbian refugees, and although the central government in Zagreb made the return of refugees a priority in accordance with the demands of the international community, its efforts have

In July 1995, upwards of 8000 Muslim men and boys were slaughtered by the Bosnian Serb Army in the Bosnian town of Srebrenica. UN Secretary General Kofi Annan described the genocide as 'the worst on European soil since the Second World War'.

Richard Holbrooke's *To End a War* (1998) recounts the events surrounding the Dayton Accords. As the American diplomat who prodded the warring parties to the negotiating table to hammer out a peace accord, Holbrooke was in a unique position to evaluate the personalities and politics of the region.

HISTORY TROUBLES IN BOSNIA & HERCEGOVINA

1993	1994	1995	2009
Bosnian Croats and Muslims, previously aligned in fighting the Bosnian Serbs, start fighting each other. Croatia's reputation is sullied by the massacre of Muslim and Serb civilians.	US-brokered talks lead to the creation of a Muslim–Croat Federation in Bosnia. Pope John Paul II visits Croatia and calls for a rejection of nationalism and a culture of peace.	The 'Oluja' military campaign sees Croatian forces reclaim lost Croatian territory in the Krajina; most of the region's Serbs flee. The Dayton Accords bring peace and confirm Croatia's borders.	Croatia officially joins NATO. Ivo Sanader suddenly resigns as prime minister. His deputy, former journalist Jadranka Kosor, takes over as the country's first female prime minister.

CORRUPTION, CRIME & PUNISHMENT

The struggle against rife corruption came into the spotlight in late 2010, when Ivo Sanader – who had stepped down from serving a second term as prime minister in July 2009 without an explanation – was charged with corruption and fled the country overnight. He denied fleeing but was arrested in Austria a few days later. He was found guilty and is currently serving an 8½-year prison term.

often been subverted by local authorities intent on maintaining the ethnic singularity of their regions. The most recent census (2011) has Serbs at 4.4% of the population, slightly down on the previous census 10 years earlier, and less than a third of their 1991 numbers.

The handover of General Ante Gotovina in 2005 to the International Court of Justice in the Hague to answer war-crimes charges was a major condition for the beginning of Croatia's negotiations to join the EU. In 2011 Gotovina and fellow ex-general Mladen Markač were sentenced to 24 and 18 years in jail respectively, but the decision was overruled in November 2012, after an appeal court ruled there had been no conspiracy to commit war crimes.

In the spring of 2008, Croatia was officially invited to join NATO at the summit in Bucharest; exactly a year later, it joined the alliance. In 2012 Croats voted in a referendum to join the EU and in 2013 the country officially became a member. In February 2015, Kolinda Grabar-Kitarović succeeded Ivo Josipović and became Croatia's first female president.

2010	2012	2013	2015
Slovenia votes in a referendum regarding a border dispute with Croatia. A narrow majority of Slovenes supports the compromise resolution, clearing way for Croatia's entry into the EU.	A referendum on whether Croatia should join the EU results in a 'yes' vote by a margin of two to one, though voter turnout is low at about 44%.	Croatia officially joins the EU, becoming the 28th member state and only the second of the former Yugoslav republics (behind Slovenia) to be admitted.	Croatia elects Kolinda Grabar-Kitarović as its first female president; she succeeds Josipović in February 2015.

People & Culture

With Germanic influences in the north and larger-than-life Mediterranean tendencies in the south, Croats aren't completely cut from the same mould. Yet from one tip of the Croatian horseshoe to the other, there are constants. Wherever you go, family and religion loom large, social conservatism is the norm and sport is the national obsession.

Croatia: West or East?

The vast majority of Croats have a strong cultural identification with Western Europe and draw a distinction between themselves and their 'eastern' neighbours in Bosnia, Montenegro and Serbia. The idea that Croatia is the last stop before the Ottoman/Orthodox east is prevalent in all segments of the population. Describing Croatia as part of Eastern Europe will not win you any friends. Some locals even baulk at the term 'Balkan', given the negative connotations that it carries. They'll be quick to point out that Zagreb is actually further west than Vienna; that the nation is overwhelmingly Catholic, rather than Orthodox; and that they use the Latin alphabet, not Cyrillic.

Despite the different alphabet used, Croatian and Serbian are more akin to related dialects than separate languages. This doesn't stop both sides stressing the differences between them though. In Croatia in particular, a French style of linguistic nationalism has seen old Yugoslav-era words like *aerodrom* (airport) dropped from signs in favour of the Croatian-derived *zračna luka* (*zrak* means air and *luka* means port – but most people still say *aerodrom* regardless). And should you ask for *hljeb* or *hleb* (the Montenegrin and Serbian words for bread, respectively) instead of *kruh* when you're dining in Dubrovnik, it won't go down well.

In 2014, a petition garnered 500,000 signatures calling for a referendum to restrict the use of Cyrillic on public signs in Croatia. At present Cyrillic is used alongside the Latin script in areas where Serbs make up more than 30% of the population, but the petition sought to increase this minimum to 50%. A court rejected the petition, stating that such a referendum would be unconstitutional. Supporters of the referendum saw this as a slap in the face for war veterans and the victims of Serbian aggression in places like Vukovar.

All of this stands in stark relief to the overwhelming popularity of Serbian turbo folk in Croatia, a type of music frowned upon and avoided during the 1990s war. It seems that ethnic tensions have eased to the point

Nikola Tesla (1856–1943), the father of the radio and alternating electric current technology, was born in the Croatian village of Smiljan to Serbian parents (his father was an Orthodox priest). Both Croatia and Serbia celebrate him as a national hero.

'NORMAL' PEOPLE

The word 'normal' pops up frequently in Croats' conversations about themselves. 'We want to be a normal country,' they might say. Croats will frequently make a distinction between rabid, flag-waving nationalists and 'normal people' who only wish to live in peace. This is among the reasons why Croatia bowed to international pressure to turn over its suspected war criminals.

where connecting Balkan elements are again being embraced in some unexpected aspects of Croatian society.

Croatia's Split Personality

With its capital inland and the majority of its big cities on the coast, Croatia is torn between a more serious *Mitteleuropean* mindset in Zagreb, Zagorje and Slavonia (with meaty food, Austrian architecture and a strong interest in personal advancement over pleasure) and the coastal Mediterranean character, which is more laid-back and open. Istrians are strongly Italian influenced and tend to be bilingual, speaking both Italian and Croatian. The Dalmatians are only slightly less Italianised and are generally a relaxed and easygoing bunch: many offices empty out at 3pm, allowing people to enjoy the long hours of sunlight on a beach or at an outdoor cafe.

Most people involved in the tourist industry speak German, English and Italian, though English is the most widely spoken language among the young.

Family Matters

Family is very important to Croats and extended-family links are strong and cherished. First cousins tend to be very close and connections are maintained with more distant cousins as well.

It's traditional and perfectly normal for children to live with their parents until well into their adult life. This extends particularly to sons, who in rural and small-town areas will often move their wives into their parents' home when they marry. The expectation that you'll stay at home until you're married makes life particularly difficult for gays and lesbians or anyone wanting a taste of independence. Many young people achieve a degree of this by leaving to study in a different town.

Most families own their own homes, bought in the postcommunist years when previously state-owned homes were sold to the tenants for little money. These properties are often passed down from grandparents, great-aunts and other relatives.

Daily Life

Etiquette Tips

. . . .

Dress modestly when visiting churches.

. . . .

Wait to be invited to use a person's first name.

. . . .

Whoever does the inviting (for dinner or drinks) pays the bill.

Lounging in cafes and bars is an important part of life here, and you often wonder how the country's wheels are turning with so many people at leisure rather than work. But perhaps it's all that coffee that makes them work twice as fast once they're back in the office.

Croats like the good life and take a lot of pride in showing off the latest fashions and mobile phones. High-end fashion labels are prized by both women and men – the more prominent the label, the better. Even with a tight economy, people will cut out restaurant meals and films in order to afford a shopping trip to Italy or Austria for some new clothes. For young men, looking good and dressing well is all part of the macho swagger. Croatian men don't like to lose face by acting stupidly in public, so although they drink, they generally don't drink to get drunk. Most local women don't drink much at all.

The cult of celebrity is extremely powerful in Croatia – the trashy tabloids are full of wannabe celebs and their latest shenanigans.

Manners & Mannerisms

Croats can come across as uninterested and rude (even those working in the tourist sector) and some people find their directness confronting. False pleasantries are regarded as just that – false. Smiles and exhortations to 'have a nice day' are reserved for people they actually care about. The idea of calling a complete stranger 'dear' at the start of a letter just

Two women on Mljet Island (p276)

seems weird to them, as does the antipodean habit of referring to people they've only just met as 'mate'.

This is just the way Croats operate, so don't take it personally. At least you'll always know where you stand. Once you graduate from the stranger category to friend, you'll find them warm, gregarious, generous and deeply hospitable. You might even make friends for life.

Never ask a Croat how they are if you don't want to know the answer. 'Fine' just doesn't cut it. Dalmatians, in particular, are prone to the dramatic: they'll either be full of the joys of life or in deep despair. Either way, if you ask, you'll hear about it.

Religion

According to the most recent census, 86.3% of the population identifies itself as Catholic, 4.4% Orthodox (this corresponds exactly with the percentage of Serbs), 4% 'other and undeclared', 3.8% atheist and 1.5% Muslim.

The main factor separating the otherwise ethnically indistinguishable Croats and Serbs is religion: Croats overwhelming adhere to the Roman Catholic faith, while Serbs are just as strongly linked to the Eastern Orthodox Church. The division has its roots in the split of the Roman Empire at the end of the 4th century. Present-day Croatia found itself on the western side, ruled from Rome, while Serbia ended up on the Greek-influenced eastern side, ruled from Constantinople (now Istanbul). As time went on, differences developed between western and eastern Christianity, culminating in the Great Schism of 1054, when the churches finally parted ways. In addition to various doctrinal differences, Orthodox Christians venerate icons, allow priests to marry and do not accept the authority of the pope.

The Croatian church once fought against Rome to retain the use of the Glagolitic alphabet, upon which Cyrillic was partially based. It continued to be used on the island of Krk until the 19th century.

The Croats pledged allegiance to Roman Catholicism as early as the 9th century and were rewarded with the right to conduct Mass and issue religious writings in the local language, using the Glagolitic script. The popes supported the early Croatian kings, who in turn built monasteries and churches to further promote Catholicism. Throughout the long centuries of Croatia's domination by foreign powers, Catholicism was the unifying element in forging a sense of nationhood.

The Church enjoys a respected position in Croatia's cultural and political life, and Croatia is the subject of particular attention from the Vatican. The Church is also the most trusted institution in Croatia, rivalled only by the military.

Croats, both within Croatia and abroad, provide a stream of priests and nuns to replenish the ranks of Catholic clergy. Religious holidays are celebrated with fervour and Sunday Mass is strongly attended.

Equality in Croatia

Croatian women weren't granted the vote until 1945. Following this election, Yugoslavia became a one-party state. Elections continued to be held but the League of Communists selected the candidates; sometimes there was only one name on the ballot.

Women continue to face some hurdles in Croatia, although the situation is improving. Under Tito's brand of socialism, women were encouraged to become politically active and their representation in the Croatian *sabor* (parliament) increased to 18%. Currently 24% of the parliament is comprised of women, and Croatia has a woman president, the first in the country's history.

More and more wives and mothers must work outside the home to make ends meet, but they still perform most household duties. Women are underrepresented at the executive level.

Women fare worse in traditional villages than in urban areas, and were hit harder economically than men after the Homeland War. Many of the factories that closed, especially in eastern Slavonia, had a high proportion of female workers.

Both domestic abuse and sexual harassment at work are quite common in Croatia, but the legal system is not yet adequate enough for women to seek redress.

Although attitudes are slowly changing towards homosexuality, Croatia is an overwhelmingly Catholic country with highly conservative views of sexuality. Most homosexuals are very closeted, fearing harassment if their sexual orientation is revealed. In 2013, a group called U ime obitelji (In the Name of the Family) campaigned for a referendum in which 65% of voters approved a constitutional ban on same-sex marriage. The following year, parliament passed a law creating civil partnerships for same-sex couples, granting limited relationship rights.

Good Sports

In 2016, Croatia was ranked the world's 10th-greatest sporting nation per head of population. Football, basketball and tennis are enormously popular, and sporty Croatia has contributed a disproportionate number of world-class players in each sport.

Football

The current crop of football stars includes Luka Modrić (who plays for Real Madrid), Dejan Lovren (Liverpool FC) and Mario Pašalić (Chelsea). The young ones to watch out for are Ante Ćorić, Nikola Vlašić and Andrija Balić.

By far the most popular spectator sport in Croatia is football (soccer), which frequently serves as an outlet for Croatian patriotism and, occasionally, as a means to express political opposition. When Franjo Tuđman came to power he decided that the name of Zagreb's football club, Dinamo, was 'too communist', so he changed it to 'Croatia'. Waves of outrage followed the decision, led by angry young football fans who used the controversy to express their opposition to the regime. Even though the following government restored the original name, you will occasionally see *Dinamo volim te* (Dinamo, I love you) graffiti in Zagreb. Dinamo's bitterest rival is Hajduk Split; there are often brawls when the two teams meet.

By far the biggest name in Croatian football, Davor Šuker scored 46 international goals by the end of his career, 45 of them for Croatia. He is the Croatian national team's all-time leading goal-scorer and the current president of the Croatian Football Federation. Back in 2004, football great Pelé named him one of the top 125 greatest living footballers.

Tennis

Croatia has produced – and continues to produce – some mighty big players, in every sense of the word. The 2001 victory of 6ft 4in Goran Ivanišević at Wimbledon provoked wild celebrations throughout the country, especially in his home town of Split. The charismatic serve-and-volley player was much loved for his engaging personality and on-court antics, and dominated the top-10 rankings during much of the 1990s. Injuries forced his retirement in 2004, but Croatia stayed on the court with a 2005 Davis Cup victory led by 6ft 4in Ivan Ljubičić and 6ft 5in Mario Ančić. One of Croatia's highest-ranked tennis players is 6ft 6in Marin Čilić, who won his first Grand Slam title, the US Open, in 2014 and was a quarterfinalist at Wimbledon the same year. A player to watch out for is Borna Ćorić, who was named in Forbes' '30 Under 30' sports list for 2016.

On the women's side, Zagreb-born Iva Majoli won the French Open in 1997 with an aggressive baseline game, but failed to follow up with other Grand Slam victories. She retired from tennis in 2004.

Tennis is more than a spectator sport in Croatia. The coast is amply endowed with clay courts. The biggest tournament in Croatia is the Umag Open in Istria, held in July.

Basketball

The most popular sport after football, basketball is followed with some reverence. The teams of Split, Zadar and Zagreb's Cibona are known across Europe, though none has yet equalled the Cibona star team of the 1980s, when they became European champions.

Skiing

If Croatia had a national goddess it would be Janica Kostelić, the most accomplished skier to have emerged from Croatia. After winning the Alpine Skiing World Cup in 2001, Kostelić won three gold medals and a silver in the 2002 Winter Olympics – the first Winter Olympic medals ever for an athlete from Croatia. Aged 20, she also became the first female skier to win three gold medals at one Olympics. In 2002, Kostelić had been plagued by a knee injury and the removal of her thyroid, but this didn't stop her from winning a gold medal in the women's combined and a silver in the Super-G at the 2006 Winter Olympics in Torino. In 2007, Kostelić announced her retirement from competitive racing.

Maybe it's in the genes. Her brother Ivica Kostelić took the men's slalom World Cup title in 2003 and brought home a silver medal in the men's combined in each of the 2006, 2010 and 2014 Winter Olympics, and a silver in the slalom in 2010.

Be like the sporty locals and keep up with Croatian football by following the fortunes of Hajduk Split (www.hajduk.hr) or Dinamo Zagreb (www.gnkdinamo.hr).

The celebrated Croatian athlete Blanka Vlašić is the second-highest-flying female high jumper of all time. She has received gold medals at various world championships and Olympic silver (Beijing) and bronze (Rio) medals.

PEOPLE & CULTURE GOOD SPORTS

The Cuisine

While holding firm to its Eastern European roots, Croatian food echoes the varied cultures that have influenced the country over its history. There's a sharp divide between the Italian-style cuisine along the coast and the flavours of Hungary, Austria and Turkey in the continental parts. From grilled sea bass smothered in olive oil in Dalmatia to robust, paprika-heavy meat stews in Slavonia, each region proudly touts its own speciality, but regardless of the region you'll find tasty food made from fresh, seasonal ingredients.

Foodie Culture

Although Croats are not overly experimental when it comes to food, they're particularly passionate about it. They'll spend hours discussing the quality of the lamb or the first-grade fish, and why it overshadows all food elsewhere. Foodie culture is on the rise here, inspired largely by the slow-food movement, which places emphasis on fresh, local and seasonal ingredients and the joy of slow-paced dining. The Istria and Kvarner regions have quickly shot to the top of the gourmet ladder, but other places aren't lagging far behind. Wine and olive-oil production have been revived, and there's now a network of signposted roads around the country celebrating these precious nectars.

A new breed of restaurants offers the opportunity to spend hours feasting on slow-food delicacies or savouring the innovative concoctions of up-and-coming chefs. There is a limit to what the local crowd can afford to pay, so restaurants still cluster in the middle of the price spectrum – few are unbelievably cheap, and few are exorbitantly expensive. Whatever your budget, you're unlikely to get a truly bad meal anywhere in Croatia. Another plus is that food is often paired with alfresco dining in warm weather.

Regional Specialities

Zagreb & Northwestern Croatia

Zagreb and northwestern Croatia favour the kind of hearty meat dishes you might find in Vienna. Juicy *pečenje* (spit-roasted and baked meat) features *janjetina* (lamb), *svinjetina* (pork) and *patka* (duck), often accompanied by *mlinci* (baked noodles) or *pečeni krumpir* (roast potatoes). Meat slow cooked under a *peka* (domed baking lid) is especially delicious, but needs to be ordered in advance at many restaurants. *Purica* (turkey) with *mlinci* is an institution on Zagreb and Zagorje menus, along with *zagrebački odrezak* (veal steak stuffed with ham and cheese, then

COOKING COURSES

Cooking courses in Croatia are becoming increasingly popular. Culinary Croatia (www.culinary-croatia.com) is a great source of information, and offers a variety of cooking classes and culinary and wine tours, mainly in Dalmatia. In Zagreb, iCroatiaTravel (p57) organises a five-hour gourmet experience. Istria-based Eat Istria (p108) offers cooking classes and wine tours around the peninsula.

DRINKS & DISHES TO TRY

Bazga Homemade elderflower juice is a classic of continental Croatia, fresh and lovely – a singular imbibing joy.

Bermet Intense herbal liqueur made only in the town of Samobor, with dried carob and figs, wormwood, orange zest, sage and mustard seeds, all soaked in red wine.

Boškarin Don't skip a taste of Istria's indigenous ox, nearly extinct by the late 20th century but brought back to life recently as a meat delicacy.

Gregada Fish stew made with different types of white fish, potatoes, white wine, garlic and spices. Hvar whips up Croatia's most famous *gregada*.

Komiška pogača Savoury focaccia-like pie from Komiža on Vis island, stuffed with onion, tomatoes and anchovies. If tomatoes are missing, then it's *viška pogača* (from the town of Vis).

Rogačica Among the many *rakija* (grappa) delights Croatia is known for, this Dalmatian liqueur made of carob is perfect if you like your drinks sweet.

Vitalac This offal delight from the island of Brač is not for the faint-hearted – think lamb intestines on a spit, grilled on hot coal.

crumbed and fried) – another calorie-laden speciality. Another mainstay is *sir i vrhnje* (fresh cottage cheese and cream), bought at local markets and paired well with bread. For those with a sweet tooth, *palačinke* (thin pancakes) with various fillings and toppings are a common dessert.

Slavonia

Spicier than the food of other regions, Slavonian cuisine uses liberal amounts of paprika and garlic. The Hungarian influence is most prevalent here: many typical dishes, such as *čobanac* (a meat stew), are in fact versions of *gulaš* (goulash). The nearby Drava River provides fresh fish, such as carp, pike and perch, which is stewed in a paprika sauce and served with noodles in a dish known as *fiš paprikaš*. Another speciality is *šaran u rašljama* (carp on a forked branch), roasted in its own oils over an open fire. The region's sausages are particularly renowned, especially *kulen,* a paprika-flavoured sausage cured over a period of nine months and usually served with cottage cheese, peppers, tomatoes and often *turšija* (pickled vegetables).

Istria

Istrian cuisine has been attracting international foodies in recent years for its long gastronomic tradition, fresh ingredients and unique specialties. Typical dishes include *maneštra,* a thick vegetable-and-bean soup similar to minestrone, *fuži,* hand-rolled pasta often served with *tartufi* (truffles) or *divljač* (game meat), and *fritaja* (omelette often served with seasonal veggies, such as wild asparagus). Thin slices of dry-cured Istrian *pršut* (prosciutto) – also excellent in Dalmatia – are often on the appetiser list; it's expensive because of the long hours and personal attention involved in smoking the meat. Istrian olive oil is highly rated and has won international awards. The tourist board has marked an olive-oil route along which you can visit local growers, tasting oils at the source. The best seasonal ingredients include white truffles, picked in autumn, and wild asparagus, harvested in spring.

For excellent reviews of restaurants all around Croatia and info about small producers, browse the excellent www. tasteofcroatia. org and download the app.

Kvarner & Dalmatia

Coastal cuisine in Kvarner and Dalmatia is typically Mediterranean, using a lot of olive oil, garlic, flat-leaf parsley and all manner of seafood. Along

PAG CHEESE

There's no other cheese quite like the distinctive *paški sir* (Pag cheese). Salty and sharp, its taste easily recalls the island that makes it. As sea winds whip through the low slopes of Pag Island, a thin deposit of salt permeates the ground and the flora it sprouts. The free-range sheep of Pag Island graze freely on the salty herbs and plants, transmitting the flavour to their meat and milk.

The milk for Pag cheese is gathered in May when the flavour is at its peak. It's left unpasteurised, which allows a stronger flavour to emerge during the fermentation process. When the cheese finally ferments, it's rubbed with sea salt, coated with olive oil and left to age for anywhere from six months to a year. The result is a tangy, firm product that matures into an aromatic, dry, crumbly cheese. As a starter, it's served in thin slices with black olives, but it can also be grated and used as a topping instead of parmesan.

Look out too for the ricotta-like *skuta,* a subtle-flavoured (though rare) soft cheese found in restaurants including Boškinac (p180), near Novalja.

The salt extracted at the Pag and Ston salt pans is considered the cleanest in the entire Mediterranean region.

the coast, look for fried *lignje* (squid) as a main course; Adriatic squid is generally more expensive than squid from further afield, and tastier for its freshness. Meals often begin with a first course of pasta such as spaghetti or *rižot* (risotto) topped with seafood. For a special appetiser, try *paški sir,* a pungent hard sheep-milk cheese from the island of Pag. Dalmatian *brodet* (stewed mixed fish served with polenta; also known as *brodetto* or *brujet*) is another regional treat, but it's often only available in two-person portions. Dalmatian *pašticada* (beef stewed in wine and spices and served with gnocchi) appears on menus on the coast as well as in the interior. Lamb from Cres and Pag is deemed Croatia's best; they feed on fresh herbs, which makes the meat delicious.

Vegetarians

A useful phrase is *Ja ne jedem meso* ('I don't eat meat'), but even then you may be served soup with bits of bacon swimming in it. That is slowly changing and vegetarians are making inroads in Croatia, but changes are mostly happening in the larger cities. Zagreb, Rijeka, Split and Dubrovnik now have vegetarian restaurants, and some restaurants in the big cities are beginning to offer vegetarian menus. Vegetarians may have a harder time in the north (Zagorje) and the east (Slavonia), where traditional fare has meat as its main focus. Specialities that don't use meat include *maneštra od bobića* (bean and fresh maize soup) and *juha od krumpira na zagorski način* (Zagorje potato soup). Other options include *štrukli* (baked cheese dumplings) and *blitva* (Swiss chard that's boiled and often served with potatoes, olive oil and garlic). Along the coast you'll find plenty of pizza, pasta and risotto dishes with various vegetable toppings and delicious cheese. If fish and seafood are part of your diet, you'll eat royally nearly everywhere.

Croatian-Style Celebrations

As in other Catholic countries, most Croats don't eat meat on Badnjak (Christmas Eve); instead they eat fish. In Dalmatia, the traditional Christmas Eve dish is *bakalar* (dried, salted cod). Christmas dinner may be roast suckling pig, turkey with *mlinci* or another meat. Also popular at Christmas is *sarma* (sauerkraut rolls stuffed with minced meat). Fresh Christmas Eve bread, also known as *badnji kruh,* is the centrepiece: it's made with honey, nuts and dried fruit. Another tradition is the Christmas braid: glazed dough made with nutmeg, raisins and almonds and shaped into a braid. It's often decorated with wheat and candles and left on the table until Epiphany (6 January), when it is cut and eaten. *Orahnjača*

Research shows that the prized oysters in the Ston area on Pelješac Peninsula have been farmed since Roman times.

(walnut cake), *fritule* (doughnuts) and *makovnjača* (poppy-seed cake) are popular desserts at celebrations.

The most typical Easter dish is ham with boiled eggs, served with fresh veggies. *Pinca*, a type of hard bread, is another Easter tradition, especially in Dalmatia.

Mealtime

Throughout former Yugoslavia, the *doručak* (breakfast) of the people was *burek* (pastry stuffed with meat, spinach or cheese). Modern Croats have opted for a lighter start to their day, usually just coffee and a pastry with some yoghurt and fresh fruit. If you're staying in hostels or private accommodation, the easiest thing to do is to get coffee at a cafe and pastries from a bakery. Otherwise, buy some bread, cheese and milk at a supermarket and have a picnic. If you're staying in a hotel you'll be served a buffet breakfast that includes cornflakes, bread, yoghurt, a selection of cold meat, powdered 'juice' and cheese. More upmarket hotels have better buffets that include eggs, sausages and homemade pastries.

Restaurants open for *ručak* (lunch) around noon and usually serve continuously until midnight, which can be a major convenience if you're arriving in town at an odd hour or just feel like spending more time at the beach. Croats tend to eat either an earlier *marenda* or *gablec* (cheap, filling lunch) or a large, late lunch. Fruit and vegetables from the market and a selection of cheese, bread and ham from a grocery store can make a healthy picnic lunch. If you ask nicely, the person behind the deli counter at supermarkets or grocery stores will usually make a *sir* (cheese) or *pršut* (prosciutto) sandwich (*sendvič,* in Croatian) and you only pay the regular price of the ingredients.

Večera (dinner) is typically a light affair, but most restaurants have adapted their schedules to the needs of tourists, who tend to load up at night. Few Croats can afford to eat out regularly; when they do, it's likely to be a large family outing on Saturday night or Sunday afternoon.

Drinks

Croatia is famous for its *rakija* (grappa), which comes in different flavours. The most commonly drunk are *loza* (made from grapes, like the Italian grappa), *šljivovica* (plum brandy) and *travarica* (herbal brandy). Istrian grappa is particularly excellent, and ranges in flavour from *medica* (honey) to *biska* (mistletoe) and various berries. The island of Vis is famous for its delicious *rogačica* (carob brandy). It's customary to have a small glass of *rakija* before a meal. Other popular drinks include *vinjak*

THE YEAR IN FOOD

While local food and wine festivals go into full swing come autumn, there's never a bad time to chow down in Croatia.

Spring (March–May) Wild asparagus and fresh berries, plus a handful of festivals like Istria's Days of Shellfish in March, Zagorje's Festival of Traditional Cakes in April and Istria's Open Cellars Wine Day in late May.

Summer (June–August) Freshly caught seafood by the sea. Beat the heat with gelato and cocktails, and check out what Croatian elders ate at the festival of traditional foods in the town of Vrbovec just northeast of Zagreb.

Autumn (September–November) Food festivals aplenty feature wine, truffles and chestnuts. Truffle and grappa lovers head to Istria while wine connoisseurs hit wine harvests in their chosen region. Don't miss Kvarner's sweet chestnut festival in October.

Winter (December–February) Time for hearty Christmas and Carnival treats.

The Zadar sour-cherry liqueur maraschino was conjured up in the early 16th century by pharmacists working in Zadar's Dominican monastery.

(cognac), maraschino (cherry liqueur made in Zadar), *prošek* (sweet dessert wine) and *pelinkovac* (herbal liqueur).

The two most popular types of Croatian *pivo* (beer) are Zagreb's Ožujsko and Karlovačko from Karlovac. The small-distribution Velebitsko has a loyal following among in-the-know beer drinkers, but only some bars and shops carry it, and they're mostly in continental Croatia. You'll want to practise saying *živjeli!* (cheers!).

Strongly brewed *kava* (espresso-style coffee), served in tiny cups, is popular throughout Croatia. You can have it diluted with milk (macchiato) or order a cappuccino. Although some places have decaf options this is considered somewhat sacrilegious, as Croats love their coffee. When locals talk of tea *(čaj),* they're usually referring to the herbal kind; black tea can be hard to find. Tap water is drinkable.

Wine

Wine from Croatia may be new to international consumers but *vino* has been an embedded part of the region's lifestyle for more than 25 centuries. Today the tradition is undergoing a renaissance in the hands of a new generation of winemakers with a focus on preserving indigenous varietals and revitalising ancestral estates. Quality is rising, exports are increasing and the wines are garnering global awards and winning the affections of worldly wine lovers thirsty for authentic stories and unique terroirs.

Croatia is roughly divided into four winemaking regions: Slavonia and the Croatian Uplands in the continental zone, with a cooler climate; and Istria, Kvarner and Dalmatia along the Adriatic with a Mediterranean climate. Within each lie multiple subregions *(vinogorje),* comprised of more than 300 geographically defined appellations.

Continental Zone

There are 17,000 registered vine growers in Croatia, 2500 wines of controlled origin and 880 wineries.

White varieties such as *graševina, traminac,* pinot blanc, chardonnay and sauvignon blanc dominate the continental zone. Styles range from fruity, mildly aromatic, refreshing wines from cool northern areas to rich, savoury, age-worthy whites from warmer Slavonia, as well as luscious dessert *(predikatno)* wines. Kutjevo is a particular sweet spot for vine growing; many wineries are located in the hamlet.

Ensconced in the pastoral hills of Međimurje, Plešivica and Zagorje, the Croatian Uplands is a land of crisp, food-friendly whites (although pinot noir does well in spots). Beside *graševina* and native *škrlet,* international varieties like chardonnay, pinot blanc, pinot gris and sauvignon blanc thrive. For ice wine *(ledeno vino),* a coveted bottle of Bodren makes a delicious souvenir.

Coastal Zone

Crowning the northern Adriatic coast is Istria, home of *malvazija istarska,* a variety capable of award-winning wines with diverse profiles: lean and light to unctuous and sweet; crisp and unoaked to acacia wood-aged and orange wines. Istria also boasts a fiery signature red: *teran.*

QUICK SNACKS

For a taste of local fast food, you can snack on *ćevapčići* (small spicy meatballs of minced beef, lamb or pork), *pljeskavica* (an ex-Yugo version of a hamburger patty), *ražnjići* (small chunks of pork grilled on a skewer) or *burek* (pastry stuffed with ground meat, spinach or cheese). These are available at fast-food outlets.

VISITING WINERIES

When planning a visit, keep in mind that most Croatian wineries are family-owned estates; not all have visitor-ready facilities. The following is a selection of recommended wineries with public tasting rooms, our pick of the best places for tastings in each of the four major winemaking regions. Appointments are highly recommended.

Slavonia

Krauthaker (p95) Top producer of *graševina*.

Vina Belje (p95) Tour a 500-year-old cellar.

Iločki Podrumi (p98) Good place to sample *traminac*.

Croatian Uplands

Bolfan Vinski Vrh (p79) Award-winning hilltop winery.

Lovrec Vineyard (p86) Top winery with a 300-year-old cellar, producing chardonnay, *graševina* and other varietals.

Cmrečnjak (p86) Family-run since 1884.

Istria/Kvarner

Cossetto (p120) Top-notch *malvazija* and reds.

Geržinić (p126) Noted particularly for its *malvazija*.

Toljanić-Gospoja (p162) An excellent place to try *žlahtina*.

Dalmatia

Boškinac (p180) Delicious cabernet merlot and the world's only producer of *gegić*.

Grgić Vina (p280) Californian wine-making legend Mike Grgich's family vineyard, producing top-flight *plavac mali* and *pošip*.

Matuško (p280) Try *plavac mali* at its best, from the Dingač appellation.

Just below Istria is Kvarner, home of *žlahtina,* a seafood-friendly white found in abundance on Krk.

Going south, the rugged beauty of Dalmatia, with its island vineyards (Hvar, Vis, Brač, Korčula), fosters a fascinating array of indigenous grape varieties that prosper in the Mediterranean climate, yielding full-bodied wines of rich character. Here *plavac mali,* scion of zinfandel *(crljenik kašteljanski)* and the obscure *dobričić,* is king of reds. Wines labelled 'Dingač' are *plavac mali* from a specific mountainside high above the sea on the Pelješac Peninsula that's widely regarded as producing Croatia's best reds. Production is tiny and good examples command premium prices.

On 1 April each year, the town of Ludbreg in the north of Croatia has wine instead of water flowing in its city fountain.

Other indigenous varieties worth seeking are *babić* (red), *pošip* (an elegant white, the best of which is from the island of Korčula), *grk* (a fruit-driven white, exclusively produced in Lumbarda on Korčula) and *malvasija* (a white from the Kvarner region, near Dubrovnik, not to be confused with *malvazija* with a 'z'). For easy-chair quaffing, the lovely rosés of Dalmatia evoke visions of the Mediterranean life.

Architecture

After they came, saw and conquered, most of Croatia's conga-line of invaders stuck around long enough to erect buildings. From the walled towns of the coast to the baroque splendour of Varaždin in the north – via Roman ruins, Gothic cathedrals, Renaissance palaces and Viennese villas – Croatia's architectural legacy is varied and extremely impressive.

Roman Riches

The Cathedral of St Domnius (3rd and 4th centuries AD) in Split is the oldest cathedral building in the world, thanks to it inhabiting the original mausoleum of the Emperor Diocletian.

No substantial buildings survive from before the Romans' arrival, but reminders of the 650 years of Roman rule are scattered all over the country: an intact archway in the centre of Rijeka; a turf-covered amphitheatre in Krka National Park; columns from the ancient forum in Zadar.

All of these pale in comparison with what is one of the best-preserved remnants of Roman architecture still standing in the world today: Diocletian's Palace (p202) in Split. This oversized complex was built by the retiring emperor at the end of the 3rd century AD, and although it was converted into a walled town and has been continuously inhabited for nearly two millennia, some parts are still wonderfully evocative of the era in which it was built. Quite unlike the crumbling ruins we associate with Roman remains, the former Mausoleum and Temple of Jupiter even have their roofs intact.

Croatia's other Roman highlights can both be found in Istria. The remarkable amphitheatre (p102) in Pula is Croatia's answer to Rome's Colosseum. This imposing 1st-century-AD arena still has a complete circuit of nearly 30m-high walls and is once again used for public entertainment – albeit of a less bloodthirsty kind than that for which it was built. The other Istrian treasure is the Euphrasian Basilica (p118) in Poreč. Built in the 6th century, this early Christian church incorporates layers of older buildings within its walls, and a precious mosaic decorates its apse.

Pre-Romanesque Churches

The first distinctively Croatian design was *pleter* (plaited ornamentation), which appeared around AD 800. Resembling the interlaced squiggles found on Celtic crosses and in medieval manuscripts, *pleter* features on church entrances and furniture from the early medieval (Old Croatian) period.

The Slavs arrived in Croatia in the early 7th century, heralding what is known in architectural terms as the Old Croatian, pre-Romanesque period. Not much survives from this time as most of it was destroyed during the Mongol invasion of the 13th century. The best remaining examples are found along the Dalmatian coast, beginning with the impressive 9th-century St Donatus' Church (p183) in Zadar, built on the ruins of the Roman forum. It has a round central structure, unique for late antiquity, and three semicircular apses.

Two other considerably smaller, but similarly curvaceous, churches survive nearby. The 11th-century Holy Cross Church in Nin has a cross-shaped plan, two apses and a dome above the centre point. Just outside of Nin, teensy St Nicholas' is a postcard-perfect fortress-like stone church perched atop a small hill.

Gothic & Renaissance

The Romanesque tradition of the Middle Ages, with its semicircular arches and symmetrical forms, persisted along the coast long after the pointy-arched Gothic style had swept the rest of Europe. In the 13th century the earliest examples of Gothic were still combined with Romanesque forms. The most beautiful work from this period is the portal of St Lawrence's Cathedral (p220) in Trogir, carved by the master artisan Radovan in 1240. The Cathedral of the Assumption of the Blessed Virgin Mary (p54) in Zagreb was the first venture into the Gothic style in northern Croatia. Although reconstructed several times, the remnants of 13th-century murals are still visible in the sacristy.

The late-Gothic period was dominated by the builder and sculptor Juraj Dalmatinac, who was born in Zadar in the 15th century. His most outstanding work was Šibenik's St James' Cathedral (p195), which marked a transition from the Gothic to the Renaissance period. Dalmatinac constructed the church entirely of stone, and adorned its outer walls with a wreath of realistically carved portraits of local people. Another beauty from this period is the 15th-century St Mark's Cathedral (p284) in Korčula.

The Renaissance flourished in Croatia, especially in independent Ragusa (Dubrovnik). By the second half of the 15th century, Renaissance influences (harking back to ancient Roman architecture) were appearing on late-Gothic structures. The Sponza Palace (p257) is a fine example of this mixed style. By the mid-16th century, Renaissance features began to replace the Gothic style in the palaces and summer residences built in and around Ragusa by the wealthy nobility. Unfortunately, much was destroyed in the 1667 earthquake.

Baroque to Brutalism

Northern Croatia is well known for the baroque style, which was introduced by Jesuit priests in the 17th century. The city of Varaždin was a regional capital in the 17th and 18th centuries, which, because of its location, enjoyed a steady interchange of artists, artisans and architects with northern Europe. The combination of wealth and creativity eventually led to Varaždin becoming Croatia's foremost city of baroque art. You'll notice the theatrical, sometimes frilly style in the elaborately restored houses, churches and especially the impressive castle.

In Zagreb, fine examples of the baroque style are found in the Upper Town, including the Jesuit Church of St Catherine (p52) and the restored mansion that is now the Croatian Museum of Naïve Art (p52). Wealthy families built their baroque mansions in the countryside around Zagreb, including at Brezovica, Miljana, Lobor and Bistra.

The influence of the Austro-Hungarian Empire is also on display in the capital, particularly in the grand neoclassical public buildings, but also in smaller art-nouveau apartments and town houses. Other examples are the former governor's palace in Rijeka and the holiday mansions of the Viennese elite scattered around neighbouring Opatija and some of the nearby islands.

During the modernist period, Croatian architecture fell in sync with the International Style. The socialist period saw many highly sophisticated and aesthetically mature examples of residential and civic architecture produced, particularly in planned suburbs such as Novi Zagreb. However, the more brutalist concrete structures, once seen as futuristic and modern, aren't to everyone's taste and many have been left to decay. Sadly, the sepia-tinged nostalgia surrounding 1970s Yugoslavia hasn't extended to preserving the wonderfully evocative hotels of the period.

St James' Cathedral in Šibenik (1431–1536) is the only building of its time that was constructed using the technique of mounting prefabricated stone elements.

ARCHITECTURE GOTHIC & RENAISSANCE

Today's Croatia has a vibrant architecture scene. In the rebuilding that followed the 1990s war, numerous open competitions were organised and young architects were suddenly given an opportunity to show their talents. Some of the more important examples of their work are the Gymnasium in Koprivnica and Hotel Lone in Rovinj.

The Natural Environment

Croatia is shaped like a boomerang, curving from the fertile farmland of Slavonia in the north, down through hilly central Croatia to the Istrian peninsula, and then south through Dalmatia along the rugged Adriatic coast. Most visitors focus their attention on the narrow coastal belt at the foot of the Dinaric Alps and the numerous gorgeous islands just offshore, but there's a whole lot more natural beauty to explore back up the boomerang.

Karst Caves & Waterfalls

The temperature of the Adriatic Sea varies greatly: it rises from an average of 7°C (45°F) in December up to a balmy 23°C (73°F) in September.

Croatia's most outstanding geological feature is the prevalent highly porous limestone and dolomitic rock called karst, which stretches along the coast and covers large parts of the hinterland. Karst is formed by acidic water dissolving the surface limestone, which then allows the water to seep into the harder layer underneath. Eventually the water forms underground streams, carving out fissures and caves before resurfacing, disappearing into another cave and eventually emptying into the sea.

Caves and springs are common interior features of karstic landscapes, which explains Croatia's Pazin Chasm, Plitvice Lakes and the Krka waterfalls, as well as the Manita Peć cave in Paklenica. When the limestone collapses, a kind of basin (known as *polje*) is formed. These are then cultivated, despite the fact that this kind of field drains poorly and can easily turn into a temporary lake.

National Parks

When the Yugoslav federation collapsed, eight of its finest national parks ended up in Croatia. The national parks cover 1.3% of the country and have a total area of 961 sq km, of which 742 sq km is land and 219 sq km is water. Around 8% of Croatia is given over to its protected areas, including nature parks and the like. The fantastic Parks of Croatia website (www.parkovihrvatske.hr) lists all 19 national and nature parks in Croatia.

On the Mainland

By far the most popular of the eight national parks is Unesco World Heritage–listed Plitvice Lakes National Park (p173), near the Bosnian border, midway between Zagreb and Zadar. Its chain of exquisitely picturesque lakes and waterfalls were formed by mosses that retained calcium carbonate as river water rushed through the karst. The falls are at their watery best in spring. The park's popularity comes at a price though: the main paths get terribly congested in the peak months.

Krka National Park (p192) is an even more extensive series of lakes and waterfalls set along the Krka River, north of Šibenik. The main access point is Skradinski Buk, where the largest cascade covers 800m. Like Plitvice, this part of the park can get uncomfortably crowded in July and August, but there are many stretches that are more peaceful. The park also includes important cultural relics in the form of a Serbian Orthodox and a Roman Catholic monastery.

The dramatically formed karstic gorges and cliffs make Paklenica National Park (p176), along the Adriatic coast near Zadar, a rock-climbing favourite. Large grottoes and caves filled with stalactites and stalagmites make it an interesting park for cave explorers, and there are many kilometres of hiking trails. Tourist facilities are well developed but there are large tracts of wilderness.

At the other end of the same mountain range, rugged Northern Velebit National Park is a patchwork of forests, peaks, ravines and ridges that backs the coast on the mainland opposite the island of Rab.

Risnjak National Park (p143), northeast of Rijeka, is the most untouched forested park, partly because the climate at its higher altitudes is somewhat inhospitable, with an average temperature of 12.6°C in July. The winters are long and snowy, but when spring finally comes in late May or early June, everything blooms at once. The park has been kept deliberately free of tourist facilities, with the idea that only mountain lovers need venture this far. The main entrance point is the motel and information facility at Crni Lug.

On the Islands

The Kornati Islands consist of 140 sparsely vegetated, uninhabited islands, islets and reefs scattered over 300 sq km, 89 of which are included in the Kornati National Park (p190). The unusual form and extraordinary rock formations of the islands make them an Adriatic highlight. Unless you have your own boat, you'll need to join an organised tour from Zadar or other places nearby.

Mljet National Park (p277), on the northwestern half of the island of the same name, incorporates two highly indented saltwater lakes surrounded by lush vegetation. Maquis shrubland is thicker and taller on Mljet than nearly anywhere else in the Mediterranean, which makes it a natural refuge for many animals.

The Brijuni Islands (p109) are the most cultivated national park, as they were developed as a tourist resort in the late 19th century. They were the getaway paradise for Tito and now attract the glitterati and their yachts. Most of the animals and plants were introduced, but the islands are lovely. Access to the islands is restricted – you can only visit on an organised tour.

Wildlife

Animals

Of the 59 mammal species present in Croatia, seven are listed as vulnerable: the garden dormouse and six species of bat. Red and roe deer are plentiful in the dense forests of Risnjak National Park, and there are also chamois, brown bears, wild cats and *ris* (Eurasian lynx), from which the park gets its name. Rarely, a grey wolf or wild boar may appear. Plitvice Lakes National Park, however, is an important refuge for wolves. The rare Eurasian otter is also protected in Plitvice Lakes National Park, as well as in Krka National Park.

Two venomous snakes are endemic in Paklenica: the nose-horned viper and the European adder. The non-venomous leopard snake, the four-lined snake, the grass snake and the snake lizard can be found in both Paklenica and Krka National Parks.

The waters around the islands of Lošinj and Cres are home to the Adriatic's only known resident pod of bottlenose dolphins. Striped dolphins and basking sharks are sometimes also sighted here. A centre devoted to

There are 1244 islands and islets along the tectonically submerged Adriatic coastline, only 50 of them inhabited. The largest are Cres, Krk, Pag and Rab in the north; Brač, Hvar, Dugi Otok and Vis in the middle; and Korčula and Mljet in the south.

Reaching up to 95cm in length, the nose-horned viper is the largest and most venomous snake in Europe. It likes rocky habitats and has a zigzag stripe on its body and a distinctive scaly 'horn' on its nose. If you're close enough to spot the horn, you're probably a little too close.

BIRDWATCHING

The griffon vulture, with a wingspan of up to 2.6m, has permanent colonies on the islands of Cres, Krk and Prvić. Paklenica National Park is rich in peregrine falcons, goshawks, sparrow hawks, buzzards and owls. Krka National Park is an important winter habitat for migratory marsh birds such as herons, wild ducks, geese and cranes, as well as rare golden eagles and short-toed eagles. Kopački Rit Nature Park, near Osijek in eastern Croatia, is an extremely important bird refuge.

rehabilitating injured loggerhead, leatherback and green turtles has been set up in Mali Lošinj.

Plants

The country's richest plant life is found in the Velebit Range, part of the Dinaric Alps, which provides the backdrop to the central Dalmatian coast. Botanists have counted around 2700 species and 78 endemic plants there, including the increasingly threatened edelweiss. Risnjak National Park is another good place to find edelweiss, along with black vanilla orchids, lilies and hairy alpenroses, which look a lot better than they sound. The dry Mediterranean climate along the coast is perfect for maquis, a low brush that flourishes all along the coast, but especially on the island of Mljet. You'll also find oleander, jasmine and juniper trees along the coast, and lavender is cultivated on the island of Hvar. Mediterranean olive and fig trees are also abundant.

Environmental Issues

The lack of heavy industry in Croatia has had the happy effect of leaving its forests, coasts, rivers and air generally fresh and unpolluted. An increase in investment and development, however, brings problems and threats to the environment.

The website of the Ministry of Environmental & Nature Protection (www.mzoip.hr) is the place to go for the latest news on Croatia's environment.

With the tourist boom, the demand for fresh fish and shellfish has risen exponentially. The production of farmed sea bass, sea bream and tuna (for export) is rising substantially, resulting in environmental pressure along the coast. Croatian tuna farms capture the young fish for fattening before they have a chance to reproduce and replenish the wild-fish population.

Coastal and island forests face particular problems. First logged by Venetians to build ships, then by local people desperate for fuel, the forests experienced centuries of neglect, which have left many island and coastal mountains barren. The dry summers and brisk *maestral* (strong, steady westerly wind) also pose substantial fire hazards along the coast. In the last 20 years, fires have destroyed 7% of Croatia's forests.

In 2014, the Croatian government called for tenders for gas- and oil-exploration licences in the Adriatic. Local environmental group Zelena Akcija (Green Action) is protesting the move due to concerns about the potentially devastating effect an oil spill would have in the relatively enclosed body of water.

The Arts

Croatia views itself very much as a cultured central European nation, steeped in the continent's finest artistic traditions and imbued with its own unique folk styles, but equally unafraid of the avant-garde. Even if they're virtually unknown elsewhere, local artists are highly regarded at home.

Literature

The Croatian language developed in the centuries following the great migration into Slavonia and Dalmatia. In order to convert the Slavs to Christianity, Greek missionaries Cyril and Methodius learnt the language and Cyril put it into writing. This became known as Glagolitic script. The earliest known example is an 11th-century inscription in a Benedictine abbey on the island of Krk.

Ivan Gundulić (1589–1638), from Ragusa (Dubrovnik), is widely considered to be the greatest Croatian poet. A more recent contender for the title is Tin Ujević (1891–1955), whose work remains extremely popular today.

Poets & Playwrights

The first literary flowering in Croatia took place in Dalmatia, which was strongly influenced by the Italian Renaissance. The works of the scholar and poet Marko Marulić (1450–1524), from Split, are still venerated in Croatia. His play *Judita* was the first work produced by a Croatian writer in his native tongue. The plays of Marin Držić (1508–67), especially *Dundo Maroje,* express humanistic Renaissance ideals and are still performed, especially in Dubrovnik. Ivan Gundulić's (1589–1638) epic poem *Osman* celebrated the Polish victory over the Turks in 1621, a victory that the Dubrovnik-based author saw as heralding the destruction of Ottoman rule.

The most significant figure in the period after the 1990s war was the lyrical and sometimes satirical Vesna Parun. Although Parun was often harassed by the government for what they considered decadent and bourgeois poetry, her published work *Collected Poems* has reached a new generation, which finds solace in her vision of wartime folly.

Novelists

Croatia's towering literary figure is 20th-century novelist and playwright Miroslav Krleža (1893–1981). Always politically active, Krleža broke with Tito in 1967 over the writer's campaign for equality between the Serbian and Croatian literary languages. Depicting the concerns of a changing Yugoslavia, his most popular novels include *The Return of Philip Latinowicz* (1932) and *Banners* (1963–65), a multivolume saga about middle-class Croatian life at the turn of the 20th century.

Mention should also be made of Ivo Andrić (1892–1975), who won the 1961 Nobel Prize for Literature for his Bosnian historical trilogy *The Bridge on the Drina, Bosnian Story* and *Young Miss.* Born as a Catholic Croat in Bosnia, the writer used the Serbian dialect and lived in Belgrade, but identified himself as a Yugoslav.

Award-winning writer Dubravka Ugrešić and four other female writers were accused of being 'witches' for not wholeheartedly supporting the Croatian war for independence.

Gold, Frankincense and Myrrh, by Slobodan Novak, was originally published in Yugoslavia in 1968, and has been translated into English. The book is set on the island of Rab, where an elderly lady is dying, and her carer – the narrator – reminisces about life, love, the state, religion and memory.

RECOMMENDED FOLK RECORDINGS

➡ *Croatie: Music of Long Ago* covers the whole gamut of Croatian music.

➡ *Lijepa naša tamburaša* is a selection of Slavonian chants accompanied by *tamburica* (a three- or five-string mandolin).

➡ *Omiš 1967–75* is an overview of *klapa* (an outgrowth of church-choir singing) music.

➡ *Pripovid O Dalmaciji* is an excellent selection of *klapa* in which the influence of church-choral singing is especially clear.

Some contemporary writers have been strongly marked by the implications of Croatian independence. Goran Tribuson uses the thriller genre to examine the changes in Croatian society after the war. In *Oblivion*, Pavao Pavličić uses a detective story to explore the problems of collective historical memory. Canadian-based Josip Novakovich's work stems from nostalgia for his native Croatia. His most popular novel, *April Fool's Day* (2005), is an absurd and gritty account of the recent wars that gripped the region. Slavenka Drakulić writes novels and essays that are often politically and sociologically provocative, and always witty and intelligent. Look out for *How We Survived Communism and Even Laughed* (1992) and *Cafe Europa* (1999).

Expat writer Dubravka Ugrešić has been a figure of controversy in Croatia and is acclaimed elsewhere. Now living in the Netherlands in self-imposed exile, she is best known for her novels *The Culture of Lies* (1998) and *The Ministry of Pain* (2006).

Miljenko Jergović, born in Sarajevo but living in Croatia, is a witty, poignant writer whose *Sarajevo Marlboro* (1994) and *Mama Leone* (1999) powerfully describe the atmosphere in prewar Yugoslavia.

Vedrana Rudan's novel *Night* (2004) perfectly illustrates the strong language and controversial antipatriarchal themes that are often ruffling feathers in the Croatian literary establishment.

Cinema

By far the most prominent person in the Croatian film industry is Branko Lustig, winner of Academy Awards for producing both *Schindler's List* and *Gladiator*. Born in Osijek to Croatian Jewish parents, he survived Auschwitz as a child and went on to work for state-owned Jadran Film alongside the likes of director Branko Bauer (1921–2001).

Another luminary is writer and director Veljko Bulajić, whose debut movie *Vlak bez voznog reda* (Train Without a Timetable) was nominated for the Golden Palm at Cannes in 1959, while *Bitka na Neretvi* (Battle of Neretva) was nominated for an Academy Award 10 years later.

More recently Vinko Brešan's *Kako je počeo rat na mom otoku* (How the War Started on My Island; 1996) and *Maršal* (Marshal Tito's Spirit; 1999) were massively popular in Croatia. Goran Rušinović's stylish *Mondo Bobo* (1997) was the first independent feature film made in Croatia, while his *Buick Riviera* (2008) went on to win awards at the Pula and Sarajevo film festivals.

On the world stage, Croatia's most famous actors are Mira Furlan (*Babylon 5, Lost*) and Goran Višnjić (*ER, The Girl with the Dragon Tattoo*). Actors of Croatian heritage include John Malkovich and Eric Bana (born Banadinović).

Music
Folk

Although Croatia has produced many fine classical musicians and composers, its most original musical contribution lies in its rich tradition of folk music. This music reflects a number of influences, many dating back to the Middle Ages when the Hungarians and the Venetians vied for control of the country. Franz Joseph Haydn (1732–1809) was born near a Croat enclave in Austria and his compositions were strongly influenced by Croatian folk songs.

The instrument most often used in Croatian folk music is the *tamburica,* a three- or five-string mandolin that is plucked or strummed. Introduced by the Turks in the 17th century, the instrument rapidly gained a following in eastern Slavonia and came to be closely identified with Croatian national aspirations. *Tamburica* music continued to be played at weddings and local festivals during the Yugoslav period, too.

Vocal music followed the *klapa* tradition. Translated as 'group of people', *klapa* is an outgrowth of church-choir singing. The form is most popular in Dalmatia, particularly in Split, and can involve up to 10 voices singing in harmony about love, tragedy and loss. Traditionally the choirs were all-male, but now women are getting involved, although there are very few mixed choirs.

Another popular strain of folk music, which is strongly influenced by music from neighbouring Hungary, emanates from the region of Medimurje in northeastern Croatia. The predominant instrument is a *citura* (zither). The tunes are slow and melancholic, frequently revolving around themes of lost love. New artists have breathed life into this traditional genre, including Lidija Bajuk and Dunja Knebl, female singers who have done much to resuscitate the music and gained large followings in the process.

For more about Croatian roots music, including the hot names on the contemporary scene, check out www.croatian rootsmusic.com.

Pop, Rock & the Rest

There's a wealth of home-grown talent in Croatia's pop and rock music scene. One of the most prominent bands is Hladno Pivo (Cold Beer), who play energetic punky music with witty, politically charged lyrics. Then there's the indie rock band Pips, Chips & Videoclips, whose breakthrough single 'Dinamo ja te volim' (Dinamo, I Love You) referred to Tuđman's attempts to rename Zagreb's football team, but whose music has generally been apolitical since.

The band Gustafi sings in the Istrian dialect and mixes Americana with local folk sounds, while the deliciously insane Let 3 from Rijeka is (in)famous for its nutty tunes and live performances at which the band members often show up naked, with only a piece of cork up their backsides (yes, really). TBF (The Beat Fleet) is Split's answer to hip hop, using Split slang to talk about current issues, family troubles, heartbreak and happy times. Bosnian-born but Croatia-based hip-hop singer Edo Maajka is another witty voice.

The fusion of jazz and pop with folk tunes is very popular in Croatia. One of the more prominent names in this scene is talented Tamara Obrovac from Istria, who sings in an ancient Istrian dialect that is no longer spoken.

The Croatian queen of pop is Severina, famous for her good looks and eventful personal life, which is widely covered by local celebrity and gossip magazines. Gibonni is another massively popular singer, and his major influence is Oliver Dragojević, a legendary singer of lovable schmaltz. All three (Severina, Gibonni and Dragojević) are from Split.

Nirvana bass player Krist Novoselic was born in California to Croatian parents and spent part of his teenage years living in Zadar.

Painting & Sculpture

The painter Vincent of Kastav was producing accomplished church frescoes in Istria during the 15th century. The small St Mary's Church near Beram contains his work, most notably the *Dance of Death*. Another notable Istrian painter of the 15th century is John of Kastav, who has left frescoes throughout Istria, mostly in the Slovenian part.

Many artists born in Dalmatia were influenced by, and in turn influenced, Italian Renaissance style. The sculptors Lucijan Vranjanin and Frano Laurana, the miniaturist Julije Klović and the painter Andrija Medulić left Dalmatia while the region was under threat from the Ottomans in the 15th century and worked in Italy. Museums in London, Paris

FOLK DANCES

Look out for the *drmeš*, a kind of accelerated polka danced by couples in small groups. The *kolo*, a lively Slavic round dance in which men and women alternate in the circle, is accompanied by Roma-style violinists. In Dalmatia, the *poskočica* is also danced by couples creating various patterns.

Like folk music, Croatian traditional dances are kept alive at local and national festivals. The best is the International Folklore Festival in Zagreb in July. If you can't make it to that, not to worry: music and folklore groups work on a circuit in the summer, hitting most coastal and island towns at one point or another. Ask at a local tourist office for a current schedule.

and Florence contain examples of their work, but few of their creations remain on display in Croatia.

Vlaho Bukovac (1855–1922) was the most notable Croatian painter in the late 19th century. After working in London and Paris, he came to Zagreb in 1892 and produced portraits and paintings on historical themes in a lively style. Early-20th-century painters of note include Miroslav Kraljević (1885–1913) and Josip Račić (1885–1908), but the most internationally recognised artist was the sculptor Ivan Meštrović (1883–1962), who created many masterpieces on Croatian themes. Antun Augustinčić (1900–79) was another internationally recognised sculptor, whose *Monument to Peace* is outside New York's UN building. A small museum of his work can be visited in the town of Klanjec, north of Zagreb.

Naive Art

Post-WWI artists experimented with abstract expressionism, but this period is best remembered for the naive art that began with the 1931 Zemlja (Soil) exhibition in Zagreb, which introduced the public to works by Ivan Generalić (1914–92) and other peasant painters. Committed to producing art that could be easily understood and appreciated by ordinary people, Generalić was joined by painters Franjo Mraz (1910–81) and Mirko Virius (1889–1943), and sculptor Petar Smajić (1910–85) in a campaign to gain acceptance and recognition for naive art.

Abstract Art

Abstract art infiltrated the postwar scene. The most celebrated modern Croatian painter is Edo Murtić (1921–2005), who drew inspiration from the countryside of Dalmatia and Istria. In 1959 a group of artists – Marijan Jevšovar (1922–88), Ivan Kožarić (b 1921) and Julije Knifer (1921–2004) – created the Gorgona group, which pushed the boundaries of abstract art. Đuro Pulitika (1922–2006), known for his colourful landscapes, was a well-regarded Dubrovnik painter, as were Antun Masle (1919–67) and Ivo Dulčić (1916–75).

Contemporary Art

For a thorough rundown of cultural events in Croatia, check out the informative www. culturenet.hr.

The post-WWII trend towards avant-garde art has evolved into installation art, minimalism, conceptualism and video art. Contemporary Croatian artists worth seeing include Lovro Artuković (b 1959), whose highly realistic painting style is contrasted with surreal settings, and video artists Sanja Iveković (b 1949) and Dalibor Martinis (b 1947). The multimedia works of Andreja Kulunčić (b 1968), the installations of Sandra Sterle (b 1965) and the video art of Zagreb-based Renata Poljak (b 1974) are attracting international attention. The performances of Dubrovnik-born multimedia artist Slaven Tolj (b 1964), including his installations and video art, have received international acclaim. Lana Šlezic (b 1973) is a Toronto-based photographer whose excellent work is often shot in Croatia.

Survival Guide

Directory A–Z

Accommodation

Croatia is traditionally seen as a summer destination and good places book out well in advance in July and August. It's also very busy in June and September.

Hotels These range from massive beach resorts to boutique establishments.

Apartments Privately owned holiday units are a staple of the local accommodation scene, especially for families.

Guesthouses Usually family-run establishments where spare rooms are rented at a bargain price – sometimes with their own bathrooms, sometimes not.

Hostels Mainly in the bigger cities and more popular beach destinations, with dorms and sometimes private rooms too.

Campgrounds Tent and caravan sites, often fairly basic.

Seasons

The tourist season generally runs from Easter to October. However, along the coast in particular, accommodation is usually priced according to four seasons:

July and August The absolute peak period, with the top rates and the highest occupancy – book ahead. Many establishments enforce minimum three-night stays or enforce a surcharge for shorter bookings (around 30%).

June and September Once the shoulder seasons, these are now busy months in their own right, so expect high prices.

April, May and October The new shoulder seasons, with rates towards the middle of their range.

November to March Many places close but for those that are open, these are the cheapest months.

Registration & Sojourn Tax

Accommodation providers will handle travellers' registration with the local police, as required by Croatian authorities. To do this, they will ask for your passport when you check in. Normally they will note the details they require and photocopy or scan the relevant page, and then hand your passport straight back.

Part of the reason for this process is so that the correct 'sojourn tax' can be paid. This is a small amount (usually less than 10KN) that is charged for every day you stay in Croatia, no matter what type of accommodation you're staying in. It's quite normal for this to be additional to the room rate you've been quoted.

Camping

Over 500 campgrounds are scattered along the Croatian coast, ranging hugely in terms of facilities and quality. Most operate from mid-April to mid-September only, although a few are open from March to October. In spring and autumn, it's best to call ahead to make sure that the campground is open. Don't go only by the opening and closing dates given by local tourist offices, travel brochures or even Lonely Planet, as these can change.

TYPES

➡ Many campgrounds in Istria are gigantic 'autocamps' with restaurants, shops and rows of caravans, but in Dalmatia they're smaller and often family owned.

➡ If you want a more intimate environment, the town tourist office should be able to refer you to smaller campgrounds (but you may have to insist upon it).

➡ Naturist campgrounds (marked FKK) are among the best because their secluded locations ensure peace and quiet.

➡ Wild camping is officially prohibited.

BOOK YOUR STAY ONLINE

For more accommodation reviews by Lonely Planet authors, check out lonelyplanet.com/croatia/hotels. You'll find independent reviews, as well as recommendations on the best places to stay. Best of all, you can book online.

➜ See www.camping.hr for camping information and links.

PRICES

The way that camping prices are calculated varies enormously and is often complicated. Some places will add up how many adults, children and pets are in your group, and then add a charge depending on whether you have a vehicle (and how big it is), how big your tent or campervan is, and whether or not you require electricity. Other places will include the vehicle and/or tent in an overall pitch charge, but add on a per-person rate at the end.

However it's calculated, expect to pay between 200KN and 300KN for two people with a smallish tent and a car in high season.

Hostels

Croatia's hostel scene is evolving at pace, although it's still mainly limited to the bigger cities and most popular destinations. The best choice is offered in Zagreb, Rijeka, Split and Hvar Town, while Osijek, Pula, Zadar, Šibenik and Dubrovnik all have at least a couple of good options.

The **Croatian YHA** (Map p48; ☑01-48 29 294; www.hfhs.hr; Savska 5, Zagreb; ⏱8.30am-4.30pm Mon-Fri) has hostels in 11 centres, the best of which are in Veli Lošinj and Pula; some of the others aren't up to much. Membership costs 60KN and provides discounts at YHAs worldwide. Nonmembers can collect a stamp per day on a welcome card; six stamps entitle you to membership.

Many of the independent hostels are small, character-filled affairs that offer communal activities such as barbecues and pub crawls. In the cities some are run out of converted apartments within larger blocks.

Not all hostels are open in winter and most aren't staffed all day. It's wise to call in advance.

Hotels

Croatian hotels are of an international standard, ranging from small family-run places to the mammoth formerly state-owned resorts on the coast. The vast majority of rooms have their own bathrooms, air conditioning and TV, and most also offer free wi-fi.

Breakfast is often included and some places, particularly in more remote locations, also offer half-board (breakfast and dinner).

In summer there may be a surcharge for short stays (fewer than three nights) along the coast and on the islands.

The star-rating system for Croatian hotels is inconsistent and not very helpful.

Private Accommodation

Private accommodation providers are an integral part of the local tourism industry and are often the best (and sometimes the only) option in more remote destinations. For budget and midrange travellers, they provide a lot more choice, especially if you're travelling in the peak season. On top of that, many of the owners go out of their way to be hospitable and some even offer the option of eating with them, which is a great way to get to know the culture.

There are two main types of private accommodation: apartments (*apartmani*) and rooms (*sobe*). Apartments always have their own bathrooms and basic cooking facilities. Rooms may share a bathroom with other guests and/or the owners.

The days of choosing your accommodation from a scrum of old ladies at the bus station are on the way out. These days you can view most options online on the websites of local tourist offices and travel agencies. Many of the best places are also listed on the big international booking websites.

Prefer on-the-fly travel? Once you've arrived in your destination, call into the tourist office or a travel agency and ask what's available. Rates are usually fixed and don't vary from agency to agency, though some agencies may not handle rooms in the cheapest category, and some only handle apartments. Stays of fewer than four nights will usually attract an agency surcharge of at least 30%; some will insist on a seven-night minimum stay in the high season.

Agencies can handle complaints (often in English) if things go wrong, but you can also deal directly with proprietors by knocking on the doors of houses with *sobe*, *zimmer* or *apartmani* ('rooms available') signs.

TIPS

➜ If you decide to book with proprietors at the bus or ferry station, or those holding signs at the side of the road, get an exact location first or you could find yourself stuck way out of town.

➜ If you've decided to door-knock until you find a room, leave your luggage in a *garderoba* (left-luggage office) before heading out – you'll be more comfortable and in a better position to negotiate a price.

➡ Clarify whether the price is per person or per room. Don't hesitate to bargain, especially if you're staying for a week.

➡ Avoid a surcharge by specifying the exact number of days you plan to stay and what time of day you plan to check out. In high season along the coast, it may be impossible to find a proprietor willing to rent you a room for one night only.

➡ If you land in a room or apartment without a blue *sobe, zimmer* or *apartmani* sign outside, the proprietor is renting illegally (ie not paying sojourn tax). They will probably be reluctant to provide their full name or phone number and you'll have absolutely no recourse if there's a problem.

Customs Regulations

➡ Travellers can bring their personal effects into the country without paying excise tax, along with 200 cigarettes, 2L of liquor over 22% proof, 1L of liquor under 22%, 4L of wine and 16L of beer.

➡ There are restrictions on food crossing into Croatia from non-EU countries.

➡ There is no quarantine period for animals brought into the country, but cats and dogs must be microchipped and you should have recent documentation from a veterinarian certifying the animal's current state of health. Otherwise, the animal must be inspected by a local veterinarian, who may not be immediately available.

Discount Cards

➡ Most museums, galleries, theatres and festivals in Croatia offer student discounts of up to 50%. For youth travel and the cards listed here, contact the travel section of the **Croatian YHA** (Map p48; ☎01-48 29 294; www.hfhs.hr; Savska 5, Zagreb; ⊕8.30am-4.30pm Mon-Fri).

➡ An International Student Identity Card (ISIC) is the best international proof of student status. People who are under the age of 26, but not students, qualify for the International Youth Travel Card (IYTC).

➡ The European Youth Card Association (www.eyca. org) offers discounts at selected shops, restaurants, sights, hostels and transport providers.

Electricity

Electrical supply is 230V, 50Hz AC. Croatia uses the standard European (round-pronged) plugs.

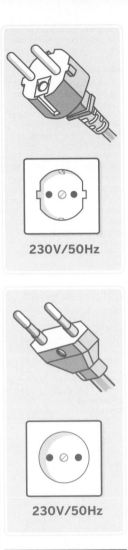

230V/50Hz

230V/50Hz

PRACTICALITIES

Newspapers Widely read newspapers include *Večernji List*, *Jutarnji List* and *Slobodna Dalmacija*.

Radio The most popular radio station is Narodni Radio, which airs only Croatian music, followed by Antena Zagreb and Otvoreni Radio. Public broadcaster Croatian Radio (Hrvatski Radio) broadcasts news in English daily at 8pm on HR1.

Smoking Smoking is, in theory at least, banned on public transport and in restaurants and most hotel rooms, bars and cafes. However, this isn't always enforced. People are generally permitted to smoke outdoors, including on the terraces of cafes and bars.

Weights & Measures Croatia uses the metric system.

LGBT Travellers

Homosexuality has been legal in Croatia since 1977 and is tolerated, but not widely accepted. Public displays of affection between same-sex couples may be met with hostility.

Gay venues are virtually nonexistent outside Zagreb. However, many towns on the coast have an unofficial gay beach – usually a rocky area at the edge of the nudist section.

➜ Split Pride is usually held on the first Saturday in June. Zagreb Pride (www.zagreb-pride.net) is usually the following Saturday.

➜ LORI (www.lori.hr) is a lesbian organisation based in Rijeka.

➜ Most Croatian websites devoted to the gay scene are in Croatian only, but www.croatia-gay.com is a good starting point.

➜ International dating apps and websites such as Grindr (www.grindr.com) and Planet Romeo (www.planetromeo.com) are very popular with local gay and bisexual men.

Health
Before You Go
HEALTH INSURANCE
Make sure you take out a comprehensive travel-insurance policy that covers you for medical expenses. When choosing a policy, check whether the insurance company will make payments directly to providers or reimburse you later for overseas health expenditures.

VACCINATIONS
No specific vaccinations are required for visiting Croatia.

In Croatia
AVAILABILITY & COST OF HEALTH CARE
Good-quality health care is readily available in Croatia. EU nationals are required to present their European Health Insurance Card (EHIC) in order to receive heavily discounted treatment in the public system (around 10KN for a doctor's visit and a maximum of 2000KN for a hospital stay). For those not covered by a reciprocal agreement, expect to pay around 250KN for a short doctor's appointment.

Pharmacists can give valuable advice and sell over-the-counter medication for minor illnesses.

The standard of dental care is usually good, but it's sensible to have a dental check-up at home before taking a long trip.

ENVIRONMENTAL HAZARDS
➜ Croatia gets scorching hot in summer and there's often little shade on mountain paths. Guard against dehydration and heat exhaustion by drinking plenty of water.

➜ Watch for sea urchins around rocky beaches. If you get some of their needles embedded in your skin, olive oil will help to loosen them. If they are not removed, the wound could become infected. As a precaution, wear rubber shoes while walking on the rocks or bathing.

➜ To avoid getting bitten by snakes, do not walk barefoot or stick your hands into holes or cracks. Half of those bitten by venomous snakes are not actually injected with poison (envenomed). If bitten by a snake, do not panic. Immobilise the bitten limb with a splint (eg a stick) and firmly apply a bandage over the site, similar to a bandage over a sprain. Do not apply a tourniquet, or cut or suck the bite. Get medical help as soon as possible so that an antivenin can be administered if necessary.

INFECTIOUS DISEASES
Tick-borne encephalitis, a serious brain infection, is spread by tick bites. Vaccination is advised for those in areas of risk who are unable to avoid tick bites (such as campers and hikers). Two doses of vaccine will give a year's protection; three doses, up to three years.

TAP WATER
Tap water in Croatia is safe to drink.

Insurance
Worldwide travel insurance is available at www.lonely planet.com/travel-insurance.

You can buy, extend and claim online any time – even if you're already on the road.

Internet Access
➜ Most cafes, restaurants and bars across Croatia have free wi-fi; just ask for the password.

➜ Hotels and private guesthouses are almost always equipped with wi-fi.

➜ Free wi-fi access has removed much of the need for internet cafes, but local tourist offices should be able to point you towards those few that remain.

Legal Matters
Although it is highly unlikely that you'll be hassled by the police, you should keep identification with you at all times as the police have the right to stop you and demand ID.

By international treaty, you have the right to notify your consular official if arrested. Embassies and consulates can normally refer you to English-speaking lawyers, although they will not pay for one.

Maps
Freytag & Berndt publishes a series of country, regional and city maps. Its 1:600,000 map of Croatia, Slovenia and Bosnia and Hercegovina is particularly useful if you're travelling in the region. If you're only staying on the coast, its 1:200,000 *Croatia Coast* sheet map is wonderfully detailed. Others include *Croatia, Slovenia* (1:800,000) by GeoCenter and *Hrvatska, Slovenija, Bosna i Hercegovina* (1:600,000) by Naklada Naprijed.

For cities other than Zagreb, Split, Zadar, Rijeka and Dubrovnik, there are few top-quality maps.

Local tourist offices usually provide helpful town maps for free. Regional tourist offices often publish good regional driving maps.

Money

ATMs

➡ Automatic teller machines (ATMs) can be found throughout Croatia and are tied in with international networks such as Cirrus and Maestro.

➡ Most ATMs also allow you to withdraw money using a credit card; note that you pay interest on the amount immediately and are charged a withdrawal fee. Privredna Banka usually has ATMs for cash withdrawals using American Express cards.

➡ All post offices will allow you to make a cash withdrawal on MasterCard or Cirrus, and a growing number work with Diners Club as well.

Credit & Debit Cards

Visa and MasterCard are widely accepted in hotels but rarely accepted in any kind of private accommodation. Diners Club and American Express are less accepted and many smaller restaurants and shops do not take any credit cards at all.

Currency

➡ Croatia uses the kuna (KN). Commonly circulated banknotes come in denominations of 500, 200, 100, 50, 20, 10 and five kuna. Each kuna is divided into 100 lipa. You'll find silver-coloured 50- and 20-lipa coins, and bronze-coloured 10-lipa coins.

➡ The kuna has a fixed exchange rate tied to the euro and the rate varies little from year to year. However,

to amass foreign currency, the government makes the kuna more expensive in summer when tourists visit. You'll get the best exchange rate from mid-September to mid-June.

➡ Many accommodation providers set their prices in euro. In Lonely Planet sleeping reviews, we list the price in either kuna or euro, depending on how the establishment sets its rates. It's often possible to pay in euro notes, but credit-card charges are invariably billed in kuna.

➡ You can sometimes pay for a meal or small services in euros, but the rate is not as good.

➡ International boat fares are priced in euros, although you pay in kuna.

Money Changers

➡ There are numerous places to change money in Croatia, all offering similar rates, including travel agencies and post offices.

➡ Most places deduct a commission of 1% to 1.5% to change cash, though some banks do not.

➡ Travellers cheques may be exchanged only in banks.

➡ Kuna can be converted into foreign currency only at a bank and only if you submit a receipt of a previous transaction.

Taxes & Refunds

Travellers from non-EU countries who spend more than 740KN in one shop are entitled to a refund of the value-added tax (VAT), which is equivalent to 25% of the purchase price.

In order to claim a VAT refund, the shop merchant must fill out a PDV-P form, which you need to present to the customs office upon leaving the country, along with the unused goods. Mail a stamped copy within six months to the shop, which will then credit your credit card with the appropriate sum.

There is also a service called Global Blue (www.globalblue.com) that will give you your refund in cash at the airport or at participating post offices.

Tipping

Tipping in Croatia is purely discretionary and is generally only done in restaurants and cafe-bars.

Restaurants Up to 10% but only for good service; leave nothing if you're dissatisfied in any way. Leave your tip in cash, even if you're paying by credit card.

Cafes & Bars Round up to the nearest round figure.

Opening Hours

Croats are early risers: by 7am there will be lots of people on the street and many places already open. Along the coast, life is more relaxed – shops and offices frequently close around noon for an afternoon break and reopen at about 4pm.

Coastal travel agencies open from 8am or 9am until 9pm or 10pm daily in high season, shortening their hours as the tourist season wanes. In continental Croatia, most agencies keep office hours.

In Zagreb and Split nightclubs are open year-round, but many places along the coast are only open in summer.

Supermarkets are open from 8am to 8pm on weekdays. Some close at 2pm on Saturdays while others stay open until 8pm. Only some supermarkets are open on Sundays during the summer season.

EATING PRICE RANGES

The following price ranges refer to a main course.

€ less than 70KN

€€ 70–120KN

€€€ more than 120KN

STREET NAMES

Particularly in Zagreb and Split, you may notice a discrepancy between the names used on maps and the names you'll actually see on the street.

In Croatian, a street name can be rendered either in the nominative or the possessive case. The difference is apparent in the name's ending. Thus, Ulica Ljudevita Gaja (street of Ljudevita Gaja) becomes Gajeva ulica (Gaja's Street). The latter version is the one most commonly seen on the street sign and used in everyday conversation. The same principle applies to a *trg* (square), which can be rendered as Trg Petra Preradovića or Preradovićev trg.

Some of the more common names are Trg Svetog Marka (Markov trg), Trg Josipa Jurja Strossmayera (Strossmayerov trg), Ulica Andrije Hebranga (Hebrangova), Ulica Pavla Radića (Radićeva), Ulica Augusta Šenoe (Šenoina), Ulica Nikole Tesle (Teslina) and Ulica Ivana Tkalčića (Tkalčićeva). Be aware also that Trg Nikole Šubića Zrinskog is almost always called Zrinjevac.

In an address, the letters 'bb' following a street name (such as Placa bb) stand for *bez broja* (without number), which indicates that the building has no street number.

Photography

Military installations may not be photographed, and you may have a lot of angry naked people after you if you try to take pictures in a naturist resort.

Post

Post services are operated by Hrvatska pošta (www.posta.hr) and are generally very reliable. Check their website for up-to-date postage rates and the location of post offices.

Public Holidays

Croats take their holidays very seriously. Shops and museums are shut and boat services are reduced. On religious holidays, the churches are full; it can be a good time to check out the artwork in a church that is usually closed.

New Year's Day 1 January

Epiphany 6 January

Easter Sunday & Monday March/April

Labour Day 1 May

Corpus Christi 60 days after Easter

Day of Antifascist Resistance 22 June

Statehood Day 25 June

Homeland Thanksgiving Day 5 August

Feast of the Assumption 15 August

Independence Day 8 October

All Saints' Day 1 November

Christmas 25 & 26 December

Safe Travel

➡ Street violence is rare and there's no particular problem with pickpocketing, but you should employ common sense regardless.

➡ During the 1990s war over a million landmines were laid in eastern Slavonia around Osijek, and in the hinterlands north of Zadar. Although the government has invested heavily in demining operations, it's a slow process. The mined areas are generally well signposted with skull-and-crossbones symbols and yellow tape. Don't go wandering off on your own in sensitive regions before checking with a local. Never go poking around an obviously abandoned or ruined house.

Telephone

➡ To call Croatia from abroad, dial your international access code, then ☑385 (the country code for Croatia), then the area code (without the initial ☑0) and the local number.

➡ To call from region to region within Croatia, start with the area code (with the initial zero; drop it when dialling within the same code).

➡ Phone numbers with the prefix ☑060 can be either free or charged at a premium rate, so watch out for the fine print.

➡ Phone numbers that begin with ☑09 are mobile-phone numbers. Calls to mobiles are billed at a much higher rate than regular numbers.

Mobile Phones

➡ If you have an unlocked 3G phone, you can buy a SIM card for between 20KN and 50KN, which includes 15 to 30 minutes of connection time. You can choose from three network providers: VIP (www.vipnet.hr), Hrvatski Telekom (www.hrvatskitelekom.hr) and Tele2 (www.tele2.hr).

➡ You can also buy a special prepaid SIM starter pack for tourists; these are available during the high season (June to September) for between 50KN and 100KN, with data and/or minutes included.

Phonecards

➡ You'll need a phonecard to use public telephones. Many phone boxes are equipped with a button on the upper left with a flag symbol. Press the button for instructions in English.

DIRECTORY A–Z TIME

➡ Phonecards are sold in post offices and newspaper kiosks.

➡ You can call from a post office without a phonecard.

Time

➡ Croatia is on Central European Time (GMT/UTC plus one hour). Daylight saving comes into effect on the last Sunday in March, when clocks are turned forward an hour. On the last Sunday in October they're turned back an hour.

➡ Croatia uses the 24-hour clock.

Toilets

➡ Most toilets are of the standard sit-down variety, although you'll sometimes come across squat toilets in some of the older ferries and public conveniences.

➡ Public toilets aren't all that common and most charge a small fee.

➡ If you're caught short, head to a cafe-bar – but it's polite to at least buy a drink.

Tourist Information

Local tourist offices have free brochures and good information on local events.

Croatian National Tourist Board (www.croatia.hr)

Dubrovnik-Neretva County (www.visitdubrovnik.hr)

Istria County (www.istra.hr)

Krapina-Zagorje County (www.tzkzz.hr)

Osijek-Baranja County (www.tzosbarzup.hr)

Primorje-Gorski Kotar (Kvarner) County (www.kvarner.hr)

Šibenik-Knin County (www.sibenikregion.com)

Split-Dalmatia County (www.dalmatia.hr)

Zadar County (www.zadar.hr)

Zagreb County (www.tzzz.hr)

Travellers with Disabilities

Mobility-impaired travellers will find the cobbled streets and endless steps of Croatia's old towns challenging. Most sights aren't well set up for wheelchair users, and specific resources for sight-impaired and hearing-impaired travellers are rare. That said, more attention is being paid to the needs of people with disabilities in Croatia due to the number of wounded war veterans. For further information, get in touch with the **Croatian Association for the Physically Disabled** (Hrvatski savez udruga tjelesnih invalida; Map p48; ☎01-48 12 004; www.hsuti.hr; Šoštarićeva 8, Zagreb).

➡ Public toilets at bus stations, train stations, airports and large public venues are usually wheelchair-accessible. Large hotels are wheelchair-accessible, but very little private accommodation is.

➡ Bus and train stations in Zagreb, Zadar, Rijeka, Split and Dubrovnik are wheelchair-accessible, but the ferries are not.

➡ Download Lonely Planet's free Accessible Travel guide from http://lptravel.to/AccessibleTravel.

Visas

Citizens of many countries, including EU member states, Australia, Brazil, Canada, Israel, Japan, New Zealand, Singapore and the USA do not need a visa for stays of up to 90 days within a 180-day period. (Note that this means that leaving the country just to get a stamp and return isn't a legal option.)

Other nationalities can check whether they need a visa and download application forms on the website of the Croatian Ministry for Foreign & European Affairs (www.mvep.hr).

Volunteering

For short-term volunteering programs, consider the **Kuterevo Refuge** (www.kuterevo-medvjedi.org) for young bears in the Velebit Range, the **Sokolarski Centre** (☎091 50 67 610; www.sokolarskicentar.com; Škugori bb) for the protection of birds of prey, near Šibenik, and the **Lošinj Marine Education Centre** (☎051-604 666; www.blue-world.org; Kaštel 24) on Lošinj Island.

Women Travellers

➡ Women face no special danger in Croatia. There have been cases in large coastal cities of some lone women being harassed and followed, but this is not common.

➡ Police will not always take reports of sexual assault by an acquaintance (aka 'date rape') very seriously. Be careful about being alone with an unfamiliar man.

➡ Topless sunbathing is tolerated, but you're better off on a nudist beach.

Work

➡ Most EU citizens can live and work in Croatia, with the exception being those from nations that restrict these rights to Croatians (at the time of research Austria, Malta, the Netherlands, Slovenia and the UK). These nationalities can work for up to 90 days with a Work Registration Certificate; if they wish to work for longer, they will need to apply for a residence and work permit.

➡ Highly qualified people from other nations can apply for an EU Blue Card.

➡ For all other categories, refer to the website of the Ministry of the Interior (www.mup.hr).

Transport

GETTING THERE & AWAY

Getting to Croatia is becoming easier, with both budget and full-service airlines flying to various airports in summer. On top of this, buses and ferries also shepherd holidaymakers into the country. Flights, cars and tours can be booked online at lonely planet.com/bookings.

Entering the Country

With an economy that depends heavily on tourism, Croatia has wisely kept red tape to a minimum for foreign visitors.

Passport

Your passport must be valid for at least another three months after the planned departure from Croatia, as well as issued within the previous 10 years.

Citizens of EU countries can enter Croatia with only their ID card.

Croatian authorities require all foreigners to register with the local police when they arrive in a new area of the country, but this is a routine matter normally handled by the hotel, hostel, campground or agency securing your private accommodation. If you're staying elsewhere (eg with relatives or friends), your host should take care of it for you.

Air

There are direct flights to Croatia from a variety of European cities year-round, with dozens of seasonal routes and charters added in summer.

Airports & Airlines

Croatia has an astonishing seven airports welcoming international flights, but only the three biggest (Zagreb, Split and Dubrovnik) do so all year round. **Croatia Airlines** (☑01-66 76 555; www.croatia airlines.hr) is the national carrier; it's part of the Star Alliance.

Brač Airport (☑021-559 711; www.airport-brac.hr) Only operates from late May until September, with the only international services being charter flights.

Dubrovnik Airport (DBV, Zračna luka Dubrovnik; ☑020-773 100; www.airport-dubrovnik. hr) Croatia Airlines and British Airways fly here year-round, with numerous other airlines joining them in the tourist season.

Pula Airport (☑060 308 308; www.airport-pula.hr) International flights in summer only.

Rijeka Airport (Zračna Luka Rijeka; ☑051-841 222; www. rijeka-airport.hr; Hamec 1, Omišalj) On the island of Krk; only used for seasonal flights from April to October.

Split Airport (Zračna Luka Split; ☑021-203 507; www. split-airport.hr; Cesta dr Franje Tuđmana 1270, Kaštel Štafilić, Kaštela) Major international airport, with year-round flights from Croatia Airlines, Germanwings and Lufthansa CityLine – along with many more in summer.

Zadar Airport (☑023-205 800; www.zadar-airport.hr)

CLIMATE CHANGE & TRAVEL

Every form of transport that relies on carbon-based fuel generates CO_2, the main cause of human-induced climate change. Modern travel is dependent on aeroplanes, which might use less fuel per kilometre per person than most cars but travel much greater distances. The altitude at which aircraft emit gases (including CO_2) and particles also contributes to their climate change impact. Many websites offer 'carbon calculators' that allow people to estimate the carbon emissions generated by their journey and, for those who wish to do so, to offset the impact of the greenhouse gases emitted with contributions to portfolios of climate-friendly initiatives throughout the world. Lonely Planet offsets the carbon footprint of all staff and author travel.

International flights in the tourist season only.

Zagreb Airport (☎01-45 62 170; www.zagreb-airport.hr) Croatia's main air hub, with various airlines flying here year-round from destinations all over Europe and the Middle East.

Land

Croatia has border crossings with Slovenia, Hungary, Serbia, Bosnia and Hercegovina, and Montenegro.

Bus

Direct bus connections link Croatia to all of its neighbours and to as far afield as Norway. In most cases, passports are collected on the bus and handed over at the border; you usually won't leave the bus unless there's an issue that needs resolving. Useful websites include www.eurolines.com, www.buscroatia.com, www.getbybus.com and www.vollo.net.

Austria Direct connections from Vienna to Zagreb, Osijek, Split and Dubrovnik; from Salzburg to Vukovar; and from Graz to Varaždin, Zagreb, Split, Makarska and Dubrovnik.

Bosnia and Hercegovina Direct buses to Sarajevo from most Croatian cities. Good connections between the Dalmatian coast and popular spots such as Mostar and Međugorje.

Czech Republic Direct buses from Prague and Brno to Zagreb, Split and Makarska.

France Coaches from Paris to Zagreb.

Germany Direct connections from various German cities to Varaždin, Zagreb and Split.

Hungary Direct services between Budapest and Zagreb.

Italy Routes include Padua, Venice and Trieste to Pula; Trieste to Dubrovnik; and Milan to Zagreb and Slavonia.

Montenegro Regular services between Dubrovnik and the Bay of Kotor, and some from Zagreb to Podgorica and from Vukovar to Ulcinj.

Serbia Buses from Belgrade to Vukovar, Osijek, Zagreb, Pula and Split.

Slovakia Direct buses from Bratislava to Zagreb, Split and Makarska.

Slovenia Buses from Ljubljana to Zagreb, Split and all the way to Dubrovnik and Slavonia.

Switzerland Direct connections from Geneva, Bern, Zürich, Lucerne and Lugano to Zagreb and Slavonia.

Train

Zagreb is Croatia's main train hub but direct international services also head to Osijek, Rijeka and, in the tourist season, Split. In most cases, passports are checked on the train. Useful websites include www.raileurope.com and www.eurail.com.

Austria Vienna, Villach and Graz to Zagreb.

Bosnia and Hercegovina Mostar, Sarajevo and Banja Luka to Zagreb.

Germany Munich to Zagreb.

Hungary Budapest to Zagreb and, from June to September, limited services to Split.

Serbia Belgrade to Zagreb.

Slovenia Ljubljana to Zagreb and Rijeka, and Maribor to Zagreb.

Switzerland Zürich to Zagreb.

Sea

Regular ferries connect Croatia with Italy. Split is the main hub, with overnight services to/from Ancona, Italy – some of which also stop in Stari Grad on Hvar. Seasonal services also head between Ancona and Zadar, Bari and Dubrovnik, and Pescara and Hvar Town. From Venice there are seasonal boats to Umag, Poreč, Rovinj and Pula, some of which also stop in Piran in Slovenia.

Blue Line (www.blueline-ferries.com)

Jadrolinija (www.jadrolinija.hr)

SNAV (www.snav.com)

Venezia Lines (www.venezialines.com)

GETTING AROUND

Air

Croatia Airlines (☎01-66 76 555; www.croatiaairlines.hr) The national carrier, with its main hub in Zagreb. Domestic services head to Brač (summer only), Dubrovnik, Osijek, Pula, Split and Zadar. There are also flights between these regional centres in summer.

Trade Air (☎091 62 65 111; www.trade-air.com) Has flights between Zagreb and Osijek, and seasonal flights between Pula, Rijeka, Split, Dubrovnik and Osijek.

European Coastal Airlines (☎021-444 813; www.ec-air.eu) Has seaplanes that fly between various coastal and island destinations from May to October.

Bicycle

Bicycles are easy to rent along the coast and on the islands, and cycling can be a great way to explore the islands. Relatively flat islands such as Pag and Mali Lošinj offer the most relaxed biking, but the winding, hilly roads on other islands offer spectacular views. Cycling on the coast or the mainland requires caution: most roads are busy, two-lane highways with no bicycle lanes.

Some tourist offices, especially in the Kvarner and Istria regions, have maps of routes and can refer you to local bike-rental agencies.

If you have some Croatian language skills, www.pedala.hr is a great reference for cycling routes around Croatia.

Boat

Numerous ferries connect the main coastal centres and islands year-round, with services extended in the tourist season. Be aware that locals use the term 'ferry' to refer exclusively to car ferries and 'catamaran' to refer to the faster, passenger-only ferry services.

G&V Line (Map p258; ☑060 100 000; www.gv-line.hr) Has a daily catamaran between Dubrovnik and the islands of Šipan and Mljet. In July and August some boats continue on to the islands of Korčula and Lastovo.

Jadrolinija (Map p204; ☑021-338 333; www.jadrolinija.hr; Gat Sv Duje bb) The main operator, with car ferries and catamarans on 34 different routes in winter and 37 in the tourist season. Only some services can be purchased in advance. Some routes get extremely busy in the holiday season, so it pays to arrive early, especially if you're transporting a car. Bicycles can be transported on car ferries for a fee. Facilities vary widely: bigger boats have restaurants and free wi-fi; most have at least a snack bar.

Kapetan Luka (Krilo; ☑021-645 476; www.krilo.hr) Fast boats between Split and the islands of Hvar, Brač and Vis, and between Rijeka and the islands of Cres, Unije, Susak, Ilovak and Lošinj. From May to October they also have a boat between Dubrovnik and Split, stopping on the islands of Mljet, Korčula, Hvar and Brač.

Bus

Bus services are excellent and relatively inexpensive. There are often a number of different companies handling each route, so prices can vary substantially. Luggage stowed in the baggage compartment under the bus costs extra (around 10KN a piece). Note that buses between Split and Dubrovnik pass through Bosnian territory so you'll need to keep your passport handy.

Bus Companies

Autoherc (☑060 301 301; www.autoherc.info) Extensive services in Dalmatia and to Zagreb.

Autotrans (☑051-660 660; www.autotrans.hr) Based in Rijeka but with services throughout most of the country, includ-

ROAD DISTANCES (KM)

	Dubrovnik	Osijek	Rijeka	Split	Zadar	Zagreb
Dubrovnik	---					
Osijek	495	---				
Rijeka	601	459	---			
Split	216	494	345	---		
Zadar	340	566	224	139	---	
Zagreb	572	280	182	365	288	---

ing Istria, Kvarner, Dalmatia, Zagreb and Slavonia.

Brioni Pula (☑052-544 537; www.brioni.hr) Based in Pula. Connections to Rovinj, Medulin, Rijeka, Split, Zagreb, Osijek and Vukovar.

Clissa (☑099 83 44 700; www.clissa-bus.hr; ☎) Only operates on the Zagreb–Trogir–Split route, but has electrical sockets, wi-fi, newspapers and water for passengers.

Croatia Bus (☑01-61 13 073; www.croatiabus.hr) Connects Zagreb with towns in Zagorje, Istria, Kvarner and Dalmatia.

Samoborček (☑01-63 21 190; www.samoborcek.hr) Connects Zagreb with towns in Dalmatia.

Tickets & Schedules

➜ At large stations, bus tickets must be purchased at the office, not from drivers.

➜ Try to book ahead to be sure of a seat, especially in summer.

➜ Departure lists above the various windows at bus stations tell you which window sells tickets for your bus.

➜ On Croatian bus schedules, *vozi svaki dan* means 'every day', and *ne vozi nedjeljom i blagdanom* means 'no service on Sunday and holidays'.

➜ Some buses travel overnight, saving you a night's accommodation. Don't expect to get much sleep, though, as the inside lights will be on and music might be blasting the whole night.

➜ Take care not to be left behind at meal or rest stops, which usually occur about every two hours.

➜ Useful websites offering schedules and bookings include www.vollo.net and www.getbybus.com.

Car & Motorcycle

Motorways connect Zagreb to Slavonia and Zagreb to Istria via Rijeka. Another major motorway heads from Zagreb to Dalmatia, with turn-offs for Zadar, Šibenik and Split; it continues in the direction of Dubrovnik, but falls short by 110km. Although the roads are in excellent condition, there are stretches where service stations and facilities are scarce.

Driving Licences

Any valid driving licence (no matter what its language) is sufficient to drive legally and rent a car; an international driving licence is not necessary.

The **Hrvatski Autoklub** (HAK; Croatian Auto Club; ☑0800 99 87; www.hak.hr) offers help, advice and a nationwide roadside assistance number (☑1987).

Hire

Car hire is available in all major towns, airports and tourist locations. Independent local companies are often much cheaper than the international chains, but the big companies offer one-way rentals. Sometimes you can

USEFUL TRAIN TERMS

Some terms you might encounter posted on timetables at train stations include the following:

brzi – fast train

dolazak – arrivals

polazak – departures

ne vozi nedjeljom i blagdanom – no service on Sunday and holidays

poslovni – business-class train

presjedanje – change of trains

putnički – economy-class/local train

rezerviranje mjesta obvezatno – compulsory seat reservation

vozi svaki dan – daily services

get a lower rate by booking the car from abroad, or by booking a fly-drive package.

In order to rent a car you must be 18, have a valid driving licence and have a major credit card to cover the insurance excess.

Insurance

Third-party public liability insurance is included by law with car rentals. If it's not covered by your travel-insurance policy, make sure your quoted price includes full collision insurance, known as a collision damage waiver (CDW).

On the Road

➡ Petrol stations are generally open from 7am to 7pm (often until 10pm in summer) and dispense Eurosuper 95 and 98 petrol and diesel.

➡ You have to pay tolls on all motorways, to use the Učka tunnel between Rijeka and Istria, to use the bridge to Krk Island, and on the road from Rijeka to Delnice. The first set of booths you come across when you enter a motorway dispenses tickets; you need to present this at the booths when you leave the motorway, where it's used to calculate the applicable toll.

➡ The radio station HR2 broadcasts traffic reports in English every hour on the hour from mid-June to August.

Road Rules

➡ In Croatia you drive on the right, and the use of seatbelts is mandatory.

➡ Unless otherwise posted, the speed limits for cars and motorcycles are as follows: 50km/h in built-up areas; 100km/h on main highways; 130km/h on motorways.

➡ On two-lane highways, it's illegal to pass long military convoys or a line of cars caught behind a slow-moving truck.

➡ It's illegal to drive with a blood-alcohol content higher than 0.05%.

➡ You are required to drive with your headlights on, even during the day; in Dalmatia, this applies only from October to June.

➡ All foreign cars must have their nationality sticker on the back, even if their EU licence plate states it.

Local Transport

The main form of local transport is bus (although Zagreb and Osijek also have well-developed tram systems). Buses in major cities such as Dubrovnik, Rijeka, Split and Zadar run about once every 20 minutes, less often on Sunday. A ride is usually 10KN to 15KN, with a small discount if you buy tickets at a *tisak* (news-stand).

Train

Croatia's train network is limited and trains are less frequent than buses but generally more comfortable. Note that delays are a regular occurrence on Croatian trains, sometimes for a number of hours. For information about schedules, prices and services, contact **HŽPP** (☑01-37 82 583; www.hzpp.hr).

No trains run along the coast and only a few coastal cities are connected with Zagreb. For travellers, the main lines of interest are the following:

➡ Zagreb–Osijek

➡ Zagreb–Varaždin

➡ Zagreb–Rijeka–Pula

➡ Zagreb–Knin–Split (change in Knin for Zadar or Šibenik)

Classes Domestic trains are either 'express' or 'passenger' (local). Prices quoted in this book are for unreserved, 2nd-class seating. Express trains have 1st- and 2nd-class cars; they are more expensive than passenger trains and a reservation is advisable.

Sleeping Cars There are no couchettes on domestic services. There are sleeping cars on overnight trains between Zagreb and Split.

Baggage Bringing luggage is free on trains; most stations have left-luggage services.

Passes Travellers who hold a European InterRail pass can use it in Croatia for free travel. Those travelling only in Croatia are unlikely to do enough train travel to justify the cost.

Language

Croatian belongs to the western group of the South Slavic language family. It's similar to other languages in this group, namely Serbian, Bosnian and Montenegrin.

Croatian pronunciation is not difficult – in the Croatian writing system every letter is pronounced and its sound does not vary from word to word. The sounds are pretty close to their English counterparts. Note that in our pronunciation guides n' is pronounced as the 'ny' in 'canyon', and zh as the 's' in 'pleasure'. Keeping these points in mind and reading our coloured pronunciation guides as though they were English, you'll be understood.

Word stress is also relatively easy in Croatian. In most cases the accent falls on the first vowel in the word – the last syllable of a word is never stressed in Croatian. The stressed syllable is indicated with italics in our pronunciation guides.

Some Croatian words have masculine and feminine forms, indicated after the relevant phrases in this chapter by 'm' and 'f'. Polite ('pol') and informal ('inf') alternatives are also shown for some phrases.

BASICS

Hello.	Bok.	bok
Goodbye.	Zbogom.	zbo·gom
Yes./No.	Da./Ne.	da/ne
Please.	Molim.	mo·leem
Thank you.	Hvala.	hva·la
You're welcome.	Nema na čemu.	ne·ma na che·moo

WANT MORE?

For in-depth language information and handy phrases, check out Lonely Planet's *Croatian Phrasebook*. You'll find it at **shop.lonelyplanet.com**, or you can buy Lonely Planet's iPhone phrasebooks at the Apple App Store.

| Excuse me. | Oprostite. | o·pro·stee·te |
| Sorry. | Žao mi je. | zha·o mee ye |

How are you?
| Kako ste/si? | | ka·ko ste/see (pol/inf) |

Fine. And you?
| Dobro. | | do·bro |
| A vi/ti? | | a vee/tee (pol/inf) |

My name is ...
| Zovem se ... | | zo·vem se ... |

What's your name?
| Kako se zovete/ | | ka·ko se zo·ve·te/ |
| zoveš? | | zo·vesh (pol/inf) |

Do you speak (English)?
Govorite/		go·vo·ree·te/
Govoriš		go·vo·reesh
li (engleski)?		lee (en·gle·skee) (pol/inf)

I (don't) understand.
| Ja (ne) razumijem. | | ya (ne) ra·zoo·mee·yem |

ACCOMMODATION

Do you have any rooms available?
| Imate li slobodnih | | ee·ma·te lee slo·bod·neeh |
| soba? | | so·ba |

Is breakfast included?
| Da li je doručak | | da lee ye do·roo·chak |
| uključen? | | ook·lyoo·chen |

How much is it (per night/per person)?
| Koliko stoji | | ko·lee·ko sto·yee |
| (za noć/po osobi)? | | (za noch/po o·so·bee) |

Do you have a ... room?	Imate li ... sobu?	ee·ma·te lee ... so·boo
single	jednokrevetnu	yed·no·kre·vet·noo
double	dvokrevetnu	dvo·kre·vet·noo
campsite	kamp	kamp
guest house	privatni smještaj	pree·vat·nee smyesh·tai

hotel	hotel	ho·tel
room	soba	so·ba
youth hostel	prenoćište za mladež	pre·no·cheesh·te za mla·dezh
air-con	klima-uređaj	klee·ma·oo·re·jai
bathroom	kupaonica	koo·pa·o·nee·tsa
bed	krevet	kre·vet
cot	dječji krevet	dyech·yee kre·vet
wi-fi	bežični internet	be·zheech·nee een·ter·net
window	prozor	pro·zor

DIRECTIONS

Where is ...?
Gdje je ...? — gdye ye ...

What's the address?
Koja je adresa? — ko·ya ye a·dre·sa

Can you show me (on the map)?
Možete li mi to pokazati (na karti)? — mo·zhe·te lee mee to po·ka·za·tee (na kar·tee)

at the corner	na uglu	na oo·gloo
at the traffic lights	na semaforu	na se·ma·fo·roo
behind	iza	ee·za
in front of	ispred	ees·pred
far (from)	daleko (od)	da·le·ko (od)
left	lijevo	lee·ye·vo
near	blizu	blee·zoo
next to	pored	po·red
opposite	nasuprot	na·soo·prot
right	desno	de·sno
straight ahead	ravno naprijed	rav·no na·pree·yed

EATING & DRINKING

What would you recommend?
Što biste nam preporučili? — shto bee·ste nam pre·po·roo·chee·lee

What's in that dish?
Od čega se sastoji ovo jelo? — od che·ga se sa·sto·yee o·vo ye·lo

That was delicious!
To je bilo izvrsno! — to ye bee·lo eez·vr·sno

Please bring the bill/check.
Molim vas donesite račun. — mo·leem vas do·ne·see·te ra·choon

KEY PATTERNS

To get by in Croatian, mix and match these simple patterns with words of your choice:

When's (the next day trip)?
Kada je (idući dnevni izlet)? — ka·da ye (ee·doo·chee dnev·nee eez·let)

Where's (a market)?
Gdje je (tržnica)? — gdye ye (trzh·nee·tsa)

Where do I (buy a ticket)?
Gdje mogu (kupiti kartu)? — gdye mo·goo (koo·pee·tee kar·too)

Do you have (any others)?
Imate li (kakve druge)? — ee·ma·te lee (kak·ve droo·ge)

Is there (a blanket)?
Imate li (deku)? — ee·ma·te lee (de·koo)

I'd like (that dish).
Želim (ono jelo). — zhe·leem (o·no ye·lo)

I'd like to (hire a car).
Želio/Željela bih (iznajmiti automobil). — zhe·lee·o/zhe·lye·la beeh (eez·nai·mee·tee a·oo·to·mo·beel) (m/f)

Can I (take a photograph of you)?
Mogu li (vas/te slikati)? — mo·goo lee (vas/te slee·ka·tee) (pol/inf)

Could you please (help)?
Molim vas, možete li (mi pomoći)? — mo·leem vas mo·zhe·te lee (mee po·mo·chee)

Do I have to (pay)?
Trebam li (platiti)? — tre·bam lee (pla·tee·tee)

I'd like to reserve a table for ...	Želim rezervirati stol za ...	zhe·leem re·zer·vee·ra·tee stol za ...
(eight) o'clock	(osam) sati	(o·sam) sa·tee
(two) people	(dvoje) ljudi	(dvo·ye) lyoo·dee

I don't eat ...	Ja ne jedem ...	ya ne ye·dem ...
fish	ribu	ree·boo
nuts	razne orahe	raz·ne o·ra·he
poultry	meso od peradi	me·so od pe·ra·dee
red meat	crveno meso	tsr·ve·no me·so

Key Words

appetiser	predjelo	pre·dye·lo
baby food	hrana za bebe	hra·na za be·be
bar	bar	bar

bottle	*boca*	*bo*·tsa
bowl	*zdjela*	*zdye*·la
breakfast	*doručak*	*do*·roo·chak
cafe	*kafić/* *kavana*	*ka*·feech/ *ka*·va·na
(too) cold	*(pre)hladno*	(pre·)*hlad*·no
dinner	*večera*	*ve*·che·ra
dish (food)	*jelo*	*ye*·lo
food	*hrana*	*hra*·na
fork	*viljuška*	*vee*·lyoosh·ka
glass	*čaša*	*cha*·sha
knife	*nož*	nozh
lunch	*ručak*	*roo*·chak
main course	*glavno jelo*	*glav*·no *ye*·lo
market	*tržnica*	*trzh*·nee·tsa
menu	*jelovnik*	*ye*·*lov*·neek
plate	*tanjur*	*ta*·nyoor
restaurant	*restoran*	re·*sto*·ran
spicy	*pikantno*	pee·*kant*·no
spoon	*žlica*	*zhlee*·tsa
with/without	*sa/bez*	*sa/bez*
vegetarian meal	*vegetarijanski obrok*	ve·ge·ta·*ree*· yan·skee *o*·brok

Meat & Fish

beef	*govedina*	*go*·ve·dee·na
chicken	*piletina*	*pee*·le·tee·na
fish	*riba*	*ree*·ba
lamb	*janjetina*	*ya*·nye·tee·na
pork	*svinjetina*	*svee*·nye·tee·na
veal	*teletina*	*te*·le·tee·na

Fruit & Vegetables

apple	*jabuka*	*ya*·boo·ka
apricot	*marelica*	ma·*re*·lee·tsa
(green) beans	*mahuna*	*ma*·hoo·na
cabbage	*kupus*	*koo*·poos
carrot	*mrkva*	*mrk*·va

SIGNS

Izlaz	Exit
Muškarci	Men
Otvoreno	Open
Ulaz	Entrance
Zabranjeno	Prohibited
Zahodi	Toilets
Zatvoreno	Closed
Žene	Women

corn	*kukuruz*	koo·*koo*·rooz
cherry	*trešnja*	*tresh*·nya
cucumber	*krastavac*	*kra*·sta·vats
fruit	*voće*	*vo*·che
grape	*grožđe*	*grozh*·je
lentils	*leća*	*le*·cha
lettuce/salad	*zelena salata*	ze·le·na sa·*la*·ta
mushroom	*gljiva*	*glyee*·va
nut	*orah*	*o*·rah
onion	*luk*	look
orange	*naranča*	na·*ran*·cha
peach	*breskva*	*bres*·kva
pear	*kruška*	*kroosh*·ka
peas	*grašak*	*gra*·shak
plum	*šljiva*	*shlyee*·va
potato	*krumpir*	*kroom*·peer
pumpkin	*bundeva*	*boon*·de·va
strawberry	*jagoda*	*ya*·go·da
tomato	*rajčica*	*rai*·chee·tsa
vegetable	*povrće*	*po*·vr·che
watermelon	*lubenica*	loo·*be*·nee·tsa

Other Foods

bread	*kruh*	krooh
butter	*maslac*	*ma*·slats
cheese	*sir*	seer
egg	*jaje*	*ya*·ye
honey	*med*	med
jam	*džem*	jem
oil	*ulje*	*oo*·lye
pasta	*tjestenina*	tye·ste·*nee*·na
pepper	*papar*	*pa*·par
rice	*riža*	*ree*·zha
salt	*sol*	sol
sugar	*šećer*	*she*·cher
vinegar	*ocat*	*o*·tsat

Drinks

beer	*pivo*	*pee*·vo
coffee	*kava*	*ka*·va
juice	*sok*	sok
milk	*mlijeko*	mlee·*ye*·ko
(mineral) water	*(mineralna)* *voda*	(*mee*·ne·ral·na) *vo*·da
tea	*čaj*	chai
(red/white) wine	*(crno/bijelo)* *vino*	(*tsr*·no/*bye*·lo) *vee*·no

LANGUAGE EATING & DRINKING

EMERGENCIES

Help!
Upomoć! oo·po·moch

I'm lost.
Izgubio/ eez·goo·bee·o/
Izgubila sam se. eez·goo·bee·la sam se (m/f)

Leave me alone!
Ostavite me na miru! o·sta·vee·te me na mee·roo

There's been an accident!
Desila se nezgoda! de·see·la se nez·go·da

Call a doctor!
Zovite liječnika! zo·vee·te lee·yech·nee·ka

Call the police!
Zovite policiju! zo·vee·te po·lee·tsee·yoo

I'm ill.
Ja sam bolestan/ ya sam bo·le·stan/
bolesna. bo·le·sna (m/f)

It hurts here.
Boli me ovdje. bo·lee me ov·dye

I'm allergic to ...
Ja sam alergičan/ ya sam a·ler·gee·chan/
alergična na ... a·ler·geech·na na ... (m/f)

SHOPPING & SERVICES

I'd like to buy ...
Želim kupiti ... zhe·leem koo·pee·tee ...

I'm just looking.
Ja samo razgledam. ya sa·mo raz·gle·dam

May I look at it?
Mogu li to pogledati? mo·goo lee to po·gle·da·tee

How much is it?
Koliko stoji? ko·lee·ko sto·yee

That's too expensive.
To je preskupo. to ye pre·skoo·po

Do you have something cheaper?
Imate li nešto ee·ma·te lee nesh·to
jeftinije? yef·tee·nee·ye

There's a mistake in the bill.
Ima jedna greška ee·ma yed·na gresh·ka
na računu. na ra·choo·noo

ATM	*bankovni automat*	ban·kov·nee a·oo·to·mat
credit card	*kreditna kartica*	kre·deet·na kar·tee·tsa
internet cafe	*internet kafić*	een·ter·net ka·feech

QUESTION WORDS

How?	*Kako?*	ka·ko
What?	*Što?*	shto
When?	*Kada?*	ka·da
Where?	*Gdje?*	gdye
Who?	*Tko?*	tko
Why?	*Zašto?*	za·shto

post office	*poštanski ured*	posh·tan·skee oo·red
tourist office	*turistička agencija*	too·ree·steech·ka a·gen·tsee·ya

TIME & DATES

What time is it?
Koliko je sati? ko·lee·ko ye sa·tee

It's (10) o'clock.
(Deset) je sati. (de·set) ye sa·tee

Half past (10).
(Deset) i po. (de·set) ee po

morning	*jutro*	yoo·tro
afternoon	*poslijepodne*	po·slee·ye·pod·ne
evening	*večer*	ve·cher
yesterday	*jučer*	yoo·cher
today	*danas*	da·nas
tomorrow	*sutra*	soo·tra

Monday	*ponedjeljak*	po·ne·dye·lyak
Tuesday	*utorak*	oo·to·rak
Wednesday	*srijeda*	sree·ye·da
Thursday	*četvrtak*	chet·vr·tak
Friday	*petak*	pe·tak
Saturday	*subota*	soo·bo·ta
Sunday	*nedjelja*	ne·dye·lya

January	*siječanj*	see·ye·chan'
February	*veljača*	ve·lya·cha
March	*ožujak*	o·zhoo·yak
April	*travanj*	tra·van'
May	*svibanj*	svee·ban'
June	*lipanj*	lee·pan'
July	*srpanj*	sr·pan'
August	*kolovoz*	ko·lo·voz
September	*rujanj*	roo·yan'
October	*listopad*	lee·sto·pad
November	*studeni*	stoo·de·nee
December	*prosinac*	pro·see·nats

TRANSPORT

Public Transport

boat	*brod*	brod
bus	*autobus*	a·oo·to·boos
plane	*avion*	a·vee·on
train	*vlak*	vlak
tram	*tramvaj*	tram·vai

NUMBERS

1	*jedan*	*ye*·dan
2	*dva*	dva
3	*tri*	tree
4	*četiri*	*che*·tee·ree
5	*pet*	pet
6	*šest*	shest
7	*sedam*	*se*·dam
8	*osam*	*o*·sam
9	*devet*	*de*·vet
10	*deset*	*de*·set
20	*dvadeset*	*dva*·de·set
30	*trideset*	*tree*·de·set
40	*četrdeset*	che·tr·*de*·set
50	*pedeset*	pe·*de*·set
60	*šezdeset*	shez·*de*·set
70	*sedamdeset*	se·dam·*de*·set
80	*osamdeset*	o·sam·*de*·set
90	*devedeset*	de·ve·*de*·set
100	*sto*	sto
1000	*tisuću*	*tee*·soo·choo

I want to go to ...
Želim da idem u ...   *zhe*·leem da ee·dem oo ...

Does it stop at (Split)?
Da li staje u (Splitu)?   da lee *sta*·ye oo (*splee*·too)

What time does it leave?
U koliko sati kreće?   oo ko·*lee*·ko sa·tee *kre*·che

What time does it get to (Zagreb)?
U koliko sati stiže   oo ko·*lee*·ko sa·tee stee·zhe
u (Zagreb)?   u (*zag*·reb)

Could you tell me when we get to (the Arena)?
Možete li mi reći   mo·zhe·te lee mee re·chee
kada stignemo kod   ka·da steeg·ne·mo kod
(Arene)?   (a·re·ne)

I'd like to get off at (Dubrovnik).
Želim izaći   *zhe*·leem ee·*za*·chee
u (Dubrovniku).   oo (*doob*·rov·nee·koo)

A ... ticket.	*Jednu ... kartu.*	*yed*·noo ... *kar*·too
1st-class	*prvorazrednu*	pr·vo·raz·*red*·noo
2nd-class	*drugorazrednu*	droo·go·raz·*red*·noo
one-way	*jednosmjernu*	*yed*·no·smyer·noo
return	*povratnu*	po·*vrat*·noo

the first	*prvi*	*pr*·vee
the last	*posljednji*	pos·lyed·nyee
the next	*sljedeći*	slye·de·chee

aisle seat	*sjedište do prolaza*	sye·deesh·te do pro·la·za
delayed	*u zakašnjenju*	oo za·kash·nye·nyoo
cancelled	*poništeno*	po·neesh·te·no
platform	*peron*	pe·ron
ticket office	*blagajna*	bla·gai·na
timetable	*red vožnje*	red vozh·nye
train station	*željeznička postaja*	zhe·lyez·neech·ka pos·ta·ya
window seat	*sjedište do prozora*	sye·deesh·te do pro·zo·ra

Driving & Cycling

I'd like to hire a ...	*Želim iznajmiti ...*	zhe·leem eez·*nai*·mee·tee ...
4WD	*džip*	jeep
bicycle	*bicikl*	bee·*tsee*·kl
car	*automobil*	a·oo·to·*mo*·beel
motorcycle	*motocikl*	mo·to·*tsee*·kl

bicycle pump	*pumpa za bicikl*	*poom*·pa za bee·*tsee*·kl
child seat	*sjedalo za dijete*	sye·da·lo za dee·ye·te
diesel	*dizel gorivo*	dee·zel go·ree·vo
helmet	*kaciga*	*ka*·tsee·ga
mechanic	*auto-mehaničar*	a·oo·to·me·*ha*·nee·char
petrol/gas	*benzin*	ben·zeen
service station	*benziska stanica*	ben·zeen·ska sta·nee·tsa

Is this the road to ...?
Je li ovo cesta za ...?   ye lee *o*·vo tse·sta za ...

(How long) Can I park here?
(Koliko dugo)   (ko·*lee*·ko doo·go)
Mogu ovdje   *mo*·goo ov·dye
parkirati?   par·*kee*·ra·tee

The car/motorbike has broken down (at Knin).
Automobil/   a·oo·to·*mo*·beel/
Motocikl   mo·to·*tsee*·kl
se pokvario   se pok·*va*·ree·o
(u Kninu).   (oo *knee*·noo)

I have a flat tyre.
Imam probušenu   ee·mam pro·boo·she·noo
gumu.   goo·moo

I've run out of petrol.
Nestalo mi je   ne·sta·lo mee ye
benzina.   ben·zee·na

I've lost the keys.
Izgubio/   eez·goo·bee·o/
Izgubila   eez·goo·bee·la
sam ključeve.   sam *klyoo*·che·ve (m/f)

GLOSSARY

(s) indicates singular and (pl) indicates plural

amphora (s), **amphorae** (pl) – large, two-handled vase in which wine or water was kept

apse – altar area of a church

autocamps – gigantic camp-grounds with restaurants, shops and row upon row of caravans

Avars – Eastern European people who waged war against Byzantium from the 6th to 9th centuries

ban – viceroy or governor

bb – in an address the letters 'bb' following a street name (such as Placa bb) stand for *bez broja* (without number), which indicates that the building has no street number

bura – cold northeasterly wind

cesta – road

crkva – church

fortica – fortress

galerija – gallery

garderoba – left-luggage offic

Glagolitic – ancient Slavonic language put into writing by Greek missionaries Cyril and Methodius

gora – mountain

HDZ – Hrvatska Demokratska Zajednica; Croatian Democratic Union

Illyrians – ancient inhabitants of the Adriatic coast, defeated by the Romans in the 2nd century BC

karst – highly porous limestone and dolomitic rock

klapa – an outgrowth of church-choir singing

konoba – the traditional term for a small, intimate dining spot, often located in a cellar; now applies to a wide variety of restaurants; usually a simple, family-run establishment

knez – duke

maestral – strong, steady westerly wind

mali – small

maquis – dense growth of mostly evergreen shrubs and small trees

muzej – museum

nave – central part of a church flanked by two aisles

NDH – Nezavisna Država Hrvatska; Independent State of Croatia

obala – waterfront

otok (s), **otoci** (pl) – island

pansion – guesthouse

plaža – beach

polje – collapsed limestone area often under cultivation

put – path, trail

restoran – restaurant

rijeka – river

sabor – parliament

šetalište – walkway

sobe – rooms available

sveti – saint

svetog – saint (genitive case – ie of saint, as in the Church of St Joseph)

tamburica – a three- or five-string mandolin

tisak – news-stand

toplice – spa

trg – square

turbo folk – a techno version of Serbian folk music

ulica – street

uvala – bay

velik – large

vrh – summit, peak

zimmer – rooms available (a German word)

Behind the Scenes

SEND US YOUR FEEDBACK

We love to hear from travellers – your comments keep us on our toes and help make our books better. Our well-travelled team reads every word on what you loved or loathed about this book. Although we cannot reply individually to your submissions, we always guarantee that your feedback goes straight to the appropriate authors, in time for the next edition. Each person who sends us information is thanked in the next edition – the most useful submissions are rewarded with a selection of digital PDF chapters.

Visit **lonelyplanet.com/contact** to submit your updates and suggestions or to ask for help. Our award-winning website also features inspirational travel stories, news and discussions.

Note: We may edit, reproduce and incorporate your comments in Lonely Planet products such as guidebooks, websites and digital products, so let us know if you don't want your comments reproduced or your name acknowledged. For a copy of our privacy policy visit lonelyplanet.com/privacy.

OUR READERS

Many thanks to the travellers who used the last edition and wrote to us with helpful hints, useful advice and interesting anecdotes:

Anthony Kay, Attila Bogdan, Bradley Carr, Elena Falzon, Gary Sheppard, Gavin Parnaby, Jean Kelly, John Bower, Marla Van Meter, Matthew Bolton, Michael Lowry, Peter Borowski, Peter Innes, Richard Bradley, Wouter Mitty.

WRITER THANKS
Peter Dragicevich

Researching in Croatia is always a joy but even more so with company – so many thanks to Robert Carpenter and Catherine Cole for joining me on the road. Once again I'm indebted to Vojko and Marija Dragičević for their wonderful hospitality.

Marc Di Duca

Big thanks go to the staff at tourist offices the length and breadth of the coast, especially those in Pula, Rab, Rijeka and Zadar; fellow LP writer Anja; Zlatko in Lopar; my wife, Tanya, and sons Taras and Kirill for their company on the trip.

Anja Mutić

A huge *hvala* to Lidija Mišćin and Andrea Pisac for their invaluable help and expertise – this book wouldn't be the same without you. To Ana Mažuran, who's the perfect companion on my research trips – thanks for being hungry at just the right times. A thank you goes to my many friends in Croatia who gave me endless tips. *Hvala*, mama, for your laughter. *Obrigada*, Kweli, for being my north star.

ACKNOWLEDGEMENTS

Climate map data adapted from Peel MC, Finlayson BL & McMahon TA (2007) 'Updated World Map of the Köppen-Geiger Climate Classification', Hydrology and Earth System Sciences, 11, 163344.

Cover photograph: Sunrise view of the Old Town in Dubrovnik, Doug Pearson/AWL ©

THIS BOOK

This 9th edition of Lonely Planet's *Croatia* guidebook was researched and written by Peter Dragicevich, Marc Di Duca and Anja Mutić. The previous two editions were written by Peter Dragicevich, Anja Mutić and Vesna Maric.

This guidebook was produced by the following:

Destination Editor Anna Tyler

Product Editor Grace Dobell

Senior Cartographer Anthony Phelan

Book Designer Wendy Wright

Assisting Editors Nigel Chin, Victoria Harrison, Kate James, Kellie Langdon, Anne Mulvaney, Gabrielle Stefanos

Cover Researcher Naomi Parker

Thanks to Cheree Broughton, Neill Coen, Daniel Corbett, Andi Jones, Lauren Keith, Claire Naylor, Karyn Noble, Kirsten Rawlings, Ellie Simpson, Angela Tinson, Tony Wheeler

Index

Map Pages **000**
Photo Pages **000**

Map Legend

Sights

- Beach
- Bird Sanctuary
- Buddhist
- Castle/Palace
- Christian
- Confucian
- Hindu
- Islamic
- Jain
- Jewish
- Monument
- Museum/Gallery/Historic Building
- Ruin
- Shinto
- Sikh
- Taoist
- Winery/Vineyard
- Zoo/Wildlife Sanctuary
- Other Sight

Activities, Courses & Tours

- Bodysurfing
- Diving
- Canoeing/Kayaking
- Course/Tour
- Sento Hot Baths/Onsen
- Skiing
- Snorkelling
- Surfing
- Swimming/Pool
- Walking
- Windsurfing
- Other Activity

Sleeping

- Sleeping
- Camping

Eating

- Eating

Drinking & Nightlife

- Drinking & Nightlife
- Cafe

Entertainment

- Entertainment

Shopping

- Shopping

Information

- Bank
- Embassy/Consulate
- Hospital/Medical
- Internet
- Police
- Post Office
- Telephone
- Toilet
- Tourist Information
- Other Information

Geographic

- Beach
- Gate
- Hut/Shelter
- Lighthouse
- Lookout
- Mountain/Volcano
- Oasis
- Park
- Pass
- Picnic Area
- Waterfall

Population

- Capital (National)
- Capital (State/Province)
- City/Large Town
- Town/Village

Transport

- Airport
- Border crossing
- Bus
- Cable car/Funicular
- Cycling
- Ferry
- Metro station
- Monorail
- Parking
- Petrol station
- S-Bahn/Subway station
- Taxi
- T-bane/Tunnelbana station
- Train station/Railway
- Tram
- Tube station
- U-Bahn/Underground station
- Other Transport

Note: Not all symbols displayed above appear on the maps in this book

Routes

- Tollway
- Freeway
- Primary
- Secondary
- Tertiary
- Lane
- Unsealed road
- Road under construction
- Plaza/Mall
- Steps
- Tunnel
- Pedestrian overpass
- Walking Tour
- Walking Tour detour
- Path/Walking Trail

Boundaries

- International
- State/Province
- Disputed
- Regional/Suburb
- Marine Park
- Cliff
- Wall

Hydrography

- River, Creek
- Intermittent River
- Canal
- Water
- Dry/Salt/Intermittent Lake
- Reef

Areas

- Airport/Runway
- Beach/Desert
- Cemetery (Christian)
- Cemetery (Other)
- Glacier
- Mudflat
- Park/Forest
- Sight (Building)
- Sportsground
- Swamp/Mangrove

OUR STORY

A beat-up old car, a few dollars in the pocket and a sense of adventure. In 1972 that's all Tony and Maureen Wheeler needed for the trip of a lifetime – across Europe and Asia overland to Australia. It took several months, and at the end – broke but inspired – they sat at their kitchen table writing and stapling together their first travel guide, *Across Asia on the Cheap*. Within a week they'd sold 1500 copies. Lonely Planet was born.

Today, Lonely Planet has offices in Franklin, London, Melbourne, Oakland, Dublin, Beijing and Delhi, with more than 600 staff and writers. We share Tony's belief that 'a great guidebook should do three things: inform, educate and amuse'.

OUR WRITERS

Peter Dragicevich

Plan Your Trip, Central Dalmatia, Southern Dalmatia After a successful career in niche newspaper and magazine publishing, both in his native New Zealand and in Australia, Peter finally gave into Kiwi wanderlust, giving up staff jobs to chase his diverse roots around much of Europe. Over the last decade he's written literally dozens of guidebooks for Lonely Planet on an oddly disparate collection of countries, all of which he's come to love. He once again calls Auckland, New Zealand his home – although his current nomadic existence means he's hardly ever there.

Marc Di Duca

Istria, Kvarner, Northern Dalmatia A travel author for the last decade, Marc has worked for Lonely Planet in Siberia, Slovakia, Bavaria, England, Ukraine, Austria, Poland, Croatia, Portugal, Madeira and on the Trans-Siberian Railway, as well as writing and updating tens of other guides for other publishers. When not on the road, Marc lives between Sandwich, Kent and Mariánské Lázně in the Czech Republic with his wife and two sons.

Anja Mutić

Understand, Survival Guide, Zagreb, Inland Croatia Born and raised in Zagreb, Croatia, Anja has travelled the globe as a professional wanderer for decades. Her travel writing career has taken her to 60+ countries, taught her several languages (she is fluent in Croatian, English and Spanish and can get by with Portuguese) and her articles have won several awards. She has lived, worked and travelled on all the continents (except Antarctica), which included 'mini lives' (stints of several months) in Buenos Aires and Lisbon. Anja's writing has been published in print and online publications such as *The Washington Post, New York Magazine, National Geographic Traveler, AFAR* and *BBC Travel*. Follow her on Instagram at Everthenomad.

Published by Lonely Planet Global Limited
CRN 554153
9th edition – April 2017
ISBN 978 1 78657 418 3
© Lonely Planet 2017   Photographs © as indicated 2017
10 9 8 7 6 5 4 3 2 1
Printed in Singapore

Although the authors and Lonely Planet have taken all reasonable care in preparing this book, we make no warranty about the accuracy or completeness of its content and, to the maximum extent permitted, disclaim all liability arising from its use.